Depreciation Systems

Depreciation

Systems

FRANK K. WOLF

W. CHESTER FITCH

IOWA STATE UNIVERSITY PRESS / AMES

Frank K. Wolf, Ph.D., P.E., is professor and past chair of the Department of Industrial Engineering at Western Michigan University where he teaches courses in operations research and statistics. He is vice president of Depreciation Programs, Inc., and has developed and presented specialized training programs and seminars in depreciation since 1971.

W. Chester Fitch, Ph.D., P.E., is dean of engineering, emeritus, Western Michigan University. He is retired after more than 40 years of conducting depreciation studies and educating and training depreciation staff. He founded a series of programs providing specialized training in depreciation in 1969 and is currently president of Depreciation Programs, Inc.

© 1994 Iowa State University Press, Ames, Iowa 50014

⊗ Printed on acid-free paper in the United States of America

First edition, 1994

Library of Congress Cataloging-in-Publication Data

Wolf, Frank K.
     Depreciation systems / Frank K. Wolf, W. Chester Fitch. — 1st ed.
        p.   cm.
     Includes bibliographical references and index.
     ISBN 0-8138-2457-5 (alk. paper)
     1. Depreciation. 2. Public utilities — United States — Accounting. 3. Economic life of fixed assets.
  I. Fitch, W. Chester.   II. Title.
HF5681.D5W65   1994
657'.73 — dc20   93–47634

Contents

Preface

THIS book grew from our recognition of the need for a systematic explanation of depreciation using simple, easy-to-follow illustrations. In particular, we examine the portion of depreciation that relates to accounting, specifically as found in public utilities. However, many of the topics covered relate to other applications of depreciation, including valuation of property and taxation. Several conceptual difficulties surround depreciation. One is the lack of understanding that the determination of depreciation involves an intricate system comprising most aspects of the operation of a company. Another is the tendency to view components of the system as being independent of one another. Finally, the use of complicated arithmetic examples, frequently requiring lengthy, time-consuming calculations when explaining ideas, distracts the reader and obfuscates the idea being illustrated.

Asset management includes four actions: (1) the decision, based on analysis of the associated costs and revenues, to acquire property; (2) its acquisition, installation, and associated accounting; (3) its use and related accounting, including the proration of capital expenses to each accounting period; and (4) its retirement and associated accounting. Each action interacts with the other. As management decisions are often based on information from these accounting records, it is essential to exercise careful control over the annual and cumulative results of the depreciation system. This means that the methods used to make estimates of the variables used in calculating and adjusting depreciation should be scrutinized, because they significantly affect the management of the assets of the company.

Investments in capital assets, such as a turbine used to turn an electrical generator, a pipeline used to carry natural gas, or a cable used to transmit communications signals, result in an initial cost for equipment that will provide service in future years. One goal of accrual accounting is to match the timing of expenses with the activities associated with the expense. Thus, the initial cost of a capital asset should be allocated to accounting periods in a way that results in a logical match of the depreciation expense with the life of the asset. These ideas lead to the concept of depreciation as a "cost of operation."

Accountants and engineers familiar with the calculation of the depreciation of a unit may believe depreciation a straightforward calculation and wonder if there is much to be said about it. The focus of this book is the depreciation of a group of property, rather than a unit. Though each unit in the group has a unique life and salvage, it is the *group* that is depreciated. This requires that the life and salvage of the group be described in statistical terms. Consequently, analysis of life and salvage data and estimation of future values of life and salvage are a major portion of a depreciation study. Proper application of these estimates when calculating depreciation requires a thorough understanding of depreciation systems. Thus, the estimation of depreciation is the result of a complex process that provides many challenges to the depreciation professional.

Many readers will be associated with the public utility industry. Because companies in this industry are characterized by large investments in capital assets, the annual accrual for depreciation represents a significant portion of the annual operating cost. The resulting cost of operation is of interest to the companies' managers, accountants, and stockholders because of its influence on the annual financial reports. The public also has an interest in depreciation. As customers they are concerned with depreciation because it affects the rates they pay for gas, water, phone, and electric service. These two groups, the company and the public, may have different estimates of depreciation, as well as other items and activities contributing to the cost of providing service. Therefore a government agency may be authorized to regulate rates. Then depreciation will be subject to periodic review by the regulatory agency. The depreciation professionals representing the utility must not only estimate depreciation but must convince others of their estimates, and the depreciation professionals representing the regulatory agency must have the expertise to evaluate the reasonableness of these estimates.

The term *estimation of depreciation* is used to emphasize that depreciation is not a single, measurable figure, but that it falls within a range that contains "reasonable" estimates. Depreciation calculations are based on accounting records, and the relationship between those calculations and the actual property in service depends on the manner in which the records reflect the physical world. Thus the accuracy and detail of accounting records (i.e., the data) affect depreciation. The calculation of depreciation takes place during the life of the property, so the life and salvage used in the calculations are forecasts. Therefore the depreciation system should allow for adjustment as forecasts are revised. There are different systems of depreciation and, even if the same estimates and data are used, each system yields different values of depreciation. Finally, management is responsible for developing and implementing a depreciation policy that reflects the needs of the company, the stockholders, and the customers. In this sense, the "correct" accrual depends on the goals of management, how management implements policy to achieve their goals, and management judgement of how the proposed accrual for depreciation meets these goals.

This book is written for those entering the field of depreciation and as a reference for those with experience in the field. Our purpose is not to prescribe solutions but to provide a sound foundation in basic ideas. The reader will be warned of computational problems and common solutions will be offered. No attempt is made to suggest operational solutions to all problems. The "best" solution varies with the situation and is the result of common sense, experience, an understanding of basic ideas, and knowledge of the organization's depreciation policy.

Jargon creeps into most areas of specialization, and attempts to create standard definitions usually fail. Many depreciation professionals have their definitions permanently recorded in the public record and find consistency of terminology a virtue, though others may find this an annoying hinderance to improvement. The terminology and definitions used in this book have been given careful thought and were developed with the hope of providing a more systematic and flexible system of describing depreciation systems. There is no intent to declare other terminology "wrong," and other terms in common use have been listed.

Many techniques, procedures, and ideas in the book are based on models. The purpose of a model is to simplify our complex world. Simplification often allows users to identify the underlying relationships between actions and the results of actions. "A penny saved is a penny earned" is a model that can be applied to our financial lives. It simplifies the complex financial decisions we are faced with and, if applied with common sense, helps us to make better decisions than we would without the model. We should have similar expectations for our mathematical models. One limit to the usefulness of a model is the availability of data. If we do not have the data necessary to make the estimates required by the model, our model does us little good. In other cases, the model may be too simple to be of help. Or the assumptions of the model may not be appropriate for the situation. Then we must remember that it is the responsibility of the analyst to choose an appropriate model and to remember its limiting assumptions when using it.

We begin by showing the assumptions, expectations, and misconceptions inherent in the basic accounting model. Next, we introduce the ideas underlying the variables used in the depreciation system. The reader's attention is then focused on the systems of depreciation. Simple arithmetic examples illustrate the calculation of depreciation for first a single vintage group of property and then a group formed by combining several vintages. Techniques used to analyze life and salvage data and use of the information to forecast life and salvage are discussed in several following chapters. The book concludes with a chapter on the organization of a depreciation study and current issues in depreciation.

Depreciation Systems continues a series of publications that began with several bulletins published by the Iowa Engineering Experiment Station at the Iowa State College. Work preceding these publications began about 1915 under the direction of Anson Marston, dean of the College of Engineering, who was involved in the valuation of industrial properties in which depreciation was a significant element. Research seeking a basis on which to estimate property lives was undertaken in the early 1920s and resulted in the publication in 1931 of Bulletin 103, *Life Characteristics of Physical Property,* by Robley Winfrey and Edwin Kurtz. This was followed by Bulletin 125, *Statistical Analysis of Industrial Property Retirements,* in 1935 and Bulletin 155, *Depreciation of Group Properties,* in 1942, both by Winfrey. *Engineering Valuation* by Marston and T. R. Agg, who had succeeded Marson as dean, was published in 1936. *Engineering Valuation and Depreciation* by Marson, Winfrey, and Jean C. Hempstead was published first in 1953 by McGraw-Hill and later by Iowa State University Press; it was written as a textbook for a course in the valuation of property. Hempstead had worked with Winfrey, who later became professor of industrial engineering at Iowa State. Work in engineering valuation continued at Iowa State University with the efforts of graduate students who were primarily under the supervision of Winfrey from 1922 to 1952 and Harold A. Cowles from 1953 to 1992.

ACKNOWLEDGEMENTS

First and foremost we are indebted to the late Robley Winfrey for his pioneering work in depreciation and life analysis of physical properties. Under his tutelage many learned the basics and subleties of the subject. We are indebted to Jean Hempstead for his work with Robley and for the enthusiasm with which he infected colleagues and students. We are indebted to our many colleagues, fellow AGA/EEI depreciation committee members, students in our seminars, presenters at the Iowa State Regulatory Conference, and attorneys and regulators who scrutinized our ideas, writings, and mathematics.

Four individuals were instrumental in the support of our work before beginning the book: B. H. Bissinger, professor of mathematics and statistics, Pennsylvania State University, who tutored many of us in the intricacies of the actuarial sciences as they are used in life analyses of property; Charles Knight, depreciation engineer, Columbia Gas Corporation, who insisted that we provide an opportunity for his company's professionals to become more knowledgeable about depreciation; E. C. Hostettler, chief of the depreciation branch, Interstate Commerce Commission, who sought the best way to assist the railroads in improving their accounting for depreciation by sponsoring the use of computers and developing software based on state-of-the-art concepts; and Charles H. Kressler, director of the valuation division and later executive vice president of Gannett Fleming Cordry and Carpenter Inc., who provided counsel in the practical aspects of making and defending studies.

We are particularly indebted to Harold Waddington, executive vice president of Gannett Fleming, for his encouragement. In addition, his insightful comments and suggestions, reflecting his many years of consulting experience, were invaluable.

Others helped in specific context while the book was being written. Harold Cowles, Anson Marston Professor at Iowa State University, provided intellectual stimulus and contact with ongoing work at Iowa State. Bob White, professor of industrial engineering at Western Michigan University, provided insight in modeling salvage. William Welke, professor of accountancy at Western Michigan University, provided the accounting expertise necessary to assure conformance to current practices in the field. Ron White, senior vice president, Foster Associates, and William Stout, vice president of the valuation and rates division of Gannett Fleming, provided helpful critiques of technical portions of the manuscript. Susan Jensen, depreciation specialist, Interstate Commerce Commission, provided an insight into the Stimulated Plant Record method. We are indebted to Karen Ponder for her help in the development of examples of calculating depreciation. Elliott Sydney and Laura Young assisted in many studies using software they developed or adapted, and Elliott helped with the many graphs and tables. Maxine Becker and Elaine Rogers were instrumental in the production of the many drafts made during the evolution of the book from notes to final copy. Countless others who have helped throughout twenty years of writing outlines, preparing lectures, and teaching in the Depreciation Programs seminars go unnamed.

Frank Wolf is indebted to Western Michigan University and the support offered in the form of a sabbatical leave during the 1990–91 academic year.

FRANK WOLF
W. C. FITCH

Depreciation Systems

Financial Aspects of Accounting for Depreciation

THE accountant from the nonregulated segment of the economy may wonder if there is much new to say about depreciation. "The question of Depreciation is one upon which so many articles have been written, and so many opinions expressed, that there would not appear to be much more which could profitably be said upon the subject" (Armstrong, 1903). Discussions about the subject are generally limited to the continual change in the tax laws, where depreciation is often used as a tool of fiscal policy.

However, because of the close relationship of depreciation to rate base, rate of return, and revenue requirements, accounting is an important topic in the regulated industries. An early legal view of depreciation as it related to public utilities came from the 1909 Supreme Court decision *Knoxville* v. *Knoxville Water Company.* This decision marked the recognition of depreciation as an item of expense and a measure of the decline of service. Much of the best early work on the depreciation concept was fostered by regulatory concerns. Apart from taxes, most of the current conceptual discussions are carried on in the regulatory area.

Major portions of this chapter rely upon a presentation at the Iowa Regulatory Conference by William Welke (1989), professor of accountancy at Western Michigan University, and on his personal notes.

3

Arguments about depreciation continue, but most of the discussions are not new. A review of the literature reveals that some of these discussions have been going on from 80 to 100 years. Hatfield's 1936 article, "What They Say about Depreciation," cites several definitions, discussions, and disagreements about the topic that are still heard over 60 years later. Grant (1952) summed it up when he said, "Writers on depreciation seem to agree on nothing except that other writers on the subject are somewhat confused."

Not only was there disagreement about the concept of *valuation* versus *allocation* in the early years, but also disagreement about who was best prepared to work with the new idea. "[Depreciation] is a difficult [item] to deal with, more particularly as it has, unfortunately, got largely into the hands of auditors and bookkeepers, who deal with it according to their own limited knowledge and entirely as a matter of account. Depreciation is much more than this, and can only be properly adjusted by an engineer who has thorough knowledge of his profession and intimate acquaintance with the particular buildings and machinery with which he is at the moment dealing" (Burton, 1905). Currently, the typical depreciation professional is most likely to be an accountant, though a significant proportion are engineers. While the difference in educational background may result in differences of opinion within the field of depreciation, it also results in a richness of ideas that might otherwise be absent.

To evaluate depreciation, we must go back to basic accounting theory. In the accounting framework, depreciation is defined as an allocation process, *not* a valuation process. This has not always been the case, and the definition remains a source of disagreement between accountants and engineers. The accountants make no pretense that the methodology used will provide any relevant measurement of value. It is unfortunate that the word *value* (i.e., book value) is used to describe the unallocated cost of an asset. If the allocation concept is accepted as the working definition of depreciation (a Generally Accepted Accounting Principle, or GAAP), then we can attempt to answer basic questions about depreciation.

Answers depend upon a set of underlying accounting assumptions and the degree to which these assumptions are met in the real world. Four basic assumptions help define the accounting framework.

The *entity assumption* forces one to recognize that to account for a set of happenings (transactions), limits must be established for the activity. These limits help decide which events should be included as a business activity and which should be excluded. The *business entity* is defined as an accounting unit that is separate and apart from the owners and their personal financial transactions. The transactions reflecting the acquisition of an asset, its use, and its retirement after its useful life need to be defined and recorded in relation to a specific entity.

The *time period assumption* says that for purposes of income determination, the life of an entity will be divided into time periods, often a year, for accounting purposes. This assumption creates problems in the area of fixed asset accounting, because the typical fixed asset has a useful life that extends over several of these one-year periods. Thus, to achieve matching and proper income, estimates of occurrences in future time periods are necessary.

The *going concern assumption* states that the entity will remain in business, and continue in business, into the future. Without this assumption, the currently employed concepts of depreciation, matching, and capital recovery would be meaningless. Valuation procedures applied under assumptions such as limited-term operations, joint ventures, or liquidation yield entirely different results than those obtained using the going concern assumption. If the entity expects a probable liquidation (i.e., the going concern assumption is not valid), the assets would be accounted for on the basis of estimated net realizable value in the marketplace, not historical cost. The ideas of cost allocation and capital recovery over time both assume that there is a future.

The *stable monetary unit assumption* holds that the dollars in all time periods are of equal purchasing power. In terms of a depreciation discussion, the assumption is that the dollars invested in an asset in the first period (acquisition cost) and the dollars recovered over the life of that asset are equal in purchasing power. Experience makes this a difficult assumption to accept.

Finally, though not one of the four basic assumptions, the *matching principle* needs to be introduced. "Accrual accounting" implies matching, and the matching principle necessitates the accrual process. The matching principle requires that all revenues earned during a given time period be matched with all the expenses incurred in that same time period to produce these revenues. The combination of these two elements results in a profit (if the revenues are greater than the expenses) or a loss (if the expenses are greater than the revenue). This process is usually called "income determination." Because of the capital-intensive nature of a public utility, depreciation is a major expense that must be calculated and brought into the matching process. Depreciation can now be defined as an "allocation process that operates within the bounds of the four basic assumptions to help accomplish income determination through matching."

Income depends on the amount of depreciation charged against the revenues in any period. Many methods of arriving at the annual depreciation charge have been developed, each providing a different amount of depreciation to be used in the matching process, and each resulting in a different amount of profit for the period. Which is the "correct," "fair," or "proper" choice? The answer may depend on your point of view. Stockholders, bondholders, consumers, regulators, and taxpayers each have a somewhat different idea of what the income ought to be. Each group makes that judgment based on its relationship to the entity. Many have been in the ambivalent position of being in two, or more, of these positions simultaneously. In the U.S. economic system it is not uncommon to be both a stockholder and a customer. The owners may want an accelerated approach that produces higher depreciation expense, lower taxable income, and faster capital recovery. But the effect on the cost of service caused by accelerating the depreciation may not appear desirable to the consumer. Because the "good" things for one group may be the "bad" things for another group, we will have continued disagreements over the "right" or "fair" method to obtain the annual accrual.

A common expectation of the depreciation system is that it will serve as a capital recovery method for the entity. Clarification is necessary at this point. Capital is recovered from revenues, and these revenues are generated by selling services. Depreciation is a noncash expense that allows the entity to retain in the business some of the revenues earned. If the revenues are adequate to cover all expenses, the amount retained will equal the amount of the depreciation expense for the period. In effect, the entity has then recovered some of the capital invested in the assets being depreciated. Because depreciation is a method of allocating historical cost, it will work as a capital recovery system if all the previous assumptions are true *and* if there are sufficient revenues in each period to cover the expenses. The depreciation system does not guarantee the adequacy of revenues to the entity, nor does it ensure against bad estimates of life or salvage that are an integral part of the depreciation calculation. Retirements earlier than estimated could mean, with group accounting, that the original cost is not recovered either by depreciation during the life or by salvage at the end of the life. Retirements later than estimated could mean that depreciation exceeds the original cost.

Depreciation, given reasonably accurate estimating procedures, will recover (when revenues are adequate) the historical costs through the allocation process. In an inflationary period, this process will not recover sufficient dollars of revenue to replace the asset when it is retired. To replace assets, capital must be recovered in terms of purchasing power. Current depreciation practices, based on original cost allocation (GAAP), will not do this task.

By examining the assumptions in the accounting model and determining where the assumptions do not hold and to what degree they do not hold, we can better understand why depreciation doesn't always work as expected. Estimates are needed for both the life of the asset and the net salvage at the end of that life, and in an uncertain world neither estimate is easy to make. Because the asset's life is longer than the accounting time period, the matching principle requires an estimate to allocate a portion of the asset cost to a specific period. If the estimate is wrong, either too long or too short, the wrong amount is charged to expense each year. If the estimate of recovery (salvage) at the end of the estimated life is wrong, then the amount allocated to each accounting period is also wrong.

Estimates of life and salvage are needed to calculate depreciation, and there will be errors, or differences, between the estimates and the actual values. The logical question, then, is, "How does the accountant compensate for these errors?" Periodic studies are necessary to decide if the current estimates of life and salvage are still reasonable or if new estimates should be used. The depreciation system should include a control mechanism that adjusts for previous accruals based on old estimates. A control mechanism that applied during the life of the asset is preferable to an adjustment that is delayed until retirement.

The first consideration for the improvement of the depreciation process should be an attempt to refine the estimating procedures for the three variables in the accrual calculation: life, gross salvage, and cost of retiring. A system of life analysis, supported by accurate historical data, provides the basis for estimating these three items.

Under GAAP, the depreciation accrual is calculated by dividing the *service cost* by the estimated useful life. The service cost component is the original historical cost minus the *net salvage*. Net salvage is the scrap value of the asset minus the related costs of retiring. Accountants have traditionally assumed net salvages to be either positive or zero. This is a simplifying assumption, and while not usually true in the real world, it was close enough for practical purposes. Note that the estimate of net salvage requires an estimate of both the residual value of the asset and the retirement costs of that asset at the *end* of the life. Often the residual value of the asset is near zero, but the retirement cost is significant. This results in negative net salvage. When the service cost is calculated as the original historical cost minus the negative net salvage, the result is a service cost factor to be allocated that is greater than the original cost. Accounting theory supports matching this total cost of using the asset against the revenues earned during the asset's life.

Negative salvage is a common occurrence. With inflation, the cost of retiring long-lived property, such as a water main, may exceed the original installed cost. Decommissioning cost of nuclear power plants is an example of large negative salvage. The matching principle specifies that all costs incurred to produce a service should be matched against the revenue produced. Estimated future costs of retiring of an asset currently in service must be accrued and allocated as part of the current expenses. While GAAP calls for accrual of such future costs, this accrual should not be hidden in the depreciation calculation. The charges to expense to provide for estimated future retirement costs may be best handled in a separate calculation and a separate subaccount. The accounting treatment of these future costs is clear. They are part of the current cost of using the asset and must be matched against revenue. While the current consumers would say they should not pay for future costs, it would be unfair to the future users if these costs were postponed. Some say that although the current consumers should pay for the future costs, the future value of the payments, calculated at some reasonable interest rate, should equal the retirement cost. Studies show that the salvage is often "more negative" than forecasters had predicted.

The matching principle requires accountants to make their best estimate of the cost of benefits of using a long-term fixed asset in any given time period. This estimate provides a better input into the profit calculation than would be obtained by expensing the asset at either the beginning or the end of its service. To paraphrase Hatfield (1936), the costs associated with providing the furnace are not different from the cost of the fuel consumed. The amounts charged to expense may be arrived at by different means, but they are all costs of the heat.

A depreciation system should be expected to recapture historical dollars only if the estimates are good and the revenues available. The dollars recovered through depreciation will not fund the replacement of the assets when the old ones are retired. Only in the most rare and unusual circumstances would the entity be able to replace the assets and maintain the same level of productive capacity with the historical cost dollar investment recovered through depreciation. Depreciation works as a capital recovery tool only in a limited sense. Given all the previous definitions and the related assumptions, it will work to recover the original historical cost of the investment. It will not recover the capital to replace assets and maintain productive capacity. Additional means of funding asset replacement must be employed.

ACCOUNTING MODELS

Depreciation accounting is one element of a much larger system of financial reporting that includes three required financial statements:

1. *Income statement:* a periodic statement of the results of operation over an accounting period that reports the revenues, expenses, gains, losses, net income, and earnings per share.
2. *Balance sheet:* a statement of financial position that reports the assets, liabilities, and owners' equity as of the end of an accounting period.

3. *Statement of cash flows:* a statement of the inflow of cash, outflow of cash, and net change in cash over an accounting period.

The financial information reported in the income statement, balance sheet, and statement of cash flows is commonly used to develop many comparative indicators of the financial condition, efficiency, and profitability of the reporting entity. It is important to understand how reporting of depreciation may affect each required financial statement and how financial statements can be used to evaluate the financial consequences of adopting alternative depreciation systems.

The basic accounting model can be viewed as three submodels, each of which represents one component of the three required financial statements. The three submodels are:

1. *Results of operations model:* a model of the income statement or statement of operating results given by

$$\text{Revenues} - \text{Expenses} = \text{Net Income}$$

2. *Financial position model:* a model of the basic content of a balance sheet or statement of financial position given by

$$\text{Assets} = \text{Liabilities} + \text{Owners' Equity}$$

3. *Cash flow model:* a model of the statement of changes in cash given by

$$\text{Net Change in Cash} = \text{Cash Inflow} - \text{Cash Outflow}$$

The results of operations model can be viewed as a change model; it describes the change in retained earnings over a specified period of operation. The financial position model, however, is not a change model; it describes the financial position of a reporting entity at a specific time. The cash flow model is a change model that describes the changes in assets, liabilities, and owners' equity (i.e., change in financial position over a specified period) measured in terms of cash flow.

The financial position model has been expressed in an algebraic format that describes the status of the resources (assets), obligations (liabilities), and residual equity (owners' equity) for a reporting entity at a specific time. Coupled with this algebraic format is an arithmetical technique known as the *debit–credit concept* that is used to report increases and decreases in specific variables in the model. The debit–credit concept can be superimposed on the algebraic model as follows:

Assets		=	Liabilities		+	Owners' Equity	
Debit for increases	Credit for decreases		Debit for decreases	Credit for increases		Debit for decreases	Credit for increases
+	−		−	+		−	+

Moreover, because revenues and investments by owners *increase* owners' equity, and expenses and withdrawals by owners *decrease* owners' equity, the algebraic model can be further expanded to include these elements. Thus,

Assets		=	Liabilities		+	Owners' Equity	
Debit for increases	Credit for decreases		Debit for decreases	Credit for increases		Debit for decreases	Credit for increases
+	−		−	+		−	+
						With- drawals by owner	Invest- ments by owner
						−	+

It is important to observe in the above diagram that debits are always on the left and credits are always on the right. But the increases and decreases are in opposite positions on each side of the equation. Thus debits represent increases to assets and decreases to liabilities and owners' equity, whereas credits represent decreases to assets and increases to liabilities and owners' equity.

Expenses are recorded as debits and revenues as credits. This algebraic arrangement forces the sum of all debits to equal the sum of all credits such that

$$\text{Assets} = \text{Liabilities} + \text{Owners' Equity} \quad \text{and}$$

$$\text{Debits} = \text{Credits}$$

This dual feature of the accounting model is often described as a *double entry system*.

ACCOUNTING FOR DEPRECIATION

Suppose a utility purchases a *utility device* for $1,000 including installation. A life of two years, a gross salvage of $100, and a cost of retiring of $300 are forecast. The depreciation professional has recommended a depreciation schedule of $700 the first year and $500 the second year. This section will follow the journal entries associated with the installation, use, and retirement of the utility device. Their effect on the accounting models also will be discussed.

Upon installation, a $1000 debit entry is made to the appropriate Plant in Service account. The specific Plant in Service account for utility devices is specified by the appropriate Uniform System of Accounts. The corresponding $1000 credit entry is to Cash, although under other circumstances the entry could be made to Accounts Payable, Construction Work in Progress, or Materials and Supplies.

The next two transactions are allocations of the initial cost. During the first year, a $700 debit is made to Depreciation Expense, and a $700 credit is made to Accumulated Provision for Depreciation. During the second year, a similar $500 transaction is made. After the $500 credit during the second year, the balance of Accumulated Provision for Depreciation is $700 + $500, or $1200.

The retirement of the utility device from service creates three transactions. First is a $1000 credit to Plant in Service, which offsets the initial $1000 debit. The $1000 debit entry is to Accumulated Provision for Depreciation, reducing the balance in that account from $1200 to $200. Second, the cost of retiring the unit from service results in a $300 debit to Accumulated Provision for Depreciation, leaving a balance of −$100. The $300 credit entry is to Cash (or Accounts Payable). Third, the $100 received for the scrapped unit is debited to Cash. The $100 credit entry is to Accumulated Provision for Depreciation, and results in a zero balance in that account.

Because our forecasts for life and net salvage proved accurate, the original cost of the asset, less net salvage, was recovered over its useful life. In this illustration, the net salvage was negative (i.e., −$200), so that a total of $1200 is recovered during the life of the property. Though we do not know the rationale behind the depreciation schedule of $700 and $500, we will assume this represents a reasonable match of expense to services rendered by the utility device.

How do these entries affect the three accounting models? The initial entry, debit the Plant in Service account and credit Cash, does not affect the operations model or the financial position model. Assets are shifted from Cash to Plant, but are unchanged. The cash flow model is affected because of the $1000 cash outflow.

The entries debiting Depreciation Expense and crediting Accumulated Provision for Depreciation affect the operations model. The net income from operations is reduced by the annual accrual for depreciation. The credit to Accumulated Provision for Depreciation reduces the *net* Plant in Service (i.e., the Plant in Service less Accumulated Provision for Depreciation, or the rate base), and this is reflected in the financial position model. The cash flow model is not affected by these transactions.

Finally, the unit is retired from service and salvage is accounted for. The entry crediting the Plant in Service account and debiting Accumulated Provision for Depreciation does not affect any of the three models. The entries reflecting cost of retirement and gross salvage affect only the cash flow model. In this illustration, the net affect on the cash flow model is a $200 cash outflow.

Note that the $1200 (i.e., $1000 + $300 − $100) cash outlay is fully recovered by the $700 and $500 accruals for depreciation. If the accruals had totaled less than $1200, then the financial position model would have been affected. After the first transaction, a debit balance would have remained in the Accumulated Provision for Depreciation. Thus, the net Plant in Service is overstated, so that an adjustment must be made to the asset side of the ledger. The financial position model requires that the owners' equity be reduced by an equal amount. This may have a significant affect on the various financial ratios used to evaluate the financial health of an organization.

CASH FLOW CONCEPTS

A statement of cash flows provides a measurement of the changes in assets, liabilities, and owners' equity over an accounting period in terms of the inflow and outflow of cash. The significance of this statement is that it requires the reporting of comprehensive information on the financing and investing activities of a reporting entity. Financing activities result in an inflow of resources and investing activities result in an outflow of resources. It is this inflow and outflow of financial resources that causes changes in the asset, liability, and owners' equity accounts over an accounting period.

Broadly speaking, commitments of capital to increase assets or decrease liabilities or owners' equity are applications of cash. In contrast, the freeing of capital through decreases in assets, or the additions of new capital through increases in liabilities or owners' equity, are sources of cash.

A simple and straightforward approach to gaining an understanding of how depreciation may affect the inflow and outflow of cash is to compare two balance sheets at the beginning and end of an accounting period. A tabulation of the changes in two balance sheets provides a basis for determining which of the cash flows (reflected by increases or decreases in assets, liabilities, and owners' equity) are sources and which are applications of cash.

The reason for showing depreciation as a "source" of cash (which is not revealed in a comparison of two balance sheets) can be understood by considering an income statement in which net income is zero. Assuming no other changes in financing or investing activities, cash or receivables is increased by the charge for depreciation and net plant is reduced by a corresponding amount. Thus, it would appear that a flow of cash has occurred by the recording of depreciation expense.

However, that depreciation expense is a noncash charge against income for the cost of operational assets acquired in the past. Depreciation, like all other expenses, reduces reported income, but the credit side of the accounting entry is to a noncurrent account (i.e., Accumulated Provision for Depreciation) that has no effect on cash or working capital. Showing net income as a source of cash implies that working capital is reduced by all operating expenses including depreciation. This misrepresentation can be corrected by adding back (or deducting) items recognized in determining income that did not use or provide working capital or cash during the accounting period. Thus, items such as depreciation expense, amortization expense, and deferred taxes are commonly shown as a source of funds from operations and labeled as "expenses not requiring an outlay of cash in the current period."

An alternative procedure that yields the same result is to start with revenue as the source of cash from operations and deduct only those operating expenses that require an outflow of cash. This approach has the advantage of not suggesting that "adjustments" to net income, such as depreciation, are sources of cash.

While the method of computation is unimportant, it cannot be overemphasized that depreciation is not a source of cash. In the first method, depreciation is added to net income to determine the cash derived from operations. But, it is operations (i.e., revenue less expenses requiring an outflow of cash or working capital) and not depreciation that provides the cash. Depreciation is neither a source nor an application of cash obtained from operations.

SUMMARY

The dictionary defines depreciation as a loss in value. Value can be measured in many ways. The valuation expert may use market value, replacement cost, reproduction cost, and even sentimental value as different approaches to establishing value. A study of the history of depreciation as applied to regulated public utilities reveals a narrowing of the meaning of depreciation to the allocation of cost concept. Some might call depreciation as defined earlier in this chapter *depreciation accounting* rather than depreciation. Nevertheless, an understanding of basic accounting is necessary to provide an understanding of what depreciation does and does not do.

2 | Data

I N the broad sense, *data* refers to any information that relates to or affects the estimation of depreciation. The topic of this chapter, however, is the data documenting the accounting transactions that increase or decrease the plant in service. These data are also called plant accounting data, service life data, life and salvage data, and retirement data. Most of these data are generated by work orders that are recorded in the continuing property records. With a computerized accounting system, the data are entered into an electronic data base. The data base provides input to software designed to provide indications of the life and salvage characteristics of the property. Another topic relating to data is the method used to price property at the time of its retirement (see Chapter 10).

The straight line, average life depreciation accrual is calculated by multiplying the plant in service times the rate $(1 - ASR)/AL$, where AL is average life and ASR is the average salvage ratio.[1] Examination of this calculation reminds us that we use life and salvage data both directly and indirectly. The plant in service is calculated directly from these data. Analysis of the life and salvage data yields indications of realized life and salvage. These indications are the basis for the estimates of AL and ASR that are used in the calculation of the accrual rate. This is an indirect use of the retirement data.

In the simple view of retirement data, there are only two transactions; units are either placed in service or retired from service. The plant in service at the start of the year is the source of all retirements, and balance at the end of the year is, using the simple view, the beginning of year balance less retirements during the year. With each retirement, there is an associated cost of retiring and, upon disposal, a gross salvage.

This simple view is not adequate to describe the actual transactions. Sales, acquisitions, transfers, and "nonregular" retirements are examples of other transactions that must be considered before constructing patterns of retirements and salvage that are helpful when estimating the averages used in the accrual rate. Occurrence of the transactions other than additions and regular retirements create two major challenges for the depreciation professional. First, the difference between the beginning and end of year balances can no longer be attributed to only regular retirements. The transactions, acquisitions, and transfers in will add to the balance during the year. If not properly accounted for, these particular transactions could produce an end of year balance that is greater than the beginning of year balance. This could result in indications that retirements are reversed, or that property is resurrected, during the year. These and other illogical outcomes can be avoided with the help of coding.

The second challenge hinges on the difference between analysis conducted to reflect what has taken place and analysis conducted to provide information used to help estimate life and salvage. When an analysis is conducted to provide information used to forecast life and salvage for accrual rates, not all transactions are treated equally. For example, historical records include retirements of insured units. Because the cost of these units is recovered through insurance payments, these retirements and their salvage should not be included in the estimates of the AL and ASR used in the accrual rate. The analyst should be able to specify which types of transaction are be included or excluded in any analysis. This requires coding the data.

CODING DATA

Coding is the process of categorizing each transaction and attaching an identifying code to it. The code allows the data to be checked for consistency and allows the analyst to include or exclude a specific category of transactions from an analysis.

Though more complicated systems are in use, this one-digit system containing 10 categories is an example of a workable system. The codes are as follows: code 0—regular retirement; code 1—reimbursed retirement; code 2—sale; code 3—transfer out; code 4—transfer in; code 5—acquisition; code 6—life span retirement; code 7—outlier retirement; code 8—balance at study data; code 9—additions or initial balance.

Regular retirement—code 0. A regular retirement occurs at the end of the useful life and excludes transactions classified as a reimbursed retirement, a sale, a transfer out, a life span retirement, or an outlier. Regular retirements are the most common transaction. They are included in an analysis to estimate the life of property whose investment is recovered through depreciation accruals.

Regular retirements are sometimes classified as either location (reusable) retirements or final retirements. The retirement of a unit of property that will be reused poses a special problem for the depreciation professional. If location life is used in the accrual rate, then the salvage ratio must also be based on location life. Thus, the unit that is retired and returned to stock to be used again must be assigned a gross salvage value. One rule is to assign salvage equal to 100% of the original cost. Consider a unit that was installed new and remained in service at the same location for 10 years. Then it was retired from that location and installed in a second location. After six years, it was retired from service at the second location. After retirement from the second location, the unit was scrapped rather than returned to stock for reuse. The net salvage at the time of its second and final retirement was zero. The "whole life" is 16 years and "whole life salvage ratio" is 0%. The average location life is (10 + 6)/2, or 8 years. If a salvage of 100% of the initial cost is assigned at the time the unit is retired from the first location, the average location life salvage ratio is (100% + 0%)/2, or 50%. Note that with either whole life or location life, the accrual rate is the same, 6.25%, i.e., 100%/16, or (100% − 50%)/8.

Multiple installations and the associated installation costs and methods of pricing reused units yielding current rather the original cost complicate capital recovery when location life is used. The use of "cradle to grave" accounting (i.e., use of whole life rather than location life) is an alternative when property is reused. Under this method, accounting location moves would not be recorded as retirements and salvage. If they are recorded, the cradle to grave effect can be achieved by considering the location salvage as a reverse retirement. Cradle to grave accounting is often favored because it is simpler than location life and avoids pricing and salvage problems created when location life is used. These advantages often result in better forecasts of life and salvage than if location life had been used.

Reimbursed retirement—code 1. A reimbursed retirement is one for which the company is fully compensated at the time of retirement, usually because the retirement occurred earlier than normal as the result of an unusual event. Compensation may be from insurance, from the party who damaged the utility by causing the retirement, or from an individual or public authority who desired or required the relocation or abandonment of the retired property. Usually reimbursed retirements should not be included in analysis to estimate the life and salvage of property whose original investment is recovered through depreciation accruals.

Sale — code 2. A retirement caused by a sale is one in which the property is not retired from service, but continues in the same service under a new owner. Typically, the sold property has not reached its normal service life and is sold for at least the book value. The sale is made to a similar company and the property continues to be used in the same or similar manner as before the sale. Because the original cost is recovered primarily via the sale, these retirements are not normally included in an analysis to estimate the life and salvage of property whose original cost is recovered through depreciation accruals.

Transfer out — code 3. A transfer out is the retirement of property from one depreciable group and concurrent assignment (i.e., transfer in) to another depreciable group. This is an accounting transaction and the property is not physically altered or removed from service. Transfers out should not be included in an analysis to estimate the life of property whose original cost is recovered through depreciation.

Transfer in — code 4. A transfer in increases the plant balance and is the result of a transfer out from another account. This code can be eliminated by defining code 3 as *Transfers*. Then a transfer out would be a code 3 with a negative value assigned to the transaction and a transfer in would be a code 3 with a positive value assigned to the transaction.

Acquisition — code 5. An acquisition results in an increase in the plant in service caused by the purchase of property from a company providing similar service. A sale for one company results in an acquisition for another. The preferred treatment, when possible, is to merge the aged data from the acquired property with the aged data for the account to which the property is added. If the record of aged data is not available, the acquired balance is incorporated into the data. If the balance is not aged, it may be necessary to statistically age the data or keep it separate from the aged data.

Life span retirement — code 6. A life span retirement is the final retirement in a life span group (see Chapter 13). This coding allows interim retirements, which are coded as regular retirements, to be analyzed separately from the final retirements. The analyst is then better able to estimate a) the interim retirement survivor curve and b) the date of the final retirement. Life span retirements must be included in analysis to estimate the life of property whose original cost is recovered through depreciation accruals.

Outlier retirement — code 7. An outlier retirement is a retirement that results from an unusual occurrence and should be excluded from consideration when forecasting service life. If the occurrence, although unusual, is one that can be expected to reoccur from time to time, the retirement should be coded as a regular retirement. If the cause of the occurrence no longer exists, then it is appropriate to code it as an outlier and exclude it from analysis when forecasting service life. The outlier retirement must be included when determining realized and average service life.

Examples of causes of retirement that can result in an outlier retirement include natural disasters such as severe floods or earthquakes and management decisions associated with a merger or a modernization program. The outlier code allows the analyst the opportunity to study the historical data with and without the outlier, so that he or she is better able to make an appropriate forecast.

Balance at Study Data — code 8. When retirements are aged, the balance at the study date will show the age distribution (i.e., the amount remaining in service by vintage). This distribution should correspond to the age distribution resulting from netting the additions (code 9) and the other transactions (codes 0 through 7).

Additions or initial balance — code 9. Additions are the property installed new during the placement year and represent the initial balance of each new vintage. If the record of aged retirements does not go back to the year during which the property was installed, then an initial balance is required. The initial balance shows the portion of the total balance allocated to each vintage. Creating the initial balance may require a physical inventory of the plant in service.

Recording errors will be made and they must be corrected. A change of the age caused by improper retirement date is made by reversing the original entry and adding the corrected data. If the error was not in the actual entry but was caused by a discrepancy in a prior year, a third date, the adjusted transaction year, should be included with the data. Such a record permits balancing the books while using the data as corrected. As it is not a Generally Accepted Accounting Principle to allow changes in prior years' records except by adjustments in the current year, the additional entry is required. It may be difficult to identify the transaction responsible for a discrepancy in the data. In this case, judgment is required to determine the transaction most likely to be responsible for the error.

The retirement ratio equals the retirements during the age interval divided by the exposures at the start of the age interval. The retirements include regular retirements plus the other retirements (i.e., reimbursed retirements, life span retirements, outlier retirements, and sales) that the depreciation professional believes are appropriate when considering the purpose of the analysis. The computer program used to analyze the life and salvage data must accommodate the particular coding system used.

A consistent and logical scheme for developing retirement ratios from coded retirement data must be developed. A helpful rule is that *exposures at the start of the age interval must be subject to retirement during the age interval.* Conversely, *retirements during the age interval must be exposed to retirement at the start of the age interval.* Usually an age interval is one year, and a natural convention is to assume that transactions occurring during the year take place at midyear. This leads to the following dilemma. Suppose a transaction increases the balance (i.e., an acquisition). If the acquired plant is included in exposures at the start of the year, then during the first six months the plant is exposed to, but not subject to, retirement. If the acquired plant is not included in the exposures until the end of the year, then during the final six months of the year it is possible to have retirements that are not included in the exposures. Thus, any convention adopted will result in misrepresentation of the retirement ratio.

Transactions that occur during the age interval and decrease the balance of the exposures in the account are included as exposures at the start of the year. Thus, no adjustment to the balance at the start of the age interval is required. Suppose an account has a balance of $1000 at the start of a year. During the year $50 is retired and coded as a regular retirement, and $100 is transferred out of the account. The transfers out are included in the exposures for the group from which they are transferred, so $1000 is exposed to retirement. Only the regular retirements are counted as retirements, so the retirement ratio for the year is 50/1000 or 5%.

One convention for transactions that occur during the age interval and increase the balance in the account is to add them to the exposures at the end of the age interval. Thus, no adjustment to the balance at the start of the age interval is required. To continue the example in the preceding paragraph, the transfer out transaction results in a $100 transfer in that increases the balance in a second account. The $100 transfer in is not included in the exposures until the end of the year, with the result that the transferred units are exposed to retirement exactly once. This convention can yield peculiar results. Suppose the transaction increasing the balance of the account is large when compared to the balance at the start of the interval (e.g., the transaction is a major acquisition). As a result of the transaction, suppose the regular retirements during the age interval *exceed* the balance at the beginning of the age interval. The resulting retirement ratio will be larger than one. Mathematically this will result in a survivor curve with a negative percent surviving. If the retirement ratio is arbitrarily set equal to one, the survivor curve will go to zero but property will remain in service. To prevent these results, adopt the convention that transactions that occur during the age interval and increase the balance in the account will be included in the exposures at the *start* of the age interval. Typically the transactions will be small when compared to the balances, and the survivor curves generated from these data will be insensitive to the convention used.

Use of the second convention yields more reasonable results in those cases when the transactions are large when compared to starting balance.

Although reimbursed retirements, sales, and transfers out are not included as exposures after the year of the transaction, they are included in the exposures in all previous years. During those years, the property was subject to regular retirement even though it was not retired. The exposures are increased, the retirement ratios are decreased, and the realized life is increased. Thus, the survival of units contributes to the indications of life.

The transactions including regular retirements, reimbursed retirements, life span retirements, sales, and outlier retirements can create salvage. When a transaction is coded, care must be taken to ensure the retirement and associated salvage are assigned the same code. The same codes should be included when analyzing life and salvage, because the estimates of life and salvage act together in the accrual rate.

The total cost concept should be considered when developing depreciation systems. The benefits resulting from the use of accurate depreciation accrual rates should not exceed the cost of generating those rates. Though the benefits of accuracy may be difficult to quantify, the magnitude of the cost of inaccurate depreciation accrual rates can be estimated, as can the potential savings caused by better estimates. The costs of generating depreciation accrual rates are relatively easy to estimate because they are primarily the salaries and overhead costs attributable to the depreciation staff or consultants.

The cost of gathering retirement data accounts for a significant portion of the cost of a study. The cost saved by gathering less data is realized immediately, while the benefits gained from gathering more data may not be realized for several years. Thus, managers must evaluate their options carefully. Decisions based entirely on short-range goals may not be the best decisions in the long run.

NOTE

1. This is the annual accrual using the SL-AL-VG system described in Chapter 5.

3 | Survivor Curves

$\mathbf{T}$HE *service life* of industrial property can be defined as the period of time from its installation until it is retired from service. Often service life, or more simply *the life,* is thought of as a single number, such as "the building has a life of 41 years." When dealing with a group of property containing many individual units, a single number becomes an inadequate description of the life characteristics of the property. With a large group of units we would expect to see a wide dispersion of life, with some units being retired soon after their installation and others providing many years of service before retirement. A complete description of life requires a description of the pattern of retirements as the property ages.

Those who first investigated life characteristics of industrial property drew on the models and vocabulary of the early actuarial scientists. A group of property installed during the same accounting period is analogous to a group of humans born during the same calendar year. A certain fraction of those born will die as infants, and the term *infant mortality* has been used to describe the retirement of industrial property soon after its installation. Deaths from the group will continue as time passes until there are no survivors. Description of the exact pattern of mortality is the task of the actuarial scientist, and this information is used to determine life insurance rates and design pension plans.

The life characteristics of industrial property can be completely described by any one of three mathematical functions: the retirement frequency curve, the survivor curve, and the retirement ratio curve. Each of these curves is dependent on the other two. That is, if one curve is known, the other two can be obtained. These curves provide the information neces-

21

sary to define the average life, probable life, equal life groups, expectancy, and other values required by various systems of depreciation.

CHARACTERISTICS OF SERVICE LIFE

To develop a simple example showing the life characteristics of industrial property, imagine a group of 100 identical units of property that are placed in service during the same year. This is a *homogeneous group of property* because all units in the group are identical.

Age Intervals

The life has been defined as the time from installation to retirement from service, but conventions must be adopted to obtain consistent statistics. A common convention is to assume that any unit installed during the year is installed on July 1, that is, at the middle of the calendar year. This is equivalent to assuming the units are installed uniformly during the year, because this would result in an average installation date at midyear. Units retired before the end of the first year will be said to have been retired at age 0.25 years, while units remaining in service at the end of the year will have reached an age of 0.5 years. These assumptions are called the *half-year convention*. Adoption of the half-year convention leads to definition of age intervals 0–0.5 years, 0.5–1.5 years, 1.5–2.5 years, through the interval containing the maximum life, with midpoints of 0.25 years, 1 year, 2 years, and extending to the maximum life. These age intervals are stated in general terms and are shown below. It is convenient to use the index i to refer to an age interval and to denote the midpoint of age interval i by the value x(i). Any unit retired during the age interval i will be assumed to have a life equal to x(i). The symbol ML represents the midpoint of the final age interval and is called the *maximum life*.[1] Use of the half-year convention results in, with the exception of the first age interval, midpoints equal to integer values with the index for an age interval equal to the midpoint.

Index	Age	Midpoint
i	Interval i	x(i)
0	0 ≤ Service Life < 0.5	0.25
1	0.5 ≤ Service Life < 1.5	1
2	1.5 ≤ Service Life < 2.5	2
•		•
•		•
ML	(ML − 0.5) ≤ Service Life < (ML + 0.5)	ML

This convention will be used throughout this text unless otherwise noted.

Frequency Curves

The *retirement frequency curve* is a graph of the frequency of retirements as a function of age. The retirement frequency is the ratio of retirements during an age interval to the original number of units installed and can be expressed as either a fraction or as a percentage. Of the 100 units in our example, suppose that the longest-lived unit was retired during the age interval 2.5–3.5 years so that the following four age intervals are necessary to describe the life characteristics.

Index	Age	Midpoint
i	Interval i	x(i)
0	$0 \leq$ Service Life < 0.5	0.25
1	$0.5 \leq$ Service Life < 1.5	1
2	$1.5 \leq$ Service Life < 2.5	2
3	$2.5 \leq$ Service Life < 3.5	3

Of the 100 units, 20 were retired during the age interval 0, 40 during age interval 1, 30 during age interval 2, and the final 10 during age interval 3. The calculations for the retirement frequency curve, Figure 3.1, are

$$f(0) = (20/100)100\% = 20\%$$
$$f(1) = (40/100)100\% = 40\%$$
$$f(2) = (30/100)100\% = 30\%$$
$$f(3) = (10/100)100\% = \underline{10\%}$$
$$100\%$$

where f(i) = the retirement frequency during age interval i. Each frequency must be positive and the sum of the frequencies must total 100%, because all property must be accounted for.

Survivor Curves

The *survivor curve* is a graph of the percent of units remaining in service expressed as a function of age. The survivor curve could be obtained by recording the number of units remaining in service at the start of each age interval. Or, if the frequency curve is known, the percent surviving at the end of an age interval can be obtained by subtracting the percent retired during the interval from the percent surviving at the start of the interval. Conversely, the frequency curve can be obtained by subtracting successive

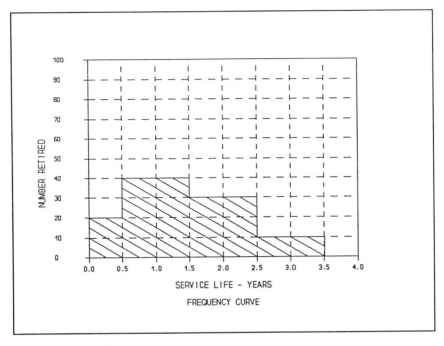

Figure 3.1. The frequency curve.

points on the survivor curve. The survivor curve for the example is shown in Figure 3.2 and is calculated from the retirement frequencies as shown below.

$$S(0) = 100\%$$
$$S(1) = S(0) - f(0) = 100\% - 20\% = 80\%$$
$$S(2) = S(1) - f(1) = 80\% - 40\% = 40\%$$
$$S(3) = S(2) - f(2) = 40\% - 30\% = 10\%$$
$$S(4) = S(3) - f(3) = 10\% - 10\% = 0\%$$

where $S(i)$ = percent of original installations remaining in service at the beginning of age interval i.

The survivor curve starts at 100% and, because the retirement frequencies must be positive or zero, the survivor curve can never be increasing. The points on the curve are connected with a straight line reflecting the assumption that retirements occur uniformly throughout the age interval.

Survivor curves also can be expressed in terms of either units or dollars surviving. The units or dollars surviving can be converted to the fraction

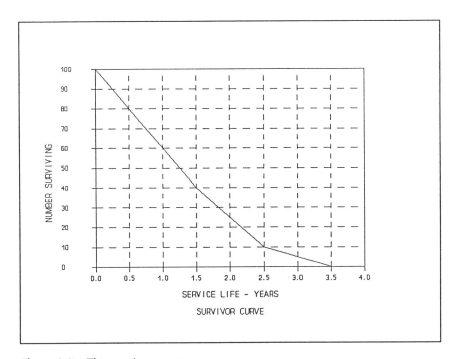

Figure 3.2. The survivor curve.

surviving by dividing by the number of units or dollars originally installed; this fraction is often expressed as a percentage.

Retirement Ratio Curves

The *retirement ratio curve* is a graph of the retirement ratio as a function of age and can be calculated by dividing the number of retirements during an age interval by the exposures, or the number of units in service, at the start of the age interval. The ratio of retirements to exposures is analogous to dividing the retirement frequency during age interval i by the fraction surviving at the start of age interval i. This ratio can be thought of as the probability that a unit that has survived until the start of a specific age interval will be retired during that age interval. The calculations for the retirement ratio curve (Figure 3.3) are

$$r(0) = f(0)/S(0) = 20\%/1.00 = \ \ 20\%$$
$$r(1) = f(1)/S(1) = 40\%/\ .80 = \ \ 50\%$$
$$r(2) = f(2)/S(2) = 30\%/\ .40 = \ \ 75\%$$
$$r(3) = f(3)/S(3) = 10\%/\ .10 = 100\%$$

where r(i) = retirement ratio for age interval i.

If a unit is not retired during the age interval, then it must still be in service at the end of the interval. The ratio of units in service at the start of the age interval i to the units in service at the end of the age interval i is equal to 1 − r(i) and is called the survivor ratio.

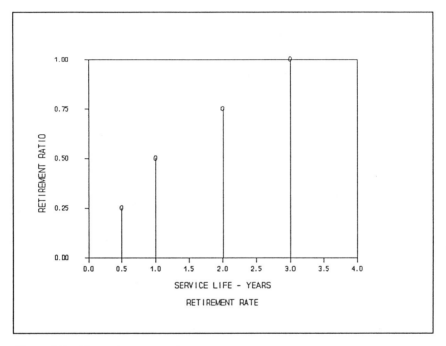

Figure 3.3. The retirement ratio curve.

The percent surviving at age zero, S(0), is 100%. The remaining points on the survivor curve can be calculated from the retirement ratio curve by using the equation S(i + 1) = S(i)[1 − r(i)]. This equation states that the percent surviving at the end of age interval i, that is, S(i + 1), equals the percent surviving at the start of the age interval, that is, S(i), multiplied by the survivor ratio for the interval. This calculation is of particular importance because it is regularly used in the calculation of life tables and it is shown below for our example.

Age Interval	Retirement Ratio	Survivor Ratio	% Surviving at Beg. of Age Interval	
0	0.20	0.80		100%
1	0.50	0.50	100% × 0.80 =	80%
2	0.75	0.25	80% × 0.50 =	40%
3	1.00	0.00	40% × 0.25 =	10%
4	—	—	10% × 0.00 =	0%

The retirement ratio must be between 0 and 1 and the ratio during the final age interval is 1. Retirement ratios tend to increase with age, though it is possible for them to remain constant or decrease during the life of the property. Both $f(i)$ and $r(i)$ describe activities that occur during age interval i, while $S(i)$ describes a condition at the start of age interval i.

Each of these three curves contains the same information presented in a different form. If any curve is known, the other two can be calculated. Historically, the survivor curve has been widely used to present life data and is of particular importance for that reason. Retirement ratios are significant because of their importance during the construction of life tables, where these ratios are created directly from the assembled data and used to calculate the corresponding survivor curve. The frequency curve is perhaps the easiest curve to understand. The widely used system of Iowa curves names the individual curves by the shape of their frequency curve.

Units versus Dollars

Property grouped for accounting purposes may be functionally similar but display a wide range of physical characteristics. In contrast to our example of a homogeneous group of property, the property in a typical accounting group consists of many different types of equipment and components. It may be possible to subdivide accounting groups into subaccounts and obtain smaller, more homogeneous groups. For example, office furniture and equipment accounts have included computers; experience would lead us to expect that the life characteristics of office desks and chairs differ from the life characteristics of computers. Division of the account into a subaccount including office desks and chairs and a subaccount including computers separates the nonsimilar property and creates groups that are more homogeneous than the original. In general, the more homogeneous the group of property, the more descriptive the life analysis and the more accurate the forecast.

If a group contains units with significantly different characteristics, then each unit should be weighted according to its importance. The most common weight given to units is dollars, so that although retirements are reported in units, as in our example, their importance is often measured in dollars. Then the percent surviving is determined by the ratio of dollars retired divided by the total dollars installed. It can be argued that because it is dollars, not units, that are the object of capital recovery, dollars are a better measure than units for use in depreciation calculations.

Average Service Life

The average life of the property can be calculated from the frequency curve by using the equation

$$AL = E(\text{life}) = \Sigma x(i)f(i)/100\% \qquad \text{for } i = 1,2,3, \ldots, ML$$

Notice that the frequency is divided by 100% to convert it to a fraction. For our example the average life is AL = (.25)(.20) + (1)(.40) + (2)(.30) + (3)(.10) = 1.35 years.

The symbol E(life) is read *expected life* and is also called the *average life*. There is a direct relationship between the survivor curve and the average life; the area beneath the survivor curve equals the average life. Because the survivor curve is measured in percent, the area under the curve must be divided by 100% to convert it from percent-years to years. The area under the survivor curve and between ages of 0–0.5 years is calculated by multiplying the average height of the curve times the width of the interval or [(1.0 + 0.8)/2](0.5) = 0.45 years. The areas under the next three intervals, each of which has a width of 1 year, are (0.8 + 0.4)/2 = 0.6, (0.4 + 0.1)/2 = 0.25, and (0.1 + 0)/2 = 0.05 respectively. Their sum is 0.45 + 0.6 + 0.25 + 0.05 = 1.35 years, which is consistent with the previous calculation. These calculations are shown graphically in Figure 3.4.

Another average that is used frequently in depreciation calculations is the expectancy, which is a function of the age. The expectancy of a unit of property is simply its remaining years of service. The expectancy of a group of units is the average number of remaining years of service of the surviving property and is calculated as follows

$$RL(i) = E(\text{remaining life at beginning of age interval } i)$$
$$RL(i) = \Sigma\,[(x(k) - i)f(x)/100\%]/S(i) \qquad \text{for } k = i, i+1, \ldots, ML$$

At age 1.5 years, the expectancy of our example property is [(2 − 1.5)(0.3) + (3 − 1.5)(0.1)]/0.4 = 0.75 years. This is also equal to the area under the survivor curve and to the right of the age 1.5 years divided by the percent surviving at age 1.5 years. Thus, this remaining service (i.e., the area under the curve) is allocated among the units remaining in service (i.e., the per-

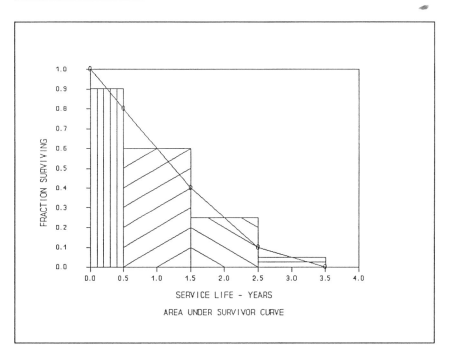

Figure 3.4. The area under the survivor curve.

cent surviving). This calculation is $[(0.4 + 0.1)/2 + (0.1 + 0)/2]/0.4 = 0.3/0.4 = 0.75$ years.

The terms *expectancy* and *average remaining life* are both commonly used to describe the E(remaining life at beginning of age interval i). The term average remaining life, which is often shortened to *remaining life*, is more descriptive and will be used in this text. The term *probable life* is used to describe the total life expectancy of the property surviving at any age and is equal to the remaining life plus the current age. The remaining life and probable life of the example property are shown below.

Age	% Surviving	Area under Curve, Right of Age, % – Years	Remaining Life, Years	Probable Life, Years
0.0	100%	135	1.35	1.35
0.5	80%	90	1.125	1.625
1.5	40%	30	0.75	2.25
2.5	10%	5	0.50	3.00
3.5	0%	0	. . .	. . .

At age zero the average life, the remaining life, and the probable life are equal.

Table 3.1 shows an example of property with service lives ranging from zero years to a maximum life of 9.5 years. This particular pattern of retirements is called an Iowa R2 curve. Column (a) shows the age at the beginning of the age interval. Note that the width of the first age interval is 0.5 years and that all other intervals are 1 year wide. The final interval is 8.5–9.5 years; after 9.5 years all property has been retired. Column (b) shows the survivors at the beginning of the age interval expressed as a percentage of the original installations; the percent surviving at age zero is defined to be 100%. Column (c) shows the frequency curve, or the percentage of the original installations retired during each age interval. The sum of the frequencies is 100%.

Table 3.1.   The life characteristics of an Iowa R2 type curve. The percent surviving, remaining life, and probable life are given at the beginning of the age interval while the frequency and retirement ratios are averages during the interval.

Age interval (a)	Surviving % (b)	Frequency % (c)	Retirement ratio % (d)	% Years service (e)	Remaining life yrs (f)	Probable life yrs (g)
0 - 0.5	100.00	1.11	1.11	500.21	5.00	5.00
0.5 - 1.5	98.89	3.56	3.60	450.49	4.56	5.06
1.5 - 2.5	95.33	6.20	6.50	353.38	3.71	5.21
2.5 - 3.5	89.13	10.12	11.35	261.15	2.93	5.43
3.5 - 4.5	79.01	15.31	19.38	177.08	2.24	5.74
4.5 - 5.5	63.70	20.30	31.87	105.72	1.66	6.16
5.5 - 6.5	43.40	21.08	48.57	52.17	1.20	6.70
6.5 - 7.5	22.32	14.99	67.16	19.31	.87	7.37
7.5 - 8.5	7.33	6.51	88.81	4.49	.61	8.11
8.5 - 9.5	.82	.82	100.00	.41	.50	9.00
9.5 -10.5	.00					

Column (d) shows the retirement ratio curve. As the property ages, the chance of surviving property being retired during the next age interval tends to increase. At age 8.5 years, the start of the final age interval, the retirement ratio is 100%. All property in service at the start of that age interval will be retired during that final period. Column (e) shows the area under the survivor curve and to the right of the age at the beginning of the interval. This is most easily understood by examining the column from the bottom up. The final portion of the curve starts at 0.82% surviving and ends at zero, forming a right triangle with a height of 0.82, a base of 1 year, and a resulting area of (0.82 × 1)/2 or 0.41 percent-years, the final entry in column (e). During age interval 7.5–8.5 years, the curve declines from 7.33% to 0.82%. The area under this section of the curve is equal to the average height, (7.33 + 0.82)/2 or 4.075 multiplied by the base of 1, which when added to the area under the curve in the age interval 8.5–9.5 years equals 4.075 + 0.41 or 4.485, which when rounded to 2 decimal places equals the next-to-last table entry of 4.49 percent-years. Continuation of this process results in an area equal to 500.21 percent-years at age zero, or an average life of 5.0 years.[2] Note that the mode, or highest frequency, occurs during the age interval 5.5–6.5 years, which is to the right of the average life, so this is called a *right modal curve*. The remaining life, shown in column (f), is column (e) divided by column (b). At age zero, the remaining life includes all future retirements, so the remaining life and average life are both 5.0 years. The remaining life declines as the property ages, and property still in service at the start of the final age interval can be expected to, on the average, last 0.5 years. Column (g), the probable life, is the remaining life plus the age. Figure 3.5 shows the relationship of these characteristics. To read the probable life at 5.5 years, find the corresponding point on the survivor curve, about 45%. Now move horizontally to the right to the probable life curve. The probable life is the age corresponding to 45% on the probable life curve, or about 7 years.

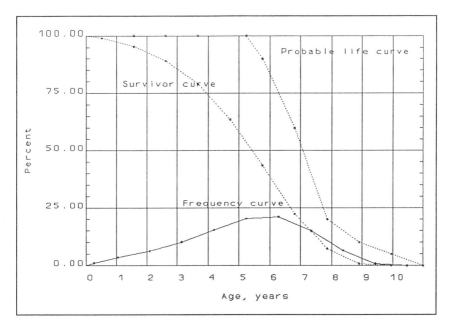

Figure 3.5. Graphs of the survivor curve, the frequency curve, and the probable life curve shown in Table 3.1.

SERVICE LIFE AS A CONTINUOUS RANDOM VARIABLE

We describe life as a continuous variable in this section, which is for those with an interest in mathematical statistics. Others can skip to the next section. So far, the life has been treated as a discrete random variable with values limited to 0.25, 1, 2, . . . to ML, and this reflects the manner in which data is collected. Development of survivor curves requires life be treated as a continuous random variable so that standard techniques of mathematical statistics can be applied.

The function f(x) is called the probability density function of x; f(x) must be nonnegative and its integral over the range 0 to maximum life must equal 1.

$$\int_0^{ML} f(x)dx = 1$$

The probability that a unit will be retired during the interval i is

$$\text{Probability } (i - 1/2 \le \text{service life} < i + 1/2) = \int_{i-1/2}^{i+1/2} f(x)dx$$

The survivor curve is

S(k) = Probability (service life is greater than k)

$$= \int_k^{ML} f(x)dx = 1 - \int_0^k f(x)dx = 1 - F(k)$$

The integral of f(x) over the range 0 to k is called the *cumulative density function* and denoted as F(k). The expectation or average life is defined as

$$E(x) = \int_0^{ML} xf(x)dx$$

and the area under the survivor curve is

$$\text{Area} = \int_0^{ML} [1 - F(x)]dx = \{x[1 - F(x)]\}_0^{ML} - \int_0^{ML} x[-f(x)]dx$$

$$= \int_0^{ML} xf(x)dx = E(x)$$

Given the set of intervals previously defined, the average retirement rate during the interval i to i + t is

$$E[r(i)] = \int_i^{i+t} f(x)dx/S(i)$$

Note that the numerator is the probability of retirement during the period i to i + t. The equation describing the instantaneous retirement rate at time x is often called the *hazard function* and is denoted as h(x). The hazard function is the slope of the survivor curve at time x divided by the fraction surviving at time x. The slope must be negative, and this accounts for the sign in the equation h(x) = [−dS(x)/dx][1/S(x)].

Calculation of the expectancy or remaining life at age k is

$$E(x/x = i) = \int_i^{ML} xf(x)dx/S(i)$$

The difficulty of performing these calculations depends on the complexity of the function f(x), and numerical integration may be required.

SURVIVOR CURVE MODELS

Survivor curve models are widely used to simplify life analysis and forecasting. A survivor curve model can be expressed as a mathematical equation that defines the percent surviving as a function of age. An important use of survivor curve models is to improve the communication of the information describing the life characteristics of industrial property. Without the help of the model, the shape of an observed survivor curve can only be described by examination of the individual points defining the survivor curve. With the aid of a survivor curve model, the life characteristics can be conveyed in a few words or symbols.

There are two general approaches to developing survivor curve models, and both have been successfully used. One approach is to develop a mathematical equation, or model, that describes the frequency, survivor, or retirement ratio curve as a function of age. This is a common scientific approach, and Newton's second law of motion, F = ma, is a simple example of a model that shows the relationship between force, mass, and acceleration. In life analysis, the Gompertz-Makeham equation describes the forces of retirement as a function of age and has been used to model life characteristics.

The second approach is the empirical method, which has also been widely used in science and engineering. This involves the gathering of data that contain information about the subject under investigation. These data are analyzed and generalizations made. Models, based on observed data, are then developed. The system of Iowa curves is the result of this approach.

In either case, the resulting model must be verified by its application and proven usefulness. Both the Iowa curve and Gompertz-Makeham models have been used successfully over long periods of time.

The Iowa Curves

Development of the curves began at the Iowa Engineering Experiment Station at what was then Iowa State College, in Ames, Iowa. Much of the early work was done under the supervision of Anson Marston, director of the Experiment Station and dean of the College of Engineering. In 1916, Edwin Kurtz, then a student at the University of Wisconsin, began to assemble data relating to the life characteristics of industrial property. He started work for the Experiment Station in 1921 and a year later was joined in his research by Robley Winfrey, a young civil engineer also employed by the Experiment Station. In 1924 the Experiment Station published in *Bulletin 70* observed life data from 52 groups of utility property. Next Kurtz (1930) described methods of compiling mortality tables and frequency curve models.

Bulletin 103 by Winfrey and Kurtz (1931) contained the forerunners to the Iowa type curves. The purpose of *Bulletin 103* is described as follows:

> The following pages present a method of calculating the mortality curve, the probable life curve, and the rate of renewals of particular examples and types of physical equipment. The method has been applied to 65 sets of original life data for property found in the following industries. . . .
>
> The 13 type curves can be used as valuable aids in forecasting the probable future service lives of individual items and of groups of items of different kinds of physical equipment. (P. 5)

The use of these curves, although recommended, was qualified:

> In view of these natural changes in character of equipment and conditions of service, mortality curves based upon the records of equipment may not give accurate pictures of what may be expected in the way of service of new equipment — equipment used to replace old items as they are retired. However, these records should indicate the general trends and when *intelligently interpreted,* offer an exceedingly valuable aid in the estimation of the service which may be expected from physical equipment. (P. 6, emphasis added.)

A total of 65 property groups were examined, and frequency and survivor curves were calculated for each group. Because the average and maximum life of the curves vary over a wide range of years, the average life was set to 100% and the curves were redrawn using an abscissa of age as a percent of average life, rather than years. The curves were then compared and the following observations were made.

> The comparison brought out three distinguishing characteristics: location of the mode (the point of maximum ordinate) relative to the average life, magnitude of the mode, and the maximum age in percent of the average life. The curves were then classified into three groups according to whether the mode was to the left, approximately coincident, or to the right of the average life, and these three groups subclassified according to the magnitude of the mode. The classification, which was almost wholly by inspection, resulted in 13 groups or types, four groups having the mode to the left of the average life, five groups having the mode to the right of the average life. (P. 27)

Next the data were smoothed by fitting them to one of the 12 types of curves developed by the statistician Karl Pearson. Professor A. W. Snedecor, who became well known for his statistical work, provided assistance with the fitting.

Winfrey continued to gather and analyze data. In 1935 he wrote *Statistical Analysis of Industrial Property Retirements, Bulletin 125,* and it became the basic reference on life analysis. Additional data, the bulk of which was from public utilities, had been gathered and the number of property groups examined now totaled 176. Types of property included waterworks boilers, telegraph and electrical poles, railroad cars, various types of crossties, farm equipment, trucks, watt hour meters, gas meters, power transformers, pavement, and culverts. Analysis of this additional data resulted in the addition of 6 more curves to bring the total to 6 left modal curves, 7 symmetrical curves, and 5 right modal curves. These became known as the Iowa curves. The *Bulletin* contains the source of the original data, the equations of the curves, tables of the curves, and a discussion of the procedures used to analyze this data. Winfrey also discussed five methods of constructing survivor curves from aged data. In the following years, Winfrey applied the Iowa curves to a wide variety of property in many parts of the world.

Harold A. Cowles (1967) revised *Bulletin 125* to correct some errors in the tables and to add 4 origin modal models, or O type curves, developed by a graduate student, Frank Couch. The original data suggested the presence of these types of curves, but they were not included in earlier publications because of the low frequency with which they occurred. Couch fit these curves and they form Appendix D of the revised *Bulletin 125.*

Winfrey (1942) also wrote *Depreciation of Group Properties, Bulletin 155*. In it he discussed various methods of group depreciation and introduced the unit summation method of depreciation, which later became known as the equal life group (ELG) method.

The appendix of *Bulletin 155* contains tables of the percent surviving and probable life of the 18 Iowa type curves. These tables contain revisions to the tables in *Bulletin 125*. Although these changes are small and mostly in the R2 and R3 type curves, only the appendix of *Bulletin 155* contains the correct values of the 18 original Iowa type curves; these tables are tabulated at 5% intervals. The appendix of this book contains tables in which the equations are evaluated at 1% intervals. These tables are reproduced from original notes of Winfrey and are consistent with the values from *Bulletin 155*. Tables of the four O type curves in the same appendix are reproduced from the revised edition of *Bulletin 125*.

Attempts to reproduce the tables using an electronic computer and the equations for the curves have been made, but the results do not exactly match the 5 decimal place figures of Winfrey's revised calculations, with the major differences occurring as the percent surviving approaches zero. The original tables were the result of tedious calculations using mechanical calculators and tables of 10-place logarithms. Winfrey needed this high degree of accuracy to achieve consistency in the renewal calculations discussed in *Bulletin 125*. There are usually differences between the original tables and the computer-generated tables. These can result from procedures used to round calculations. Also, a function evaluated from tables of logarithms and the same function evaluated from an algorithm used by the computer may have different values. Current computer programs requiring values from the Iowa curves often store the table values of the 22 curves and use a table lookup procedure to obtain points on the survivor curve and the probable life curve.

The estimates made by the life forecaster do not require the five-decimal accuracy found in these tables. Yet, two identical sets of calculations, both using the same input data but done on different computers, should generate identical results. Failure to obtain this consistency may create undeserved reservations about the results of the computer programs. This, in turn, could cast doubts on the soundness of a report that uses the output in question.

The Iowa curves have become widely used models of the life characteristics of industrial property and they have been used for a variety of applications other than depreciation. Their repeated use has served as a test of their validity as a model. One criticism of the Iowa curves was that because their roots were in property installed near the turn of the century, new technology might bring with it new types of curves. The counterargument was that the Iowa type curves represent a wide range of patterns and though the technology may change, the underlying patterns of retirements remain relatively constant and can be adequately described by the 22 Iowa type curves.

In the late 1970s, John Russo, a graduate student working under the supervision of Cowles, conducted research that reproduced the original development of the Iowa curves. Data from more than 2000 property accounts reflecting observations during the period 1965 to 1975 were collected. From these, 490 accounts from a wide range of industries were selected for analysis. They were grouped into 33 clusters that were designated as the Russo curves. Then 56 accounts, selected from the approximately 1500 remaining, were fit to both the Russo curves and to the Iowa curves. Russo (1980, 15) drew three major conclusions:

1. No evidence was produced to conclude that the Iowa curve set, as it stands, is not a valid set of standard curves.

2. No evidence was found to conclude that new curve shapes could be produced at this time that would add to the validity of the Iowa curve set. A very small percentage of industrial account data could not be well fit by Iowa curves. The vast majority were well fit within the current Iowa array. The occasional data not easily fit appeared to reflect random management or economic situations that did not fall within the norms of any particular industry. No pattern, however, was evident that would lead to an expansion of the array that would be useful over a large amount of data experience. By far the most prevalent types of accounts that could not be easily fit were multi-modal accounts. Because of the diversity of locations and magnitudes of the modes between multi-modal accounts, no discernable patterns were found that might lead to an expansion of the Iowa set or the formulation of a set of standard multi-modal curves. Additional study and research in this area is definitely in order.

3. No evidence was found to suggest that the number of curves within the Iowa set should be reduced, although some Iowa curves, especially in the symmetrical modal group, were not utilized to produce fits during the fitting of the 56 curves. A general review of the overall account data used in the study suggested that these curves would be utilized to some degree with larger sample sizes. Because some reasonably substantial usage of these curves can be expected in industrial practice and because the elimination of selected curves would interrupt a well-spaced existing array, it appeared unreasonable to reduce the number of curves within the Iowa set based on the evidence produced in this study.

The System of Iowa Curves

The equations for the frequency curves of the 22 Iowa curves and tables of the percent surviving and probable average service lives can be found in *Bulletin 125*. The curves are classified by three variables: the average life, the location of the mode, and the variation of the life. Because the tables are organized by percent average life, each type of curve represents a family of survivor curves, each with the same shape but with a different average life.

Four modal characteristics are used: the left modal, symmetrical, right modal, and origin modal. The mode is the percent life that results in the highest point on the frequency curve and represents the life most likely to occur.

The variation is measured by both the variance and the maximum life. In the classification of the Iowa curves, each curve is given an interval number, 0, 1, 2, 3, 4, 5, or 6, that is a measure of the variation. The lower the number, the lower the mode, the larger the variation, and the larger the maximum life. The appendix contains the standard deviation and variance for the Iowa curves.

Iowa curves are identified by specifying the modal characteristics, the variation, and the average life in years. The letters L, S, R, and O refer to the left modal, symmetrical, right modal, and origin modal type curves respectively. R3–32 indicates a right modal curve (R) with a medium variation (3) and a 32-year life. If the average life is not given, the reference R3 is to the family of curves.

The mode of the L type curves is to the left of the average life. Because the average life can be thought of as the center of gravity of the frequency curve, the large area under the curve and to the left of the average life must be counterbalanced by the area under the tail of the curve, which extends to the right and must be relatively long to balance the large area to the left of the average life. The left mode reflects many retirements during the early life of the property. This results in a survivor curve in which the percent surviving drops quickly from 100%. At the same time, a significant portion of the property survives far beyond the average life.

There are six L type curves ranging from L0 to L5. The maximum life of the L0 type curve is 408% of the average life, and this is the largest maximum life of the original 18 Iowa curves. To contrast the large variation of the L0 type curve with the smaller variation of the L5 type curve, the ages at which 75% are surviving and 25% are surviving can be compared. These ages will include the middle 50% of the retirements. Ages 50% to 140% of average life include the middle of 50% of the L0 curves, while the range is only 90% to 109% for the L5 curves.

There are seven S type curves starting with the low modal S0 and ranging to the high modal S6. Because these curves are symmetrical, their mode is at 100% of life; the maximum life cannot exceed 200%. The S2 type curve is similar to the familiar normal distribution. The middle 50% of retirements occur between the ages of 62% to 137% of average life for the S0 type curve compared with 95% to 105% of average life for the higher modal S6 type curve.

The five right modal R curves range from the R1 to the R5. These curves are characterized by few retirements early in life, followed by heavy retirements soon after the average life. Because the tail of the curve extends to the left and is bounded at zero, the tails of R curves are shorter than those of the L curves and the maximum lives of the R curves are less than those of the L curves. The R1 has a maximum life of 201% while the R5 has a maximum life of 137% of average age. Fifty percent of the retirements of the R1 occur between the ages of 65% and 136% of average life compared with 92% and 109% for the higher modal R5 curve.

Four curves, denoted O1 through O4, are included in the origin modal group, whose mode occurs at age zero. The indexing of this set of curves is opposite to that used for the L, S, and R types, because the O1 has the least variability and the O4 the most. The O1 curve, also called the SC curve, is uniformly distributed and ranges from 0% to 200% of average life. Each life is equally likely and the resulting survivor curve is a straight line reaching 0% surviving at 200% of average life. The O3 curve is similar to the exponential distribution. The difference between points on the O3 curve and the survivor curve of the exponential distribution are less than 1% for ages less than 300% of average life.

Variations of the Iowa curves include "half curves" denoted, for example, as the R1.5 curve. This would be a curve halfway between the R1 and R2 curves, and the percent surviving at age 10% of average life would be calculated by averaging the percent surviving at that age for the R1 and the R2 curves. Lower mode curves, such as the L0.5, L1.5, L2.5, S0.5, S1.5, S2.5, R1.5, R2.5, and R3.5 are often added to the original set of curves.

Table 3.2.   A summary of the 22 Iowa curve types showing the maximum age (age at which 5% remain in service). Age is given as a percent of average life.

Modal location	Modal index						
	0	1	2	3	4	5	6
L	408 (217)	315 (195)	281 (180)	238 (163)	215 (143)	192 (130)	X X
S	200 (176)	200 (163)	198 (151)	192 (140)	174 (128)	155 (119)	138 (112)
R	X X	201 (171)	186 (155)	169 (140)	153 (130)	137 (120)	X X
O	X X	200 (190)	309 (242)	386 (305)	440 (361)	X X	X X

Using the Iowa Curve Tables

The Iowa curves were developed using the single parameter of age expressed as a percent of the average life, which was necessary if the curves were to be of practical value. Any particular Iowa curve type can be thought of as a family of curves, where each member of the family has the same form and follows the same mathematical function but has a different average life. Each member of the family can be obtained from the same table.

Find the table for the Iowa R2 curve in the appendix. The first column measures the life as a percentage of the average life. Note that entries have been calculated at 1% intervals and that the percent surviving entries shown in the second column are carried to 5 decimal places. The final column shows the probable life; the remaining life can be calculated by subtracting the age from the probable life.

Suppose that the points of a particular survivor curve, say an Iowa R2 with an average life of 5 years, are needed. To calculate a specific survivor curve, it is necessary to express the age as a percent of the average life. Suppose that the percent surviving at age 2.5 years is needed. This is (2.5/5.0) × 100% or 50.0% of the average life. Enter the table at 50 and read 89.12668 percent surviving and 108.45 as the probable life, measured in percent of average life. Multiply 1.0845 by 5.0 years or 5.4225 years probable life or 5.4225 − 2.5 or 2.9225 years remaining life. The maximum life for the R2 is 186% of average life or 5.0 × 1.86 or 9.3 years.

The Gompertz-Makeham Model

In 1825 the Royal Society of London published a paper by Benjamin Gompertz in which he postulated that human death may be the result of either of two causes. One is chance, where the cause is independent of age so that young and old are at equal risk. The other is a cause that is related to an increasing inability to survive, so that as one ages he or she becomes more likely to succumb to death by disease and injury. Gompertz theorized that the rate of change of the force of mortality is proportional to the force of mortality, so the older a person is, the faster the forces of mortality increase. He noted that if this was not true, there would be no limit to the age of man. Letting $h(x)$ represent the force of mortality at age x, Gompertz's theory can be stated mathematically as $dh(x)/dx = kh(x)$, which can be rewritten $dh(x)/h(x) = kdx$. Integrating yields

$$\ln h(x) = kx + \text{constant of integration}$$
$$h(x) = Be^{kx} = Bc^x$$

Previously h(x) has been called the hazard function, but the actuarial scientists call it the *mortality function* and its value the force of mortality.

The resulting survivor curve function can be calculated from the mortality function using the definition of the hazard function.

$$-[1/S(x)][dS(x)/dx] = Bc^x$$
$$-dS(x)/S(x) = Bc^x dx$$

Integration yields

$$-\ln S(x) = Bc^x + \text{constant of integration}$$
$$S(x) = ke^{Bc^x} = kg^{c^x}$$

It is interesting that although Gompertz postulated two elements in the mortality function, only one appeared in his final formula.

Modification of Gompertz's model was left to William Matthew Makeham (1860), whose paper was published in *The Assurance Magazine and Journal of the Institute of Actuaries*. While comparing the Gompertzian theory to observed data, Makeham noticed that there was a systematic difference between the observed and theoretical points, and that adding a constant to the logarithm of the probabilities resulted in a better fit in three different sets of data. This is shown below where the term Ax is added to Gompertz's formula.

$$-\ln S(x) = Ax + Bc^x + \text{constant of integration}$$

The resulting mortality function is then

$$h(x) = A + Bc^x$$

which is consistent with Gompertz's belief that the force of mortality could be divided into two causes, one that is constant with time and one that increases with time. Integrating yields the survivor curve function

$$-\ln S(x) = Ax + Bc^x + \text{constant of integration}$$
$$S(x) = ke^{Ax}e^{Bc^x}$$

which is commonly written

$$S(x) = ks^x g^{c^x}$$

This model, known as the Gompertz-Makeham formula, has been widely used by actuaries to smooth human life tables. The constant s, which is equal e^A, should not be confused with the function $S(x)$, the value of the survivor curve at age x.

Those studying the life characteristics of industrial property in the 1920s looked to the work of the actuarial scientists. Winfrey investigated the use of the Gompertz-Makeham formula to describe the life characteristics of property for which he had gathered data, but discarded this idea and continued development of the Iowa curves. AT&T engineers, however, adopted the Gompertz-Makeham formula and have successfully used this model in life analysis and forecasting since the 1920s. The Bell companies continue to use this model.

Estimating the Gompertz-Makeham Parameters

If the Gompertz-Makeham formula is adopted, it is necessary to estimate the parameters s, g, and c that will result in the best fit between the observed data and the points on the smoothed curve defined by the formula. This challenging mathematical problem is complicated by tedious calculations resulting from the complexity of the formula. For those working on the problem before the arrival of electronic computers, the computational problems were a major concern. Kurtz (1930) developed a graphical method for estimating the parameters and described it in *Life Expectancy of Industrial Property*. Winfrey used a method by King that he described in *Bulletin 125*.

A technique used by AT&T Company engineers, described in *Depreciation Engineering Practices,* equates the area under the observed survivor curve to the area under the theoretical curve and also equates the first moment of the observed survivor curve to the first moment of the corresponding points on the theoretical curve. These two equations can be solved simultaneously so that s and g can be expressed in terms of c.

First the value of the constant k can be found by evaluating $S(0)$. Remember that $S(0)$ equals 1.

$$S(0) = ks^0g^{c^0} = kg$$

so that

$$k = S(0)/g$$

and

$$S(x) = S(0)s^xg^{c^x-1}$$

The Gompertz-Makeham formula can be simplified by taking the logarithm of both sides and applying the notations $L(x) = \log S(x)$, $LS = \log s$, $LG = \log g$.

$$\log S(x) = \log S(0) + x\log s + (c^x - 1)\log g$$
$$L(x) = L(0) + xLS + (c^x - 1)LG \qquad (3.1)$$

Set the first and second moments of the observed data equal to the first and second moments of the theoretical curve. The superscript ° is used to denote the observed survivor curve.

First let $S°(x)$ = the point on the observed life table at age x, $L°(x)$, = $\log S°(x)$, $S(x)$ = point on the Gompertz-Makeham curve at age x, and $L(x)$ = $\log S(x)$. Then equate the sum of the points on the observed and theoretical curves and the sum of the first moments of the observed and theoretical curves.

$$\Sigma\, L°(x - .5) = \Sigma\, L(x - .5) \qquad (3.2)$$
$$\Sigma\, (x - 1)L°(x - .5) = \Sigma\, (x - 1)L(x - .5) \qquad (3.3)$$

summed for x = 1, 2, 3, . . ., t. Note that the argument (x − .5) will take on values .5, 1.5, 2.5, etc., which is consistent with the half-year convention.

The moments selected are shown in equation (3.3). The left-hand side of equations (3.2) and (3.3) are calculated directly from the observed survivor curve, while the right-hand sides can be rewritten in terms of equation (3.1). First write the right-hand side of equation (3.2) as

$$\begin{aligned}
\Sigma\, L(x -.5) &= \Sigma\, L(0) + \Sigma\, LS\, (x - .5) + \Sigma\, LG(c^{x-.5} - 1)\\
&= tL(0) + LS\, \Sigma\, (x - .5) + LG\, \Sigma\, c^{(x-.5)} - LGt\\
&= tL(0) + LS(t^2/2) + LG[(c^{t+.5} - c^{.5})/(c - 1) - t]
\end{aligned}$$

and then for equation (3.3)

$$\begin{aligned}
\Sigma\, &(x - 1)L(x -.5)\\
&= \Sigma\, (x - 1)L(0) + \Sigma(x - 1)LS(x - .5) + \Sigma(x - 1)\, LG(c^{x-.5} - 1)\\
&= L(0)\, \Sigma\, (x - 1) + LS\, \Sigma\, (x - .5)(x - 1) + LG[\Sigma(x - 1)c^{x-.5} - \Sigma\, (x - 1)]\\
&= L(0)[(t^2 - t)/2] + LS[(4t^3 - 3t^2 - t)/12] + LG\, \{(tc^{t+.5})/(c - 1) - [c(c^{t+.5} - c^{.5})\, /(c - 1)^2] - (t^2 - t)/2\}
\end{aligned}$$

Now the two equations permit solution of the constants LG and LS in terms of c, t (the number of points on the observed survivor curve), and the points on the observed survivor curve.

$$\begin{aligned}
a &= \Sigma\, L°(x - .5) - tL(0)\\
b &= \Sigma\, (x - 1)L°(x - .5) - L(0)(t^2 - t)/2\\
d &= [(4t^3 - 3t^2 - t)/12]/(t^2/2)
\end{aligned}$$

$$i = (c^{t+.5} - c^{.5})/(c - 1) - t$$
$$j = (tc^{t+.5})/(c - 1) - c(c^{t+.5} - c^{.5}) /(c-1)^2 - (t^2 - t)/2$$
$$LG = (da - b)/(di - j)$$
$$LS = (a - iLG)/(t^2/2)$$

The constant LG must be positive.

Now an initial value of c is arbitrarily selected; experience has shown that a value of c equal to 1.01 is a good choice. The value of c is varied, often in steps of size 0.01, until the value that minimizes the sum of squares is found. Experience shows that the sum of squares as a function of c is concave, so that when a local minimum is found, it can be assumed to be the global minimum. When c is found, LG and LS can be determined and the points on the theoretical curve can be calculated. Then the differences between the observed and theoretical curves are calculated, squared, summed, and used as a measure of fit.

Other Curves

The *square survivor curve* describes a single unit. The curve remains at 100% until the age equals the average life, then it drops to zero. The actual life is equal to the average life. Mathematical properties of this curve, in spite of its simplicity, are the same as more complex curves.

Bimodal curves are characterized by a frequency curve with two modes. Although there may be property with this inherent characteristic, it is more likely that the bimodal characteristics are the result of combining two types of property, each with different life characteristics, into a single group. Consider a group of 500 units whose life characteristics are described by an Iowa S3–10 curve combined with a group of 500 units whose life characteristics are described by an Iowa S3–20 curve. The resulting curve would have an average life of 15 years and have one mode at 67% of average life (10 years) and a second at 133% of average life (20 years). An infinite number of curves can be constructed in this manner. The best method of analysis is to divide the larger group into smaller, more homogeneous groups that can be analyzed separately and are likely to exhibit more common life characteristics.

The *New York h-curves,* developed by Bradford Kimball of the New York Public Service Commission and reported in 1947, are used by that commission. They are based on the normal curve with the left tail truncated. A complete description of the curves can be found in "A system of life tables for physical property based on the truncated normal distribution" by Kimball (1947b).

Lawrence S. Patterson, a statistician for the New York Public Service Commission, developed a system of one parameter, symmetrical curves in about 1937. The parameter is a function of the variance of the life table and can be calculated from the observed data. *Patterson curves* have been little used in life analysis. A description of these curves can be found in Kimball (1947b).

In 1992 Ronald White proposed a new set of generalized survivor tables including the Iowa curves, curves generated using the Gompertz-Makeham model, and New York h-curves. The generalized Iowa curves differ slightly from those in the appendix in this book. The Gompertz-Makeham survivor curves were generated using specific coefficients developed by AT&T engineers called the Bell curves. Adoption of a standard set of tables of survivor curves provides an easy way for different computer programs to generate identical survivor curves, thus eliminating a source of differences in depreciation calculations. Sets of curves are easily transferred on magnetic disks.

SMOOTHING, FITTING, AND EXTRAPOLATING

Survivor curves from observed data are often irregular rather than smooth. Often they are incomplete in the sense that the final percent surviving is some number larger than zero. To classify the data, it is first necessary to select a survivor curve model and then find the specific curve that best fits the observed data.

Statisticians often recommend smoothing observed data before fitting it to a curve. The smoothing process eliminates the point-to-point variation and simulates data that could be expected if a larger sample had been taken. An argument against smoothing is that it alters the original data, perhaps misrepresenting them. Either the survivor curve or the retirement ratio curve can be smoothed.

The mathematical process of calculating the survivor curve from the retirement ratios is itself a smoothing process. Retirement ratios that have significant point-to-point variation will create a relatively smooth survivor curve.

Smoothing can be done visually or mathematically. Visual smoothing relies on the judgment of the analyst to capture the essence of the points and reduce them to a smooth curve. Mathematical curve fitting removes judgment from the fitting process. If the retirement ratio curve is smoothed and the smoothed points are used to calculate a survivor curve, then the result is a curve that has been smoothed twice.

A common method of mathematical smoothing is to fit the observed retirement ratios to a polynomial curve of a high enough order to provide a good fit; usually a third-order curve is sufficient. In the equation below, Y represents the smoothed curve and X the observed values.

$$Y = a_0 + a_1X + a_2X^2 + a_3X^3 + \ldots + a_nX^n$$

Standard regression techniques and computer programs can be used to find the regression coefficients a_i. Although this technique works well for smoothing, the polynomial function should only be used with great care to extrapolate data. In *Statistical Theory with Engineering Applications* Abraham Hald (1952:559) states, "From a purely statistical point of view the regression curve provides a description of the interrelation between the two variables within the limited range of the observations, and extrapolations, i.e., computations or values outside this range are in principle not justifiable as perhaps it is not possible to represent the interrelation outside the observed range by the function utilized. It is therefore absolutely necessary that extrapolation be firmly based on professional knowledge concerning the data." A polynomial curve may not be a good function to use for the difficult task of extrapolation.

If the Iowa curves are adopted as a model, an underlying assumption is that the process describing the retirement pattern is one of the 22 processes described by the Iowa curves. The problem is then to decide which specific type of Iowa curve "best" fits the observed data. *Best* can take on different meanings, each with subtle differences; here it will refer to the curve that most accurately represents the observed data.

One method is to fit the data visually. Until recently, this required a set of curves printed on translucent paper. Printed on each sheet is a family of a specific type Iowa curve. Each member of the family represents a different average life, typically running from 10 to 50 years in steps of 2 years. Traditionally these curves were scaled to 4 years/inch and 10% surviving/inch, but sets of curves scaled to one-half or double this size were also common. These scales can be multiplied or divided by a constant to accommodate observed data with very long or very short lives. If, for example, the observed curve had an average life of about 80 years, the scale could be doubled so that the curves would run from 20 to 100 years. The observed curve was plotted on graph paper using the same scale, and a translucent sheet of paper with the printed curves was then placed over the observed curve, allowing the analyst to compare visually the empirical and observed curves.

After plotting the observed curve, the analyst should first visually examine the plotted data to make an initial judgment about the type curves that may be good fits. The analyst also must decide which points or sections of the curve should be given the most weight. Points at the end of the curve are often based on fewer exposures and may be given less weight than points based on larger samples. The weight placed on those points will depend on the size of the exposures. Often the middle section of the curve (that section ranging from approximately 80% to 20% surviving) is given more weight than the first and last sections. This middle section is relatively straight and is the portion of the curve that often best characterizes the survivor curve.

Begin fitting with the left modal curves and identify the two or three curves that appear to best fit the data. Note the curve type and the corresponding average life, which is typically estimated to the nearest year. Continue with the symmetrical, right modal, and origin modal curves. Some groups may not give a suitable fit.

Continue by reexamining the contenders selected during the first pass. Often the choice between two or three tentative selections is difficult to make. The conservative choice is toward the lower life and right modal curve.

An alternative to visual fitting is mathematical fitting. Usually the least squares method is used. This method is time consuming if done by hand, and is not practical unless a computer is used. Typical logic for a computer program is as follows. First a type curve is arbitrarily selected. If the observed curve goes to zero percent surviving, calculate the area under the curve and designate this the average life.

If the observed curve is a stub curve (i.e., if it does not go to zero), calculate the area under the curve and up to the age at final data point. Call this area the *realized life*. Then systematically vary the average life of the theoretical survivor curve and calculate its realized life at the age corresponding to the study date. This trial and error procedure ends when you find an average life such that the realized life of the theoretical curve equals the realized life of the observed curve. Call this the *average life.*

Once the average life is found, calculate the difference between each percent surviving point on the observed survivor curve and the corresponding point on the Iowa curve. Square each difference and sum them. The sum of squares is used as a measure of goodness of fit for that particular Iowa type curve. This procedure is repeated for the remaining 21 Iowa type curves. The "best fit" is declared to be the type of curve that minimizes the sum of differences squared.

On the surface, the removal of judgment from the fitting process may appear to be an advantage, but blind acceptance of mechanical fitting processes will occasionally but consistently result in poor results. A better procedure is to use the least squares method to select candidates for the best fit. Comparison of the sum of squares will reveal situations where the difference between the best choices is small. The analyst should then visually examine the observed data and compare them to the theoretical curves. This can be done quickly on a computer with graphic capabilities so that the analyst need not use time to plot the observed curve by hand. The analyst can consider single points that may contribute significantly to the sum of squares but that may deserve less weight than other points. Fits at

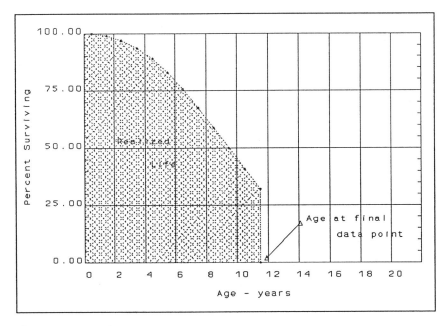

various sections on the curve can be evaluated and weighted using the judgment of an experienced analyst.

The results of mathematical curve fitting serve as a guide for the analyst and speed the visual fitting process. But the results of the mathematical fitting should be checked visually and the final determination of the best fit be made by the analyst. Computer systems that will mathematically fit the data and provide graphical curve fitting are widely available. Wisely used, these systems are a powerful tool for the depreciation professional.

Fitting Stub Survivor Curves

Stub curves, which are survivor curves for which the data end before the curve reaches 0% surviving, are frequently encountered. The realized life of the property is the area under the curve and to the left of the final point on the survivor curve as shown in Figure 3.6. Unless the remaining property is retired immediately, the average life of the property will exceed the realized life.

The process of fitting stub survivor curves to an Iowa or other type curve is essentially the same as fitting a complete survivor curve. The obvious and critical difference is that the fit is valid only to the final observed point on the survivor curve.

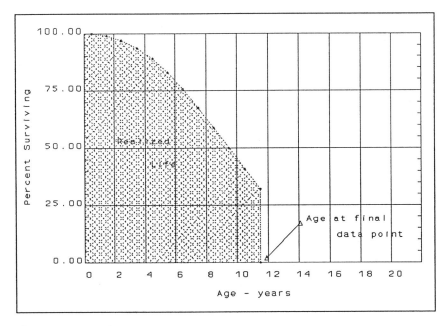

Figure 3.6. A stub survivor curve and the realized life.

Stub curves contain the essence of the shape of the curve and can be accurately fit even though the curve is not complete. To clarify this, think about conducting the following experiment. Gather several complete survivor curves and fit them to Iowa curves. Then truncate the observed survivor curves and fit the truncated curves to Iowa curves. Compare the fits of the complete and stub curves to see if consistent results are obtained. The experiment could be repeated by successively truncating more of the curve until only a short stub remained. Analysis of the results of the experiment will reveal how short the stub curve can be before the results of fitting the stub curves differ from the fit to the entire curve. This experiment was performed by Cowles (1957), who concluded that reasonably good fits were obtained for stub curves that ended at a point as high as 70% surviving. Longer stub curves (i.e., those with 40% or less surviving) were fit with a high degree of accuracy. This shows that the upper portions of the various types of Iowa curves are distinctive enough to identify the curve.

When reporting the results of fitting a stub curve, the analyst must be careful to say the fit applies to the observed data and not beyond. This can be done by appending the length of the stub to the results of the fit. This notation is suggested:

Type − life [S(b) − S(e)]

where S(b) = largest observed percent surviving (usually 100%) and S(e) = the smallest, or ending, percent surviving.

An example of the use of this notation is R2 − 30 [100% − 46%], which would show that the analyst believed the best fit of the observed data was an Iowa R2 type curve with a 30-year average life, and that the observed curve started at 100% surviving but was a stub curve whose final point was at 46% surviving. The average life of the property will be 30 years only if the future forces of retirement continue to follow those of a R2–30 Iowa curve.

A method of estimating the parameters g, s, and c of the Gompertz-Makeham equation to observed data has been described and can be applied to either a stub or complete curve. Once the parameters are estimated, the complete, smoothed curve can be plotted, and the area under the curve (i.e., the average life) can be calculated. Again, the reports of the results of the analysis must include the length of the stub curve. Only the realized life (i.e., the area under the stub curve) is known, and the estimate of life obtained from extrapolation of the survivor curves assumes that future forces of retirement will remain unchanged. The forces can be thought of as measured by the constants in the hazard function

$$h(x) = A + Bc^x$$

If these parameters remain constant, then the estimate of the average life will be correct.

Given the proper combination of parameters, it is possible for the Gompertz-Makeham equation to turn upward, so that the number of survivors increases with age and, possibly, exceeds 100%. If the curve exceeds 100% for a short period, then turns downward, the common solution is to set all points greater than 100% to 100%. If the curve takes in a continuous, upward trend, the parameters must be adjusted.

NOTES

1. This treatment assumes retirements occur uniformly during the final age interval and that the life of the longest lived unit is ML + .5 years. If the life of the longest lived unit is known, this value can be used as the end of the final age interval and can be used to calculate the midpoint of the final interval.

2. The maximum life for this Iowa R2 curve is 9.0 years. If the final age interval had been defined to be 8.5 to 9.0 years, the corresponding area would have been 0.21 percent-years, and the total area would have been 500.00 percent-years. See note 1.

4 | Salvage Concepts

SALVAGE can be divided into two components: gross salvage and cost of retiring. *Gross salvage* is the value of a unit retired from service resulting from its sale for scrap or reuse. *Cost of retiring,* also called cost of removal, is the expense incurred to remove the unit from service, including expenses necessary to return the environment to an acceptable condition. Thus, *net salvage* is the gross salvage less the cost of retiring.

The original cost less net salvage is called the *depreciable base.* It represents the capital consumed during the life of the unit and the amount to be recovered through depreciation. If the net salvage is positive, then the capital consumed is less than the original cost. If the net salvage is negative, the capital consumed is greater than the original cost.

When net salvage is zero or near zero, its effect on the depreciable base is nil. However, industrial property exhibits a wide range of salvage, and the effect of salvage on the annual accrual is often substantial. Examples of property yielding positive salvage include land, which is generally assumed to be fully recoverable; buildings and vehicles, which often have significant resale value; and aluminum or copper wire, which has a gross salvage value determined by the intrinsic value of the material. Utility poles and railroad track are often reused, and if the accounting system defines a unit as retired when it is removed from a location, its salvage is determined by its value when it is installed in a new location. On the other hand, underground pipe used for transportation or distribution of gas or water must first be disconnected and then may be filled and capped, or even removed from the ground. These activities are costly because they require significant labor

51

and heavy equipment, while the gross salvage is nil or negligible. The result is a net salvage that is often both large and negative. Decommissioning costs of a nuclear generating plant are a contemporary example of an investment with a significant negative net salvage.

Basic salvage concepts must be understood before either the analysis of realized salvage or the forecasting of future salvage can be discussed. Most of these concepts can be applied equally well to either gross salvage or cost of removal, so the term *salvage* is used generically to apply to net salvage, gross salvage, or cost of retiring.

Property placed in service during the same year forms a *vintage group*. The fraction of the vintage group remaining in service is a function of its age and is described by a survivor curve. An underlying functional relationship between the age at retirement and salvage is assumed. A formal development of how salvage changes as property ages is necessary to understand the effect of salvage on depreciation.

A salvage curve is the graph of the salvage ratio versus age. The salvage ratio is the ratio of the salvage to the original cost of the retired unit. The salvage received during any age interval is found by multiplying the salvage ratio for that interval by the dollars retired during that interval. The net salvage ratio is the gross salvage ratio less the cost of retiring salvage ratio.

As one example of a salvage curve, consider property that is easily removed from service and is still functional after retirement. Gross salvage of early retirements will be high if the property is in good condition and the technology is current, because the property will be valuable for sale or reuse. Older retirements would be less valuable because, besides their added wear, they would be competing for use with property that has a more current technology. If the cost of retiring is assumed to be near zero, this model would lead to a net salvage schedule where the salvage ratio is initially near one, but then decreases with age. This example could be expanded to include retirements resulting from damage from an accident or mechanical failure. Because of their physical condition, these units would have a salvage ratio near zero and would lower the overall salvage ratio.

A salvage curve need not decrease with age. The gross salvage of scrap copper, steel, or aluminum typically, because of inflation, increases with age. A cost of retiring that is labor and equipment intensive is another example of a salvage curve that, because of inflation, increases with age. Because this element of salvage is a cost, the term "increases with age" means the salvage becomes more negative with age. Retirement of a utility pole is an example of an activity for which the hours required to remove the pole might remain relatively constant, but the hourly labor rate, and therefore the cost of retirement, would increase as the pole ages.

There are three reasons why it is important to consider salvage as a function of age, rather than simply using an overall average salvage. First, though the average life (AL) procedure uses an accrual rate based on the average net salvage, the equal life group (ELG) procedure uses the net salvage associated with each equal life group (i.e., salvage by age). Second, the calculated accumulated depreciation (CAD) model must reflect the change in salvage with age if it is to approximate the accumulated provision for depreciation. Because the CAD is the feedback measure used to determine the adequacy of the accumulated provision for depreciation, it is important that the model used be as lifelike as possible. When the remaining life method of adjustment is used, the amount to be recovered is found by adjusting for the future salvage. These first two reasons show that regardless of the system of depreciation used, both the average and the future salvage are required. Finally, considering salvage as a function of age results in a more realistic model and therefore enhances understanding of the depreciation process and aids in forecasting.

THE SALVAGE RATIO

One inherent characteristic of the salvage ratio is that the numerator and denominator are measured in different units; the numerator is measured in dollars at the time of retirement, while the denominator is measured in dollars at the time of installation. Inflation is an economic fact of life and although both numerator and denominator are measured in dollars, the timing of the cash flows reflects different price levels. Consider the pattern of installations and retirements illustrated in Figure 4.1 (see end of chapter).

Two replacement cycles are represented. The installation cost of the first unit is B dollars, it lasts K years, and has a net salvage of V dollars. The salvage ratio of the first unit is SR(present) = V/B. If the cost of the replacement when measured in constant dollars is equal to the cost of the first unit, then the replacement cost measured in inflated dollars is $B \times (1 + p)^K$. The factor $(1 + p)^K$ is called the compound amount factor and equals the value of \$1 after K years when the annual rate of inflation is p. Suppose the life of the replacement unit is L years and during its life the annual rate of inflation is f. Then the future salvage of the replacement is $V \times (1 + f)^L$. The salvage ratio of the replacement is SR(future) = $V \times (1 + f)^L/B \times (1 + p)^K$. If the past inflation rate p equals the future inflation rate f, and if the life of the original equals that of the replacement, so that K equals L, then the two inflation factors will be equal. The salvage ratio for the replacement will equal V/B, unchanged from the original ratio.

This simple model illustrates two important characteristics of the salvage ratio when the uninflated original cost and uninflated salvage remain constant. One is that a change in the inflation rate will cause a change in the salvage ratio. The other is that a change in service life will change the salvage ratio.

The magnitude of the change in salvage ratio depends on p, f, K, and L. As an example, assume that the past inflation rate, p, has been 3% during the past K years, that $V/B = 10\%$, and that the life of the replacement is also K years. Future salvage ratios are determined by the function $10\% \times [(1 + f)^K/(1 + p)^K]$. Table 4.1 (see end of chapter) shows future salvage ratios for different values of f, the inflation rate during the life of the replacement, and different lives. Notice that if the inflation rate does not change, then the salvage remains unchanged regardless of the life. But if the inflation rate increases, the salvage ratio increases. The longer the life and the greater the change in inflation rate, the more the future salvage ratio deviates from the present 10% ratio. Also note the nonlinear relationship between the salvage ratio and the variables f and K.

Table 4.1 uses future inflation rates that are equal to or greater than the inflation rate during the life of the first unit. If a similar table is constructed using future inflation rates that are equal to or less than the inflation rate during the life of the first unit, then the salvage ratios will be equal to or less than the 10% ratio experienced by the first unit.

Inflation does not affect all segments of the economy equally. The cost of construction, capital equipment, and labor can all increase at different rates. Because the cost of retiring is often labor and equipment intensive, this element of salvage may be closely tied to indexes that reflect labor and equipment costs. Gross salvage values may be closely tied to used equipment costs and are likely to inflate at a different rate than the cost of retiring. Allowing for different inflation rates for capital equipment, gross salvage, and cost of retiring requires modification to the model just presented.

Assume the inflation rates affecting the cost of replacing the first unit and the gross salvage are equal and constant during the replacement cycle; call this rate h. Assume that the cost of retiring inflates at a different rate; call this rate j. After L years the net salvage, V, will equal the (uninflated gross salvage) $\times (1 + h)^L$ − (uninflated cost of retiring) $\times (1 + j)^L$. We can use this model to find how the net salvage ratio is affected when these two inflation rates differ.

As an example, assume that the current gross salvage ratio is 20% and that the current cost of retiring ratio is 10%, so that the net salvage ratio is 20% − 10% or 10%. The future net salvage ratio will be the net salvage at the end of the life of the replacement unit divided by the installed cost of the replacement unit, or $[20\% \times (1 + h)^L - 10\% \times (1 + j)^L]/(1 + h)^L$. Assume that h is 3% and that the lives of the initial unit and the replacement unit both equal L years. Table 4.2 (see end of chapter) shows future salvage ratios for various values of L and j. Notice that as the difference between h and j becomes larger, the cost of retiring increases faster than the gross salvage. In our example, the cost of retiring catches and exceeds the gross salvage for the larger values of j and the longer lives. The result is negative net salvage.

The salvage ratio as a function of age and inflation rate can be modeled using the equation $(V/B) \times (1 + p)^A$. Table 4.3 (see end of chapter) shows that if the net salvage at time of installation remains constant except for inflation, the observed salvage ratio will vary significantly with time. For example, if the inflation rate was 6% and the salvage ratio at age zero is equal to 10%, the salvage ratio at age 5 would be 13.38% and by age 20 would have increased to 32.07% simply because of inflation. Because the value of the function $(1 + p)^A$ increases rapidly as A becomes large, the factors for a large age (e.g., 40 years) are significantly greater than the 10% initial value.

Recognition of the effect of inflation on salvage will influence the analysis and forecasting of salvage. To find the effect of inflation, it is necessary to understand and calculate the time value of money.

THE SALVAGE CURVE

A salvage curve has been defined as the graph of the salvage ratio as a function of the life of the property. To calculate the average salvage ratio, or the future average salvage ratio at any age, *both the salvage curve and the survivor curve must be known.*

The net salvage curve is the gross salvage curve less the cost of retiring curve. The method of calculating the average salvage ratio (ASR) is to calculate a weighted average of the salvage ratios for each age interval as shown below.

$$\text{ASR} = \text{E(salvage ratio)} = \Sigma \ f(i)g(i) \quad \text{for i} = 1,2,3, \ldots , \text{ML}$$

where $f(i)$ = the retirement frequency during age interval i and $g(i)$ = the salvage ratio during age interval, or the ratio evaluated at the midpoint of interval i, where the age intervals and indexes i are defined as

i	interval i	x(i)
0	$0.0 \leq$ service life <0.5	.25
1	$0.5 \leq$ service life <1.5	1.00
2	$1.5 \leq$ service life <2.5	2.00
3	$2.5 \leq$ service life <3.5	3.00
ML	$\text{ML} - .5 \leq$ service life $<\text{ML} + .5$	ML

where x(i) = the midpoint of age interval i and ML = the maximum service life.

The functions f(i) and g(i) also can be described as continuous functions and the equation written in integral form, but this offers little computational advantage. Discrete functions and the age intervals defined above are consistent with the methods used to describe service life.

Two more measures of salvage are

RSR(i) = the realized salvage ratio at the start of age interval i
= Σ f(k)g(k) / Σ f(k)   for k = 1, 2, 3, . . . , i − 1
FSR(i) = the future salvage ratio at the start of age interval i
= Σ f(k)g(k) / Σ f(k)   for k = i, i + 1, i + 2, . . . , ML

Suppose that the frequency curve and the salvage curve of a group of property are as shown below. The units are retired at ages 0.25, 1, 2, or 3 years with corresponding salvage ratios of 15%, 10%, 5%, or 0%.

Retirement Frequency Curve	Salvage Ratio Curve
f(0) = .20	g(0) = .15
f(1) = .30	g(1) = .10
f(2) = .40	g(2) = .05
f(3) = .10	g(3) = .00
Total = 1.00	

The average salvage ratio is then calculated as

ASR = Σ f(i)g(i)   for i = 1,2,3,4
= (.20)(.15) + (.30)(.10) + (.40)(.05) + (.20)(0) = 0.08 or 8.0%

Suppose it is the start of the age interval 1.5 to 2.5 years, so that the index i equals 2. The realized salvage ratio at age 1.5 years, RSR(2), is determined by salvage realized during the first two age intervals, so that.

RSR(2) = [(.20)(.15) + (.30)(.10)]/[.20 + .30] = 0.12 or 12%
FSR(2) = [(.40)(.05) + (.10)(.00)]/[.40 + .10] = 0.04 or 4%

Note that the weighted average of the realized and future salvage ratios equals the average salvage ratio:

Weight for RSR(2) = .20 + .30 = .50
Weight for FSR(2) = .40 + .10 = .50
Weighted average salvage = ASR = .50 × 12% + .50 × 4% = 8%.

Table 4.4 (see end of chapter) shows the salvage calculations for an Iowa R2 curve with a 5-year average life (R2–5). Column (c) is the percent retired during the age interval and is found by subtracting successive points on the survivor curve shown in column (b). Column (d) shows the average salvage ratio during the age interval. Note that the salvage ratios in this schedule increase with age.

The salvage observed during the age interval depends on both the salvage per unit and the number of units retired. Column (e) is the product of the salvage ratio and the fraction retired. It equals the salvage during the age interval as a percent of the initial cost. During the age interval 2.5 to 3.5 years, the salvage equals 1.21% of the initial cost. The sum of these amounts is the total salvage over the life of the group expressed as a percent of the initial cost; this is the average salvage ratio, which is 13.46%.

Column (f) is the realized salvage ratio and represents the average that would result if an observer recalculated the average salvage ratio at the start of each age interval or each year. The average salvage at age 2.5 years depends on the salvage during each of the preceding three age intervals. The salvage during these intervals is summed to obtain 0.11% + 0.38% + 0.70% or 1.19%. This amount must be divided by the fraction retired by that age, or 1 − 0.8913 or 0.1087, to obtain 1.19%/0.1087 or 10.92%. The realized salvage ratio at the start of the second age interval equals the average during the first age interval. As the age increases, the realized salvage ratio approaches the average salvage ratio. At the end of the final age interval the realized salvage ratio, 13.46%, equals the average salvage ratio.

Column (g) is the future salvage ratio, or salvage expectancy, at the start of each age interval. The future salvage ratio at any age is the average salvage ratio observers would calculate if they recorded the salvage from that time on. At age zero the future salvage ratio and the average salvage ratio are equal because both averages include all future salvage ratios. At age 6.5 years, future salvage depends on the salvage during each of the three remaining age intervals. The salvage during these intervals is summed to obtain 2.25% + 1.04% + 0.14% or 3.43%. This amount must be divided by the future amount to be retired, which is the fraction in service at age 6.5, or 22.32%, to obtain 3.43%/0.2232 or 15.37%. Because the ratios in this salvage schedule increase with age, the future salvage ratios also increase with age.

At any time, the average of the realized and future salvage ratios will equal the overall average salvage. At age 3.5 years, the weighted average of the realized and future salvage ratios is 11.40% × (1 − .7901) + 14.01% × (.7901) or 13.46%. Figure 4.2 (see end of chapter) is a graph of the salvage ratio, future salvage ratio, and realized salvage ratio versus age.

Salvage Schedule Models

A survivor curve must start at 100% and decrease monotonically to zero, but there are no similar constraints for the salvage schedule. The salvage curve can be either increasing or decreasing and need not be monotonic. It need not start at 100% nor end at 0%. There are, however, several basic models that approximate actual patterns and are therefore useful to the analyst and forecaster. We will describe each first in constant dollars and then add inflation. The curve with inflation represents the salvage curve that would be constructed from observed data. The curve without inflation shows the underlying model and is therefore useful when analyzing salvage data.

The first model is a salvage ratio that, when measured in constant dollars, remains constant. This model could reflect the gross salvage of property whose major value is as scrap so that the gross salvage would equal the intrinsic value of the material. It also could be applied to the cost of retiring when the method of removal remains unchanged with time. Table 4.5 (see end of chapter) shows a salvage curve with ratios equal to 10% at all ages. The survivor curve in column (b) is an Iowa R2–5. The salvage curve is shown in column (c); all ratios are equal to 10%. Column (d) is the product of the fraction retired during the age interval and the salvage ratio shown in column (c), and when these are summed the average salvage is found to be 10%. Because the future salvage is needed when calculating depreciation, the future salvage ratios are shown in column (e).

Columns (f), (g), and (h) contain the inflated curves. The inflated ratio is found by multiplying the corresponding, uninflated ratio by the compound amount factor $(1 + i)^{AGE}$ where i is the inflation rate. The salvage curve for the constant model with inflation increases exponentially with age. The 6% inflation rate increases the average salvage ratio from 10% to 13.46% and the salvage ratio at the maximum life, 9 years, to 16.89%. Figure 4.3 (see end of chapter) is a graph of these salvage ratios both with and without inflation. Remember that the difference between the uninflated and inflated salvage ratios increases with age. If an example using a survivor curve with an average life longer than 5 years had been used, the difference between the two ratios would be even larger.

The second model is one in which the salvage ratio decreases uniformly with age. The linear model shown in Table 4.6 and Figure 4.4 (see end of chapter) starts at 100% at age zero (and averages 97.37% during the first age interval) and ends at 0% at age 9.5 years with a resulting annual decrease of 100%/9.5 or 10.53%. The initial value need not be 100%. Suppose, for example, that 20% of the capitalized cost was installation cost. If the property was removed immediately after installation, installation cost would be lost and, if the full price of the unit was recovered, the salvage ratio would be 80%.

If the survivor curve is symmetrical, the average salvage ratio for the constant dollars model will be the salvage ratio at the midpoint of the curve, which here is the average of the initial and final salvage ratios. Because the survivor curve is the right modal R2 curve, more weight is given to early retirements and the average salvage is less than 50%.

The linear model with inflation also decreases, but in a nonlinear fashion. The shape of the linear model with inflation depends on slope of the line and the inflation rate. The constant model can be considered a special case of the linear model.

The third model reflects an accelerated rate early in life. This model would be particularly applicable to gross salvage when the value falls rapidly early in life and then decreases more slowly later in life. Property such as automobiles and electronic equipment are examples that might follow this pattern. Several mathematical functions could be used to describe this pattern, but a function similar to that used to calculate sum-of-years–digit depreciation was chosen.

To obtain an accelerated curve, first identify the maximum life, ML, and then sum the digits $1 + 2 + 3 + \ldots + ML = (ML)(ML + 1)/2 = D$. Next find the total amount by which the salvage ratio will decrease, which is $S(0) - S(ML)$. Then find the numerator of the rate for each age interval i. For age interval 0 to 0.5 years, this is $ML/2$. For all other age intervals it is $ML - i + 0.5$. The annual decrease of salvage during age interval i is the product of the total amount of decrease times $(ML - i + .5)/D$.

Table 4.7 (see end of chapter) shows the calculation of the average salvage ratio curve using the accelerated model. The initial salvage ratio, $S(0)$, was chosen to equal 100% and the salvage ratio at the maximum life was chosen to equal zero, so that $S(ML) = 0\%$. The maximum life of the R2–5 occurs during age interval $i = 9$, or during the age interval 8.5 – 9.5 years. The sum of digits 1 through 9 is 45. Column (b) shows the numerator of the rate, which is $L/2 = 9/2 = 4.5$ for the first interval and $9 - (i + 0.5)$ thereafter. The numerator decreases by 1 each year and the value during the final age interval is always 0.5. Each year the salvage decreases by an amount equal to the total decrease, 100%, times the weight in column (b) divided by 45. During age interval 2.5 – 3.5 this amount is $100\% \times (9 - 3 + 0.5)/45$ or 14.44%. Because the salvage at age zero is 100%, the value at the end of the first age interval, column (e), is 100% less the decrease of $(4.5/45) \times 100\%$ or 10%, or 90%. This amount is carried forward to the start of the next age interval. The average salvage during the age interval is shown in column (f).

Table 4.8 (see end of chapter) shows the salvage ratios that would result if life characteristics are described by the Iowa R2–5 survivor curve and the salvage shown in Table 4.7 is used; the table also shows the salvage ratios with an inflation rate of 6% applied. Figure 4.5 (see end of chapter) shows the salvage ratios without and with inflation plotted versus age.

Aged Data

Salvage curves reflecting historical salvage can be constructed from aged retirement data using the same techniques used to develop life tables. Because the forces affecting gross salvage and cost of retiring are often independent, these two costs should be recorded, analyzed, and forecasted separately. The net salvage is obtained by subtracting the cost of retiring from the gross salvage.

The requirements for aged salvage data are similar to the requirements for aged retirement data. As with aged retirement data, aged salvage data can be organized in a matrix with rows designating placement years and columns designating experience years.

Data from two sources are necessary to calculate the salvage curve for a vintage group. One set of data is the total salvage dollars during each experience year for the vintage under consideration. The salvage is either the gross salvage or the cost of retiring, depending on which salvage curve is being developed. The second set of data is the annual dollars retired during each experience year of the vintage under consideration. The salvage ratios are calculated directly from these data. The total salvage during the year depends on both the total number of retirements per year and the salvage per unit. The quotient of the total salvage divided by the original cost of the retirements equals the salvage ratio for that experience year.

The first three rows in Table 4.9 (see end of chapter) show the gross salvage, the cost of retiring, and the dollars retired from a 1982 vintage. Remember that the retirements are measured in original cost dollars (i.e., 1982 dollars), but the gross salvage and cost of retiring are measured in experience-year dollars. The ratios are the salvage dollars divided by the dollars retired for the same year. The survivor curve for this placement group shows about 22% of the property installed in 1982 is still in service at the end of 1988, so the resulting survivor curves do not reflect the complete history of the vintage group.

Conversion to Constant Dollars

An observed salvage ratio is a ratio of dollars at time x + age over dollars at time x, where x represents the year in which the property was installed. This ratio of mixed dollars often obscures underlying salvage patterns. For example, in the constant model presented in the previous section, the ratios were uniform only when measured in constant dollars, and the shape of the inflated, or observed, curve concealed the uniform pattern. The underlying patterns are also concealed in the linear and accelerated models. Conversion of the inflated ratios to ratios of constant, or uninflated, dollars reveals the underlying model and is therefore of value to the analyst.

The examples shown in Tables 4.5 through 4.9 assumed inflation at a constant annual rate of 6%. A more accurate view would be that each year is associated with a unique inflation factor and that the product of the annual factors, rather than an average, should be used in the discounting or adjusting process.

An important question centers on which inflation factor to use. Perhaps the most common index is the consumer price index (CPI), which is familiar because it reflects changes in the weighted price of goods and services used by the typical U.S. consumer. It recognizes that different segments of the economy, (e.g., health care, food, housing, energy) have different rates of inflation and that the result is a weighted average of these.

It is desirable to obtain specialized indexes that reflect the inflation rates in special segments of the economy, and in fact firms specialize in estimating these factors. Different indexes may apply to gross salvage and cost of retiring, and the appropriate index for gross salvage in one account will generally differ from that of another account. Once the historical indexes are obtained, they can be stored in the data base and updated each year.

The matrix containing the salvage dollars can be adjusted to convert all entries to a common year or reference point. Most indexes have a base year at which the index is set to 1, and other years are measured in reference to it.

Table 4.9 contains an example of salvage data. Suppose that during the period 1982 to 1988 the annual inflation rate was 6%. Table 4.10 (see end of chapter) shows the salvage values introduced in Table 4.9 converted to 1982 dollars, so that salvage and original cost are measured at the same price level. The resulting salvage ratios now have the inflation removed. The annual salvage dollars can be converted to 1982 dollars by dividing by the factor $(1 + .06)^{AGE}$. In 1985 the age is 3, and the factor is $1/(1.06)^3 = 1/1.19$ or 0.840. The observed gross salvage during 1985 was $768 and the observed cost of retiring was $329; multiplying by 0.840 yields 1982 price level values of $645 and $276 respectively.

The underlying patterns can now be seen more easily. Examine the gross salvage ratio and observe that it is approximately linear and declines by about 6% each year. With inflation removed, the cost of retiring ratio is constant and equals 17%.

A first step in salvage analysis is to convert the observed dollars to constant dollars. Then the constant dollar salvage curves can be examined and fit to a model.

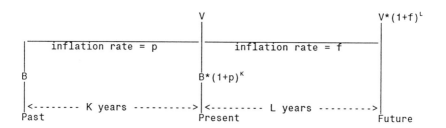

Figure 4.1. A cash flow diagram of investment and salvage costs.

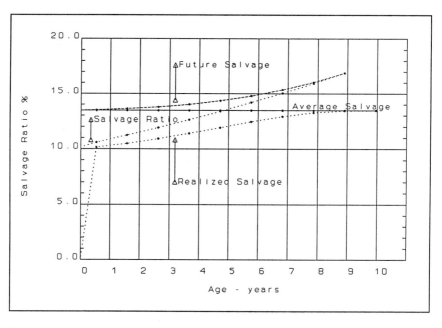

Figure 4.2. A graph of the salvage ratios and the realized and future salvage ratios versus age are for the data shown in Table 4.4.

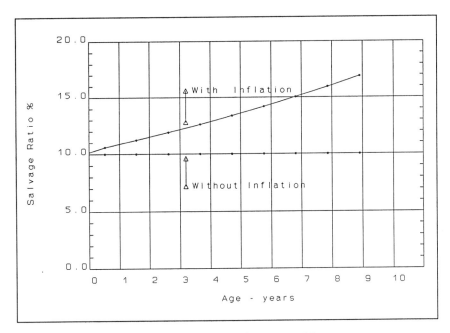

Figure 4.3. A graph of the salvage ratios shown in Table 4.5.

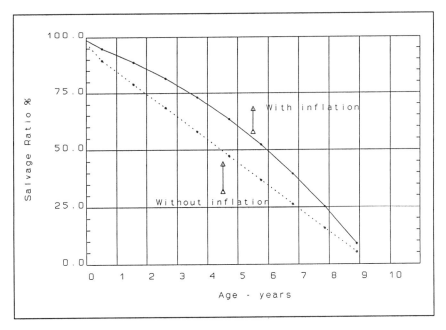

Figure 4.4. A graph of the salvage ratios shown in Table 4.6.

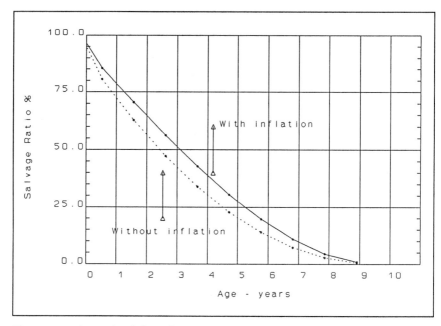

Figure 4.5. A graph of the salvage ratios shown in Table 4.8.

Table 4.1. Future salvage ratios as a function of the future inflation rate,
f, and the life of the unit, K.
The salvage ratio of the first
unit is V/B = 10% and p, the annual rate of inflation during its
life, is 3%. The life of the first
unit equals the life of the replacement unit (i.e., K = L).

K	Inflation rate - f			
Years	3%	6%	10%	12%
5	10.00%	11.54%	13.89%	15.20%
10	10.00%	13.33%	19.30%	23.11%
20	10.00%	17.76%	37.25%	53.41%
40	10.00%	31.53%	138.75%	285.25%

Table 4.2. Future salvage ratios as a func-
            tion of the cost of retiring in-
            flation rate, j, when p = 3%, the
            current gross salvage = 20% of
            first cost, and the present cost
            of retiring = 10% of first cost.
            The life of the first unit equals
            the life of the replacement unit.

L	Inflation rate - j			
Years	3%	6%	10%	12%
5	10.00%	8.46%	6.11%	4.80%
10	10.00%	6.67%	.70%	-3.11%
20	10.00%	2.24%	-17.25%	-33.41%
40	10.00%	-11.53%	-118.75%	-265.25%

Table 4.3. Salvage ratios as a function of
            life and inflation rate when V/B =
            10%.

Life	Inflation rate - p			
Years	3%	6%	10%	12%
0	10.00%	10.00%	10.00%	10.00%
5	11.59%	13.38%	16.11%	17.62%
10	13.44%	17.91%	25.94%	31.06%
20	18.06%	32.07%	67.27%	96.46%
40	32.62%	102.86%	452.59%	930.51%

Table 4.4. Calculation of average, realized, and future salvage ratios for
            the salvage schedule shown in column (d) and with life charac-
            teristics described by an Iowa R2-5 survivor curve. The percent
            surviving, realized salvage ratio, and future salvage ratio are
            all shown at the start of the age interval.

	Constant rate w/inflation						
Age interval (a)	Percent survive (b)	Percent retired (c)	Salvage ratio % (d)	Weighted ratio % (e)	Realized salvage % (f)	Future salvage % (g)	Average salvage % (h)
0- 0.5	100.00	1.11	10.15	.11	.00	13.46	13.46
.5- 1.5	98.89	3.56	10.60	.38	10.15	13.50	13.46
1.5- 2.5	95.33	6.20	11.24	.70	10.49	13.61	13.46
2.5- 3.5	89.13	10.12	11.91	1.21	10.92	13.77	13.46
3.5- 4.5	79.01	15.31	12.62	1.93	11.40	14.01	13.46
4.5- 5.5	63.70	20.30	13.38	2.72	11.91	14.34	13.46
5.5- 6.5	43.40	21.08	14.19	2.99	12.44	14.79	13.46
6.5- 7.5	22.32	14.99	15.04	2.25	12.91	15.37	13.46
7.5- 8.5	7.33	6.51	15.94	1.04	13.26	16.05	13.46
8.5- 9.5	.82	.82	16.89	.14	13.43	16.89	13.46
9.5-10.5	.00	--	--		13.46	--	13.46
			Average = 13.46%				

Table 4.5. A salvage curve with a constant rate and 6% inflation.

		*	Constant rate		* Constant rate w/inflation *		
Age interval (a)	Percent survive (b)	Salvage ratio % (c)	Weighted ratio % (d)	Future salvage ratio % (e)	Salvage ratio % (f)	Weighted ratio % (g)	Future salvage ratio % (h)
.0- 0.5	100.00	10.00	.11	10.00	10.15	.11	13.46
.5- 1.5	98.89	10.00	.36	10.00	10.60	.38	13.50
1.5- 2.5	95.33	10.00	.62	10.00	11.24	.70	13.61
2.5- 3.5	89.13	10.00	1.01	10.00	11.91	1.21	13.77
3.5- 4.5	79.01	10.00	1.53	10.00	12.62	1.93	14.01
4.5- 5.5	63.70	10.00	2.03	10.00	13.38	2.72	14.34
5.5- 6.5	43.40	10.00	2.11	10.00	14.19	2.99	14.79
6.5- 7.5	22.32	10.00	1.50	10.00	15.04	2.25	15.37
7.5- 8.5	7.33	10.00	.65	10.00	15.94	1.04	16.05
8.5- 9.5	.82	10.00	.08	10.00	16.89	.14	16.89
9.5-10.5	.00	--	--	--	--	--	--
		Average	= 10.00%		Average	= 13.46%	

Table 4.6. A linear salvage curve starting at 100% and declining to 0%, with 6% inflation.

		*	Linear rate		* Linear rate w/inflation *		
Age interval (a)	Percent survive (b)	Salvage ratio % (c)	Weighted ratio % (d)	Future salvage ratio % (e)	Salvage ratio % (f)	Weighted ratio % (g)	Future salvage ratio % (h)
.0- 0.5	100.00	97.37	1.08	47.35	98.80	1.10	60.94
.5- 1.5	98.89	89.47	3.19	46.79	94.84	3.38	60.51
1.5- 2.5	95.33	78.95	4.89	45.19	88.71	5.50	59.23
2.5- 3.5	89.13	68.42	6.92	42.84	81.49	8.25	57.18
3.5- 4.5	79.01	57.89	8.86	39.57	73.09	11.19	54.07
4.5- 5.5	63.70	47.37	9.62	35.16	63.39	12.87	49.49
5.5- 6.5	43.40	36.84	7.77	29.45	52.26	11.02	42.99
6.5- 7.5	22.32	26.32	3.94	22.47	39.57	5.93	34.24
7.5- 8.5	7.33	15.79	1.03	14.61	25.17	1.64	23.35
8.5- 9.5	.82	5.26	.04	5.26	8.89	.07	8.89
9.5-10.5	.00	--	--	--	--	--	--
		Average	= 47.35%		Average	= 60.94%	

Table 4.7. Calculation of an accelerated salvage curve starting at 100% and declining to 0%.

Age interval (a)	Weight (b)	Change (c)	Salvage at start (d)	Salvage at end (e)	Average salvage (f)
0 - .5	4.5	10.00	100.00	90.00	95.00
.5 - 1.5	8.5	18.89	90.00	71.11	80.56
1.5 - 2.5	7.5	16.67	71.11	54.44	62.78
2.5 - 3.5	6.5	14.44	54.44	40.00	47.22
3.5 - 4.5	5.5	12.22	40.00	27.78	33.89
4.5 - 5.5	4.5	10.00	27.78	17.78	22.78
5.5 - 6.5	3.5	7.78	17.78	10.00	13.89
6.5 - 7.5	2.5	5.56	10.00	4.44	7.22
7.5 - 8.5	1.5	3.33	4.44	1.11	2.78
8.5 - 9.5	.5	1.11	1.11	.00	.56

Table 4.8. A salvage curve with the accelerated model shown in Table 4.7 and with 6% inflation.

		*	Accelerated rate		*Accelerated rate w/inflation*		
Age interval (a)	Percent survive (b)	Salvage ratio % (c)	Weighted ratio % (d)	Future salvage ratio % (e)	Salvage ratio % (f)	Weighted ratio % (g)	Future salvage ratio % (h)
0- 0.5	100.00	95.00	1.05	26.60	96.39	1.07	32.99
.5- 1.5	98.89	80.56	2.87	25.83	85.39	3.04	32.28
1.5- 2.5	95.33	62.78	3.89	23.79	70.54	4.37	30.29
2.5- 3.5	89.13	47.22	4.78	21.08	56.24	5.69	27.50
3.5- 4.5	79.01	33.89	5.19	17.73	42.78	6.55	23.81
4.5- 5.5	63.70	22.78	4.62	13.85	30.48	6.19	19.25
5.5- 6.5	43.40	13.89	2.93	9.67	19.70	4.15	14.00
6.5- 7.5	22.32	7.22	1.08	5.68	10.86	1.63	8.62
7.5- 8.5	7.33	2.78	.18	2.53	4.43	.29	4.04
8.5- 9.5	.82	.56	.00	.56	.94	.01	.94
9.5-10.5	.00	--	--	--	--	--	--
		Average = 26.60%			Average = 32.99%		

Table 4.9. Partial retirement and salvage data from the 1982 vintage group. The upper portion of the table shows the gross salvage dollars, cost of retiring, and dollars retired for a vintage group. The lower portion of the table shows the resulting salvage ratios.

	Experience year						
	82	83	84	85	86	87	88
Gross salvage	94	357	470	768	1053	1191	1021
Cost of retiring	27	113	183	329	552	721	784
Annual retirements	157	627	941	1568	2508	3135	3292
Gross salvage ratio	.60	.57	.50	.49	.42	.38	.31
Cost of retir- ing ratio	.17	.18	.20	.21	.22	.23	.24
Net salvage ratio	.43	.39	.30	.28	.20	.15	.07

Table 4.10.   Conversion of salvage in Table 4.9 to 1982 dollars.

	Experience year						
	82	83	84	85	86	87	88
Gross salvage	94	337	418	645	834	890	720
Cost of retiring	27	106	163	276	437	539	553
Annual retirements	157	627	941	1568	2508	3135	3292
Gross salvage ratio	.60	.54	.44	.41	.33	.28	.22
Cost of retiring ratio	.17	.17	.17	.18	.17	.17	.17
Net salvage ratio	.43	.37	.27	.23	.16	.11	.05

5 | Depreciation Systems

$\mathbf{T}$HE recovery of capital through depreciation accruals may be thought of as a dynamic system. A system is an arrangement of things that are connected to form a complete organization of integrated parts. The state of the system at any time is defined by current values of the characteristics that define the system. A dynamic system is one where the state of the system depends on the history of the input variables. To define and study a system is to better understand the system so that more efficient methods of control can be designed to accomplish the desired ends.

There are two methods of controlling a system. One is to select an input and wait for the result or final output. If a different output is desired, the input is changed and the new output is obtained. The other method of control is to select an initial input, monitor the process, and when necessary, alter the input to achieve the desired goal. The first method is called an open control loop and the second a closed control loop. A necessary feature of the closed control loop is the feedback resulting from the monitoring of the system. A home heating system is a common and simple example of a dynamic system with a closed feedback loop. The parts of the system are a furnace and a thermostat. The thermostat monitors the room temperature and creates feedback, in the form of electrical signals, when the room temperature rises above or falls below the desired temperature. The electrical signals turn the furnace off or on to achieve the desired goal, a constant, predetermined room temperature.

Think of a depreciation accounting system as a dynamic system controlled with a closed feedback loop. Estimates of life and salvage and the amount of plant in service are inputs to the system, and the accumulated provision for depreciation is a measure of the state of the system at any time. The process of calculating the accumulated provision for depreciation is determined by the factors needed to define the system. The initial input to the system is estimates of the life and salvage, which are combined in an accrual rate. Dynamic forces affect the life and salvage, and revision of the original life and salvage estimates are the result of the monitoring process. These revisions to the initial input initiate feedback in the form of adjustments to the accumulated provision for depreciation. The goal of the system is recovery of capital in a timely manner.

One consideration that complicates this discussion is that many options can be combined to form many different depreciation systems. Whether the depreciation is for book, tax, valuation, or other purposes, each of these factors must be considered when discussing and defining a depreciation system.

DEFINING A DEPRECIATION SYSTEM

Below is a list of the factors needed to define a depreciation system. Each factor contains two or three options, and the complete definition of a system requires the selection of one option from each factor. The order of the list is arbitrary, but the last four factors are those whose options are varied when discussing depreciation systems commonly used to calculate book depreciation.

1. The depreciation concept, including (a) physical condition, (b) decrease in value, or (c) cost of operation
2. Depreciation over (a) time or (b) units of production
3. Depreciation of (a) a unit of property or (b) a group of property
4. Methods of allocation, including (a) the straight line method, (b) an accelerated method, or (c) a decelerated method
5. Procedures for applying the method of allocation including (a) the average life procedure, (b) the equal life group procedure, or (c) the probable life procedure
6. Adjustment using (a) the amortization method or (b) the remaining life method
7. Use of (a) the broad group model or (b) the vintage group model

The mathematically astute reader who multiplies the number of options in each factor will find that there are 432 combinations of options, each of which is a potential depreciation system. However, not all of these combinations are feasible, and some are unimportant. Only a few of these combinations are of major interest when considering systems of book depreciation currently being used.

Concepts of Depreciation

Three options are available when defining the concept of depreciation. These include (a) physical condition, (b) decrease in value, or (c) cost of operation. Though all have been used by utilities to determine book value, the cost of operation is, with few exceptions, the concept in current use.

Physical condition is, perhaps, the first option a lay person would think of if asked to define depreciation. An early reference to the relationship between depreciation and physical condition is from the 1588 textbook by John Mellis who referred to a debit to the profit and loss account because "implements of householde I doe find at this day to be consumed and worn." A later reference is in the 1833 annual report of the Baltimore and Ohio Railroad, which reported that an annuity was established "to provide for the replacement of oak sills and sleepers and yellow pine stringpieces."

Two problems arise when using the concept of physical condition as a measure of depreciation. First, wear and tear do not account for all retirements; in fact, they are often a minor reason for the retirement of property. Second, physical condition can be difficult to measure. Though it is possible to measure directly the wear of railroad track and the corrosion of cast iron pipe, easily measurable wear is not characteristic of most industrial property.

The concept of loss of value is also a common depreciation concept, and the lay person often uses it to explain the difference between the purchase price and the current market value of an automobile or major household appliance. The definition from the Supreme Court case *Lindheimer v. Illinois Bell Telephone* (1934) is often quoted: "Broadly speaking, depreciation is the loss, not restored by current maintenance, which is due to all the factors causing the ultimate retirement of the property. These factors embrace wear and tear, decay, inadequacy, and obsolescence."

In contrast to the concept of physical depreciation, the Lindheimer definition recognizes that factors other than wear and tear cause or contribute to the retirement of property. The definition refers to the "loss" but does not clearly state what is "lost" or how the "loss" should be measured. A 1935 definition by the Federal Communications Commission was similar to the Lindheimer definition but referred to "loss in service value," where service value is equated to the original cost less salvage.

Use of the concept of loss of value to determine annual depreciation charges might imply the need for an annual valuation of the property owned by the organization, particularly if the rate of loss in value was not uniform or readily defined. The process of determining a value is complex, depending on the purpose of the valuation and type of property. Thus, an annual valuation of a utility could be such an expensive and time-consuming process that it would not be a practical approach to use in determining annual depreciation.

Many types of property provide a constant level of service until they are retired. The intrinsic physical value of this type of property is only that it functions. A gas meter is a common example of a type of property that may provide a constant level of service throughout its life. If value is measured by the level of service provided, the meter would retain full value until retirement because its value to the utility would depend on its function rather than its age. This concept ignores the consumption of future service and would result in an annual depreciation charge that would be zero until the final year of service. Then the charge would equal the full value and would result in deferring all depreciation charges until the final year of service. A concept that better matches depreciation to service rendered and weighs it in relation to the total service potential might be preferable for purposes of both book and valuation depreciation. That is, a quantitative measure of value, such as service-years, is generally preferable to a functional measure.

The third concept is that depreciation represents an allocated cost of capital to operation. This concept recognizes that depreciation is a cost of providing service and that an organization should recover the capital invested in equipment and other property needed to provide the required service. In fact, the term *capital recovery* is often used in connection with depreciation. An early reference to depreciation is by the Roman Marcus Vitrurius Pollio, who in 27 B.C. wrote of "walls which are built of soft and smooth-looking stone, that will not last long." He calculated that the walls would not last more than eighty years and suggested that, for purposes of valuation, one-eightieth part of their original cost be deducted each year. Pollio not only raised several issues concerning depreciation but seemed to be equating depreciation to a cost of operation.

The definition of *depreciation accounting* by the American Institute of Certified Public Accountants (1961, par. 56) reflects the concept of depreciation as a cost: "Depreciation accounting is a system of accounting that aims to distribute cost or other basic value of tangible capital assets, less salvage (if any), over the estimated useful life of the unit (which may be a group of assets) in a systematic and rational manner. It is a process of allocation, not of valuation." This definition does not use the term *loss of service value* because it is defining depreciation accounting rather than depreciation itself. The definition emphasizes that the purpose of depreciation accounting is a means of distributing cost in a rational manner during the service life, in turn providing for the systematic recovery of capital. By use of the term *useful life,* the definition encompasses all causes of retirement. By referring to the distribution of cost less salvage, this definition recognizes that salvage should be considered when developing depreciation charges.

Historically, all three concepts of depreciation have been used by utilities to determine the book value of industrial property. Of these, the concept of depreciation as the allocation of cost has proven to be the most useful and most widely used concept.

Time versus Unit of Production

Useful life can be measured in units of time or units of production (also called units of service). Measurement of life in years is a common and familiar concept. Measurement of life in units of production can be applied to some types of property such as a truck, whose life can be measured in miles (e.g., a useful life of 100,000 miles). A feeder pipeline connecting an oil field to a transmission line will be in service until the field is no longer productive. If the only function of the feeder line is to transport oil from the field to the transmission line, the life of the feeder line is determined by the reserves of the oil field that must eventually pass through the pipeline. Annual depreciation could be measured in units of production, such as barrels of oil. A railroad might depreciate rail as a function of the accumulated weight that the rail has carried.

Suppose a truck is to be depreciated over its life as measured in miles. First, the life must be estimated, say 100,000 miles. Second, the number of miles the truck will be driven during the next year, say 27,000 miles, must be forecast to have sufficient information to budget the annual depreciation charge. Third, at the end of the year when the budgeted annual depreciation becomes an accounting entry, the amount would be calculated to reflect the actual miles driven.

The most common measure of life is in units of time rather than units of production. Most types of property (e.g., poles, buildings, wire) do not have a measure of production associated with them. If the life can be measured in some unit of production and the rate of production is constant from year to year, measurement of life in either units of time or production will result in the same annual accruals. The unit of production has strong appeal in situations where use varies significantly over time and the life can be measured in units of production. But these two conditions are not often met, and usually life is measured over time.

Depreciation of an Individual Unit versus a Group

Accounting records of transactions relating to depreciable property can be kept on either a unit or a group basis. An individual unit of property has a single life, while the units in a group of property display a range, or dispersion, of lives. Grouping many units of property into a single account simplifies the accounting system but also creates a complexity not encountered in the depreciation of an individual unit. The resulting complications provide a major challenge to the depreciation analyst.

A vintage group refers to a group of property placed in service during the same year. The plant in service decreases until all units are retired from service. The individual unit and the vintage group are similar because each has well-defined life characteristics. The life of an individual unit is described by a single number and the life of a vintage group is described by a survivor curve, which is a statistical description of the lives of the units of property in the group.

Methods of Allocation

To fully recover capital invested in plant and equipment, the total depreciation charge must equal the depreciation base. When using the allocation of cost concept, the depreciation base is the initial, or original, cost less net salvage. The annual depreciation accrual rate for a unit of property can be (a) constant over life (straight line), (b) high during early years and low in later years (accelerated), or (c) low in early years and high in later years (decelerated). Most methods of allocation fall into one of these three classifications, although it would be possible to develop a method that is a combination of them. The straight line method of allocation is the method of allocation most often used when calculating book depreciation. Accelerated methods of allocation are commonly used for tax purposes. Decelerated methods of allocation are not in common use for book or tax purposes, but they are of historical interest and are used in valuation problems.

Average Life, Equal Life Group, or Probable Life Procedures

The average life and equal life group procedures are two ways of applying a method of allocation to determine the annual accrual. The probable life procedure is similar to the average life procedure, but is not appropriate for depreciation accounting.

A group of property displays a wide range of lives, and the life characteristics of the group must be described statistically. This is in contrast to a unit of property, whose life can be described as a single number. When depreciating a group of property, rather than a unit of property, a major decision must be made whether to base the depreciation accrual rate on the average life of the group (the average life procedure) or whether to divide the group into subgroups of equal life (the equal life group procedure).

In the average life procedure, a constant annual accrual rate based on the average life of all property in the group is applied to the surviving property. Most retirements occur either before or after, rather than at, the average life, but both short- and long-lived property are depreciated at the same rate. Property having a shorter life than the average will not be fully depreciated by the time of its retirement. Because the accrual rate is based on the average life of the group, the difference between accruals for early retirements and the full cost of the early retirements will be balanced during the life of the property having lives longer than the average. The result is that the group will be fully depreciated by the time of the final retirement.

In the equal life group procedure the property is divided into subgroups that each have a common life. Each subgroup is then depreciated as a unit using an accrual rate based on the common life of the group. Each unit is fully depreciated by the time it is retired. Application of the equal life group procedure is generally considered to better match the consumption of capital with service provided than does application of the average life procedure.

Any of the three methods of allocation (i.e., straight line, accelerated, or decelerated) can be applied to an individual unit or to group property. When the average life procedure is applied, the straight line method of allocation is easily used; application of either an accelerated or a decelerated method becomes more complicated. When the equal life group procedure is used, any of the three methods of allocation can be easily used.

The probable life procedure is a variation of the average life procedure. It is not valid for depreciation accounting or capital recovery because it does not fully depreciate the group. The depreciation charges are allocated over the average life of the property remaining in service (i.e., over the probable life), so that the continually decreasing rate is inadequate to fully recover the depreciable base. Use of this procedure should be restricted to those special situations where it is applicable; for example, it may used in the valuation process.

Methods of Adjustment

Depreciation accrual rates are calculated using estimates of the service life and salvage. Over time, new events that provide additional information occur, and the existing estimates are revised. A revision of the estimates of life and salvage results in the recognition that the accumulated provision for depreciation may now be either higher or lower than necessary, depending upon the magnitude and direction of the revised estimates. This recognition may justify an adjustment to the accumulated provision for depreciation, an adjustment to the annual depreciation rate, or both.

Adjustments to the accumulated provision for depreciation[1] can be made using either a fixed amortization period or the remaining life basis. The term *amortization method of adjustment* is used to describe a general approach in which the first step is the estimation of the required adjustment to the accumulated provision for depreciation and the second step is the determination of the timing and amount of the adjustment. In the remaining life method of adjustment, adjustments to the accumulated provision for depreciation are amortized over the remaining life of the property and are automatically included in the annual accrual.

The amortization method of adjustment uses the revised estimates of life and salvage characteristics to compute the calculated accumulated depreciation (CAD) to serve as a guide when determining the appropriate adjustment. The CAD is compared to the accumulated provision for depreciation; a significant difference between the two shows that an adjustment to the accumulated provision for depreciation may be advisable. The adjustment can be allocated in several ways, which might include (1) a lump sum equal to the adjustment made immediately, (2) amortization of the adjustment over a fixed period (e.g., over 5 years), or (3) amortization of the adjustment over the remaining life of the property. A lump sum adjustment is not an amortization but will be considered an option in the amortization method of adjustment (i.e., the amortization method could be more accurately called the amortization or lump sum method of adjustment). The difference between the CAD and the accumulated provision for depreciation is only an estimate of the required adjustment. The need for, the magnitude of, and the timing of the actual adjustment should be based upon the recommendation of the depreciation professional. This recommendation requires professional judgment and should consider several factors: the characteristics of the account; the cause of the difference; estimates of future events that will affect the property; the year-to-year volatility of the accumulated provision for depreciation; and the depreciation policies of the organization. A revised forecast of life or salvage normally leads to a revised depreciation rate even when an adjustment to the accumulated provision for depreciation is not considered necessary.

When using the remaining life method of adjustment, emphasis is placed upon forecasting the remaining life of the property in service. A change in the estimate of either life or salvage characteristics automatically triggers an adjustment to the accumulated provision for depreciation, and the adjustment will be spread over the remaining life of the property.

Broad Group or Vintage Group Model

Typically, property depreciated as a group provides a service to the organization over a long period of time. Each year property in the group is retired from service, but new property is added to the group to replace that retired or to increase the capacity of the group. Thus, over time vintage groups are continually being retired from and added to the group. A group such as this is called a *continuous property group,* though the term *open-ended group* is also used. The life and salvage characteristics of the vintages in the continuous property group must be specified in some systematic manner. The broad group model views each vintage in the continuous group as having identical life and salvage characteristics. The vintage group model views each vintage as having different life and salvage characteristics.

UNIT DEPRECIATION

Depreciation of a unit of property is a concept more readily understood than depreciation of a group of property. This section will present a brief discussion of the three methods of allocating the depreciable cost of a unit of property among accounting periods. An understanding of unit depreciation, particularly the straight line method of allocation, is necessary when considering depreciation for a group of property. In all examples, the cost of operation depreciation concept will be used, and depreciation will be over time (i.e., years). The depreciation base will equal the original cost less net salvage. This base represents the amount of capital to be consumed and, therefore, the amount of capital to be recovered through depreciation accruals.

Methods of Allocation

The three general methods of allocation are straight line, accelerated, and decelerated. An example of each will be applied to a unit of property that has an initial cost of $4000, a life of 4 years, and a net salvage value of $800 at retirement. The net salvage is commonly expressed in terms of the *salvage ratio* (SR), $800/$4000 or 0.20 or 20%.

Straight Line Method of Allocation

The straight line method of allocation is used almost exclusively by regulated, capital-intensive companies when calculating depreciation accruals for book accounting purposes. The straight line method applies a constant annual accrual rate to the cost of the unit, thus yielding a constant annual depreciation charge. The net book value (i.e., the original cost less the accumulated provision for depreciation) plotted versus time is a straight line.

The straight line rate is $(1 - SR)/\text{life}$. The factor $(1 - SR) = (1 - 0.20) = 0.80$, or 80%, represents the fraction of the original investment consumed during the life of the property, or the depreciable base. In this example that amount is $0.80 \times \$4000$, or $3200. The accrual rate is $0.80/4$

or 20%. The equal annual accruals are obtained by multiplying the original cost by the accrual rate. The figures in Table 5.1 (see end of chapter) are based on the assumption that this property was installed on January 1, 1974, and show the resulting accumulated provision for depreciation by year for this system. In the final year, the credit to the accumulated provision for depreciation equals the annual depreciation charge of $800 plus the net salvage of $800 for a total credit of $1600.

A major reason for the popularity of the straight line method is its simplicity. In addition, it occupies a middle ground between the accelerated and decelerated methods. Implicit in the use of the straight line method is the suggestion that the level of service provided by industrial property is independent of its age, and therefore the annual depreciation rate also should be independent of age (i.e., constant). Examples can be given where property such as poles, pipelines, cable, and meters provides a constant level of service throughout its life, but examples where the service provided by these types of property varies with age also can be given.

Accelerated Methods of Allocation

Any method that results in annual accruals that are higher early in life than late in life is called an accelerated method of allocation. Accelerated methods are allowed for calculating depreciation for tax purposes and are often used because of the rapid recovery of capital that they provide. Sometimes industrial property provides more service during early years than later years. An electrical generating unit begins its life as a base load generator operating continuously except for scheduled maintenance. As more efficient generators are installed, the base load generator becomes a peak load generator and operates only several hours each day. Eventually the generator is not used regularly but is used on a standby basis. Thus the service it provides changes significantly with age.

One accelerated method is the sum-of-years–digits method. Applying it to the $4000, 4 years, 20% salvage ratio example leaves the depreciable base unaffected at $3200, but the annual accruals vary with age rather than staying constant. To calculate the annual rate during year i, first sum the digits from 1 through the maximum life. In the example the sum is $1 + 2 + 3 + 4 = 10$. (A useful equation is that the sum of digits from 1 to n is $[(n)(n + 1)/2]$ or in the example $[(4) \times (5)/2] = 10$.) The rate during year i is $(1 - SR)(\text{life} - i + 1)/(\text{sum-of-years–digits})$. Applied to the example, the annual accrual rates are calculated as follows:

Year	Sum	Life − Year + 1	Annual Rate	
			No Salvage	With Salvage
1	10	4 − 1 + 1 = 4	40%	32%
2	10	4 − 2 + 1 = 3	30%	24%
3	10	4 − 3 + 1 = 2	20%	16%
4	10	4 − 4 + 1 = 1	10%	8%
			100%	80%

Note that with no salvage the accrual rates sum to 100% and that with salvage the accrual rates sum to 100%(1 − SR) or 80%, so that the depreciable base is recovered. Table 5.2 (see end of chapter) shows the application of the sum-of-years–digits method to the example.

The annual accruals of $1280 and $960 during the first two years are larger than the $800 annual accrual when using the straight line method of allocation, but the $640 and $320 for the final two years are less. When matching depreciation to service, an accelerated method of allocation would be appropriate if the property yields significantly more service early in life than it does later in life.

The declining balance method is another example of an accelerated method of allocation and it is widely used for tax depreciation. This method applies a constant rate to the declining balance of the book value, so that the annual accruals decrease even though the rate is constant. The rate is equal to a constant/life; if the constant is two, the rate is double the straight line rate and results in the double declining balance method. Rather than double declining balance, we will use 1.5 declining balance, so that the rate is 1.5/4 or 37.5%. Table 5.3 (see end of chapter) shows the calculations using the 1.5 declining balance method and illustrates a complexity inherent in the method. Because salvage was not included in the rate, it is necessary to switch to a straight line rate late in life so that the final value of the accumulated provision for depreciation is zero. In this example, the book value is $976 at the beginning of the fourth year; continuation of the 37.5% rate will result in a fourth-year accrual of $366 and total accruals of $3390, which is $190 more than the $3200 capital that has been consumed. We will switch to a straight line rate that will yield a final accrual of $976 − $800 or $176 during the final year as shown in Table 5.3. Details on switching rules should be obtained from the IRS if using this method for tax depreciation.

The equation $1 - (SR)^{1/N}$ calculates the declining balance rate that will yield a final book value equal to a nonzero salvage. In our example that rate is $1 - 0.2^{1/4}$ or $1 - 0.67$ or 33%. Applying that rate to the book balance yields total annual accruals of $3200 without resorting to switching rules at the end of the life.

Decelerated Methods of Allocation

Any method that results in annual accruals that are lower early in life than later in life is called a decelerated method of allocation. The sinking fund method is an example of a decelerated method. To apply it to our example, the sinking fund factor (also called the A/F factor) must be calculated; the sinking fund factor is $\{r/[(1 + r)^n - 1]\}$, where r is an interest rate and n is the life. Tables of this factor as a function of r and n are included in most books on business finance and engineering economics. If r = 10% and n = 4, the sinking fund factor is $\{0.10/[(1.10)^4 - 1]\}$ or 0.2155. This means that if 100×0.2155 or $21.55 is invested at the end of each year for four years and returns an annual effective return of 10% compounded annually, the value of the sinking fund at the end of the fourth year will be $100. But in order for the four annual payments of $21.55 to total $100, each payment must be compounded by $(1 + r)$, or 1.10 in the example, each year. The accrual rate without salvage is 21.55% the first year, $1.1 \times 21.55\%$ or 23.70% the second year, $1.1 \times 23.70\%$ or 26.07% the third year, and $1.1 \times 26.07\%$ or 28.68% the fourth year. The annual accrual rates without and with 20% salvage are summarized as follows:

Year	Annual Rate	
	No Salvage	With Salvage
1	21.55%	17.24%
2	23.70%	18.96%
3	26.07%	20.85%
4	28.68%	22.95%
	100.00%	80.00%

The accrual rates with salvage are used in Table 5.4 (see end of chapter).

The annual accruals of $690 and $758 during the first two years are less than the $800 annual accrual resulting from the straight line method of allocation, and the $834 and $918 during the final two years are more. A larger rate of interest results in a larger difference between annual accruals. A negative interest rate will result in accelerated depreciation. A zero interest rate results in a straight line rate.

Another decelerated method of allocation is the present worth method. It results in annual accruals that are identical with the sinking fund method, although the rationale leading to the calculation of the annual accruals is different. The present worth method is often used in the economic valuation and comparison of capital investments.

GROUP DEPRECIATION SYSTEMS WITH NO SALVAGE

The remainder of this chapter is devoted to the depreciation of a vintage group of property. First, the systems described and examples presented will assume zero salvage. Then the modifications to these systems when salvage is not zero will be introduced and discussed.

Four of the seven factors of depreciation listed at the beginning of the chapter will be limited to one option during the following discussion. Only the cost of operation concept of depreciation will be considered. Depreciation will be over time. Depreciation will be of a group, not a unit. Only the straight line method of allocation will be used. Both the average life and equal life group procedures, and the amortization and remaining life methods of adjustments will be examined. A discussion of the broad group and vintage group models will be deferred to a following chapter.

The Average Life Procedure Applied to a Vintage Group

Calculation of the Annual Accrual

One system of calculating the annual accrual incorporates the straight line method of allocation (SL) and applies the average life procedure (AL) to a vintage group. It is denoted by the initials SL-AL. As defined, this system lacks a feedback loop to control the system. A method of adjustment must be added to design a controlled, closed loop depreciation system.

The average life procedure applies the constant rate of 1/AL to the average plant in service during the year. Note that because the balance is averaged over a year, the AL must be measured in years. If the estimate of the average life is accurate, the vintage will be fully depreciated (i.e., the accumulated provision for depreciation will equal zero) after the final retirement.

It may not be immediately clear that this system will work (i.e., that the sum of the accruals will equal the original cost of the initial installations). The left side of the equation below equals the sum of the annual accruals when a rate of 1/AL is used and is set equal to the amount to be recovered (i.e., the original cost or initial balance).

$$\Sigma \text{ (average plant in service during age interval j)}/AL = \text{original cost}$$
$$\text{summed for } j = 0, 1, 2, \ldots, ML \text{ (the maximum life)}$$

The average plant in service during the age interval times the one-year width of the age interval equals the dollar-years service provided during the year. The sum of the values (average plant in service during age interval j) is

equal to the area under the survivor curve and may be written (area under
the survivor curve)/AL = original cost, or by rearranging this equation,
AL = (the area under the survivor curve)/(original cost). The average life
has been shown to equal the area under the survivor curve divided by the
original cost (true whether the survivor curve is measured in dollars or
units), so the original equality is true. We can conclude that this system will
fully recover the initial investment regardless of the shape of the survivor
curve.

This equation also shows that if the AL used in the accrual rate is not
equal to the actual average life, the sum of the accruals will not equal the
original cost. Suppose that the actual life was 8 years, but a life of 6 years
was forecast and used in the depreciation rate. The total accruals would
equal 8/6 or 133% of the original cost, and the accumulated provision for
depreciation would show an overaccrual equal to 133% − 100% or 33% of
the original cost at the time of the final retirement. Similarly, a forecast of a
life of 10 years would result in total accruals of 8/10 or 80% of the original
cost. At the time of the final retirement the accumulated provision for
depreciation would show an underaccrual equal to 100% − 80% or 20% of
the original cost.

Consider a property group having the survivor curve shown in Figure
5.1. This curve could result from the grouping of two units, one with a cost
of $4000 and a 4-year life and the second with a cost of $6000 and an 8-year
life. The average life (AL) is the area under the survivor curve divided by
the original cost or the AL = [(4000 × 4) + (6000 × 8)]/10000 or 6.4
years. The straight line, average life annual accrual rate is 1/6.4 or
15.625%.

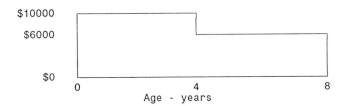

Figure 5.1. A survivor curve with an average life of 6.4 years.

*NOTE: To simplify calculations in this section, age intervals will be
0–1, 1–2, 2–3, etc., installations will be assumed to occur at the
start of the age interval, and retirements will be assumed to occur
at the end of the age interval. The average plant in service during
the age interval will then equal the balance at the start of the
interval, so that applying the annual accrual rate to the plant in*

service at the start of the interval is equivalent to applying it to the average balance. In all tables in this section, the balance, accumulated provision for depreciation, and calculated accumulated depreciation are calculated at the beginning of the year. Note that the accumulated provision for depreciation is zero at the beginning of the initial year. Examples using the half-year convention will be shown later.

Table 5.5 (see end of chapter) shows the annual accruals and accumulated provision for depreciation that result from the SL-AL system. Column (b) shows beginning of year balances of $10,000 for the four years 1974 to 1977, and balances of $6000 for the next four years, 1978 to 1981. This follows the survivor curve shown in Figure 5.1. Column (c) shows a $4000 retirement at the end of 1977 and a $6000 retirement at the end of 1981. The annual accrual, column (e), is the product of the rate, column (d), and the plant balance at the start of the year, column (b). As described in the preceding note, retirements are assumed to take place at the end of the year, so that the plant balance at the start of the year is also the average balance during the year. The accumulated provision for depreciation, column (f), is zero at the start of the first year and is then increased by the annual accruals and reduced by the annual retirements. At the time of the final retirement, the accumulated provision for depreciation is zero, showing that the sum of the annual accruals and the annual retirements equals zero and that the property is fully depreciated.

Suppose that at the time of the initial installation of the property, the estimate of the average life was 7.4 years. If the rate 1/7.4 is used throughout the life of the property but the actual life is 6.4 years, then only (6.4/7.4)($10000) or $8649 will be depreciated and $10000 − $8649 or $1351 of invested capital will not be recovered. This is verified by the calculations shown in Table 5.6 (see end of chapter).

An Adjustment Problem—AL Procedure

Now suppose that in January 1977, because of events and activities occurring since 1974, the original forecast of 7.4 years average life is revised to 6.4 years. Table 5.7 (see end of chapter) shows the accumulated provision for depreciation at the start of 1977 is $4054. Unless some corrective action is taken, the annual accruals will not equal the $10,000 original cost, and at the time of the final retirement a total of $1351 will remain unrecovered. The SL-AL system of calculating the annual accruals must be augmented to include a method of adjustment to define a depreciation system that will adapt to the almost certain circumstance that forecasts are revised from time to time.

When there is a revision of the original forecast of service life, it becomes necessary to consider a method of augmenting the SL-AL system of calculating annual accruals. Either of two methods of adjustment, the amortization method (AM) or the remaining life method (RL), can be added to the system of calculating annual accruals to construct a depreciation system with a closed feedback loop.

Amortization Method of Adjustment (SL-AL-AM)

Use of the amortization method of adjustment does not result in the prescription of an adjustment, but places the responsibility of recommending the magnitude and timing of the adjustment in the hands of the depreciation professional. Control focuses on the calculated accumulated depreciation (CAD). The CAD is normally a reasonable and valid estimate of an adequate level of the accumulated provision for depreciation. The depreciation professional will examine the variation between the CAD and the accumulated provision for depreciation to determine if adjustments to the annual accrual are necessary.

DEVELOPMENT OF THE CALCULATED ACCUMULATED DEPRECIATION. Two approaches can be used to develop the calculated accumulated depreciation. One, a retrospective approach, is to reconstruct the past accruals and retirements to determine what the accumulated provision for depreciation would have been given the current estimate of the life characteristics. The other, a prospective approach, is to estimate the sum of the future additions to and subtractions from the accumulated provision for depreciation. The sum of these additions and subtractions also is an estimate of the accumulated provision for depreciation that would be desirable to have on the books.

The retrospective approach appears to be straightforward. In fact, Table 5.5 shows that if property had the service life characteristics shown in Figure 5.1, the accumulated provision for depreciation at the start of the fourth year would be $4688. Comparison of this figure to the accumulated provision for depreciation of $4054 shown in Table 5.7 shows that an adjustment of $634 is necessary. In practice, however, the retrospective approach has a major shortcoming. The history of the account may go back many years and include accounting transactions, such as transfers, sales, acquisitions, and adjustments, which have been recorded in the accumulated provision for depreciation account. Use of the retrospective approach requires complete knowledge of these transactions as they must be considered for inclusion in the construction of the CAD. Because of the difficulties likely to be encountered in reconstructing the accumulated provision for depreciation, the retrospective approach is usually discarded in favor of the prospective approach.

The prospective approach to the CAD is based on estimates of the future accruals and retirements. Estimates of future accruals and retirements can be made if the survivor characteristics of the property have been estimated. The following relationship states that the calculated accumulated depreciation plus all future accruals, less all future retirements, equals zero. If this relationship holds, the cost of the property will be fully allocated at the time of the final retirement.

$$\text{CAD(i)} + \text{future accruals} - \text{future retirements} = 0$$

or

$$\text{CAD(i)} = \text{future retirements} - \text{future accruals}$$

The future retirements equal the current balance of the plant in service, because all property currently in service must eventually be retired. The future accruals is the sum of the annual future accruals when the SL-AL system of calculating the annual accruals is used. Thus, CAD(i) = current balance − Σ (average balance during year j)(1/AL) = current balance − (1/AL)Σ (average balance during year j) summed for j from year i to year of final retirement, where CAD(i) = calculated accumulated depreciation at the start of year i.

The average balance during each year is determined by the survivor curve used to describe the life characteristics of the vintage. The sum of the average balances during the year, starting with the current year and continuing through all years until the year of the final retirement, is equal to the area under the survivor curve and to the right of the current age. This area represents the remaining service and is measured, in this case, in dollar-years. The remaining service divided by the plant in service is defined as the average remaining life (also called the expectancy). Dividing both sides of the equation above by the current balance yields the following definition and equation for the calculated accumulated depreciation ratio, which will be abbreviated as CADR[2]:

$$\text{CAD(i)/current balance} = \text{current balance/current balance} - \text{(area under the survivor curve/current balance)/AL}$$

$$\text{CAD(i)/current balance} = \text{CADR(i)} = 1 - \text{RL(i)/AL}, \text{where CADR(i)} = \text{calculated accumulated depreciation ratio at age i and RL(i)} = \text{remaining life at age i}$$

Tables of the Iowa survivor curves contain values of the calculated accumulated depreciation ratios.

Table 5.8 (see end of chapter) shows the calculation of the RL, the

CADR, and the CAD for the survivor curve shown in Figure 5.1. The 64,000 dollar-years of remaining service at age zero, column (d), is equal to the sum of the annual balances shown in column (c) and also equal to the area under the survivor curve. (Remember that the width of each interval is one year, so that the balance at the start of the year multiplied by the width of the interval, one year, is the area under the survivor curve attributable to that year.) The amount in column (d) represents the remaining service contained in the existing plant. Each year the amount in column (d) is reduced by the average plant balance during that year times the one-year period (i.e., the service provided during the year) to calculate the service, measured in dollar-years, remaining at the beginning of the next year. The remaining life, column (e), is the remaining service divided by the balance or column (d)/column (c). The CADR, column (f), is 1 − remaining life/ average life. The CAD, column (g), equals the CADR multiplied by the plant in service. This calculation shows that the CADR is sensitive to both the average life *and* the shape of the survivor curve.

AN AMORTIZATION SOLUTION TO THE AL ADJUSTMENT PROBLEM.   Now return to the problem raised in the scenario shown in Table 5.7. Table 5.8 shows that if the estimate of a 6.4-year average life is accurate, the current value of the accumulated provision for depreciation would be $4688 rather than the recorded $4054, and this results in an apparent deficit of $634. If the depreciation professional believes this variation is significant, then an adjustment to the accumulated provision for depreciation should be made.

The adjustment to the accumulated provision for depreciation can be made in several ways, ranging from a lump sum adjustment of $634 to amortizing the $634 over a period less than the remaining life, equal the remaining life, or longer than the remaining life. For example, suppose it is decided to amortize the $634 over two years; then the accumulated provision for depreciation would be credited an additional $317 in 1978 and 1979. In addition, the annual rate would be changed to 1/6.4 to reflect the revised forecast. Table 5.9 (see end of chapter) shows that these adjustments will result in a recovery of the $10,000 initial investment as reflected by the final zero balance of the accumulated provision for depreciation.

The CAD is not a precise measurement. It is based on a model that only approximates the complex chain of events that occur in an actual property group and depends upon forecasts of future life and salvage. Thus, it serves as a guide to, not a prescription for, adjustments to the accumulated provision for depreciation.

Remaining Life Method of Adjustment (SL-AL-RL)

In 1953 the California Public Utilities Commission issued *Determina-*

tion of Straight-line Remaining Life Depreciation Accruals, also called *Standard Practice U-4.* This document, which was revised in 1961, presents the steps required in determining the annual accrual when using the straight line method of allocation, the average life procedure, and the remaining life method of adjustment.

Though the term *remaining life* is often thought of as a basis for calculating the annual accrual, it is more appropriately considered a method of adjustment used with a system of calculating annual accruals. As discussed in the preceding paragraphs, a revision of the forecast of average life may lead to an adjustment to the accumulated provision for depreciation. When the remaining life method of adjustment is used, the variation between the CAD and the accumulated provision for depreciation is amortized over the remaining life of the plant in service. This adjustment is automatic in the sense that it is built into the remaining life calculations.

Table 5.5 shows the calculation of annual accruals using the SL-AL system applied to property described by the survivor curve of Figure 5.1. Remember that the annual accrual is the average balance during the year times the straight line rate 1/AL. Use of the remaining life method of adjustment requires different calculations even though the same annual accruals will result. Before calculating the accruals, the remaining life rates for the survivor curve used to estimate the life characteristics must be determined, and these calculations are shown in Table 5.10 (see end of chapter).

The remaining life calculations can be viewed in two ways. One is that the rate 1/RL is applied to the future accrual, which is the current plant in service less the accumulated provision for depreciation. The future accrual (i.e., the amount remaining to be accrued) is allocated over the remaining life of the vintage group using the straight line method. The procedure used to apply the straight line method assumes each unit in service has a remaining life equal to the average remaining life. Thus the AL procedure is used. Table 5.11 (see end of chapter) shows the remaining life calculations using the survivor curve in Figure 5.1. Column (d), the future accruals, is the balance less the accumulated provision for depreciation, column (b) − column (g). The remaining life rates, taken from Table 5.10, are shown in column (e). The annual accruals, the product of columns (d) and column (e), are in column (f). Note that the annual accruals resulting from the remaining life calculations are identical with those obtained by applying the rate 1/AL to the average plant in service and shown in Table 5.5.

A second way of viewing the remaining life calculation is to consider the annual accrual as the SL-AL accrual plus an adjustment to reduce the variation between the CAD and the accumulated provision for depreciation. The following calculations show that the amortization method, SL-AL-AM, and the remaining life method, SL-AL-RL, yield identical annual accruals when the variation between the CAD and the accumulated provision for depreciation is either (a) zero or (b) amortized over the remaining life.[3]

Let:[4] B   = plant balance
        AL   = average life
        RL   = remaining life
        APD   = the accumulated provision for depreciation
        APDR = the ratio APD/B
        CAD   = the calculated accumulated depreciation
        CADR = the ratio CAD/B
        AARL = the annual accrual using the RL method of adjustment
        AAAM = the annual accrual using the AM method of adjustment

The annual accrual will be calculated for both methods of adjustment, and the two annual accruals will then be compared. First, the annual accrual using the remaining life method of adjustment (the AARL) is the total amount remaining to be depreciated (i.e., the future accrual) divided by the remaining life or AARL = (B − APD)/RL = B[(1 − APDR)/RL].

Next, the annual accrual using the amortization method of adjustment (the AAAM) will be written as the sum of the straight line, average life accrual plus the annual adjustment of the variation between the CAD and the accumulated provision for depreciation. The following calculations assume the variation is amortized over the remaining life and make use of the fact that the CADR = 1 − RL/AL.

$$
\begin{aligned}
\text{AAAM} &= \text{annual accrual} + \text{adjustment} \\
&= \text{annual accrual} + \text{variation/remaining life} \\
&= B/AL + (CAD − APD)/RL \\
&= B/AL + [B(CADR) − B(APDR)]/RL \\
&= B[1/AL + CADR/RL − APDR/RL] \\
&= B[1/AL + (1 − RL/AL)/RL − APDR/RL] \\
&= B[1/AL + 1/RL − 1/AL − APDR/RL] \\
\text{AAAM} &= B[(1 − APDR)/RL]
\end{aligned}
$$

but this is the same as the annual accrual using the RL method of adjustment so AARL = B[(1 − APDR)/RL] = AAAM.

If the variation is zero, then the accumulated provision for depreciation (APDR) equals the CAD. Because the CAD equals 1 − RL/AL, the annual accruals using the remaining life method of adjustment can be written

$$
\begin{aligned}
\text{AARL} &= B[(1 − APDR)/RL] \\
&= B[(1 − CADR)/RL]
\end{aligned}
$$

$$= B[(1 - 1 + RL/AL)/RL]$$
$$= B[1/AL]$$
$$= AAAM$$

Thus, when the variation is zero, the remaining life accrual can be expressed as the balance divided by the AL.

EFFECTS OF USING AN IMPROPER REMAINING LIFE.   Calculation of the remaining life requires knowledge of the survivor curve; survivor curves with the same average life but different shapes will have different remaining lives. This raises the question of the result of applying the remaining life method of adjustment when the average life is correct but the shape of the survivor curve used to calculate the remaining lives differs from the actual retirement pattern. To examine this question, suppose the survivor curve shown in Table 5.12 (see end of chapter) is used to estimate the life characteristics of the property to be depreciated. Though the average life of this curve is 6.4 years, the same as the survivor curve shown in Figure 5.1, its retirement pattern is significantly different from the pattern shown in Figure 5.1.

Note that, as shown during 1981 in Table 5.12, calculation of the remaining life can be puzzling. Confusion arises because the final retirement takes place not at the end of the year, but 1/3 of the way through the year. At the start of the year, the remaining life is 2000/6000 or 1/3 year. However, a remaining life of 1 is needed to obtain a final rate of 100%. An explanation is the choice of one-year intervals to calculate accruals. Suppose that accruals were calculated every 1/3 year, so that a unit of time is 1/3 year rather than 1 year. The average life would then be 6.4 × 3 or 19.2 units (i.e., 19.2 one/third years). These calculations would show the sum of the three 1/3-year accruals equal the annual accruals shown in Table 5.12. However, at the start of 1981, the remaining life is 1 unit, and the corresponding rate is 100%.

Table 5.13 (see end of chapter) shows the result of applying the accrual rates from Table 5.12 to property whose survivor curve is described in Figure 5.1. That is, we will use the correct average life but the incorrect remaining lives. Though the total accruals equal the $10,000 original cost, the annual accruals are not identical with those of Table 5.11. In this example, the maximum life of the survivor curve used to calculate the remaining life rates (7.33 years) is less than the maximum life of the property (8 years), so the final, 100% accrual rate of Table 5.12 assures the accruals will total $10,000.

Now suppose that the survivor curve used to describe the life characteristics of the property being depreciated still has an average life of 6.4 years but the maximum life is greater than 8 years, as shown in Table 5.14

(see end of chapter). When the accrual rates shown in Table 5.14 are applied to property whose life characteristics are shown in Figure 5.1, an under-accrual of $1875 results, because the final retirement was forecast to occur in 1983 but actually occurred in 1981. This emphasizes the fact that when using the remaining life method of adjustment, estimates of the shape of the survivor curve may need to be revised, even though estimates of the average life are unchanged. See Table 5.15 at the end of this chapter.

How does the remaining life adjustment behave when life estimates are revised? Again, the scenario shown in Table 5.7 can be used to observe the results of applying the remaining life method of adjustment. Let the initial forecast of service life be the survivor curve shown in Table 5.16 (see end of chapter); it has an average life of 7.4 years, the same life used to generate the accrual rate shown in Table 5.6.

The remaining life rates of Table 5.16 are used to calculate annual accruals and the accumulated provision for depreciation shown in Table 5.17 (see end of chapter). Because the actual average life is 6.4 years but the forecast life is 7.4 years, the total accruals are $1351 less than the required $10,000.

A REMAINING LIFE SOLUTION TO THE AL ADJUSTMENT PROBLEM. Table 5.7 presented a scenario where accrual rates based on a forecast life of 7.4 years were used for the years 1974, 1975, and 1976. Then in January 1977, the forecast was revised to an average life of 6.4 years. From our discussion of the amortization method of adjustment, we know that in 1977 the accumulated provision for depreciation is $634 less than it would be had the revised forecast been used during 1974, 1975, and 1976. Unless some adjustment is made, that difference will grow to $1351.

The remaining life method of adjustment shown in Table 5.18 (see end of chapter) will amortize the $634 in the following manner. At the start of 1977 the remaining life is 3.4 years, so the adjustment during that year is $634/3.4 or $186. This amount is the difference between the $1749 accrual shown in Table 5.18 and the $1563 accrual (i.e., the average life accrual $10000/6.4) shown in Table 5.5. It reduces the adjustment to $643 − $186 or $448 at the start of 1978. Then the remaining life is 4 years, so the adjustment during 1978 is $448/4 or $112, which is again the difference between the accruals for 1978 as shown in Tables 5.17 and 5.5. In this manner the adjustments for 1979, 1980, and 1981 can be shown to be $112, $112, and $112. Thus, the $1634 variation is amortized over the remaining life. The adjustments are "automatic"; that is, they result automatically when the remaining life calculations are used to determine the annual accruals.

Summary

When comparing the amortization and remaining life methods of adjustment, remember that the magnitude and timing of the annual accruals depend upon the method of allocation and the procedure for applying the method of allocation. The difference between the two methods of adjustment only becomes apparent when the forecast is revised. The remaining life method amortizes the variation between the CAD and the accumulated provision for depreciation over the remaining life and the adjustment is included in the annual accrual. The amortization method allows the variation to be amortized over any period, but requires that the annual amount to be amortized be calculated separately and then added to the calculated accrual. If the depreciation professional chooses to amortize the variation over the remaining life, the two methods result in equal annual accruals.

Neither method of adjustment will properly recover the depreciable base unless accurate forecasts are made. It could be argued that the remaining life method requires only an estimate of the remaining life, while the amortization method requires an estimate of the average life. Remember that at age zero the remaining life is also the average life, and that at any time, the average life can be partitioned into the realized life and the remaining life. The realized life can be obtained from historical records while the remaining life must be forecast. From that point of view, there is no difference between the difficulty of forecasting the remaining life and the average life, because the average life depends on the realized life (which is known) and the remaining life (which must be forecast).

Both methods of adjustment require a forecast of the survivor curve describing the property. The amortization method requires only the average life when calculating the annual accruals, but requires the shape of the survivor curve to calculate the CAD. The remaining life method requires the average life and the shape of the curve to calculate the remaining life and the annual accruals.

The Equal Life Group Procedure Applied to a Vintage Group

The next system of calculating the annual accrual uses the straight line method of allocation and applies the equal life group procedure to a vintage group (SL-ELG). Both the AM and RL methods of adjustment are combined with the ELG procedure.

History of the Equal Life Group Procedure

Allocation using the equal life group procedure was discussed as early as March, 1928, during an ICC hearing (*Telephone Engineer and Management,* 1967, p. 55). Robley Winfrey studied it during the 1930s and in 1942 published a detailed discussion of the procedure in *Depreciation of Group Properties, Bulletin 155*. Winfrey considered it "the only mathematically correct procedure" (p. 71) and called it the unit summation procedure. The procedure was primarily of academic interest until the 1970s.

The major objection to the everyday use of the equal life group procedure was the large number of computations necessary to calculate the annual depreciation. When done manually, these calculations consumed enough time to make the equal life group procedure impractical. As computers became more common and computer time less expensive, this objection gradually disappeared. Another objection focused on the fact that in a growing account, the change from the average life to the equal life group procedure typically was accompanied by a significant increase in annual accruals. Though this increase was coupled with a similar decrease as the account matured, the increase created a bias against the procedure. In the early 1970s, the Bell System began to espouse the equal life group procedure in both the United States and Canada. Bell's informational campaign speeded acceptance first by regulators in Canada and then in the United States. The major argument for equal life group procedure is that it more closely matches depreciation charges with the service rendered during the life of the property than does the average life procedure.

The ELG Procedure

To find the accrual rate when using the equal life group procedure, the life characteristics (the average service life and the shape of the survivor curve) must be estimated. Then the original cost is subdivided into equal life groups. Typically, the equal life groups are formed by specifying the life of each group in one-year increments, and the survivor curve is used to find the proportion of the original cost assigned to each equal life group. Though it is not possible to physically identify the individual units in each ELG, it is possible to statistically identify the fraction of the plant in service in each ELG. Each equal life group is treated as a unit of property and is depreciated using the straight line method of allocation. Note that any method of allocation that can be applied to an individual unit can be applied in the same manner to an equal life group. The total annual accrual for the vintage is found by summing the annual accruals for each equal life group remaining in service. The ELG accrual rate is the total annual accrual divided by the average plant in service during the year.

The $10,000 original cost of the survivor curve shown in Figure 5.1 can be divided into two groups. The first group has a life of 4 years and contains $4000 of the original cost. The second group has a life of 8 years and contains $6000 of the original cost. These will be identified as group A and group B respectively. Note that each dollar in group A has a life of 4 years, therefore the name *equal life group*. Each group will be depreciated using the straight line method of allocation, so that the first group will be depreciated at a rate of 1/4 for 4 years and the second group at a rate of 1/8 for 8 years. Table 5.19 (see end of chapter) shows the calculation of the annual accruals for each equal life group and then sums them to obtain the total accruals and accrual rates. For the year 1974, the annual accruals of $1000 and $750 total $1750, which results in a composite annual rate of $1750/$10000 or 17.50%. For this survivor curve, the ELG rates are constant during the first 4 years (17.50%) and during the last 4 years (12.50%).

The annual accrual rates developed in Table 5.19 are used in Table 5.20 (see end of chapter), which shows the SL-ELG method of calculating the annual accruals and accumulated provision for depreciation for property described by the survivor curve shown in Figure 5.1.

Comparison of the AL and ELG Procedure

Compare the annual accruals and the accumulated provision for depreciation resulting from the use of the SL-ELG system, which are shown in Table 5.20, with the annual accruals and accumulated provision for depreciation resulting from the use of the SL-AL system, which are shown in Table 5.5. When contrasted with the average life procedure, the equal life group procedure results in annual accruals that are higher during the early years and lower in the later years. After the first retirement, which reduces the 1977 balance by $4000, the accumulated provision for depreciation using the average life procedure is $2250 as contrasted with $3000 using the equal life group procedure. With the equal life group procedure, the first unit has been fully depreciated and retired, and $3000 has been accumulated against the eventual (in 4 years) retirement of the $6000 life group, which has a life of 8 years. The $6000 life group is halfway through its life and is half depreciated. The accumulated provision for depreciation with the average life procedure is only $2250, so the $4000 unit was not fully depreciated at the time of its retirement. The $750 difference in the accumulated provision for depreciation between the two procedures will be made up over the life of the longer-lived unit. This is not to imply that the average life procedure is incorrect, only that it is different.

Both procedures are "systematic and rational" as required by the definition of depreciation accounting. Use of the average life procedure matches the depreciation charges to the service provided by the average-lived unit. That is, the shorter-lived units contribute fewer units of service than the longer-lived units, and therefore, the total accrual associated with a short-lived unit is less than that associated with a long-lived unit.

The AL procedure treats each unit as though its life is equal to the average life of the group. The ELG procedure treats each unit in the group as though its life was known. This is the basis for the argument that the equal life group procedure better matches depreciation charges with the life of the units in the group.

Effect of Improper Forecast of Curve Shape

What happens if the shape of the curve used to calculate the equal life group rates differs from the shape of the curve describing the property, even though the estimate of the average service life is correct? Table 5.14 shows a survivor curve with an average life of 6.4 years and with units of $4000 and $6000 but with a different shape than the survivor curve shown in Figure 5.1. Table 5.21 (see end of chapter) shows the application of the ELG rates (see Table 5.19) for the survivor curve shown in Figure 5.1 to property whose survivor curve is shown in Table 5.14. The accruals total only $9400, leaving $600 of the original cost unrecovered. This shows that the shape of the survivor curve affects the capital recovery when using the ELG procedure.

Effect of Improper Average Life Forecast

Now recall the survivor curve with an average life of 7.4 years that was used to show the result of overestimating the service life when using the SL-AL system. The annual accrual rates for this curve when using the SL-ELG system are shown in Table 5.22 and these accrual rates are applied to property with an average life of 6.4 years to obtain the annual accruals shown in Table 5.23. (See end of chapter for both tables.) The results are similar to those shown in Table 5.6. The property lacks $1034 of being fully recovered; this is a smaller deficit than if the average life procedure had been used because of the higher early accrual rates resulting from the use of the equal life group procedure.

An Adjustment Problem — The ELG Procedure

As before, suppose that during 1974, 1975, and 1976 annual accruals were obtained from rates based on a 7.4 year life and shown in Table 5.22. In January 1977, the original forecast is revised to the survivor curve shown in Figure 5.1. Table 5.24 (see end of chapter) shows the accumulated depreciation at the time of the revised forecast to be $4863. The SL-ELG system must be augmented to include a method of adjusting the accumulated provision for depreciation to correct for the accruals made during 1974, 1975, and 1976.

Either the amortization or the remaining life method of adjustment can be used to add a feedback loop to the SL-ELG system of calculating annual accruals. Much of the previous discussion of adjustments to the SL-AL system is applicable to the SL-ELG system, and this section will address only the additional information needed when the equal life group procedure is substituted for the average life procedure.

Amortization Method of Adjustment (SL-ELG-AM)

The discussion of the purpose of, approach to, and estimation of the accumulated provision for depreciation in a preceding section is germane to the CAD calculation when using the SL-ELG-AM system. The calculation of the calculated accumulated depreciation ratio at age i using the equation CADR(i) = 1 − RL(i)/AL is still correct, but the terms RL(i) and the AL now apply to each equal life group rather than the total vintage group. As such, the RL and the AL are no longer averages but are simply the remaining life and the life of a single ELG. The CADR is calculated for each equal life group and is then multiplied by the number of dollars in that equal life group to find the CAD for that equal life group. The CAD for the vintage group is then obtained by summing the CAD for each equal life group remaining in service.

Calculation of the CADR(i) is simplified because the remaining life of an equal life group is the life of the equal life group minus its age. This is true because the survivor curve of a unit is the square survivor curve. If the life of an equal life group is 8 years and its age is 3 years, the remaining life is 5 years, and the calculated accumulated depreciation ratio is CADR(3) = 1 − 5/8 or 3/8, which simplifies to the age/AL.

Table 5.25 (see end of chapter) shows the CAD calculations for the survivor curve shown in Figure 5.1. At the end of the third year, both equal life groups remain in service and their age is 3 years. The $4000 equal life group has an age of 3 years, a CADR of 3/4 or 0.75, and the CAD for this unit is $4000 × 0.75, or $3000. The $6000 equal life group has an age of 3 years, a calculated accumulated depreciation ratio of 3/8 or 0.375, and the CAD for this unit is $6000 × 0.375 or $2250. The CAD of the vintage is $3000 + $2250 or $5250. Because the balance at that time is $10,000, the calculated accumulated depreciation ratio for the vintage is 0.525.

AN AMORTIZATION SOLUTION TO THE ELG ADJUSTMENT PROBLEM. Now return to the scenario summarized in Table 5.24. The accumulated provision for depreciation is $4863 and it is now the start of 1977; the original forecast has been revised and the CAD, based on the revised forecast, calculated. Had the revised forecast been used starting in 1974, the current amount of the accumulated provision for depreciation would be $5250. An adjustment of $5250 − $4863 or $387 is needed to fully recover the initial $10,000 investment.

The amortization method of adjustment allows the $387 to be amortized over a period recommended by the depreciation professional. Suppose that it is decided to make the entire adjustment as a lump sum during 1977. An argument for an immediate adjustment of $387 is that this timing places the increase in the cost of service nearest to the customers who benefitted by the under-accruals during 1974, 1975, and 1976. Deferral of this adjustment until later in the life of the property may be more likely to assess customers who had not benefitted by the service provided by the property during 1974, 1975, and 1976.

Table 5.26 (see end of chapter) shows the resulting accruals if an immediate, lump sum adjustment is made and the revised rates adopted. As anticipated, the accumulated provision for depreciation is zero at the time of the final retirement.

Remaining Life Method of Adjustment (SL-ELG-RL)

The remaining life method of adjustment can be used with the ELG procedure to form the SL-ELG-RL system of depreciation. The general comments concerning the SL-AL-RL system of depreciation apply when using the ELG procedure, rather than the AL procedure. This section will discuss the differences between the two systems and will focus on the equal life groups formed from the vintage group.

When using the SL-ELG-RL system of depreciation, the annual accruals, as shown in Table 5.20, are determined by the SL-ELG system. But the remaining life method of adjustment requires that the annual accruals be calculated by dividing the future accrual by the remaining life. Application of the remaining life method of adjustment to the ELG procedure requires calculations be made for each ELG. The accruals for each ELG are obtained by dividing the future accrual of the ELG by the remaining life of the ELG and summing over all ELGs to obtain the annual accrual for the vintage. These calculations are shown in Table 5.27 (see end of chapter), where the first section of the table shows the calculations for the $4000 and the $6000 units, and the second portion of the table totals the accruals from each ELG to obtain the vintage accrual. As expected, the annual accruals and the accumulated provision for depreciation are equal to those shown in Table 5.20.

Note that column (e) of the final section of Table 5.27, labeled 1/RL and equaling the composite rate, was calculated by dividing the annual accruals by the future accrual (i.e., the vintage accrual rate was calculated after the annual accrual was calculated).

These accrual rates also can be viewed as a weighted average, where the remaining life for an ELG is weighted by the balance/life of the ELG. In 1976 both unit A and B are in service and their remaining lives are 2 and 6 years respectively. The weight for A is $4000/4 (the balance/life of the ELG) or $1000; for B it is $6000/8 or $750. The remaining life using the average service life weighting is then [$1000(2) + $750(6)]/$1750 or 3.71 years. Note that the numerator ($6500) equals the future accrual and the denominator equals the annual accrual, so that these calculations are equivalent to those shown in Table 5.27.

ALLOCATION OF THE ACCUMULATED PROVISION FOR DEPRECIA-
TION. The calculation of the annual accruals when there is a variation
between the CAD and the accumulated provision for depreciation raises the
question of how the accumulated provision for depreciation should be allocated among the equal life groups. Any accrual rate used to calculate the
annual accrual either explicitly or implicitly allocates the accumulated provision for depreciation (and the variation) among the ELGs. Suppose that
at the start of 1976 the accumulated provision for depreciation is $2500,
resulting in a variation between the CAD and the accumulated provision
for depreciation of $3500 − $2500 or $1000, so that future accrual must
include adjustments that will total $1000.

Any method that allocates the accumulated provision for depreciation
to each ELG could be used (e.g., the accumulated provision for depreciation could be spread equally among the ELGs, or $1250 to unit A and
$1250 to unit B). Logically, the method used should be based on a rational
scheme that is consistent with the goals of the depreciation system.

Two methods of allocation will be considered: (a) allocation proportional to the CAD and (b) allocation proportional to the balance less the
CAD, which will be called the calculated future accrual (CFA). In either
case, we must divide the $2500 accumulated provision for depreciation into
two parts and assign one part to unit A and the other to unit B.

The first method considered will be an allocation proportional to the
CAD. The calculations are shown below, with columns (b) and (c) taken
from Table 5.27. Column (d) shows that ratio of the CAD associated with
unit A to the total CAD is 2000/3500 or 57.14%, so that portion of the
accumulated provision for depreciation will be allocated to unit A and the
remaining 1500/3500 or 42.86% to unit B. Column (e) shows the results of
using these percentages to allocate the $2500 accumulated provision for
depreciation to the two units. Column (f) is obtained by subtracting the
accumulated provision for depreciation allocated to the unit, column (e),
from the balance, column (b), and is divided by the remaining life to obtain
the annual accrual, column (h), for the ELG. These calculations are equivalent to allocating the $1000 variation proportionally to the CAD; note that
57.14% of $1000 is $571 and that the CAD for unit A, $2000 less $571 is
$1429. The total annual accrual is $2107, the resulting composite rate is
2107/7500 or 28.09%, and the composite remaining life is 1/0.2809 or 3.56
years.

Unit (a)	Bal (b)	CAD (c)	% CAD (d)	Accum depr (e)	Future accrual (f)	RL (g)	Accrual (h)
A	4000	2000	57.14	1429	2571	2	1286
B	6000	1500	42.86	1071	4929	6	821
		3500		2500	7500		2107

The preceding example assumed a variation of +$1000. Now suppose the accumulated provision for depreciation is $4500 as shown below. The resulting variation is $3500 − $4500 or −$1000; the future accrual will be reduced by $1000. The calculations below show allocation of this variation proportional to the CAD. The annual accrual is now only $1393, the composite rate is 25.32%, and the composite remaining life is 1/0.2532 or 3.95 years. Note that when using this method of allocation, the composite rate varies with the variation. The larger the variation the larger the rate (and the smaller the composite remaining life), while the smaller the variation the smaller the rate (and the larger the composite remaining life).

Unit	Bal	CAD	% CAD	Accum depr	Future accrual	RL	Accrual
(a)	(b)	(c)	(d)	(e)	(f)	(g)	(h)
A	4000	2000	57.14	2571	1429	2	714
B	6000	1500	42.86	1929	4071	6	679
		3500		4500	5500		1393

The second method allocates the variation proportional to the CFA. The calculations are shown below. Column (d) shows the balance less the CAD and column (e) shows these figures as a percentage of the total. The $7500 actual future accrual is then allocated to each unit using these percentages and the results are shown in column (f). This is equivalent to allocating the $1000 variation by assigning 30.77% to unit A and 69.23% to unit B. The total accrual is $2019, the composite rate is 2019/7500 or 26.92%, and the composite remaining life is 3.71 years. Note that the composite rate is the same as that used when there was a zero variation and is shown in Table 5.27. If this example was carried out assuming an accumulated provision for depreciation of $4500 resulting in a variation of −$1000, the composite rate would remain at 26.92% and the composite remaining life would remain at 3.71 years.

Unit	Bal	CAD	CFA	% CFA	Future Accrual	RL	Accrual
(a)	(b)	(c)	(d)	(e)	(f)	(g)	(h)
A	4000	2000	2000	30.77	2308	2	1154
B	6000	1500	4500	69.23	5192	6	865
			6500		7500		2019

An important insight into the difference between the two methods is gained by observing the contribution of each ELG to the total annual accrual. The variation can be expressed as $1000/6500 or 15.38% of the

CFA; the future accrual is 15.38% more than it should be if the most recent forecast is correct. Had the accumulated provision for depreciation been $6500, the annual accrual would have been $1750. If the accumulated provision for depreciation is allocated proportionally to the CAD (i.e., the first method), the total annual accrual is increased by $(2107 - 1750)/1750$ or 20.40%; also, the accrual due to unit A is increased by $(1286 - 1000)/1000$ or 28.60%, and the accrual due to unit B is increased by $(821 - 750)/750$ or 9.5%. In contrast, allocation proportional to the CFA (i.e., the second method) yields an increase in the annual accrual of $(2019 - 1750)/1750$ or 15.38%; also, the accrual due to unit A and unit B are both increased by 15.38%. Allocation proportional to the CAD results in accruals associated with units with a smaller remaining life receiving a proportionally larger share of the variation. Allocation proportional to the CFA yields accruals that are uniformly proportional to the variation.

Use of the method of allocation in which the variance is proportional to the CAD is supported by these arguments.

1. Each ELG will be fully depreciated by the end of its service life.
2. Adjustments (either positive or negative) to past accruals are more rapid, thus placing the added costs or savings on the rate payers closest to the past.
3. The composite rate will increase or decrease as the size of the variation increases or decreases. The larger the variation, the more rapid the rate of adjustment.
4. Typically the allocation of the accumulated provision for depreciation among accounts is proportional to the CAD, and this method extends that concept to the vintage group.

Arguments for allocation proportional to the CFA are listed below:

1. The accrual for each ELG is increased (or decreased) by the same proportion.
2. Adjustments to past accruals are spread over a longer period, thus the magnitude of change in the annual accrual is minimized.
3. The composite rate remains constant despite the size of the variation, thus simplifying both the concept and the calculations.
4. This method is currently widely used when allocating the accumulated provision for depreciation among ELGs within a vintage group.

Strong arguments exist for both methods of allocation. In all future examples, the variation within a vintage group will be allocated proportionally to the CFA, thus allowing use of a constant composite rate despite the magnitude of the variation. This does not imply that this method is better, only that in this case it is more convenient because the composite rate can be calculated without knowledge of the variation.

Again, return to the problem raised in the scenario shown in Table 5.24. First, duplicate the results of Table 5.23 using the remaining life calculations. This requires calculation of the composite remaining life of the survivor curve shown in Table 5.16, which had an average life of 7.4 years; these calculations are shown in Table 5.28 (see end of chapter).

A REMAINING LIFE SOLUTION TO THE ELG ADJUSTMENT PROB-LEM.   Next, apply these accrual rates to the example problem, as shown in Table 5.29 (see end of chapter). Note that the annual accruals and accumulated provision for depreciation are the same as in Table 5.23 because both use the same forecast. If the forecast is not revised, $1034 of the initial investment will not be recovered.

Now apply the remaining life method of adjustment to the problem presented in Table 5.24. Starting in 1977, use the accrual rates shown in Table 5.27. The results, shown in Table 5.30 (see end of chapter), are that the −$387 difference between the accumulated provision for depreciation and the CAD at the start of 1977 is amortized over the remaining life of the property, and the accumulated provision for depreciation, after the final retirement, is $0.

How does the remaining life method of adjustment allocate the $387 deficit? Table 5.27 shows that the CFA, at the start of 1977, is $1000 for unit A and $3750 for unit B, for a total of $4750, and that the remaining lives are 1 and 5 years respectively. Unit A accounts for 1000/4750 or 21% of the total while unit B accounts for 3750/4750 or 79%. The method of calculating the composite rate shown in Table 5.27 prorates the $387 deficit so that 21% or 0.21 × $387 or $82 is added to the future accrual of unit A and 79% or 0.79 × $387 or $305 is added to the future accrual of unit B. The $82 is amortized over the remaining life of 1 year, so that the 1977 accrual includes ($1000 + $82)/1 or $1082 for unit A. The $305 is amortized over the remaining life of 5 years, so that the 1977 accrual includes 750 + $305/5 or $811 for unit B. The total 1977 accrual is then $1082 + $811 or $1893. The annual accruals from 1978 through 1981 include the $750 and a $305/5 or $61 adjustment.

GROUP DEPRECIATION SYSTEMS WITH SALVAGE

The preceding discussion of systems of depreciation of a vintage group of property assumed there was no salvage (i.e., the net salvage was zero). These systems can be modified to include salvage so that the annual accruals are a function of the estimates of both life and salvage. In this section the term *salvage* will always refer to salvage used in the accrual rate, which is the net salvage (i.e., the gross salvage less the cost of retiring). An important concept is that a depreciation system should consider the change in salvage as the property ages.

Aged Salvage

Examine the salvage schedule shown in Table 5.31 (see end of chapter) as it will be used in the examples that follow. The salvage ratios of units A and B are 30% and 10% respectively so the salvage is 0.30 × $4000 or $1200 for unit A and 0.10 × $6000 or $600 for unit B. The average salvage ratio (ASR) is (1200 + 600)/10000 or 18%. Column (b) shows the age at the start of the year and reminds us that the salvage ratio changes with age. The term *aged salvage* is used to express this concept. Column (c) is the survivor curve and column (e) shows the salvage ratio for each year in which the plant is retired. Column (f) is the salvage ratio times the retirement frequency. The salvage ratio during the fourth year is 30% and the retirement frequency is 4000/10000 or 0.40, yielding a weighted ratio of 30% × 0.40 or 12% to show that salvage during that year equals 12% of the original investment. The sum of column (f), 18%, is the total salvage expressed as a percentage of the initial cost and is called the average salvage ratio (ASR). The product of the average salvage ratio and the original cost equals the total salvage dollars for the vintage group. Column (g) is the total salvage to that time divided by the total retirements to that time and equals the (average) realized salvage ratio[5] at that age. At age 4, the total salvage realized thus far is $1200 and retirements have totaled $4000; the ratio 1200/4000 yields the realized salvage ratio of 30%. Column (h) is the total salvage remaining to be collected divided by plant remaining to be retired and equals the (average) future salvage ratio. At age 4, the remaining salvage is $600 and the plant remaining to be retired is the $6000 plant in service; the ratio 600/6000 yields the future salvage ratio of 10%. Column (i) is the average salvage ratio. It is the sum of the product of the realized salvage ratio, column (g), times the percent of the plant that has been retired, plus the product of the future salvage ratio, column (h), times the percent of the plant in service. At age 5, 40% of the plant has been retired with a realized salvage ratio of 30%, while 60% remains in service with a future salvage ratio of 10%; the average salvage ratio is 30% × 0.4 + 10% × 0.6 or 18%. Though the realized and future salvage ratios vary with time, the average salvage ratio for the salvage schedule is constant.

It is important to remember that the future salvage ratio changes with the age of the plant. At the time of the initial installation, the future salvage ratio and the average salvage ratio are both 18%. But after unit A is retired, the future salvage depends only on the remaining plant in service, unit B, and that salvage ratio is 10%. A positive salvage was used in the example, but negative salvage could have been selected just as easily. This schedule also reflects salvage that decreases with age, but an example where salvage increases with age could have been used.

The Average Life Procedure Applied to a Vintage Group

Calculation of the Annual Accrual

When applying the SL-AL system of calculating annual accruals, the rate 1/AL is applied to the plant in service to recover the initial investment. Only the original cost less salvage, or 1 − ASR, may be recovered through annual accruals. In our example the original cost is $10,000 and the ASR is 18%, so $10000 × 1.00 − 0.18 or $8200 is recovered through annual accruals and the remaining 18% or $1800 is recovered as salvage at the time of the retirement.

In the section that assumed no salvage, it was shown that original cost = Σ (average plant in service during age interval j)/AL, when summed over j = 0,1,2, . . ., ML. The equation below shows both sides multiplied by the fraction of the original cost to be recovered, (1 − ASR), so that the rate, on the righthand side, will now be (1 − ASR)/AL. The total accruals, the lefthand side, will be the original cost times (1 − ASR), which equals the capital consumed. This shows that application of the rate (1 − ASR)/ AL will fully recover the original cost less the salvage.

(original cost)(1 − ASR) = Σ (average plant in service during age interval j)(1 − ASR)/AL when summed over j = 0,1,2, . . ., ML

Table 5.32 (see end of chapter) shows the result of applying this rate to the example used in the previous section to obtain the annual accruals.

The accumulated provision for depreciation is $2325 after the first retirement. The accumulated provision for depreciation at the start of the previous year, $3844, is increased by the annual accrual of $1281, decreased by the $4000 original cost, and increased by the $1200 salvage to yield the accumulated provision for depreciation of $2325 at the start of 1978.

Note that any other salvage schedule with an average salvage ratio of 18% will yield the same annual rate and result in the same annual accruals shown in Table 5.32. However, the accumulated provision for depreciation will vary from Table 5.32 because the timing of the salvage between the two schedules will differ. If, for example, the salvage ratio is 18% for *both* units (so that the average salvage remains at 18%), the annual accruals will remain at $1281 for the first 4 years and $769 for the last 4 years. But, the accumulated provision for depreciation at the start of 1978 will equal $3844

+ \$1281 − \$4000 × (1.00 − 0.18) or \$1845 rather than \$2325. This difference would continue until the final retirement, when the accumulated provision for depreciation becomes zero.

Modifying the annual accrual rate (1/AL) by the factor (1 − ASR) is an extension of the average life procedure to include salvage. The factor (1 − ASR) in the accrual rate is a constant used throughout the life of the property regardless of the actual salvage ratio at each age. All units are treated as though their salvage ratio was equal to the average salvage ratio even though the actual salvage for that year is, depending on the salvage schedule, above or below the average.

Effect of Error in the Estimate of Average Salvage

If the estimate of average salvage is wrong, then the total accruals will not equal the capital consumed. Suppose the estimate of average salvage is \$0; then \$10,000 rather than \$8200 is recovered and the accumulated provision for depreciation will equal \$1800 after the final retirement. Or suppose the original estimate is a salvage ratio of 40% for unit A and 15% for unit B, resulting in an average salvage ratio of [(40% × 4000) + (15% × 6000)]/10000 or 25%, as shown in Table 5.33 (see end of chapter).

If a correct life estimate of 6.4 years is assumed, the resulting rate using this schedule is (100% − 25%)/6.4 or 11.719%. Table 5.34 (see end of chapter) shows that the total accruals will equal only \$7500, leaving \$7500 − \$8200 or −\$700 in the accumulated provision for depreciation after the final retirement because an ASR of 25% rather than 18% was used.

An Adjustment Problem—The AL Procedure

Assume that our initial estimate of the salvage schedule is that shown in Table 5.33 and that the annual accruals for 1974 through 1977 were based on the 11.719% rate. Now suppose that in January 1978, because of events and activities occurring since 1974, the original salvage forecast of 25% average salvage is revised to 18% as shown in the salvage schedule in Table 5.31, which will turn out to be a correct estimate. Table 5.35 (see end of chapter) shows the accumulated provision for depreciation at the start of 1978 is \$1888 and presents the problem of adjusting the future accruals in light of the revised forecast.

When you use either the amortization (AM) or remaining life (RL) method of adjustment, the distinction between the average salvage and future salvage plays an important role in the calculation of the adjustment to the accumulated provision for depreciation. Since both the CAD and remaining life calculations are based on future events, they require estimates of future, rather than average, salvage. Though at age zero the average and future salvage ratios are equal, the difference between these two averages typically increases as the property ages.

Amortization Method of Adjustment (SL-AL-AM)

The underlying relationship used to develop the CAD when there was no salvage was CAD = future retirements − future accruals. Future salvage will affect the future value of the accumulated provision for depreciation. The relationship should be modified to read CAD = future retirements − future gross salvage + future cost of retiring − future accrual, or CAD = future retirements − future net salvage − future accrual. This shows that positive future salvage reduces the required accumulated provision for depreciation, because a portion of the original cost is recovered through salvage. Future retirements equal the current balance, the future salvage can be expressed as the future salvage ratio times the current balance, and the straight line rate (1 − ASR)/AL is used to calculate future accruals so that

$$CAD(i) = B(i) − B(i)[(FSR(i)] − [(1 − ASR)/AL] \Sigma \text{ (average balance}$$
during year j) when summed over j from year i to final year of retirement

where B(i) = balance at age i (i.e., the current balance)
    CAD(i) = calculated accumulated depreciation at age i
    CADR(i) = calculated accumulated depreciation ratio at age i, CAD(i)/B(i)
    FSR(i) = future salvage ratio at age i
    RL(i) = remaining life at age i
    AL = average life

The term Σ (average balance during year j)/B(i) has been shown to equal the remaining life, RL(i), so RL(i) × B(i) = Σ (average balance during year i). Making this substitution and dividing both sides of the equation by B(i) yields the equation CADR(i) = [1 − FSR(i)] − (1 − ASR)[RL(i)/AL]. The first term is the fraction of the plant in service to be recovered and the second is the future accruals expressed as a fraction of the plant in service. Another form of this equation is CADR(i) = (1 − ASR)[1 − RL(i)/AL] + ASR − FSR(i). This form emphasizes the sensitivity of the CADR(i) to the difference between the average and future salvage. If the average and future salvages are equal, or if they are assumed to be equal, the above equation reduces to CADR(i) = (1 − ASR) − (1 − ASR)[RL(i)/AL] = (1 − ASR)[1 − RL(i)/AL].

Table 5.36 (see end of chapter) shows the CAD for the example problem when the salvage schedule shown in Table 5.31 is used. Column (e) is 1 − FSR(i), which represents the percentage of the current plant in service that must be recovered through annual accruals. Initially this is 82%, but after the first retirement it changes to reflect the fact that 90% of plant now in service must be recovered via depreciation. Column (f) is the straight line rate (100% − 18%)/6.4 or 12.81%. Column (g) is the remaining life, which was obtained from Table 5.8. These factors are combined using the equation [1 − FSR(i)] − (1 − ASR)[RL(i)/AL] to compute the calculated accumulated depreciation ratios shown in column (h). At the end of 1978, the remaining life is 4 years and the future salvage ratio is 10%. If the first form of the equation for the CADR(4)−note that at this time both the age and the remaining life happen to be 4 years−is used, the calculation is (1 − 0.10) − (1 − 0.18)(4/6.4) or 38.75%. If the second form is used, the calculation is (1 − 0.18)(1 − 4/6.4) + (0.18 − 0.10), which also equals 38.75%. Finally, the CADR(4) is multiplied by the current balance, B(4), to obtain the CAD(4), which is shown in column (i).

AN AMORTIZATION SOLUTION TO THE AL ADJUSTMENT PROBLEM.   A comparison of the CAD shown in Table 5.36 with the accumulated provision for depreciation shown in Table 5.35 shows that at the start of 1978 the plant is underaccrued by $2325 − $1888 or $437. With the amortization method of adjustment, this deficit is amortized over a period recommended by the depreciation professional. Suppose it was decided to amortize the deficit over the remaining 4 years of life, or $437/4 or $109 each year. The results are shown in Table 5.37 (see end of chapter).

Remaining Life Method of Adjustment (SL-AL-RL)

The remaining life method of adjustment requires an estimate of future salvage to calculate the future accrual. When the salvage is not zero, the future accrual (i.e., the total amount remaining to be recovered) equals the current balance less the *future* salvage less the accumulated provision for depreciation. As before, the annual accrual is the future accrual divided by the remaining life or

$$AARL(i) = [B(i) − FS(i) − APD(i)]/RL(i)$$
$$= B(i)[1 − FSR(i) − APDR(i)]/RL(i)$$

where: B(i)   = balance at age i
   FS(i)   = future salvage at age i
   FSR(i) = future salvage ratio at age i
   APD(i) = the accumulated provision for depreciation at age i
   APDR(i) = the ratio APD(i)/B(i)
   RL(i)   = remaining life at age i
   AARL(i) = the annual accrual at age i using the RL method of adjustment

When there is no salvage, the annual accrual resulting from use of the RL method of adjustment equals the annual accrual resulting from use of the AM method of adjustment if the variation between the CAD and the accumulated provision for depreciation is zero or if the variation is amortized over the remaining life. This is also true when the salvage is not zero and can be proven using the arguments presented in the preceding section. Remember both methods of adjustment require use of the future salvage; the RL method requires it to calculate the future accrual and the amortization method requires it to calculate the CAD.

Table 5.38 (see end of chapter) shows the remaining life calculations for the example problem; the future accrual, column (d), is calculated by subtracting the future salvage and the accumulated provision for depreciation from the balance. At the start of 1978 this calculation is $6000 − $600 − $2325 or $3075. Because the variation between the CAD and the accumulated provision for depreciation is zero, the annual accruals equal those calculated using the SL-AL method and shown in Table 5.32.

Table 5.39 (see end of chapter) shows the remaining life calculations when the salvage schedule shown in Table 5.33 is used as a forecast. Because the salvage forecast is incorrect, the original cost is not fully recovered. When using the remaining life method of adjustment, the actual salvage for unit A, $1200, was reflected in the accumulated provision for depreciation at the start of 1978. The difference between the actual and forecast salvage for unit A, $(0.40 − 0.30) × 4000 or $400, was amortized over the remaining four years, accounting for the $100 a year difference between annual accruals shown in Table 5.34 and those shown in Table 5.39 during the years 1978 to 1981. Because the final salvage is misestimated by $300, total accruals in Table 5.39 are $300 less than the required $8200.

A REMAINING LIFE SOLUTION TO THE AL ADJUSTMENT PROBLEM. Now return to the problem presented in Table 5.35 and use the revised forecast of future salvage to calculate annual accruals starting in 1978. The remaining life calculations will amortize the $437 deficit over the remaining 4 years. The 1978 annual accrual of $878 shown in Table 5.40 (see end of chapter) is composed of a $769 accrual and a $437/4 or $109 adjustment. The annual adjustment for the next year is the variation, which is now $437 − $109, divided by the remaining life of 3 years, which again yields an adjustment of ($437 − $109)/3 or $109. In the same manner the adjustments for the next 2 years can each be shown to be $109. Table 5.37 shows the results of using the amortization method of adjustment to distribute the $437 variation over 4 years. The annual accruals for both methods of adjustment are the same (see Tables 5.37 and 5.40) because the 4-year amortization period chosen for the AM method of adjustment equals the remaining life (4 years).

The Equal Life Group Procedure Applied to a Vintage Group

Calculation of the Annual Accrual

A previous section illustrated the division of the survivor curve shown in Figure 5.1 into ELGs, each of which had zero salvage and were depreciated as a unit using the annual rate of 1/AL. When salvage is not zero, the annual rate (1 − ASR)/AL is applied to each ELG. The average salvage ratio (ASR) and the average life (AL) both refer to a specific ELG rather than to the average of the vintage group. Table 5.41 (see end of chapter) shows the calculation of annual accrual rates using the SL-ELG system of calculating annual accruals. The rate of (100% − 30%)/4 or 17.5% is applied to unit A and results in annual accruals of $700 for 4 years; the rate of (100% − 10%)/8 or 11.25% applied to unit B results in annual accruals of $625 for 8 years. The ELG rate for the vintage group is 13.75% for the first 4 years and 11.25% for the final 4 years.

Table 5.42 (see end of chapter) shows the application of the rates developed in Table 5.41 to obtain the annual accruals and the accumulated provision for depreciation.

Now compare the accruals using the ELG procedure with those obtained using the AL procedure and shown in Table 5.32. The ELG procedure again results in higher annual accruals early in life and lower accruals later in life. The ELG procedure with zero salvage was shown to yield the same accruals that would result if each equal life group was depreciated as an individual unit, so that each unit is fully depreciated at the time of its retirement. The same principle applies with nonzero salvage; each equal life group is assigned the salvage ratio associated with that particular group, thus assuring that the dollars in each ELG will be fully depreciated at retirement. In contrast, the AL procedure uses the average salvage ratio in the accrual rate. The salvage ratio during any year may be above or below the average ratio used in the accrual rate. Retirements with a large salvage ratio are averaged with those with a small ratio so that the depreciation for a particular retirement is averaged over the life of the vintage group.

Table 5.33 is a schedule with an average salvage ratio of 25% and was used to show the results of misestimating salvage when using the AL procedure. Table 5.43 (see end of chapter) shows the ELG rates that result from using that same salvage schedule.

The higher average salvage ratio yields lower accrual rates. When these rates are applied, as shown in Table 5.44, the original cost is not fully recovered. After the final retirement the accumulated provision for depreciation is −$700, which is the difference between the actual salvage of $1600 and forecast salvage of $2500. This is the same deficit that resulted when using the AL procedure (see Table 5.34). In both procedures, the depreciable base was underestimated by $700, so the total annual accruals were $700 less than required to fully recover the original cost.

An Adjustment Problem — ELG Procedure

Again suppose that the rates shown in Table 5.43 are used from 1974 through 1977. Then in January 1978, the original salvage ratio estimate of 40% for unit A and 15% for unit B is revised to 30% for unit A and 10% for unit B. Table 5.45 (see end of chapter) shows the current accumulated provision for depreciation at the start of 1978 is $2150. The future accrual must be adjusted to ensure recovery of the $8200 of capital used to provide service during the years 1974 to 1982.

Both the amortization (AM) and remaining life (RL) methods of adjustment used with the ELG procedure and with no salvage were discussed in a previous section. That discussion will now be extended to include salvage.

Amortization Method of Adjustment (SL-ELG-AM)

The first step when using the amortization method of adjustment is to calculate the current value of the CAD as shown in Table 5.46 (see end of chapter). Unit A has a life of 4 years and a salvage of 30% so that (1.00 − 0.30) × $4000 or $2800 must be recovered through the annual accruals. The first row shows the accumulated provision for depreciation for unit A at the start of years 1, 2, 3, and 4. At the start of year 5, the sum of the previous accruals equals the original cost less salvage ($2800), so the retirement of unit A reduces the CAD to zero. In a similar manner, the (1.00 − 0.10) × $6000 or $5400 depreciable cost associated with unit B is recovered over 8 years as shown in the second row. The annual CAD is the sum of the CAD over all ELGs, 2 in this case, and the calculated accumulated depreciation ratio is, by definition, the CAD/plant in service.

The CAD at age 4 is $2700, but the accumulated provision for depreciation at the start of 1977 and shown in Table 5.45 is $2150, which results in a variation of $550. The depreciation professional must decide if this is a significant variation and, if so, how an adjustment should be made.

Note that at the start of 1978 unit A has been retired and is no longer an element in the calculation of the CAD. Any estimates relating to the age or salvage of unit A do not affect the calculation of the CAD from 1978 on. In general, equal life groups that have been retired do not affect the CAD. When calculating the CAD for a system using the ELG procedure, future, rather than past or average, estimates of life and salvage are needed.

AN AMORTIZATION SOLUTION TO THE ELG ADJUSTMENT PROBLEM.   At the start of 1978 only unit B remains in service and the estimate of its life remains at 8 years, while its salvage ratio is now estimated to be 10% rather than 15%. Even if the annual accrual rate is immediately re-

vised to 11.25% (see Table 5.41) to reflect this change in the salvage forecast, the existing deficit of $550 will remain in the accumulated provision
for depreciation. By amortizing this variation over 3 years, $550/3 or $183
per year will be added to the annual accruals during the next 3 years, as
shown in Table 5.47 (see end of chapter).

Remaining Life Method of Adjustment (SL-ELG-RL)

The remaining life method of adjustment requires the future salvage
and the life of each ELG to calculate the annual accrual. Each ELG has a
single life and a single salvage, so the average and future salvage for each
ELG are the same. Table 5.48 (see end of chapter) shows the calculation of
the annual accruals for each ELG using the salvage schedule shown in Table
5.31. The future accrual equals the plant in service less the future salvage
less the accumulated provision for depreciation and must be calculated for
each ELG remaining in service. The initial value of the future accrual for
unit A is $(1.00 - 0.30) \times \$4000$ or $2800, the remaining life is 4 years, and
the annual accrual is $700. For unit B the future accrual is $(1.00 - 0.10) \times
\$6000$ or $5400, the remaining life is 8 years, and the annual accrual is $675.

The future accrual and the annual accrual for each ELG are combined
in the bottom portion of the table to obtain the totals shown in columns (d)
and (f). The annual accrual rate shown in column (e) of Table 5.48 was
obtained by dividing the annual accrual shown in column (f) by the future
accrual shown in column (d) (i.e., the annual accruals were calculated first
and then divided by the future accrual to find the annual rate). As mentioned previously, the reciprocal of the rate is called the composite remaining life.

The annual rate also can be calculated using the weighted average
referred to in the discussion of depreciation systems with no salvage. Calculation of this average when there is salvage requires calculating the
weighted average of the remaining life times $(1 - ASR)$. In 1976, both
units A and B are in service and their remaining lives are 2 and 6 years
respectively, while their salvage ratios are 30% and 10% respectively. The
numerator of the weight for A is the balance over the average life, $4000/4
years, and this weight is independent of salvage. The numerator of the
weight for B is $6000/8. The composite remaining life is $\{[\$4000 \times (1 -
0.30)/4] \times 2 + [\$6000 \times (1 - 0.10)/8] \times 6\}$ divided by the sum of the
weights, $[\$4000 \times (1 - 0.30)/4 + \$6000 \times (1 - 0.10)/8]$ or $[(\$700 \times 2)
+ (\$675 \times 6)]/\$1375$ or 3.964 or 25.229%, which agrees with the rate
shown in Table 5.48.

ALLOCATION OF THE VARIATION.   In the section on depreciation systems with no salvage, we discussed the calculation of annual accruals when
there is a variation between the CAD and the accumulated provision for

depreciation. That discussion will now be expanded to include salvage.

In the section with no salvage we assumed a $1000 variation and then calculated the 1976 accrual. We will now repeat that calculation with salvage. Assume the accumulated provision for depreciation at start of 1976 is $1750 (i.e., from Table 5.46 we see the CAD at the start of 1976 is $2750, the variation is $2750 − $1750 or $1000). First allocate the variation in proportion to the CAD as shown below. Column (e) uses the percentages in column (d) to allocate the $1750 accumulated provision for depreciation to units A and B. The future accrual, column (f), is obtained by subtracting the accumulated provision for depreciation and the salvage ($1200 and $600 for units A and B respectively) from the balance, column (b). Dividing the future accrual by the remaining life yields the annual accrual for each ELG, column (h). The accruals total $1712. This results in a composite rate of $1712/$6450 or 26.54% and a composite remaining life of 3.77 years.

Unit	Bal	CAD	% CAD	Accum depr	Future accrual	RL	Accrual
(a)	(b)	(c)	(d)	(e)	(f)	(g)	(h)
A	4000	1400	50.91	891	1909	2	955
B	6000	1350	49.09	859	4541	6	757
		2750		1750	6450		1712

Now consider the same circumstances but make the allocation in proportion to the calculated future accrual, as shown in the following calculations. For unit A the calculated future accrual (CFA), column (d), is the balance less the CAD less the salvage or $4000 − $1400 − $1200 or $1400. Column (f) is obtained by first calculating the total future accrual, which is $10000 − ($1200 + $600) − $1750 or $6450; this amount is then prorated to units A and B using the percentages shown in column (e). Totaling the accruals for each ELG yields $1627 and a composite rate of $1627/$6450 or 25.229% and a composite remaining life of 3.96 years. This is the same as the composite rate when the variation is zero (see Table 5.48).

Unit	Bal	CAD	CFA	% CFA	Future accrual	RL	Accrual
(a)	(b)	(c)	(d)	(e)	(f)	(g)	(h)
A	4000	1400	1400	25.69	1657	2	829
B	6000	1350	4050	74.31	4793	6	798
			5450		6450		1627

Now the composite rates shown in Table 5.48 are applied to the example problem and the results are shown in Table 5.49 (see end of chapter). At the start of 1979, the estimated future salvage is $600, so the future accrual is $6000 − $600 − $3375 or $2025, and applying the composite annual remaining life rate of 33.33% results in an annual accrual of $675. Because the life and salvage estimates used in Table 5.48 were correct, no adjustments are required and the remaining life accruals are equal those obtained using the SL-ELG system of calculating annual accruals and shown in Table 5.42.

Table 5.50 (see end of chapter) shows the calculation of the composite annual rates when the estimated salvage ratios are 40% and 15% for units A and B respectively. The balance to be depreciated for unit A is (1.00 − 0.40) × $4000 or $2400; the balance for unit B is (1.00 − 0.15) × $6000 or $5100. Composite rates are shown in the bottom portion of the table. Note that the rates during ages 5 through 8 are identical with those in Table 5.48 although the salvage ratios differ. To explain this, remember that the composite rate is the sum of the balance less salvage divided by the annual accrual. During the final 4 years of the example problem, only one ELG survives. The numerator and the denominator of the composite rate both contain the factor (1 − ASR); these cancel, so in this example the composite rates for the final 4 years are independent of the salvage ratios.

Table 5.51 (see end of chapter) shows application of these rates to the example problem. Future salvage ratio estimates of 25% from 1974 to 1977 and 15% from 1978 to 1981 are used to calculate the future accrual. As with the SL-AL-RL system (see Table 5.39), the misestimation of future salvage results in an under-accrual of $300.

A REMAINING LIFE SOLUTION TO THE ADJUSTMENT PROBLEM. Return to the ELG adjustment problem presented in Table 5.45. When the 1978 forecast of future salvage is changed from 15% to 10% and the depreciation process is carried forward, the entire $8200 is, as shown in Table 5.52 (see end of chapter), fully recovered.

A COMMENT. Hypothetical examples of survivor curves and salvage schedules have been used to show basic concepts of depreciation. Be careful when making generalizations based on these examples. The only generalization that can be drawn from the preceding examples is that incorrect forecasts can result in improper capital recovery. The magnitude and direction of the error depends on the particular example. Estimates of life can be too short or too long and the shape of the curve can vary while keeping the average life constant. The shape of the curve determines the remaining life and therefore affects the CAD calculations and the remaining life rates. The salvage ratio can be positive or negative, though only positive salvage was used in the preceding examples. When considering aged salvage, the ratios can increase or decrease with age, and the consequences of using average rather than aged salvage depend on the pattern of the salvage. Any generalizations concerning the variation between the calculated accumulated depreciation and the accumulated provision for depreciation because of errors in estimation of parameters should carefully state the assumptions made.

Use of Average, Rather than Aged, Salvage

Salvage is sometimes viewed as though it remains constant as the property ages, as opposed to the more realistic view that the salvage varies with age. The former view equates average and future salvage, while the latter view recognizes that the salvage ratio may change each year and that it is necessary to estimate the salvage schedule. This section will examine the results of not recognizing that salvage varies with age by illustrating the use of the average salvage ratio rather than a salvage schedule.

The Average Life Procedure

The average life procedure requires estimates of future salvage to assure proper adjustments. When using the amortization method of adjustment, the future salvage enters the CAD calculation; when using the remaining life method of adjustment, the future salvage is needed to calculate the future accrual.

First consider the amortization method of adjustment. The CAD equation $CADR(i) = (1 - ASR)[1 - RL(i)/AL] + ASR - FSR(i)$ reduces to $CADR(i) = (1 - ASR)[1 - RL(i)/AL]$ when the future salvage ratio, $FSR(i)$, is set equal to the average salvage ratio, ASR. The annual values of the CAD using the second equation are shown in Table 5.53 (see end of chapter), and these values should be compared to those in Table 5.36, which were calculated using the correct future salvage. Though the CAD starts and ends at zero in both tables, there is a significant difference between the two after the first retirement. In Table 5.53 the calculations for the CAD at the start of year 5 anticipate a salvage ratio of 18%, which is $4000 × 0.18 or $720 for unit A, rather than the actual salvage of $1200. This difference of $1200 − $720 or $480 equals the difference between the CAD at the start of year 5 in the two tables.

If the CAD shown in Table 5.53 is used as a guide in analyzing the problem posed in Table 5.35, the variation between the calculated accumulated depreciation and the accumulated provision for depreciation is $1845 − $1888 or −$43. This suggests that the future accrual should be *reduced* by a total of $43. The potential $437 deficit is concealed by the failure of the depreciation professional to forecast the salvage schedule. The salvage of the final retirement is estimated to be $6000 × 0.18 or $1080 rather than the actual $600, and this difference of $480 is the difference between the CAD calculated using the salvage schedule and the CAD calculated using the average salvage during the final 4 years.

The net impact of not distinguishing between average and future salvage depends on the amount of the change in salvage ratios as the account matures. Forecasters may tend to associate realized salvage with average salvage, thus presupposing that future salvage ratios will be close to those observed early in the life of the vintage. The result may be a poor forecast of the average salvage ratio used in the accrual rate.

Results of using the average salvage rather than the future salvage with the remaining life method of adjustment are shown in Table 5.54 (see end of chapter). The annual accruals during the first 4 years are the same as in Table 5.38 (which uses the correct value of future salvage), because the future and average salvage are equal until the time of the first retirement. During the remaining 4 years, the system assumes that only 82% of the plant in service must be recovered. Actually 90% is needed, so a deficit of (82% − 90%) × $6000 or −$480 results.

When using the AL procedure and either method of adjustment, accurate estimates of the salvage schedule are needed to fully recover invested capital in a timely manner. Use of the average, rather than aged salvage, will result in incorrect estimates of the CAD and may result in accruals that do not equal the capital consumed.

The Equal Life Group Procedure

The equal life group procedure requires the salvage ratio for each life group in order to calculate the annual accrual. The future salvage is the weighted average of all ELGs remaining in service. Table 5.55 (see end of chapter) shows the calculation of annual accrual rates using the 18% average salvage ratio for both ELGs. Unit A is assigned a rate of (100% − 18%)/4 or 20.5% and unit B a rate of (100% − 18%)/8 or 10.25%.

Table 5.56 (see end of chapter) shows the application of these rates. Note that the accruals total $8200, as they should, but the timing of the accruals differs from those shown in Table 5.42, which use the correct aged salvage. Because the first retirement had a higher than average salvage ratio, the total annual accruals generated by unit A, 4 × $820 or $3280, are $480 greater than the $4000 − $1200 or $2800 to be depreciated, while the total annual accruals for unit B, 8 × $615 or $4920, are $480 less than the $6000 − $600 or $5400 to be depreciated. The fact that the two differences cancel each other is not coincidence, but the result of using the average salvage ratio.

In this example, use of the average salvage resulted in higher early rates than would have resulted if the salvage schedule had been used. If the salvage schedule had reflected salvage ratios that increased with age, the early rates would have been lower than those resulting from using the average.

Use of the average salvage rather than the aged salvage associated with each ELG results in the use of the AL procedure for the salvage portion of the annual accrual rate. This combination of the ELG procedure for life and the AL procedure for salvage fully recovers the initial investment less salvage, but it partially negates the major attribute of the ELG procedure. Use of the average salvage in the ELG accrual rate will not match the annual depreciation charges with the consumption of capital. When the ELG procedure is used with a salvage schedule, the units comprising the ELG are fully accrued at the time of their retirement. This is not true if the average salvage is used. The magnitude of the difference in timing resulting from using the average salvage rather than the salvage schedule depends on two factors. First, if the salvage ratio is zero or near zero, then the difference is also zero or near zero. Second, if the salvage ratio is constant, or nearly constant, the annual retirement ratios will be close to the average salvage ratio and the difference will be small. These two factors interact to determine the magnitude of the difference.

Suppose the average salvage ratio of 18%, rather than the aged salvage, had been applied to each ELG when calculating the CAD. The resulting CADs and CADRs are shown in Table 5.57 (see end of chapter).

The CAD at the start of 1978 calculated using the average salvage is $2460 as compared to the CAD of $2700 obtained using the salvage schedule. If the average salvage is used, the variation between the CAD and the accumulated provision for depreciation of $2150 shown in Table 5.45 would be $310 rather than the correct value of $550. If the adjustment was based on the CAD calculated using the average salvage, a deficit of $240 would result. This shows that when the salvage varies with age, use of the average salvage with the ELG procedure will affect the accuracy of the CAD.

Now examine the effects of using the average salvage rather than the aged salvage when the remaining life method of adjustment is used. Table 5.58 at the end of the chapter (which is constructed in the same manner as Table 5.48) shows the calculation of the composite rates using average salvage. The balances for both units A and B are calculated by multiplying the initial cost by (100% − 18%) or 82%, yielding balances of $3280 and $4920 respectively.

Table 5.59 (see end of chapter) shows the results of using average rather than aged salvage with the remaining life method of adjustment. Note that the total accruals were $480 less than necessary to recover the $8200 of capital consumed. After the first retirement, the system expected a future salvage of 0.18 × $6000 or $1080 and accruals were based on that assumption. When only $600 was received, a deficit in accumulated provision for depreciation of $480 resulted.

SUMMARY

The two preceding sections discussed depreciation systems for group property. All the systems discussed applied the straight line method of allocation to a vintage group. First it was assumed that there was no salvage, and then the consideration of salvage was added.

Two procedures for applying the straight line method of depreciation were used. The average life procedure treats each member of the group as though it will have a life and salvage equal to the group average. Though we know that each member of the group will not behave as the average member, our assumption works because the variation between members brings us back to the average. The equal life group procedure statistically divides the vintage group into smaller, equal life groups so that each member of the equal life group will have the same life and salvage. Each equal life group is then depreciated as a unit using the life and salvage associated with the ELG. This yields two systems of calculating annual accruals, the SL-AL system and the SL-ELG system.

These systems are incomplete until a method of control is included in the system. There are two methods of creating a closed loop feedback system. One method is labeled the amortization (AM) method of adjustment. This term describes a system in which the calculated accumulated depreciation (CAD) is used as a measure against which the (book) accumulated provision for depreciation is compared. The depreciation analyst uses this feedback as a guide in determining the necessary adjustment to the annual accruals or, if necessary, to the accumulated provision for depreciation. The remaining life (RL) method of adjustment automatically amortizes the variation between the CAD and the accumulated provision for depreciation over the remaining life of the property.

Combining both methods of allocation with both methods of adjustment yields four depreciation systems. Two use the average life procedure, SL-AL-AM and SL-AL-RL, and two use the equal life group procedure, SL-ELG-AM and SL-ELG-RL. Because the methods of allocation for purpose of book depreciation are almost exclusively limited to the straight line method, these four choices represent the systems available for the depreciation of a vintage group.

Table 5.1.   Calculation of the annual accruals and the accumulated provision
              for depreciation for a unit of property using the straight line
              method of allocation. The unit has a life of 4 years and a 20%
              salvage ratio.

| Year | Balance Jan 1 | Retired | Rate% | Annual accrual | * Accumulated depreciation * | | |
					Net Jan 1	Debit	Credit
1974	$4000		20.0	$800	$0	$0	$800
1975	4000		20.0	800	800	0	800
1976	4000		20.0	800	1600	0	800
1977	4000	$4000	20.0	800	2400	4000	1600
1978	0				0		
				$3200		$4000	$4000

Table 5.2.   Calculation of the annual accruals and the accumulated provision
              for depreciation for a unit of property using the sum-of-years-
              digits (accelerated) method of allocation. The unit has a life
              of 4 years and a 20% salvage ratio.

| Year | Balance Jan 1 | Retired | Rate% | Annual accrual | * Accumulated depreciation * | | |
					Net Jan 1	Debit	Credit
1974	$4000		32.0	$1280	$0	$0	$1280
1975	4000		24.0	960	1280	0	960
1976	4000		16.0	640	2240	0	640
1977	4000	$4000	8.0	320	2880	$4000	1120
1978	0				0		
				$3200		$4000	$4000

Table 5.3.   Calculation of the annual accruals and the accumulated provision
              for depreciation for a unit of property using the declining
              balance (accelerated) method of allocation. The unit has a life
              of 4 years and a 20% salvage ratio. The rate is 1.5/4 or 37.5%.

| Year | Declining balance Jan 1 | Retired | Rate% | Annual accrual | * Accumulated depreciation * | | |
					Net Jan 1	Debit	Credit
1974	$4000		37.5	$1500	$0	$0	$1500
1975	2500		37.5	938	1500	0	938
1976	1562		37.5	586	2438	0	586
1977	976	$4000	*	176	3024	4000	976
1978	0				0		
				$3200		4000	$4000

* Switch to straight line rate. This yields a final accrual of $176.

Table 5.4. Calculation of the annual accruals and the accumulated provision for depreciation for a unit of property using the sinking fund (decelerated) method of allocation with i=10%. The unit has a life of 4 years and a 20% salvage ratio.

Year	Balance Jan 1	Retired	Rate%	Annual accrual	* Accumulated depreciation * Net Jan 1	Debit	Credit
1974	$4000		17.24	$690	$0	$0	$690
1975	4000		18.96	758	690	0	758
1976	4000		20.86	834	1448	0	834
1977	4000	$4000	22.95	918	2282	4000	1718
1978	0				0		
				$3200		4000	$4000

Table 5.5. Calculation of annual accruals and accumulated provision for depreciation using the SL-AL system and a rate of 1/6.4 or 15.625%.

Year (a)	Balance (b)	Retired (c)	Rate % (d)	Annual accrual (e)	Accum depr (f)
1974	$10000		15.625	$1563	$0
1975	10000		15.625	1563	1563
1976	10000		15.625	1563	3125
1977	10000	$4000	15.625	1563	4688
1978	6000		15.625	938	2250
1979	6000		15.625	938	3188
1980	6000		15.625	938	4125
1981	6000	6000	15.625	938	5063
1982	0				0

Table 5.6. Calculation of annual accruals and accumulated provision for depreciation using the SL-AL system and a rate of 1/7.4 or 13.514%.

Year (a)	Balance (b)	Retired (c)	Rate % (d)	Annual accrual (e)	Accum depr (f)
1974	$10000		13.514	$1351	$0
1975	10000		13.514	1351	1351
1976	10000		13.514	1351	2703
1977	10000	$4000	13.514	1351	4054
1978	6000		13.514	811	1405
1979	6000		13.514	811	2216
1980	6000		13.514	811	3027
1981	6000	6000	13.514	811	3838
1982	0				-1351

Table 5.7. Calculation of annual accruals and accumulated provision for depreciation using the SL-AL system. A rate of 1/7.4 or 13.514% was used during the first three years.

	Year (a)	Balance (b)	Retired (c)	Rate % (d)	Annual accrual (e)	Accum depr (f)
P	1974	$10000		13.514	$1351	$0
A	1975	10000		13.514	1351	1351
S	1976	10000		13.514	1351	2703
T						4054
F	1977	0000	$4000			
U	1978	6000				
T	1979	6000				
U	1980	6000				
R	1981	6000	6000			
E	1982	0				

Table 5.8. Calculation of the CAD for the survivor curve shown in Figure 5.1.

Year (a)	Age (b)	Balance (c)	Service in $-yrs (d)	Remaining life (e)	CADR (f)	CAD (g)
1974	0	$10000	64000	6.40	.0000	$0
1975	1	10000	54000	5.40	.1563	1563
1976	2	10000	44000	4.40	.3125	3125
1977	3	10000	34000	3.40	.4688	4688
1978	4	6000	24000	4.00	.3750	2250
1979	5	6000	18000	3.00	.5313	3188
1980	6	6000	12000	2.00	.6875	4125
1981	7	6000	6000	1.00	.8438	5063
1982	8	0	0		1.0000	0

Table 5.9. Application of the amortization method of adjustment to the problem presented in Table 5.7. The $634 deficit is amortized over two years and the rate is increased to 15.63%.

Year (a)	Balance (b)	Retired (c)	Rate % (d)	Annual accrual (e)	Accum depr (f)
1974	$10000		13.51	$1351	$0
1975	10000		13.51	1351	1351
1976	10000		13.51	1351	2702
1977	10000	$4000	15.63	1880*	4054
1978	6000		15.63	1255**	1933
1979	6000		15.63	938	3187
1980	6000		15.63	938	4125
1981	6000	6000	15.63	938	5062
1982	0				0

* Includes a $1563 annual accrual plus a $317 adjustment.

** Includes a $938 annual accrual plus a $317 adjustment.

119

Table 5.10. Calculation of the remaining life and the rate for the survivor curve shown in Figure 5.1.

Year (a)	Age (b)	Balance (c)	Retired (d)	Remaining service $-yrs (e)	Remaining life (f)	Rate % 1/RL (g)
1974	0	$10000		$64000	6.40	15.63
1975	1	10000		54000	5.40	18.52
1976	2	10000		44000	4.40	22.73
1977	3	10000	$4000	34000	3.40	29.41
1978	4	6000		24000	4.00	25.00
1979	5	6000		18000	3.00	33.33
1980	6	6000		12000	2.00	50.00
1981	7	6000	6000	6000	1.00	100.00
1982	8	0				

Table 5.11. Calculation of the annual accrual and the accumulated provision for depreciation using the SL-AL-RL system of depreciation and the accrual rates shown in Table 5.10.

Year (a)	Balance (b)	Retired (c)	Future accrual (d)	Rate % 1/RL (e)	Annual accrual (f)	Accum depr (g)
1974	$10000		$10000	15.625	$1563	$0
1975	10000		8438	18.519	1563	1563
1976	10000		6875	22.727	1563	3125
1977	10000	$4000	5313	29.412	1563	4688
1978	6000		3750	25.000	938	2250
1979	6000		2813	33.333	938	3188
1980	6000		1875	50.000	938	4125
1981	6000	6000	938	100.000	938	5063
1982	0					0

Table 5.12. Remaining life of a survivor curve in which $4000 is retired after 5 years and $6000 after 7.33 years, resulting in an average life of 6.4 years.

Year (a)	Age (b)	Balance (b)	Retired (c)	Remaining service $-yrs (e)	Remaining life (f)	Rate % (g)
1974	0	$10000		$64000	6.40	15.63
1975	1	10000		54000	5.40	18.52
1976	2	10000		44000	4.40	22.73
1977	3	10000		34000	3.40	29.41
1978	4	10000	$4000	24000	2.40	41.67
1979	5	6000		14000	2.33	42.86
1980	6	6000		8000	1.33	75.00
1981	7	6000	6000	2000*	1.00*	100.00
1982	8	0				

* $6000 is retired 1/3 of the way through the final year so the average balance during 1981 is $2000 and the remaining life at the start of the year is 1.00 year.

Table 5.13. Calculation of the annual accrual and the accumulated provision for depreciation using the SL-AL-RL system and accrual rates developed in Table 5.12.

Year (a)	Balance (b)	Retired (c)	Future accrual (d)	Rate % 1/RL (e)	Annual accrual (f)	Accum depr (g)
1974	$10000		$10000	15.625	$1563	$0
1975	10000		8438	18.519	1563	1563
1976	10000		6875	22.727	1563	3125
1977	10000	$4000	5313	29.412	1563	4688
1978	6000		3750	41.667	1563	2250
1979	6000		2188	42.857	938	3813
1980	6000		1250	75.000	938	4750
1981	6000	6000	313	100.000	313	5688
1982	0					0

Table 5.14. Remaining life for a survivor curve in which $4000 is retired after 1 year and $6000 after 10 years, resulting in an average life of 6.4 years.

Year (a)	Age (b)	Balance (c)	Retired (d)	Remaining service $-yrs (e)	Remaining life (f)	Rate % (g)
1974	0	$10000	$4000	$64000	6.40	15.63
1975	1	6000		54000	9.00	11.11
1976	2	6000		48000	8.00	12.50
1977	3	6000		42000	7.00	14.29
1978	4	6000		36000	6.00	16.67
1979	5	6000		30000	5.00	20.00
1980	6	6000		24000	4.00	25.00
1981	7	6000		18000	3.00	33.33
1982	8	6000		12000	2.00	50.00
1983	9	6000	6000	6000	1.00	100.00
1984	10	0				

Table 5.15. Calculation of the annual accrual and the accumulated provision for depreciation using the SL-AL-RL system and accrual rates developed in Table 5.14.

Year (a)	Balance (b)	Retired (c)	Future accrual (d)	Rate % 1/RL (e)	Annual accrual (f)	Accum depr (g)
1974	$10000		$10000	15.625	$1563	$0
1975	10000		8438	11.111	938	1563
1976	10000		7500	12.500	938	2500
1977	10000	$4000	6563	14.286	938	3438
1978	6000		5625	16.667	938	375
1979	6000		4688	20.000	938	1313
1980	6000		3750	25.000	938	2250
1981	6000	6000	2813	33.333	938	3188
1982	0			50.000		-1875
1983				100.000		

Table 5.16.   Remaining life for a survivor curve in which $4000 is retired after 4 years, $6000 after 9.67 years, with an average life of 7.4 years.

Year (a)	Age (b)	Balance (b)	Retired (c)	Remaining service $-yrs (e)	Remaining life (f)	Rate % (g)
1974	0	$10000		$74000	7.40	13.51
1975	1	10000		64000	6.40	15.63
1976	2	10000		54000	5.40	18.52
1977	3	10000	$4000	44000	4.40	22.73
1978	4	6000		34000	5.67	17.65
1979	5	6000		28000	4.67	21.43
1980	6	6000		22000	3.67	27.27
1981	7	6000		16000	2.67	37.50
1982	8	6000		10000	1.67	60.00
1983	9	6000*	6000	$4000*	1.00*	100.00
1984	10	0				

* $6000 is retired two-thirds of the way through the final year, so the average balance during 1983 is $4000 and the remaining life is 1.00 year.

Table 5.17.   Calculation of the annual accrual and the accumulated provision for depreciation using the SL-AL-RL system and accrual rates developed in Table 5.16.

Year (a)	Balance (b)	Retired (c)	Future accrual (d)	Rate % 1/RL (e)	Annual accrual (f)	Accum depr (g)
1974	$10000		$10000	13.514	$1351	$0
1975	10000		8649	15.625	1351	1351
1976	10000		7297	18.519	1351	2703
1977	10000	$4000	5946	22.727	1351	4054
1978	6000		4595	17.647	811	1405
1979	6000		3784	21.429	811	2216
1980	6000		2973	27.273	811	3027
1981	6000	6000	2162	37.500	811	3838
1982	0			60.000		-1351
1983				100.000		

Table 5.18.   Application of the remaining life method of adjustment to the problem presented in Table 5.7.

Year (a)	Balance (b)	Retired (c)	Future accrual (d)	Rate% 1/RL (e)	Annual accrual (f)	Accum depr (g)
1974	$10000		$10000	13.514	$1351	$0
1975	10000		8649	15.625	1351	1351
1976	10000		7297	18.519	1351	2703
1977	10000	$4000	5946	29.410*	1749	4054
1978	6000		4197	25.000*	1049	1803
1979	6000		3148	33.333*	1049	2852
1980	6000		2099	50.000*	1049	3901
1981	6000	6000	1049	100.000*	1049	4951
1982	0					0

* Accrual rates from Table 5.10.

Table 5.19. Calculation of the annual accrual rates for the survivor curve shown in Figure 5.1 using the SL-ELG system.

Group (a)	Group amount (b)	Group life (c)	Group rate % (d)	Annual accrual 1974-77 (e)	Annual accrual 1978-81 (f)
A	$4000	4	25.00	$1000.00	
B	6000	8	12.50	$750.00	$750.00
Annual accruals				$1750.00	$750.00
Balance during interval				$10000	$6000
Annual accrual rate %				17.50	12.50

Table 5.20. Calculation of annual accruals and accumulated provision for depreciation using the SL-ELG system using the rates calculated in Table 5.19.

Year (a)	Balance (b)	Retired (c)	Rate % (d)	Annual accrual (e)	Accum depr (f)
1974	$10000		17.50	$1750	$0
1975	10000		17.50	1750	1750
1976	10000		17.50	1750	3500
1977	10000	$4000	17.50	1750	5250
1978	6000		12.50	750	3000
1979	6000		12.50	750	3750
1980	6000		12.50	750	4500
1981	6000	6000	12.50	750	5250
1982	0				0

Table 5.21. Calculation of annual accruals and accumulated provision for depreciation using the SL-ELG system and the accrual rates calculated in Table 5.19. The survivor curve for the property is shown in Table 5.14.

Year (a)	Balance (b)	Retired (c)	Rate % (d)	Annual accrual (e)	Accum depr (f)
1974	$10000	$4000	17.50	$1750	$0
1975	6000		17.50	1050	-2250
1976	6000		17.50	1050	-1200
1977	6000		17.50	1050	-150
1978	6000		12.50	750	900
1979	6000		12.50	750	1650
1980	6000		12.50	750	2400
1981	6000		12.50	750	3150
1982	6000		12.50	750	3900
1983	6000	6000	12.50	750	4650
1984	0				-600

Table 5.22.   Calculation of the annual accrual rates for the survivor curve shown in Table 5.16 using the SL-ELG system.

Group (a)	Group amount (b)	Group life (c)	Group rate % (d)	Annual accrual 1974-78 (e)	Annual accrual 1979-81 (f)
A	$4000	4	25.00	$1000.00	
B	6000	9.67	10.34	620.69	$620.69
Annual accruals				$1621.00	$621.00
Balance during interval				$10000	$6000
Annual accrual rate %				16.21	10.34

Table 5.23.   Calculation of annual accruals and accumulated depreciation using the SL-ELG system and the accrual rates calculated in Table 5.22.

Year (a)	Balance (b)	Retired (c)	Rate % (d)	Annual accrual (e)	Accum depr (f)
1974	$10000		16.21	$1621	$0
1975	10000		16.21	1621	1621
1976	10000		16.21	1621	3242
1977	10000	$4000	16.21	1621	4863
1978	6000		10.34	620	2484
1979	6000		10.34	620	3104
1980	6000		10.34	620	3725
1981	6000	6000	10.34	620	4345
1982	0				-1034

Table 5.24.   Calculation of annual accruals and ac-cumcumulated depreciation using the SL-ELG system. The accrual rates shown in Table 5.22 are used for the first three years.

	Year (a)	Balance (b)	Retired (c)	Rate % (d)	Annual accrual (e)	Accum depr (f)
P	1974	$10000		16.21	$1621	$0
A	1975	10000		16.21	1621	1621
S	1976	10000		16.21	1621	3242
T						4863
F	1977	10000	$4000			
U	1978	6000				
T	1979	6000				
U	1980	6000				
R	1981	6000	6000			
E	1982	0				

Table 5.25. Calculation of the calculated accumulated depreciation and the calculated accumulated depreciation ratios for the survivor curve shown in Figure 5.1.

		CAD At Start of Year								
Life	Amount	1	2	3	4	5	6	7	8	9
4	4000	0	1000	2000	3000	0				
8	6000	0	750	1500	2250	3000	3750	4500	5250	0
Annual CAD		0	1750	3500	5250	3000	3750	4500	5250	0
Start of year balance		10000	10000	10000	10000	6000	6000	6000	6000	0
CADR		.000	.1750	.3500	.5250	.5000	.6250	.7500	.8750	1.000

Table 5.26. Application of the amortization method of adjustment to the problem presented in Table 5.24. The $387 deficit is amortized over a 1-year period and the accrual rates are changed to those shown in Table 5.19.

Year (a)	Balance (b)	Retired (c)	Rate % (d)	Annual accrual (e)	Accum depr (f)
1974	$10000		16.21	$1621	$0
1975	10000		16.21	1621	1621
1976	10000		16.21	1621	3242
1977	10000	$4000	17.50	2137*	4863
1978	6000		12.50	750	3000
1979	6000		12.50	750	3750
1980	6000		12.50	750	4500
1981	6000	6000	12.50	750	5250
1982	0				0

* Includes a $1750 accrual and a $387 adjustment.

Table 5.27. Calculation of the annual accruals and accumulated provision for depreciation using the SL-
ELG-RL system of depreciation and the survivor
curve shown in Figure 5.1.

Accruals by ELG

Year (a)	Balance (b)	Retired (c)	Future accrual (d)	Rate % 1/RL (e)	Annual accrual (f)	Accum depr (g)
Unit A						
1974	$4000		$4000	25.000	$1000	$0
1975	4000		3000	33.333	1000	1000
1976	4000		2000	50.000	1000	2000
1977	4000	$4000	1000	100.000	1000	3000
						0
Unit B						
1974	$6000		$6000	12.500	$750	$0
1975	6000		5250	14.286	750	750
1976	6000		4500	16.667	750	1500
1977	6000		3750	20.000	750	2250
1978	6000		3000	25.000	750	3000
1979	6000		2250	33.333	750	3750
1980	6000		1500	50.000	750	4500
1981	6000	$6000	750	100.000	750	5250
						0

Total accruals

Year (a)	Balance (b)	Retired (c)	Future accrual (d)	Composite rate % (e)	Annual accrual (f)	Accum depr (g)
1974	$10000		$10000	17.50	$1750	$0
1975	10000		8250	21.21	1750	1750
1976	10000		6500	26.92	1750	3500
1977	10000	$4000	4750	36.84	1750	5250
1978	6000		3000	25.00	750	3000
1979	6000		2250	33.33	750	3750
1980	6000		1500	50.00	750	4500
1981	6000	6000	750	100.00	750	5250
1982	0					0

Table 5.28. Calculation of the composite annual accrual rates
using the SL-ELG-RL system of depreciation and
the survivor curve shown in Table 5.16.

Year (a)	Balance (b)	Retired (c)	Future accrual (d)	Rate % 1/RL (e)	Annual accrual (f)	Accum depr (g)
Unit A						
1974	$4000		$4000	25.000	$1000	$0
1975	4000		3000	33.333	1000	1000
1976	4000		2000	50.000	1000	2000
1977	4000	$4000	1000	100.000	1000	3000
						0
Unit B						
1974	$6000		$6000	10.341	$620	$0
1975	6000		5380	11.534	620	620
1976	6000		4759	13.037	620	1240
1977	6000		4139	14.992	620	1860
1978	6000		3518	17.637	620	2480
1979	6000		2898	21.413	620	3100
1980	6000		2277	27.248	620	3720
1981	6000		1657	37.453	620	4340
1982	6000		1036	59.880	620	4960
1982	6000	$6000	416	100.000	416	5580
1983	0					0

Total accruals

Year (a)	Balance (b)	Retired (c)	Future accrual (d)	Composite rate % (e)	Annual accrual (f)
1974	$10000		$10000	16.205	$1621
1975	10000		8379	19.339	1621
1976	10000		6758	23.975	1621
1977	10000	$4000	5137	31.536	1621
1978	6000		3516	17.637	620
1979	6000		2816	21.413	620
1980	6000		2276	27.248	620
1981	6000		1656	37.453	620
1982	6000	6000	1036	59.880	620
1983	0		416	100.000	416

Table 5.29. Calculation of the annual accrual and the
accumulated provision for depreciation using the SL-ELG-RL system of depreciation
and the accrual rates shown in Table 5.28.

Year (a)	Balance (b)	Retired (c)	Future accrual (d)	Rate % 1/RL (e)	Annual accrual (f)	Accum depr (g)
1974	$10000		$10000	16.205	$1621	$0
1975	10000		8379	19.339	1621	1621
1976	10000		6758	23.975	1621	3242
1977	10000	$4000	5137	31.536	1621	4863
1978	6000		3516	17.637	620	2484
1979	6000		2896	21.413	620	3104
1980	6000		2276	27.248	620	3724
1981	6000	6000	1656	37.453	620	4344
1982	0			59.880		-1034
1983				100.000		

Table 5.30. Application of the remaining life method of adjustment to the problem presented in Table 5.24.

Year (a)	Balance (b)	Retired (c)	Future accrual (d)	Rate % 1/RL (e)	Annual accrual (f)	Accum depr (g)
1974	$10000		$10000	16.205	$1621	$0
1975	10000		8379	19.339	1621	1621
1976	10000		6758	23.975	1621	3242
1977	10000	$4000	5137	36.842*	1893	4863
1978	6000		3244	25.000*	811	2756
1979	6000		2433	33.333*	811	3567
1980	6000		1622	50.000*	811	4378
1981	6000	6000	811	100.000*	811	5189
1982	0					0

* Accrual rates from Table 5.27.

Table 5.31. The salvage schedule for the survivor curve shown in Figure 5.1 and having an average salvage ratio of 18%.

Year (a)	Age (b)	Balance (c)	Retired (d)	SR % (e)	% of orig cost (f)	Realized salvage ratio % (g)	Future salvage ratio % (h)	Average salvage ratio % (i)
1974	0	$10000				.00	18.00	18.00
1975	1	10000				.00	18.00	18.00
1976	2	10000				.00	18.00	18.00
1977	3	10000	$4000*	30.00	12.00	.00	18.00	18.00
1978	4	6000				30.00	10.00	18.00
1979	5	6000				30.00	10.00	18.00
1980	6	6000				30.00	10.00	18.00
1981	7	6000	6000*	10.00	6.00	30.00	10.00	18.00
1982	8	0				18.00		18.00
					18.00			

* Salvage for these units is $1200 and $600 respectively.

Table 5.32. Calculation of annual accruals and accumulated provision for depreciation using the SL-AL system and a rate of (100%-18%)/6.4 or 12.813%.

Year (a)	Balance (b)	Retired (c)	Rate % (d)	Annual accrual (e)	Accum depr (f)
1974	$10000		12.813	$1281	$0
1975	10000		12.813	1281	1281
1976	10000		12.813	1281	2563
1977	10000	$4000*	12.813	1281	3844
1978	6000		12.813	769	**2325
1979	6000		12.813	769	3094
1980	6000		12.813	769	3863
1981	6000	6000*	12.813	769	4631
1982	0				***0

* Salvage for these units is $1200 and $600 respectively.

** 2325 = 3844 + 1281 - 4000 + 1200

*** 0 = 4631 + 769 - 6000 + 600

Table 5.33. Salvage schedule for survivor curve shown in Figure 5.1 and having an average salvage ratio of 25%.

Year (a)	Age (b)	Balance (c)	Retired (d)	SR % (e)	% of orig cost (f)	Realized salvage ratio % (g)	Future salvage ratio % (h)	Average salvage ratio % (i)
1974	1	$10000				.00	25.00	25.00
1975	2	10000				.00	25.00	25.00
1976	3	10000				.00	25.00	25.00
1977	4	10000	$4000*	40.00	16.00	.00	25.00	25.00
1978	5	6000				40.00	15.00	25.00
1979	6	6000				40.00	15.00	25.00
1980	7	6000				40.00	15.00	25.00
1981	8	6000	6000*	15.00	9.00	40.00	15.00	25.00
1982	9	0			25.00	25.00		25.00

* Salvage for these units is $1600 and $900 respectively.

Table 5.34. Calculation of annual accruals and accumulated provision for depreciation using the SL-AL system using a rate of (100%-25%)/6.4 or 11.719%.

Year (a)	Balance (b)	Retired (c)	Rate % (d)	Annual accrual (e)	Accum depr (f)
1974	$10000		11.719	$1172	$0
1975	10000		11.719	1172	1172
1976	10000		11.719	1172	2344
1977	10000	$4000*	11.719	1172	3516
1978	6000		11.719	703	1888
1979	6000		11.719	703	2591
1980	6000		11.719	703	3294
1981	6000	6000*	11.719	703	3997
1982	0				-700

* Salvage for these units is $1200 and $600 respectively.

Table 5.35. Calculation of annual accruals and accumulated provision for depreciation using the SL-AL system. A rate of (100%-25%)/6.4 or 11.719% was used during the first four years.

	Year (a)	Balance (b)	Retired (c)	Rate % (d)	Annual accrual (e)	Accum depr (f)
P	1974	$10000		11.719	$1172	$0
A	1975	10000		11.719	1172	1172
S	1976	10000		11.719	1172	2344
T	1977	10000	$4000*	11.719	1172	3516
						1888
F	1978	6000				
U	1979	6000				
T	1980	6000				
U	1981	6000	6000			
R	1982	0				
E						

* Salvage for this unit is $1200.

Table 5.36. Calculation of the CAD for the SL-AL system using the survivor curve shown in Figure 5.1 and the salvage schedule shown in Table 5.31.

Year (a)	Age (b)	Balance (c)	Retired (d)	1-FSR (e)	Rate % (f)	RL (g)	CADR (h)	CAD (i)
1974	0	$10000		82.00	12.81	6.40	.00	$0
1975	1	10000		82.00	12.81	5.40	12.81	1281
1976	2	10000		82.00	12.81	4.40	25.63	2563
1977	3	10000	$4000*	82.00	12.81	3.40	38.44	3844
1978	4	6000		90.00	12.81	4.00	38.75	2325
1979	5	6000		90.00	12.81	3.00	51.56	3094
1980	6	6000		90.00	12.81	2.00	64.38	3863
1981	7	6000	6000*	90.00	12.81	1.00	77.19	4631
1982	8	0						0

* Salvage for these units is $1200 and $600 respectively.

Table 5.37. Application of the amortization method of adjustment to the problem presented in Table 5.35. The $437 deficit is amortized over 4 years and the rate is increased to 12.813%.

Year (a)	Balance (b)	Retired (c)	Rate % (d)	Annual accrual (e)	Accum depr (f)
1974	$10000		11.719	$1172	$0
1975	10000		11.719	1172	1172
1976	10000		11.719	1172	2344
1977	10000	$4000*	11.719	1172	3516
1978	6000		12.813	878**	1888
1979	6000		12.813	878**	2766
1980	6000		12.813	878**	3644
1981	6000	6000*	12.813	878**	4522
1982	0				0

* Salvage for these units is $1200 and $600 respectively.

** Includes a $769 accrual and a $109 adjustment.

Table 5.38. Calculation of the annual accruals and the accumulated provision for depreciation using the SL-AL-RL system of depreciation. The rates are shown in Table 5.10 and the future salvage is shown in Table 5.31.

Year (a)	Balance (b)	Retired (c)	Future accrual (d)	Rate % 1/RL (e)	Annual accrual (f)	Accum depr (g)
1974	$10000		$8200	15.625	$1281	$0
1975	10000		6919	18.519	1281	1281
1976	10000		5638	22.727	1281	2563
1977	10000	$4000*	4356	29.412	1281	3844
1978	6000		3075	25.000	769	2325
1979	6000		2306	33.333	769	3094
1980	6000		1538	50.000	769	3863
1981	6000	6000*	769	100.000	769	4631
1982	0					0

* Salvage for these units is $1200 and $600 respectively.

Table 5.39.   Calculation of the annual accrual and the accumulated provision for depreciation using the SL-AL-RL system of depreciation with the rates shown in Table 5.10 and the salvage schedule shown in Table 5.33.

Year (a)	Balance (b)	Retired (c)	Future accrual (d)	Rate % 1/RL (e)	Annual accrual (f)	Accum depr (g)
1974	$10000		$7500	15.625	$1172	$0
1975	10000		6328	18.519	1172	1172
1976	10000		5156	22.727	1172	2344
1977	10000	$4000*	3984	29.412	1172	3516
1978	6000		3213	25.000	803	1888
1979	6000		2409	33.333	803	2691
1980	6000		1606	50.000	803	3494
1981	6000	6000*	803	100.000	803	4297
1982	0					-300

* Salvage for these units is $1200 and $600 respectively.

Table 5.40.   Application of the SL-AL-RL system of depreciation to the problem presented in Table 5.35.

Year (a)	Balance (b)	Retired (c)	Future accrual (d)	Rate % 1/RL (e)	Annual accrual (f)	Accum depr (g)
1974	$10000		$7500	15.625	$1172	$0
1975	10000		6328	18.519	1172	1172
1976	10000		5156	22.727	1172	2344
1977	10000	$4000*	3984	29.412	1172	3516
1978	6000		3513**	25.000	878	1888
1979	6000		2634**	33.333	878	2766
1980	6000		1756**	50.000	878	3644
1981	6000	6000*	878**	100.000	878	4522
1982	0					0

* Salvage for these units is $1200 and $600 respectively.

** A future salvage of 10% ratio is used.

Table 5.41.   Calculation of the annual rates for the survivor curve shown in Figure 5.1 and the salvage schedule shown in Table 5.31 using the SL-ELG system of calculating annual accruals.

Group (a)	Group amount (b)	Group life (c)	Group salvage % (d)	Group rate % (e)	Annual accrual 1974-77 (f)	Annual accrual 1978-81 (g)
A	$4000	4	30.00	17.50	$700.00	
B	6000	8	10.00	11.25	675.00	$675.00
Annual accruals					$1375.00	$675.00
Balance during interval					$10000	$6000
Annual accrual rate %					13.75	11.25

Table 5.42.   Calculation of annual accruals and accumulated provision for depreciation using the SL-ELG system of calculating annual accruals and the rates shown in Table 5.41.

Year (a)	Balance (b)	Retired (c)	Rate % (d)	Annual accrual (e)	Accum depr (f)
1974	$10000		13.750	$1375	$0
1975	10000		13.750	1375	1375
1976	10000		13.750	1375	2750
1977	10000	$4000*	13.750	1375	4125
1978	6000		11.250	675	2700
1979	6000		11.250	675	3375
1980	6000		11.250	675	4050
1981	6000	6000*	11.250	675	4725
1982	0				0

* Salvage for these units is $1200 and $600 respectively.

Table 5.43.   Calculation of the annual rates for the survivor curve shown in Figure 5.1 and the salvage schedule shown in Table 5.33 using the SL-ELG system.

Group (a)	Group amount (b)	Group life (c)	Group salvage % (d)	Group rate % (e)	Annual accrual 1974-77 (f)	Annual accrual 1978-81 (g)
A	$4000	4	40.00	15.00	$600.00	
B	6000	8	15.00	10.63	638.00	$638.00
Annual accruals					$1238.00	$638.00
Balance during interval					$10000	$6000
Annual accrual rate %					12.38	10.63

Table 5.44.   Calculation of annual accruals and accumulated provision for depreciation using the SL-ELG system and the rates shown in Table 5.43.

Year (a)	Balance (b)	Retired (c)	Rate % (d)	Annual accrual (e)	Accum depr (f)
1974	$10000		12.375	$1238	$0
1975	10000		12.375	1238	1238
1976	10000		12.375	1238	2475
1977	10000	$4000*	12.375	1238	3713
1978	6000		10.625	638	2150
1979	6000		10.625	638	2788
1980	6000		10.625	638	3425
1981	6000	6000*	10.625	638	4063
1982	0				-700

* Salvage for these units is $1200 and $600 respectively.

Table 5.45. Calculation of annual accruals and accumulated provision for depreciation using the SL-ELG system. Rates shown in
Table 5.43 were used during the first 4
years.

	Year (a)	Balance (b)	Retired (c)	Rate % (d)	Annual accrual (e)	Accum depr (f)
P	1974	$10000		12.375	$1238	$0
A	1975	10000		12.375	1238	1238
S	1976	10000		12.375	1238	2475
T	1977	10000	$4000*	12.375	1238	3713
						2150
F	1978	6000				
U	1979	6000				
T	1980	6000				
U	1981	6000	6000			
R	1982	0				
E						

* Salvage for this unit is $1200.

Table 5.46. Calculation of the calculated accumulated depreciation and the
calculated accumulated depreciation ratios for the survivor
curve shown in Figure 5.1 and the salvage schedule shown in
Table 5.31.

		CAD at start of year								
Life	Amount	1	2	3	4	5	6	7	8	9
4	2800	0	700	1400	2100	0				
8	5400	0	675	1350	2025	2700	3375	4050	4725	0
Annual CAD		0	1375	2750	4125	2700	3375	4050	4725	0
Start of year balance		10000	10000	10000	10000	6000	6000	6000	6000	0
CADR		.000	.1375	.2750	.4125	.4500	.5625	.6750	.7875	1.000

Table 5.47. Application of the amortization
method of adjustment to the problem
presented in Table 5.45. The $550
variation is amortized over a 3-
year period and rates are changed
to those shown in Table 5.41.

Year (a)	Balance (b)	Retired (c)	Rate % (d)	Annual accrual (e)	Accum depr (f)
1974	$10000		12.375	$1238	$0
1975	10000		12.375	1238	1238
1976	10000		12.375	1238	2475
1977	10000	$4000*	12.375	1238	3713
1978	6000		11.250	858**	2150
1979	6000		11.250	858**	3008
1980	6000		11.250	858**	3867
1981	6000	6000*	11.250	675	4725
1982	0				0

* Salvage for these units is $1200 and $600
respectively.

** Includes $675 annual accrual and $183
adjustment.

Table 5.48. Calculation of the composite annual accrual rates using the SL-ELG-RL system of depreciation, the survivor curve shown in Figure 5.1, and the future salvage shown in Table 5.31.

Year (a)	Balance (b)	Retired (c)	Future accrual (d)	Rate % 1/RL (e)	Annual accrual (f)	Accum depr (g)
Unit A						
1974	$4000		$2800	25.000	$700	$0
1975	4000		2100	33.333	700	700
1976	4000		1400	50.000	700	1400
1977	4000	$4000	700	100.000	700	2100
						0
Unit B						
1974	$6000		$5400	12.500	$675	$0
1975	6000		4725	14.286	675	675
1976	6000		4050	16.667	675	1350
1977	6000		3375	20.000	675	2025
1978	6000		2700	25.000	675	2700
1979	6000		2025	33.333	675	3375
1980	6000		1350	50.000	675	4050
1981	6000	$6000	675	100.000	675	4725
						0

Total accruals

Year (a)	Balance (b)	Retired (c)	Future accrual (d)	Composite rate % (e)	Annual accrual (f)
1974	$10000		$8200	16.768	$1375
1975	10000		6825	20.147	1375
1976	10000		5450	25.229	1375
1977	10000	$4000*	4075	33.742	1375
1978	6000		2700	25.000	675
1979	6000		2025	33.333	675
1980	6000		1350	50.000	675
1981	6000	6000*	675	100.000	675
1982	0				

* Salvage for these units is $1200 and $600 respectively.

Table 5.49. Calculation of the annual accruals and accumulated provision for depreciation using the SL-ELG-RL system of depreciation and the rates shown in Table 5.48 and the future salvage shown in Table 5.31.

Year (a)	Balance (b)	Retired (c)	Future accrual (d)	Rate % 1/RL (e)	Annual accrual (f)	Accum depr (g)
1974	$10000		$8200	16.768	$1375	$0
1975	10000		6825	20.147	1375	1375
1976	10000		5450	25.229	1375	2750
1977	10000	$4000*	4075	33.742	1375	4125
1978	6000		2700	25.000	675	2700
1979	6000		2025	33.333	675	3375
1980	6000		1350	50.000	675	4050
1981	6000	6000*	675	100.000	675	4725
1982	0					0

* Salvage for these units is $1200 and $600 respectively.

Table 5.50. Calculation of the composite rates for the survivor curve shown in Figure 5.1 and the salvage schedule shown in Table 5.33.

Year (a)	Balance (b)	Retired (c)	Future accrual (d)	Rate % 1/RL (e)	Annual accrual (f)	Accum depr (g)
Unit A						
1974	$4000		$2400	25.000	$600	$0
1975	4000		1800	33.333	600	600
1976	4000		1200	50.000	600	1200
1977	4000	$4000	600	100.000	600	1800
						0
Unit B						
1974	$6000		$5100	12.500	$638	$0
1975	6000		4463	14.286	638	638
1976	6000		3825	16.667	638	1275
1977	6000		3188	20.000	638	1913
1978	6000		2550	25.000	638	2550
1979	6000		1913	33.333	638	3188
1980	6000		1275	50.000	638	3825
1981	6000	$6000	638	100.000	638	4463
						0

Total accruals

Year (a)	Balance (b)	Retired (c)	Future accrual (d)	Composite rate % (e)	Annual accrual (f)
1974	$10000		$7500	16.500	$1238
1975	10000		6263	19.760	1238
1976	10000		5025	24.627	1238
1977	10000	$4000	3788	32.673	1238
1978	6000		2550	25.000	638
1979	6000		1913	33.333	638
1980	6000		1275	50.000	638
1981	6000	6000	638	100.000	638
1982	0				

Table 5.51. Calculation of annual accruals and accumulated provision for depreciation using the SL-AL-RL system of depreciation with the rates shown in Table 5.50 and future salvage shown in Table 5.33.

Year (a)	Balance (b)	Retired (c)	Future accrual (d)	Rate % 1/RL (e)	Annual accrual (f)	Accum depr (g)
1974	$10000		$7500	16.500	$1238	$0
1975	10000		6263	19.760	1238	1238
1976	10000		5025	24.627	1238	2475
1977	10000	$4000*	3788	32.673	1238	3713
1978	6000		2950	25.000	738	2150
1979	6000		2213	33.333	738	2888
1980	6000		1475	50.000	738	3625
1981	6000	6000*	738	100.000	738	4363
1982	0					-300

* Salvage for these units is $1200 and $600 respectively.

Table 5.52. Application of the SL-ELG-RL depreciation system to the problem presented in Table 5.45.

Year (a)	Balance (b)	Retired (c)	Future accrual (d)	Rate % 1/RL (e)	Annual accrual (f)	Accum depr (g)
1974	$10000		$7500	16.500	$1238	$0
1975	10000		6263	19.760	1238	1238
1976	10000		5025	24.627	1238	2475
1977	10000	$4000*	3788	32.673	1238	3713
1978	6000		3250**	25.000***	813	2150
1979	6000		2438**	33.333***	813	2963
1980	6000		1625**	50.000***	813	3775
1981	6000	6000*	813**	100.000***	813	4588
1982	0					0

* Salvage for these units is $1200 and $600 respectively.

** A future salvage of 10% is used.

*** Accrual rates from Table 5.48.

Table 5.53. Calculation of CAD for the SL-AL system using the survivor curve shown in Figure 5.1 and a future and average salvage ratio of 18%.

Year (a)	Age (b)	Balance (c)	Retired (d)	1-ASR (e)	RL (f)	CADR (g)	CAD (h)
1974	0	$10000		82.00	6.40	00.00	$0
1975	1	10000		82.00	5.40	12.81	1281
1976	2	10000		82.00	4.40	25.63	2563
1977	3	10000	$4000*	82.00	3.40	38.44	3844
1978	4	6000		82.00	4.00	30.75	1845
1979	5	6000		82.00	3.00	43.56	2614
1980	6	6000		82.00	2.00	56.38	3383
1981	7	6000	6000*	82.00	1.00	69.19	4151
1982	8	0					0

* Salvage for these units is $1200 and $600 respectively.

Table 5.54. Application of the SL-AL-RL system of depreciation using the average salvage ratio of 18% rather than the future salvage ratio.

Year (a)	Balance (b)	Retired (c)	Future accrual (d)	Rate % 1/RL (e)	Annual accrual (f)	Accum depr (g)
1974	$10000		$8200	15.625	$1281	$0
1975	10000		6919	18.519	1281	1281
1976	10000		5638	22.727	1281	2563
1977	10000	$4000*	4356	29.412	1281	3844
1978	6000		2595	25.000	649	2325
1979	6000		1946	33.333	649	2974
1980	6000		1298	50.000	649	3623
1981	6000	6000*	649	100.000	649	4271
1982	0					-480

* Salvage for these units is $1200 and $600 respectively.

Table 5.55. Calculation of the annual accrual rates for the survivor curve shown in Figure 5.1 and an average salvage ratio of 18% using the SL-ELG system of calculating annual accruals.

Group (a)	Group amount (b)	Group life (c)	Group salvage % (d)	Group rate % (e)	Annual accrual 1974-77 (f)	Annual accrual 1978-81 (g)
A	$4000	4	18.00	20.50	$820.00	
B	6000	8	18.00	10.25	$615.00	$615.00
Annual accruals					$1435.00	$615.00
Balance during interval					$10000	$6000
Annual accrual rate %					14.35	10.25

Table 5.56. Calculation of annual accrual rates and accumulated provision for depreciation using the SL-ELG system with rates based on average salvage and shown in Table 5.55.

Year (a)	Balance (b)	Retired (c)	Rate % (d)	Annual accrual (e)	Accum depr (f)
1974	$10000		14.350	$1435	$0
1975	10000		14.350	1435	1435
1976	10000		14.350	1435	2870
1977	10000	$4000*	14.350	1435	4305
1978	6000		10.250	615	2940
1979	6000		10.250	615	3555
1980	6000		10.250	615	4170
1981	6000	6000*	10.250	615	4785
1982	0				0

* Salvage for these units is $1200 and $600 respectively.

Table 5.57. Calculation of the calculated accumulated depreciation and calculated accumulated depreciation ratios using the SL-ELG-AM depreciation and an average salvage ratio of 18% for all ELGs.

Life	Amount	CAD at start of year 1	2	3	4	5	6	7	8	9
4	3280	0	820	1640	2460	0				
8	4920	0	615	1230	1845	2460	3075	3690	4305	0
Annual CAD		0	1435	2870	4305	2460	3075	3690	4305	0
Start of year balance		10000	10000	10000	10000	6000	6000	6000	6000	0
CADR		.000	.1445	.2870	.4305	.4100	.5125	.6150	.7175	1.000

Table 5.58. Calculation of composite rates using the survivor curve shown in Figure 5.1 and letting the salvage ratio for all retirements equal the average salvage ratio of 18%.

Year (a)	Balance (b)	Retired (c)	Future accrual (d)	Rate % 1/RL (e)	Annual accrual (f)	Accum depr (g)
Unit A
1974	$4000		$3280	25.000	$820	$0
1975	4000		2460	33.333	820	820
1976	4000		1640	50.000	820	1640
1977	4000	$4000	820	100.000	820	2460
						0
Unit B
1974	$6000		$4920	12.500	$615	$0
1975	6000		4305	14.286	615	615
1976	6000		3690	16.667	615	1230
1977	6000		3075	20.000	615	1845
1978	6000		2460	25.000	615	2460
1979	6000		1845	33.333	615	3075
1980	6000		1230	50.000	615	3690
1981	6000	$6000	615	100.000	615	4305
						0

Total accruals

Year (a)	Balance (b)	Retired (c)	Future accrual (d)	Composite rate % (e)	Annual accrual (f)
1974	$10000		$8200	17.500	$1435
1975	10000		6765	21.212	1435
1976	10000		5330	26.923	1435
1977	10000	$4000	3895	36.842	1435
1978	6000		2460	25.000	615
1979	6000		1845	33.333	615
1980	6000		1230	50.000	615
1981	6000	6000	615	100.000	615
1982	0				

Table 5.59. Application of the SL-AL-ELG-RL system of depreciation using the rates shown in Table 5.58 and a future salvage ratio of 18% rather than the future salvage shown in Table 5.31.

Year (a)	Balance (b)	Retired (c)	Future accrual (d)	Rate % 1/RL (e)	Annual accrual (f)	Accum depr (g)
1974	$10000		$8200	17.500	$1435	$0
1975	10000		6765	21.212	1435	1435
1976	10000		5330	26.923	1435	2870
1977	10000	$4000*	3895	36.842	1435	4305
1978	6000		1980	25.000	495	2940
1979	6000		1485	33.333	495	3435
1980	6000		990	50.000	495	3930
1981	6000	6000*	495	100.000	315	4425
1982	0					-480

* Salvage for these units is $1200 and $600 respectively.

NOTES

1. Gas (FERC), electric (FERC), and water companies (NARUC) use the title Accumulated Provision for Depreciation, while telecommunications (FCC) and railroads (ICC) use the title Accumulated Depreciation. Telecommunications used the title Depreciation Reserve until 1986. We will use the term *Accumulated Provision for Depreciation*. It refers to the net balance of either of these accounts.

2. The CADR is also called reserve ratio or the accrued ratio.

3. The balance, usually shown in column (b) of the tables at the end of this chapter, can be defined as the balance at the start of the year or the average balance during the year. The convention used in this chapter results in the start-of-year balance equaling the average balance. When other conventions are used, a small difference between the two annual accruals may result because the remaining life calculation typically applies the rate to the beginning-year balance while the amortization calculation typically applies the rate to the average balance during the year.

4. All of these variables except AL are a function of the age of the property, and a complete notation would include an index for the age. For example, rather than RL, use RL(i) = the remaining life at age i. The following calculations all refer to the same year so the index i is dropped.

5. Remember that both the realized and future salvage ratios are averages. Both the survivor curve and the salvage ratio at each age from zero to the maximum life are required to calculate these average ratios. For convenience, we will use the terms realized or future salvage ratio rather than *average* realized or *average* future salvage ratio.

6 Continuous Property Groups

C HAPTER 5 used elementary survivor curves, a single vintage group, and a simplified format to illustrate the calculation of the annual accrual for depreciation for several systems of depreciation. This chapter will use Iowa survivor curves and formats characteristic of those found in industrial practice to illustrate the application of these systems of depreciation to continuous property groups. The illustrations will include the use of both average salvage and salvage that varies with age.

A continuous property group[1] is created when vintage groups are combined to form a common group. Each year property is removed from service for many reasons and, at the same time, property may be added either to replace property that was retired or to increase service capacity. Over time the operating and physical characteristics of the property change, but the continuous property group continues as long as the service it provides is needed. If new vintages are no longer added, the continuous property group becomes closed, or bounded, and over time becomes smaller and finally vanishes. The continuous property group, which is usually recorded as a plant account or subaccount, is of interest because it represents the most common method of grouping assets for depreciation.

The method of allocation, the procedure for applying the method of allocation, and the method of adjustment (e.g., SL-AL-AM) specify the factors that define a depreciation system for a vintage group. The terms broad group and vintage group describe two ways of viewing the life and salvage characteristics of the vintage groups that have been combined to form a continuous property group for purposes of depreciation. One approach is to view the continuous property group as a collection of vintage

139

groups each of which have the same life and salvage characteristics. This is called the *broad group model*. The other approach is to view the continuous property group as a collection of vintage groups each of which can have different life and salvage characteristics. This is called the *vintage group model*. The model being used will be identified by either stating that the broad or vintage group model is being used or by adding the initials BG or VG to those defining the depreciation system (e.g., SL-AL-AM-BG).

THE BROAD GROUP MODEL

The broad group model requires that a single survivor curve and a single salvage schedule be chosen to represent all the vintages in the continuous property group. Though it is likely that individual vintages will have different life and salvage characteristics, the broad group model makes the simplifying assumption that all vintages in the continuous property group have identical life and salvage characteristics. Thus, if the broad group model is used, it must be reasonable to represent the life and salvage characteristics of each vintage with a single survivor curve and salvage schedule.

The Average Life Procedure

The average life (AL) procedure is discussed in this section. First the amortization (i.e., the SL-AL-AM-BG system) and then the remaining life method of adjustment (i.e., the SL-AL-RL-BG system) will be illustrated.[2] Both the life and salvage characteristics must be chosen in a manner consistent with the assumptions of the broad group model to provide reasonable estimates of depreciation. When using the average life procedure, the reasoning used to choose the life and salvage characteristics of the broad group is the same for both the AM and RL methods of adjustment.

Figure 6.1 represents the realized (historical) and future (forecast) life characteristics of a continuous property group. Each row represents a vintage group. The first row represents the oldest surviving vintage and the final row the most recent vintage. Each column represents a calendar year. The first column is the year during which the oldest surviving vintage was installed. The space dividing the realized life and the future life marks the end of the most recent year, and the last column is the year the last unit from the last surviving vintage is retired. Let each cell represent the vintage surviving plant at the end of the calendar year, so that the cells in any row form a survivor curve reflecting the life characteristics of that vintage.

Tables 8.1 and 8.2 in Chapter 8 contain the schedule of additions, retirements, and plant balances for the continuous property group called Account 897 — Utility Devices. This property group is used to illustrate the

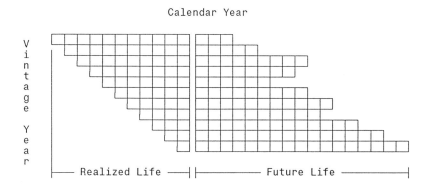

Figure 6.1. A representation of the realized and future life of a continuous property group.

calculation of the annual accrual for depreciation. Tables 8.1 and 8.2 contain the data necessary to construct the triangular-shaped, realized life portion of Figure 6.1. Place yourself in time at the end of the final year for which there is data (i.e., for Account 897 this is December 31, 1990). Look back in time and see the historical record of additions and retirements. Now imagine moving forward in time. As the years pass, visualize the declining vintage balances, with some vintages becoming completely retired while others remain in service. Finally, the last unit of the last vintage is retired. The record of the future balances, contained in the righthand side of the figure, defines the future life. Each row (i.e., each vintage survivor curve) can be divided into either realized life or future life. Older vintages are mostly realized life and newer vintages are mostly future life. The realized life is documented in the aged data while the future life is a forecast. The product of the age at retirement times the amount of the retirement, summed over all retirements and divided by the total retirements is the average life. The job of the depreciation professional is, first, to determine the realized life and, second, to forecast the future life. Then when using the AL procedure and the broad group model, he or she must select the survivor curve that best describes the life characteristics (i.e., a single curve that describes both the realized life and the future life) of the single group of property formed by combining the vintage groups shown in Figure 6.1. The Iowa S1−10 survivor curve will be used to describe the life characteristics of Account 897 for use with the average life procedure and the broad group model.

Figure 6.1 also can be used to help explain the method of estimating the average salvage ratio and the future salvage ratios. For this purpose, let each cell in Figure 6.1 represent the net salvage for the corresponding vintage and calendar years. The sum of all salvage, realized and future, divided by the original cost of all retirements, realized and future, is the average salvage ratio. This average contains salvage associated with early retirements from older vintages, later retirements from newer vintages, and all other combinations of vintage and calendar years. The salvage for any vintage contains both realized salvage and future salvage. The future salvage ratio is the total forecast future salvage divided by the future retirements. The future retirements, assuming all transactions will be regular retirements, must equal the plant in service at the time of the study. The average salvage ratio used in the illustration is -25%, and the future salvage ratio is -30%. This implies the realized salvage ratio is larger (i.e., nearer zero) than -25%.

The annual accrual using the straight line method, the average life procedure, and the broad group model is the product of the SL-AL rate and the average annual balance. The SL-AL accrual rate is $[1 - (-0.25)]/10$ or 12.50%. The 1990 accrual is the 12.50% rate times the average balance during 1990, $4791.00,[3] and is $598.88. This method of calculating the annual accrual is sometimes called "broad group depreciation." However, this system does not include a method of adjustment that reflects the value of the recorded accumulated provision for depreciation. If the amortization (AM) method of adjustment is used, the calculated accumulated depreciation (CAD) for the continuous property group must be found.

The broad group assumption that the life and salvage characteristics of all vintages in the continuous property group are the same does not affect the calculation of the $598.88 annual accrual; the 10-year life and -25% salvage describe the characteristics of the combined vintages, but not necessarily any specific vintage. To calculate the CAD, it is necessary to divide the continuous property group into vintages and assign a remaining life, an average salvage ratio, and a future salvage ratio to each vintage. If the data are unaged, the $4791.00 average balance must be aged (see Chapter 12). The data for Account 897 are aged, so the vintage balances are known. The assumption that all vintages have the same life and salvage characteristics allows the use of a single survivor curve to find the RL for each vintage and allows the assignment of the same average salvage ratio to each vintage.

Table 6.1 presents the calculation of the 1990 accrual and the CAD on January 1, 1990, for Account 897. The calculations are made at the vintage level and use the Iowa S1–10 curve, an average salvage ratio of -25%, and a future salvage ratio of -30% for all vintage calculations. Column (a) designates the vintage year and column (b) shows the average plant in service during the year. The beginning of and end of year balances for the 1982 vintage are $390.00 and $380.00 respectively, so the average balance during the year is $385.00. Columns (c) and (d) show the average life and average salvage ratio used to calculate the accrual rate. When the broad group model is used, the same rate, 12.50%, is applied to each vintage. Column (e) shows the future salvage ratio, and the estimate of -30% represents a weighted average that is applied to all vintages. The annual accrual, column (f), equals the annual rate times the average annual balance. The 1990 balance is zero during the first half of the year and $90.00 during the last half of the year (Tables 8.1 and 8.2 show additions of $90.00 and no retirements during 1990). This yields a $45.00 average during the year. Column (g) shows the remaining life of each vintage on January 1, 1990. The age of the 1982 vintage on January 1, 1990, is 7.5 years, and the corresponding value from the table of Iowa curves is 4.36 years. The calculated accumulated depreciation ratio (CADR) on January 1, 1990, column (h), is $(1 - \text{ASR})(1 - \text{RL}/\text{AL}) + (\text{ASR} - \text{FSR})$.[4] For 1982, this calculation is $[1 - (-0.25)](1 - 4.36/10.0) + [-0.25 - (-0.30)]$ or 0.755. The calculated accumulated depreciation (CAD), column (j), is the product of the January 1, 1990, balance, column (i), and the CADR, column (h). The

Table 6.1. Calculation of the 1990 annual accrual for depreciation and the January 1, 1990, calculated accumulated depreciation for Account 897 using the SL-AL-AM system of depreciation and the broad group model. The Iowa S1-10 curve is used to describe the life characteristics of the broad group.

Inst year (a)	Average balance (b)	Avg life (c)	Salvage Avg% (d)	Fut% (e)	Annual accrual (f)	RL ******** (g)	CADR 1/1/1990 (h)	Balance ****** (i)	CAD ******* (j)
1966	22.50	10.0	-25.0	-30.0	2.81	.00	1.300	30.00	39.00
1967	.00	10.0	-25.0	-30.0	.00	.00	1.300	.00	.00
1968	.00	10.0	-25.0	-30.0	.00	.00	1.300	.00	.00
1969	6.50	10.0	-25.0	-30.0	.81	.00	1.300	8.00	10.40
1970	30.00	10.0	-25.0	-30.0	3.75	.14	1.283	36.00	46.19
1971	45.00	10.0	-25.0	-30.0	5.63	.40	1.250	45.00	56.24
1972	111.00	10.0	-25.0	-30.0	13.88	.68	1.215	117.00	142.17
1973	93.50	10.0	-25.0	-30.0	11.69	.97	1.179	99.00	116.73
1974	13.50	10.0	-25.0	-30.0	1.69	1.27	1.142	16.00	18.27
1975	94.00	10.0	-25.0	-30.0	11.75	1.58	1.103	94.00	103.66
1976	286.00	10.0	-25.0	-30.0	35.75	1.91	1.062	292.00	310.03
1977	112.00	10.0	-25.0	-30.0	14.00	2.25	1.019	112.00	114.09
1978	190.00	10.0	-25.0	-30.0	23.75	2.62	.973	190.00	184.87
1979	546.50	10.0	-25.0	-30.0	68.31	3.01	.924	553.00	511.11
1980	203.00	10.0	-25.0	-30.0	25.38	3.42	.872	206.00	179.66
1981	138.00	10.0	-25.0	-30.0	17.25	3.87	.816	138.00	112.59
1982	385.00	10.0	-25.0	-30.0	48.13	4.36	.755	390.00	294.40
1983	295.50	10.0	-25.0	-30.0	36.94	4.90	.688	296.00	203.65
1984	340.00	10.0	-25.0	-30.0	42.50	5.48	.615	340.00	208.97
1985	465.00	10.0	-25.0	-30.0	58.13	6.13	.533	465.00	247.96
1986	220.00	10.0	-25.0	-30.0	27.50	6.86	.443	220.00	97.46
1987	139.00	10.0	-25.0	-30.0	17.38	7.66	.343	140.00	47.99
1988	430.00	10.0	-25.0	-30.0	53.75	8.54	.232	430.00	99.81
1989	580.00	10.0	-25.0	-30.0	72.50	9.50	.112	580.00	65.11
1990	45.00	10.0	-25.0	-30.0	5.63	10.00	--	0.00	0.00
	4791.00				598.88			4797.00	3210.35

Composite accrual rate   12.50%
CADR   66.92%

annual accrual, $598.88, and the CAD, $3210.35, for the account are the sum of the vintage accruals and vintage CADs. The composite annual accrual rate is 598.88/4791.00 or 12.50% and the CADR is 3210.35/4797.00 or 66.92%. Application of the 12.50% rate to each vintage and summing the accruals is equivalent to applying that rate to the average balance for the account; either method yields a $598.88 annual accrual.

The calculation of the annual accrual for the years before 1970 requires special consideration. The maximum life of the S1–10 survivor curve is 20 years. If the retirements exactly followed the S1–10 curve, property installed before 1970 would be fully retired by the start of 1990 and property installed during 1970 would be fully retired during the 1990 calendar year. This can be seen by observing that the remaining life on January 1, 1990, for all vintages installed before 1970 is zero. However, both the 1966 and 1969 vintages have nonzero balances during 1990. This does not necessarily mean that the S1–10 is a poor choice of curves to describe the broad group life characteristics. The broad group model requires that one curve be selected to describe the life characteristics of the combined vintages. An Iowa type curve can only be expected to approximate the actual survivor curve. In this case, the tail of the theoretical curve does not reflect the long lives of a small amount of property from the early vintages. The S1–10 curve is used to represent all of the property in Account 897, though individual vintages may be better described by other curves.

Though it could be argued that the 1966 and 1969 vintages are fully accrued and should not contribute to the accrual, a common practice is to apply the accrual rate to all surviving plant. This reflects the view that even though the average vintage lives vary, the average life of the combined group (i.e., the continuous property group) is 10 years. On an individual basis, some vintages may appear to be overaccrued and others underaccrued, but the combined group will be properly accrued. Application of the annual accrual to the average annual balance of the continuous property group applies the rate to all vintages.

Now consider the remaining life method of adjustment (e.g., the SL-AL-RL-BG system of depreciation). The annual accrual is equal the future accrual divided by the remaining life. The future accrual and the remaining life are calculated at a specific time.[5] A common convention is to base all calculations on the balance, the accumulated provision for depreciation (i.e., the book depreciation, or book reserve, or depreciation reserve), the future salvage, and the remaining life, at *the start of the year.* This convention will be used in the following illustrations. On January 1, 1990, the future accrual for Account 897 is the plant in service, $4842.00, less the future salvage, less the accumulated provision for depreciation. If we set the accumulated provision for depreciation equal to $3210.35 (i.e., the value of the CAD calculated in Table 6.1), the variation between the accumulated provision for depreciation and the CAD will equal zero and the remaining life accrual should (approximately) equal the SL-AL-AM accrual of $598.88.

Two approaches to find the annual accrual for the SL-AL-RL system of depreciation can be used. Both require that balance be aged (i.e., divided into vintages), and that each vintage be assigned a future salvage ratio and a remaining life. The first approach allocates the $3210.35 accumulated provision for depreciation to the vintages, calculates the accrual for each vintage, and sums the vintage accruals to find the accrual for the depreciable group. The second approach calculates a weighted average remaining life, which is divided into the $3082.00 future accrual to find the annual accrual for the depreciable group.

Table 6.2 shows the calculation of the 1990 annual accrual and the January 1, 1990, CAD using the first approach. Column (b) shows the plant balance, column (c) the accumulated provision for depreciation, column (d) the future salvage ratio, and column (f) the remaining life, all on January 1, 1990. The $3210.35 accumulated provision for depreciation has been allocated to the vintages in proportion to the vintage CAD shown in Table 6.1. The rationale for this method of allocation is discussed later. The future accrual, column (e), is the balance less the future salvage less the accumulated provision for depreciation. For the 1982 vintage, the future accrual is 390.00 − (−117.00) − 294.40 or $212.60. The RL of the Iowa S1−10 curve at age 7.5 years is 4.36 years, so the accrual is 212.60/4.36 or $48.76.

A modification to the calculation of the annual accrual for the 1990 vintage is required because it has no January 1, 1990 balance. A common convention is to multiply the average balance during the year by the SL-AL rate of 12.50% (i.e., use the accrual calculated in Table 6.1). Summation of the vintage accruals yields an annual accrual of $600.34 for the account, and the resulting composite accrual rate is 600.34/4842.00 or 12.40%.

When the accruals are made during the year, the current year additions (i.e., $90.00 during 1990) are not yet known and must be estimated. At the end of the year, a "true up" is necessary to adjust for the difference between the actual and estimated additions. Some consider it practical to calculate the composite rate based on the activity up to the beginning of the current year (i.e., the composite rate would exclude 1990 balance and accrual and be 594.71/4797.00 or 12.40%). This rate[6] is applied to the monthly balances, so that the accruals take on the new additions as they are added. The 12.40% rate, rather than the theoretically correct 12.50% rate, will be applied to the 1990 additions. This is considered acceptable because the resulting difference is normally less than the error inherent in the model, and it will be corrected over the remaining life of the additions. This approach is practical because it eliminates the need to estimate additions for the current year.

We assumed the accumulated provision for depreciation was main-

Table 6.2. Calculation of the 1990 annual accrual using the SL-
           AL-RL system of depreciation and the broad group mod-
           el. An Iowa S1-10 curve is used to describe the broad
           group life characteristics. The accumulated provision
           for depreciation is set equal to the CAD when
           calculated using an average salvage ratio of -25% and
           a future salvage ratio of -30.0%.

Inst year (a)	Balance 1/1/1990 (b)	Acc depr 1/1/1990 (c)	Fut sal ratio % (d)	Future accrual (e)	RL 1/1/1990 (f)	Annual accrual (g)
1966	30.00	39.00	-30.0	.00	.00	.00
1967	.00	.00	-30.0	.00	.00	.00
1968	.00	.00	-30.0	.00	.00	.00
1969	8.00	10.40	-30.0	.00	.00	.00
1970	36.00	46.19	-30.0	.61	.14	4.36
1971	45.00	56.24	-30.0	2.26	.40	5.65
1972	117.00	142.17	-30.0	9.93	.68	14.60
1973	99.00	116.73	-30.0	11.97	.97	12.34
1974	16.00	18.27	-30.0	2.53	1.27	2.00
1975	94.00	103.66	-30.0	18.54	1.58	11.75
1976	292.00	310.03	-30.0	69.57	1.91	36.50
1977	112.00	114.09	-30.0	31.51	2.25	14.00
1978	190.00	184.87	-30.0	62.13	2.62	23.75
1979	553.00	511.11	-30.0	207.79	3.01	69.13
1980	206.00	179.66	-30.0	88.14	3.42	25.75
1981	138.00	112.59	-30.0	66.81	3.87	17.25
1982	390.00	294.40	-30.0	212.60	4.36	48.76
1983	296.00	203.65	-30.0	181.15	4.90	37.00
1984	340.00	208.97	-30.0	233.03	5.48	42.50
1985	465.00	247.96	-30.0	356.54	6.13	58.13
1986	220.00	97.46	-30.0	188.54	6.86	27.50
1987	140.00	47.99	-30.0	134.02	7.66	17.50
1988	430.00	99.81	-30.0	459.19	8.54	53.75
1989	580.00	65.11	-30.0	688.90	9.50	72.50
1990	45.00*	0.00	-25.0*	56.25	10.00	5.63
	4842.00	3210.35		3082.00		600.34

            Composite accrual rate   12.40%
            Composite remaining life   5.134 years

* The 1990 calculations are based on the average balance and SR.

tained at the account level.[7] If the accumulated provision for depreciation is maintained at a broader level, it is necessary to allocate it to the depreciable group or account level. The allocation process will most likely spread any indicated deficiency or excess in the accumulated provision for depreciation in one account among all the accounts, thus obscuring the source of the variation. Better feedback and control are obtained when the accumulated provision for depreciation is maintained at the same level as the depreciable group rather than at a broader level.

A discussion in Chapter 5 pointed out that if the variation between the CAD and the accumulated provision for depreciation is zero, then the SL-AL-AM and the SL-AL-RL systems will yield identical vintage accruals. Comparison of the vintage accruals in Tables 6.1 and 6.2 show they are close, $598.88 versus $600.34, but not equal. This is the result of using the average balance during the year in one case and the beginning of year balance in the other. To show that the vintage accruals are the same for both systems if the same reference points are used, calculate the accrual for the 1982 vintage using the AM method of adjustment, but base the calculations on the beginning of year balance rather than on the average balance. The annual accrual is then 390.00×0.1250 or \$48.76, the same as the RL accrual. Or, if the RL calculation was made at midyear, rather than at the beginning of the year, the resulting RL accrual would equal the \$48.13 shown in Table 6.1. When the variation is zero and the same computational convention is used, the systems will yield identical annual vintage accruals.

A statistic called the *composite remaining life* can be calculated by dividing the future accrual by the annual accrual, or $3082.00/600.34$ or 5.134 years. This composite remaining life also can be viewed as the reciprocal of the weighted average of $1/RL$ for each vintage, where the weight is the vintage future accrual. Note that this composite remaining life depends on the survivor curve, the salvage, the balances, and the provision for accumulated depreciation. *It cannot be directly estimated.*

Adjustments

Suppose the accumulated provision for depreciation on January 1, 1990, for Account 897 is \$2900.00. When the amortization method of adjustment is used, the \$2900.00 is compared with the \$3210.35 CAD shown in Table 6.1, and a variation of \$310.35 is found. Is this an indication that the account may be underaccrued significantly? If so, over what period should this variation be amortized? Remember that the CAD is sensitive to the estimates of average life, curve type, average salvage, and future salvage. The "deficit" of \$310.35 could be the result of changes in accounting policy, unforeseen events, a deviation from the forecast, random deviations from the averages the CAD is based on, or on combinations of these. The CAD must be viewed as an estimate, not as a "fact." Whether or not an adjustment is made to the annual accrual rests heavily on the judgment of the depreciation professional. That judgment is guided by management policy.

When the RL method of adjustment is used in combination with the approach of allocating the accumulated provision for depreciation to the vintages, the variation (e.g., the \$310.35) is often allocated to each vintage in proportion to the vintage CAD. Mathematically this is the same as allocating the accumulated provision for depreciation (e.g., the \$2900.00) in proportion to the CAD. Because the CAD is the product of the CADR and the balance, allocation in proportion to the CAD gives more weight to older vintages, because they will have larger CADRs, and more weight to vintages with larger balances left to recover. This method of allocation is logical and appropriate if the factors causing the variation are associated with previous estimates or past activities such that, over time, the cumulative vintage variation is approximately proportional to the age of the vintage. When the variation is known to have a different source, a different basis for allocation may be justified.

Table 6.3 shows the allocation of the $2900 accumulated provision for depreciation in proportion to the CAD. One way to compute the allocation is to focus on the $310.35 variation. For the 1982 vintage, the total allocation is the original $294.40 CAD less the allocated proportion of the variation. This equals 310.35 × (294.40/3210.35) or $28.46, so the 1982 allocation is $294.40 − $28.46 or $265.94. Or, more simply, the $265.94 can be calculated as 2900.00 × (294.40/3210.35). The 1982 accrual is the future accrual of $241.06 divided by the remaining life of 4.36 years or $55.29. Or the $55.29 accrual can be viewed as the original $48.76 accrual plus a remaining life adjustment of $28.46/4.36 or $6.53. The annual accrual for the account increases from $600.34 to $759.10, reflecting an adjustment of $158.76 for the 1990 year. The composite accrual rate increases from

Table 6.3. Calculation of the annual accrual using the SL-AL-RL system of depreciation and the broad group model. An Iowa S1-10 curve is used to describe the broad group life characteristics and a future salvage of -30.0% is estimated. Allocation of the $2900.00 accumulated provision for depreciation is in proportion to the vintage CADs shown in Table 6.1.

Inst year (a)	Balance 1/1/1990 (b)	Acc depr 1/1/1990 (c)	Fut sal ratio % (d)	Future accrual (e)	RL 1/1/1990 (f)	Annual accrual (g)
1966	30.00	35.23	-30.0	3.77	.00	.00
1967	.00	.00	-30.0	.00	.00	.00
1968	.00	.00	-30.0	.00	.00	.00
1969	8.00	9.39	-30.0	1.01	.00	.00
1970	36.00	41.71	-30.0	5.09	.14	36.38
1971	45.00	50.81	-30.0	7.69	.40	19.22
1972	117.00	128.42	-30.0	23.68	.68	34.83
1973	99.00	105.42	-30.0	23.28	.97	24.00
1974	16.00	16.50	-30.0	4.30	1.27	3.39
1975	94.00	93.64	-30.0	28.56	1.58	18.10
1976	292.00	280.06	-30.0	99.54	1.91	52.22
1977	112.00	103.06	-30.0	42.54	2.25	18.90
1978	190.00	167.00	-30.0	80.00	2.62	30.58
1979	553.00	461.72	-30.0	257.18	3.01	85.54
1980	206.00	162.29	-30.0	105.51	3.42	30.82
1981	138.00	101.71	-30.0	77.69	3.87	20.06
1982	390.00	265.94	-30.0	241.06	4.36	55.29
1983	296.00	183.96	-30.0	200.84	4.90	41.02
1984	340.00	188.77	-30.0	253.23	5.48	46.18
1985	465.00	223.99	-30.0	380.51	6.13	62.03
1986	220.00	88.04	-30.0	197.96	6.86	28.87
1987	140.00	43.35	-30.0	138.65	7.66	18.11
1988	430.00	90.17	-30.0	468.83	8.54	54.88
1989	580.00	58.81	-30.0	695.19	9.50	73.16
1990	45.00*	0.00	-25.0*	56.25	10.00	5.63
	4842.00	2900.00		3392.35		759.10

Composite accrual rate   15.68%
Composite remaining life   4.47 years

* The 1990 calculations are based on the average balance and SR.

12.40% to 15.68%, and the composite remaining life decreases from 5.13 years to 4.47 years. A comparison of Tables 6.2 and 6.3 shows that when the variation is $310.35, the older vintages receive a relatively larger portion of the total accrual than when the variation is zero. This reduces the composite remaining life.

The Weighted Average Remaining Life

The second approach to the calculation of the annual accrual when using the SL-AL-RL system is to divide the future accrual of the continuous property group by a *weighted average remaining life.* This approach simplifies the calculations by circumventing the need to allocate the accumulated provision for depreciation to each vintage and is of particular interest because it is widely used.

A basic reference to the remaining life method of adjustment is *Determination of Straight-line Remaining Life Depreciation Accruals* by the California Public Utilities Commission. Originally issued in 1952, a more recent revision is dated 1961. Subtitled *Standard Practice U-4,* this guide covers a wide range of topics including accounting for depreciation, life estimation, determination of salvage, staff procedures, and tables of the Iowa curves. Application of the remaining life method to both a unit of property and to mass property groups is discussed. Several methods of estimating remaining life are identified and examined. The following (italics added) is from Chapter 5, paragraph 11, of the 1961 revision:

SELECTING A METHOD OF WEIGHTING
In selecting a method of weighting, several considerations apply. First, *it is desired that the method of weighting used shall produce the same results as though the book reserve had been prorated to the various age groups or classes of property on the basis of the applicable reserve requirement.* Secondly, it is desirable that the result obtained by weighting be in conformance with the provisions of certain of the uniform systems of accounts, that the accrual computed for an account as a whole shall be the same as if separate accruals had been computed for each class of property and the total obtained. Under these considerations, direct weighting produces proper results if the average service life of each age group or class of property weighted is approximately the same. Reciprocal weighting produces proper results if the reserve for the various classes of property or groups weighted is distributed in proportion to the plant dollars, a condition which is more likely in stable plant with slow growth. Average service life weighting produces proper results if the book reserve and the reserve requirement are closely the same. From these considerations it is concluded that direct or future dollar weighting is the proper method to use between age groups, whereas either reciprocal weighting or average service life weighting will usually yield the better approximation between classes of property. *In very large accounts where individual classes of property*

exceed $100,000 of plant, occasionally a utility may prefer to prorate the book reserve within the account according to a reserve requirement between each class of property rather than to attempt any of the other weighting methods. Such a proration is used only infrequently, is made only at the time of a periodic review for weighting purposes within a very large account, and is normally not carried forward from the date of the calculation.

The italicized sections indicate that allocation of the accumulated reserve for depreciation (i.e., the book reserve) in proportion to the CAD (i.e., the reserve requirement) is the preferred method of application, but use of a weighted remaining life may be a reasonable alternative. At the time of the initial issue of *Standard Practice U-4* (1952), property records contained less detail than now and computers were not in general use. It seems likely that the lack of detailed accounting data and need to minimize computations may have motivated the development of the alternative of calculating a weighted average remaining life.

The three types of weighting described in Chapter 5, paragraph 10, of *Standard Practice U-4* are called *direct weighting, reciprocal weighting, and average service life weighting.* Each is a weighted average of the vintage remaining lives (RL), where the weights are combinations of the vintage balances (Bal) and the vintage average lives (AL). The direct weighted remaining life is $\Sigma(\text{Bal} \times \text{RL})/\Sigma(\text{Bal})$. The reciprocal weighted remaining life is $\Sigma[(\text{Bal})/\Sigma(\text{Bal}/\text{RL})$. Finally, the average service life weighted remaining life is $\Sigma[(\text{Bal}/\text{AL}) \times \text{RL}]/\Sigma(\text{Bal}/\text{AL})$. In each case, the Σ is over all vintages.

A fourth weighted remaining life is the straight line, average life weighted remaining life. This weighting includes the average salvage ratio (ASR) and is the vintage balance times vintage accrual rate, or $\text{Bal} \times (1 - \text{ASR})/\text{AL}$. Thus the straight line, average life weighted remaining life is $\Sigma\{[\text{Bal} \times (1 - \text{ASR})/\text{AL}] \times \text{RL}\}/\Sigma[\text{Bal} \times (1 - \text{ASR})/\text{AL}]$. The importance of this weighted remaining life is that *when the variation between the accumulated provision for depreciation and the CAD is zero, calculation of the annual accrual either by allocating the accumulated provision for depreciation to each vintage in proportion to the vintage CAD or using the straight line, average life weighted remaining life yields the same result.*[8] If the ASR is the same for each vintage, the straight line, average life weighted remaining life reduces to the average service life weighted remaining life. Furthermore, if the AL is the same for each vintage, the average service life weighted remaining life reduces to the direct weighted remaining life. Thus, if the broad group model is used, the straight line, average life weighted remaining life equals the direct weighted remaining life.

The straight line, average life weighted remaining life for Account 897 can be calculated from the balances and remaining lives shown in Table 6.3.

Each RL is weighted by the balance times the rate $[(1-ASR)/AL]$. The numerator is the $\Sigma\{[Bal \times (1 - ASR)/AL] \times RL\}$ or $[45.00 \times (1.25/10) \times 10.00 + 580.00 \times (1.25/10) \times 9.5 + 430.00 \times (1.25/10) \times 8.54 + \ldots + 36.00 \times (1.25/10) \times 0.14]$ or 3082.00. The denominator is the $\Sigma[Bal \times (1 - ASR)/AL]$ or $[45.00 \times (1.25/10) + 580.00 \times (1.25/10) + 430.00 \times (1.25/10) + \ldots + 36.00 \times (1.25/10]$ or 600.34. The straight line, average life weighted remaining life is then 3082.00/600.34 or 5.134 years. Calculation of the direct weighted remaining life also yields 5.134 years. If the accumulated provision for depreciation is $3210.35, then the future accrual, from Table 6.2, is $3082.00 and the annual accrual is 3082.00/5.134 or $600.34.

Table 6.4 summarizes the results of using allocation of the accumulated provision for depreciation, shown in Tables 6.2 and 6.3, and two types of weighting. Column (a) shows three values of the accumulated provision for depreciation. The value in the second row, $3210.35, is from Table 6.2 and represents a zero variation from the CAD, as noted in column (b). The first and third rows represent a $310.35 variation above and below the CAD. Column (c) shows the future accrual of $3082.00, from Table 6.2, when the variation is zero. Columns (d) and (e) are the results of allocation in proportion to the CAD, columns (f) and (g) the results of direct weighting, and columns (h) and (i) the results of reciprocal weighting. The accrual is the future accrual divided by the RL.

When the variation is zero, the two approaches (allocation of the accumulated provision for depreciation to vintages in proportion to the CAD and calculation of direct weighted remaining life) result in the same accrual. However, if the variation is $310.35 (i.e., a deficit), and the first approach is used, the composite RL is reduced to 4.47 and the rate is increased to 22.4%. A variation of -$310.35 (i.e., an excess) increases the RL to 6.28 years and decreases the rate to 15.9%. The more the variation varies from zero, the more the rate varies from 1/5.13 or 19.5%. Because

Table 6.4. Results of allocating the accumulated provision for depreciation in proportion to the CAD, direct weighting, and reciprocal weighting when calculating the annual accrual. Calculations are made for the three values of the accumulated provision for depreciation shown in column (a).

Accum depr (a)	Varia- tion (b)	Future accrual (c)	Allocation		Direct wt*		Reciprocal wt	
			RL (d)	Accrual (e)	RL (f)	Accrual (g)	RL (h)	Accrual (i)
2900.00	310.35	3392.35	4.47	759.10	5.13	661.29	2.78	1220.29
3210.35	.00	3082.00	5.13	600.34	5.13	600.34	2.78	1108.65
3520.70	-310.35	2771.65	6.28	441.35	5.13	540.29	2.78	997.01

* Same as either average service life or straight line, average life weighted remaining life. This is the result of using the same AL and ASR for each vintage.

the direct weighted remaining life is independent of the variation, it remains a constant 5.134 years. Thus, the two approaches may yield significantly different accruals when the variance is not close to zero.

Regardless of the variation, the results of reciprocal weighting do not appear to be reasonable. In this example, when the variation is zero the accrual resulting from use of the reciprocal weighted remaining life is almost twice the annual accrual using the SL-AL rate (i.e., from Table 6.4, $1108.65 versus $600.34). These results are consistent with the warning in *Standard Practice U-4* that reciprocal weighting produces proper results only if the accumulated provision for depreciation is distributed in proportion to plant balances.

Because the two approaches used to calculate the annual accrual may yield different results, the question, "Is one approach better than the other?" is raised. Both require the same data and estimates. Both require the assumption that all vintages have the same life and salvage characteristics. The calculations for either approach are quickly made on a small computer. The first approach requires calculation of the CAD, while the second does not. It can be argued that the CAD should be calculated even though the RL method of adjustment is used, so that the depreciation professional is aware of the degree of adjustment included in the remaining life accrual. If the second approach is, as suggested in *Standard Practice U-4,* an approximation to the more desirable procedure of allocation of the accumulated provision for depreciation to each vintage, then the first approach is preferred.

Life Cycle Depreciation

Earlier in this chapter the SL-AL accrual rate was multiplied by the plant in service to find the annual accrual, and it was noted that this is sometimes called broad group depreciation. Thus, only the life and salvage for the continuous property group, and not each vintage, need be estimated. However, if the life and salvage characteristics change from vintage to vintage, then forecasting the required life and salvage is an imposing challenge. Not only must the life and salvage of property currently in service be forecast, but the magnitude, life, and salvage of all future additions must also be forecast. If the life of the continuous property group continues far into the future, then this is a difficult and perplexing task. If the end of the life of the continuous group is in the near future, then the task may be manageable.

Life cycle depreciation is based on the concept that the average life and salvage of a continuous property group can be forecast. The continuous property group must consist of units with a common technology. Thus, by the end of the life cycle of the technology (i.e., the time starting with the introduction of the technology until the time it is replaced with a new technology), all of the property in the group will have been retired. Methods used to forecast the life cycle of technology include the Fisher-Pry model, which is used to forecast the rate at which one technology is substituted for another. Estimates of the life cycle of the technology provide the basis for forecasting future additions and retirements to the group. Once the forecasts are made, plot the plant in service versus each calendar year, starting at the time of the first additions of the new technology, continuing through observed and then forecast balances, and ending with a zero balance when the technology has been replaced with a newer technology. The area under this curve divided by the total additions during the life of the group equals the average life of the continuous property group needed to calculate the broad group depreciation accrual rate. This approach eliminates the need to estimate the life characteristics of each vintage. An objection to the use of this system of depreciation is that it averages lives of property in service with lives of property not yet placed in service. An alternative approach to life cycle depreciation is offered in the discussion of technological obsolescence in Chapter 13.

The Equal Life Group Procedure

In this section we replace the AL procedure with the equal life group (ELG) procedure and consider the SL-ELG-AM and SL-ELG-RL systems. Because the broad group model is used, a single survivor curve and salvage schedule are used to describe the life and salvage characteristics of each vintage group. However, the reasoning used to select the life and salvage characteristics for the ELG procedure is significantly different from the reasoning used for the AL procedure.

While the AL rate used to calculate the vintage accruals is a constant value, the ELG rate varies with the age of the property. Figure 6.2 shows a survivor curve for a vintage group whose current age is marked by a vertical line. The lightly shaded area includes the ELGs with lives less than the current age; if the proper rates have been used, then these ELGs will be fully accrued. The heavily shaded area includes the ELGs with lives longer than the current age; these ELGs are not yet fully accrued. Because the ELGs with lives shorter than the current age are fully accrued and retired, the shape of the survivor curve from age zero to the current age no longer affects the ELG rates. The rate at the indicated age is determined by the surviving ELGs and therefore depends *only* on the shape of the survivor curve to the right of the current age.

The shape of the heavily shaded portion of Figure 6.2 is defined by the shape of that portion of the survivor curve to the right of the current age. The life of a vintage group can be divided into the realized life and the future life. Because we are concerned with the surviving ELGs, only the

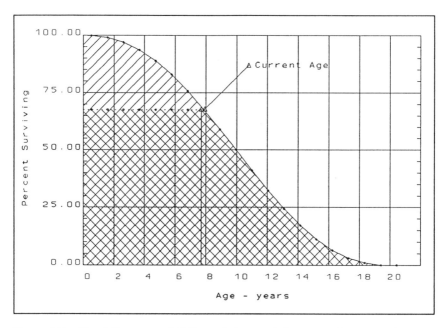

Figure 6.2. The fully accrued ELGs and the partially accrued ELGs at the current age.

future life characteristics are needed when using the ELG procedure. Under the ELG procedure, the task of the depreciation professional is to select the single survivor curve that best describes the future life characteristics of the group of property formed by combining all future retirements. Though knowledge of the realized life is valuable when forecasting the future life, the shape of the realized life portion of the vintage survivor curve does not affect the future ELG rates.

When the broad group model is used, the survivor curve selected to describe the life characteristics when using the ELG procedure often can be expected to differ from the survivor curve selected to describe the life characteristics when using the AL procedure. We will, for illustrative purposes, continue to use the Iowa S1–10 survivor curve to describe both the total life characteristics (for the AL procedure) and the future life characteristics (for the ELG procedure) of Account 897. This will allow us to directly compare the results of the AL and ELG procedures.

The ELG salvage also differs from the AL salvage. Extending the reasoning in the preceding two paragraphs, the salvage used to calculate the ELG rates should be the salvage that occurs when the ELGs remaining in service are retired, that is, the *future salvage*. The estimate of the average salvage, used with the AL procedure, does not directly affect the ELG rates. Thus, the average future salvage ratio of -30% is used to describe the salvage characteristics.

Table 6.5 shows the calculation of the annual ELG accrual rates for the Iowa S1–10 survivor curve. Column (a) shows the interval defining each of the 21 ELGs. The ELGs are defined by specifying a minimum age of zero and the maximum ages of 0.5, 1.5, 2.5, 3.5 and continuing by 1-year intervals until the maximum life of 20.5 years. Column (b) shows the percent of the initial investment assigned to each ELG and is obtained by subtracting consecutive points on the survivor curve. Column (c) shows the future salvage ratio (FSR). Column (d) shows the product of the percent retired and $(1 - \text{FSR})$; this is the capital to be recovered expressed as a percent of the initial investment.

The 21 remaining columns are used to calculate the composite rate for each age interval, where each age interval is defined by its age at the start of the interval. Because of space limitations, only the columns for the first 6 age intervals are shown. All property retired during the 2.5–3.5 year age interval is placed in the ELG defined by the 0.0–3.5 year interval and is assigned a life of 3 years (i.e., assume all retirements take place at midyear).

Table 6.5. Calculation of annual accrual rates using the straight line method and ELG procedure, an Iowa S1-10 survivor curve, and an average future salvage ratio (FSR) of -30%. The portion of the table for age intervals greater than 4.5-5.5 years is not shown.

				***	Age at start of age interval				***
ELG interval (a)	% Retired (b)	FSR % (c)	% Recovered (d)	0.0 (e)	0.5 (f)	1.5 (g)	2.5 (h)	3.5 (i)	4.5 (j)
0.0- 0.5	.02	-30.0	.03	.03					
0.0- 1.5	.46	-30.0	.58	.29	.29				
0.0- 2.5	1.41	-30.0	1.84	.46	.92	.46			
0.0- 3.5	2.66	-30.0	3.46	.58	1.15	1.15	.58		
0.0- 4.5	4.01	-30.0	5.21	.65	1.30	1.30	1.30	.65	
0.0- 5.5	5.37	-30.0	6.98	.70	1.39	1.40	1.40	1.39	.70
0.0- 6.5	6.59	-30.0	8.57	.71	1.43	1.43	1.43	1.43	1.43
0.0- 7.5	7.63	-30.0	9.92	.71	1.42	1.42	1.42	1.42	1.42
0.0- 8.5	8.42	-30.0	10.94	.68	1.37	1.37	1.37	1.37	1.37
0.0- 9.5	8.90	-30.0	11.57	.64	1.29	1.29	1.29	1.29	1.29
0.0-10.5	9.06	-30.0	11.77	.59	1.18	1.18	1.18	1.18	1.18
0.0-11.5	8.90	-30.0	11.57	.53	1.05	1.05	1.05	1.05	1.05
0.0-12.5	8.42	-30.0	10.94	.46	.91	.91	.91	.91	.91
0.0-13.5	7.63	-30.0	9.92	.38	.76	.76	.76	.76	.76
0.0-14.5	6.59	-30.0	8.57	.31	.61	.61	.61	.61	.61
0.0-15.5	5.37	-30.0	6.98	.23	.47	.47	.47	.47	.47
0.0-16.5	4.01	-30.0	5.21	.16	.33	.33	.33	.33	.33
0.0-17.5	2.66	-30.0	3.46	.10	.20	.20	.20	.20	.20
0.0-18.5	1.41	-30.0	1.84	.05	.10	.10	.10	.10	.10
0.0-19.5	.46	-30.0	.58	.02	.03	.03	.03	.03	.03
0.0-20.5	.02	-30.0	.03	.00	.00	.00	.00	.00	.00
Total	100.00		130.00	8.29	16.21	15.45	14.42	13.19	11.84
Average percent surviving				49.99	99.75	98.82	96.78	93.45	88.76
Composite rate %				16.58	16.25	15.64	14.90	14.12	13.34

Column (d) shows that 2.66 × 1.30 or 3.46% of the original cost must be recovered during the life of the ELG; using the straight line method of allocation, 3.46/3 or 1.15% will be recovered each year. Applying the half-year convention results in recovery of 0.58% during the installation year, 1.15% during each of the next two years, and 0.58% during the retirement year. Note that the rates in this table are rounded to two decimal places and that the exact values for this ELG are 0.575% and 1.155%. These amounts are shown in the row for the 0.0–3.5 ELG in columns (e) through (h) and their sum is 3.46%. For any row, the sum of the entries in column (e) and all columns to the right equals the amount in column (d).

The column sums are shown in the row labeled "Total." The sum of the retirement frequencies, column (b), must equal 100%, and the total amount to be recovered, column (d), must equal 130% of the initial investment. The sum of any of the remaining columns, i.e, columns (e) through (j), is the sum of the accruals for all ELGs surviving to the end of the associated age interval. The sum of these accruals (i.e., 8.29 + 16.21 + 15.45 + 14.47 + 13.19 + 11.84 + . . .) is 130%. Because the ELG rate will be multiplied by the plant remaining in service, not the total original investment, each accrual is divided by the average balance during that age interval to obtain a rate that can be applied to the average balance during the year. During the 2.5–3.5 year age interval, 14.42% of the initial investment should be recovered. The average balance[9] during the 2.5–3.5 year age interval is (98.11 + 95.45)/2 or 96.78% and the resulting ELG rate is 14.42/0.9678 or 14.90%.

Table 6.6 shows the calculation of the CADR and uses the same format as Table 6.5, except that the columns to the right of column (d) show the CADR at the indicated age rather than the accrual during the age interval. For any ELG, the accumulated depreciation at any age is the sum of the accruals during all previous age intervals. The accumulated depreciation at age 1.5 years for the 0.0–3.5 year ELG is 0.58 + 1.15 or 1.73%. At the end of the final age interval, the addition of the final accrual and the simultaneous subtraction of the amount recovered because of the retirement of the ELG reduces the accumulated depreciation to zero. The sum of column (e), or any column to its right, is the accumulated depreciation at the corresponding age as a percent of the initial investment. Divide that total by percent surviving at that age to find the CADR. Thus these values are the CADRs at the beginning of the age interval.

Table 6.7 shows the calculation of the 1990 accrual and the CAD on January 1, 1990, for Account 897. The average annual balances by vintage are shown in column (b) and the ELG rates, from Table 6.5, are shown in column (c). The vintage accruals are the products of the average balance and the rate and are shown in column (d). In this illustration, a zero rate is applied to the 1969 and 1966 balances, though it could be argued, as in the

Table 6.6. Calculation of CADR using the straight line method and ELG
            procedure, an Iowa S1-10 survivor curve, and an average fu-
            ture salvage of 30%. The portion of the table for ages great-
            er than 4.5 years is not shown.

ELG interval (a)	% Retired (b)	FSR % (c)	% Recovered (d)	*********** Age - years **********						
				0.0 (e)	0.5 (f)	1.5 (g)	2.5 (h)	3.5 (i)	4.5 (j)
0.0- .5	.02	-30.0	.03	.00					
0.0- 1.5	.46	-30.0	.58	.00	.29				
0.0- 2.5	1.41	-30.0	1.84	.00	.46	1.37			
0.0- 3.5	2.66	-30.0	3.46	.00	.58	1.73	2.88		
0.0- 4.5	4.01	-30.0	5.21	.00	.65	1.95	3.26	4.56	
0.0- 5.5	5.37	-30.0	6.98	.00	.69	2.09	3.49	4.89	6.28
0.0- 6.5	6.59	-30.0	8.57	.00	.71	2.14	3.57	5.00	6.43
0.0- 7.5	7.63	-30.0	9.92	.00	.71	2.13	3.54	4.96	6.38
0.0- 8.5	8.42	-30.0	10.94	.00	.68	2.05	3.42	4.79	6.16
0.0- 9.5	8.90	-30.0	11.57	.00	.64	1.93	3.21	4.50	5.79
0.0-10.5	9.06	-30.0	11.77	.00	.59	1.77	2.94	4.12	5.30
0.0-11.5	8.90	-30.0	11.57	.00	.53	1.58	2.63	3.68	4.73
0.0-12.5	8.42	-30.0	10.94	.00	.46	1.37	2.28	3.19	4.10
0.0-13.5	7.63	-30.0	9.92	.00	.38	1.14	1.91	2.67	3.43
0.0-14.5	6.59	-30.0	8.57	.00	.31	.92	1.53	2.14	2.75
0.0-15.5	5.37	-30.0	6.98	.00	.23	.70	1.16	1.63	2.09
0.0-16.5	4.01	-30.0	5.21	.00	.16	.49	.81	1.14	1.46
0.0-17.5	2.66	-30.0	3.46	.00	.10	.31	.51	.71	.92
0.0-18.5	1.41	-30.0	1.84	.00	.05	.15	.26	.36	.46
0.0-19.5	.46	-30.0	.58	.00	.02	.05	.08	.11	.14
0.0-20.5	.02	-30.0	.03	.00	.00	.00	.00	.01	.01
Total	100.00		130.00	.00	8.25	23.87	37.49	48.45	56.43

Percent surviving	100.00	99.97	99.52	98.11	95.45	91.44
Composite CADR	.0000	.0825	.2398	.3821	.5076	.6172

preceding section, that a nonzero rate should be applied to all balances for which the remaining life is zero. The vintage accruals total $571.11. The CADRs in column (e) are from Table 6.6, and are multiplied by the beginning of year balances, column (f), to obtain the CAD on January 1, 1990.

The AL composite accrual rate shown in Table 6.1 is 12.50%. Compare that rate with the ELG vintage rates shown in Table 6.7. The ELG rates from 1984 to 1990 are higher than 12.50%, while those for earlier years are lower; note that the average ELG rate for the surviving plant during 1990 is 11.92%. In general, with a growing property group the ELG procedure will result in larger annual accruals than the AL procedure, because the higher rates will be applied to significantly larger balances. The opposite is true for a property group in which the annual additions are becoming smaller. Though the annual additions to Account 897 are erratic, there appears to be little, if any, annual growth. This results in the ELG and AL accruals being about the same, $571.11 and $598.88. While the 1990 accruals are about the same, the past accruals under the ELG procedure have been larger than under the AL procedure. Evidence for this is that the CAD for the ELG procedure is $3531.59, while it is only $3210.35 for the AL procedure.

Table 6.7.   Calculation of the 1990 accrual for depreciation and
              the January 1, 1990, calculated accumulated provision
              for depreciation for Account 897 using the SL-ELG-AM
              system of depreciation and the broad group model. The
              Iowa S1-10 curve and a future salvage ratio of -30.0%
              are used to describe the life and salvage character-
              istics of the broad group.

Inst year (a)	Average balance (b)	Accrual rate % (c)	Annual accrual (d)	CADR ********* (e)	Balance 1/1/1990 (f)	CAD ********* (g)
1966	22.50	0.00	.00	1.3000	30.00	39.00
1967	.00	0.00	.00	1.3000	.00	.00
1968	.00	0.00	.00	1.3000	.00	.00
1969	6.50	0.00	.00	1.3000	8.00	10.40
1970	30.00	6.50	1.95	1.2675	36.00	45.63
1971	45.00	6.81	3.06	1.2628	45.00	56.82
1972	111.00	7.06	7.84	1.2463	117.00	145.82
1973	93.50	7.34	6.86	1.2258	99.00	121.35
1974	13.50	7.64	1.03	1.2019	16.00	19.23
1975	94.00	7.97	7.49	1.1753	94.00	110.48
1976	286.00	8.33	23.83	1.1454	292.00	334.47
1977	112.00	8.72	9.77	1.1119	112.00	124.54
1978	190.00	9.15	17.38	1.0743	190.00	204.11
1979	546.50	9.61	52.52	1.0318	553.00	570.57
1980	203.00	10.11	20.53	.9836	206.00	202.62
1981	138.00	10.66	14.71	.9288	138.00	128.18
1982	385.00	11.26	43.35	.8664	390.00	337.88
1983	295.50	11.91	35.18	.7946	296.00	235.21
1984	340.00	12.60	42.84	.7121	340.00	242.13
1985	465.00	13.34	62.04	.6172	465.00	286.98
1986	220.00	14.12	31.06	.5076	220.00	111.68
1987	139.00	14.90	20.71	.3821	140.00	53.50
1988	430.00	15.64	67.25	.2398	430.00	103.13
1989	580.00	16.25	94.23	.0825	580.00	47.86
1990	45.00	16.58	7.46	.0000	.00	.00
	4791.00		571.11		4797.00	3531.59

Composite accrual rate   11.92%
CADR   73.62%

Now consider the RL method of adjustment. Much of the preceding
discussion of the SL-AL-RL system also applies when using the ELG procedure. Because the selection of life and salvage characteristics depend on the
method of allocation and procedure for applying the method of allocation,
and not on the method of adjustment, the Iowa S1–10 survivor curve and a
future salvage of -30% will continue to be used to describe the future life
and salvage characteristics of the continuous property group.

First, the ELG composite remaining life for each vintage must be calculated. In Chapter 5, the composite vintage RL at any age was shown to be
the sum of the ELG future accruals, calculated at the start of the age
interval, divided by the sum of the ELG accruals during the age interval.
These calculations for Account 897 are shown in Table 6.8. The age is
shown in column (a), the future salvage ratio is shown in column (b), and
the CADR, from Table 6.7, is shown in column (c). The calculated future
accruals ratio (CFAR) is $1 -$ CADR $-$ FSR. At age 2.5 years this is [1.00

Table 6.8. Calculation of the composite ELG remaining lives
for ages zero through 5.5 years. The values of
the annual accrual rates and CADRs are from Tables 6.5 and 6.6 respectively.

Age (a)	FSR % (b)	CADR (c)	CFAR (d)	Annual accrual rate (e)	Composite RL years (f)
0.0	-30	.0000	1.3000	.1658	7.84
0.5	-30	.0825	1.2175	.1625	7.49
1.5	-30	.2398	1.0602	.1564	6.78
2.5	-30	.3821	.9179	.1490	6.16
3.5	-30	.5076	.7924	.1412	5.61
4.5	-30	.6172	.6828	.1334	5.12
5.5	-30	.7121	.5879	.1260	4.67

$- (-0.30) - .3821]$ or 0.9179. The RL, column (f), is the CFAR divided
by the accrual rate, from column (e). The resulting composite vintage remaining life is 0.9179/0.1490 or 6.16 years.

Table 6.9 shows the calculation of the annual accruals using the SL-
ELG-RL-BG system and is in the same format as Table 6.2, which showed
the calculations for the SL-AL-RL-BG system. The accumulated provision
for depreciation equals the CAD values from Table 6.7 and the RLs are
calculated as shown in Table 6.8. Since the accumulated provision for depreciation equals the CAD, the annual accruals for both the AM ($571.11)
and RL ($574.72) methods of adjustment (Tables 6.7 and 6.9) are, as ex-
pected, (about) the same. Remember that in Table 6.7 we applied the ELG
rate to the average balance during 1990 while in Table 6.9 we applied the RL
rate to the future accruals on January 1, 1990. The average accrual rate is
11.87% and the composite remaining life is 4.81 years.

Adjustments

Now assume that the accumulated provision for depreciation for Account 897 is $3100.00 so that the variation from the CAD is $3531.59 −
$3100.00 or $431.59. Again, if the variation is judged to be significant, it
may be amortized over an appropriate period when the AM method of
adjustment is used.

Use of the RL method of adjustment with the ELG procedure adds
complexity to the calculations. With either the AL or the ELG procedure,
the variation between the CAD and the accumulated provision for depreciation is allocated, either explicitly or implicitly, to the vintages. With the
ELG procedure, a second allocation is needed. The accumulated provision
for depreciation allocated to a vintage must then be allocated among the
ELGs. Allocation of the variation to each vintage in proportion to the
vintage CAD was advocated in the preceding section and was used to con-

Table 6.9.   Calculation of the 1990 annual accrual using the SL-
ELG-RL system of depreciation and the broad group
model. An Iowa S1-10 curve is used to describe the
broad group future life characteristics. The vintage
accumulated provision for depreciation equals that
shown in Table 6.7.

Inst year (a)	Balance 1/1/1990 (b)	Accum depr (c)	Future salvage (d)	Future accrual (e)	RL (f)	Annual accrual (g)
1966	30.00	39.00	-30.0	.00	.00	.00
1967	.00	.00	-30.0	.00	.00	.00
1968	.00	.00	-30.0	.00	.00	.00
1969	8.00	10.40	-30.0	.00	.00	.00
1970	36.00	45.63	-30.0	1.17	.50	2.34
1971	45.00	56.82	-30.0	1.68	.55	3.06
1972	117.00	145.82	-30.0	6.28	.76	8.26
1973	99.00	121.35	-30.0	7.35	1.01	7.27
1974	16.00	19.23	-30.0	1.57	1.28	1.22
1975	94.00	110.48	-30.0	11.72	1.56	7.49
1976	292.00	334.47	-30.0	45.13	1.86	24.33
1977	112.00	124.54	-30.0	21.06	2.16	9.77
1978	190.00	204.11	-30.0	42.89	2.47	17.38
1979	553.00	570.57	-30.0	148.33	2.79	53.14
1980	206.00	202.62	-30.0	65.18	3.13	20.83
1981	138.00	128.18	-30.0	51.22	3.48	14.71
1982	390.00	337.88	-30.0	169.12	3.85	43.91
1983	296.00	235.21	-30.0	149.59	4.24	35.24
1984	340.00	242.13	-30.0	199.87	4.67	42.84
1985	465.00	286.98	-30.0	317.52	5.12	62.04
1986	220.00	111.68	-30.0	174.32	5.61	31.06
1987	140.00	53.50	-30.0	128.50	6.16	20.86
1988	430.00	103.13	-30.0	455.87	6.78	67.25
1989	580.00	47.86	-30.0	706.14	7.49	94.23
1990	45.00*	00.00	-30.0	58.50	7.84	7.46
	4842.00	3531.59		2763.01		574.72

Composite accrual rate   11.87%
Composite remaining life   4.81 years

* The 1990 calculations are based on the average balance.

struct Table 6.10. The $296.59 allocation to the 1982 vintage is the $337.88
CAD (see Table 6.7) less the portion of the variation allocated to the vintage, which is 431.59 × (337.88/3531.59) or $41.29. Now the $41.29 vintage variation must be allocated to the ELGs, divided by the RL of the
ELG, and incorporated into the composite rate.

In Chapter 5 we discussed two methods of allocating the vintage variation to the ELGs. One was in proportion to the CAD and the other was in
proportion to the calculated future accruals (CFA). That section presented
arguments supporting both methods of allocation. One point that favors
allocation in proportion to the CFA is that the resulting composite vintage
RLs are independent of the magnitude of the variation. The composite RLs
shown in Table 6.8 were computed using a variation of zero. Use of these
RLs when the variation is not zero is equivalent to allocation of the vintage
variation to the ELGs in proportion to the CFA. An advantage of this
method of allocation is that the ELG composite RLs need not be calculated
using the accumulated provision for depreciation for the specific deprecia-

Table 6.10. Calculation of the 1990 annual accrual using the SL-ELG-RL system of depreciation and the broad group model. An Iowa S1-10 curve is used to describe the broad group future life characteristics. The $3100.00 accumulated depreciation is allocated to the vintages in proportion to the CAD.

Inst year (a)	Balance 12/31/90 (b)	Accum depr (c)	Future salvage (d)	Future accrual (e)	RL (f)	Annual accrual (g)
1966	30.00	34.23	-30.0	4.77	.00	.00
1967	.00	.00	-30.0	.00	.00	.00
1968	.00	.00	-30.0	.00	.00	.00
1969	8.00	9.13	-30.0	1.27	.00	.00
1970	36.00	40.05	-30.0	6.75	.50	13.49
1971	45.00	49.88	-30.0	8.62	.55	15.76
1972	117.00	128.00	-30.0	24.10	.76	31.69
1973	99.00	106.52	-30.0	22.18	1.01	21.92
1974	16.00	16.88	-30.0	3.92	1.28	3.05
1975	94.00	96.98	-30.0	25.22	1.56	16.17
1976	292.00	293.59	-30.0	86.01	1.86	46.36
1977	112.00	109.32	-30.0	36.28	2.16	16.13
1978	190.00	179.17	-30.0	67.83	2.47	27.49
1979	553.00	500.84	-30.0	218.06	2.79	78.13
1980	206.00	177.86	-30.0	89.94	3.13	28.75
1981	138.00	112.52	-30.0	66.88	3.48	19.21
1982	390.00	296.59	-30.0	210.41	3.85	54.63
1983	296.00	206.47	-30.0	178.33	4.24	42.01
1984	340.00	212.54	-30.0	229.46	4.67	49.19
1985	465.00	251.91	-30.0	352.59	5.12	68.90
1986	220.00	98.03	-30.0	187.97	5.61	33.49
1987	140.00	46.96	-30.0	135.04	6.16	21.92
1988	430.00	90.53	-30.0	468.47	6.78	69.11
1989	580.00	42.01	-30.0	711.99	7.49	95.01
1990	45.00*	0.00	-30.0	58.50	7.84	7.46
	4842.00	3100.00		3194.60		760.55

Composite accrual rate   15.71%
Composite remaining life   4.20 years

* The 1990 calculations are based on the average balance.

ble group. The combination of methods of allocation (i.e., allocation among vintages in proportion to the CAD and allocation among the ELGs in proportion to the CFA) is common practice and is used in the calculations shown in Table 6.10.

Though the combination of methods of allocation could be criticized as inconsistent, it has two advantages. First it is simple; the composite vintage RLs depend only on the survivor curve. Second, use of constant RLs dampens the magnitude of the RL adjustment. This dampening effect is considered an advantage, because the activities that result in debits or credits to the accumulated provision for depreciation frequently occur in lumps rather than being spread over several years. Hence, the RL adjustments may be an overreaction to random events rather than a systematic adjustment to an excess or deficiency in the accumulated provision for depreciation. The dampening effect would reduce the randomness in the annual accruals.

The annual accrual of $760.55 reflects an RL adjustment of $760.55 −

$574.72 or $185.83, reducing the variation from $431.59 to $245.76. The composite accrual rate increased from 11.87% to 15.71% while the composite remaining life decreased from 4.81 years to 4.20 years.

THE VINTAGE GROUP MODEL

The calculation of the annual accrual for depreciation for a continuous property group using the vintage group model is discussed in this section. The vintage group model allows each vintage in the continuous property group to be described by different life and salvage characteristics. This relaxation of the broad group requirement that the life and salvage characteristics of all vintages be described by a single survivor curve and a single salvage schedule enables the vintage group model to approximate the actual world more closely. The details of application differ for the AL and ELG procedures, and use of the vintage group model is more commonly associated with the AL than the ELG procedure. Use of the vintage group model and AL procedure requires aged data.

Describing Life Characteristics

In Figure 6.1, each vintage is divided into realized and future life. When aged data are available, the surviving plant in service from each vintage is known, and a survivor curve reflecting the realized life of each vintage can be constructed. Thus, with the *vintage group model* and *either the AL or ELG procedure,* only the *future* life of each vintage need be estimated. Frequently a single survivor curve is used to represent the future life characteristics of all vintages. However, a different future curve can be used for each vintage.

Changes in life characteristics over eras (i.e., periods of time spanning several vintages) can often be identified. An era can include vintages that share a common technology. An account for gas services might be divided into an era when most services were steel and an era when most were plastic. An account for utility poles might be divided into an era when wood poles were treated to prevent rot and into an earlier era when they were not treated. All vintages in an era will be assigned common life and salvage characteristics that are appropriate to that era. The decision to divide a continuous property group into eras requires knowledge of the property and a thorough analysis of the historical life. Suppose a continuous property group is divided into two or more eras. The depreciation professional may then either divide the continuous property group into two depreciable groups, each with common life and salvage characteristics or, as in the following illustration, maintain a single depreciable group but use two or more survivor curves to describe future life.

An actuarial analysis of Account 897 data reveals a difference between the life characteristics of the early vintages and the recently installed vintages. Rather than select a single curve that attempts to reflect the average future life of all vintages, Account 897 has been divided into two eras. During the first era, 1966 through 1975, the future life characteristics are described by the Iowa L1–10 survivor curve. During the second era, 1976 through 1990, the future life characteristics are described by the Iowa S0–12 survivor curve.

The Salvage Schedule

The salvage schedule shown in Table 6.11 is used in the remaining illustrations. Aged salvage is preferable to average salvage, because it more realistically represents the accounting entries associated with gross salvage and cost of retiring. Aged salvage can be used with systems incorporating either the broad group or the vintage group model. The illustrations in this chapter combine average salvage with the broad group model and aged salvage with the vintage group model.

Table 6.11. The salvage schedule for an Iowa S0-12 survivor curve, an initial net salvage of -15%, and an annual rate of increase of 5%.

Age (a)	% Surviving (b)	% Retired (c)	SR % (d)	Wtd SR (e)	Realized salvage (f)	Future salvage (g)
.0	100.00	.26	-15.00	-.04	.00	-28.00
.5	99.74	1.45	-15.75	-.23	-15.00	-28.02
1.5	98.29	2.38	-16.54	-.40	-15.64	-28.20
2.5	95.91	3.12	-17.36	-.54	-16.16	-28.49
3.5	92.79	3.73	-18.23	-.68	-16.68	-28.86
4.5	89.06	4.22	-19.14	-.81	-17.21	-29.31
5.5	84.84	4.66	-20.10	-.94	-17.71	-29.76
6.5	80.18	5.02	-21.11	-1.06	-18.33	-30.38
7.5	75.16	5.30	-22.16	-1.17	-18.89	-30.99
8.5	69.86	5.53	-23.27	-1.28	-19.46	-31.66
9.5	64.33	5.67	-24.43	-1.38	-20.05	-32.39
10.5	58.66	5.76	-25.66	-1.49	-20.65	-33.15
11.5	52.90	5.80	-26.94	-1.56	-21.26	-33.97
12.5	47.10	5.76	-28.28	-1.63	-21.89	-34.84
13.5	41.34	5.67	-29.70	-1.68	-22.51	-35.75
14.5	35.67	5.53	-31.18	-1.72	-23.15	-36.71
15.5	30.14	5.30	-32.74	-1.74	-23.78	-37.72
16.5	24.84	5.02	-34.38	-1.73	-24.41	-38.78
17.5	19.82	4.66	-36.10	-1.69	-25.04	-39.89
18.5	15.16	4.22	-37.90	-1.61	-25.65	-41.06
19.5	10.94	3.73	-39.80	-1.48	-26.23	-42.29
20.5	7.21	3.12	-41.79	-1.30	-26.78	-43.58
21.5	4.09	2.38	-43.88	-1.04	-27.26	-44.94
22.5	1.71	1.45	-46.07	-.67	-27.66	-46.42
23.5	.26	.26	-48.38	-.12	-27.93	-48.38
24.5	.00			- -	-28.00	
			Average =	-28.00%		

Column (b) of Table 6.11 shows the percent surviving from the Iowa S0–12 survivor curve at the age shown in column (a). The Iowa S0–12 curve represents the future life characteristics of the 1976 to 1990 era. Column (c) shows the retirement frequency during each age interval, where the age at the start of the interval is shown in column (a). During the 3.5–4.5 year age interval, 92.79–89.06 or 3.73% of the original installation is retired. Column (d) shows the (net) salvage ratio during the age interval. The salvage ratio during the 0.0–0.5 year age interval is estimated to be −15%. This ratio is expected to inflate (i.e., become more negative) at an annual rate of 5%. Column (e) shows the weighted salvage ratios obtained by multiplying columns (c) and (d), and the sum of column (e), −28%, is the average salvage ratio. Columns (f) and (g) show the realized and future salvage as a function of age.

These ratios will be applied to all vintages from 1976 forward. Similar calculations, but using the Iowa L1–10 survivor curve, must be made to obtain salvage ratios for all vintages installed during and before 1975.

The Average Life Procedure

The SL-AL-AM-VG system uses aged data to construct the realized portion of the vintage survivor curve. The curve is extended using the survivor ratios from the survivor curve chosen to represent the future life characteristics of the vintage. The resulting survivor curve is a combination of observed and estimated retirement ratios and is unique to the vintage, as are the associated average and remaining lives.

Table 6.12 shows the calculation of the survivor curve for the 1981 vintage. Column (a) shows the age at the start of the age interval. Column (b) shows the exposures at the start of the age interval, and column (c) shows the retirements during the age interval. These exposures and retirements are taken from Tables 8.1 and 8.2 in Chapter 8. Column (d) contains the retirement ratios. For ages 0–7.5 years (i.e., from 1981 through 1989), these are observed ratios derived from the observed retirements divided by the observed exposures, i.e., column (c)/column (b). The retirement ratios starting with the age interval 8.5–9.5 years are from the Iowa S0–12 survivor curve, which was selected to represent *the future life of the vintage*. The retirement ratio for the 8.5–9.5 year age interval can be obtained from columns (b) and (c) in Table 6.11. The exposures at age 8.5 years are 69.86% of the initial additions, and the retirements during the 8.5–9.5 year age interval are 5.53% of the initial additions. The resulting retirement ratio is 5.53/69.86 or 7.9%. The percent surviving shown in column (e) is the survivor curve constructed from the retirement ratios in column (d). Column (f) shows the average fraction surviving during the year. At 8.5 years, 73.02% survives, and one year later, at age 9.5 years, 67.25% sur-

Table 6.12. Construction of the survivor curve for the 1981 vintage.
The Iowa SO-12 survivor curve is used to describe the
future life.

	Observed		Ret	Percent	Avg fraction	Areas Realized	Future
Age (a)	Exp (b)	Ret (c)	ratio (d)	surviving (e)	surviving (f)	life (g)	life (h)
0	189	6	.032	100.00	0.9841	.492	
.5	183	0	.000	96.83	0.9683	.968	
1.5	183	2	.011	96.83	0.9630	.963	
2.5	181	4	.022	95.77	0.9471	.947	
3.5	177	3	.017	93.65	0.9286	.929	
4.5	174	6	.034	92.06	0.9048	.905	
5.5	168	10	.060	88.89	0.8624	.862	
6.5	158	9	.057	83.60	0.8122	.812	
7.5	149	11	.074	78.84	0.7593	.759	
8.5			.079	73.02	0.7013		.701
9.5			.088	67.25	0.6429		.643
10.5			.098	61.33	0.5832		.583
11.5			.110	55.31	0.5228		.523
12.5			.122	49.24	0.4623		.462
13.5			.137	43.22	0.4026		.403
14.5			.155	37.30	0.3441		.344
15.5			.175	31.52	0.2876		.288
16.5			.202	25.99	0.2337		.234
17.5			.235	20.74	0.1830		.183
18.5			.279	15.86	0.1364		.136
19.5			.341	11.43	0.0948		.095
20.5			.433	7.53	0.0590		.059
21.5			.581	4.27	0.0303		.030
22.5			.848	1.79	0.0103		.010
23.5			1.000	.27	0.0014		.001
24.5				.00			
					Total	7.638	4.696

Average life   = 7.638 + 4.696 = 12.334 years
Remaining life = 4.696/0.7302 = 6.431 years

vives. The average during the year is (73.02 + 67.25)/2 or 70.13%. It is convenient to convert this to the fraction 0.7013.

A graph of the 1981 survivor curve is shown in Figure 6.3. The lefthand portion of the curve is constructed from the observed retirement ratios and the righthand portion from the forecast retirement ratios. The realized life is the heavily shaded area under the curve,[10] and is found by summing the areas in column (g) of Table 6.12. The area associated with each age interval is the width, 1 year, multiplied by the average fraction surviving during the age interval, column (f). An exception is the first age interval, which is a half year wide. These areas are shown in column (g). The future life is the lightly shaded area under the curve and is found by summing the areas shown in column (h). The average life for the 1981 vintage is the realized life plus the future life, or 7.638 + 4.696 or 12.334 years. The remaining life at age 8.5 years is the future life divided by the percent surviving at age 8.5 years or 4.696/.7302 or 6.431 years. Once the average life and remaining life for each vintage are found, calculation of the annual accrual for the continuous property group can proceed.

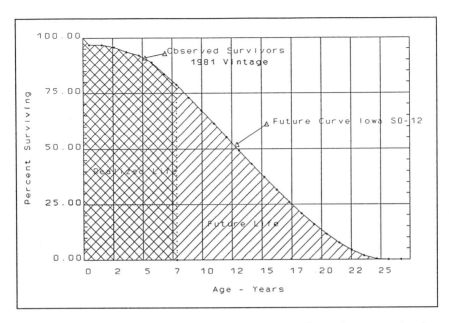

Figure 6.3. The survivor curve for the 1981 vintage. The retirement ratios for the future portion of the curve are from the Iowa S0–12 survivor curve.

Table 6.13 shows the calculation of the 1990 accrual and January 1, 1990, CAD for Account 897 using the SL-AL-AM depreciation system and the vintage group model. The format and calculations are the same as those shown in Table 6.1 for the broad group model. However, with the vintage group model the lives and salvage now vary from vintage to vintage. Column (c) contains the average life for each vintage. Note the 12.3-year average life and 6.4-year remaining life for the 1981 vintage. The average salvage ratio from 1976 through 1990 is −28%, as shown in Table 6.11, and for 1975 and earlier it is −25.3%. The future salvage ratio, column (d), depends on the age of the vintage. The age of the 1981 vintage on January 1, 1990, is 8.5 years, and the corresponding future salvage ratio from Table 6.11 is 31.7%. The SL-AL accrual rate is calculated for each vintage and multiplied by the average vintage balance to obtain the annual accrual. For the 1981 vintage, the annual rate is [1 − (−0.28)]/12.3 or 10.41% and the vintage accrual is 138.00 × 0.1041 or $14.36. The CADR on January 1, 1990, is [1 − (−1.28)](1 − 6.4/12.3) + [−.280 − (−.317)] or 0.651. The sum of the vintage accruals is $493.61 and the CAD on January 1, 1990, is $2653.95.

The average life of the continuous property group (12.40 years) is the

Table 6.13. Calculation of the 1990 annual accrual for depreciation and the January 1, 1990, calculated accumulated depreciation for Account 897 using the SL-AL-AM system of depreciation and the vintage group model. The Iowa L1-10 curve is used from 1966 through 1975 and the Iowa SO-12 curve from 1976 through 1990.

Inst year (a)	Average balance (b)	Avg life (c)	Salvage Avg% (d)	Fut% (e)	Annual accrual (f)	RL (g)	CADR (h)	Balance 1/1/1990 (i)	CAD (j)
1966	22.50	12.5	-25.3	-50.9	2.26	1.3	1.379	30.00	41.36
1967	.00	.0	-25.3	-48.4	.00	.0	.000	.00	.00
1968	.00	.0	-25.3	-47.1	.00	.0	.000	.00	.00
1969	6.50	10.7	-25.3	-45.3	.76	1.9	1.231	8.00	9.84
1970	30.00	13.7	-25.3	-43.6	2.74	2.1	1.244	36.00	44.78
1971	45.00	13.6	-25.3	-42.0	4.15	2.3	1.208	45.00	54.36
1972	111.00	12.5	-25.3	-40.4	11.13	2.5	1.153	117.00	134.95
1973	93.50	12.1	-25.3	-39.0	9.68	2.7	1.110	99.00	109.93
1974	13.50	10.3	-25.3	-37.6	1.64	2.9	1.023	16.00	16.37
1975	94.00	13.4	-25.3	-36.3	8.79	3.8	1.008	94.00	94.72
1976	286.00	11.4	-28.0	-35.8	32.11	4.1	.898	292.00	262.11
1977	112.00	11.5	-28.0	-34.8	12.47	4.6	.836	112.00	93.63
1978	190.00	12.0	-28.0	-34.0	20.27	5.0	.807	190.00	153.27
1979	546.50	13.9	-28.0	-33.2	50.33	5.5	.826	553.00	456.52
1980	203.00	10.8	-28.0	-32.4	24.06	5.9	.625	206.00	128.70
1981	138.00	12.3	-28.0	-31.7	14.36	6.4	.651	138.00	89.84
1982	385.00	13.7	-28.0	-31.0	35.97	6.9	.665	390.00	259.48
1983	295.50	13.2	-28.0	-30.4	28.65	7.5	.577	296.00	170.71
1984	340.00	12.7	-28.0	-29.8	34.27	8.0	.492	340.00	167.18
1985	465.00	12.1	-28.0	-29.3	49.19	8.6	.383	465.00	178.21
1986	220.00	12.5	-28.0	-28.9	22.53	9.3	.337	220.00	74.07
1987	139.00	11.9	-28.0	-28.5	14.95	9.9	.220	140.00	30.82
1988	430.00	11.8	-28.0	-28.2	46.64	10.7	.121	430.00	52.17
1989	580.00	12.0	-28.0	-28.0	61.87	11.5	.053	580.00	30.93
1990	45.00	12.0	-28.0	-28.0	4.80	12.0	.000	.00	.00
	4791.00				493.61			4797.00	2653.95

Composite accrual rate   10.30%
CADR   55.33%
Average life   12.40 years
Average salvage   -27.77%

reciprocal of the average of 1/AL weighted by the average vintage balance (i.e., $\Sigma[\text{Bal}]/\Sigma[\text{Bal}/\text{AL}]$, where the sum is over all vintages). The average salvage ratio (-27.77%) is the average of the vintage salvage ratios weighted by the average balance, i.e., $\Sigma(\text{Bal} \times \text{SR})/\Sigma(\text{Bal})$. The significance of these two averages is that if each vintage AL is replaced by the average 12.40 years, and each vintage SR is replaced by the average -27.77%, the total annual accrual remains \$493.61, even though the vintage accruals would differ from those shown in Table 6.13. The composite accrual rate can be found either by dividing the annual accrual by the average balance, 493.61/4791.00, or by using the averages in the equation $(1 - \text{SR})/\text{AL}$, or $[1 - (-0.278)]/12.40$; both calculations yield a 10.30% accrual rate.

The construction of a unique survivor curve for each vintage by combining the observed and forecast survivor ratios rather than using a single survivor curve for each vintage is the major difference between the vintage group model and the broad group model when using the SL-AL-AM system of depreciation. The SL-AL-AM-VG system commonly is called the *vintage group procedure*. An advantage of the vintage group model is that it properly includes any erratic behavior in the historical retirement ratios. Suppose that property in all vintages in a continuous property group suffered heavy retirements during a single calendar year. This could be the result of an unusually severe storm, an urban renewal project, or any other force of retirement that tended to be related to a calendar year rather than to age. The resulting drop in the survivor curve occurs at a different age for each vintage. If the broad group model is used, the requirement that a single curve be used to describe the life characteristics of all vintages may result in a poor approximation of the actual retirements. With the vintage group model, the use of a unique survivor curve for each vintage can provide a good representation of the actual retirements.

Often a single survivor curve will adequately describe the future life characteristics of all vintages. But the vintage group model allows a continuous property group to be divided into eras, as shown in Table 6.13. This is a second difference between the two models. The use of two or more curves allows the depreciation professional to associate different curves with property from eras that have different life characteristics. This avoids the broad group requirement that the two or more future curves, each with different shapes and lives, be represented by a single, average curve.

Next consider the RL method of adjustment. Table 6.14 shows the calculation of the 1990 accrual using the SL-AL-RL-VG system. The format and calculations are the same as those shown in Table 6.2 for the broad group model, but each vintage RL is calculated in the same manner as shown in Table 6.12 for the 1981 vintage. Because the salvage is aged, the FSR varies from vintage to vintage. The values in column (c), the accumulated provision for depreciation, equal the vintage CAD shown in Table 6.13 so that the variation between the CAD and the accumulated provision for depreciation is zero. The FSRs and RLs are from columns (d) and (f) of Table 6.13. Calculations are based on the January 1, 1990, balances rather than the average balance during the year, so, as before, the annual accruals differ slightly between the two methods of adjustment even though the variation between the CAD and the accumulated provision for depreciation is zero.

Adjustments

The comments concerning adjustments made in this chapter are valid when using the vintage group model. Because the vintage group model allows differences in vintage life and salvage characteristics, this model can better reflect the accounting transactions, including those associated with salvage, that are linked with the retirement of property from a continuous property group. If all other factors are equal, use of the vintage group

Table 6.14. Calculation of the 1990 annual accrual using the SL-
AL-RL system of depreciation and the vintage group
model. The Iowa L1-10 curve is used from 1966 through
1975 and the Iowa S0-12 curve from 1976 through 1990.
The accumulated depreciation equals the CAD shown in
Table 6.13.

Inst year (a)	Balance 1/1/1990 (b)	Acc depr 1/1/1990 (c)	Fut sal ratio % (d)	Future accrual (e)	RL 1/1/1990 (f)	Annual accrual (g)
1966	30.00	41.36	-50.9	3.91	1.3	3.01
1967	.00	.00	-48.4	.00	.0	.00
1968	.00	.00	-47.1	.00	.0	.00
1969	8.00	9.84	-45.3	1.78	1.9	.94
1970	36.00	44.78	-43.6	6.91	2.1	3.29
1971	45.00	54.36	-42.0	9.54	2.3	4.15
1972	117.00	134.95	-40.4	29.32	2.5	11.73
1973	99.00	109.93	-39.0	27.68	2.7	10.25
1974	16.00	16.37	-37.6	5.64	2.9	1.95
1975	94.00	94.72	-36.3	33.40	3.8	8.79
1976	292.00	262.11	-35.8	134.42	4.1	32.79
1977	112.00	93.63	-34.8	57.34	4.6	12.47
1978	190.00	153.27	-34.0	101.33	5.0	20.27
1979	553.00	456.52	-33.2	280.08	5.5	50.92
1980	206.00	128.70	-32.4	144.05	5.9	24.41
1981	138.00	89.84	-31.7	91.91	6.4	14.36
1982	390.00	259.48	-31.0	251.42	6.9	36.44
1983	296.00	170.71	-30.4	215.27	7.5	28.70
1984	340.00	167.18	-29.8	274.14	8.0	34.27
1985	465.00	178.21	-29.3	423.03	8.6	49.19
1986	220.00	74.07	-28.9	209.51	9.3	22.53
1987	140.00	30.82	-28.5	149.08	9.9	15.06
1988	430.00	52.17	-28.2	499.09	10.7	46.64
1989	580.00	30.93	-28.0	711.47	11.5	61.87
1990	45.00*	.00	-28.0	57.60	12.0	4.80
	4842.00	2653.95		3717.94		498.81

Composite accrual rate   10.30%
Composite remaining life   7.45 years

* The 1990 calculations are based on the average balance.

model and aged salvage results in a better estimate of depreciation than if the broad group model and average salvage are used.

When the remaining life method of adjustment is used, the straight line, average life weighted remaining life will yield the same result as allocating the accumulated provision for depreciation in proportion to the CAD. The weight is the balance times the rate $(1 - ASR)/AL$, where the ASR and the AL can vary with each vintage. The numerator is [45.00 × (1.28/12.0) × 12.0 + 580.00 × (1.28/12.0) × 11.5 + 430.00 × (1.28/11.8) × 10.7 + . . . 30.00 × (1.253/12.5) × 1.3] or 3717.94. The denominator is [45.00 × (1.28/12.0) + 580.00 × (1.28/12.0) + 430.00 × (1.28/11.8) + . . . 30.00 × (1.253/12.5)] or 498.81. The resulting weighted remaining life is 7.45 years, which equals the composite remaining life shown in Table 6.14. Note that this weighting incorporates both the different vintage average lives as well as the difference in the average salvage ratios between the two eras.

The ELG Procedure

Table 6.15 shows the calculation of the annual ELG accrual rates for an Iowa S0–12 survivor curve and the salvage schedule shown in Table 6.11. Table 6.15 is in the same format as Table 6.5. However, Table 6.5 shows the calculation of the ELG rates using an Iowa S1–10 curve and an average future salvage ratio of −30% for all ELGs. The FSR in column (c) is the aged SR shown in column (d) of Table 6.11, and is matched with the ELG retired during that age interval. Using aged salvage is consistent with the ELG goal of fully accruing each ELG by the time of its retirement.

With both the broad group and vintage group models, the ELG procedure requires only the future life characteristics to calculate the annual accrual and CAD. This raises the question of how the ELG rates differ between the broad group and vintage group models. Consider the survivor curve for the 1981 vintage shown in Table 6.12. At the time of the study, its age is 8.5 years and 73.02% of the original additions remain in service, but the Iowa S0–12 survivor curve shows 69.86% surviving at that age, i.e.,

Table 6.15. Calculation of annual accrual rates using the straight line method and ELG procedure, an Iowa S0-12 survivor curve, and salvage ratios from Table 6.11. The portion of the table for age intervals greater than 4.5-5.5 years is not shown.

ELG interval (a)	% Retired (b)	SR % (c)	% Recovered (d)	0.0 (e)	0.5 (f)	1.5 (g)	2.5 (h)	3.5 (i)	4.5 (j)
0.0- .5	.26	-15.0	.30	.30					
0.0- 1.5	1.45	-15.8	1.68	.84	.84				
0.0- 2.5	2.38	-16.5	2.77	.69	1.39	.69			
0.0- 3.5	3.12	-17.4	3.66	.61	1.22	1.22	.61		
0.0- 4.5	3.73	-18.2	4.40	.55	1.10	1.10	1.10	.55	
0.0- 5.5	4.22	-19.1	5.04	.50	1.01	1.01	1.01	1.01	.50
0.0- 6.5	4.66	-20.1	5.60	.47	.93	.93	.93	.93	.93
0.0- 7.5	5.02	-21.1	6.08	.43	.87	.87	.87	.87	.87
0.0- 8.5	5.30	-22.2	6.47	.40	.81	.81	.81	.81	.81
0.0- 9.5	5.53	-23.3	6.82	.38	.76	.76	.76	.76	.76
0.0-10.5	5.67	-24.4	7.06	.35	.71	.71	.71	.71	.71
0.0-11.5	5.76	-25.7	7.24	.33	.66	.66	.66	.66	.66
0.0-12.5	5.80	-26.9	7.36	.31	.61	.61	.61	.61	.61
0.0-13.5	5.76	-28.3	7.39	.28	.57	.57	.57	.57	.57
0.0-14.5	5.67	-29.7	7.35	.26	.53	.53	.53	.53	.53
0.0-15.5	5.53	-31.2	7.25	.24	.48	.48	.48	.48	.48
0.0-16.5	5.30	-32.7	7.04	.22	.44	.44	.44	.44	.44
0.0-17.5	5.02	-34.4	6.75	.20	.40	.40	.40	.40	.40
0.0-18.5	4.66	-36.1	6.34	.18	.35	.35	.35	.35	.35
0.0-19.5	4.22	-37.9	5.82	.15	.31	.31	.31	.31	.31
0.0-20.5	3.73	-39.8	5.21	.13	.26	.26	.26	.26	.26
0.0-21.5	3.12	-41.8	4.42	.11	.21	.21	.21	.21	.21
0.0-22.5	2.38	-43.9	3.42	.08	.16	.16	.16	.16	.16
0.0-23.5	1.45	-46.1	2.12	.05	.09	.09	.09	.09	.09
0.0-24.5	.26	-48.4	.39	.01	.02	.02	.02	.02	.02
Total	100.00		127.98	8.07	14.71	13.17	11.87	10.71	9.66
Average percent surviving				49.94	99.02	97.10	94.36	90.94	87.18
Composite rate				.1617	.1485	.1357	.1258	.1178	.1108

100% minus the sum of column (b) for ELG intervals from 0.0–0.5 through 0.0–8.5 equals 69.86%, not 73.02%. If the ELG rates were calculated using the observed 73.02% surviving rather than 69.86%, would these rates differ from those shown in Table 6.15? The answer is that if the 73.02% surviving is allocated to the future ELG intervals in proportion to the percent retired shown in column (b) of Table 6.15, the resulting ELG accrual rates will equal[11] those shown in Table 6.15. Thus, using this method of allocation, the ELG rates depend only on the survivor curve, not on the observed percent surviving, and the rates for the broad group and vintage group models are the same.

In practice, when the ELG procedure is used, a single survivor curve almost always is used to describe the future life of the continuous property group. This implies use of the broad group model. Table 6.16 shows the calculation of the 1990 accrual and CAD on January 1, 1990, using the SL-ELG-RL depreciation system and the vintage group model. It differs from

Table 6.16. Calculation of the 1990 accrual for depreciation and the January 1, 1990, calculated accumulated provision for depreciation for Account 897 using the SL-ELG-AM system of depreciation and the vintage group model. The Iowa L1-10 curve is used from 1966 through 1975 and the Iowa SO-12 curve from 1976 through 1990. The estimates of aged salvage are shown in Table 6.11.

Inst year (a)	Average balance (b)	Accrual rate % (c)	Annual accrual (d)	CADR ********* (e)	Balance 1/1/1990 (f)	CAD ******** (g)
1966	22.50	6.00	1.35	1.42	30.00	42.60
1967	.00	6.12	.00	1.39	.00	.00
1968	.00	6.25	.00	1.36	.00	.00
1969	6.50	6.40	.42	1.32	8.00	10.56
1970	30.00	6.55	1.97	1.29	36.00	46.44
1971	45.00	6.73	3.03	1.26	45.00	56.70
1972	111.00	6.92	7.68	1.23	117.00	143.91
1973	93.50	7.12	6.66	1.19	99.00	117.81
1974	13.50	7.35	.99	1.16	16.00	18.56
1975	94.00	7.60	7.14	1.12	94.00	105.28
1976	286.00	7.73	22.11	1.06	292.00	308.88
1977	112.00	7.97	8.92	1.01	112.00	113.18
1978	190.00	8.23	15.63	.96	190.00	182.62
1979	546.50	8.52	46.54	.91	553.00	502.77
1980	203.00	8.83	17.93	.85	206.00	176.01
1981	138.00	9.19	12.68	.80	138.00	109.86
1982	385.00	9.58	36.89	.73	390.00	286.17
1983	295.50	10.03	29.63	.67	296.00	197.30
1984	340.00	10.50	35.70	.59	340.00	200.70
1985	465.00	11.08	51.51	.51	465.00	238.70
1986	220.00	11.78	25.91	.42	220.00	93.44
1987	139.00	12.58	17.49	.33	140.00	45.55
1988	430.00	13.57	58.34	.21	430.00	91.01
1989	580.00	14.85	86.15	.08	580.00	45.20
1990	45.00	16.17	7.27	.00	.00	.00
	4791.00		501.96		4797.00	3133.24

Composite accrual rate   10.48%
CADR   65.40%

the broad group model in that Account 897 has been divided into eras, each having different future life characteristics. The Iowa L1–10 curve is used from 1966 through 1975 and the Iowa S0–12 curve is used from 1976 through 1990.

If the broad group model was used, the two curves would be replaced by a single survivor curve that properly weighted the two curves to represent the future life of all vintages in the continuous property group. That curve would be used to calculate the ELG rates for all vintages.

Calculations for the remaining life method of adjustment (i.e., the SL-ELG-RL-VG system) are not shown because the mechanics are identical with those for the SL-ELG-RL-BG system. Illustration of the vintage group model would require calculation of the ELG rates and CADRs using the survivor curve and salvage schedule associated with each era.

SUMMARY

The smallest depreciable group is a vintage group. One way to develop an understanding of the factors that define a depreciation system is to apply the system to a vintage group, as was done in Chapter 5. Though in practice the depreciable group may be a vintage group, it is typically a continuous property group.

When vintage groups are aggregated to form a continuous property group, the practical problem now facing the depreciation professional is not how to depreciate the vintage group but how to economically and realistically describe the life and salvage characteristics of the continuous property group, which often includes many vintages. The available data describing the continuous property group affects the solution to this problem. Unaged retirement data contain less information about the life and salvage characteristics than do aged retirement data. With unaged data, the vintage balances are not known and must be estimated, and the historical life characteristics are more difficult to determine (see Chapter 11). This lack of information leads to the broad group model and the simplifying assumption that all vintages share the same life and salvage characteristics.

When the life and salvage characteristics change slowly from one vintage to the next, the error created by assuming each vintage has the same characteristics is likely to be small, and the broad group model will likely provide a reasonable estimate of depreciation. When the life and salvage characteristics of a continuous property group change significantly and quickly, or when the characteristics are erratic, the broad group model may not provide an adequate estimate of depreciation. Whether the estimate of depreciation is adequate is a matter of judgment. Factors that should be considered when making this judgment include the rate and magnitude of the change, the importance of the depreciable group under consideration when compared to other depreciable groups, the accuracy of the continuing property records, the ability to forecast future life and salvage, and the importance placed on estimates of depreciation. If the use of the broad group model in a depreciation system yields results that are not satisfactory because of the dynamic or erratic characteristics of the account, the vintage group model should be used.

If data are aged, movement from the broad group model to the vintage group model is straightforward. If data are unaged, the accounting system must be modified to age data. Though it may take several years for the aged data of the new system to accumulate to the point of becoming useful, it may be possible to statistically age the existing data and accelerate the benefits of switching from the broad group to the vintage group model.

The advantage of the vintage group model is that it can more realistically reflect the actual world. Because each vintage is allowed its own life and salvage characteristics, changes in the characteristics of the continuous property group are incorporated into the calculation of the estimate of depreciation.

NOTES

1. In *Bulletin 155,* page 12, Winfrey defined a continuous property group to be "composed wholly of separate, like units whose separate retirement and renewal from time to time enable the property group to be continued in service for as long as desired." In that *Bulletin,* he examined continuous property groups in which each retirement generated a replacement, so that the total number of units in the group remained constant. Winfrey used this definition while studying renewals, and it is more restrictive than the definition used in this chapter.

2. These two systems are often referred to as the "whole life-broad group" or "broad group" method and the "remaining life" method respectively. See Chapter 7.

3. See Tables 8.1 and 8.2 in Chapter 8 to obtain the beginning and end of year balance for each vintage.

4. This equation was developed in Chapter·5. The variables are average salvage ratio (ASR), remaining life (RL), average life (AL), and future salvage ratio (FSR).

5. This differs from the calculations in Table 6.1 where an average annual rate was applied to the average annual balance.

6. Because the average and remaining lives are given in years, the resulting rates are annual rates. The average monthly rate is 1/12 the annual rate.

7. The continuous property group is important because it is often a depreciable group. In this illustration, the property in the functional Account 897 is also a continuous property group and a depreciable property group.

8. Prove this by substituting the formula for the CADR in the equation for the future accrual, FA = Bal × (1 − CADR − FSR). The result is FA = RL × [Bal × (1 − ASR)/AL]. Thus, Σ[RL × Bal × (1 − ASR)/AL]/Σ[Bal × (1 − ASR)/AL] = Σ(FAR)/Σ(Accrual) = Composite Remaining Life.

9. This average was found by averaging the beginning of year and end of year balances. This assumes the survivor curve segment is a straight line during the age interval. A more accurate method is to use the table value of the percent surviving at the midpoint of the age interval.

10. The area under the curve in Figure 6.3 is measured in percent-years and must be divided by 100% to convert to years.

11. The percent retired for each ELG interval will be adjusted by a factor of 73.02/69.86 or 1.045. The percent surviving at each age will be adjusted by the same factor. When the accrual for the age interval is divided by the average percent surviving, the adjustments cancel each other and the resulting rates are the same as shown in Table 6.15.

7 | Defining Depreciation Systems

THIS chapter will define terms commonly used to describe depreciation systems. There is no single source of standard definitions of depreciation systems. Several terms have been commonly used to express the same meaning, and sometimes a term may have multiple meanings, depending on the user or the context in which it is used.

The field of depreciation is small and fragmented. It includes capital-intensive enterprises such as public utilities and railroads, as well as many regulatory bodies at both the state and federal levels. Further, the concept of depreciation varies with the application, which can include capital recovery, taxes, damage claims and insurance recoveries, condemnations, and acquisitions and sales.

This fragmentation has contributed to the difficult task of adopting a standard vocabulary and definitions. Those working in depreciation should be familiar with terms that are often used to describe depreciation systems and what these terms do or do not imply. The terminology described in this chapter relates primarily to capital recovery and valuation concepts within the regulated utility and railroad industries.

Chapter 5 introduced depreciation systems that are specified by three factors. These include the method of allocation, e.g., straight line (SL), the procedure for applying the method of allocation, average life (AL) or equal life group (ELG), and the method of adjustment, amortization (AM) or remaining life (RL). This yields four possible combinations of depreciation systems. Chapter 6 added a fourth factor that included either the broad group, BG, or the vintage group, VG, models.

We normally assume that the same depreciation system will be used for both salvage and life, although combinations that further complicate the problems of definition are possible. For example, the ELG procedure is sometimes used with the average salvage, rather than aged salvage, applied to each equal life group. The result is a combination of the ELG procedure applied to life and the AL procedure applied to salvage. The high cost of decommissioning nuclear power plants has resulted in a system that combines the straight line method of allocation for life with the sinking fund method of allocation for salvage.

The terms *whole life, vintage group, broad group, ELG,* and *remaining life* are widely used to describe depreciation systems. These terms do not explicitly define the system, although each term carries with it certain implications. Unfortunately, the implications of the terms vary from user to user, so the following definitions reflect only the most common usage.

Whole life[1] depreciation is a general term used to describe any system not using the remaining life method of adjustment. Though whole life describes the length of time from initial installation to final retirement, the average life is used to calculate the accrual rate. Whole life depreciation commonly, but not necessarily, implies use of the amortization method of adjustment. As previously discussed, the amortization method of adjustment requires calculation of the variation between the calculated accumulated depreciation and accumulated provision for depreciation. *Reserve requirement* and *theoretical reserve* are synonymous with the term *calculated accumulated depreciation.* In this context, the term *ratio* refers to the calculated accumulated depreciation divided by the plant in service. This results in the terms *reserve ratio, theoretical reserve ratio,* and *calculated accumulated depreciation ratio.*

Both the American Gas Association and the Edison Electric Institute have standing committees on depreciation that have been an important industry forum for the discussion of depreciation. In 1972, the committees published a training manual titled *An Introduction to Depreciation.* A feature of the manual was the use of a pedagogical tool called the depreciation cube to help define depreciation systems. Three of the contiguous faces of the cube were labeled *methods, procedures,* and *techniques.* Each face was divided into four layers, so that the cube was divided into 64 smaller cubes. Each of the smaller cubes was characterized by one of the four methods, procedures, and techniques.

The label "methods" had the same meaning as methods of allocation as defined in Chapter 5. The label "procedures" was divided into four layers including (1) individual unit procedures; (2) equal life group procedures; (3) vintage group procedures; and (4) broad group procedures. This use of the term procedures is different from the term procedure for applying the method of allocation as defined in Chapter 5. The label "techniques" included either (1) the whole life technique or (2) the remaining life technique. Technique has a meaning that is partially similar to the term adjustment method as defined in Chapter 5. The manual describes the whole life technique as an approach that, when the forecast of life and/or salvage is revised, changes the accrual rate to reflect the new forecasts but does *not* adjust for the fact the past accruals were calculated using the previous forecasts. Thus, the whole life technique does not require the use of the calculated accumulated depreciation. The remaining life technique and remaining life method of adjustment have the same meaning. The technique face of the depreciation cube divides both techniques into whole life and location life, so that there are four layers. However, the definition of service life as either whole life or location life is independent of the depreciation system.

The terms *broad group depreciation* and *vintage group depreciation* both imply use of the average life procedure. Both terms often, but not always, define a system that includes the amortization method of adjustment. Broad group depreciation usually refers to the SL-AL-AM system and use of the broad group model. A single average life and average net salvage ratio are chosen to represent all vintage groups in the continuous property group.

When calculating the calculated accumulated depreciation for broad groups, the difference between the average and future salvage is often ignored or assumed to equal zero. The last term of the equation $CADR(i) = (1 - ASR)[1 - RL(i)/ASL] + [ASR - FSR(i)]$ is then zero and the equation becomes $CADR(i) = (1 - ASR)[1 - RL(i)/AL]$. When the difference between the average and future salvage is significant, and the equation $CADR(i) = (1 - ASR)[1 - RL(i)/ASL] + [ASR - FSR(i)]$ is used, a single future salvage ratio is usually chosen to represent all vintages (i.e., rather than estimating a salvage schedule for the broad group and using it at age i to calculate FSR(i), a single FSR is used for all ages).

Vintage group depreciation usually refers to the SL-AL-AM system and use of the vintage group model. The term *generational arrangement* is also used, primarily by the Bell Companies, to describe the vintage group model. Aged data are required. The survivor curve for each vintage is found by using observed retirement ratios from age zero to the age at study date, then using retirement ratios from the forecast curve to complete the survivor curve. Typically, a single forecast curve (often called the future curve) is used to extend all vintages, although a different curve could be used for each vintage. If a salvage schedule has been forecast, the future salvage ratio as a function of age is calculated and used in the calculation of the CAD. It is common, however, to apply a single future salvage ratio to each vintage.

The term *ELG depreciation* typically refers to the SL-ELG-AM system. Usually a single future curve is used for all vintages (i.e., the broad group model is used), though a different future curve could be used for each vintage. Emphasis is placed on forecasting the "future curve" (i.e., the survivor curve used to describe the life characteristics of the property from the study date forward), because, under the ELG procedure, property should be fully depreciated at retirement and the accrual rate depends only on the shape of the survivor curve from the age at the study date to maximum life. It is not unusual to estimate a single average net salvage ratio and apply it to each ELG, rather than to use aged salvage with a different salvage ratio for each ELG. The use of an average salvage ratio is often the result of the lack of aged salvage data and the lack of models to estimate future salvage ratios by age.

Remaining life depreciation usually refers to the SL-AL-RL system of depreciation; use of the AL procedure is implied as is use of the same survivor curve for all vintages. Emphasis is placed on forecasting the remaining life or future curve. When calculating the future accruals, the same future salvage ratio is often used for all vintages.

Users of remaining life depreciation often do not explicitly calculate the CAD. As previously discussed, calculation of the CAD is implicit in the use of the remaining life method of adjustment, because the variation between the CAD and the accumulated provision for depreciation is automatically amortized over the remaining life. Explicit calculation of the CAD will allow the depreciation professional to find the portion of the annual accrual associated with amortization of the variation (either positive or negative).

When the ELG procedure is used with the remaining life method of adjustment, a term such as *ELG − remaining life depreciation* may be used to describe the SL-ELG-RL system. A single future survivor curve and future salvage ratio usually are applied to all vintages, although the future curve could be varied. Several pages in Chapter 6 were devoted to a discussion of the allocation of the accumulated provision for depreciation to each vintage when using this depreciation system. It was shown that allocation in proportion to the calculated future accruals resulted in a composite remaining life that is independent of the variation between the CAD and the accumulated provision for depreciation. Then the composite ELG accrual rate is calculated based on that composite remaining life.

Specify each of the four factors of a depreciation system to ensure communication. It is not safe to assume that life and salvage are treated in the same manner. Take care to indicate differences in the manner in which they are treated.

NOTE

1. *Whole life* is also used in a second context in which it is used in contrast to *location life*. When property is reused, the location life is the length of time from installation at a particular location to retirement from that location. The whole life can then be divided into a series of location lives.

8 | Actuarial Methods of Developing Life Tables

FOUR basic methods of developing a life table can be used when aged data are available. These include the placement band method,[1] the experience band method, the multiple original group method, and the individual unit method. Each provides special insight to the life characteristics of the property and each has its limitations.

DATA REQUIREMENTS

The term *aged data* is used to describe the information reflecting the initial age distributions, annual additions, and the changes to that property for each year in the history of the account. Original data include the annual additions, retirements, transfers, sales, acquisitions, and other transactions. These data must be checked to ensure they are consistent, accurate, and coded so that they can be used to find the exposures and retirements for each age interval.

The aged data base used in this chapter is an account labeled Account 897–Utility Devices and is shown in Tables 8.1 and 8.2 (see end of chapter). These data contain the initial age distribution and have been simplified by assuming that the only two transactions can occur—the addition of new property and the retirement of installed property. Table 8.1 displays the plant in service, or exposures, at the start of each calendar year from 1968 until 1991. The first placement year is 1962 and the last is 1990. The half-year convention is used, so all installations are treated as though they occurred at midyear. Note that the table is incomplete; no experience describing the 1962–1967 placement years before 1968 is available. The first placement with experience starting at age zero is 1968. For some years the initial placements have been completely retired (e.g., 1968), while most still have plant in service. Table 8.2 is the companion to Table 8.1 and contains the retirements during each year. Given these two tables, retirement ratios can be obtained by dividing the retirements during the year by the exposures, or plant in service, at the start of the year.

The period during which transactions are grouped is typically one year, the accounting period most commonly associated with these records. The following ideas could, however, be based on any periods of any length of time.

Figure 8.1 (see end of chapter) is a simplified, graphical description of the source of the exposures and retirements used to calculate the retirement ratios. It will be used to illustrate the methods of combining these ratios to obtain a survivor curve.

Each column in Figure 8.1 represents a calendar year, and groups of one or more columns will be called *experience bands*. This term reflects the realization that, during each calendar year, all property, regardless of its age, is subjected to common forces of retirement that are the result of the particular activities or experiences occurring during that specific period. Each row represents property added, or placed in service, during a particular year. The terms *vintage group* and *original group* are used to describe the group of property placed in service during a single year. Groups of one or more rows are called *placement bands*.

Each table entry in Figure 8.1 represents a retirement ratio. The retirement ratio is a statistic that can be used to estimate the probability that a unit of property in service at the start of an age interval is retired during that same age interval. The experience band determines the age at which the particular retirement ratio applies. Consider, for example, the retirement data for the 1968 placement band shown in Tables 8.1 and 8.2. This band includes all property installed during the 1968 calendar year. The half-year convention, which assumes that all property is installed midyear, or on July 1, is applied. The retirement ratio for the 1968 placement band and 1968 experience band describes the average rate of retirement during the age interval 0.0–0.5 years. On January 1, 1969, property installed during 1968 is 0.5 years old, so the age interval for the 1969 experience band is 0.5–1.5 years. The age interval corresponding to the 1968 placement band and 1990 experience band, which is the oldest experience band in this data base, is 21.5–22.5 years.

The entries on a diagonal row are retirement ratios from the same age interval. For example, the entries on the diagonal starting at the upper left corner and ending at the lower right corner contain retirement ratios for the age interval 0.0–0.5 years.

The concept of placement bands, experience bands, and the corresponding retirement rates is fundamental to life analysis. When viewing a placement band, visualize a group of property installed during the same year or during several consecutive years. This group of property will often have similar physical characteristics. As time passes, the property ages and is retired. The forces of retirement acting on the property, including weather, economic conditions, and management policy, may vary from year to year, but the group of property being observed remains constant. Observations start during the year the property is installed and continue until the final retirement.

When viewing an experience band, visualize a picture of retirements taken during a single year or several consecutive years. All property in service is observed, and the age of the property ranges from the most recent vintage to property from the oldest surviving vintage. Thus, the physical characteristics of the property may span several technologies, but the forces of retirement are limited to those acting during the experience band.

THE PLACEMENT AND EXPERIENCE BAND METHODS

Placement and experience band analyses of retirement ratios are the most important methods of obtaining life tables. A life table contains the data necessary to graph a survivor curve and also may include the exposures and retirements used in the calculations as well as the retirement and survivor ratios. Table 8.3 (see end of chapter) is a life table. Heading information includes the account number, the method of analysis, and the placement and experience bands used to construct the table.

Column (a) defines the age interval. Because the half-year convention is used, the first age interval, 0.0–0.5 year, is one-half year, and all others (e.g., 0.5–1.5 years) are one year.

Columns (b) and (c) contain the exposures at the start of the age interval and retirements during the age interval specified in the first column. The exact procedure for selecting the exposures from Table 8.2 is defined by the method of analysis. Exposures and retirements are measured in either dollars or units.

Calculate the retirement ratio, shown in column (d), by dividing the retirements during the period by the exposures at the beginning of the period. For example, during the age interval 8.5–9.5 years, $123.00 was exposed to retirement and $6.00 was retired, which yields a retirement ratio of 6.00/123.00 or 0.0488. Any property that was exposed but not retired during the age interval must have survived or still have been in service at the end of the age interval. Therefore, the survivor ratio, shown in column (e), is 1 minus the retirement ratio. For age interval 8.5–9.5 years the survivor ratio is 1 − 0.0488 or 0.9512.

Column (f) contains the percent surviving at the beginning of the interval. At age 0, 100% of the property is in service and the retirement ratio for the age interval 0.0–0.5 years shows that survivor ratio for the interval is 1 − 0 or 1, leaving 1 × 100.00% or 100.00% surviving at age 0.5 years. During age interval 0.5–1.5 years, the survivor ratio is 1 − 0.0137 or 0.9863, so that the percent surviving at age 1.5 years is 0.9863 × 100.00% or 98.63%. In general, the percent surviving at the beginning of an interval is the percent surviving at the beginning of the previous interval multiplied by the survivor ratio during the interval.

In this example, all the original $146.00 has been retired from service. Often plant is still in service at the start of the oldest age interval resulting in an incomplete or stub survivor curve. The survivor curve is plotted by graphing the percent surviving shown in column (f) as a function of the age, shown in column (a).

The retirement ratios show a tendency to increase with age, although there is randomness as the ratios fluctuate from year to year. The retirement ratio during the age interval 13.5–14.5 years appears significantly larger than its neighbors. Look to the forces of retirement during 1982 for a possible explanation of this large ratio. During the year 1988, all the remaining plant in service is retired and the resulting retirement ratio of 1 brings the percent surviving to zero. Figure 8.2 (see end of chapter) is a graph of this survivor curve.

Placement Band Method

Perhaps the most intuitive method of constructing a life table is by the placement band method. First, consider a placement band consisting of a single year, 1968. Experience for this placement band starts in 1968 and ends in 1990, as shown in Figure 8.3 (see end of chapter).

Table 8.3 is the life table developed using the 1968 placement band. Note that in the table heading the placement band is defined 1968–1968, while the experience band runs from 1968, the first year in which property was installed, to 1990, the most recent experience.

When using the placement band method, the resulting survivor curve describes the life characteristics of the group of property installed during that placement year. Suppose there had been no transfers, sales, acquisitions, and other entries, but only the initial installations followed by the regular retirements each year. The survivor curve obtained from the single placement year would be identical with that obtained by plotting the dollars surviving at the end of each year. Examination of the placement band method when only additions and retirements are considered emphasizes that this method traces the history of the particular group of property installed during a specific placement year or band of years.

Usually placement bands include more than one year, defining a group of property installed during a specific period or era, rather than a single year. Construction of a band of more than one year raises two computational questions. To identify and help answer these questions, consider the placement band formed by combining the 1968, 1969, and 1970 placement years. This band is shown graphically in Figure 8.4 and the resulting life table is shown in Table 8.4 (see end of chapter for figures and tables).

For the typical age interval, retirements and exposures from each of the three placement bands must be combined to obtain a single retirement ratio, and this raises the first computational problem. Two possible methods of combining these numbers come to mind, but first the retirement ratio for each of the three placement bands must be calculated. For the age interval 6.5–7.5 years in the 1968–1970 placement band, retirements come from (a) the 1968 placement band and the 1975 experience year—5 units, (b) the 1969 placement band and the 1976 experience band—2 units, and (c) the 1970 placement band and the 1977 experience band—8 units. These retirements all occur during the same age interval, 6.5–7.5 years. Exposures of 133, 69, and 102 for each of the three years are obtained in a similar manner and retirement ratios of 5/133 or 0.0376, 2/69 or 0.0290, and 8/102 or 0.0784 can then be calculated. The first method to combine these ratios, and the method used in all remaining examples, is to weight each ratio by its exposures/total exposures and calculate a weighted average of (133 × 0.0376 + 69 × 0.0290 + 102 × 0.0784)/(133 + 69 + 102) or 0.0493. This is equivalent to dividing the sum of the retirements by the sum of the exposures, or (5 + 2 + 8)/(133 + 69 + 102) or 0.0493.

The second method is to calculate an unweighted average of the three rates to obtain (0.0375 + 0.0289 + 0.0784)/3 or 0.0483. This weights each placement year equally regardless of the number of units involved, and this method should be considered when it is desirable to give each vintage equal weight. As a practical matter, the two methods will typically yield approximately the same results. The first method is most commonly used because it gives equal weight to each unit.

The second computational problem occurs near the end of the survivor curve. Through the first 19 age intervals, each of the three years contributes exposures and retirements to be included in the calculation of the retirement ratio. However, during the age interval 17.5–18.5 years, the exposures and retirements from the 1970 placement band are from the final experience year, 1990, and this placement cannot contribute information for the calculation of the next age interval. The common solution, and the one used in most computer programs, is to calculate the next retirement ratio using the two remaining placement years. Next, the 1969 placement band drops out and the final retirement ratio uses information from only the oldest placement year in the band. Because the band is three years wide, the final two points are "different" from all preceding points, and this should be considered when analyzing curves from bands wider than one year. The wider the placement band, the greater the problem, because the number of different points is always the band width less one. Because of this computational problem, it is often desirable to limit placement band analysis to relatively narrow bands that trace the history of a particular group of property installed during a particular era.

Experience Band Method

Figure 8.5 (see end of chapter) graphically contrasts a one-year placement band with a one-year experience band. The placement band method results in a survivor curve that describes the life characteristics of an actual group of property over a period of experience starting at the date of installation and continuing until the study date. This is represented by the row of asterisks in Figure 8.5. In contrast, the experience band method results in a survivor curve that describes a hypothetical group of property with exposures ranging from the oldest vintage to the most recent vintage. The survivor curve describes a hypothetical group of property, because no single vintage group with these life characteristics existed.

This hypothetical group is described by the retirement ratios represented by the column of asterisks in Figure 8.5. One retirement ratio comes from each placement; each retirement ratio comes from the same experience band. The importance of this is that each placement band experiences common forces of retirement. The activities and events occurring during the experience band act on all property. Suppose an unusually severe ice storm occurred during the calendar year defined by the experience band. Destruction caused by the storm would act equally on property of all ages, that is from each placement, and the likely result would be large retirement ratios during that year, or experience band, for property from all placements. The survivor curve generated from the experience band defined by the year of the storm is likely to be significantly different from other one-year bands that did not suffer from this unusual experience. In contrast, a typical placement band would show a large retirement ratio during that particular calendar year. Weather is only one of the forces of retirement that may be associated with a specific experience band.

Table 8.5 (see end of chapter) is a life table developed using the 1990 experience band. To include retirement ratios from all placements, the placement band starts with the first year for which data is available, 1962, and ends with the latest year in the experience band, 1990. The experience band is shown graphically in Figure 8.6 (see end of chapter).

Experience bands usually include more than one year, and Table 8.6 is a life table developed from the 1986–1990 experience band. Combining these five years of experience into one experience band presents the same computational problems that were raised during the placement band discussion, and their solutions are the same. Retirement ratios are obtained by adding the retirements during the same age interval over the five placement bands and dividing by the sum of the exposures during the same age interval and over the five placement bands. Because the band is five years wide, the last four points in the survivor curve are different from the others; the retirements and exposures used to calculate the retirement ratio for these points include, as explained before, fewer than five sets of exposures and retirements. This is shown graphically in Figure 8.7 (see end of chapter).

Choice of Bands for Analysis

One decision the life analyst must make is the choice of bands to be run during analysis. Suppose the forces of retirement and the life characteristics of the property have been constant during the life of an account. Then the retirement ratio for a specific age interval would be the same regardless of which placement band or retirement band is chosen, and the same survivor curve would result regardless of the method of analysis. This situation rarely, if ever, occurs. Forces of retirement are continually changing, as are the characteristics of industrial property. Life analysis requires that the account be taken apart and examined to find the magnitude and rate of these changes, and the placement and experience band are two of the major tools for doing this.

Placement band analysis is particularly useful in comparing the survivor characteristics of properties with different physical characteristics. Typically, technological change is reflected by the difference in the characteristics of property installed in different eras. An early placement band may consist of property based on a now-outdated technology, while a more recent placement would consist of property of a newer technology. By comparing the survivor curves from the two eras, the analyst may be able to draw conclusions about the relative survivor characteristics of the two technologies.

The placement band reflects the life characteristics of a specific group of installed property and should be used to estimate the shape of the survivor curve. Whether heavy early retirements yield a left modal curve, or heavy retirements late in life result in a right modal curve, the placement band gives the best estimate of curve shape.

A characteristic of the placement band is that the more recent the placement, the less the experience and the shorter the survivor curve. Recent placement bands may be too short to give significant information about either the life or the general shape of the curve. In contrast, the most recent experience bands yield the longest life tables.

Recent experience bands yield the most recent retirement ratios, providing the forecaster with valuable information about the current retirement ratios for all ages. The analyst may examine the influence of a specific force of retirement by using the experience band method. For example, the effect of a recent change in a company's maintenance policy could be examined by comparing the survivor curve from an experience band that ends at the last year in which the old policy was in effect with the survivor curve from an experience band that starts with the first year during which the new policy was used.

Choosing the width of either the experience band or the placement band is an important decision that the analyst must make. A band of only one year will typically exhibit significant randomness, resulting in a survivor curve that may be difficult to analyze. Combining several years in a single band will result in an average curve that is smoother; that is, it shows less randomness than the curves from the one-year bands. This smoothing, or averaging, effect is a primary motivation for combining single years into multiple bands. Although widening a band has the advantage of smoothing the data, it has the disadvantage of obscuring or hiding differences between the individual bands.

The analyst must use good judgment when determining band widths. Many empirical procedures governing this choice have been developed. These include the selection bands of fixed width, often 3, 5, or 10 years; rolling bands, in which one band overlaps the next; and shrinking bands, in which the width of the band systematically decreases.

A preferred approach is to select the bands based on the history and the activities that occurred during the period defined by the bands. Because placement bands are often used to describe property of a particular technology, a band could be chosen that will be wide enough to include all property of a similar technology. Experience bands may be chosen to include the calendar years during which a single force of retirement was of particular interest.

Bands may be chosen to detect change in the survivor characteristics. Suppose, for example, that an experience band covering the past 12 years had been selected because it was believed that the economic forces had been somewhat constant during this period. To test for change during this period, the 12 years can be subdivided into nonoverlapping intervals. Division of these 12 years into the first five years and the last seven years would be an example. The life characteristics of the single 12-year period can be compared to the five-year and the seven-year periods. The mean service life indicated by the survivor curve constructed from the 12-year band is a weighted average of the curve from the five-year and seven-year bands, and a comparison of the shorter periods will show whether the service life has been constant during the 12-year period.

The ultimate combination of bands is the overall band, which combines all individual placement and experience bands into a single, overall band. The major attribute of the survivor curve obtained from this band is that it uses every available exposure and retirement. On the other hand, this grand average obscures the dynamic characteristics of the life characteristics of the property. In addition, it is difficult to define the meaning of the resulting survivor curve. Each individual retirement ratio is based on a different group of property. The first retirement ratio will include observations from all vintages and the second retirement ratio from all but the most recent. This pattern continues until the final point is based on observations from only one vintage. It is difficult to figure out the exact meaning of the overall band, and, in spite of the fact it does include all the data points, it should be given limited significance.

Incomplete Actuarial Data

Notice that the Account 897 data are incomplete. There are no data for the 1962 through 1967 placements before 1968, and this type of gap in data is not unusual. Legislation enacting the Uniform System of Accounts passed in the mid 1930s, and implementation in some industries started in the late 1930s. The start of implementation also depended on the size of the company, and some companies have started only recently. Companies were faced with the problem of initiating retirement records for property that had been in service for some time. The usual solution was to conduct a physical inventory so that, with the examination of records and information obtained from accounting and operating personnel, the age of the property currently in service could be estimated and recorded. From that point on, exposure and retirement data were kept. Figure 8.8 (see end of chapter) represents a data matrix that is missing data from the first two vintages.

Consider the construction of a survivor curve from the data in the experience band shown in Figure 8.8. Retirement ratios from early placement years are available even though the early history from those placements, indicated by the question marks, is unavailable. But construction of a survivor curve for an early placement band is not possible unless additional data, the fraction surviving from each vintage with missing data, are obtained or estimated. In Account 897, all years before 1968 are missing data. For example, the 1963 vintage is missing data for the age interval 0–

4.5 years. Although the remaining retirement ratios are available, the survivor curve cannot be calculated without additional information. When the percent surviving from the 1963 placement at age 4.5 years is estimated, the remainder of the survivor curve, from 4.5 years on, can be calculated. Many computer programs allow this point to be entered so that the lower portion of the curve can be determined.

TWO ADDITIONAL METHODS

Although the placement band and experience band methods are the primary techniques used by the life analyst to construct life tables, two additional methods are useful. These are called the *individual unit method* and the *multiple original group method*.

Individual Unit Method

The individual unit method is a useful tool for the life analyst. Many of the survivor curves used in developing the Iowa curves were constructed using this method as only retirements were available. The method has an intuitive appeal and is frequently used by field personnel. In addition, it is helpful when attempting to establish a lower bound for the service life.

The individual unit method can be applied to retirements from either a placement or an experience band. When using this method, the first step is to select the band, which may be one or more years, to be analyzed. Table 8.7 (see end of chapter) shows a life table developed from the 1980 placement band using the individual unit method. First column (c) is developed by obtaining the retirements during each age interval from the 1980 placement band. These are summed to obtain the total retirements. Here the total retirements from the 1980 placement band, which includes experience from 1980 through 1990, are $218.00. The $218.00 is assumed to represent 100% of the initial installations, and the figure is entered in row one of column (b). Find the cumulative retirements at the beginning of the next age interval by subtracting the retirements during the previous interval from the cumulative retirements at the start of the interval. The cumulative retirements act as a surrogate for the plant in service. Retirement ratios, shown in column (d), are the retirements during the interval divided by the cumulative retirements (i.e., the exposures) at the start of the interval. The percent surviving, shown in column (f), is the cumulative retirements at the start of the interval divided by the sum of the retirements. Because the sum of the retirements is used to represent the initial installations, the survivor curve created using the individual unit method always ends at zero percent surviving.

Contrast the life table obtained using the 1980 placement band and the placement band method, shown in Table 8.8 (see end of chapter), with the life table just discussed. Table 8.8 shows 200/418 or 47.85% of plant still in service at the end of 1990. In both tables the average age of retirements is 6.5 years, but the placement band method clearly shows that almost 50% of the original units are still in service. Because the individual unit method ignores the future retirement of plant that is still in service, the average age of retirements of 6.5 years can be considered a lower bound of the service life. As a placement band matures, the life tables obtained using the individual unit method and the placement band method become more alike. Table 8.3 is the life table from the 1968 placement band and was developed using the placement band method. For this placement year, 146 units were initially installed and the retirement of the final unit was made in 1988; this is reflected by the fact that 0% are surviving at the beginning of age interval 20.5–21.5, which is on January 1, 1989. Compare this with the life table in Table 8.9 (see end of chapter), which was constructed using the 1968 placement band and the individual unit method. Because all units are retired, the sum of the retirements equals 146, the number of installations during 1968, so the two life tables are identical.

As mentioned earlier, the data in Account 897 include only original installations and regular retirements. Because the individual unit method considers only retirements, while the placement band method is based on the ratio of retirements/exposures, the life tables from the two methods will converge as the placement band matures, but, contrary to the example in the preceding paragraph, the columns containing the percent surviving will be similar but not identical. The larger the magnitude of transfers, sales, and other transactions, the more significant the difference.

Be careful when interpreting the survivor curve that results from application of the individual unit method to an experience band. The number of retirements depends on both the retirement ratio and the magnitude of original installations. With a placement band the number of original installations remains constant, but with an experience band the original installations change with each age interval. The life table resulting from the application of the individual unit method can be significantly affected by factors such as growth in the account.

If the placement band is wider than one year, the retirements during the final age intervals come from a reduced number of placement years. As with the placement and experience band methods, this results in the final points on the survivor curve being different, because they come from fewer placement years than the earlier points.

Multiple Original Group Method

The multiple original group method uses data from the entire data matrix with each placement year contributing one point to the survivor curve. The percent surviving from the most recent placement supplies the percent surviving at the 0.5 years, the second most recent supplies the percent surviving at age 1.5 years, and so on. Table 8.10 (see end of chapter) is the life table developed using the multiple original group method and a placement band of 1968–1990. Because 1968 is the earliest year for which the initial installations are known, the span from 1968 to 1990 will provide the longest possible survivor curve. Column (a) denotes the placement year used to construct all information contained on that line. For example, the 1984 placement year corresponds to the age interval 7.5–8.5 years; of the $420 originally installed during 1984, $380 or 380/420 × 100% or 90.48% remain in service.

A peculiarity of this method is that because each point is independent of all others, the percent surviving can increase from one year to the next, and this happens several times in Table 8.10.

The survivor curve resulting from the multiple original group method represents a group of hypothetical property. Each placement year has equal weight despite the magnitude of the original installations.

Because the survivor curve is developed using only the original installations and plant surviving at the date of the study for each placement, knowledge of the annual retirements during the intervening years is not necessary. This is important because under these circumstances the multiple original group method could represent the only method of constructing a life table. Comparison of a survivor curve constructed by this method to a specific Iowa curve may allow the analyst to draw conclusions that recent or older placements appear to match or deviate from the pattern indicated by the Iowa curve. These observations would help the analyst draw inferences about the changing characteristics of a group of property from a single life table.

NOTE

1. *Retirement rate method* is a term often used to describe both the placement and experience band methods. If this terminology is used, the placement and experience band methods are subgroups of the retirement rate method.

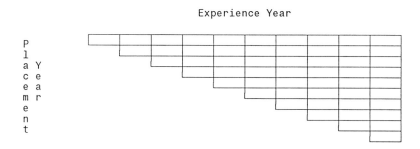

Figure 8.1. The simplified retirement ratio matrix.

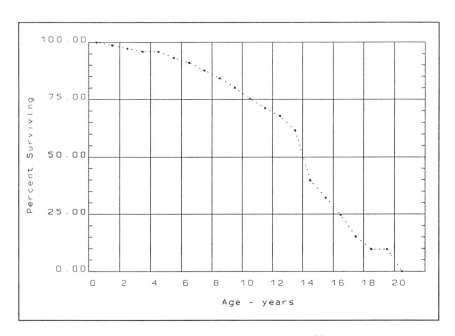

Figure 8.2. A graph of the survivor curve shown in Table 8.3.

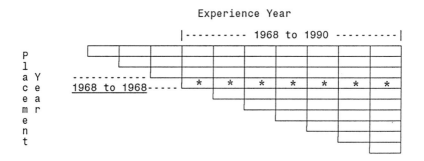

Figure 8.3. The retirement ratios for the 1968 placement band.

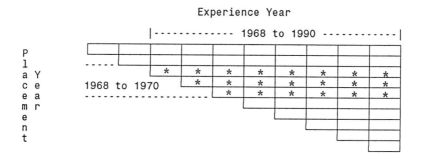

Figure 8.4. The retirement ratios for the 1968–1970 placement band.

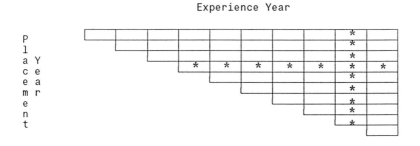

Figure 8.5. One-year placement band contrasted with a one-year experience band.

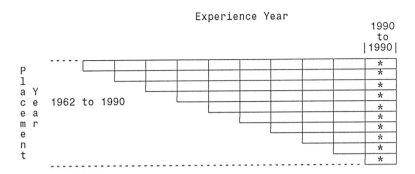

Figure 8.6.   The retiement ratios for the 1990 experience band.

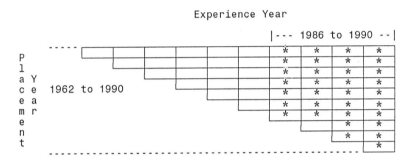

Figure 8.7.   Retirement ratios for the 1986–1990 experience band.

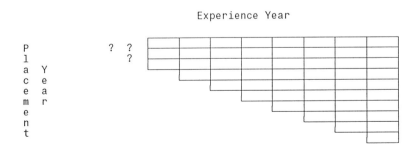

Figure 8.8.   An incomplete actuarial data matrix.

Table 8.1. Plant retired during the calendar year for Account 897.

Account 897 - Utility Devices

Plant Retired during the Calendar Year

Calendar Year → Year installed	68	69	70	71	72	73	74	75	76	77	78	79	80	81	82	83	84	85	86	87	88	89	90
1962	8	6	11	2	7	9	13	2	0	0	0	5	0	0	0	0	0	0	0	0	0	0	0
1963	0	4	14	6	12	8	17	12	16	22	5	9	7	6	5	5	6	0	0	0	0	0	0
1964	3	2	4	7	4	8	9	23	51	44	30	3	8	8	0	0	0	0	0	0	0	0	0
1965	0	6	0	13	8	10	9	5	4	0	5	7	4	24	8	5	0	19	6	13	0	0	15
1966	7	8	7	11	22	12	16	32	18	2	38	6	6	43	4	2	3	9	0	0	0	0	0
1967	0	2	4	15	13	37	13	17	19	9	7	24	5	24	8	15	10	14	8	0	14	0	0
1968	0	2	2	2	0	4	3	5	5	6	7	6	5	9	32	11	11	0	0	0	0	4	0
1969		0	0	1	0	0	0	0	2	0	29	0	17	0	0	0	13	3	6	4	0	20	3
1970			0	1	1	7	3	3	3	8	5	6	8	7	4	6	5	0	17	8	15	8	12
1971				0	4	3	9	5	6	9	10	11	7	14	2	10	10	12	7	31	0	0	12
1972					5	2	5	10	11	23	28	18	19	25	10	44	9	51	21	7	0	10	11
1973						8	0	0	0	8	37	19	14	9	43	22	20	6	3	4	9	8	5
1974							0	1	3	0	2	8	6	7	11	11	7	10	6	25	8	13	0
1975								0	0	15	7	0	5	6	26	24	16	20	54	63	20	20	12
1976									0	8	7	37	33	61	21	86	26	80	53	26	55	20	0
1977										8	0	0	4	3	7	12	11	32	23	39	25	25	0
1978											0	4	0	8	0	16	0	85	19	38	30	29	13
1979												0	0	0	0	7	20	3	6	10	34	11	6
1980													3	0	0	4	4	0	6	6	9	10	0
1981														6	0	2	0	2	4	2	2	8	10
1982															5	5	0	0	0	5	7	35	1
1983																0	0	10	4	0	0	15	0
1984																	0	3	4	8	0	8	0
1985																		0	0	0	0	6	2
1986																			0	0	8	0	0
1987																				0	0	8	0
1988																					0	6	0
1989																						0	2
1990																							0

Table 8.2. Plant remaining in service at the beginning of the calendar year.

Account 897 - Utility Devices

Plant Remaining in Service at Beginning of Year

Calendar Year → / Year installed ↓	(installed)	68	69	70	71	72	73	74	75	76	77	78	79	80	81	82	83	84	85	86	87	88	89	90	91
1962		63	55	49	38	36	29	20	7	5	5	5	5	0	0	0	0	0	0	0	0	0	0	0	0
1963		154	154	150	136	130	118	110	93	81	65	43	38	29	22	16	11	6	0	0	0	0	0	0	0
1964		204	201	199	195	188	184	176	167	144	93	49	19	16	8	0	0	0	0	0	0	0	0	0	0
1965		108	108	102	102	89	81	71	62	57	53	53	48	41	37	13	5	0	0	0	0	0	0	0	0
1966		305	298	290	283	272	250	238	222	190	172	170	132	126	120	77	73	71	68	49	43	30	30	30	15
1967		231	231	229	225	210	197	160	147	130	111	102	95	71	66	42	34	19	9	0	0	0	0	0	0
1968	146		146	144	142	140	140	136	133	128	123	117	110	104	99	90	58	47	36	22	14	14	8	0	0
1969	80			80	80	69	69	69	69	69	67	67	38	38	21	21	21	21	8	8	8	8	8	8	5
1970	120				120	119	118	111	108	105	102	94	89	83	75	68	64	58	53	50	44	40	40	36	24
1971	222					222	218	215	206	201	195	186	176	165	158	144	142	132	122	122	105	80	65	45	45
1972	364						359	357	352	342	331	308	280	262	243	218	208	164	155	143	143	135	125	117	105
1973	382							374	374	374	374	366	329	310	296	287	244	222	202	151	130	99	99	99	88
1974	115								115	114	111	103	101	93	87	80	69	58	51	45	42	35	26	16	11
1975	207									207	207	207	207	207	202	196	170	146	130	130	114	110	102	94	94
1976	710										710	695	688	651	618	557	536	450	424	404	350	325	305	292	280
1977	368											360	360	360	356	353	346	334	323	303	250	187	132	112	112
1978	392												392	388	388	380	380	364	364	284	261	235	210	190	190
1979	725													725	725	725	718	698	698	666	647	608	578	553	540
1980	418														415	415	415	411	411	326	307	269	235	206	200
1981	189															183	183	181	177	174	168	158	149	138	138
1982	420																415	410	410	410	404	402	400	390	380
1983	322																	322	322	320	316	311	304	296	295
1984	375																		375	375	375	375	375	340	340
1985	512																			502	498	490	480	465	465
1986	224																				220	220	220	220	220
1987	148																					148	148	140	138
1988	444																						436	430	430
1989	580																							580	580
1990	90																								90

Table 8.3. The life table for the 1968 placement band.

Account 897 - Utility Devices
Actuarial Band Analysis

Placement band 1968 - 1968   Experience band 1968 - 1990

Age at begin of interval (a)	Exposures at begin of age interval (b)	Retmt during age interval (c)	Retmt ratio (d)	Surv ratio (e)	Pct surv begin of interval (f)
0	146.00	.00	.0000	1.0000	100.00
.5	146.00	2.00	.0137	.9863	100.00
1.5	144.00	2.00	.0139	.9861	98.63
2.5	142.00	2.00	.0141	.9859	97.26
3.5	140.00	.00	.0000	1.0000	95.89
4.5	140.00	4.00	.0286	.9714	95.89
5.5	136.00	3.00	.0221	.9779	93.15
6.5	133.00	5.00	.0376	.9624	91.10
7.5	128.00	5.00	.0391	.9609	87.67
8.5	123.00	6.00	.0488	.9512	84.25
9.5	117.00	7.00	.0598	.9402	80.14
10.5	110.00	6.00	.0545	.9455	75.34
11.5	104.00	5.00	.0481	.9519	71.23
12.5	99.00	9.00	.0909	.9091	67.81
13.5	90.00	32.00	.3556	.6444	61.64
14.5	58.00	11.00	.1897	.8103	39.73
15.5	47.00	11.00	.2340	.7660	32.19
16.5	36.00	14.00	.3889	.6111	24.66
17.5	22.00	8.00	.3636	.6364	15.07
18.5	14.00	.00	.0000	1.0000	9.59
19.5	14.00	14.00	1.0000	.0000	9.59
20.5					.00

Table 8.4. The life table for the 1968-1970 placement band.

Account 897 - Utility Devices
Actuarial Band Analysis

Placement band 1968 - 1970   Experience band 1968 - 1990

Age at begin of interval (a)	Exposures at begin of age interval (b)	Retmt during age interval (c)	Retmt ratio (d)	Surv ratio (e)	Pct surv begin of interval (f)
0	346.00	.00	.0000	1.0000	100.00
.5	346.00	3.00	.0087	.9913	100.00
1.5	343.00	14.00	.0408	.9592	99.13
2.5	329.00	9.00	.0274	.9726	95.09
3.5	320.00	3.00	.0094	.9906	92.49
4.5	317.00	7.00	.0221	.9779	91.62
5.5	310.00	6.00	.0194	.9806	89.60
6.5	304.00	15.00	.0493	.9507	87.86
7.5	289.00	10.00	.0346	.9654	83.53
8.5	279.00	41.00	.1470	.8530	80.64
9.5	238.00	15.00	.0630	.9370	68.79
10.5	223.00	30.00	.1345	.8655	64.45
11.5	193.00	9.00	.0466	.9534	55.78
12.5	184.00	15.00	.0815	.9185	53.18
13.5	169.00	37.00	.2189	.7811	48.84
14.5	132.00	27.00	.2045	.7955	38.15
15.5	105.00	17.00	.1619	.8381	30.35
16.5	88.00	18.00	.2045	.7955	25.43
17.5	70.00	8.00	.1143	.8857	20.23
18.5	62.00	4.00	.0645	.9355	17.92
19.5	58.00	26.00	.4483	.5517	16.76
20.5	8.00	3.00	.3750	.6250	9.25
21.5					5.78

Table 8.5. The life table for the 1990 experience band.

Account 897 - Utility Devices
Actuarial Band Analysis

Placement band 1968 - 1990   Experience band 1990 - 1990

Age at begin of interval (a)	Exposures at begin of age interval (b)	Retmt during age interval (c)	Retmt ratio (d)	Surv ratio (e)	Pct surv begin of interval (f)
0	90.00	.00	.0000	1.0000	100.00
.5	580.00	.00	.0000	1.0000	100.00
1.5	430.00	.00	.0000	1.0000	100.00
2.5	140.00	2.00	.0143	.9857	100.00
3.5	220.00	.00	.0000	1.0000	98.57
4.5	465.00	.00	.0000	1.0000	98.57
5.5	340.00	.00	.0000	1.0000	98.57
6.5	296.00	1.00	.0034	.9966	98.57
7.5	390.00	10.00	.0256	.9744	98.24
8.5	138.00	.00	.0000	1.0000	95.72
9.5	206.00	6.00	.0291	.9709	95.72
10.5	553.00	13.00	.0235	.9765	92.93
11.5	190.00	.00	.0000	1.0000	90.75
12.5	112.00	.00	.0000	1.0000	90.75
13.5	292.00	12.00	.0411	.9589	90.75
14.5	94.00	.00	.0000	1.0000	87.02
15.5	16.00	5.00	.3125	.6875	87.02
16.5	99.00	11.00	.1111	.8889	59.82
17.5	117.00	12.00	.1026	.8974	53.18
18.5	45.00	.00	.0000	1.0000	47.72
19.5	36.00	12.00	.3333	.6667	47.72
20.5	8.00	3.00	.3750	.6250	31.82
21.5					19.88

Table 8.6. The life table for the 1986-1990 experience band.

Account 897 - Utility Devices
Actuarial Band Analysis

Placement band 1968 - 1990   Experience band 1986 - 1990

Age at begin of interval (a)	Exposures at begin of age interval (b)	Retmt during age interval (c)	Retmt ratio (d)	Surv ratio (e)	Pct surv begin of interval (f)
0	1486.00	12.00	.0081	.9919	100.00
.5	1886.00	10.00	.0053	.9947	99.19
1.5	1671.00	16.00	.0096	.9904	98.67
2.5	1545.00	16.00	.0104	.9896	97.72
3.5	1801.00	26.00	.0144	.9856	96.71
4.5	1729.00	50.00	.0289	.9711	95.31
5.5	1540.00	39.00	.0253	.9747	92.56
6.5	1827.00	77.00	.0421	.9579	90.21
7.5	1739.00	117.00	.0673	.9327	86.41
8.5	1545.00	138.00	.0893	.9107	80.60
9.5	1673.00	173.00	.1034	.8966	73.40
10.5	1420.00	119.00	.0838	.9162	65.81
11.5	806.00	47.00	.0583	.9417	60.29
12.5	720.00	49.00	.0681	.9319	56.78
13.5	702.00	60.00	.0855	.9145	52.91
14.5	484.00	35.00	.0723	.9277	48.39
15.5	405.00	46.00	.1136	.8864	44.89
16.5	356.00	38.00	.1067	.8933	39.79
17.5	252.00	40.00	.1587	.8413	35.55
18.5	107.00	4.00	.0374	.9626	29.90
19.5	58.00	26.00	.4483	.5517	28.79
20.5	8.00	3.00	.3750	.6250	15.88
21.5					9.93

198

Table 8.7. The life table for the 1980 placement band developed using the individual unit method.

Account 897 - Utility Devices
Individual Unit Analysis

Placement band 1980 - 1980   Experience band 1980 - 1990

Age at begin of interval (a)	Exposures at begin of age interval (b)	Retmt during age interval (c)	Retmt ratio (d)	Surv ratio (e)	Pct surv begin of interval (f)
0	218.00	3.00	.0138	.9862	100.00
.5	215.00	.00	.0000	1.0000	98.62
1.5	215.00	.00	.0000	1.0000	98.62
2.5	215.00	4.00	.0186	.9814	98.62
3.5	211.00	.00	.0000	1.0000	96.79
4.5	211.00	85.00	.4028	.5972	96.79
5.5	126.00	19.00	.1508	.8492	57.80
6.5	107.00	38.00	.3551	.6449	49.08
7.5	69.00	34.00	.4928	.5072	31.65
8.5	35.00	29.00	.8286	.1714	16.06
9.5	6.00	6.00	1.0000	.0000	2.75
10.5					.00

Table 8.8. The life table for the 1980 placement band developed using the placement band method.

Account 897 - Utility Devices
Actuarial Band Analysis

Placement band 1980 - 1980   Experience band 1980 - 1990

Age at begin of interval (a)	Exposures at begin of age interval (b)	Retmt during age interval (c)	Retmt ratio (d)	Surv ratio (e)	Pct surv begin of interval (f)
0	418.00	3.00	.0072	.9928	100.00
.5	415.00	.00	.0000	1.0000	99.28
1.5	415.00	.00	.0000	1.0000	99.28
2.5	415.00	4.00	.0096	.9904	99.28
3.5	411.00	.00	.0000	1.0000	98.33
4.5	411.00	85.00	.2068	.7932	98.33
5.5	326.00	19.00	.0583	.9417	77.99
6.5	307.00	38.00	.1238	.8762	73.44
7.5	269.00	34.00	.1264	.8736	64.35
8.5	235.00	29.00	.1234	.8766	56.22
9.5	206.00	6.00	.0291	.9709	49.28
10.5					47.85

Table 8.9. The life table for the 1968 placement band developed using the individual unit method.

Account 897 - Utility Devices
Individual Unit Analysis

Placement band 1968 - 1968   Experience band 1968 - 1990

Age at begin of interval (a)	Exposures at begin of age interval (b)	Retmt during age interval (c)	Retmt ratio (d)	Surv ratio (e)	Pct surv begin of interval (f)
0	146.00	.00	.0000	1.0000	100.00
.5	146.00	2.00	.0137	.9863	100.00
1.5	144.00	2.00	.0139	.9861	98.63
2.5	142.00	2.00	.0141	.9859	97.26
3.5	140.00	.00	.0000	1.0000	95.89
4.5	140.00	4.00	.0286	.9714	95.89
5.5	136.00	3.00	.0221	.9779	93.15
6.5	133.00	5.00	.0376	.9624	91.10
7.5	128.00	5.00	.0391	.9609	87.67
8.5	123.00	6.00	.0488	.9512	84.25
9.5	117.00	7.00	.0598	.9402	80.14
10.5	110.00	6.00	.0545	.9455	75.34
11.5	104.00	5.00	.0481	.9519	71.23
12.5	99.00	9.00	.0909	.9091	67.81
13.5	90.00	32.00	.3556	.6444	61.64
14.5	58.00	11.00	.1897	.8103	39.73
15.5	47.00	11.00	.2340	.7660	32.19
16.5	36.00	14.00	.3889	.6111	24.66
17.5	22.00	8.00	.3636	.6364	15.07
18.5	14.00	.00	.0000	1.0000	9.59
19.5	14.00	14.00	1.0000	.0000	9.59
20.5					.00

Table 8.10. The life table using the multiple original group method.

Account 897 - Utility Devices

Multiple Original Group Analysis
Placement Band 1968 - 1990

Place-ment year (a)	Age 12/31/74 (b)	Placement during yr dollars (c)	Survivors dollars (d)	Survivors 12/31/74 percent (e)
1990	.5	90	90.00	100.00
1989	1.5	580	580.00	100.00
1988	2.5	444	430.00	96.85
1987	3.5	148	138.00	93.24
1986	4.5	224	220.00	98.21
1985	5.5	512	465.00	90.82
1984	6.5	375	340.00	90.67
1983	7.5	322	295.00	91.61
1982	8.5	420	380.00	90.48
1981	9.5	189	138.00	73.02
1980	10.5	418	200.00	47.85
1979	11.5	725	540.00	74.48
1978	12.5	392	190.00	48.47
1977	13.5	368	112.00	30.43
1976	14.5	710	280.00	39.44
1975	15.5	207	94.00	45.41
1974	16.5	115	11.00	9.56
1973	17.5	382	88.00	23.04
1972	18.5	364	105.00	28.85
1971	19.5	222	45.00	20.27
1970	20.5	120	24.00	20.00
1969	21.5	80	5.00	6.25
1968	22.5	146	.00	.00

9 | Renewals

R*ENEWALS* are the annual additions required to "renew" a continuous property group[1] so that the plant in service remains constant from one year to the next. Thus, the annual additions (i.e., the renewals) must equal the annual retirements from the previous year. An understanding of the characteristics of such a continuous property group can provide insight into the characteristics of continuous property groups with other patterns of growth.

A continuous property group with a constant balance will be created to illustrate renewal characteristics. Assume all renewals have the same life characteristics as the initial installations. The life characteristics are such that of a group of additions, 60% survive exactly 1 year, 30% survive exactly 2 years, and 10% survive exactly 3 years. Their average life is $(1 \times 0.6) + (2 \times 0.3) + (3 \times 0.1)$ or 1.5 years. Call this curve 1. Start the account by installing 1000 units, as shown in column (b) of Table 9.1 (see end of chapter). The row for year 1 contains the initial 1000-unit balance and shows, in columns (c), (d), and (e), that 600 of the units will be retired at the end of the first year, 300 at the end of the second year, and 100 at the end of the third year. Renewals at the start of the second year equal the 600 retirements at the end of the first year and are shown as the total of column (c). Of these 600 renewals, 60% or 360 will be retired at the end of the second calendar year, 30% or 180 at the end of the third calendar year, and 10% or 60 at the end of the fourth calendar year. These figures are shown in the second row under columns (d), (e), and (f). To find the renewals at the start of the third year, sum the retirements at the end of the second year, as shown in column (d). These include the 300 retirements from the initial

200

1000 units installed and the 360 retirements from the 600 first-year renewals, for a total of 660 units retired at the end of the second year. Thus,
660 additions are required at the start of the third year to maintain the
1000-unit balance. By the end of the third year, retirements are generated
from all previous additions and include the final 100 units from the initial
1000 units installed, 180 units from the first-year renewals, and 396 units
from second-year renewals. These retirements are shown in column (e) and
account for the 676 renewals at the start of the fourth year. These calculations are repeated for the following years, and the pattern of retirements
eventually stabilizes at 667 units each year.

The average age of the annual retirements is shown in the bottom row
of Table 9.1. The retirements at the end of the first year are all 1 year old.
At the end of the second year, 300 of the retirements are 2 years old, and
360 are 1 year old. Their average age is $[(360 \times 1) + (300 \times 2)]/660$ or
1.45 years. At the end of the third year, 100, 180, and 396 units are retired
at ages 3, 2, and 1 years respectively, so their average age is $[(100 \times 3) +
(180 \times 2) + (396 \times 1)]/676$ or 1.56 years.

Look at the pattern of annual renewals. Starting at 600, renewals increase to 676, decrease to 664, and finally stabilize at 667. Renewals follow
a dampened, cyclic pattern regardless of the shape of the survivor curve,
and other statistics (i.e., the average age of retirements and the average age
of the plant in service) follow a similar pattern. Renewals stabilize at an
amount equal to the balance/average life or, in our example, 1000/1.5 or
667 units. The turnover method of life estimation is based on this fact.
Notice the average age of retirements stabilizes at the average life, or 1.5
years. The age distribution of the retirements stabilizes at 400 retired at age
1, 200 at age 2, and 67 at age 3. Taken as a fraction of the total 667
renewals, these retirements are 400/667 or 60%, 200/667 or 30%, and 67/
667 or 10%, which are the retirement frequencies of curve 1. The age
distribution of the annual retirements always stabilizes at that of the original survivor curve. In this example, the renewals stabilized after 6 years or
two life cycles, where a life cycle is the time from age zero until the maximum life of a unit.

Table 9.2 (see end of chapter) shows the distribution of the plant in
service. The average age of the plant in service at the end of the year is
shown in the bottom row. At the end of the first year, 400 of the initial 1000
units remain in service, as shown in the column (c). Their age is now 1 year,
and this is the average age shown in the bottom row. The age distribution at
the end of the second year is shown in column (d). There are 100 units from
the original 1000 additions, and their age is 2 years and 240 units from the
first year renewals, and their age is 1 year. The average age of the balance of
the plant in service is $[(100 \times 2) + (240 \times 1)]/340$ or 1.29 years. When the
plant in service stabilizes at 333 units, 267 units have an age of 1 and 67

units an age of 2, so the average age is 1.2 years. Winfrey (1935) called this the *normal age*. You may have expected the age to stabilize at 1.5 years, but the average age of the stabilized plant (i.e., the normal age) is always less than average life. The end of year balances stabilize at an amount equal to the initial balance times (1 − 1/average life), or 1000 × (1 − 1/1.5) or 333 units.

Now consider the depreciation[2] of the continuous property group created by the renewals model. First use the straight line, average life rate of 1/1.5 or 66.67%, as shown in Table 9.3 (see end of chapter). The annual accrual is the rate, column (d), times the average balance, column (b), and is shown in column (e). The accumulated provision for depreciation at the start of the year is shown in column (f). Though the accruals are constant, the accumulated depreciation cycles before stabilizing at 67 units. The stabilized end of year balance is 333 units (i.e., 1000 − 667), so the ratio of the accumulated provision for depreciation to the end of year balance is 67/333 or 20%. In Winfrey's time, the accumulated provision for depreciation was called the reserve for depreciation, and the 20% ratio would have been called the reserve ratio. The value of this ratio depends on the shape of the survivor curve.

Now use the equal life group (ELG) procedure, rather than the average life (AL) procedure, for applying the straight line method of allocation. The ELG procedure divides the vintage additions into equal life groups and applies the straight line method of allocation to each ELG. The ELG accrual rate varies with the age of the vintage, so, unlike the AL procedure, the annual accruals follow a dampened cyclic pattern, as shown in Table 9.4 (see end of chapter). Though the ELG accruals must stabilize at an amount equal to the AL accruals, the difference in the accruals before stabilization results in the accumulated depreciation stabilizing at 167, rather than 67, units. The ratio of the stabilized accumulated provision for depreciation to the plant in service (i.e., the reserve ratio) is 167/333 or 50%.

In *Bulletin 155,* Winfrey (1942, 81) observed that "the service life remaining in the group of units comprising a stable property group is exactly 50 percent of the service available in the same units when new." Under stable conditions, Table 9.2 shows the plant in service has 267 units that are 1 year old and 67 units that are 2 years old. Of the 267 units that are 1 year old, 75% or 200 units will provide one additional year of service and the remaining 25% or 67 units will provide 2 years service, for a total of 200 × 1 + 67 × 2 or 334 years service. The 67 units that are 2 years old will provide one additional year of service. The service life *remaining* in the 333 surviving units is 334 + 67 or 401 service years. If these *same units were new,* each of the 267 1-year-old units would have one additional year of service, and each of the 67 2-year-old units would have two additional years of service. The total years of additional service is 267 × 1 + 67 × 2 or 401 service years. Thus, when new, the 333 surviving units had 802 service years ahead of them. Notice that their remaining service is 401/802 or 50% of their remaining service when new. This supports Winfrey's observation that in any stable account, *the remaining service of the balance is 50% of the remaining service when the same units were new.*

Winfrey "could think of no reason why the unit summation method [i.e., the ELG procedure] should not be used by public utilities, private industries, for tax purposes and other uses."[3] A major reason he espoused the ELG procedure was that, in a stabilized account, the service to be rendered by the remaining plant in service is 50% of the service when new and, with the ELG procedure, *the accumulated provision for depreciation is 50% of the balance.* The AL procedure results in a system in which the accumulated provision for depreciation stabilizes at less than 50% of the balance.

The length of time, often measured in life cycles, until the renewals stabilize depends on the shape of the survivor curve. Table 9.5 (see end of chapter) shows the renewals for survivor curves called curve 2 and curve 3. Both have 3-year life cycles. The format of this table is similar to that of Table 9.1 except that rows are compressed. For any row, columns (b), (c), and (d) show the retirements at ages 1, 2, and 3 years respectively. Thus, the sum of columns (b), (c), and (d) equal column (a). Read diagonally to find the end of year retirements. The 100 additions at the start of year 2 equal the 100 retirements from year 1 additions. The 310 additions at the start of year 3 equal the 300 retirements from year 1 plus the 10 retirements from year 2. The 661 additions at the start of year 4 equal the 600 retirements from year 1, the 30 retirements from year 2, and the 31 retirements from year 3.

Survivor curve 2, on the left, is the opposite of the earlier example; the percent retired at the end of years 1, 2, and 3 is 10%, 30%, and 60% respectively, and the average life is 2.5 years. With survivor curve 2, it takes about 28 years, or more than nine life cycles, for the renewals to stabilize. In general, right modal curves (e.g., curve 2) take longer to stabilize than left modal curves (e.g., curve 1). Remember that curve 1 was left modal and stabilized at less than two life cycles. Curve 3, on the righthand side of Table 9.5, is symmetrical. The percent retired at the end of years 1, 2, and 3 is 10%, 80%, and 10% respectively, and the average life is 1.5 years. This curve can be described as having a high mode (i.e., the 80% retired in the second year is larger than the 60% maximum for curves 2 and 3), and renewals stabilize after 29 years. In general, high modal curves take longer to stabilize than lower modal curves.

Winfrey (1967, 41–47) studied the renewal characteristics associated with the Iowa curves.[4] In our example we made the simplifying assumption that all retirements occurred at the end of the year. Winfrey made the more realistic assumption that retirements occurred uniformly during the year. This complicated the calculations, because he then had to account for the renewals of the units retired during the same year they were installed (i.e., renewal of the renewals). To do this, he calculated a "renewal multiplier" that depends on the retirement frequency of the adjacent half-year intervals. Figure 9.1 shows the renewals pattern for three Iowa curves, and the data are taken from Winfrey's (1967, 107–108) calculations. The renewals are measured in 10% intervals of average life, which is the same as 1-year intervals and a 10-year average life.

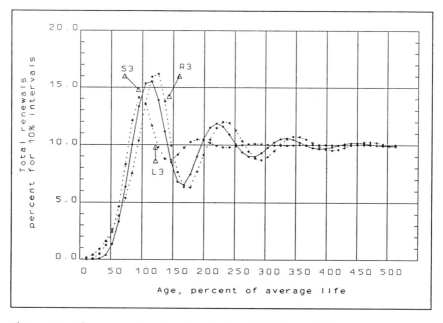

Figure 9.1. The renewal pattern for the Iowa R3, S3, and L3 survivor curves.

The behavior of renewals in a growing account is also of interest. Table 9.6 (see end of chapter) shows an account in which the annual renewals increase at a constant rate. The life characteristics of the renewals are defined by curve 1. Columns (e), (f), and (g) show the retirements at ages 1, 2, and 3, respectively. Column (b) shows the annual retirements from the previous year, which are the diagonal sum of the retirements in columns (e), (f), and (g). The additions, column (c), equal the previous year's retirements plus 10% of the preceding year's balance. Thus the balance, column (d), increases at a constant rate of 10% each year. Column (h) shows the average age of the retirements. The average age stabilizes at 1.46 years, less than the average life of 1.50 years. Note that of the 1170 retirements at the end of year 7, 735 were generated from the 1225 units added at the start of year 7 and have an age of 1 year. This is 735/1170 or 62.8% of the retirements, slightly more than the 60% that would be observed if the process had stabilized and there was no growth. The growing balances result in a stabilized average age of retirements that is *less* than the average life of the vintage.

If a stabilized account has a zero growth rate, then the ratio of the balance over either the additions or the retirements equals the average life. In an actual account, this ratio may provide a useful estimate of the average life. The average life estimator changes when the growth rate is not zero. Column (i) shows the balance at the start of the year divided by the retirements at the end of the year, and the ratio stabilizes at 1.51 years, slightly more than the average life. The ratio of the balance at the start of the year to the additions at the start of the year is shown in column (j). When there is growth, this ratio stabilizes at less than the average life and is 1.45 years in this example. The square root of the product of these two indicators, i.e., $\sqrt{1.51 \times 1.45}$, is used as an indication of average life, even though it stabilizes at 1.48 years, slightly less than the average life. See Chapter 11 for a discussion of turnover methods, which use these statistics to develop life analysis models.

Table 9.7 (see end of chapter) is reproduced from *Statistical Analysis of Industrial Property Retirements* (Winfrey, 1967, 76) and shows the characteristics of 18 of the Iowa curves. Columns (f) and (g) are of particular interest because they relate to properties of renewals. Our example shows that the higher the mode, the longer until the renewals stabilize. Examine column (f) and note that for each of the three types of curves, the age at which renewals stabilize usually increases as the mode increases (i.e., the R5 type curve has a higher mode and takes longer to stabilize than a R1 type curve). In our examples, the left modal curve stabilized faster than the symmetrical or right modal curves. This is also true of the Iowa curves and can be seen by comparing the values in column (f) for the L2 curve with those for the S2 and R2 curves. We saw that the normal age, column (g), is the average age of the plant in service and is always less than the average life. Table 9.7 shows the normal age decreases as the mode increases.

Tables 9.3 and 9.4 show the accumulated provision for depreciation for a continuous property group using the AL and ELG procedures. When the AL procedure is used, the accumulated provision for depreciation stabilized at 20% of the end of year balance, but with the ELG procedure it stabilized at 50%. Winfrey calculated the stabilized value of the accumulated provision for depreciation (which he called the *normal reserve*) for a continuous property group for each of the 18 Iowa type curves. The calculations are based on a continuous property group with a constant balance of 100,000 units and an average service life of 10 years. The results for the AL procedure (Winfrey, 1942, 78) are shown in Table 9.8 (see end of chapter). The stabilized value of the accumulated provision for depreciation for the ELG procedure is 50,000 units regardless of the survivor curve.

The depreciation of mass property usually involves a continuous property group. Actual continuous property groups can be expected to differ from the theoretical continuous property group created to study the behavior of renewals. An actual group can be expected to have dynamic rather than constant life characteristics, and the growth from year to year will tend to be erratic rather than zero or constant. Nonetheless, the renewals model is often a reasonable representation of an actual continuous property group, and knowledge of the characteristics of renewals will provide insight into the characteristics of a more complex group. This knowledge is valuable when analyzing or forecasting life and salvage, predicting annual retirements, and understanding the difference between the AL and ELG procedures. Actual continuous property groups with a long history may be close to stability. If so, the properties of a stabilized renewals account will help us understand the relationship between the age distribution of retirements and the underlying life characteristics of the continuous property group. Renewals of a newly formed continuous property group will display cyclic properties characteristics that are predictable to those familiar with renewal theory. A final use of renewal theory is that it requires us to examine the difference between the AL and ELG procedures by considering the relationship between the stabilized remaining service and the accumulated provision for depreciation. Generally the difference between the two procedures is approached by examining the accrual rate. Thus, the study of the renewals model is a valuable prelude to the study of both life analysis and of depreciation systems.

Table 9.1.　Calculation of annual renewals for curve 1. Initially 1000 units are installed and the probability of surviving exactly 1, 2, or 3 years is 0.6, 0.3, or 0.1 respectively.

Year (a)	Renewals Jan 1 (b)	1 (c)	2 (d)	3 (e)	4 (f)	5 (g)	6 (h)	7 (i)	8 (j)	9 (k)
			Retirements at the end of the year							
1	1000	600	300	100						
2	600		360	180	60					
3	660			396	198	66				
4	676				406	203	68			
5	664					398	199	66		
6	667						400	200	67	
7	667							400	200	67
8	667								400	200
9	667									400
Total		600	660	676	664	667	667	667	667	667
Avg age of retirements		1.00	1.45	1.56	1.48	1.50	1.50	1.50	1.50	1.50

Table 9.2. Calculation of the average age of plant in service for the property group shown in Table 9.1.

Year (a)	Balance Dec 31 (b)	Plant remaining in service at the end of year								
		1 (c)	2 (d)	3 (e)	4 (f)	5 (g)	6 (h)	7 (i)	8 (j)	9 (k)
1	400	400	100							
2	340		240	60						
3	324			264	66					
4	336				270	68				
5	333					265	66			
6	333						267	67		
7	333							267	67	
8	333								267	67
9	333									267
Total		400	340	324	336	333	333	333	333	333
Avg age of plant		1.00	1.29	1.19	1.20	1.20	1.20	1.20	1.20	1.20

Table 9.3. Calculation of the annual accruals and accumulated depreciation using the SL-AL-AM system. Additions and retirements are shown in Table 9.1.

Year (a)	Balance Jan 1 (b)	Retired (c)	Rate % (d)	Annual accrual (e)	Accum depr Jan 1 (f)
1	1000	600	66.67	667	0
2	1000	660	66.67	667	67
3	1000	676	66.67	667	74
4	1000	664	66.67	667	63
5	1000	667	66.67	667	66
6	1000	667	66.67	667	67
7	1000	667	66.67	667	67
8	1000	667	66.67	667	67
9	1000	667	66.67	667	67

Table 9.4. Calculation of the annual accruals and accumulated depreciation using the SL-ELG-AM system. Additions and retirements are shown in Table 9.1.

Year (a)	Balance Jan 1 (b)	Retired (c)	Rate % (d)	Annual accrual (e)	Accum depr Jan 1 (f)
1	1000	600	78.33	783	0
2	1000	660	65.33	653	183
3	1000	676	66.03	660	177
4	1000	664	67.05	671	161
5	1000	667	66.58	666	168
6	1000	667	66.66	667	167
7	1000	667	66.68	667	167
8	1000	667	66.66	667	167
9	1000	667	66.67	667	167

Table 9.5. Calculation of annual renewals for survivor curves 2 and 3.

	Curve 2					Curve 3			
Age at retirement	1	2	3		Age at retirement	1	2	3	
Probability	10%	30%	60%		Probability	10%	80%	10%	
Yr	Additions	Retirements				Additions	Retirements		
	(a)	(b)	(c)	(d)		(a)	(b)	(c)	(d)
1	1000	100	300	600		1000	100	800	100
2	100	10	30	60		100	10	80	10
3	310	31	93	186		810	81	648	81
4	661	66	198	397		261	26	209	26
5	219	22	66	131		684	68	547	68
6	406	41	122	244		358	36	287	36
7	503	50	151	302		609	61	487	61
8	304	30	91	182		416	42	333	42
9	425	42	127	255		565	56	452	56
10	435	44	131	261		450	45	360	45
11	353	35	106	212		538	54	431	54
20	397	40	119	238		496	50	397	50
21	404	40	121	242		503	50	402	50
22	399	40	120	239		498	50	398	50
23	399	40	120	239		502	50	401	50
24	402	40	120	241		499	50	399	50
25	399	40	120	239		501	50	401	50
26	400	40	120	240		499	50	399	50
27	401	40	120	240		501	50	400	50
28	399	40	120	240		500	50	400	50
29	400	40	120	240		500	50	400	50
30	400	40	120	240		500	50	400	50

Table 9.6. Calculation of annual renewals when the beginning-of-year balance increases by 10% each year. The probability of survival for exactly 1, 2, or 3 years is 0.60, 0.30, or 0.10 respectively (i.e., curve 1).

Year (a)	Retired (b)	Added (c)	Balance (d)	Retired at age 1 (e)	2 (f)	3 (g)	Average age of retirement (h)	d/b (i)	d/c (j)	Age estimate* (k)
1		1000	1000	600	300	100	1.00			
2	600	700	1100	420	210	70	1.42	1.67	1.57	1.62
3	720	830	1210	498	249	83	1.51	1.53	1.46	1.49
4	808	929	1331	557	279	93	1.44	1.50	1.43	1.46
5	876	1010	1464	606	303	101	1.46	1.52	1.45	1.48
6	967	1114	1611	668	334	111	1.46	1.51	1.45	1.48
7	1064	1225	1772	735	368	123	1.46	1.51	1.45	1.48
8	1170	1347	1949	808	404	135	1.46	1.51	1.45	1.48
9	1287	1482	2144	889	445	148	1.46	1.51	1.45	1.48
10	1416	1630	2358	978	489	163	1.46	1.51	1.45	1.48
11	1558	1793	2594	1076	538	179	1.46	1.51	1.45	1.48
12	1713	1973	2853	1184	592	197	1.46	1.51	1.45	1.48
13	1885	2170	3138	1302	651	217	1.46	1.51	1.45	1.48
14	2073	2387	3452	1432	716	239	1.46	1.51	1.45	1.48
15	2280	2626	3797	1575	788	263	1.46	1.51	1.45	1.48

* Column (c) = Sqrt[column(i) x column(j)]

Table 9.7. Characteristics of the 18 type curves from <u>Bulletin 125</u> (p. 76, Winfrey, 1967), courtesy of Iowa State University College of Engineering.

| Type curve (a) | Location of mode, percent of average life (b) | Frequency at mode, percent for 10% of average life (c) | Maximum age, percent of average life | | Age, percent of average life at stability* (f) | Normal age, percent of average life (g) |
			Zero frequency ordinate (d)	0.00001 life at ordinate (e)		
L-0	49.40	6.243	445.53	408.50	230.5	69.88
L-1	60.00	7.451	324.18	316.50	210.5	63.65
L-2	78.10	10.204	286.86	282.50	190.5	59.21
L-3	86.90	14.089	240.55	238.55	250.5	55.59
L-4	94.30	20.914	227.19	217.50	520.5	52.79
L-5	97.13	30.308	206.04	191.50	1020.5	51.36
S-0	100.00	6.952	200.00	200.00	330.5	61.16
S-1	100.00	9.080	200.00	199.99	290.5	57.55
S-2	100.00	11.911	200.00	198.75	360.5	54.85
S-3	100.00	15.611	200.00	192.75	490.5	53.02
S-4	100.00	22.329	190.00	175.50	880.5	51.55
S-5	100.00	33.220	180.00	156.50	1820.5	50.74
S-6	100.00	52.473	170.00	139.50	4400.0**	50.32
R-1	118.80	7.838	200.83	200.83	380.5	60.91
R-2	114.03	11.010	185.82	185.21	400.5	56.87
R-3	109.60	15.528	164.51	164.50	520.5	53.89
R-4	106.00	21.823	153.08	152.65	810.5	52.16
R-5	103.75	30.992	137.48	137.30	1490.5	50.94

*   Stability occurs when calculated value is within $\pm$ 0.1 of ordinate
** Estimated

Table 9.8. The stabilized accumulated provision for depreciation for a continuous property group when the AL procedure is used. The continuous property group has a constant balance of 100,000 units and the survivor curve has an average life of 10 years. Results are shown for 18 Iowa type curves. From <u>Bulletin 155</u> (p. 78, Winfrey, 1942), courtesy of Iowa State University College of Engineering.

Curve	Normal reserve	Curve	Normal reserve	Curve	Normal reserve
L-0	30,140	S-0	38,800	R-1	39,160
L-1	36,320	S-1	42,320	R-2	43,140
L-2	40,650	S-2	45,152	R-3	46,130
L-3	44,270	S-3	46,870	R-4	48,000
L-4	47,100	S-4	48,500	R-5	
L-5	48,700	S-5	49,200		
		S-6	49,600		

NOTES

1. See Chapter 6 for a definition of a continuous property group.

2. See Chapter 5 for an explanation of methods of calculating the annual accrual.

3. This quotation is from a letter to W. C. Fitch and is reproduced in *Estimation of Depreciation* (Fitch et al., 1975, 51).

4. Winfrey's calculations can easily be reproduced with an electronic computer. He had none, but carried out calculations by hand, using survivor curves with the percent surviving carried to 10 decimal places.

10 | Pricing Retirements

EACH unit of property removed from service must be assigned a price representing its original cost for inclusion in the continuing property records. This accounting task may appear to be a perfunctory act that has little to do with depreciation. The appearance is deceptive, and the price placed on retirements affects figures found in the major annual financial reports. The system to price retirements should be considered part of the depreciation system, and the choice of a pricing system should be made with full knowledge of the costs and consequences associated with it.

The price placed on a retirement determines the debit entry to the accumulated provision for depreciation account and the credit entry to the plant account. Thus, one consequence of the pricing system is that, because it directly affects the plant balance to which the accrual rate is applied, it affects the annual accrual for depreciation and the net book value of plant in service. A second consequence of the pricing system chosen is that it affects the amount of data collected. The amount of data determines which techniques the depreciation professional can use to analyze life and salvage characteristics. A third consequence is that because the pricing system affects the record of plant in service, it also affects the historical indications of service life and salvage.

A pricing system is often biased in the sense that the price placed on retirements is consistently over or consistently under the actual price. The short-run effect may not be important. But small annual errors in an account can accumulate to create significant long-run errors in the estimate of average life, salvage, and recorded plant in service and, in turn, errors in the estimated rate base and annual accrual for depreciation.

PRICING BASED ON AGED RETIREMENTS

Pricing based on aged retirements requires identification of the age of the unit of property retired and uses historical costs to price the unit. One method is to attach a unique identifying mark (e.g., a serial number) to each unit and record the identifying mark and original cost. Upon retirement, the original cost of the unit can be recovered. Motor vehicles or other large pieces of equipment are priced in this manner. This method requires detailed records but perfectly matches retirement cost with original cost.

Another method of pricing based on age is to attach a mark identifying the year in which the unit was installed. Record the number of units installed during the year and their total original cost, and calculate the average unit cost for the vintage. At retirement, the unit of property is assigned a price equal to the average unit cost for the associated vintage. Though the average unit cost will not exactly match the original cost of the retired unit, the averaging process will ensure that when the final unit in the vintage is retired, the total vintage dollars retired will equal the original cost of the vintage additions. This significantly reduces the amount of information needed. Only the vintage year, not a unique identification, is required, and only the average unit cost for each vintage, not the cost of each unit, need be recorded.

These two methods require acquisition of information that either identifies the unit or the year it was installed. Field personnel removing the unit from service must be trained to report that information. Property such as poles, transformers, and meters can be physically tagged so that the year of installation can be read visually. A bar code identification can be read and recorded electronically. The installation year of property that is difficult to tag physically, such as aerial or underground wire, services, and distribution lines, can be recorded on the maps identifying their location. Digital mapping makes recovery of this information more accurate and less costly.

When discussing the importance of good records, NARUC (1968, 41) noted that "accurate and complete historical data are vital to the proper determination of retirement unit costs and to each factor considered in determining property depreciation rates." Pricing by age is the only method that provides accurately priced retirements and a record of aged retirements.

PRICING BASED ON STATISTICALLY AGED RETIREMENTS

Statistical aging is a term that describes the general process of using a survivor curve to simulate the manner in which additions in one year generate retirements in following years. The term Statistical Aging System

(STAGE) was given to a computer program developed for the Interstate Commerce Commission (1985), and the documentation for that program provides reference material about a comprehensive statistical aging system. STAGE can be used to price retirements and to convert unaged data to statistically aged data.

Unaged data includes the number of units in service at the start of the year and the number of units retired during the year. Statistical aging simulates the ages of the retired units. The simulation requires that *the life characteristics of the retired units be estimated.* The average life of the curve type specified is varied until the simulated retirements during the year equal the actual retirements. The cost of the annual retirements can be calculated from (a) the simulated number of retirements from each vintage and (b) the average unit cost from each vintage. Thus, pricing is based on the *statistically* aged retirements.

If a method of pricing based on unaged retirement data has been used, a computer program such as STAGE can be used to convert unaged data reflecting the annual additions and balances and measured in dollars to (statistically) aged data. Note that in the preceding paragraph, retirements and balances referred to units, while in this paragraph they refer to dollars. Thus, some method of pricing has been used. The record of additions and balances is used to simulate aged retirements. That is, each annual balance is aged. Given a type curve, this can be done by varying the average life and successively aging each vintage balance. Options that allow more than one type survivor curve to be used and that allow the number of retirements in a specific vintage to be assigned are desirable. Though only regular retirements have been mentioned, parallel calculations are made for other transactions such as reimbursed retirements, sales, and transfers. The process of aging unaged data reflecting the additions and retirements measured in dollars is also called *computed mortality* and is discussed in Chapter 12.

PRICING BASED ON UNAGED RETIREMENTS

Several systems of pricing retirements that do not require aging retirements are in widespread use. An advantage of these systems is that they generally require less effort to maintain than systems that require the retired unit to be aged. Their disadvantage is that they provide less information than systems that age retirements. The short-run savings resulting from the reduced effort required by systems that do not require aging are offset by factors that result in long-term, indirect costs that are difficult to estimate. The consequences of the lack of information were discussed at the beginning of this chapter. This section discusses the effects of inflation on pricing and four pricing systems based on unaged retirements.

Inflation and Pricing

If prices remain constant from year to year, any method of pricing yields the same result. However, prices change from year to year. They may rise because of general increases in the price of materials and labor or fall because of increased competition or improved manufacturing methods. Changing technology and improved design can change the physical attributes of property in a functional account, thus changing the characteristics of a unit and the unit price. Unless there is an event that causes a major price shift, prices can often be observed to steadily increase over time.

A simple yet helpful model is to assume that prices increase at a constant annual rate. Inflation is inherent in our economy. The urban consumer price index (CPI-U) is a familiar example of an inflation index, but more specialized indices are available. During the 30-year period 1961 through 1990, the annual CPI-U rate ranged from 0.7% to 13.3%. For 21 of the 30 years, it was between 3% and 9%; the overall annual rate during this 30-year period was 5.1%, though the annualized rate during the 1970s and 1980s was more than 6%. At a 6% annual rate of inflation, prices double every 12 years, and over 30 years prices would increase almost six times. Because of the long life of much of the property used by utilities and the history of a significant positive inflation rate, we can often expect a large difference between the original cost of a retirement and the current cost of its replacement. With our model, a unit price in a base year, and a historical price index appropriate to the property, we can reconstruct prices from previous years, forecast prices in future years, and make generalizations about the results of using different methods of pricing retirements.

FIFO Pricing

FIFO (first in, first out) pricing is based on a method used by accountants to price goods removed from inventory. The retired unit is assumed to be the oldest unit in service. The unit retired is priced using the average cost for the oldest surviving vintage. Three factors influence the variation between the FIFO price and the actual price. One factor is the inflation rate. The closer the rate is to zero, the smaller the variation. A second factor is the shape of the survivor curve. If the survivor curve is square (i.e., the life of each unit is equal to the average life, which is also the maximum life), then the retired unit *is* the oldest unit and FIFO pricing is correct. For any other curve, the average life is less than the maximum life, and the retired unit is probably not the oldest unit. In general, the lower the mode of the survivor curve, the larger the variation associated with FIFO pricing. The third factor is the rate of growth of the account. In Chapter 9, it was shown that the average age of the annual retirements stabilized at the average life when additions equaled retirements. When a property group is growing, the average age of the annual retirements is less than the average life of the property. Thus, the greater the growth in an account, the poorer the assumption that the retirement is the oldest unit. In most cases, the FIFO system will *overestimate* the age and, assuming a *positive* rate of inflation, will *underprice* the retirement. The FIFO pricing variation depends on the combination of the inflation rate, the curve shape, and the growth rate of the account.

LIFO Pricing

LIFO (last in, first out) pricing is similar to the FIFO system except that it assumes the retired unit is the most recent addition. The age of the retirement is *underestimated* so that with a positive inflation rate, LIFO pricing will *overprice* retirements. Factors that affect FIFO pricing also affect LIFO pricing. This method is seldom used to price retirements.

Lag Pricing

Lag pricing requires an estimate of the *average age* of the retirements. The average age of the retirements is the *price lag,* and the retirement is priced by using the unit cost from the vintage associated with the price lag. If the average age of the retirements was estimated to be 12 years, the unit price would be set equal to the average unit cost 12 years ago. When the vintage unit costs are not known, the current price can be deflated over a period equal to the price lag to estimate the original cost. Lag pricing can be refined to account for the shape of the survivor curve and the inflation rate by adjusting the lag period from the average life. The effect of these factors on the lag period is discussed and correction factors are given in a report to NARUC (1946). The accuracy of lag pricing depends on the ability of the depreciation professional to estimate the average age of the retirements. If the lag is overestimated, retirements will be underpriced, and vice versa. Lag pricing is easy to use and, given a reasonable estimate of the lag period, will usually give better estimates of original cost of the retired unit than either FIFO or LIFO.

Cumulative Average Pricing

A common method of pricing unaged retirements is based upon a calculation of the average unit cost of plant in service. Start with the current dollars and units in the account, and use these to calculate the initial average unit cost. During the following year identify the number of units and dollars added to the account. Record the number of units retired and calculate the dollars retired by multiplying the number of retirements by the *current average unit cost*. Then calculate the new end of year balance in units by adding additions to and subtracting retirements from the start of year balance in units. Make the same calculation for the end of year balance in *dollars*. Calculate the new average unit cost by dividing the end of year dollar balance by the end of year unit balance.

Table 10.1 illustrates these calculations. On January 1, 1985, there are 1647 units and $2011.95 in service. The average unit cost at the start of 1985 is $1.2216. During 1985, 322 units costing $527 were placed in service. One hundred and twenty-four units were retired during the year and, priced at $1.2216 each, resulted in a total retirement cost of $151.48. On January 1, 1986, the new balance is the old balance plus additions less retirements. In units, this is 1647 + 322 − 124 or 1845 and in dollars it is $2011.95 + $527.00 − $151.48 or $2387.47. The new average unit cost is $2387.47/ 1845 or $1.2940. The new average can be viewed as a weighted average of the old average and the most recent unit price.

Table 10.1. Calculation of the average price of retirements.

	Start of year balances			Additions		Retirements	
Year (a)	Units (b)	Cost $ (c)	Avg $ (d)	Units (e)	Cost $ (f)	Units (g)	Cost $ (h)
1980	0	.00	1.0000	364	364.00	5	5.00
1981	359	359.00	1.0000	207	223.00	10	10.00
1982	556	572.00	1.0288	368	436.00	43	44.24
1983	881	963.76	1.0939	725	938.00	75	82.05
1984	1531	1819.72	1.1886	189	279.00	73	86.77
1985	1647	2011.95	1.2216	322	527.00	124	151.48
1986	1845	2387.47	1.2940	512	907.00	134	173.40
1987	2223	3121.07	1.4040	224	423.00	253	355.21
1988	2194	3188.86	1.4534	388	802.00	358	520.33
1989	2224	3470.53	1.5605	490	1100.00	316	493.11
1990	2398	4077.42	1.7003				

Unit costs are weighted by the number of additions but not their age. In a growing account and with a positive inflation rate, this average will tend to *underestimate* the retirement cost. As with FIFO pricing, the variation depends on the inflation rate, the shape of the survivor curve, and the growth of the account.

Summary

Pricing systems can be divided into those that require the retired unit to be aged and those that do not. A generalization is that though pricing systems based on the age of the retirement require more effort, they provide more information than systems that do not require the age of the retirement. The amount of extra effort required to age retirements depends on the type of property in the account and the specific procedures and activities used to recover the age. Thus, the added cost of aging retirements depends on the physical characteristics of the property and the efficiency of the record-keeping system used to recover the age of the retirement. The difference between the price established using a system not based on age and the actual price (i.e., a price based on age) is a complicated interaction of the pricing system, the rate at which the price inflates, the shape of the survivor curve, and the rate of growth of the account. Finally, the importance of the difference between the two types of systems (i.e., the accuracy of the system) depends on factors that include the amount of the difference in the price of the retirement, the additional cost of aging the retirements, the relative dollar value of the account, and the importance management places on estimates of depreciation. The error associated with pricing retirements is often cumulative. Though the immediate effect may be small, over time the cumulative error can become large, and the effort required to evaluate and correct it can be time-consuming and expensive.

11 | Analysis of Unaged Data

RETIREMENT data reflecting the amount of property in service can be either aged or unaged. When aged retirement data are available, actuarial methods can be used to develop life tables. When only unaged retirement data are available, other methods must be used to analyze the historical life characteristics of the property. This chapter will describe these methods.

Figure 11.1 is a graphical representation of the information contained in unaged data. The rows represent placement years (the terms placement and vintage can be used interchangeably) and the columns experience years. The A values (i.e., A1, A2, etc.) represent the annual additions or the original amount of each vintage installation. The B values (i.e., B1, B2, etc.) represent the total plant in service at the beginning of each year. The total plant in service at the start of year 5 is the sum of the remaining plant in service from the installations during years 1 through 4. Fifth-year additions are assumed to be installed at midyear and do not affect the balance at the start of that year. In contrast with aged data, the interior elements of the unaged data matrix are unknown. Though the total plant in service at the start of each year is known, its distribution by placement year (i.e., its age distribution) is unknown. An age distribution is derived by associating each unit of the total plant in service with a specific placement year.

The depreciation professional faces two new problems when required to use unaged, rather than aged, data. The problems result because unaged data contain less information than aged data. One problem is that life analysis becomes more difficult because actuarial methods cannot be used to develop life tables. Other methods of analysis must be used, and because

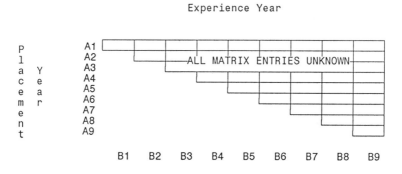

Figure 11.1. The simplified retirement ratio matrix for unaged data.

unaged data contain less information than aged data, those methods will provide less information about the historical life characteristics of the property. This, in turn, makes forecasting life more difficult. The second problem is that the age distribution of the plant in service is unknown. To apply any depreciation system, the total plant in service must be aged[1]. This requires that the age distribution be estimated so that depreciation calculations can be made.

This chapter will describe methods of analysis, including several turnover methods and the simulated plant record (SPR) method.

TURNOVER METHODS

Before the 1950s, turnover methods were the predominate means of analysis used to provide indications of service life when only unaged data were available. These methods have been replaced by the SPR method and are now of primarily historical interest, so we will discuss them only briefly.

Four turnover methods that were in common use include the turnover period method, the half-cycle ratio method, the asymptotic method, and the geometric mean method. Both the National Association of Railroad and Utilities Commissioner's Report (1943) and *Methods of Estimating Utility Plant Life* by the Edison Electric Institute (1952) provide detailed descriptions of these methods. Either is a good reference if you want more information about turnover methods.

Turnover methods are based on the renewals concept. Start with any initial balance of newly installed property. Each year "renew" the property group by replacing all retirements with property having identical life characteristics. Because additions equal retirements, the balance will remain constant. Over time, the renewals (i.e., the annual additions) will stabilize at an amount equal to the balance divided by the average life. A summary of characteristics of renewals is presented in Chapter 9.

The turnover period method calculates the time to "turn over" the balance. One way to do this is to select a starting year and sum the retirements backward. Find the year when the cumulative retirements equal the balance. The time between the starting year and the year the cumulative retirements equal the balance is the turnover period. During this period, the total retirements equal the initial balance, so the balance has "turned over." Remember that in the renewals model the annual retirements stabilize at an amount equal to the balance/average age, so that during a period equal to the average life, the total renewals will equal the balance.

Two hypothetical groups of property, Accounts 900 and 800, will be used to illustrate turnover methods. Table 11.1 shows unaged data for Account 900. The balance is constant at 15000 and the annual renewals are about 1500. Column (e) sums the retirements backward from 1990. After summing backward 10 years, the cumulative retirements (15070) are about equal to the 1980 end of year balance (15000). The 10-year turnover period is an indication of the historical life. Other calendar years could be used to find the turnover period. For example, the summation could start at the end of 1988 rather than 1990. Examination of the Account 900 data shows the turnover period will be about 10 years for any starting point.

Notice that if the renewals have stabilized, an indication of the average life is the balance/annual renewals. For 1990 this would be 15000/1560 or 9.6 years. Statistics based on a single year tend to be erratic, and the turnover period method provides a more consistent indication by including many years' retirements in the calculation.

Table 11.1.   Unaged data from Account 900. The reverse cumulated retirements shown in column (e) show the turnover period to be 10 years.

Year (a)	Additions during year (b)	Retirements during year (c)	End of year balance (d)	Reverse cumulative retirements (e)
1978	1500	1500	15000	
1979	1490	1490	15000	
1980	1510	1510	15000	15070
1981	1510	1510	15000	13560
1982	1480	1480	15000	12080
1983	1530	1530	15000	10550
1984	1530	1530	15000	9020
1985	1480	1480	15000	7540
1986	1490	1490	15000	6050
1987	1520	1520	15000	4530
1988	1500	1500	15000	3030
1989	1470	1470	15000	1560
1990	1560	1560	15000	0

Now examine Table 11.2, which is data for Account 800. The unadjusted turnover period, calculated by summing retirements backward from 1990, is 9.7 years. Note that this account shows growth from one year to the next, and this violates the assumption that the balance remains constant. However, the turnover period can be adjusted to compensate for the growth. From figures[2] not reproduced here, an adjustment factor can be obtained for each type Iowa curve as a function of the growth ratio. The growth ratio is the balance at the start of the turnover period divided by the balance at the end of the period, or 12935/7697 or 1.7. The adjustment factor for an Iowa R3 type curve and a growth ratio of 1.7 is about 1.05, so the indicated life is 9.7 × 1.05 or 10.2 years.

Table 11.2. Unaged data for Account 800. The reverse cumulated retirements shown in column (e) show the turnover period to be 9.7 years.

Year (a)	Additions during year (b)	Retirements during year (c)	End of year balance (d)	Reverse cumulative retirements (e)
1971	600	6	594	
1972	656	13	1237	
1973	711	14	1934	
1974	745	33	2646	
1975	799	41	3404	
1976	861	56	4209	
1977	903	84	5028	
1978	956	114	5870	
1979	1011	201	6680	
1980	1065	264	7481	7798
1981	1111	391	8201	7407
1982	1143	485	8859	6922
1983	1196	621	9434	6301
1984	1234	705	9963	5596
1985	1288	797	10454	4799
1986	1343˙	859	10938	3940
1987	1397	909	11426	3031
1988	1457	960	11923	2071
1989	1522	1011	12434	1060
1990	1561	1060	12935	0

The half-cycle method is a variation of the turnover period method. Instead of requiring a full turnover period equal to the average life, a half-cycle (i.e., a period equal to one-half the average life) is estimated. Adjustment for the type curve and growth are the same as for the turnover period method.

The asymptotic and geometric mean methods do not require an adjustment for the type curve. In Account 800 there are 1561 additions and 1060 retirements during 1990, and the average balance during 1990 is 12683. An indication of the life based on additions is 12683/1561 or 8.1 years, while an indication based on the retirements is 12683/1060 or 12.0 years. If the renewals have stabilized and the growth rate is constant, then the average life is the square root of the product of the two statistics. Here that indication is $\sqrt{8.1 \times 12.0}$ or 9.9 years. The asymptotic method does not assume stability but uses statistical methods to smooth the data and provide an indication of the life at stability. The geometric mean assumes stability and provides an indication of the life as shown above (i.e., 9.9 years).

The turnover methods have two weaknesses. First, they provide an indication of average life but not curve type. Second, they require either a constant balance or a balance that increases at a constant rate each year. The SPR method, discussed next, does everything the turnover methods do, and more.

SIMULATED PLANT RECORD (SPR) METHOD

The SPR method is the only technique available to analyze unaged data that provides an indication of both the service life and the curve type, and this accounts for its widespread use for analyzing unaged data. Though a powerful tool, its usefulness is often limited by the characteristics of the account being analyzed. These limits are reflected in the SPR literature by many references to "idiosyncrasies" and "anomalies" and emphasis on the importance of judgment when using SPR.

History

Cyrus Hill is generally credited with first developing the principles used in the SPR method. He developed a simulation-based technique while analyzing the life of various classes of telephone plant and reported it in a 1922 article in *Telephony*.

Twenty-five years later Alexander E. Bauhan (1947) presented his classic paper *Life Analysis of Utility Plant for Depreciation Accounting Purposes by the Simulated Plant Record Method* at the National Conference of Electric and Gas Utility Accountants. This paper has been frequently reprinted and is recommended reading for those interested in the method. About this time, Whiton (1947) was developing a similar model.

Though Bauhan conducted his developmental work using hand calculations, the SPR method is computer-oriented because it requires time-consuming trial-and-error calculations. As computers became more available after the early 1950s, the SPR method gained popularity and quickly replaced the turnover methods. Continued application of and research on the SPR method has extended knowledge, understanding, and acceptance of the technique.

How SPR Works

The model requires the history of the annual additions and retirements and/or balances for the property group being simulated. Some computer programs require additions, retirements, and balances. The balances, as calculated by adding the observed additions and subtracting the observed retirements, are compared with the observed balances to check the consistency of the data.

The SPR model has two variations. Either the balances or the retirements can be simulated. Bauhan (1947) simulated balances while Whiton (1947) simulated retirements.

Simulation of plant balances will be described first. Before the calculations can start, a test band must be specified. The factors that should be considered when defining the test band, which defines the years in which balances are to be simulated, will be discussed later. The set of survivor curves that will be used to simulate balances or retirements also must be specified. Though the Iowa curves are used almost exclusively, other sets of curves can be used.

To start the simulation, select a specific type curve from the specified set of curves. Eventually all the curve types will be used, so the selection of the first curve type to be used does not affect the results. An initial value of the average life also must be selected. Various values of the average life will be tried until the life resulting in a curve that best matches the observed data is found, so the initial value will not affect the final answer. However, a good initial estimate of life will reduce the number of trials required to find the best fit.

A specific survivor curve (i.e., the curve type and average life) specifies the fraction surviving at any age, and the product of the fraction surviving times the initial additions is a simulated balance. Thus, the surviving balance from each vintage at the end of each age interval can be simulated, and an estimate of the interior of the matrix shown in Figure 11.1 can be obtained. The sum of the simulated balances for any experience year is the simulated plant balance for that year. Only the experience years included in the test band, and not the entire matrix, need be simulated.

Simulate means to "look or act like" and is used to describe many models in fields of engineering, mathematics, and the social sciences. In the current context, the simulated balances "look like" those that would result if the survivor curve used to calculate the simulated balances also described the life characteristics of the observed property.

The simulated balances are compared with the observed balances to see how closely they match. The SPR model is based on the logic that *the closer the simulated balances are to the observed balances, the better the survivor curve used to simulate the balances describes the life characteristics of the observed property.*

The simulation continues as follows. First, the type curve (e.g., an Iowa R1) is fixed, and, using a trial-and-error procedure, the life is varied until an average life that yields the closest match of the simulated and actual balances is found. Those results are saved and the analyst, or computer program, moves to the next type curve (e.g., an Iowa R2) where the trial and error search for the average life that yields the closest match is repeated. Each type curve that the analyst believes may produce reasonable results is examined. Computer programs usually simulate balances for all curves in the set, though an option to include only specified curves is desirable. The results include the average life for each type curve and statistics that measure the closeness of the fit. The analysis will center on the curves with the best fits of simulated to actual balances. The results are used to help estimate the survivor curve that best describes the historical life characteristics of the property under analysis. This estimation is not simply a matter of calculating certain statistics and selecting the "best" fit. It requires familiarity with the property, knowledge of the SPR method, and the application of judgment.

In his search for the best fit, Bauhan initially plotted the simulated balances on a graph with the observed balances. He then visually selected the best-fitting curve type and average life. Bauhan also suggested that a statistic, the sum of squared deviations between the simulated and observed balances, could be used to obtain a more precise and objective result than could be obtained by visual matching. Other statistics measuring the goodness of fit between the simulated and observed balances have been developed and applied since the time of Bauhan's original work. Yet, a visual examination of the simulated and observed balances often provides insight that statistics do not.

Simulated Balances—An Example

An example will be used to show the necessary calculations and present the principles of the SPR method when simulating balances. Statistics typically included in the results will be introduced and calculated. Table 11.2 contains the unaged data for Account 800. These data were previously used to illustrate the turnover period. Notice that the first addition to the account was in 1971 and that the annual additions have been increasing by about 5% each year. Assume that the only transactions were additions and retirements (i.e., there were no transfers, sales, or other transactions).

This hypothetical account was generated by using an Iowa R3−10 curve to generate retirements. Then random amounts were added or subtracted to the retirements to represent the random fluctuations from the

average that would be observed in an actual account. This knowledge of the
life characteristics underlying the data will allow you to evaluate the per-
formance of the model.

A test band, often called the term of comparison, starting in 1974 and
extending to 1990 and with 4 years between each test year, will be used. This
results in test years of 1974, 1978, 1982, 1986, and 1990. Table 11.3 shows
the calculation of the simulated balances using an Iowa R3 curve and an
average life of 9 years. There is a row for each placement year. Columns (a)
and (b) are data from Table 11.2. Column (c) contains points from the Iowa
R3-9 survivor curve. The last number, 99.89%, is the percent surviving at
age 0.5 years, and the next to last, 99.47%, is the percent surviving at 1.5
years. This pattern continues in 1-year age intervals until the top number,
0.09%, which is the percent surviving at age 14.5 years. Columns (d)
through (h) contain the simulated balances for each of the 5 test years. To
calculate the simulated plant balance at the end of 1974, visually move
column (c) up until the bottom number, 99.89, is in the row containing the
year 1974. Of the $745 added during 1974, 99.89% or $744 will be surviving
at the end of 1974 with an age of 0.5 years, as shown in column (d). Of the

Table 11.3. Calculation of the simulated balances and the sum of squared deviations for Account 800. An Iowa R3-9 survivor curve was used for the simulation.

			Simulated balances for each test year				
Year (a)	Add (b)	Surv % (c)	1974 (d)	1978 (e)	1982 (f)	1986 (g)	1990 (h)
1971	600		582	452	90	0	
1972	656		647	552	190	1	
1973	711		707	642	336	10	
1974	745		744	703	469	44	
1975	799			776	601	120	
1976	861	.09		849	725	250	1
1977	903	1.46		898	816	427	13
1978	956	5.90		955	902	602	56
1979	1011	14.96			981	761	151
1980	1065	29.02			1050	897	309
1981	1111	47.31			1105	1004	526
1982	1143	62.93			1142	1079	719
1983	1196	75.28				1161	900
1984	1234	84.19				1217	1039
1985	1288	90.35				1281	1164
1986	1343	94.40				1342	1268
1987	1397	97.08					1356
1988	1457	98.63					1437
1989	1522	99.47					1514
1990	1561	99.89					1559
Simulated Balances			2681	5828	8409	10194	12013
Observed Balances			2646	5870	8859	10938	12935
Deviation (Ob-Sim)			-35	42	450	744	922
Squared Deviation			1218	1792	202712	552806	850468

Sum of Squared Deviations = 1608997

$711 added during 1973, 99.47% or $707 will be surviving at the end of 1974 with an age of 1.5 years. The surviving plant from the 1972 and 1971 additions is simulated in the same way. The sum of the four values is $2681 and represents the simulated plant balance at the end of 1974. This process is repeated for each remaining year in the test band. For each test year, move the bottom value in column (c) into the row matching the placement year with the test year. The value in column (c) then represents the percent of the additions from the vintage indicated in column (a) surviving at the end of the specified test year.

The deviations between the simulated balances and the observed balances are shown at the bottom of Table 11.3 for each test year. Note that the deviation is the observed balance minus the simulated balance. Each deviation is squared and then added to yield a sum of squared deviations of 1,608,997; this statistic will be used to measure the fit between the simulated and observed balances in this example, but other statistics will be discussed later in this chapter. Note that, except for 1974, the simulated balances are less than the observed balances (i.e., the deviations are positive). We have underestimated the balances, and this suggests we have underestimated the average service life. Our next step is to increase the average service life from 9 to 10 years and repeat the simulation as shown in Table 11.4. Table 11.4 differs from Table 11.3 in that column (c) now contains points from the Iowa R3–10 survivor curve, and this changes the simulated balances.

A life of 10 years yields a sum of squared deviations of 44283, which is less then 1/3 of the value when the life is 9 years. Perhaps a life of 11 years will produce even a better fit. See Table 11.5 for the calculation of the sum of squared deviations when an Iowa R3–11 survivor curve is used to simulate the balances.

The sum of squared deviations increased to over 2 million. The sequence of the sum of squared deviations (1,608,997; 44,283; 2,391,401) decreased and then increased as the life was increased from 9 to 10 to 11 years. We conclude that the life that will minimize the sum of the squared deviations is between 9 and 11 years. Examining the deviations from Table 11.4, we notice they are all negative. This suggests a life of less than 10 years. The deviations also are small, and this suggests a life near 10 years. If we were to repeat the simulation with lives of 9.8, 9.9, and 10.0 years, we would find the sum of squared deviations would be minimized at 9.9 years.

Table 11.6 shows the deviations for best fitting R2, R3, and R4 type curves. The life that yields the best fit varies from 9.7 to 10.1 years, depending on the curve type. The middle curve, the R3, may be judged to be the best fit because its sum of squared deviations is lower than those on either side. Though the R3 is probably the best fit of all the R type curves, we

Table 11.4. Calculation of the simulated balances and the sum of squared deviations for Account 800. An Iowa R3-10 survivor curve was used for the simulation.

Simulated balances for each test year

Year (a)	Add (b)	Surv % (c)	1974 (d)	1978 (e)	1982 (f)	1986 (g)	1990 (h)
1971	600		587	492	192	3	
1972	656		649	580	310	20	
1973	711		708	660	438	61	
1974	745	.01	744	714	546	137	0
1975	799	.56		781	656	256	4
1976	861	3.00		852	761	407	26
1977	903	8.59		899	838	557	78
1978	956	18.34		955	916	701	175
1979	1011	31.98			988	830	323
1980	1065	47.31			1053	941	504
1981	1111	61.63			1106	1031	685
1982	1143	73.30			1142	1095	838
1983	1196	82.06				1169	981
1984	1234	88.38				1221	1091
1985	1288	92.81				1282	1195
1986	1343	95.81				1342	1287
1987	1397	97.75					1366
1988	1457	98.92					1441
1989	1522	99.57					1515
1990	1561	99.90					1559
Simulated Balances			2688	5933	8947	11052	13069
Observed Balances			2646	5870	8859	10938	12935
Deviation (Ob-Sim)			-42	-63	-88	-114	-134
Squared Deviation			1732	3929	7738	12963	17921

Sum of Squared Deviations = 44283

Table 11.5. Calculation of the simulated balances and the sum of squared deviations for Account 800. An Iowa R3-11 survivor curve was used for the simulation.

Simulated balances for each test year

Year (a)	Add (b)	Surv % (c)	1974 (d)	1978 (e)	1982 (f)	1986 (g)	1990 (h)
1971	600		589	520	293	29	
1972	656		650	598	404	43	
1973	711	.19	708	672	514	148	1
1974	745	1.46	744	720	600	261	11
1975	799	4.79		784	693	390	38
1976	861	6.51		853	785	531	56
1977	903	20.81		899	853	653	188
1978	956	35.00		955	924	770	335
1979	1011	48.83			992	877	494
1980	1065	61.63			1055	972	656
1981	1111	72.27			1107	1049	803
1982	1143	80.52			1142	1105	920
1983	1196	86.70				1174	1037
1984	1234	91.23				1223	1126
1985	1288	94.46				1283	1217
1986	1343	96.69				1342	1299
1987	1397	98.16					1371
1988	1457	99.08					1444
1989	1522	99.61					1516
1990	1561	99.92					1560
Simulated Balances			2692	6003	9363	11848	14071
Observed Balances			2646	5870	8859	10938	12935
Deviation (Ob-Sim)			-46	-133	-504	-910	-1136
Squared Deviation			2075	17612	253907	827385	1290422

Sum of Squared Deviations = 2391401

have no mathematical guarantee that this is true (i.e., we have not tried the R1 and R5 type curves).

Table 11.6 shows the R3 type curve to be a good fit not only because it results in the minimum sum of squared deviations, but because each deviation is about the same value. The computer program used to generate these results calculated the life to the nearest tenth of a year. The five negative deviations suggest that a shorter life, one between 9.80 and 9.90 years, could be found that would result in even smaller deviations. Though the extra calculations would result in a fit that is mathematically better (i.e., results in smaller deviations), carrying the indication of the life to the nearest 1/100 of a year would not provide any useful additional information to the analyst.

Table 11.6. Deviations and sum of squared deviations for the best fitting Iowa R2, R3, and R4 type curves.

Year (a)	Bal (b)	Iowa R2-10.1 Dev (c)	Iowa R2-10.1 Sq Dev (d)	Iowa R3- 9.9 Dev (e)	Iowa R3- 9.9 Sq Dev (f)	Iowa R4- 9.7 Dev (g)	Iowa R4- 9.7 Sq Dev (h)
1974	2646	9	81	-42	1764	-62	3844
1978	5870	153	23409	-54	2916	-189	35721
1982	8859	175	30625	-41	1681	-102	10404
1986	10938	-35	1225	-28	784	56	3136
1990	12935	-93	8649	-31	961	101	10201
Sum of Squared Deviations			63989		8106		63306

The R2 curves have a lower mode than the R3 curves, so the middle portion of an R2 survivor curve has a shallower slope than an R3 curve with the same average life. Examine the deviations when an R2–10.1 survivor curve was used to simulate the balances. For the first 3 years in the test band the simulated balances are underestimated and positive deviations result. In the last 2 years, the shallower curve overestimates the balances and negative deviations result. In contrast, the R4 curve, which is steeper than either the R2 or R3 curves, overestimates early balances and underestimates later balances so that the early deviations are negative and the later deviations are positive.

Thus, examination of the pattern of the deviations over the years in the test band may provide clues about the fit of a particular type curve. A pattern of approximately constant deviations suggests the type curve is a good match but that the life should be changed; if the deviations are negative, a shorter life will yield a better fit, and if positive, a longer life will be better. If the deviations associated with early test years are positive but become smaller and then negative for recent test years, a higher modal curve (i.e., a steeper curve) is suggested. The opposite pattern suggests a curve with a lower mode will result in a better fit.

Table 11.7 contains the complete SPR results for Account 800. The curves simulated by the computer program used to generate this output include the original 18 Iowa curves, the 4 origin modal, or O type curves, and 9 half curves (e.g., S1.5). The sum of squared deviations is replaced by a statistic called the *residual measure*. The residual measure is the square root of the average squared deviations. It is proportional to the sum of squared deviations, so the curve that minimizes one also minimizes the other. The sum of squared deviations for the R4–9.7 curve is, from Table 11.6, 63306 and, because there are five deviations, the average deviation is 63306/5 or 12661. The square root of 12661 is 113 and corresponds to the residual measure[3] shown in Table 11.7.

Table 11.7.   Results of the SPR simulated balance model for Account 800, shown in Table 11.2. The test years are 1974, 1978, 1982, 1986, and 1990.

Account 800

Summary of Simulated Plant Balance Results
Term of Comparison 1974-1990

Survivor curve	Average book balance	Residual measure	Conformance index	Experience Beg	End
10.5-S0	8,250	291	28.4	9.0	97.9
10.3-S0.5	8,250	231	38.7	6.8	99.3
10.1-S1	8,250	143	57.7	4.4	99.9
10.0-S1.5	8,250	88	93.8	2.9	100.0
9.9-S2	8,250	52	158.7	1.4	100.0
9.9-S2.5	8,250	55	150.0	0.8	100.0
9.8-S3	8,250	82	100.6	0.2	100.0
9.7-S4	8,250	147	56.1	0.0	100.0
9.7-S5	8,250	181	45.6	0.0	100.0
9.6-S6	8,250	189	43.7	0.0	100.0
10.7-R0.5	8,250	405	20.4	13.3	94.7
10.4-R1	8,250	290	28.4	10.7	99.1
10.3-R1.5	8,250	201	41.0	8.2	99.7
10.1-R2	8,250	113	73.0	5.8	100.0
10.0-R2.5	8,250	48	171.9	4.1	100.0
9.9-R3	8,250	40	206.3	2.3	100.0
9.7-R4	8,250	113	73.0	0.5	100.0
9.7-R5	8,250	168	49.1	0.0	100.0
11.7-L0	8,250	471	17.5	13.0	84.1
11.2-L0.5	8,250	394	20.9	10.5	88.2
10.6-L1.5	8,250	243	34.0	5.5	94.2
10.3-L2	8,250	174	47.4	3.3	96.6
10.2-L2.5	8,250	117	70.5	2.2	98.0
10.0-L3	8,250	78	105.8	1.0	99.4
9.8-L4	8,250	103	80.1	0.1	100.0
9.7-L5	8,250	155	53.2	0.0	100.0
11.1-01	8,250	522	15.8	15.8	87.8
12.4-02	8,250	544	15.2	15.9	81.4
16.3-03	8,250	653	12.6	17.5	70.6
20.6-04	8,250	702	11.8	18.6	66.6

The *conformance index* (CI) was developed by Bauhan and is the statistic most often used to measure goodness of fit. The conformance index is the average observed plant balance for the years in the test band divided by the residual measure. For this example, the average plant balance is (2646 + 5870 + 8859 + 10938 + 12935)/5 or 8250; this is shown as the average book balance in Table 11.7. The CI for the R4–9.7 curve is 8250/113 or 73.0. Because the observed plant balance is independent of the curve used to simulate the balances, the conformance index is inversely proportional to the sum of squared deviations. The curve that *minimizes* the sum of squared deviations will *maximize* the conformance index.

Either the sum of squared deviations or the CI can be used to measure the fit of the simulated balance. The sum of the squared deviations will increase as the number of test years in the test band increases. Also, the deviations would be expected to increase as the plant balances increase (i.e, the average deviation would remain constant, but the magnitude of the deviations would increase). The advantage of the CI is that, because both the numerator and denominator are averages, it does not depend on either the number of years in the test band or the size of the plant balances. Thus, conformance indexes from two simulations can be compared.

White and Cowles (1970) suggested the use of a statistic called the *index of variation* (IV) to measure the fit of the simulated balance. The index of variation is 1000/CI or (residual measure/average balance) × 1000, so a CI of 200 would equal an IV of 5. Divide the IV by 10 and the result is the variation (ie., the residual measure) expressed as a percent of the average balance, so an IV of 5 signifies the variation is 0.5% of the average balance.

The average absolute deviation is the average of the absolute value of each deviation and, for the R4–9.7 curve, is (62 + 189 + 102 + 56 + 101)/5 or 102. That is, the average distance between the observed and simulated balances is 102. This relationship is mentioned because it may be easier to understand the meaning of the average absolute deviation than the square root of the average squared deviation, though both are measures of the difference between the simulated and actual balances.

There is a mathematical relationship between the average absolute deviation and the residual measure. The relationship requires the residual measure to be calculated by dividing the sum of squared deviations by n − 1 rather than n. Thus the residual measure of the R4–9.7 curve, 113, is revised by multiplying it by the $\sqrt{(n-1)/n}$. This yields $\sqrt{(5/4)} \times 113$ or 126. Divide the revised residual mean by 1.25 and you will have 126/1.25 or 101, which serves as an estimate of the average absolute deviation[4] (the exact value is 102).

Examination of Table 11.7 reveals that the largest conformance index, 206.3, is obtained using a R3–9.9 curve. The next best, 171.9, is the R2.5–

10.0; because of the similarity of the two curves, this is not surprising. The S2–10.0, with a conformance index of 158.7, is third best. The left modal curves provide relatively poor fits. This is not unexpected because the life characteristics of the property are right, not left, modal. The origin modal O curves are shaped quite differently than the R curves, and this is reflected in the small conformance indexes for these curves.

Another important statistic is the *retirements experience index* (REI), shown under the heading Experience in Table 11.7. The retirements experience index is the percent of the property retired from the oldest vintage in the test year at the end of the test year. Refer to Table 11.4 and observe that the R3–10 curve reaches 0.01% surviving at 16.5 years and 0% surviving at 17.5 years. The oldest vintage year is 1971. The ending test year is 1990, and survivors from the 1971 vintage at the end of 1990 would be 19.5 years old. Zero percent of the 1971 vintage is surviving at the end of 1990, so the percent retired from the oldest vintage, or the REI, is 100%. Now look at the beginning year in the test band, 1974. Only the first four points on the survivor curve are used to simulate the balance at the end of 1974. There are 97.75% surviving from the 1971 vintage at the end of 1974, so the retirements experience index is 100% − 97.75% or 2.25%. This corresponds to the figure of 2.3% associated with the R3–9.9 curve shown in Table 11.7. If the REI was calculated for the 1978, 1982, or 1986 test years, it would fall between 2.3% and 100%.

An REI of less than 100% can be compared to a stub survivor curve. A small REI implies that the history of the account may be too short to distinguish between type curves. However, an REI of 100% does not imply there is not a problem. If the older additions were small and later installations large, the 100% index would be based on the small amounts and would not reflect the experience of the larger (more important) amounts.

Simulated Retirements—An Example

Simulation of retirements requires only a slight modification of the procedure used to simulate plant balances. The same statistics are used to analyze the results of both models.

Table 11.8 shows the simulated retirements from Account 800 using a R3–10 survivor curve and the same test band used in the simulated balances example. The format of Table 11.8 is the same as that used for Table 11.4. Because the R3–10 curve is used in both simulations, the survivor curve, column (c) is the same in both tables. Rather than simulate the balances at the end of a year, we now simulate retirements during the year. Column (d) shows the simulated retirements for 1974. Again, visually move column (c) up until the 99.90% is in the 1974 row. Calculate the percent of retirements during 1974 by subtracting the percent surviving at the end of the year, 99.90%, from the percent surviving at the start of the year, 100.00% (because this is the 0–0.5 age interval, the 100% represents the midyear additions). This difference, 0.10% or 0.001, is multiplied by the 745 additions to simulate 0.745 or 1 retirement. The simulated retirements from the 1973 vintage during 1974 are (0.9990 − 0.9957) × 711 or 2.34, which is rounded to 2. The simulated retirements for 1974 is the sum of the retirements in column (d), 14. Retirements for the remaining test years are simulated in the same way, the deviations are calculated, squared, and summed to yield a sum of squared deviations of 539. Note that the steepest portion of the survivor curve, the middle portion, produces the largest number of retirements. This is most evident in the 1986 and 1990 test years.

Table 11.8. Calculation of the simulated retirements and the sum of squared deviations for Account 800. An Iowa R3-10 survivor curve was used for the simulation.

			Simulated retirements for each test year				
Year (a)	Add (b)	Surv % (c)	1974 (d)	1978 (e)	1982 (f)	1986 (g)	1990 (h)
1971	600		7	38	92	15	
1972	656		4	29	94	37	
1973	711		2	21	83	69	0
1974	745	.01	1	14	65	102	4
1975	799	.56		9	50	122	19
1976	861	3.00		6	38	123	48
1977	903	8.59		3	27	105	88
1978	956	18.34		1	19	84	130
1979	1011	31.98			12	64	155
1980	1065	47.31			7	47	153
1981	1111	61.63			4	33	130
1982	1143	73.30			1	22	100
1983	1196	82.06				14	76
1984	1234	88.38				8	55
1985	1288	92.81				4	39
1986	1343	95.81				1	26
1987	1397	97.75					16
1988	1457	98.92					9
1989	1522	99.57					5
1990	1561	99.90					2

Simulated Retirements	14	122	492	851	1055
Observed Retirements	33	114	485	859	1060
Deviation (Ob-Sim)	19	-8	-7	8	5
Squared Deviation	347	58	49	59	26

Sum of Squared Deviations = 539

Table 11.9 shows the results of simulating the annual retirements. For the R3 curve, the life of 10.0 yielded the best fit and the highest conformance index. Though the deviations for the retirements (19, −8, −7, 8, 5) are smaller than the deviations for the balances (−42, −63, −88, −114, −134), the average observed retirements (510) are also smaller than the average observed balances (8250). The net result is that the conformance indexes are higher for the simulated balances than for the simulated retirements.

Table 11.9. Results of the SPR simulated retirement model for Account
            800, shown in Table 11.2. The test years are 1974, 1978,
            1982, 1986, and 1990.

Account 800

Summary of Simulated Plant Retirement Results
Term of Comparison 1974-1990

Survivor curve	Average book balance	Residual measure	Conformance index	Experience Beg	End
9.9-S0	510	67	7.6	9.9	99.9
9.9-S1	510	42	12.1	4.7	100.0
10.0-S2	510	22	23.2	1.3	100.0
10.1-S3	510	19	26.8	0.2	100.0
10.3-S4	510	40	12.8	0.0	100.0
10.5-S5	510	56	9.1	0.0	100.0
10.8-S6	510	60	8.5	0.0	100.0
9.9-R1	510	60	8.5	11.3	99.9
9.9-R2	510	29	17.6	6.0	100.0
10.0-R3	510	10	51.0	2.2	100.0
10.1-R4	510	25	20.4	0.5	100.0
10.5-R5	510	48	10.6	0.0	100.0
10.2-L0	510	101	5.0	15.6	90.5
10.1-L1	510	77	6.6	8.8	94.6
10.2-L2	510	54	9.4	3.4	96.9
10.1-L3	510	32	15.9	1.0	99.3
10.2-L4	510	32	15.9	0.0	100.0
10.4-L5	510	49	10.4	0.0	100.0
9.8-01	510	99	5.2	17.9	99.5
10.4-02	510	109	4.7	18.9	88.2
12.4-03	510	143	3.6	22.7	79.2
15.6-04	510	160	3.2	24.1	73.3

There are two variations to the simulated retirements model. The example just shown is the older variation suggested by Bauhan (1947) and Whiton (1947) and is called the simulated *annual* retirements model. Garland (1967) suggested a simulated *period* retirements model. With this model, the life is found so that during the specified period the total of the simulated retirements equal the total observed retirements. The regular statistics can then be calculated.

Analysis of SPR Results

Depreciation professionals have found the SPR method often produces results that are difficult to interpret. Analysts may view the same output and reach different conclusions about the historical life characteristics of the property. Though legitimate differences of opinion are expected, a qualified opinion should be based on a thorough understanding of the SPR model.

The SPR model produces balances that simulate those that would result if the observed additions followed specific life characteristics. The simulated balances are compared to the observed balances that result from the unknown life characteristics we are trying to estimate. If a particular set of simulated balances matches the observed balances better than those from other curves, we might conclude that the life characteristics used to create the simulated balances match the unknown life characteristics that resulted in the observed balances. Before we make this conclusion, several questions should be answered.

1. If the simulated balances are not close to the observed balances, can we conclude the life characteristics used to simulate the balances differ from the actual life characteristics?
2. If the simulated balances are close to the observed balances, can we conclude the life characteristics used to simulate the balances are the same as the actual life characteristics?
3. How close must the simulated and observed balances be to be considered "close?"

Topics that help answer these questions include the data requirements, the test band chosen, the statistics used to measure the results (e.g., the CI or REI), the properties of stable accounts, and the dynamics of life characteristics.

Data

Poor data result in misleading output. One of the first steps in any analysis is checking the data for consistency and for characteristics that may signal a need to adjust the data. Failure to examine the data for even small problems can cast doubts on the SPR output and, consequently, on the final conclusions of your study.

The data shown in Table 11.2 are the history of additions, retirements, and balances for Account 800. These data should be reconciled to ensure that the start of year balance plus the annual additions less the annual retirements equal the end of year balances. If there are other transactions (i.e., an increase in the balances because of acquisition of property or reduction because of a sale), they should be included in the reconciliation, reflected in the adjusted data, and considered when interpreting the results.

Account 800 shows a balance of zero before the initial 1971 additions. Often, however, the data starts with a nonzero initial balance. The record of the previous additions that led to this initial balance was never recorded, was lost, or is unavailable for other reasons. The additions that led to the initial balance also contribute to the succeeding balances, and those contributions must be included in the simulated balances. This requires that the additions that led to the initial balance be estimated and added to the data. The SPR model can then include their contributions in the simulated balances.

Because the life characteristics of the property are not well known, the estimate of the size and years of the additions before the initial balance rests heavily on the judgment of the analyst. One general question is whether the additions were recent or old. In the first case, we would assign relatively large additions during the years immediately preceding the initial balance. In the second case, smaller additions would be assigned to a larger number of years preceding the initial balance. Any information concerning the age distribution of the property in the initial balance will be helpful. This information, with a rough estimate of the life characteristics, can be used to work backward and estimate the historical additions. Some computer programs have a method of using an initial balance to allocate prior additions, and the user must be familiar with that logic when using the allocation options.

Fortunately, in many accounts the output is not sensitive to the adjustments to the initial balance. The annual additions often increase with time, so that the more recent additions are several times larger than the early additions. The result is that the contribution of the early additions to the simulated balances is relatively small. A second factor is the length of time between the initial addition and the simulated balance and how that time compares to the life of the property. Look at Table 11.3, column (h), which contains the contribution of each vintage to the 1990 simulated balance. Additions before 1975 are 100% retired and make no contribution to the simulated balance. If there had been an initial balance, it would not have affected the simulated 1990 balance. The longer the time from the initial balance to the year of the simulated balance, and the shorter the maximum life of the survivor curve used in the simulation, the less sensitive the simulated balance is to adjustments made because of an initial balance.

Adjustments also are needed whenever a transaction other than an addition or retirement occurs. Suppose an acquisition of property increases the plant balance. Then, depending on the data accompanying the acquired property, there may be property in the balance for that and the following years for which there were no additions. This results in simulated balances that will be less than the observed balances when the proper life characteristics (i.e., the actual life characteristics of the property) are used. If a transaction, such as a sale of operating plant, reduced rather than increased the balance, the simulated balance would be greater than the observed balance.

There are two approaches to adjusting for these transactions. Assume the transaction increased the balance (e.g., an acquisition). One approach is to adjust, in this case reduce, all future balances by an amount equal to the estimated contribution of the acquired property. A second approach is to adjust, in this case increase, prior additions by an amount equal to the estimated amount necessary to compensate for the increased balance. It is most common to adjust the prior additions. If we reduce future balances, the adjustment must continue each year we add new data. But if prior additions are increased, no additional adjustments are necessary.

Suppose we decide to adjust by increasing the additions for the years before the transaction. How should the size of the adjustments be determined? Even if the size of the transaction is small, an adjustment is recommended. A transaction that causes a significant change in the balance requires an adjustment.

In the case of an acquisition or sale and when data are available, the ideal solution is to segregate the historical data for the acquired or sold property and either merge it with or delete it from the data under study. However, if the complete history of the property included in the transaction is not known, the lack of information requires the exercise of judgment. Again, many computer programs have options to adjust for these transactions, and the analyst must be familiar with the program options.

How Close Is Close?

If the life characteristics of the observed property are the same as the life characteristics used to simulate the balances, will the simulated balances equal the observed balances? We have implied the answer is, "No, because the observed balances include random deviations from the average. But the two should be close." Then we may ask, "How close is close? Is close a matter of judgment or are there statistical tests that will help us answer this question?" We will first explore the variability of the difference between the simulated and observed balances and then review the status of statistical tests and guidelines for defining "close."

In his 1947 paper, Bauhan proposed the following rating scale for the conformance index:

Conformance Index	Rating
over 75	Excellent
50 to 75	Good
25 to 50	Fair
under 25	Poor

Bauhan characterized these ratings as "arbitrary" apparently because they were based on the experience he gained while developing and applying the model. Though practitioners sometimes find the ratings to conflict with their experience, no other rankings have been widely accepted. Bauhan's ratings are frequently referenced and are helpful when trying to define "close."

The simulated balances can be viewed as the *average* balances that result from the given additions and a specific survivor curve. The observed balances can be viewed as the *random* balances that actually occurred. Thus, even if the survivor curve used to simulate the balances was the same as the survivor curve that describes the life characteristics of the observed property, the observed balances would not exactly equal the simulated balances. Instead, the observed balances would fluctuate randomly about the simulated balances generating a series of positive and negative deviations with an average deviation near zero. The sum of squared deviations would not equal zero, but would presumably be "small" and suggest an excellent fit.

The survival or retirement of a unit of property is analogous to the coin flipping example often used by the instructor in a statistics or probability course. Two outcomes are possible when a coin is tossed: heads or tails. The probability of the outcome being a head, assuming a fair coin, is 0.5, and the probability of not a head (i.e., a tail) is $1 - 0.5$ because the sum of the two probabilities must equal one. Two outcomes are possible when a unit of property is placed in service and then observed for a length of time x: the property can be retired before it reaches age x or it can be in service at age x. The probability of survival until age x is the point on the survivor curve $S(x)$, and the probability of not surviving (i.e., being retired before age x) is $1 - S(x)$. We can use the analogy between coin tossing and the retirement of industrial property to better understand the deviations between the simulated and observed balances.

When a second coin is tossed, the probability of heads remains 0.5 regardless of whether the first outcome was heads or tails. If a second unit of property from the same vintage is observed, its probability of survival is $S(x)$ regardless of whether the first unit was retired or survived. In both cases the second outcome is independent of the first.

Now consider the similarity between tossing n coins and counting the number of heads and observing the installation of n units of property and counting the number of survivors at age x. Suppose 100 coins are tossed (i.e., let n = 100). To simulate the outcome, we can multiply 100 times the average rate for heads, 0.5 per toss, and obtain a simulation of 50 heads. We realize this is an average and that most likely the observed number of heads will be close to, but not equal, 50. The standard deviation[5] of the number of heads is given by $\sqrt{n \times p \times (1-p)}$, where p is the probability of the outcome head. In this case p is 0.5 and the standard deviation is $\sqrt{100 \times 0.5 \times 0.5}$ or 5. Knowledge of the binomial distribution allows us to conclude that more than 95% of the time the number of heads would be between 40 and 60. If a deviation was greater than 10 (i.e., there were 39 or fewer heads, or 61 or more heads), we might want to inspect the coin or keep a closer watch on the counting process, because a deviation of more than 10 is large if the coin is fair. A statistician could design a hypothesis test to make a formal test of whether the coin was fair.

Now suppose that 100 units of property are installed, and that at age x the survivor curve describing the property shows S(x) equal to 90%. The simulated balance at age x is 100×0.90 or 90 units. The standard deviation of the simulated balance is $\sqrt{100 \times 0.90 \times 0.10}$ or 3. The residual measure is a statistic that estimates the standard deviation between the simulated and observed balances, and the conformance index (CI) is the average balance divided by the residual measure. Here the CI is 90/3 or 30. If the size of observed deviation was significantly larger than 3, making the CI significantly less than 30, we might suspect that the probability of survival of the observed property was not equal to 90%.

If the survivor curve of the observed property is known, then the average conformance index for a single year can be calculated.[6] The actual conformance index is a random variable that depends on the observed retirements, but calculation of the average conformance index, shown in Table 11.10, will allow us to draw general conclusions about the magnitude of the CI for different values of n and S(x).

Table 11.10. The average conformance index for a single balance for S(x) equal to 0.1, 0.5, and 0.9.

	S(x)		
n	0.1	0.5	0.9
100	3	10	30
1000	11	32	95
10000	33	100	300
100000	105	316	949
1000000	333	1000	3000

Table 11.10 shows the CI for a single vintage, but the simulated balance for a test year is the sum of balances from all previous vintages. To obtain the standard deviation for the sum of the balances, we must find the variance (i.e., the standard deviation squared) for each vintage, add them, and take their square root. These calculations are shown in Table 11.11. Columns (a) through (d) are from Table 11.4. The variance, column (e), is n $\times$ S(x) $\times$ [1 $-$ S(x)] or, for 1981, $1111 \times 0.6163 \times 0.3837$ or 262.72. The sum of column (e) is the variance of the simulated balance. Note that the largest variance occurs when S(x) is near 0.5.

The discussion so far has shown that when the life characteristics used in the simulation and those of the observed property are the same, the CI will increase in proportion to the square root of the number of units in the average balance. The CI also becomes larger as S(x) approaches 1. From Table 11.11, we see that the growth patterns of the property and the shape of the survivor curve affect the CI. With growth, the newer vintages have a

Table 11.11.   Calculation of the conformance index for
               the data from Table 11.4 and the 1990 test
               year.

Year (a)	Additions (b)	S(x) % (c)	Simulated balance (d)	Variance (e)	CI by year (f)
1971	600				
1972	656				
1973	711				
1974	745	.01	0	.07	0
1975	799	.56	4	4.45	2
1976	861	3.00	26	25.06	5
1977	903	8.59	78	70.90	9
1978	956	18.34	175	143.17	15
1979	1011	31.98	323	219.92	22
1980	1065	47.31	504	265.48	31
1981	1111	61.63	685	262.72	42
1982	1143	73.30	838	223.70	56
1983	1196	82.06	981	176.07	74
1984	1234	88.38	1091	126.73	97
1985	1288	92.81	1195	85.95	129
1986	1343	95.81	1287	53.91	175
1987	1397	97.75	1366	30.73	246
1988	1457	98.92	1441	15.57	365
1989	1522	99.57	1515	6.52	594
1990	1561	99.90	1559	1.56	1249
			$\overline{13069}$	$\overline{1712.51}$	

Residual measure = SQRT(1712.51) =   41.38
Overall conformance index = 13069/41.38 = 316

larger value of n and values of S(x) nearer 1, and these factors combine to yield larger CIs.

R. E. White (1968) examined the statistical characteristics of the variation between the simulated and observed balances. The result was a test of the hypothesis that the life characteristics used to simulate the balances are the same as the life characteristics of the observed property. The test, also described in White and Cowles (1970), uses the additions, observed balances, and the survivor curve used to simulate the balances to calculate a chi squared statistic used to decide whether to accept or reject the hypothesis.

Though the development of a test of the deviations represented an important step in answering the "how close is close" question, it proved to be of little practical help. When applied to industrial data, the test rejected the conclusion that the simulated and observed life characteristics were the same for all but the most regular data (e.g., the hypothetical Account 800 is regular because of the way it was created). Rose (1972) and Rippe (1969) provided examples of observed data rejected by the test. Typically the variation of the observed balances from the average is more than allowed for in the test, and this would cause a statistician to describe the test as too powerful. Examination of the assumptions of the statistical test will provide some insight to the sources of this variation.

The test assumes each unit in a vintage group is identical in the sense that at any age, each unit has the same probability of retirement. Often property that serves the same functional purpose but includes units with different physical characteristics is included in a single group. Thus, each unit is not identical, and the variation of the observed balances is increased.

Many accounts are measured in dollars rather than units, and this places a major limitation on the application of the model. Karen Ponder (1978) modified White's test so it could be used on accounts measured in dollars. Ponder required the unit price as input so that dollars could be converted to units. The price was allowed to vary from vintage to vintage. Application of the modified test has been limited.

A second assumption is that retirements from one vintage are independent of retirements from all other vintages. White and Cowles (1970) say evidence suggests retirements are not independent. They cite highway relocation requiring removal of transmission lines and causing retirements across vintages independent of age as an example. In Chapter 8 placement and experience bands were discussed. Experience bands were used to examine forces of retirement during specific periods or eras of interest. Forces of this type result in statistical dependence between vintages and increase the variation of the deviations. Ponder also examined the dependence between vintages.

A third assumption is that each vintage has the same life characteristics. This follows from the application of the same survivor curve to each addition when simulating balances. It is difficult to find an example of a functional group of property whose physical characteristics have not changed over time, and this is a source of changing life characteristics. Because the SPR model applies the same survivor curve to additions that probably have different life characteristics, the best fitting curve represents a compromise or some sort of average. The rate of change of service life and change in the shape of the survivor curve from one vintage to another will increase the variation of the deviations and reduce the conformance index.

Choosing the Test Band

The test band specifies the calendar years for which balances will be simulated. Specification of the test band requires two decisions. One is the choice of the earliest and latest years in the test band. This defines the width of the band, or the time between the first and last years. The other decision is the number of additional test years between the first and last year, and this is typically resolved by including all the years in the test band.

A major consideration is that the band width not be too narrow. Consider a test band consisting of only 1 year.[7] By varying the life, the simulated balance for any type curve can be made to equal the observed balance.

Table 11.12 shows the SPR results for Account 800 when a test band of 1990–1990 (i.e., a single year) is used. Note the low residual measures and high conformance indexes. The difference in residual measures is caused by chance rather than curve type. The computer program that generated the output shown in this chapter fit to the nearest 0.1 of a year; if the fit had been to a smaller value (e.g., 0.01 of a year), the residual measure for each type curve would have been nearer zero.

Table 11.12. Results of the SPR simulated balance model for Account 800 using a one-year test band.

Account 800

Summary of Simulated Plant Balance Results
Term of Comparison 1990-1990

Survivor curve	Average book balance	Residual measure	Conformance index	Experience Beg	End
10.2-S0	12,935	26	497.5	99.1	99.1
10.0-S1	12,935	43	300.8	100.0	100.0
9.9-S2	12,935	15	862.3	100.0	100.0
9.8-S3	12,935	33	392.0	100.0	100.0
9.8-S4	12,935	33	392.0	100.0	100.0
9.7-S5	12,935	42	308.0	100.0	100.0
9.7-S6	12,935	25	517.4	100.0	100.0
10.2-R1	12,935	14	923.9	99.5	99.5
10.0-R2	12,935	7	1,847.9	100.0	100.0
9.9-R3	12,935	31	417.3	100.0	100.0
9.8-R4	12,935	5	2,587.0	100.0	100.0
9.7-R5	12,935	50	258.7	100.0	100.0
11.0-L0	12,935	2	6,467.5	87.2	87.2
10.4-L1	12,935	35	369.6	93.5	93.5
10.1-L2	12,935	47	275.2	97.1	97.1
10.0-L3	12,935	48	269.5	99.4	99.4
9.8-L4	12,935	25	517.4	100.0	100.0
9.8-L5	12,935	39	331.7	100.0	100.0
10.6-01	12,935	22	588.0	92.0	92.0
11.6-02	12,935	5	2,587.0	84.2	84.2
14.4-03	12,935	9	1,437.2	74.7	74.7
17.8-04	12,935	2	6,467.5	70.3	70.3

We know that the property in Account 800 is described by an R3–10 survivor curve. Note the curves with a higher mode than the R3 tend to underestimate the life, while those with a lower mode tend to overestimate life.

A band width of 1 year provides little information about the life characteristics of the property. Narrow bands, even if wider than 1 year, will not provide adequate discrimination between type curves and should not be used. The minimum band width depends on the average life and the regularity of the data. The longer the average life, the larger the minimum band width. The more regular the data (i.e., the smaller the variation between the observed balances and the average balance), the narrower the minimum width. Bauhan (1947) stated that "the analysis [should] include comparisons over a fairly extended period." He discussed the 1-year band and stated that the indeterminate results would "probably not [be] much improved by using a span of only four or five years." Finally, he suggested that when dealing "with the wider dispersions typical of utility plant accounts, it is believed the indeterminateness will be avoided if the comparison term is made not less than 20 years." This guideline appears to be based on average lives of 20 to 40 years.

Practitioners frequently use band widths equal to or smaller than the average life. Thus, a band width of 10 years may be adequate if the service life is near 10 years. If narrow bands are used, it may be prudent to also use a wider band or bands. The analyst can compare the results and observe the effect of the narrower bands. Large conformance indexes for many type curves could be an indication that the test band is too narrow.

Once the band width has been determined, the number of test years (i.e., the additional test years between the first and last years) must be specified. Bauhan (1947) suggested "that, ordinarily, balance comparisons made every fourth or fifth year will give a result not importantly different than comparisons made on the basis of every year." Because Bauhan was working with band widths of 20 years or more, this would suggest four or more test years in a test band. Bauhan's calculations were made by hand. Today's analyst, armed with a personal computer, finds it expedient to include every year in the band rather than to speculate on the maximum interval between years that would yield the same result as including every year.

The test band can be chosen to reflect specific eras of interest. By comparison of an early era with a later era, the SPR method can be used to detect trends in the service life. However, if the average service life is long and the history short, it is not possible to detect trends.

The Retirements Experience Index

The REI is the percent of the property retired from the oldest vintage in the test year by the end of the test year. Thus, it can range from 0% to 100%. If most of the property from the oldest vintage remains in service, then no pattern of retirements will have been revealed, and it is likely that for each type curve a life can be found that will result in a high CI. The REI will be low (i.e., closer to 0% than to 100%) and will warn us that the data do not contain enough history to uncover the life characteristics of the property. Under these circumstances, the life indications may have little meaning in spite of the high CIs.

Bauhan (1947) discussed the importance of the REI and suggested the following ratings:

Rating	REI
Excellent	more than 75%
Good	from 50% to 75%
Fair	from 33% to 50%
Poor	from 17% to 33%
Valueless	from 0% to 17%

He noted that in growing accounts the magnitude of the earliest vintage in the test year might be small when compared to more recent vintages, and the REI could be misleading. He suggested using the first vintage year with "substantial additions" rather than the oldest vintage. Again, the analyst must be familiar with the manner in which the computer program being used calculates the REI.

Table 11.4 provides an example where the beginning and ending REIs range from low to high. The REIs for the 1974 and the 1990 test years are 2.3% and 100% respectively. The 2.3% REI suggests that the 1974 test year does not contribute as much information to the SPR model as the later test bands and may cast doubt on the results of the simulation. But the test band is 17 years wide, almost twice the average life. The REI is about 18% for the 1978 test year and 68% for the 1982 test year. Thus, the low beginning REI does not, in this example, cause concern about the results. Still, there are only 5 test years in the test band and 2 have low REIs. This suggests either reducing the band to 9 or 10 years and eliminating the low REI years, or spacing the test years 1 year apart, so that there are 17 test years rather than 5.

This example showed that when the beginning REI is low, the width of the test band should be examined. A low beginning REI with a narrow test band probably will not discriminate between type curves. A low beginning REI with a wide test band may not be a matter for concern if other test years yield high REIs.

If the test band does not include the most recent observation year, then more current experience can be gained by widening the test band to include it. If the REI remains too low, the account is too young to provide reliable indications of its life characteristics.

Stable Accounts

An account that maintains a constant balance by replacing annual retirements with an equal number of annual additions is of special interest when discussing the SPR model. The additions are called renewals and the characteristics of such an account were discussed earlier.

Account 900, shown in Table 11.13, illustrates a stable account with an annual balance of 15000. The additions equal the retirements and average about 1500 each year, though there is some random variation from year to year. For a stable account, the average life is equal to the balance divided by the annual retirements. Knowing this, we can estimate the average life of Account 900 as 15000/1500 or 10 years. Though we can estimate the average life, note that *any* survivor curve with an average life of 10 years could have generated the average of 1500 retirements each year. Account 900 will be used to show the response of the SPR method to a stable account.

Table 11.13. Data for Account 900. Initial balance is 15000 and annual additions equal the annual retirements.

Year	Retr	Add	Balance	Year	Retr	Add	Balance
1960			15000	1976	1520	1520	15000
1961	1520	1520	15000	1977	1480	1480	15000
1962	1510	1510	15000	1978	1500	1500	15000
1963	1470	1470	15000	1979	1490	1490	15000
1964	1510	1510	15000	1980	1510	1510	15000
1965	1490	1490	15000	1981	1510	1510	15000
1966	1530	1530	15000	1982	1480	1480	15000
1967	1480	1480	15000	1983	1530	1530	15000
1968	1500	1500	15000	1984	1530	1530	15000
1969	1490	1490	15000	1985	1480	1480	15000
1970	1510	1510	15000	1986	1490	1490	15000
1971	1470	1470	15000	1987	1520	1520	15000
1972	1520	1520	15000	1988	1500	1500	15000
1973	1490	1490	15000	1989	1470	1470	15000
1974	1470	1470	15000	1990	1560	1560	15000
1975	1470	1470	15000				

Before using the model, we should examine the data more closely. Note that the initial record is a 15000 balance at the end of 1960. The additions during and before 1960 that contributed to this balance are not recorded, and this requires an adjustment to the data. But first we will use the data as they are, and this will allow us to observe the effects of eschewing the adjustment.

Table 11.14 shows the simulated balances for the R4 and L0 type curves for a test band of the even years from 1974 through 1990. These two curves were chosen for comparison because they have contrasting maximum lives. The high modal R4–10 has a maximum life of 15 years while the low modal L0–10 has a maximum life of 41 years. It is 14 years from the initial balance until the first year of the test band, 1974. This results in an REI of 98% for the R4 curve; the lack of adjustments for additions before 1960 has little effect on the simulated balances for this curve. The REI for the L0 curve is 70.7%, so 29.3% of the property from the L0–10.3 curve has a life greater than 14 years. No additions before 1961 are recorded, so when using the L0 type curve the SPR model underestimates the 1974 balance (i.e., the simulated balance of 13408 is 1592 less than the observed 15000 balance). To compensate, the average life is increased to 10.3 years so

Table 11.14.   Simulated balances for Account 900 with no adjust-
                ment made for the additions before 1961.

Simulated Plant Balances Based on Survivor Curve

		10.0-R4		10.3-L0	
Year	Book balance	Simulated balance	Diff	Simulated balance	Diff
1974	15,000	14,948	52	13,408	1,592
1976	15,000	14,939	61	14,098	902
1978	15,000	14,923	77	14,580	420
1980	15,000	14,932	68	14,921	79
1982	15,000	14,936	64	15,135	-135
1984	15,000	15,015	-15	15,327	-327
1986	15,000	15,005	-5	15,373	-373
1988	15,000	15,036	-36	15,432	-432
1990	15,000	15,068	-68	15,482	-482

	Average book balance	Residual measure	Conformance index	Experience beg	end
10.0-R4	15,000	55	272.7	98.0	100.0
10.3-L0	15,000	684	21.9	70.7	99.5

that balances in later test years are about 400 units greater than 15000. The result is that the simulated balances using the R4–10.0 curve closely match the 15000 balance and produce a high CI of 272.7, while the unadjusted data cause a poor match and a low CI of 21.9 for the L0–10.3 curve.

Now let's adjust the Account 900 data to include an estimate of the additions that resulted in the 15000 balance at the end of 1960. Presume that the account has been in existence for at least 30 years and that there are no indications of events that would have caused major changes in the life characteristics of the property during that time. One assumption that can be made is that the observable pattern of an average of 1500 additions each year existed during and before 1960. The assumption was adopted and the following adjustment was made to Account 900: 1500 additions were made during each year from 1940 through 1960. The results of the SPR program using adjusted data are shown in Table 11.15.

Compare Table 11.15 with Table 11.14. Note that the simulated balances using the R4 curve are not affected by the adjustment to the data. Though the beginning REI changed from 98% to 100%, this change was not large enough to change the simulated balances. With the L0 type curve, many survivors in 1974 come from additions before 1961. Consequently, the adjustment allowed significantly larger simulated balances in 1974 and 1976, so the match was improved and the CI increased to 108.7.

The summary of output from the SPR model using the adjusted data is shown in Table 11.16. Observe that the indicated lives are 10.0 or 10.1. The smallest CI is 81, most are over 100, and many are over 250. We have a clear picture of the average service life and no indication of the shape of the

Table 11.15. Simulated balances for Account 900 with adjustments
of 1500 additions each year from 1940 to 1960 added
to the data.

Simulated Plant Balances Based on Survivor Curve

		10.0-R4		10.1-L0	
Year	Book balance	Simulated balance	Diff	Simulated balance	Diff
1974	15,000	14,948	52	14,768	232
1976	15,000	14,939	61	14,859	141
1978	15,000	14,923	77	14,922	78
1980	15,000	14,932	68	14,987	13
1982	15,000	14,936	64	15,030	-30
1984	15,000	15,015	-15	15,128	-128
1986	15,000	15,000	-5	15,119	-119
1988	15,000	15,036	-36	15,153	-153
1990	15,000	15,068	-68	15,189	-189

	Average book balance	Residual measure	Conformance index	Experience beg	end
10.0-R4	15,000	55	272.7	100.0	100.0
10.1-L0	15,000	138	108.7	100.0	100.0

Table 11.16. Results of the SPR simulated balance model for the adjusted
data for Account 900.

Account 900

Summary of Simulated Plant Balance Results
Term of Comparison 1974-1990

Survivor curve	Average book balance	Residual measure	Conformance index	Experience Beg	End
10.0-S0	15,000	142	105.6	100.0	100.0
10.0-S1	15,000	105	142.9	100.0	100.0
10.0-S2	15,000	77	194.8	100.0	100.0
10.0-S3	15,000	61	245.9	100.0	100.0
10.0-S4	15,000	57	263.2	100.0	100.0
10.0-S5	15,000	57	263.2	100.0	100.0
10.0-S6	15,000	57	263.2	100.0	100.0
10.0-R1	15,000	131	114.5	100.0	100.0
10.0-R2	15,000	85	176.5	100.0	100.0
10.0-R3	15,000	60	250.0	100.0	100.0
10.0-R4	15,000	55	272.7	100.0	100.0
10.0-R5	15,000	57	263.2	100.0	100.0
10.1-L0	15,000	138	108.7	100.0	100.0
10.1-L1	15,000	138	108.7	100.0	100.0
10.0-L2	15,000	129	116.3	100.0	100.0
10.0-L3	15,000	96	156.3	100.0	100.0
10.0-L4	15,000	66	227.3	100.0	100.0
10.0-L5	15,000	58	258.6	100.0	100.0
10.1-01	15,000	169	88.8	100.0	100.0
10.1-02	15,000	131	114.5	100.0	100.0
10.3-03	15,000	108	138.9	97.0	100.0
10.1-04	15,000	185	81.1	93.7	100.0

survivor curve. Had the variation been removed from the data (i.e., if all retirements and additions equalled 1500), the residual measure would have been reduced to zero, or very near zero, for all type curves.

The SPR technique will provide an indication of historical life but not curve shape when the account is stable (i.e., the additions and retirements are approximately equal and the balance is relatively constant).

When an estimate of the curve shape is necessary, additional information must be obtained. One approach is to take a random sample of the retired property and estimate the age of each unit sampled. If the number of annual renewals has stabilized, the age distribution of the retirements reflects the survivor curve defining the life characteristics of the additions, and this curve can be estimated from the ages of the sampled property.

Simulated Balances or Retirements?

Most computer programs allow simulation of either the balances or the retirements, and there are advocates of both variations of the SPR model. Yet, the simulated balances model is used more often and is the subject of more research than the simulated retirements model. Either model provides reasonable results when the life characteristics are constant from year to year, and this is reflected in Tables 11.7 and 11.9. Though the results of the two simulations of Account 800 are similar, Tables 11.4 and 11.8 show differences in the simulation process. Look at column (h) in both tables. The 1990 simulated balance is most influenced by recent additions, while the 1990 simulated retirements are most influenced by retirements from placements during the period 1978 to 1982, when the survivor curve was steepest. Thus, if the life characteristics from year to year are not constant, the two models can be expected to yield different results.

A major disadvantage of the simulated retirements method is that the magnitude of the retirements is much less than the magnitude of the balances. The deviations between the observed and simulated retirements are much more sensitive to the randomness in the annual transactions than are the deviations between the observed and simulated balances. Because of this, the results of the simulated retirements method are often characterized as erratic, and conformance indexes tend to be much lower than with the simulated balances model. Fitch, Jensen, and Young (1982) compared the simulated balances, simulated retirements, and simulated period retirements models for periods of growth, stability, and decline. They concluded that the balances model provided the best results and warned that caution is needed when using the simulated retirements models.

Analysis of Dynamic Accounts

A simple view of the life characteristics of property is that they remain constant both from one vintage to the next and throughout the life cycle.

This is the view that the SPR model takes when simulating balances. A more realistic, but more complicated, view is that the life characteristics may change from one vintage to the next or from one time to another. Adoption of the view that life characteristics are constantly changing raises the question of how the SPR model responds when applied to dynamic accounts.

The answer to this question is complicated because both the curve type and average life can change across both vintage years and calendar years. The change can be gradual or rapid, systematic or random, and positive or negative. These variables combine to create many combinations. Whether the SPR model can provide reasonable indications of the life characteristics of the property depends on the particular combination of variables present in the property group under examination.

The common research approach used to examine the responses of the SPR model to an account with changing life characteristics is to select a pattern of change that is of interest to the researcher. Then create a set of additions and balances that could have resulted from such a pattern, apply the SPR to the data, and draw conclusions based on the output. This technique has been used in this chapter. Accounts 800 and 900 each had certain characteristics. The SPR model was applied to this data, and we learned about response of the model to specific data by studying the results.

Others have used this approach. Garland (1967, 1968) examined the ability of the retirements method to detect changes in the life characteristics. Shelbourn (1969) compared SPR results with those obtained using actuarial methods. Chopp (1971) examined the impact of increased variation from a known pattern. Ponder's (1978) work centered on the statistical characteristics of the results and their sensitivity to the number of units, or size of the balance. Singh (1980) examined the differences between the balances and retirement models.

Fitch, Jensen, and Young (1982) generated balances from the Iowa O1 and S2 curves using lives ranging from 10 to 15 years. They created accounts in which the lives were constant, varied randomly, increased from 5 to 15 in steps of 0.5, and decreased from 15 to 5 in steps of 0.5. Their study confirmed that all the curves result in a good fit of simulated to actual balances when a 1-year band is used or when the balance is stable. The method detected changes in life by comparing the results from test bands covering an early period, a middle period, and a later period in the account life. As might be predicted, the life indications in the later test bands lagged the average life of the additions. Though the life indicators suggested changing average lives, the conformance indexes were low. High conformance indexes occurred in the early test bands, but they were associated with low REIs. Those models with trends in average life produced conformance indexes that fell mostly in Bauhan's "poor" classification.

Susan Jensen (1983) extended this research and it became the topic of her Ph.D. dissertation, which represents the most extensive report of the SPR method to date. She examined data generated from the Iowa O1, S0, S2, S4, S6, R4, and L2 curves. Vintage lives followed random, increasing, and decreasing trends. Among her findings were the conclusions that when the curve type was constant but the life had a trend, the SPR measures of fit were highest for either curves with a high mode and low average life or curves with a low mode and high average life.

Table 11.17 shows the SPR output for Account 897. A placement band analysis of this account will show the curve type and service life vary significantly from vintage to vintage, and the low conformance indexes reflect this. All conformance indexes are less than 20, which rates "poor" on Bauhan's scale. Life indications range from 11 to 30 years. Note that the lower modal curves have higher lives (e.g., 13.4–S0, 13.2–R1, 15.5–L0, and 30.3–O4) and the higher modal curves have lower lives (e.g., 11–S6, 11.8–R5, 11.9–L5, and 15.0–O1). A choice of a single curve to represent this account will require additional knowledge about the characteristics of the account and the application of judgment.

Table 11.17. Results of the SPR simulated balance model for Account 897.

Account 897

Summary of Simulated Plant Balance Results
Term of Comparison 1976-1990

Survivor curve	Average book balance	Residual measure	Conformance index	Experience Beg	End
13.4-S0	3,986	252	15.8	30.2	94.6
12.7-S1	3,986	221	18.0	28.0	99.5
12.3-S2	3,986	224	17.8	24.6	100.0
12.1-S3	3,986	242	16.5	19.7	100.0
11.9-S4	3,986	268	14.9	12.6	100.0
11.8-S5	3,986	290	13.7	5.0	100.0
11.8-S6	3,986	302	13.2	0.5	100.0
13.2-R1	3,986	270	14.82	8.5	97.2
12.5-R2	3,986	234	17.0	25.0	100.0
12.1-R3	3,986	237	16.8	20.7	100.0
11.9-R4	3,986	255	15.6	16.2	100.0
11.8-R5	3,986	282	14.1	8.5	100.0
15.5-L0	3,986	295	13.5	32.3	79.1
14.0-L1	3,986	243	16.4	31.4	88.3
13.1-L2	3,986	212	18.8	29.0	94.8
12.5-L3	3,986	220	18.1	23.9	98.9
12.0-L4	3,986	251	15.9	16.7	100.0
11.9-L5	3,986	276	14.4	9.5	100.0
15.0-O1	3,986	334	11.9	31.7	78.3
16.8-O2	3,986	334	11.9	31.8	75.5
23.4-O3	3,986	356	11.2	32.0	64.4
30.3-O4	3,986	366	10.9	32.6	61.0

SUMMARY

Unaged retirement data contain less information than aged retirement data. No amount of analysis can restore the information lost when data are recorded in unaged, rather than aged, form. The usefulness of the SPR model is affected by the growth characteristics of the account and the changing life characteristics of the property; under some circumstances, the SPR results are of limited help when attempting to estimate the historical life characteristics of the property being analyzed. However, the SPR model is the best technique available to analyze unaged data.

The following items summarize the previous comments and can be used as a check list when using the SPR model.

1. Gather all available information about the history of the account. Establish preliminary estimates, or ranges of estimates, of the life and curve types.
2. Check the data and adjust as necessary. Adjust for the initial balance and for annual transactions other than additions of new plant and regular retirements.
3. Carefully select the test band or bands. Be concerned about the width of the band in comparison to preliminary estimates of service life.
4. Check the retirements experience index. Is there sufficient experience in the test band to yield reliable indications of life? If not, widen the test band.
5. Do the results show many high conformance indexes? If so, be suspicious, and:
   a. Check the band width. Is it wide enough? Are there enough years in the test band? If not, rerun with different test bands.
   b. Check for a stable account. If the additions and the balance show little change from year to year, the simulated lives will be close to each other and provide a reasonable indication of life. The curve type estimate will be unreliable because the model is limited by the stable characteristics of the account.
   c. Recheck the retirements experience indexes. If they are small, the account may be too young to provide useful life estimation information.
6. Do the results show all low conformance indexes? Uniformly low conformance indexes most often result because the life characteristics of the property have changed over time. A less likely cause is that the survivor curve describing the experienced life characteristics is not included in the set of curves simulated (e.g., the Iowa

curves contain no bimodal curves). When all conformance indexes are low, resist the temptation to choose the curve with the highest CI. One conformance index will be larger than the others, but that does not mean that those life characteristics provide a good fit to the observed characteristics or that those characteristics are an appropriate representation of the property. The analyst must rely on judgment to select a curve type and average age that are consistent with other knowledge about the property in the account.

7. Do the results show a curve, or two or three similar curves, with high conformance indexes? If so, and if these results are consistent with other knowledge about the property, then the SPR results provide useful information about the historical life characteristics.

NOTES

1. When using the SL-AL-BG-AM system, the annual accruals can be obtained by multiplying the rate by the total plant in service. But vintage balances must be known in order to calculate the CAD for feedback and control. The remaining life method of adjustment also requires vintage balances to calculate annual accruals.

2. See Figures 3.1, 3.2, and 3.3 of *Methods of Estimating Utility Plant Life,* Edison Electric Institute (1952).

3. The residual measure is similar to the statistic called the standard deviation and is often denoted by the symbol S. The denominator of the standard deviation is the number of observations minus 1, or, here, the number of years tested minus 1. The standard deviation for the R4–9.7 curve is the square root of 63306/4 or 126.

4. This relationship requires that the deviations be distributed by the normal distribution. See Brown (1963).

5. The distribution of the number of heads is described by the binomial distribution. References can be found in a basic text in probability or statistics.

6. The CI is $S(x) \times n/\sqrt{S(x) \times n \times [1 - S(x)]}$, which can be simplified to $\sqrt{S(x) \times n/[1 - S(x)]}$.

7. The use of one year is same as the "Indicated Survivor" method, a forerunner of the Simulated Plant Balances method.

12 | Aging Balances

A NALYSIS of unaged retirement data yields an estimate of the historical life characteristics of the property group. This estimate serves two purposes. One is to provide the basis for forecasting life characteristics. The second, which is the topic of this chapter, is to provide information to age the balance of plant in service. To age the balance, the surviving balance from each vintage must be estimated so that the sum of the surviving vintage balances equals the unaged (total) balance. The vintage balances are called an age distribution.

DIRECT AGING

The term *direct aging* is used to describe the following two methods of modifying a simulated balance so it will equal the observed balance. The principles used to develop the SPR model are useful when aging balances. Suppose we have analyzed Account 800[1] and selected the Iowa R3–10 curve to describe its life characteristics. Table 11.4 of the preceding chapter shows the simulated balances for Account 800 when an Iowa R3–10 survivor curve is used. Column (h) contains the December 31, 1990, simulated balances from each vintage. However, as is commonly the case, the simulated total balance does not exactly equal the observed balance. Here the 1990 simulated balance is 13069 and the observed balance is 12935, a difference of −134. Thus, the balances in column (h) do not provide an age distribution that is consistent with the actual balance.

One method of aging the balance is to simulate the balances using the

251

R3 type curve and a test band consisting of the single year 1990. Table 12.1 shows the output from a computer program that ages the balance in this way. Because the test band is a single year, an average life can be found that yields a perfect fit such that the simulated balance equals the observed balance. In the example, the simulated life of 9.9 years differs from the life of 10.0 years chosen to represent the historical life characteristics. The reason for the difference between the two lives can be explained by the random variation of the annual retirements. The magnitude of the difference between the life used to age the balance and the age used to describe the life characteristics will vary with the data. In this example the difference is small and can be attributed to random variation, but a large difference raises questions about the reasonableness of the estimated life characteristics. Also, in cases where the estimated future life characteristics differ from the historical life indications, the aging of the balances should be based on the historical life.

Table 12.1.   The age distribution of the 1990 balance of Account 800 using an Iowa R3-9.9 survivor curve and a 1990 test band.

Year (a)	Calculated additions (b)	Survivors (c)	Year (a)	Calculated additions (b)	Survivors (c)
1971	00	.00	1981	1,111	761.00
1972	656	.00	1982	1,143	828.00
1973	711	.00	1983	1,196	975.00
1974	745	.00	1984	1,234	1,086.00
1975	799	.00	1985	1,288	1,193.00
1976	861	.00	1986	1,343	1,285.00
1977	903	62.00	1987	1,397	1,365.00
1978	956	161.00	1988	1,457	1,441.00
1979	1,011	306.00	1989	1,522	1,515.00
1980	1,065	487.00	1990	1,561	1,560.00
			Total	21,559	12,935.00

This aging procedure is repeated annually using the current observed balance. When a new depreciation study is made, a new estimate of the life characteristics may result in the choice of a different type of curve to represent the life characteristics. This new curve type would then be used as the basis on which to age the plant in service.

An alternative method of aging the balance is to adjust each simulated balance in column (h) of Table 11.5 by the factor 12935/13069 or 0.9897. Multiplying each simulated vintage balance by this factor will result in a total aged balance of 12935. Note that under this method the factor can exceed 1.0, so it is possible to calculate an aged vintage balance that exceeds the original vintage additions. The first method is preferable to the alternative method, though both are used and accepted.

STATISTICAL AGING AND COMPUTED MORTALITY

For many years, when dealing with unaged data the Bell System used a method of statistical aging they called *computed mortality.*[2] Bell called aged data *mortality data,* so computed mortality describes a system that converts unaged data to aged data. Chapter 3 of *Depreciation Engineering Practices,* published by AT&T (1957), describes the system. Articles by Alfar (1986) and Carver (1989) also discuss the system. The Interstate Commerce Commission *User Documentation for the Statistical Aging System* (1985) used the term *statistical aging* to describe a system that has some similarities to computed mortality but differs because it incorporates a procedure for statistically aging retired units. The method of pricing the retirements is based on the statistical age of the unit.

The implementation of a system of statistical aging can be divided into two phases. The first phase starts the system and the second phase maintains the system. The objective of the first phase is to obtain an aged initial balance. This can be done using direct aging methods. Suppose that the December 31, 1989, balance for Account 800 has been aged with the results shown in column (b) of Table 12.2, thus completing phase one. It is now one year later. The 1990 retirements and additions are known and the new balance, 12935, has been calculated. The property must now be aged.

The second phase starts with the aged initial balance (i.e., the January 31, 1989 balance) and, given the type of curve, finds the life that will yield a simulated balance equal to the observed balance. The calculations shown in Table 12.2 assume the life characteristics are described by an Iowa R3 type curve (if the Gompertz-Makeham equation is used to describe the life characteristics, the constants c, g, and s must be specified). Column (c) is the R3–9 survivor curve; the last figure is the percent surviving at age 0.5 years. Column (d) shows the survivor ratios for the R3–9 survivor curve (e.g., the survivor ratio for the 1985 vintage is 90.35/94.40 or 0.9571). The simulated end-of-year balance shown in column (e) is the initial balance times the survivor rate during the year. The sum of column (e), 12505, is the simulated balance when an average life of 9 years is used. Because this is less than the actual balance of 12935, a larger average life must be used. Columns (f), (g), and (h) repeat the previous calculations using a R3–10 survivor curve; the resulting simulated balance is 12981, larger than the actual balance. Interpolation between the two computed balances yields an indicated life of 9.86 years. The final computed balance, or the age distribution, in column (i) is an interpolation of columns (e) and (h). A plot of the indicated average life versus the calendar year will often show random annual changes with an underlying trend. Because of its squiggly shape, this plot is called a *worm curve.*

Table 12.2. Calculation of computed mortality for 1990 for Account 800.

Year (a)	Balance 12/31/89 (b)	Using a R3-9 curve			Using a R3-10 curve			Final computed balance 12/31/90 (i)
		% Surv (c)	Surv ratio % (d)	Computed balance 12/31/90 (e)	% Surv (f)	Surv ratio % (g)	Computed balance 12/31/90 (h)	
1974	0				0.00			
1975	0				0.01	1.79		
1975	0	0.00			0.56	18.66		
1976	57	0.09	6.16	4	3.00	34.92	20	18
1977	152	1.46	24.75	38	8.59	46.61	71	66
1978	289	5.90	39.44	114	18.43	57.63	167	160
1979	462	14.96	51.55	238	31.98	67.60	312	302
1980	643	29.02	61.34	394	47.31	76.76	494	480
1981	805	47.31	75.19	605	61.63	84.08	677	667
1982	931	62.92	83.58	778	73.30	89.32	832	825
1983	1053	75.28	89.42	942	82.06	92.85	978	973
1984	1143	84.19	93.18	1065	88.38	95.23	1088	1085
1985	1233	90.35	95.71	1180	92.81	96.87	1194	1192
1986	1312	94.40	97.24	1276	95.81	98.02	1286	1285
1987	1382	97.08	98.43	1360	97.75	98.82	1366	1365
1988	1451	98.63	99.16	1439	98.92	99.35	1442	1441
1989	1521	99.47	99.49	1513	99.57	99.67	1516	1516
1990	1561	99.98	99.98	1559	99.90	99.90	1559	1559
	12434*			12505			12981	12935

* This total does not include the 1990 additions.

The aged balance is permanently recorded, so that the data that were initially unaged are now aged. Further, the computed aged data (i.e., the computed mortality data) can now be analyzed using actuarial techniques. The results of the analysis can be used to determine if another type curve should be used for future calculations. Proponents of this system argue that because the aged balances represent the best estimates of the data matrix at the time of the calculation, these estimates of aged data should be permanently recorded as aged data. Arguments against this system are that the results depend on the type of curve used, and that treating the estimates of aged data as observed aged data will compound any error made in the initial estimate of the curve type.

NOTES

1. Account 800 was introduced in Chapter 11.
2. Although the word mortality is widely used by depreciation professionals, it refers to the death of a human being, and its use to describe the retirement of a unit of industrial property is contrary to its definition. In general, *retirement* can be substituted for *mortality* in the context of depreciation; the term *computed retirement* is preferable to *computed mortality*.

13

Life Span Groups

A *LIFE SPAN* is the span of time between the birth and death of humans or other living organisms. Its meaning is often broadened to include inanimate objects. Kendig and Hutton (1979) called their book *Life Spans, Or How Long Things Last,* and this subtitle is a good working definition of the term life span when applied to industrial property.

Depreciation professionals use the term life span to describe both a unit of property and a group of property that will be retired as a unit. Examples of a unit of property are a hydroelectric dam or the building housing electrical generating equipment. Examples of a group of property that will be retired as a unit include the turbines, generators, and other equipment used to generate electrical power and housed in either the dam or building. In either case, the life of the dam or building and the life of the equipment housed in the facility are tied together, because the retirement of one usually causes the retirement of the other. The dispersion pattern of retirements from a group of life span property differs from the pattern of other property, because much of the life span property is retired simultaneously. The resulting survivor curve is truncated rather than gradually curving to zero percent surviving.

It is not unusual for life span groups to account for a significant portion of the total plant. They require special consideration when coding retirements, describing life characteristics, forecasting life and salvage, and calculating accruals for depreciation.

Figure 13.1 shows a survivor curve used to describe the life characteristics of a life span group of property. The life span shown in Figure 13.1 is

255

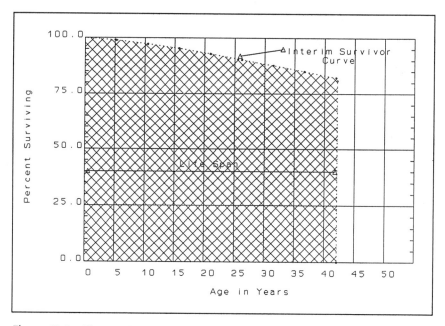

Figure 13.1. The survivor curve for a vintage group with a life span of 42 years and an Iowa L0–105 interim retirement curve.

42 years. The life span for a vintage group is defined by specifying the calendar year of the retirement. Typically, a part of the life span group of property, or vintage group, is retired before the end of the life span. These are called interim retirements. The pattern of interim retirements is often described by a portion of an Iowa curve, referred to as the interim retirement curve. The Iowa L0–105 interim survivor curve provides a good fit to the interim retirements shown in Figure 13.1. By age 42 years, interim retirements have totaled 20% of the initial installation. All the 80% remaining in service are retired during the forty-second year. The life characteristics of the life span group of property are described by an Iowa L0–105 survivor curve *truncated* at 42 years. The average life of the life span property should not be confused with the 105-year parameter of the interim survivor curve; the average life can not exceed the 42-year life span.

The average life of the property is the area under the survivor curve. One way to find the average life is to sum the areas associated with each age interval. The average life can be found more quickly by using information from the table of the Iowa curves. At age 42 (i.e., at 42/105 or 40% of the average life), the table value of the probable life of an L0–105 curve is 118.14% of the average life. Thus, the remaining life is 118.14% − 40% or approximately 78% of the average life. The remaining life is the area under the survivor curve and to the right of the current age divided by the fraction surviving at the current age (i.e., 78% = area/80%). Thus, this area is 78% × 0.80 or 62.4% of the average life. The total area under the Iowa curve is 100% of the average life, so the area under the curve shown in Figure 13.1 is 100% − 62.4% or 37.6% of the average life. Thus, the average life of the group of life span property shown in Figure 13.1 is 105 × 0.376 or 39 years.

The vintage group installed the year before the vintage group shown in Figure 13.1 shares the same retirement date, so its life span is 43 years. The vintage group installed the year after the vintage group shown in Figure 13.1 has a life span of 41 years. Accordingly, the average lives of these two vintage groups are slightly longer and slightly shorter than 39 years.

The special shape of the life span survivor curve must be considered when making depreciation calculations for a life span group of property. Figure 13.2 shows survivor curves representing three typical vintages from a depreciable group of property that will be retired in the year 2012. Usually the same curve is used to describe the interim retirements for each vintage, but each vintage has a different average life. The survivor curve for the 1970 vintage is the same curve shown in Figure 13.1 and has an average life

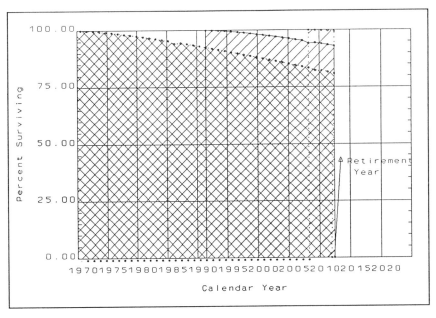

Figure 13.2. Survivor curves from three vintages in a continuous property group. Each vintage group will be retired during the same calendar year.

of 39 years. Even though the survivor curve for the 2008 vintage uses the L0–105 curve to describe the interim retirements, the installations during 2008 have an average life of slightly less than 4 years. Thus, description of the calendar year during which the property will be retired and the survivor curve describing the interim retirements provide the information needed to calculate the life characteristics of the property.

FORECASTING LIFE SPANS

Two general forces of retirement can be associated with life spans. Understanding these two forces may aid the depreciation professional when forecasting the life span.

One force includes any single event that can cause a facility to be retired. An example is the expiration of a required license or lease. Hydro-electric dams are often operated under a long-term license for the site on which the dam is constructed. Factors relating to economics, safety, or the environment, including concern for endangered species of fish or other wildlife, can result in failure to renew the license. Thus, an entire facility, including many components that could otherwise continue in operation for some time, is retired from service. Failure to renew the operating license of a nuclear power plant is another example of a single force that causes retirement at a predetermined date. In these examples, the date of the event that may cause retirement is easy to find. The forecasting challenge is to determine whether or not the license or lease will be renewed. If renewal is likely, the forecaster must predict the events that could result in retirement during the life of the renewed lease or license.

The other general force of retirement is a combination of factors that render continued use of the facility uneconomical. The terms *defender* and *challenger*[1] are useful here. Defender refers to the facility currently in serv-ice. With each passing year, the incremental costs of keeping the facility in service for one more year tend to increase. Maintenance and operational costs tend to increase with age. Compliance with governmental regulations relating to safety or protection of the environment may require modifica-tions that increase the annual cost of keeping the defender. Each year the service provided by the defender may become less adequate, resulting in additional direct costs of providing additional service or intangible costs resulting from customer dissatisfaction.

The challenger is a new facility that can be purchased or constructed to replace the defender. The challenger represents the most efficient design, the newest technology, and provides for the current operational needs. Al-though acquisition of the challenger requires a large capital expense, it provides better service and lower annual maintenance and operational costs than the defender. As each year passes, design and technology improve and operational needs change, and the gap between the efficiencies of the defender and the challenger widens. Eventually, potential savings associated with the difference in annual costs between the defender and challenger offset the annualized initial cost of the challenger, so that it becomes more economical to construct a new facility than to continue to operate the current facility. An economic analysis that considers these factors will result in an estimate of the time when it is no longer economical to continue operation of the current facility. This will not be a specific year, but a period when the incremental cost of keeping the defender one more year is about equal to the annualized cost of a new facility. The life span of the current facility falls in the period.

TECHNOLOGICAL OBSOLESCENCE

The life span idea and the computer programs that perform life span depreciation calculations can be used for mass property groups on which the major force of retirement is technological obsolescence. Though the obsolescence does not cause the entire group to be retired during a single year, it often results in a group of the property sharing a common technology being completely retired during a period of only several years. Retirements are related to the calendar year rather than age; old technology is replaced by new technology. Think of the midpoint of the period of heavy retirements because of technological obsolescence as defining the life span. Then the depreciation calculation for the group of property retired due to technological obsolescence is closely approximated by the life span model.

NOTE

1. The terms *challenger* and *defender* were popularized by George Terbough (1967) in his work addressing the economical replacement of manufacturing property.

14

Salvage Analysis and Forecasting

$\mathbf{T}$HIS chapter discusses the analysis of aged salvage data and illustrates the use of a mathematical model to help estimate future salvage. Table 8.1 at the end of Chapter 8 shows the aged retirements for Account 897, Utility Devices. These data will be needed in this chapter. For convenience, Table 8.1 will be called the *retirement matrix*.

Net salvage is composed of gross salvage and cost of retiring.[1] Data reflecting these two categories often are kept separately. Different economic forces act on each, so that the pattern of gross salvage versus age differs from the pattern of cost of retiring versus age. If separate records are kept, each pattern can be analyzed. If the records are combined, the separate patterns may be obscured.

Though the patterns of gross salvage and cost of retiring versus age may be different, the general process for analyzing the patterns is the same. The gross salvage for Utility Devices will be assumed to be zero. This will simplify our illustration, and the cost of retiring will provide an example on which to base a discussion of analyzing and forecasting salvage.

Table 14.1 (see end of chapter) shows the cost of retiring by age for Account 897. Each row represents a vintage (or placement or installation) year, and each column represents an experience (or calendar) year. Each entry in the table is the total cost of retiring units from that vintage during that experience year. Vintage years run from 1962 through 1990 and experience years from 1968 through 1990.

260

Table 14.2 (see end of chapter) shows the salvage ratios (SR) for Account 897. The SR is the salvage divided by the original cost of the retirements and usually is expressed as a percentage. During 1974, $9.00 from the 1971 vintage was retired (see the retirement matrix). The cost of retiring these dollars, shown in Table 14.1, was $2.03, and the resulting SR is −2.03/9.00 or −22.6%.

SALVAGE ANALYSIS

Salvage analysis starts with an examination of the data reflecting the total annual costs. Often these are the only data available. The final row in Table 14.1 shows the sum of each column and equals the total cost of retiring during the calendar year. The original cost of all retirements during the calendar year is shown in the retirement matrix. Table 14.3 (see end of chapter) combines these annual retirement amounts. Column (a) shows the calendar year, column (b) shows the total dollars retired during the year, and column (c) shows the total cost of retiring during the year. Column (d) is the salvage ratio (SR) for the year (i.e., column (c)/column (b) times 100%). Statistics based on single years are often erratic, making any underlying pattern difficult to detect. The final four columns are used in the calculation of SRs for 3-year "rolling bands" or moving averages. This averaging process smooths the pattern of ratios. Column (e) defines the rolling bands. Each band has 2 years in common with the bands on either side of it. The retirements, column (f), during the 1968–1970 band equal 18.00 + 30.00 + 42.00 or $90.00, and the cost of retiring, column (g), is (−4.28) + (−7.65) + (−10.42) or −22.35. Column (h) is the average SR during the 3-year rolling band.

The average realized salvage is the total cost of retiring divided by the total retirements, or −1452.28/3833.00 or −37.9%. The SRs steadily become more negative, from about −24% during the early years to about −40% during the most recent years. One reason for this trend is that the average age of the annual retirements has increased. The first additions were made in 1962. The average life of the property in Account 897 is known to be about 10 years. During 1969 the account was "young," because a retired unit could not have been older than 7 years (i.e., a retirement from the 1962 vintage), and most retirements were younger than 7 years (i.e., retirements from more recent vintages). The average age of the units retired during 1969 was 4.8 years (the age and number of dollars retired during 1969 can be found in the retirement matrix). As time passed, the average age of the retirements increased. By 1989 the average age of retirements was 10.2 years.

In a stable account with zero growth (see Chapter 9), the average age of the retirements equal the average life. Though the annual additions to

Account 897 vary from year to year, the net growth in the account is near zero. By 1989 the account is "mature." The oldest vintage was installed more than 25 years ago, so the age of retirements can range from less than a year to the maximum life. Thus, the average age of the retirements during 1989 would be expected to be near the average life, and they are. If no more additions were made to the account, the average age of retirements would increase with time, and, as the plant remaining in service becomes less and less, the average age of the retirements will increase and approach the maximum life. The sum of all future costs of retiring divided by the sum of future retirements (i.e., the current balance) is the future salvage ratio (FSR). The average salvage ratio (ASR) is the sum of the realized cost and the future cost of retiring, divided by the original cost of all additions.

The data in Table 14.3 show that the cost of retiring increases with the age of the retired unit. Though the average cost of retiring all units retired to date is known, the future cost of retiring must be estimated before the ASR can be estimated. Without additional data or adoption of a retirement model, it is difficult to describe how to estimate the future cost of retiring.

Before attempting to forecast the future cost of retiring, the depreciation professional should become familiar with the physical characteristics of the property in the account and with the manner of retiring the property from service. This knowledge will provide the basis for developing a preliminary model describing the relationship between age and salvage. One cost of retiring model is based on the observation that the cost of retiring a unit is often independent of the age of the unit. For example, the process of removing a gas service or a utility pole typically has little to do with the age of the service or pole. This model can be extended by assuming that the process of retiring the unit is labor intensive, and that the hours of labor required to retire a unit have remained constant during the history of the account. This implies the technology used to retire a unit has remained constant.

This model will be adopted and applied to Account 897. Remember that this is one of many possible models, and the depreciation professional cannot adopt a model unless he or she is familiar with the property involved and the company operations that affect the method of retirement. The logic of the mathematical model must reflect the actual world. Whether the model reflects reality is a judgment made by the analyst.

If the model just described reflects the cost of retiring a utility device, then, during periods of inflation, the SRs can be expected to increase as a unit becomes older. Though the hours of labor required to retire the unit remain constant, labor rates can be expected to inflate each year. Thus, the SR for a group of property installed during the same year can be expected to increase (i.e., become more negative) each successive year in direct proportion to the annual rate of inflation. A more comprehensive analysis of the aged data will reveal the historical relationship between age and salvage ratio and may provide support for the model. Chapter 8 introduced the idea of placement bands and experience bands. A placement band follows the history of a vintage through different experience years, while an experience band follows the history over all vintages during the specified experience years.

These ideas are used to construct a graph of the SR versus age for the placement band consisting of the 1970, 1971, and 1972 vintages. Table 14.4 (see end of chapter) reproduces part of the annual cost of retiring during 1970, 1971, and 1972 from Table 14.1. The cost of retiring is shown in the upper portion of Table 14.4.

Table 14.5 (see end of chapter) shows how the data are used to construct salvage ratios by age. Column (a) of Table 14.5 shows the age interval and column (b) shows the sum of retirements from the 1970, 1971, and 1972 vintages during each age interval. Column (c) shows the corresponding cost of retiring. To obtain the total cost of retiring during the 0.0–0.5 year age interval, refer to the upper portion of Table 14.4. Sum the first entry in each row, $0 + 0 + (-1.02)$ or -1.02. These are the costs of retiring during 1970 from the 1970 vintage, during 1971 from the 1971 vintage, and during 1972 from the 1972 vintage, respectively. Column (d) is the SR, or the cost of retiring divided by the original cost expressed as a percentage. Observe that the SR during the initial age interval is about -20%, and that the SRs steadily become more negative as the property ages. After 20 years, the SR is almost -70%. Because these figures represent costs, the costs increase but the SRs decrease (become more negative).

Because the SR is the quotient of dollars in different price levels (i.e., the retirement year price level is reflected in the numerator and the installation year price level is reflected in the denominator), it may be helpful to calculate the SR using a constant price level. This removes inflation from the ratio so that the salvage schedule adjusted for inflation[2] can be analyzed.

To calculate the adjusted SR shown in column (f) of Table 14.5, return to Table 14.4 and note the row labeled CPI-U. These data are the July consumer price indexes for all urban consumers (CPI-U) from the U.S. Bureau of Labor Statistics for the years 1970 through 1977. The July figures were chosen because both additions and retirements are assumed to take place at midyear. During 1975, the cost of retiring units placed in service during 1971 totaled $-\$1.49$. To adjust 1975 dollars to 1971 dollars, multiply the 1975 dollars by the ratio of the 1971 index/1975 index. This is $-1.49 \times (40.70/54.20)$ or $-\$1.12$ measured in July 1971 dollars. The lower portion of the table shows the salvage from the upper portion of the table after being adjusted to dollars during the placement year. The adjusted cost of retiring can now be used to calculate the adjusted cost of retiring shown in column (e) of Table 14.5. The original cost of the retirements shown in column (b) and the salvage shown in column (e) are measured in dollars of the same price level. Column (f) shows the adjusted SR, i.e., column (e)/column (b) × 100%.

Figure 14.1 is a graph of columns (d) and (f). Observe the graph of the SRs with inflation. If the SRs are increasing in proportion to inflation, they will form a pattern that is curved upward, reflecting the exponential growth of the price levels. However, it is difficult to tell the underlying shape of this curve. Observe the graph of the SRs when inflation is removed. The pattern of constant SRs, with a value of about −20%, is clear. Though a formal statistical test of the relationship can be made, such a test is not necessary because the graph is strong evidence that when inflation is removed, the cost of retiring is independent of age. Thus, the data supports, or verifies, the model that the time required to retire a unit is constant and that the increased cost of retiring is proportional to the rate of inflation.

Can this model be used to forecast future cost of retiring? *If* the depreciation professional believes that the same procedure for retiring that has been used in the past will continue to be used in the future, *then* the model can be used to forecast future cost of retiring. Under this model, future SRs

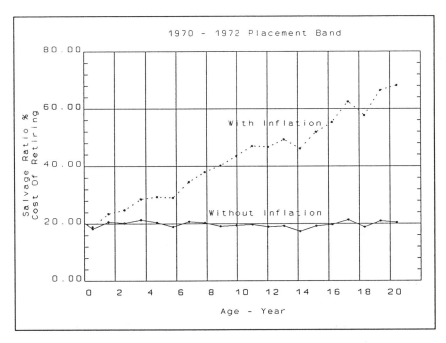

Figure 14.1. Salvage ratios versus age both with and without inflation. Data are from Table 14.3.

can be derived if three parameters are estimated. They are (a) the SR during the 0.0–0.5 year age interval, (b) the annual rate of inflation, and (c) the life characteristics of the property.

Table 14.6 (see end of chapter) shows the construction of the salvage schedule for the 1981 vintage. Construction of the survivor curve for this vintage is shown in Table 6.12 of Chapter 6, and the survivor curve from that table is shown in column (b) of Table 14.6. The values from age 0.0–8.5 years are based on the observed exposures and retirements. The values from age 8.5–21.5 years are based on the estimate that the future life characteristics will be described by an Iowa S0–12 survivor curve. The SRs, column (d), from age 0.0–8.5 years are the observed values shown in Table 14.2. The forecast for all age intervals beyond 8.5 years is the SR from the previous age interval inflated by 5% (i.e., the SR during age interval 9.5–10.5 is 29.72 × 1.05 or 31.20%). The 5% rate is the estimate of the future inflation rate. Column (e) is the SR weighted by the fraction retired, i.e., column (c) × column (d)/100%, and the sum of column (e) is the ASR, −34.81%. The realized salvage ratio is shown in column (f) and the future salvage ratio (FSR) is shown in column (g). Because the observed SRs were used during the early age intervals, it was not necessary to estimate the initial SR.

THE BROAD AND VINTAGE GROUP MODELS

Depreciation calculations require an estimate of the average salvage ratio (ASR) and the future salvage ratio (FSR) for each vintage. The method of determining these ratios depends on whether the broad group or vintage group model is used.

If the broad group model is used, the same salvage schedule is applied to each vintage. Chapter 6 contains an illustration of the application of a single salvage schedule to each vintage. Table 6.11 of that chapter is a salvage schedule used in the calculation of the annual accrual using both the AL and ELG procedures. The salvage ratio during the 0.0–0.5 year age interval is −15%, and it increases (becomes more negative) at an annual rate of 5%. These ratios are used with the ELG procedure. The Iowa S0–12 curve describes the life characteristics of each vintage. The resulting ASR, −28%, is used with the AL procedure. The FSR at the start of each age interval is matched to the appropriate vintage. Depending on the depreciation system, the CAD of the future accrual is then calculated using the proper FSR. Thus, a single salvage schedule provides the information to calculate the annual accrual for each vintage.

If the vintage group model is applied to salvage, a different salvage schedule is applied to each vintage. The calculation of the schedule for the 1981 vintage is shown in Table 14.6. It results in the ASR and the FSR for the 1981 vintage, and similar calculations must be made for all other vintages. The vintage group model, which uses observed life and observed salvage data to construct the realized portion of the schedule, is a refinement of the broad group model. It has the advantage of more accurately reflecting the actual world transactions then does the broad group model.

THE SIMULATION OF SALVAGE BY AGE

It is not uncommon to record only the total salvage during the year. The data shown in Table 14.3 are of this type. Estimates of the ASR and an average FSR must be based on the unaged salvage data. When retirements are recorded by age, an alternate method of using this data is available. The alternative requires the depreciation professional to adopt a salvage model and use it to allocate the total annual salvage to each vintage. The result is salvage by age, as shown in Table 14.1, except the data are simulated rather than observed. The simulated data can be used in the manner described earlier in this chapter. However, the simulated data cannot be used to verify the model because to do so would be circular logic.

Table 14.7 (see end of chapter) shows how the $10.42 cost of retiring during 1970 can be allocated to the 1962 through 1970 vintages *if* the cost of retiring model discussed earlier in this chapter is adopted. The depreciation professional must be familiar with the account Utility Devices so that he or she can judge whether the model will result in a reasonable representation of the cost of retiring. Column (a) shows the vintage year and column (b) shows the original cost of the retirements during the 1970 calendar year. Column (c) shows the consumer price index (CPI-U) for July of the vintage year. Column (d) shows the ratio of the CPI-U for the vintage year to the CPI-U for the 1970 calendar year. For 1963, the ratio 61.0/39.0 or 1.56 suggests that a dollar spent in 1963 would purchase 1.56 times as much as a dollar spent in 1970. Column (e) is the product of column (b) times column (d), and represents a restatement of the vintage dollars to 1970 price level dollars. The $14.00 retired in 1963 are restated as $21.90 in the 1970 price level.

Thus, entries in column (e) are proportional to the *units* retired during 1970 *if* the model is applicable *and* the CPI-U is an appropriate index. The entries in column (e) are used as weights to allocate the $10.42 cost of retiring. Column (f) is the entry from column (e) divided by the sum of column (e). The fraction of the $10.42 allocated to the 1963 vintage is 21.90/61.84 or 0.3541. The allocation to the 1962 vintage is 0.3541 × 10.42 or $3.69, as shown in column (g). If this process is repeated for each calendar year, the result is the simulated cost of retiring by age. The simulated data can be used to construct salvage schedules similar to the schedule shown in Table 14.5.

SUMMARY

It is desirable to analyze gross salvage and cost of retiring separately. The two salvage schedules can be combined to find the average net salvage ratio and the future net salvage ratios by age. Data that reflect salvage by age, rather than only the total annual salvage, provide valuable information.

In practice, the procedure for estimating salvage varies widely. The depreciation professional's judgment of whether a procedure is reasonable is based on several variables. These include the magnitude of the salvage ratio, the available data, and the importance of the depreciable group. It is not unusual for a mass property account of a utility to exhibit large negative salvage. In such cases, the depreciation accrual rate may be more sensitive to the salvage estimate than to the life estimate.

If both the realized gross salvage and realized cost of retiring are near zero, extensive analyses may not be productive because the depreciation calculations are not sensitive to salvage ratios near zero. In such cases, the key to forecasting is predicting whether there will be a significant change in future operations that will change the levels of gross salvage or cost of retiring.

Often the only available data are the total annual gross salvage and cost of retiring. An example of this type of data is shown in Table 14.3. When analyzing unaged salvage, remember that realized salvage depends on the age of the retirements. Realized salvage starts at zero and does not reach the average until the final unit in the group is retired. Thus, the average age of the annual retirements and the average life of the group are important variables. Continuous property groups showing growth typically have large differences between the average age of the retirements and the average life of the group.

Salvage ratios are a function of inflation. For long-lived property, the salvage associated with the longest-lived property is affected most. However, this effect may not be reflected in the data for some time. A mathematical model that includes the effect of salvage can be a valuable forecasting tool. Salvage data by age contains information helpful for constructing and verifying a mathematical model.

NOTES

1. Cost of retiring is also called cost of removal.
2. See Chapter 4 for a discussion of inflation and salvage ratios.

Table 14.1   The cost of retiring by age for Account 897.

Calendar Year	68	69	70	71	72	73	74	75	76	Account 897 - Cost of 77
Year installed										
1962	1.92	1.87	3.21	.72	2.42	2.77	5.04	.87	.00	.00
1963	.00	.89	3.17	1.84	2.75	2.51	5.34	4.37	5.06	9.89
1964	.66	.50	1.00	1.94	1.06	2.35	2.99	6.77	18.36	15.50
1965	.00	1.54	.00	2.93	2.21	2.66	2.74	1.76	1.40	.00
1966	1.71	1.96	1.75	2.88	4.88	3.20	4.68	11.57	5.82	.77
1967	.00	.44	.89	3.26	3.70	8.84	4.14	6.40	6.67	2.99
1968	.00	.44	.40	.50	.00	.89	.95	1.58	1.76	2.33
1969		.00	.00	2.25	.00	.00	.00	.00	.56	.00
1970			.00	.20	.19	1.58	.80	.81	.88	2.48
1971				.00	.71	.63	2.03	1.49	1.57	2.79
1972					1.02	.41	1.30	2.83	3.13	7.03
1973						1.72	.00	.00	.00	2.11
1974							.00	.22	.73	1.86
1975								.00	.00	.00
1976									.00	3.29
1977										1.46
1978										
1979										
1980										
1981										
1982										
1983										
1984										
1985										
1986										
1987										
1988										
1989										
1990										
Total	4.28	7.65	10.42	16.51	18.93	27.57	30.02	38.67	45.94	52.48

Utility Devices

Retiring

78	79	80	81	82	83	84	85	86	87	88	89	90
.00	2.51	.00	.00	.00	.00	.00	.00	.00	.00	.00	.00	.00
2.29	4.13	3.96	4.00	3.16	3.07	4.09	.00	.00	.00	.00	.00	.00
11.02	1.33	4.63	3.93	.00	.00	.00	.00	.00	.00	.00	.00	.00
2.40	3.15	2.12	13.34	5.10	3.61	.00	.00	.00	.00	.00	.00	.00
14.60	2.59	3.08	26.85	2.27	1.23	1.70	12.56	3.94	9.68	.00	.00	12.45
2.64	10.61	2.50	12.68	4.68	8.78	6.71	5.44	.00	.00	.00	.00	.00
2.24	2.50	2.46	4.79	19.23	6.67	6.79	8.46	4.55	.00	10.78	.00	.00
10.12	.00	7.55	.00	.00	.00	7.25	.00	.00	.00	.00	.00	2.13
1.73	2.35	3.64	3.15	1.93	2.81	2.30	1.70	3.83	2.39	.00	2.66	8.18
3.19	4.26	2.95	5.85	.87	4.47	4.92	.00	8.62	13.47	9.09	11.60	.00
7.97	6.78	7.29	9.98	4.44	20.88	4.34	6.09	.00	4.20	5.40	5.38	6.88
11.54	7.09	5.56	3.41	15.67	10.23	9.82	24.77	10.68	16.94	.00	.00	6.73
.56	2.48	2.01	2.86	4.97	4.59	3.20	2.80	1.37	3.44	4.86	5.19	2.29
.00	.00	1.54	2.00	9.31	8.46	5.52	3.94	2.52	1.78	3.73	3.61	.00
1.65	10.88	8.86	20.24	7.16	27.59	9.78	7.55	23.88	10.28	8.16	5.71	5.34
.00	.00	1.10	.85	2.13	4.15	3.82	6.49	20.16	24.95	23.93	7.00	.00
.00	.99	.00	2.02	.00	5.39	.00	26.01	7.82	9.10	8.52	7.06	.00
	.00	.00	.00	.00	1.91	5.92	8.76	5.36	11.44	9.95	8.95	4.38
		.64	.00	.00	.95	.00	22.51	4.96	11.11	9.96	9.82	1.89
			1.22	.00	.45	.90	.66	1.39	2.57	2.39	3.11	.00
				1.05	1.14	.00	.00	1.48	.44	.51	2.67	2.40
					.00	.00	.46	.92	1.24	1.64	2.30	.27
						.00	.00	.00	.00	.00	8.11	.00
							2.18	.93	1.48	2.28	3.66	.00
								.75	.00	.00	.00	.00
									.00	1.43	1.15	.45
										.00	1.69	.00
											.00	.00
												.00
71.96	61.65	59.89	117.16	81.97	116.39	77.04	140.41	103.17	124.50	102.63	89.68	53.38

Table 14.2. The salvage ratios (SR) by age for Account 897.

Account 897 - Utility Devices

Salvage Ratios ** All Ratios Are Negative

Calendar Year → Year installed	68	69	70	71	72	73	74	75	76	77	78	79	80	81	82	83	84	85	86	87	88	89	90
1962	23.9	31.2	29.2	35.8	34.5	30.8	38.8	43.3	.0	.0	.0	50.3	.0	.0	.0	.0	.0	.0	.0	.0	.0	.0	.0
1963	.0	22.2	22.6	30.6	22.9	31.4	31.4	36.4	31.6	44.9	45.7	45.9	56.6	66.7	63.2	61.4	68.2	.0	.0	.0	.0	.0	.0
1964	22.0	25.1	25.0	27.7	26.6	29.4	33.2	29.4	36.0	35.2	36.7	44.4	57.9	49.1	63.8	.0	.0	.0	.0	.0	.0	.0	.0
1965	.0	25.6	25.0	22.6	27.6	26.6	30.5	35.2	35.0	.0	48.0	45.0	52.9	55.6	56.7	72.2	.0	.0	65.6	74.5	.0	.0	83.0
1966	24.4	24.5	22.3	26.2	22.2	26.7	29.2	36.2	32.3	38.4	38.4	43.2	51.3	62.4	58.4	61.4	56.7	66.1	.0	.0	77.0	.0	.0
1967	.0	22.2	20.2	21.7	28.4	23.9	31.9	37.6	35.1	33.2	37.7	44.2	50.1	52.8	60.1	58.5	67.1	60.4	56.9	.0	.0	66.5	70.9
1968	.0	22.0	.0	24.8	.0	22.2	31.8	31.6	35.3	38.8	32.1	41.7	49.2	53.2	.0	60.7	61.7	60.5	.0	59.8	60.6	58.0	68.2
1969		.0	.0	20.5	.0	.0	.0	.0	28.1	.0	34.9	.0	44.4	.0	48.2	.0	55.7	.0	63.8	53.9	54.0	67.2	57.3
1970				20.2	19.1	22.6	26.7	27.1	29.2	31.0	34.6	39.2	45.5	45.0	43.5	46.8	46.1	56.8	50.7	52.5	53.9	51.9	61.2
1971				.0	17.8	21.0	22.6	29.8	26.1	31.0	31.9	38.8	42.1	41.8	44.4	44.7	49.2	.0	.0	54.7	46.7	45.1	45.8
1972					20.3	20.5	25.9	28.3	28.5	30.6	28.4	37.7	38.4	39.9	36.4	47.5	48.2	50.8	50.0	49.1	40.8	44.0	44.5
1973						21.5	.0	.0	.0	26.4	31.2	37.3	39.7	37.8	45.2	46.5	49.1	48.6	54.7	44.5	43.5	35.0	.0
1974							.0	22.1	24.4	23.3	27.8	31.0	33.4	40.8	35.8	41.7	45.7	46.7	45.8	40.6	34.1	35.3	33.7
1975								.0	.0	.0	.0	.0	30.8	33.3	34.1	35.2	34.5	39.4	42.1	39.6	33.2	33.9	31.4
1976									.0	21.9	23.6	29.4	26.8	33.1	30.5	34.6	37.6	37.8	44.2	35.0	29.3	33.9	24.0
1977										18.2	.0	.0	27.4	28.5	.0	33.7	34.7	32.4	38.0	35.3	25.4	26.7	26.8
1978											.0	24.7	.0	25.2	.0	27.3	.0	32.5	34.0	29.3	23.5	28.8	.0
1979												.0	.0	.0	.0	23.8	29.6	27.4	28.2	29.2	22.8	23.2	22.5
1980													21.5	.0	.0	22.7	.0	26.5	26.1	25.7	.0	24.4	.0
1981														20.4	20.9	22.8	22.4	22.0	24.6	21.9	17.9	21.1	.0
1982															20.9	22.8	.0	.0	23.1	24.9		19.2	22.5
1983																22.8	22.4	23.1	.0	18.5		.0	
1984																	.0	.0	23.3	.0			
1985																		21.8	18.8				
1986																			18.8				
1987																				18.5			
1988																					17.9		
1989																						19.2	
1990																							.0

Table 14.3. Salvage ratios by calendar year for Account 897, Utility Devices. Column (d) is the SR for a single year and column (h) is the average SR for 3-year rolling bands.

Year (a)	Dollars retired (b)	Cost of retiring (c)	SR % (d)	Years (e)	Dollars retired (f)	Cost of retiring (g)	SR % (h)
1968	18.00	-4.28	-23.8				
1969	30.00	-7.65	-25.5	1968-70	90.00	-22.35	-24.8
1970	42.00	-10.42	-24.8	1969-71	140.00	-34.57	-24.7
1971	68.00	-16.51	-24.3	1970-72	186.00	-45.86	-24.7
1972	76.00	-18.93	-24.9	1971-73	252.00	-63.01	-25.0
1973	108.00	-27.57	-25.5	1972-74	281.00	-76.51	-27.2
1974	97.00	-30.02	-30.9	1973-75	320.00	-96.25	-30.1
1975	115.00	-38.67	-33.6	1974-76	350.00	-114.62	-32.7
1976	138.00	-45.94	-33.3	1975-77	415.00	-137.09	-33.0
1977	162.00	-52.48	-32.4	1976-78	510.00	-170.38	-33.4
1978	210.00	-71.96	-34.3	1977-79	535.00	-186.08	-34.8
1979	163.00	-61.65	-37.8	1978-80	524.00	-193.49	-36.9
1980	151.00	-59.89	-39.7	1979-81	574.00	-238.69	-41.6
1981	260.00	-117.16	-45.1	1980-82	597.00	-259.01	-43.4
1982	186.00	-81.97	-44.1	1981-83	733.00	-315.51	-43.0
1983	287.00	-116.39	-40.6	1982-84	644.00	-275.40	-42.8
1984	171.00	-77.04	-45.1	1983-85	834.00	-333.84	-40.0
1985	376.00	-140.41	-37.3	1984-86	806.00	-320.62	-39.8
1986	259.00	-103.17	-39.8	1985-87	943.00	-368.09	-39.0
1987	308.00	-124.50	-40.4	1986-88	823.00	-330.31	-40.1
1988	256.00	-102.63	-40.1	1987-89	814.00	-316.81	-38.9
1989	250.00	-89.68	-35.9	1988-90	608.00	-245.69	-40.4
1990	102.00	-53.38	-52.3				
Total	3833.00	-1452.28	-37.9				

Table 14.4. Aged cost of retiring for the 1970 through 1972 vintage, as extracted from Table 14.1. The lower portion of the table adjusts the annual cost of retiring to the price level during the year the property was installed using the consumer price index for all urban consumers (CPI-U) from the U.S. Bureau of Labor Statistics, 1982-1984 = 100.

	70	71	72	73	74	75	76	77	78
1970	.00	-.20	-.19	-1.58	-.80	-.81	-.88	-2.48	-1.73
1971		.00	-.71	-.63	-2.03	-1.49	-1.57	-2.79	-3.19
1972			-1.02	-.41	-1.30	-2.83	-3.13	-7.03	-7.97
CPI-U	39.00	40.70	41.90	44.30	49.40	54.20	57.10	61.00	65.70
1970	.00	-.19	-.18	-1.39	-.63	-.59	-.60	-1.58	-1.03
1971		.00	-.69	-.58	-1.67	-1.12	-1.12	-1.86	-1.98
1972			-1.02	-.39	-1.10	-2.19	-2.30	-4.83	-5.08

Table 14.5. The salvage ratio schedule for the 1970-1992
placement band. The nonadjusted retirement cost
is measured in dollars during the year of
retirement. The adjusted retirement cost is
measured in dollars during the year of installation.

Age interval (a)	Dollars retired (b)	Non-adj cost of retiring (c)	Non-adj SR (d)	Adjusted cost of retiring (e)	Adjusted SR (f)
0- 0.5	5.00	-1.02	-20.3	-1.02	-20.3
.5- 1.5	7.00	-1.32	-18.9	-1.27	-18.2
1.5- 2.5	9.00	-2.12	-23.5	-1.86	-20.6
2.5- 3.5	26.00	-6.44	-24.8	-5.25	-20.2
3.5- 4.5	19.00	-5.43	-28.6	-4.05	-21.3
4.5- 5.5	32.00	-9.41	-29.4	-6.53	-20.4
5.5- 6.5	40.00	-11.63	-29.1	-7.54	-18.9
6.5- 7.5	36.00	-12.45	-34.6	-7.45	-20.7
7.5- 8.5	35.00	-13.29	-38.0	-7.10	-20.3
8.5- 9.5	38.00	-15.28	-40.2	-7.27	-19.1
9.5-10.5	32.00	-13.93	-43.5	-6.22	-19.4
10.5-11.5	53.00	-24.90	-47.0	-10.46	-19.7
11.5-12.5	23.00	-10.74	-46.7	-4.34	-18.9
12.5-13.5	28.00	-13.81	-49.3	-5.39	-19.2
13.5-14.5	5.00	-2.30	-46.1	-.86	-17.3
14.5-15.5	28.00	-14.52	-51.9	-5.37	-19.2
15.5-16.5	41.00	-22.69	-55.3	-8.09	-19.7
16.5-17.5	27.00	-16.86	-62.5	-5.75	-21.3
17.5-18.5	32.00	-18.47	-57.7	-6.00	-18.8
18.5-19.5	4.00	-2.66	-66.5	-.83	-20.9
19.5-20.5	12.00	-8.18	-68.2	-2.45	-20.4

Table 14.6. The salvage schedule for the 1981 vintage. Observed values
are used through age 8.5 years. The future survivor curve
is an Iowa SO-12 curve. Future salvage ratios are found
by inflating the SR from the previous year by 5%.

Age interval (a)	Percent surviving (b)	Percent retired (c)	SR % (d)	Wtd SR (e)	Realized SR% (f)	Future SR% (g)
0.0- 0.5	100.00	3.17	-20.40	-.65	.00	-34.81
0.5- 1.5	96.83	.00	.00	.00	-20.40	-35.29
1.5- 2.5	96.83	1.06	-22.40	-.24	-20.40	-35.29
2.5- 3.5	95.77	2.12	-22.00	-.47	-20.90	-35.43
3.5- 4.5	93.65	1.59	-23.20	-.37	-21.27	-35.73
4.5- 5.5	92.06	3.17	-25.70	-.82	-21.65	-35.95
5.5- 6.5	88.89	5.29	-26.60	-1.41	-22.81	-36.32
6.5- 7.5	83.60	4.76	-28.30	-1.35	-24.03	-36.93
7.5- 8.5	78.84	5.82	.00	.00	-24.99	-37.45
8.5- 9.5	73.02	5.77	-29.72	-1.71	-19.60	-40.44
9.5-10.5	67.25	5.92	-31.20	-1.85	-21.38	-41.36
10.5-11.5	61.33	6.02	-32.76	-1.97	-22.89	-42.34
11.5-12.5	55.31	6.06	-34.40	-2.09	-24.22	-43.38
12.5-13.5	49.24	6.02	-36.12	-2.18	-25.43	-44.48
13.5-14.5	43.22	5.92	-37.92	-2.24	-26.57	-45.65
14.5-15.5	37.30	5.78	-39.82	-2.30	-27.64	-46.88
15.5-16.5	31.52	5.53	-41.81	-2.31	-28.67	-48.17
16.5-17.5	25.99	5.25	-43.90	-2.30	-29.65	-49.52
17.5-18.5	20.74	4.88	-46.10	-2.25	-30.59	-50.94
18.5-19.5	15.86	4.43	-48.40	-2.15	-31.49	-52.44
19.5-20.5	11.43	3.90	-50.82	-1.98	-32.34	-54.00
20.5-21.5	7.53	3.26	-53.36	-1.74	-33.12	-55.65
21.5-22.5	4.27	2.48	-56.03	-1.39	-33.81	-57.39
22.5-23.5	1.79	1.52	-58.83	-.89	-34.37	-59.28
23.5-24.5	.27	.27	-61.78	-.17	-34.74	-61.78
24.5-25.5	.00	.00	-64.86	.00	-34.81	
				-34.81		

Table 14.7. Allocation of the total cost of retiring during 1970, $10.42, to each vintage.

Year (a)	Retired (b)	CPI-U (c)	Ratio of CPI-U to 39.00 (d)	Adjusted retired (e)	Factor (f)	Allocated cost of retiring (g)
1962	11.00	65.7	1.68	18.53	.2996	3.12
1963	14.00	61.0	1.56	21.90	.3541	3.69
1964	4.00	57.1	1.46	5.86	.0947	.99
1965	0.00	54.2	1.39	.00	.0000	.00
1966	7.00	49.4	1.27	8.87	.1434	1.49
1967	4.00	44.3	1.14	4.54	.0735	.77
1968	2.00	41.9	1.07	2.15	.0347	.36
1969	0.00	40.7	1.04	.00	.0000	.00
1970	0.00	39.0	1.00	.00	.0000	.00
	42.00			61.84		10.42

15 | Forecasting Service Life

LIKE it or not, the accrual rates used to calculate annual depreciation charges are based on forecasts of the service lives and salvage values of the plant in service. Industrial property often has average lives of 15 to 40 years, with the longer-lived units surviving 80 years or more. Prediction this far into the future of the many factors that will ultimately affect the retirement of the plant currently in service places the depreciation analyst in an uncomfortable position. The analyst is required to forecast events that will not culminate for many years, very likely after his or her retirement from the forecasting business. Furthermore, that forecast of service life may be used to calculate a depreciation rate to three-decimal accuracy that, in turn, will be applied to the plant in service to calculate the millions of dollars of annual depreciation charge. The depreciation professional may wish for an easier route to the calculation of depreciation, but it remains true that reasonable forecasts are a requisite to timely capital recovery. Although forecasting the service life of industrial property is an imprecise art, there are systematic approaches to forecasting that will lead to reasonable predictions.

Forecast has several synonyms, including foretell and predict. One dictionary states that "foretell is the general term for a telling or indicating beforehand and does not itself suggest the means used." Predict "more often suggests deduction from facts already known or the use of scientific calculation." To forecast is "to estimate or calculate in advance; predict or seek to predict." Prophesy "implies prediction by divine inspiration or occult knowledge." The depreciation analyst can be said to require either a forecast or a prediction but would do well to avoid prophesies.

274

It is important to remember forecasters in the public utilities industry must not only develop a reasonable forecast, but they also must be able to convince others that the forecast is reasonable. The accuracy of a forecast is not known until time passes and the forecast can be compared with outcome of events under consideration. A forecast must be judged on, in very general terms, its reasonableness. Thus, the forecaster must use a forecasting process that both convinces others of its validity and has a good chance of eventually proving reasonably accurate.

This chapter will discuss the relationship of forecasting to life analysis, identify forces of retirement to be forecast, attempt to develop a general approach to forecasting, and outline specific forecasting procedures and the circumstances under which they might be applicable.

LIFE ANALYSIS

Life analysis is the historical foundation on which a foretelling of the future is based and precedes the process of life forecasting. Life analysis may be defined as the process of separating and examining all information that may add to the understanding of the forces that affect the life characteristics of the property under consideration. The major results of life analysis are summarized in the following list.

1. Identification of the life characteristics of installed property;
2. Identification of the historical trends in the life characteristics of installed property;
3. Identification of those factors that have affected the life characteristics of retired property. These factors can be divided into two categories: (a) those factors primarily associated with the technology and physical attributes of the property, and (b) those factors associated with the environment in which the property operates.

The identification of these characteristics, trends, and factors is based on historical evidence. While conducting a life analysis, the analyst may become aware of information concerning events that may occur in the future and, therefore, be of importance to the forecaster. For example, the life analyst might find that lack of a comprehensive maintenance plan has been an important factor in historical retirements, but that management is considering increasing expenditures for maintenance and plans to install a comprehensive maintenance plan. Though this is a possible future event rather than a historical fact, the analyst would be expected to include this extra information in the life analysis report. So, a fourth result of life analysis could be added to our list.

4. Identification of special activities or events that may, in the future, affect retirement of property. This will include only those activities that the analyst encountered during the life analysis process and would not be a comprehensive list.

Life analysis necessarily precedes life forecasting. Analysis of historical data and events gives the forecaster the raw material on which the forecast will be based.

RETIREMENT: A MANAGEMENT DECISION

Early work in the analysis of service life of industrial property was based on models, developed by actuarial scientists, that described age characteristics of human populations. *Forces of mortality* is a descriptive term used by these scientists, and, although "mortality" properly refers to humans, the term has been applied to industrial property. Forces of retirement is perhaps a better phrase to use to describe the various conditions that lead to the retirement of industrial property. Many useful categories of forces of retirement have been made, and the following list is from *Engineering Valuation and Depreciation* (Marston, Winfrey, and Hempstead, 1953).

A. Physical condition
   1. Accident
   2. Catastrophe
   3. Deterioration from time
   4. Wear and tear from use
B. Functional situations
   5. Inadequacy
   6. Obsolescence
      a. Economic
      b. Style and mode
C. Situations unrelated to the property
   7. Termination of the need
   8. Abandonment of the enterprise
   9. Requirement of the public authority

Retirement of industrial property is the result of a management decision. Some of these are easy decisions. When a car, for example, runs into and destroys a telephone pole, management has little choice but to retire and replace the pole. The decision to retire an electric generating system in more difficult and its timing is critical to the financial health of the company.

Decisions to replace industrial property are, to some extent, a function of the laws of nature that determine the physical characteristics and properties of materials and processes used to provide services. Many models used in engineering reflect natural phenomena and are based on the work of mathematicians, physicists, chemists, and other scientists. For example, failure of railroad track caused by wear may be a highly predictable function of the cumulative tons of traffic carried by the track. Models that develop this functional relationship can be very useful in developing maintenance policy, planning operations, and, to some extent, predicting service life.

However, most retirements are more subtle functions of factors such as the economy, changing technology, or government regulations, all of which significantly influence management decisions. Other factors such as maintenance policy or organizational goals are a direct result of management decisions. It is accurate to think of retirement as a management decision and realize that when forecasting service life, the various factors that mold management thought and action must be identified.

FORECASTING: A SYSTEMATIC APPROACH

The process used for developing a forecast of service life characteristics is heavily dependent on the circumstances surrounding the specific group of property under consideration. The appropriate forecasting approach can range from a traditional, well-defined, highly mechanical process to a nontraditional, loosely defined process involving newly developed forecasting techniques. In addition, because forecasting involves significant portions of judgment, experts may disagree upon which process is appropriate.

Most of the forecasting problems encountered in public utilities can be classified into several general categories. One method of developing a systematic approach to forecasting is to define the general categories and then prescribe a forecasting approach to each. When necessary, additional categories can be defined and appropriate forecasting approaches developed. Sometimes new techniques may be needed. The set of categories and prescriptions then defines a systematic approach to forecasting.

Seven Major Categories

This section defines seven general categories of forecasting problems. The characteristics of each category are defined by the results or output from the life analysis process. Each category is broad enough to maintain its own distinct characteristics. Although these seven categories are not exhaustive, they do include a significant proportion of the forecasting situations encountered in the public utilities industry.

Category 1 includes those situations where the property has a long life history that has been well documented. Usually this documentation would include record keeping by vintage so that aged data are available and actuarial techniques of analysis can be applied.

Starting in 1939 the Uniform Systems of Accounts required systematic recording of accounting data for many regulated public utility companies. If aged data from that time were available, then the property would be described by a lengthy history. For many property groups, plant installed in the early forties would be nearly fully retired, and the survivor curves of vintages installed during that era would show only a small portion of the original installations still surviving. Analysis of data from these groups would provide the forecaster with abundant and reliable information concerning the property.

Besides the life history requirement, there is a second prerequisite that must be met before property is placed in this category. This is the historical rate of change in the life characteristics of the property. The life analysis must show that the life characteristics have been relatively stable over the life history and particularly over recent history, if the property is to fall into category 1.

Category 2 is similar to category 1 in that it includes those situations where the property has a long and well-documented life history, but it differs in that it includes those cases where life analysis shows moderate changes in the life characteristics.

The rate of change of the service life is of particular interest. Let the annual rate of change of the average service life be an indicator of the relative annual rate of change. For example, if analysis indicated that the recent average annual change in life was about $+1$ years per year, and that during this time the average service life was about 35 years, then the relative annual rate of change, expressed as a percentage, would be $+1/35 \times 100\%$ or about $+3\%$. Relative annual rates of change between -5% to -2% and $+2\%$ to $+5\%$ may be considered "moderate" and place the property group into this category. Property falling into the first two categories would often include meters, poles, services, office furniture, vehicles, and work equipment.

Category 3 is similar to categories 1 and 2 in that it also requires a long and well-documented life history but differs because the relative annual rate of change of the life characteristics can be defined as "high" rather than "low" or "medium." A high annual average rate of change will be considered any rate that exceeds $\pm 5\%$. Note that an annual rate of change of $\pm 5\%$ carried over only 3 years will change the average service life by 15%, and property with an average service life of 30 years would decrease to 25.5

years or increase to 34.5 years. A higher rate of change of, say, ±10% over a 3-year period would result in a decrease to 21 years or an increase to 39 years for the same property, a dramatic change in the life characteristics. In recent years, rapidly changing technology in the telecommunications industry has provided examples of property with a high rate of change in the service life. Telephone switching equipment is an example.

The values ±2% and ±5% are to be used as guidelines rather than absolute boundaries. The focus is on the identification of a trend in the service life or gradual change in the shape of the survivor curve. Judgment is required when determining if recent changes in either of these attributes represent temporary fluctuations or a permanent change. If the attributes are determined to be in a state of change, the determination of the magnitude of the rate of change also requires the application of judgment.

Category 4 is similar to the first two categories in that the life history is well documented. The difference is that the life history is short when compared to the average service life, so that the survivor curves of the earliest vintages still show a large fraction of the original installations to be in service. An example would be long-lived property such as gas or water mains. Property of this type may have an average service life of more than 50 years; after 50 years over half the property from early vintages may still be in service, and the maximum life could exceed 150 years. In this case, not enough time has passed to obtain reasonably complete historical information concerning the life characteristics of the earliest vintages.

Category 5 includes groups of property that will be retired at a single time. The length of time from a reference point, typically the date of installation, until the time when all the property will be retired is often called the life span of the property. The documentation of the data, length of the life history, and recent life trends are not used as distinguishing characteristics for this category. These factors are important and will affect the analysis, but the life span consideration dominates these factors. Because the remaining property from all vintages will be retired simultaneously, special care must be taken when calculating the depreciation for this property.

Suppose that a utility's nonrenewable license to operate on the property site of a hydroelectric facility expires in 1999. All the property installed at the facility may be expected to be retired from service in 1999, the end of the life span. Because this includes recently installed property that would, under other conditions, have a long remaining service life, forecasters must be careful not to overlook or ignore the imminent retirement of newly installed property that falls into this category.

Category 6 includes property for which the historical data go back some time in history, but the records are incomplete. Typically, unaged retirement data fall into this category. The life analyst must use nonactuarial techniques that cannot accurately identify or quantify trends in the service life or changes in the shape of the survivor curve. Though the presence or absence of trends may be suggested, the rate or type of change cannot be accurately identified or quantified. Thus, the property cannot be placed into categories 1, 2, or 3. Accounting procedures, rather than characteristics of the property, will determine if the property falls into this category.

Category 7 includes property using new technology for which there is no history. The first communications satellites would be one recent example. Another would be large facilities to liquify natural gas. In both cases, the use of a new technology denied the forecaster a significant body of historical information.

The purpose of these categories is to identify the characteristics that will be likely to affect the approach to forecasting that is most appropriate. If a property does not clearly fit into a specific category, then it may be associated with more than one category, and more than one forecasting approach will need to be considered. Figure 15.1 summarizes the characteristics of the seven categories.

Characteristics	Category						
	1	2	3	4	5	6	7
Well Documented	Y	Y	Y	Y	N/A	N	N
Long Life History	Y	Y	Y	N	N/A	Y	N
Trends	LOW	MED	HIGH	NK*	N/A	NK*	N/A
Life Span	N	N	N	N	Y	N	N

*Not Known

Figure 15.1. Seven categories of forecasting characteristics.

Categories 1, 2, and 3 are the same except for the trends in the life characteristics, while trends are not a distinguishing factor in the remaining categories. Category 4 is similar to the first three categories, except that the life history is short when compared to the average life, and trends in the life characteristics cannot be detected. Category 5 is unique because it requires a future, or forecasted event, for classification. Both categories 6 and 7 lack well-documented history. Category 6 includes those situations that have a history but are lacking full documentation, while category 7 includes new technology with no history.

Forecasting Approaches

The systematic approach to forecasting suggested here first requires the forecaster to place the property under consideration into one, or possibly more, of the seven categories. This, in turn, will define a general approach to developing a forecast of the life characteristics of the property.

Category 1 presents the easiest forecasting situation, because the future appears to be a continuation of the past. History is well documented. Analysis will have shown indications of life characteristics to be independent of the placement and experience bands chosen, indicating the forces of retirement acting on the property have shown little change during the life of the property.

The major concern of the forecaster is whether the future holds events significantly different from those of the past, and whether those events will affect the life characteristics of the property. The forecaster must estimate the future forces of retirement. If there are no major changes in view, then the forecast seems clear; the future will be similar to the past and future life will mirror historical life.

If future events that will alter the historical forces of retirement appear likely, then the forecast becomes more difficult. Except in the most dramatic circumstances, future changes in the forces of retirement would be expected to be reflected by gradual changes in the life characteristics of the property group. The forecaster would concentrate on the direction and magnitude of these changes.

Supporting evidence for the forecast rests with the historical life described by the life analysis. If the forecaster believes the future will mirror the past, there will be sufficient data to support the life analysis, and there should be little difficulty in convincing others of the validity of the forecast.

If, on the other hand, changes in the forces of retirement from the historical patterns of retirement are forecast, the job of convincing others becomes more difficult. First, evidence must be shown that the future will differ from the past. Then the expected effect of these changes on the life characteristics must be explained.

Category 2 is similar to category 1, with the exception that more recent history has shown trends in the life characteristics, such as a gradual change in the shape of the survivor curve, a gradual lengthening or shortening of the average service life, or both.

If the future is expected to reflect the past, these trends can be expected to continue and forecasters would indicate future lives that are reflections of continuation of the trend. The forecaster must be aware of two concerns. First, as in the previous category, he or she must be assured that the future forces of retirement will not significantly differ from those of the past; that is, the trend will continue at the same rate and in the same direction. As before, a significant change in the future forces of retirement will alter the equation between the past and the future.

Secondly, he or she must be careful when extrapolating trends. Trends are often measured in terms of change in life over a given span of years, with the implication that the trend is linear. Extrapolation of a linear trend over a long enough period will often lead to insupportable forecasts. A negative linear trend will eventually lead to zero or negative life, while a positive linear trend will lead to infinite life.

Because the trends are moderate, they can be assumed to continue into the immediate future before the extrapolation becomes questionable. The forecaster should analyze the forces that appear responsible for the trends and estimate how long the trends will continue.

Supporting evidence rests heavily with results of the life analysis. A historical trend can be expected to continue, but not forever; the forecaster must estimate the length of time during which this trend will continue. Knowledge of historical life, current trends, and estimation of the length of time over which the trend will continue will determine the life forecast. A convincing forecast must examine the forces causing the trend in the life characteristics and examine their likelihood of continuing into the future.

Category 3 is an extension of category 2, but with a major difference. The rate of change in the category is so high that extrapolation over short periods will result in dramatic changes in the average life. In the discussion of the definition of this category, it was noted that a continuing change of 10% per year will reduce the life by one-half in only 5 years. That is, property with a historical life of 15 years might be expected, in only 5 years, to have an average service life of 7.5 years. This dramatic rate of change is difficult to support without additional evidence. Because property in this category reflects the effects of a dynamic environment, the analyst must examine all possible directions that the future may take to reach an informed conclusion whether the trend will continue at the same rate, disappear, or even change direction.

Specialized forecasting techniques are often appropriate in this case. Some models have focused on separation of the forces of retirement into two or more categories, each of which is forecast separately, and then recombined to obtain a single forecast for the retirement rate. Technological forecasting has provided new insights into methods of predicting future technology, as well as the development and verification of new forecasting models that can be applied to the estimation of service life characteristics. Technological substitution models are used to forecast the life of a particular technology.

Category 4 requires a careful estimation of the future forces of retirement. Life analysis does provide a stub survivor curve, but one in which the remaining survivors represent a significant percentage of the original installations in the vintages for which full history is available. Typically the realized life has given indications that the lower bound, or minimum estimate of service life is large, perhaps in the area of 50 years. The forecaster may be faced with the task of predicting forces of retirement during the next 50 to 100 years. Estimation of the forces of retirement this far into the future is difficult and involves much judgment, and heavy reliance on experts' opinions of future forces may be necessary.

Category 5 is commonly called the life span situation. Because all property will be retired at the same time, or date, the major task is to estimate that date. The event that will cause retirement of all property is one that has not occurred to any members of the group in the past. But historical events may influence the date at which the property will be retired. The analyst must carefully examine the scheduled events that will determine the life span and estimate the date of retirement.

The term *interim retirements* is used to describe those retirements that take place before the final retirement of all property. These retirements typically can be analyzed by standard methods to derive an interim survivor curve. The surviving property follows that curve until the end of the life span, when it drops to zero percent surviving. The resulting survivor curve for each vintage can be described as a truncated survivor curve. The average life of a vintage will be forecast by estimating the pattern of interim survivors, estimating the date of final retirement, and calculating the area under the truncated survivor curve.

A convincing forecast must be based on sound evidence of complete retirement at or near the estimated date marking the end of the life span. In general, the further the end of the life span is into the future, the more difficult it is to forecast the retirement date.

Category 6's forecasting problems focus on the lack of detailed information brought forward from the life analysis activity. Unaged retirement data include initial installations, total annual retirements, and end of year balances but exclude the history of the individual vintages. Models associated with unaged retirement data include the simulated plant record method of analysis, statistical aging, and computed mortality. Though these are sophisticated models, their power to indicate service life characteristics is limited by the narrow amount of information, or data, input. In addition, these models cannot provide reliable information concerning trends in service life characteristics, because an assumption of stable survivor characteristics is inherent to their design. This means that estimates of future trends in the service life must be made without the benefit of reliable indications of past trends. The analyst must depend extensively on judgment when forecasting life characteristics of a property group that is experiencing change in life characteristics. Experience with similar property may provide information of value to the analyst.

Category 7 may not be encountered as frequently as the other categories, but when a new technology is installed the initial cost may be great. One source of data for consideration would be from engineers responsible for the design of the system. Also the life of new technology may be indicated by the lives of past technology, although the lives of successive technologies tend to become successively shorter. Economic factors, such as those relating to future demand for the product produced by the installation, will often have a greater influence on the service life than the physical characteristics of the property.

16 | Making a Depreciation Study

THIS chapter describes the steps a depreciation professional should consider following when conducting an initial depreciation study. Other topics include the use of consultants when making a study and managing a study.

FLOWCHART OF A STUDY

Figure 16.1 shows a flowchart identifying the activities comprising a depreciation study. Arrows show the sequence of the activities. This flowchart is created on the assumption that this is the first time the depreciation professional has made a study for this company. Studies should be made periodically, often every three to five years. If the depreciation professional had previously made a study and was now making another study, the flow chart should be modified. Though not all the activities would need to be repeated in detail, previously completed steps should be reviewed for continued applicability. The flowchart can be easily modified to serve as a guide to a periodic study.

The flowchart divides the activities comprising a study into three phases. They are (1) planning; (2) data assembly; and (3) analysis, forecasting, review, and support.

Phase One

Careful planning is necessary to coordinate the activity of the individuals contributing to the study to ensure that the study is completed in a

285

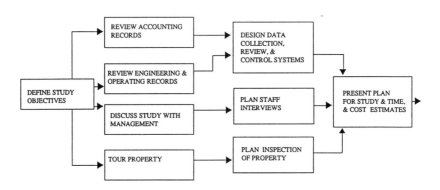

Figure 16.1A. A flowchart of making a depreciation study. Phase I.

timely and efficient manner. The planning phase starts with a statement of the study goals. The goals determine the scope of the study and affect the assignment of resources to the project. These goals, including completion time, should be reviewed with management to ensure that the party responsible for conducting the study and the party responsible for authorizing the study are in agreement about the conduct of the study.

The type and amount of retirement data available will dictate the methods of life and salvage analysis used in the study. Before data can be analyzed, they must be entered into an electronic data base so that they can be read into the computer programs used for analysis. Assembling the data can be a lengthy and time-consuming activity, and a review of the accounting data provides a basis for estimating the time necessary for data collection and control. A tour or similar in-depth review of the property gives the depreciation professional firsthand information and provides valuable background information about the property to be studied.

After these initial activities have been completed, the depreciation professional should have the information necessary to design a detailed plan for the study. The plan should state who will accomplish each task and how long it will take. The Gantt chart and critical path method (CPM) are management tools helpful when planning projects that require the coordination of people and equipment. An important part of the plan is the estimated cost and time required to complete the study. It is recommended that the plan be reviewed with the party responsible for authorizing the study to ensure that the estimated time and cost are acceptable. The plan should specify the times when key staff are scheduled to work on the study in order that any conflicts with their other assignments may be resolved by management without jeopardizing the progress of the study. The first phase ends with approval of the plan.

Phase Two

There are two tasks to be accomplished during the second phase. One is to assemble the data that will be used to analyze and forecast life and salvage. The other is to start the written report that will document the study.

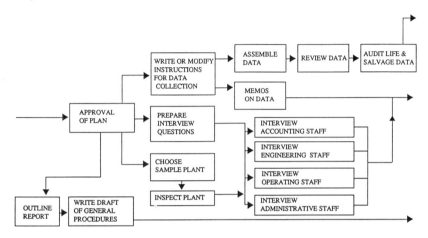

Figure 16.1B. A flowchart of making a depreciation study. Phase II.

In the broad sense, the term "data" includes all information used when analyzing past life and salvage and when forecasting future life and salvage. Most of the statistical data are retirement and salvage data that must be in a form that can be readily processed by a computer.

Analysis of either aged retirement data using actuarial techniques or unaged retirement data using simulation techniques requires careful attention to the information required by the computer program. Even though standard techniques are used, each computer system has its unique options, features, and characteristics. Whether the software is inherited from a predecessor, purchased new from a vendor, or developed in-house, the depreciation professional should schedule time to become familiar with its operation.

The assembled data are used to calculate the depreciation accrual as well as to analyze life and salvage data. Errors or inconsistencies in the data can undermine the validity of your results. Inconsistencies that may appear minor or insignificant during analysis may become major problems when defending your report on the witness stand. Ideally, the data assembled for a study should reconcile with the transactions recorded in the continuing property records, and these should, in turn, reconcile with the entries in the general ledger. Software used for analysis and for depreciation calculations should include programs that audit the consistency of the data.

Preparation of data for entry into computer programs can be expensive and time consuming. Though studies are not conducted annually, data should be updated each year rather than waiting several years until the time of the next study. This will minimize the time and effort spent on data preparation.

Interviews with accounting, engineering, and operations staff should be designed to obtain information that will be helpful when analyzing the output from the life and salvage programs. A change in accounting rules, such as a change in the definition of a retirement unit, can result in a change in the indications of life and salvage. Operational changes, such as a new maintenance program, can have the same effect. The staff interviewed also may be aware of future events that may affect life and salvage characteristics. Information of this type lies at the heart of many forecasting problems.

Before preparing for staff interviews, identify accounts that are of particular interest because of their magnitude, high accrual rates, or changing characteristics. It is prudent to inspect the property in these accounts and talk firsthand with the operating staff familiar with it.

Field trips are an important part of the data assembly phase. They provide firsthand information on the operation of the system, the physical characteristics of the plant under study, the attitudes of operating and management personnel, and other characteristics that cannot be obtained in any other way. This information can be useful when interpreting historical data as well as when forecasting. The vivid impressions acquired through a field inspection often are useful when supporting as well as formulating conclusions reached during the course of a study.

The object of a formal report is to clearly present the results of the depreciation study to management and the regulatory agency. Forecasts of life and salvage are at the heart of a study. Forecasts are subjective, and the forecaster must not only make a good forecast but must convince others of the validity of the forecast. Thus, your analysis and forecasting procedures must be sound, logical, *and clearly documented*. A well-written report is the result of planning, editing, and rewriting. Submitting your first draft as your final report will guarantee a poor report. Start writing each portion of the report as soon as possible. The outline and general procedures can be written when the study is approved. Document your interviews and field trips. Record the data collection process while it is fresh in your mind. Document all corrections and adjustments made to the original data. These and other activities that will be summarized in the written report and testimony should be documented as the study progresses. This is the key to a convincing report and persuading testimony.

Information collection and data preparation required for the computer programs used to analyze life and salvage and to calculate depreciation accruals leads to analysis and forecasting.

Phase Three

The activities during the third phase of the study include applications of actuarial or simulation techniques to analyze retirement data, forecasting life and salvage, calculation of depreciation, completion and review of the draft report, and presentation of the report to management and to the regulatory agency.

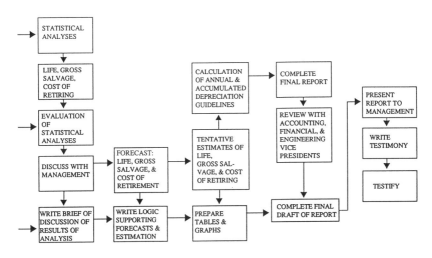

Figure 16.1C. A flowchart of making a depreciation study. Phase III.

Analysis is the process of separating and examining all information that adds to the understanding of the forces that shape the life characteristics and salvage values of the industrial property under consideration. Analysis provides indications of the historical life characteristics, gross salvage values, and cost of retiring and is the prerequisite to forecasting service life characteristics, gross salvage values, and cost of retiring. All knowledge of the forces of retirement is contained in history, so a thorough understanding of the past is the foundation of a sound forecast.

One method of organizing an analysis of life and salvage is to group the property by accounts. An account can be divided into two or more subaccounts or, as with buildings, into individual units. The process of analyzing, forecasting, and documenting life and salvage estimates can be applied to the smallest group of property for which separate records are kept. The report can be organized by assigning each account a section in the report.

Depreciation studies are conducted under limited resources that include time, budget, personnel, and ancillary facilities including computer resources. One management task is to allocate the resources available in an efficient manner.

Equal resources could be allocated to each account, but because each account has characteristics that differ significantly, this is not an efficient method of allocation. One characteristic that may be used as a measure of the importance of the account is the current balance or plant in service for the account. Balances will vary significantly from account to account. If the accounts are ranked by balance, you can expect that a small fraction of the total accounts will comprise a large portion of the total plant in service. This generalization, called the *Pareto principle,* is widely used to identify and rank problems.

Two randomly selected companies were analyzed using this approach and the results are shown in Table 16.1. The original data included several subaccounts, but to keep the example compact, these were not separated.

The telephone company consists of 11 accounts. The first three, or 27% of the accounts, include 70% of the plant in service. The first five, or 45% of the accounts, include 88% of the plant in service. The situation is even more dramatic in the gas company, where the first 20% of the accounts include 86% of the plant in service.

Other factors to be considered when allocating analysis time to each account are the complexity of the account, recent activities affecting the account, and the accrual rate. In fact, the annual accruals (i.e., the accrual rate times the plant in service) may be a better measure of the importance of the account than simply the plant in service. Still, a Pareto analysis of the plant in service is a good starting place when determining the "proper" amount of effort to expend on each account.

A good starting point for an analysis of retirement data is the examination of graphs showing the balances, additions, and retirements plotted for each calendar year. Sometimes these graphs are included in the report. The results of actuarial analysis can be examined by viewing life tables and graphic displays of the survivor curves on a computer screen. This reduces the need for printing intermediate results but increases the need to record your observations and conclusions during the computer-oriented portion of the analysis. These notes become the basis for the section of the report documenting the life analysis for the account. Analysis of salvage data can be performed at this time and in a similar manner. Tables and figures used to support the life and salvage analysis to be included in the report can be selected and printed at this time.

Table 16.1. A Pareto analysis of the account balances for a telephone
           company and a gas company.

A typical telephone company

Acct no	Name of account	Plant in service	* * Cumulative Plant in service	* % of plant	* % of accts
221	Central Office Equipment	1,693,095	1,693,095	39%	9%
242	Cable	879,204	2,572,299	59%	18%
232	Station Connectors	502,505	3,074,804	70%	27%
231	Telephone Station Apparatus	480,670	3,555,474	81%	36%
212	Buildings	286,344	3,841,818	88%	45%
244	Underground Conduit	198,454	4,040,272	92%	55%
234	Large Private Branch Exchange	139,593	4,179,865	95%	64%
264	Vehicles & Other Equipment	99,809	4,279,674	98%	73%
241	Pole Lines	70,684	4,350,358	99%	82%
261	Furniture & Office Equipment	20,175	4,370,533	100%	91%
243	Aerial Wire	7,134	4,377,667	100%	100%

A typical gas company

Acct no	Name of account	Plant in service	* * Cumulative Plant in service	* % of plant	* % of accts
359	Mains	2,576,339	2,576,339	65%	7%
361	Services	441,614	3,017,953	77%	13%
362	Meters	366,271	3,384,224	86%	20%
364	House Regulators	84,357	3,468,581	88%	27%
357	Distribution System Land	67,441	3,536,022	90%	33%
373	Autos/Trucks/Trailers	62,191	3,598,213	91%	40%
365	House Regulator Installation	59,543	3,657,756	93%	47%
367	Other Distb Equipment	47,233	3,704,989	94%	53%
372	Office Furniture/Equipment	46,579	3,751,568	95%	60%
363	Meter Installations	46,299	3,797,867	96%	67%
366	Distb Lg Vol Meas & Reg In	41,102	3,838,969	98%	73%
360	Measuring & Regulating Equip	39,529	3,878,498	99%	80%
377	Work Equipment	27,710	3,906,208	99%	87%
358	Measuring & Regulating Str	27,475	3,933,683	100%	93%
379	Other General Equipment	2,515	3,936,198	100%	100%

Forecasting follows analysis. The appropriate forecasting model depends on the characteristics of the account. Questions concerning past or future activities may arise, and staff who might provide answers should be interviewed. The forecasting portion of the report should be written as the forecasts are made. The thought process leading to the forecast should be explained, and the connection between the results of the analysis and the forecast should be made clear. Writing the first draft of the report concurrently with the analysis and forecasting activity reduces the need for notes and working papers and allows the depreciation professional to put his or her ideas on paper while they are still fresh.

Calculation of depreciation follows the forecasting activity. Tables of computations associated with each account and summary tables including all accounts will be prepared and those to be included in the report must be specified. Well-designed computer systems will print tables that can be included in the report with little or no modification.

After the forecasts are reviewed and the depreciation calculations made, the report can be assembled and edited. Though the analysis proceeds on an account-by-account basis, those reviewing the results of the study may be most interested in the total accruals and overall accrual rate. Thus, the summary portions of the report are of particular importance.

The final tasks of the study are review and approval of the report and formal presentation to the regulatory agency. Those responsible for providing information used in the report should review the draft, particularly those sections for which they provided information. After final changes, the report is submitted to management for approval. The approved report is then formally presented to the regulatory agency.

USE OF CONSULTANTS

Because of the specialized and periodic nature of depreciation studies, an organization may find it impractical or uneconomical to continuously employ professional personnel who are qualified to conduct a depreciation study. Therefore, when it is time for a study, a depreciation consultant often is hired. The consultant's level of participation may range from providing education and informal review of a study to assuming complete responsibility for the study.

An organization has several strategies to choose from when deciding who will make a study. One alternative is to do the entire study in-house. This requires trained, experienced personnel and computer software that can be used to analyze life and salvage data, make the required depreciation calculations, and create the tables needed in the report. Larger organizations often find this strategy workable and economical. This is particularly true for service companies providing support to affiliated companies. A consultant may be used to provide training and to work with company personnel during the initial studies.

Another alternative is to retain a consultant to be responsible for making the entire study. Under this alternative, company personnel familiar with the process of making the study should serve as a link between the consultant and the other members of the company. A depreciation study does not lend itself to a "turnkey" approach. If company personnel understand how the data they record are used in a depreciation study, they can assemble and audit it in less time, and for less cost, than can a consultant. Efficient use of a consultant requires persons at the company be knowledgeable of basic concepts of depreciation, the type of information required by the consultant for analysis and forecasting purposes, and the basic regulatory review process.

A third alternative is to hire a consultant to work with company personnel to make the study. In the case, the responsibilities of each party must be clearly defined. If the report is to be submitted under the consultant's name, they will expect full control over the conduct of the study.

MANAGING A STUDY

Many organizations conduct periodic in-house studies, and the depreciation professional may find himself or herself responsible for managing a study. The complexity of the study will vary with the size of the company, the time since the last study, and the purpose of the study. However, all managers of a study face similar problems.

Identification of the tasks necessary to complete the study is perhaps the first activity of a manager preparing to undertake a new study. The flowchart of a depreciation study, shown in Figure 16.1 and discussed in the first section of this chapter, provides a starting point for identifying these tasks. A similar chart, but one with more detail, would identify specific staff to be interviewed, plant to be inspected, and accounts to be analyzed.

The Gantt chart is a technique for managing projects. It identifies each activity to be done, the activities that must be completed before others may start, and the time each activity will take. Activity times are plotted on an axis showing calendar time. The critical path method (CPM) and program evaluation and review techniques (PERT) provide similar help but are more sophisticated than the Gantt chart. Computer software supporting these techniques is widely available.

As with most projects, all tasks of a depreciation study cannot be performed at the same time. Adding personnel or working overtime may shorten the completion time, but the sequential relationship results in an overall completion time that is substantially greater than the length of the most time-consuming task. Though some large organizations separate their plant accounts into segments to be studied and supported by several different professionals, a more common practice is to place the entire study under the direction of a single expert. The resulting sequential relationship results in a greater time for completion.

Frequently the professional staff involved in the study has other continuing responsibilities, and cannot spend 40 hours a week on the study. The manager of the study must coordinate staff activities with operating, engineering, planning, accounting, and regulatory and other managers. If a consultant is used, the in-house manager must coordinate the staff activities with those of the consultant.

17 | Current Issues in Depreciation

EACH year brings with it new issues and concerns to professionals working in their field of interest. It is difficult to predict the specific issue or issues that will capture the interest of the practitioner during the coming year, but it is safe to predict that new issues will arise. The field of depreciation is no exception.

A wide range of factors can influence the work of the depreciation professional. In a broad view, each national election has the potential to result in a philosophical change that may produce a shift in the extent of regulation. Changes in the economy and the marketplace are factors that often place organizations in a position where they must improve their efficiency. Organizational change is a common response to this challenge, and these changes typically alter the resources available to the depreciation professional. Technology is another factor that generates new issues for the depreciation professional. The adoption of new technology brings greater uncertainty about the future lives and salvage of both new and old technology, and forecasting these changes is often at the heart of current issues. Another factor that has changed the manner in which studies are conducted is the computer revolution. The evolution of hardware and software will continue to affect the manner in which studies are conducted and the manner in which they are reviewed by other parties.

A commentator observing the seventieth anniversary of the *Harvard Business Review* examined the premier issue of that magazine, which compared issues of interest then with issues of interest now. That publication contained articles on the capital gains tax and business ethics; both are concerns that have periodically resurfaced as "hot" issues during the past 70 years. In this case, current issues were not new but were old issues that attracted renewed interest or old issues raised in a contemporary environment. An investigation of the papers and talks relating to depreciation supports the supposition that a "current" issue is not necessarily a "new" issue. Thus, a review of the literature is often a good starting point when seeking solutions to new problems. This chapter identifies six areas that may create current issues in depreciation.

CONCEPTS OF DEPRECIATION

Three concepts of depreciation are physical condition, decrease in value, and cost of operation. The cost of operation concept is well established and widely used when estimating book depreciation. When this concept is applied, the allocation of the original cost over the life of the asset becomes a goal of depreciation. In addition, the fairness issue implies a matching relationship between the annual accrual and the service an asset provides. A change from original cost and from the cost of operation concept is an issue that is raised periodically. For example, price level depreciation would recover an amount other than the original cost. A period of high interest rates may increase the interest in this sort of proposal because it can affect internal funding. Because depreciation is only one part of the rate-setting process, consideration of a different goal for depreciation should be done in concert with other changes in the system.

DEPRECIATION SYSTEMS

Depreciation systems can be defined by describing the method of allocation, the procedure for applying the method of allocation, and the method of adjustment. Currently, the straight line method of allocation is used almost exclusively for book depreciation. An issue that could significantly change accrual rates is the change from straight line to an accelerated or decelerated method of allocation. Also, the ELG procedure is not universally accepted, and its use remains an issue in some jurisdictions.

RECORDS AND DATA

Data are generally derived from property records that include additions, retirements, and other transactions. These records may include detailed information about the transaction, or they may include generalized information about a group of transactions. Detail is lost when only generalized information is recorded, so these records yield unaged retirement and salvage data. This loss of information makes forecasting life and salvage more difficult and, in general, less accurate. The issues created by the lack of information resulting from using unaged data typically focus on methods of analysis and forecasting models. However, an underlying issue is the decision not to record more detailed data.

One cost of not collecting aged retirement data is related to the extra work required because of the loss of information. Two strategies are available when dealing with unaged data. One strategy is to analyze the data using models that do not require aged data. The simulated plant retirement (SPR) method is an example. Another example, relating to salvage, is to assume salvage is independent of age and to use an average annual salvage ratio to analyze salvage.

A second strategy is to "age" the unaged data, record them as aged data, and then analyze them using actuarial methods. The result is simulated aged data rather than observed aged data. The simulation process requires assumptions concerning the life characteristics. The shape of the survivor curve may be *assumed,* and the age simulated. When the resulting simulated aged data are analyzed, and the results of the analysis are used as the basis for estimating the curve shape the following period, a circular logic results. The difference between the simulated ages and the actual, but unknown, ages that result from this strategy depends on the characteristics of the account and the assumptions made by the analyst. Little is known about the cumulative effects of this procedure. A current concern is that simulated data may be given the same status as observed data and the uncertainty associated with it neglected.

SALVAGE

The estimation of salvage has historically been given less importance than the estimation of life. This may be justified when the net salvage is near zero. However, when the cost of retirement is large, the accrual rate will be sensitive to the salvage. A knowledge of salvage by age would allow development and use of models that would be helpful when forecasting salvage.

Cost of retirement models based on aged salvage and retirement data provide the most reliable and dependable route to good forecasting models. Because data only becomes useful after they are accumulated for several years, the wise manager may be the one who invests in the careful collection of potentially useful data now, even though the full benefits of that investment may not be realized until later. A continuing issue is the amount of data collected.

LIFE ANALYSIS

Depreciation professionals have typically used the survivor curve, rather than the frequency curve or retirement ratio curve, to fit observed curves to theoretical curves. Before the widespread use of personal computers, visual curve fitting was done manually. Better computers and accompanying progress in software resulted in the wide availability of systems that graphically display the observed survivor curve along with any desired theoretical curve, eliminating time-consuming, manual fitting. In addition, mathematical curve fitting is now easily done. Movement from manual to computer fitting did not affect the reliance on the survivor curve as the focus of attention. Thus, the characteristic shapes of the left, right, and origin modal curves or the symmetrical curves are familiar to those using this general approach to life analysis.

During the time of change from manual plotting to computer plotting, new emphasis was placed on reliability engineering. The reliability engineer is interested in the life characteristics of mechanical and electrical components used in products ranging from automobiles to spacecraft. Reliability engineers focus on the retirement rate curve, rather than the survivor curve, when developing statistical models and tests for reliability. Techniques used by reliability engineers are applicable to the life analysis of industrial property and have placed new interest on fitting the retirement rate curve. One caveat must be made when considering the transfer of models used by reliability engineers to the area of depreciation. Reliability testing is often conducted under laboratory conditions. Thus, the environment under which the property operates can be held constant so that the causes of failure are limited to mechanical causes. In contrast, retirement data collected for industrial property reflect varying environmental conditions. To the depreciation professional, environmental conditions include not only forces of retirement such as the weather, but the economy, technology, regulation, and other factors related to the experience band. This factor may limit the value of reliability models when analyzing the service of industrial property.

Nonetheless, the depreciation professional may be wise to consider fitting of observed retirement ratio curves, rather than or in addition to the survivor curves, to theoretical curves. Software that fits survivor curves can be easily modified to also display retirement ratio curves. Some patterns and trends may be more easily identified on the retirement ratio curve than on the survivor curve.

FORECASTING

Forecasting life and salvage is perhaps the central and, to many, the most interesting activity of the depreciation professional. Many of the activities performed during a depreciation study are in preparation for the forecasting activity. Because the actual life or salvage is not known until well after the forecast is made, the validity of the forecast must be judged on the manner in which the forecast is developed. Because the very nature of forecasting leads to controversy, forecasting methods and models are often at issue.

Though forecasting concerns are frequently directed at a specific type of property, the underlying issue is often not the actual forecast but the logic and the model used to arrive at the forecast. The Fisher-Pry (1970) substitution model is used to predict the rate at which an existing technology will be replaced by a new technology. The life cycle model was developed by marketing experts to aid in strategic planning. This model described the life history of a particular product from development to phase-out. Rapid changes in technology in the telecommunications industry had resulted in dramatic rates of change in the service life of central office equipment. During the 1980s, these two models were adapted for use in forecasting the life of this type of equipment. The models were not only available but were creditable, because they had been successfully used in other areas. The adaption of well-accepted models from outside the field of depreciation proved a valuable tool.

A forecasting model suggested by Fitch and Wolf (1985) centered on the identification of specific forces of retirement and on the resulting retirement ratio curve. Sometimes a single force of retirement may dominate all others, and this model outlined a way to combine two or more forces of retirement into a single survivor curve. Thus, the retirement ratio curve can be helpful in both analyzing retirement data and in forecasting life.

SUMMARY

Current issues facing the depreciation professional range from allocation of resources to routine accounting activities to challenging technical problems. Current issues vary between industries as well as between regulatory jurisdictions. Often current issues are not new but simply recurring. The heart of an issue may not rest with the proposed solution, but with convincing others that the path to the solution was sound. Depreciation professionals should look to models and other tools used by others and adapt them to their own needs.

Bibliography

Accounting Research and Terminology Bulletins. (1961). Final edition, "Accounting Terminology Bulletins, No. 1, Review and Resume." New York, NY, American Institute of Certified Public Accountants.

Alfar, Aly. (1986). The use of the computed mortality method. Ames, IA, *Proceedings, Iowa State Regulatory Conference,* pp. 287–299.

American Gas Association Depreciation Committee and Edison Electric Depreciation Accounting Committee. (1975). *An introduction to depreciation.* Arlington, VA, American Gas Association – Edison Electric Institute.

American Gas Association Depreciation Committee and Edison Electric Depreciation Accounting Committee. (1989). *Simulated plant-record applications task force report.* Arlington, VA, American Gas Association – Edison Electric Institute.

American Telephone and Telegraph Company. (1957). *Depreciation engineering practices: Development of depreciation rates in the Bell system.* New York, NY, American Telephone and Telegraph Company.

Armstrong, John H. (1903). Depreciation Reserves. *The Accountant,* August 8, p. 1014.

Bauhan, A.E. (1947). *Life analysis of utility plant for depreciation accounting purposes by the simulated plant-record method.* Paper presented at the AGA-EEI National Conference of Electric and Gas Utility Accountants, Buffalo, NY.

Brown, R.G. (1963). *Smoothing forecasting and prediction of discrete time series.* Englewood Cliffs, NJ, Prentice Hall.

Burton, Frances G. (1905). *The Commercial Management of Engineering Works.* Manchester, England, The Scientific Publishing Co.

California Public Utilities Commission. (1952). *Determination of Straight-line Remaining Life Depreciation Accruals. Standard Practice U-4.* San Francisco, CA, California Public Utilities Commission, Utilities Division.

California Public Utilities Commission. (1961). *Determination of Straight-line Remaining Life Depreciation Accruals. Standard Practice U-4.* San Francisco,

CA, California Public Utilities Commission, Utilities Division. Revised edition.

California Public Utilities Commission. (1962). *Determination of Straight-line Remaining Life Depreciation Accruals.* Excerpts from 1961 *Standard Practice U-4.* San Francisco, CA, California Public Utilities Commission, Utilities Division.

Carver, Linda. (1989). Computed Mortality. *Journal of the Society of Depreciation Professionals.* Vol. 1, No. 1, pp. 55–59.

Chopp, Charles C. (1969). Probability techniques in forecasting plant life. *Proceedings, National Conference of Electric and Gas Utility Accountants,* pp. E42–E47.

Chopp, Charles C. (1971). One measure of bias in life analysis. *Proceedings of National Conference of Electric and Gas Utility Accountants,* pp. F9–F16.

Cowles, Harold Andrews. (1957). Prediction of mortality characteristics of industrial property groups. (Doctoral dissertation, Iowa State University). *Dissertation Abstracts International.*

Edison Electric Institute. (1952). *Methods of estimating utility plant life.* New York, NY, Edison Electric Institute.

Engineering Experiment Station. (1924). *Condition per cent tables.* Ames, IA, Iowa State College of Agriculture and Mechanic Arts Official Publication, Vol. XXIII, No. 5, July 2, 1924.

Fisher, J.C., and Pry, R.H. (1970). A simple substitution model of technological change. Technical Information Series #70-C-215. Schenectady, NY, General Electric Research and Development Center.

Fitch, W. Chester. (1950). Fundamental aspects of depreciation theory. (Doctoral dissertation, Iowa State University). *Dissertation Abstracts International.*

Fitch, W. Chester, Bissinger, Bernard H., and Greene, Edward D. (1971). *Methods of estimating service life and depreciation.* Kalamazoo, MI, Western Michigan University, Center for Depreciation Studies.

Fitch, W. Chester, Bissinger, Bernard H., and Wolf, Franklin K. (1975). *The Estimation of Depreciation.* Kalamazoo, MI, Western Michigan University, Center for Depreciation Studies.

Fitch, W. Chester, Jensen, Susan Diane, and Young, Laura J. (1982). *A preliminary study of simulated methods in life analysis.* Washington, DC, Interstate Commerce Commission.

Fitch, W. Chester, and Wolf, Franklin K. (1985). A conceptual framework for the forecasting of the useful life of industrial properties. Ames, IA, *Proceedings, Iowa State Regulatory Conference.*

Garland, William D. (1967). Proposal of a simulated plant record period retirements method for plant mortality analysis. *Proceedings, National Conference of Electric and Gas Utility,* E45–E63.

Garland, William D. (1968). Simulated plant retirements method: Criteria for mortality pattern evaluation. *Proceedings, National Conference of Electric and Gas Utility,* F51–F52.

Gompertz, Benjamin. (1825). On the Nature of the Function Expressive of the Law of Human Mortality and on a New Mode of Determining the Value of Life

Contingencies. *Abstracts of The Papers Printed in the Philosophical Transactions of the Royal Society of London, from 1800 to 1830 inclusive,* Vol. 2, pp. 513–529.

Grant, Eugene L. (1952). Fundamental Aspects of the Depreciation Problem. In David Solomons, *Studies in Costing,* Sweet & Maxwell, p. 292.

Grant, Eugene L., and Norton, Paul T. (1949). *Depreciation.* New York, NY, The Ronald Press.

Hald, Abraham. (1952). *Statistical theory with engineering applications.* New York, NY, John Wiley & Sons.

Hatfield, Henry R. (1936). What they say about depreciation, *The Accounting Review,* March, pp.18–26.

Hill, Cyrus G. (1922). Depreciation of Telephone Plants. Part I. *Telephony,* March 18, Vol. 82, No. 11, pp. 12–16.

Hill, Cyrus G. (1922). Depreciation of Telephone Plants. Part II. *Telephony,* March 25, Vol. 82, No. 12, pp. 21–26.

Interstate Commerce Commission. (1979). *FASB-33 Users Manual Computer Assisted Inflation Accounting System, developed in response to Statement No. 33, Financial Accounting Standards Board.* Prepared under contract by Susan D. Jensen. Washington, DC, ICC Depreciation Branch, Bureau of Accounts.

Interstate Commerce Commission. (1979). *User Documentation for the Computer Assisted Depreciation and Life Analysis System.* Prepared under contract by Susan D. Jensen. Washington, DC, ICC Depreciation Branch, Bureau of Accounts.

Interstate Commerce Commission. (1980). *User Documentation for the Report System to Summarize a Depreciation Study.* Prepared under contract by Susan D. Jensen. Washington, DC, ICC Depreciation Branch, Bureau of Accounts.

Interstate Commerce Commission. (1980). *User Documentation for the Simulated Computer Program.* Prepared under contract by Susan D. Jensen. Washington, DC, ICC Depreciation Branch, Bureau of Accounts.

Interstate Commerce Commission. (1982). *User Documentation for the Renewals Forecasting System.* Prepared under contract by Susan D. Jensen. Washington, DC, ICC Depreciation Branch, Bureau of Accounts.

Interstate Commerce Commission. (1985). *User Documentation for the Statistical Aging System (STAGE).* Prepared under contract by Susan D. Jensen. Washington, DC, ICC Depreciation Branch, Bureau of Accounts.

Interstate Commerce Commission. (1985). *User Documentation for the Salvage System.* Prepared under contract by Susan D. Jensen. Washington, DC, ICC Depreciation Branch, Bureau of Accounts.

Interstate Commerce Commission. (1986). *User Documentation for the Equal Life Group Depreciation and Valuation System (ELG).* Prepared under contract by Susan D. Jensen. Washington, DC, ICC Depreciation Branch, Bureau of Accounts.

Jensen, Susan Diane. (1983). Investigation of the simulated plant-record (SPR) balances life analysis model. (Doctoral dissertation, Iowa State University). *Dissertation Abstracts International.*

Kendig, Frank, and Hutton, Richard. (1979). *Life-Spans Or How Long Things*

Last. New York, NY, Holt, Rinehart and Winston.

Kimball, Bradford F. (1947a). *System of Life Tables Based on the Truncated Normal Distribution.* Chicago, IL, University of Chicago Press.

Kimball, Bradford F. (1947b). A System of life tables for physical property based on the truncated normal distribution. *Econometrica,* Vol. 15, pp. 342–360.

King, George. (1902). *Institute of Actuaries Text Book, Part II, Life Contingencies,* 2d ed. London, England, Charles and Edwin Layton.

Knoxville v. Knoxville Water Company. (1909). 212 U.S. 1 (U.S. Supreme Court).

Kurtz, Edwin B. (1930). *Life expectancy of physical property based on mortality laws.* New York, NY, Ronald Press.

Lamp, George Emmett. (1968). Dispersion effects in industrial property life analysis. (Doctoral dissertation, Iowa State University). *Dissertation Abstracts International.*

Lindheimer et al. v. Illinois Bell Telephone Co. (No. 440), *Illinois Bell Telephone Co. v. Lindheimer et al.* (No. 548), 292 U.S. 151, 167, 175, 3 P.U.R. (N.S.) 337 (U.S. Sup. Ct. Apr. 30, 1934).

Makeham, William Matthew. (January 1860). On the law of mortality and the construction of annuity tables. *The Assurance Magazine, and Journal of the Institute of Actuaries,* Vol. 8, pp. 301–310.

Marston, Anson, and Agg, Thomas R. (1936). *Engineering valuation,* New York, NY, McGraw Hill.

Marston, Anson, Winfrey, Robley, and Hempstead, Jean. (1953). *Engineering valuation and depreciation,* 2d ed. Ames, IA, Iowa State University Press.

Moulton, J.S. (1932). Report on estimated service lives and corresponding sinking fund annuities for the electric property of the San Joaquin Light and Power Corporation.

National Association of Railroad and Utilities Commissioners. (1938). *Report of Special Committee on Depreciation.* Washington, DC, National Association of Railroad and Utilities Commissioners.

National Association of Railroad and Utilities Commissioners. (1943). *Report of Special Committee on Depreciation.* Washington, DC, National Association of Railroad and Utilities Commissioners.

National Association of Railroad and Utilities Commissioners. (1944). *Report of Committee on Depreciation.* Washington, DC, National Association of Railroad and Utilities Commissioners.

National Association of Railroad and Utilities Commissioners. (August 1946). Unpublished report prepared by the Ad Hoc Committee (commonly known as the Lag Method of Pricing Retirements). Washington, DC, National Association of Railroad and Utilities Commissioners.

National Association of Railroad and Utilities Commissioners. (1968). *Public Utility Practices.* Washington, DC, National Association of Railroad and Utilities Commissioners.

Pidock, Wayne L. (May 1966). The depreciation mystery. Paper presented at the national conference of Electric and Gas Utility Accountants, New Orleans, LA.

Ponder, Karen A. (1978). Some aspects of statistically modeling the simulated plant record method of life analysis. (Doctoral dissertation, Iowa State University). *Dissertation Abstracts International.*

Rippe, R.D. (1969). Service life expectation of institutional china tableware by life analysis. Unpublished master's thesis. Library, Iowa State University of Science and Technology, Ames, IA.

Rose, R.G. (1972). Life analysis of institutional china tableware. Unpublished master's thesis. Library, Iowa State University of Science and Technology, Ames, IA.

Russo, John G. (1978). Iowa type survivor curve revalidation. (Doctoral dissertation, Iowa State University). *Dissertation Abstracts International.*

Russo, John G., and Cowles, Harold Andrews. (1980). Revalidation of the Iowa type survivor curves. *The Engineering Economist,* Vol. 26, No. 1, pp. 1–16.

Shelburn, William W., Jr. (1969). Applications of simulated retirement experience of limited-life industrial property. *Proceedings, National Conference of Electric and Gas Utility Accountants,* pp. E35–E41.

Singh, V. (1980). Preliminary study of a simulated plant-record method for life analysis. Unpublished technical paper for Master's Degree. Iowa State University, Ames, IA.

Smith, Gerald W. (1973). *Engineering Economy: Analysis of Capital Expenditures,* 2d ed. Ames, IA, Iowa State University Press.

Suelflow, James E. (1973). *Public Utility Accounting: Theory and Application.* Lansing, MI, Institute of Public Utilities, Graduate School of Business Administration, Michigan State University.

Telephone Engineer and Management. (1967). June 15, p. 55.

White, Bob E. (1986). Economic forces of retirement. Ames, IA. *Proceedings, Iowa State Regulatory Conference,* pp. 271–286.

White, Bob E., and Welke, William. (1992). Accounting for negative net salvage in public utilities. *Journal of the Society of Depreciation Professionals,* Vol. 4, No. 1, pp. 7–10.

White, Ronald Eugene. (1968). The multivariate normal distribution and the simulated plant-record method of life analysis. Unpublished master's thesis, Iowa State University, Ames, IA.

White, Ronald Eugene. (1992). A new set of generalized survivor tables. *Journal of the Society of Depreciation Professionals,* Vol. 4, No. 1, pp. 90–95.

White, Ronald Eugene, and Cowles, Harold Andrews. (1970). Test procedure for the simulated plant record method of life analysis. *Journal of American Statistical Association,* Vol. 65, pp. 1204–1212.

Whiton, Harry R. (1947). The indicated retirement approach to the simulated plant-record method of estimating lives of mass accounts of utility property for depreciation accounting purposes. Paper presented at the National Conference of Electric and Gas Utility Accountants, American Gas Association, Edison Electric Institute, Buffalo, NY.

Winfrey, Robley. (1942). *Condition percent tables for depreciation of unit and group properties (Bulletin 156).* Ames, IA, Iowa Engineering Experiment Station.

Winfrey, Robley. (1942). *Depreciation of group property (Bulletin 155).* Ames, IA,

Iowa Engineering Experiment Station.

Winfrey, Robley. (1935). *Statistical analysis of industrial property retirements (Bulletin 125)*. Ames, IA, Iowa Engineering Experiment Station.

Winfrey, Robley. (1967). *Statistical analysis of industrial property retirements (Bulletin 125)*. Revised edition. Ames, IA, Iowa Engineering Experiment Station.

Winfrey, Robley, and Kurtz, Edwin B. (1931). *Life characteristics of physical property (Bulletin 103)*. Ames, IA, Iowa Engineering Experiment Station.

Wolf, Franklin K. (1985). Forecasting forces of mortality. Ames, IA, *Proceedings, Iowa State Regulatory Conference.*

APPENDIX I

Iowa Curve Tables

SOURCE: The table values for the L, S, and R type curves are based on calculations using 10 place logarithms and made under the supervision of Robley Winfrey. The values at 5% intervals were first published in *Depreciation of Group Properties*, Iowa Engineering Experiment Station Bulletin 155, published in 1942 and republished 1969 by the Iowa State University Engineering Research Institute. Winfrey's complete tables, with values at 1% intervals, were first published in *The Estimation of Depreciation* by Fitch, Bissinger, and Wolf in 1975. The values for the O type curves are from Winfrey's *Statistical Analysis of Industrial Property Retirements*, Bulletin 125 as revised in April 1967 by Harold A. Cowles.

Table A

Age %AL	Iowa Type curve LO Percent Surviving	Remaining Life	CAD Ratio	Prob. Life	Age %AL	Iowa Type curve LO Percent Surviving	Remaining Life	CAD Ratio	Prob. Life
0	100.00000	100.00000	0.0000	100.00	100	44.81457	57.4317	0.4257	157.43
1	99.87056	99.1198	0.0088	100.12	101	44.26652	57.1366	0.4286	158.14
2	99.68038	98.3080	0.0169	100.31	102	43.72131	56.8428	0.4316	158.84
3	99.44834	97.5362	0.0246	100.54	103	43.17898	56.5505	0.4345	159.55
4	99.18298	96.7958	0.0320	100.80	104	42.63958	56.2596	0.4374	160.26
5	98.88950	96.0816	0.0392	101.08	105	42.10313	55.9700	0.4403	160.97
6	98.57147	95.3900	0.0461	101.39	106	41.56968	55.6818	0.4432	161.68
7	98.23157	94.7183	0.0528	101.72	107	41.03927	55.3950	0.4460	162.40
8	97.87191	94.0646	0.0594	102.06	108	40.51194	55.1096	0.4489	163.11
9	97.49419	93.4271	0.0657	102.43	109	39.98773	54.8255	0.4517	163.83
10	97.09985	92.8045	0.0720	102.80	110	39.46666	54.5427	0.4546	164.54
11	96.69011	92.1956	0.0780	103.20	111	38.94879	54.2613	0.4574	165.26
12	96.26604	91.5996	0.0840	103.60	112	38.43413	53.9812	0.4602	165.98
13	95.82657	91.0173	0.0898	104.02	113	37.92274	53.7024	0.4630	166.70
14	95.37855	90.4425	0.0956	104.44	114	37.41463	53.4249	0.4658	167.42
15	94.91874	89.8782	0.1012	104.88	115	36.90985	53.1487	0.4685	168.15
16	94.44381	89.3277	0.1067	105.33	116	36.40843	52.8738	0.4713	168.87
17	93.96040	88.7847	0.1122	105.78	117	35.91039	52.6002	0.4740	169.60
18	93.46710	88.2506	0.1175	106.25	118	35.41577	52.3278	0.4767	170.33
19	92.96443	87.7251	0.1227	106.73	119	34.92459	52.0567	0.4794	171.06
20	92.45291	87.2077	0.1279	107.21	120	34.43690	51.7868	0.4821	171.79
21	91.93301	86.6981	0.1330	107.70	121	33.95270	51.5182	0.4848	172.52
22	91.40618	86.1949	0.1381	108.19	122	33.47204	51.2509	0.4875	173.25
23	90.86982	85.7007	0.1430	108.70	123	32.99494	50.9847	0.4902	173.98
24	90.32735	85.2124	0.1479	109.21	124	32.52142	50.7198	0.4928	174.72
25	89.77813	84.7306	0.1527	109.73	125	32.05150	50.4561	0.4954	175.46
26	89.22254	84.2551	0.1574	110.26	126	31.58522	50.1935	0.4981	176.19
27	88.66092	83.7857	0.1621	110.79	127	31.12260	49.9322	0.5007	176.93
28	88.09361	83.3220	0.1668	111.32	128	30.66365	49.6721	0.5033	177.67
29	87.52092	82.8639	0.1714	111.86	129	30.20840	49.4131	0.5059	178.41
30	86.94316	82.4113	0.1759	112.41	130	29.75687	49.1553	0.5084	179.16
31	86.36064	81.9638	0.1804	112.96	131	29.30908	48.8987	0.5110	179.90
32	85.77364	81.5213	0.1848	113.52	132	28.86504	48.6432	0.5136	180.64
33	85.18246	81.0836	0.1892	114.08	133	28.42478	48.3889	0.5161	181.39
34	84.58736	80.6505	0.1935	114.65	134	27.98832	48.1357	0.5186	182.14
35	83.98860	80.2219	0.1978	115.22	135	27.55566	47.8836	0.5212	182.88
36	83.38647	79.7976	0.2020	115.80	136	27.12683	47.6327	0.5237	183.63
37	82.78120	79.3774	0.2062	116.38	137	26.70184	47.3829	0.5262	184.38
38	82.17306	78.9611	0.2104	116.96	138	26.28070	47.1341	0.5287	185.13
39	81.56228	78.5487	0.2145	117.55	139	25.86343	46.8865	0.5311	185.89
40	80.94912	78.1399	0.2186	118.14	140	25.45004	46.6400	0.5336	186.64
41	80.33381	77.7346	0.2227	118.73	141	25.04053	46.3946	0.5361	187.39
42	79.71659	77.3326	0.2267	119.33	142	24.63493	46.1502	0.5385	188.15
43	79.09766	76.9337	0.2307	119.93	143	24.23324	45.9069	0.5409	188.91
44	78.47734	76.5379	0.2346	120.54	144	23.83547	45.6646	0.5434	189.66
45	.77.85578	76.1450	0.2386	121.14	145	23.44162	45.4235	0.5458	190.42
46	77.23323	75.7547	0.2425	121.75	146	23.05171	45.1833	0.5482	191.18
47	76.60992	75.3670	0.2463	122.37	147	22.66573	44.9442	0.5506	191.94
48	75.98606	74.9817	0.2502	122.98	148	22.28371	44.7062	0.5529	192.71
49	75.36190	74.5986	0.2540	123.60	149	21.90563	44.4691	0.5553	193.47
50	74.73764	74.2175	0.2578	124.22	150	21.53151	44.2331	0.5577	194.23
51	74.11342	73.8384	0.2616	124.84	151	21.16135	43.9981	0.5600	195.00
52	73.48930	73.4612	0.2654	125.46	152	20.79514	43.7641	0.5624	195.76
53	72.86534	73.0860	0.2691	126.09	153	20.43290	43.5311	0.5647	196.53
54	72.24160	72.7127	0.2729	126.71	154	20.07462	43.2991	0.5670	197.30
55	71.61815	72.3413	0.2766	127.34	155	19.72030	43.0681	0.5693	198.07
56	70.99504	71.9719	0.2803	127.97	156	19.36994	42.8381	0.5716	198.84
57	70.37234	71.6043	0.2840	128.60	157	19.02354	42.6090	0.5739	199.61
58	69.75010	71.2386	0.2876	129.24	158	18.68110	42.3809	0.5762	200.38
59	69.12840	70.8748	0.2913	129.87	159	18.34261	42.1538	0.5785	201.15
60	68.50728	70.5128	0.2949	130.51	160	18.00807	41.9276	0.5807	201.93
61	67.88682	70.1527	0.2985	131.15	161	17.67748	41.7023	0.5830	202.70
62	67.26707	69.7945	0.3021	131.79	162	17.35082	41.4780	0.5852	203.48
63	66.64809	69.4380	0.3056	132.44	163	17.02810	41.2547	0.5875	204.25
64	66.02994	69.0834	0.3092	133.08	164	16.70931	41.0322	0.5897	205.03
65	65.41269	68.7306	0.3127	133.73	165	16.39443	40.8107	0.5919	205.81
66	64.79639	68.3795	0.3162	134.38	166	16.08347	40.5901	0.5941	206.59
67	64.18110	68.0303	0.3197	135.03	167	15.77640	40.3704	0.5963	207.37
68	63.56689	67.6828	0.3232	135.68	168	15.47323	40.1515	0.5985	208.15
69	62.95380	67.3371	0.3266	136.34	169	15.17394	39.9336	0.6007	208.93
70	62.34191	66.9931	0.3301	136.99	170	14.87851	39.7166	0.6028	209.72
71	61.73127	66.6508	0.3335	137.65	171	14.58695	39.5005	0.6050	210.50
72	61.12193	66.3103	0.3369	138.31	172	14.29923	39.2852	0.6071	211.29
73	60.51396	65.9715	0.3403	138.97	173	14.01534	39.0708	0.6093	212.07
74	59.90741	65.6343	0.3437	139.63	174	13.73527	38.8573	0.6114	212.86
75	59.30233	65.2989	0.3470	140.30	175	13.45901	38.6447	0.6136	213.64
76	58.69880	64.9652	0.3503	140.97	176	13.18653	38.4329	0.6157	214.43
77	58.09686	64.6331	0.3537	141.63	177	12.91783	38.2219	0.6178	215.22
78	57.49656	64.3027	0.3570	142.30	178	12.65288	38.0118	0.6199	216.01
79	56.89797	63.9739	0.3603	142.97	179	12.39168	37.8025	0.6220	216.80
80	56.30114	63.6468	0.3635	143.65	180	12.13419	37.5940	0.6241	217.59
81	55.70613	63.3213	0.3668	144.32	181	11.88041	37.3864	0.6261	218.39
82	55.11298	62.9974	0.3700	145.00	182	11.63032	37.1796	0.6282	219.18
83	54.52176	62.6751	0.3732	145.68	183	11.38389	36.9736	0.6303	219.97
84	53.93250	62.3544	0.3765	146.35	184	11.14111	36.7684	0.6323	220.77
85	53.34528	62.0353	0.3796	147.04	185	10.90195	36.5640	0.6344	221.56
86	52.76014	61.7178	0.3828	147.72	186	10.66640	36.3605	0.6364	222.36
87	52.17713	61.4018	0.3860	148.40	187	10.43444	36.1577	0.6384	223.16
88	51.59631	61.0874	0.3891	149.09	188	10.20603	35.9557	0.6404	223.96
89	51.01772	60.7745	0.3923	149.77	189	9.98117	35.7544	0.6425	224.75
90	50.44141	60.4631	0.3954	150.46	190	9.75982	35.5540	0.6445	225.55
91	49.86744	60.1533	0.3985	151.15	191	9.54197	35.3543	0.6465	226.35
92	49.29585	59.8450	0.4016	151.84	192	9.32758	35.1554	0.6484	227.16
93	48.72669	59.5382	0.4046	152.54	193	9.11664	34.9573	0.6504	227.96
94	48.16001	59.2329	0.4077	153.23	194	8.90912	34.7599	0.6524	228.76
95	47.59585	58.9290	0.4107	153.93	195	8.70500	34.5632	0.6544	229.56
96	47.03427	58.6267	0.4137	154.63	196	8.50425	34.3673	0.6563	230.37
97	46.47530	58.3258	0.4167	155.33	197	8.30684	34.1722	0.6583	231.17
98	45.91900	58.0263	0.4197	156.03	198	8.11275	33.9777	0.6602	231.98
99	45.36541	57.7283	0.4227	156.73	199	7.92195	33.7840	0.6622	232.78

Table A continued

	Iowa Type curve L0					Iowa Type curve L0			
Age %AL	Percent Surviving	Remaining Life	CAD Ratio	Prob. Life	Age %AL	Percent Surviving	Remaining Life	CAD Ratio	Prob. Life
200	7.73441	33.5911	0.6641	233.59	300	0.23719	17.2586	0.8274	317.26
201	7.55011	33.3989	0.6660	234.40	301	0.22560	17.1196	0.8288	318.12
202	7.36902	33.2073	0.6679	235.21	302	0.21449	16.9804	0.8302	318.98
203	7.19111	33.0165	0.6698	236.02	303	0.20384	16.8415	0.8316	319.84
204	7.01636	32.8264	0.6717	236.83	304	0.19363	16.7032	0.8330	320.70
205	6.84472	32.6370	0.6736	237.64	305	0.18385	16.5651	0.8343	321.57
206	6.67618	32.4483	0.6755	238.45	306	0.17448	16.4278	0.8357	322.43
207	6.51071	32.2603	0.6774	239.26	307	0.16552	16.2901	0.8371	323.29
208	6.34827	32.0729	0.6793	240.07	308	0.15694	16.1533	0.8385	324.15
209	6.18884	31.8863	0.6811	240.89	309	0.14874	16.0163	0.8398	325.02
210	6.03239	31.7003	0.6830	241.70	310	0.14089	15.8808	0.8412	325.88
211	5.87888	31.5150	0.6848	242.52	311	0.13340	15.7444	0.8426	326.74
212	5.72828	31.3304	0.6867	243.33	312	0.12624	15.6090	0.8439	327.61
213	5.58057	31.1464	0.6885	244.15	313	0.11940	15.4745	0.8453	328.47
214	5.43571	30.9632	0.6904	244.96	314	0.11288	15.3395	0.8466	329.34
215	5.29368	30.7805	0.6922	245.78	315	0.10666	15.2049	0.8480	330.20
216	5.15443	30.5985	0.6940	246.60	316	0.10073	15.0705	0.8493	331.07
217	5.01795	30.4172	0.6958	247.42	317	0.09508	14.9364	0.8506	331.94
218	4.88419	30.2365	0.6976	248.24	318	0.08969	14.8039	0.8520	332.80
219	4.75313	30.0564	0.6994	249.06	319	0.08457	14.6699	0.8533	333.67
220	4.62473	29.8770	0.7012	249.88	320	0.07969	14.5376	0.8546	334.54
221	4.49897	29.6982	0.7030	250.70	321	0.07505	14.4055	0.8559	335.41
222	4.37580	29.5201	0.7048	251.52	322	0.07064	14.2736	0.8573	336.27
223	4.25521	29.3425	0.7066	252.34	323	0.06645	14.1421	0.8586	337.14
224	4.13714	29.1656	0.7083	253.17	324	0.06247	14.0113	0.8599	338.01
225	4.02159	28.9893	0.7101	253.99	325	0.05870	13.8791	0.8612	338.88
226	3.90850	28.8136	0.7119	254.81	326	0.05512	13.7480	0.8625	339.75
227	3.79785	28.6385	0.7136	255.64	327	0.05172	13.6189	0.8638	340.62
228	3.68961	28.4640	0.7154	256.46	328	0.04851	13.4870	0.8651	341.49
229	3.58374	28.2901	0.7171	257.29	329	0.04546	13.3583	0.8664	342.36
230	3.48021	28.1168	0.7188	258.12	330	0.04258	13.2280	0.8677	343.23
231	3.37898	27.9441	0.7206	258.94	331	0.03985	13.1000	0.8690	344.10
232	3.28004	27.7720	0.7223	259.77	332	0.03727	12.9722	0.8703	344.97
233	3.18333	27.6005	0.7240	260.60	333	0.03484	12.8421	0.8716	345.84
234	3.08884	27.4295	0.7257	261.43	334	0.03254	12.7145	0.8729	346.71
235	2.99653	27.2591	0.7274	262.26	335	0.03037	12.5873	0.8741	347.59
236	2.90636	27.0893	0.7291	263.09	336	0.02833	12.4577	0.8754	348.46
237	2.81830	26.9201	0.7308	263.92	337	0.02640	12.3318	0.8767	349.33
238	2.73233	26.7514	0.7325	264.75	338	0.02459	12.2027	0.8780	350.20
239	2.64840	26.5833	0.7342	265.58	339	0.02288	12.0774	0.8792	351.08
240	2.56649	26.4158	0.7358	266.42	340	0.02128	11.9479	0.8805	351.95
241	2.48657	26.2487	0.7375	267.25	341	0.01977	11.8222	0.8818	352.82
242	2.40860	26.0823	0.7392	268.08	342	0.01835	11.6984	0.8830	353.70
243	2.33255	25.9163	0.7408	268.92	343	0.01702	11.5735	0.8843	354.57
244	2.25838	25.7511	0.7425	269.75	344	0.01578	11.4436	0.8856	355.44
245	2.18608	25.5862	0.7441	270.59	345	0.01461	11.3200	0.8868	356.32
246	2.11560	25.4219	0.7458	271.42	346	0.01351	11.2010	0.8880	357.20
247	2.04692	25.2581	0.7474	272.26	347	0.01249	11.0749	0.8893	358.07
248	1.98000	25.0949	0.7491	273.09	348	0.01154	10.9454	0.8905	358.95
249	1.91481	24.9322	0.7507	273.93	349	0.01064	10.8290	0.8917	359.83
250	1.85133	24.7700	0.7523	274.77	350	0.00981	10.7029	0.8930	360.70
251	1.78951	24.6084	0.7539	275.61	351	0.00904	10.5720	0.8943	361.57
252	1.72934	24.4472	0.7555	276.45	352	0.00831	10.4567	0.8954	362.46
253	1.67078	24.2866	0.7571	277.29	353	0.00764	10.3299	0.8967	363.33
254	1.61380	24.1264	0.7587	278.13	354	0.00701	10.2133	0.8979	364.21
255	1.55837	23.9668	0.7603	278.97	355	0.00643	10.0895	0.8991	365.09
256	1.50446	23.8077	0.7619	279.81	356	0.00589	9.9687	0.9003	365.97
257	1.45204	23.6491	0.7635	280.65	357	0.00539	9.8470	0.9015	366.85
258	1.40109	23.4909	0.7651	281.49	358	0.00493	9.7192	0.9028	367.72
259	1.35157	23.3333	0.7667	282.33	359	0.00450	9.6001	0.9040	368.60
260	1.30345	23.1763	0.7682	283.18	360	0.00410	9.4879	0.9051	369.49
261	1.25671	23.0196	0.7698	284.02	361	0.00374	9.3531	0.9065	370.35
262	1.21132	22.8635	0.7714	284.86	362	0.00340	9.2384	0.9076	371.24
263	1.16726	22.7076	0.7729	285.71	363	0.00309	9.1151	0.9088	372.12
264	1.12448	22.5525	0.7745	286.55	364	0.00280	9.0073	0.9099	373.01
265	1.08297	22.3978	0.7760	287.40	365	0.00254	8.8782	0.9112	373.88
266	1.04270	22.2435	0.7776	288.24	366	0.00230	8.7524	0.9125	374.75
267	1.00364	22.0897	0.7791	289.09	367	0.00208	8.6253	0.9137	375.63
268	0.96577	21.9363	0.7806	289.94	368	0.00187	8.5377	0.9146	376.54
269	0.92905	21.7835	0.7822	290.78	369	0.00169	8.3938	0.9161	377.39
270	0.89347	21.6311	0.7837	291.63	370	0.00152	8.2767	0.9172	378.28
271	0.85900	21.4790	0.7852	292.48	371	0.00137	8.1282	0.9187	379.13
272	0.82560	21.3277	0.7867	293.33	372	0.00122	8.0661	0.9193	380.07
273	0.79327	21.1766	0.7882	294.18	373	0.00110	7.8915	0.9211	380.89
274	0.76197	21.0259	0.7897	295.03	374	0.00098	7.7965	0.9220	381.80
275	0.73167	20.8760	0.7912	295.88	375	0.00087	7.7191	0.9228	382.72
276	0.70236	20.7263	0.7927	296.73	376	0.00078	7.5521	0.9245	383.55
277	0.67402	20.5767	0.7942	297.58	377	0.00069	7.4719	0.9253	384.47
278	0.64660	20.4281	0.7957	298.43	378	0.00062	7.2591	0.9274	385.26
279	0.62010	20.2797	0.7972	299.28	379	0.00054	7.2604	0.9274	386.26
280	0.59449	20.1318	0.7987	300.13	380	0.00048	7.1055	0.9289	387.11
281	0.56975	19.9843	0.8002	300.98	381	0.00042	7.0492	0.9295	388.05
282	0.54586	19.8370	0.8016	301.84	382	0.00037	6.9342	0.9307	388.93
283	0.52279	19.6903	0.8031	302.69	383	0.00033	6.7141	0.9329	389.71
284	0.50052	19.5442	0.8046	303.54	384	0.00029	6.5713	0.9343	390.57
285	0.47904	19.3981	0.8060	304.40	385	0.00025	6.5427	0.9346	391.54
286	0.45831	19.2529	0.8075	305.25	386	0.00022	6.3668	0.9363	392.37
287	0.43833	19.1077	0.8089	306.11	387	0.00019	6.2931	0.9371	393.29
288	0.41906	18.9633	0.8104	306.96	388	0.00017	5.9747	0.9403	393.97
289	0.40050	18.8190	0.8118	307.82	389	0.00014	6.1479	0.9385	395.15
290	0.38262	18.6750	0.8132	308.68	390	0.00012	6.0893	0.9391	396.09
291	0.36540	18.5316	0.8147	309.53	391	0.00011	5.5975	0.9440	396.60
292	0.34882	18.3886	0.8161	310.39	392	0.00009	5.7304	0.9427	397.73
293	0.33286	18.2464	0.8175	311.25	393	0.00008	5.3842	0.9462	398.38
294	0.31752	18.1037	0.8190	312.10	394	0.00007	5.0820	0.9492	399.08
295	0.30276	17.9619	0.8204	312.96	395	0.00006	4.8458	0.9515	399.85
296	0.28857	17.8206	0.8218	313.82	396	0.00005	4.7151	0.9528	400.72
297	0.27493	17.6799	0.8232	314.68	397	0.00004	4.7690	0.9523	401.77
298	0.26184	17.5388	0.8246	315.54	398	0.00003	5.1921	0.9481	403.19
299	0.24926	17.3987	0.8260	316.40	399	0.00003	4.1925	0.9581	403.19

Table A continued

	Iowa Type curve LO					Iowa Type curve L1			
Age %AL	Percent Surviving	Remaining Life	CAD Ratio	Prob. Life	Age %AL	Percent Surviving	Remaining Life	CAD Ratio	Prob. Life
400	0.00002	5.0390	0.9496	405.04	0	100.00000	100.0000	0.0000	100.00
401	0.00002	4.0396	0.9596	405.04	1	99.94205	99.0636	0.0094	100.06
402	0.00002	3.0402	0.9696	405.04	2	99.87728	98.1275	0.0187	100.13
403	0.00001	4.1190	0.9588	407.12	3	99.80521	97.1980	0.0280	100.20
404	0.00001	3.4820	0.9652	407.48	4	99.72534	96.2755	0.0372	100.28
405	0.00001	2.4831	0.9752	407.48	5	99.63717	95.3602	0.0464	100.36
406	0.00001	1.4843	0.9852	407.48	6	99.54020	94.4526	0.0555	100.45
407	0.00001	0.4855	0.9951	407.49	7	99.43392	93.5531	0.0645	100.55
408	0.00000	0.0000	1.0000	408.00	8	99.31755	92.6621	0.0734	100.66
					9	99.19147	91.7792	0.0822	100.78
					10	99.05431	90.9056	0.0909	100.91
					11	98.90588	90.0413	0.0996	101.04
					12	98.74570	89.1865	0.1081	101.19
					13	98.57331	88.3416	0.1166	101.34
					14	98.38828	87.5068	0.1249	101.51
					15	98.19015	86.6824	0.1332	101.68
					16	97.97853	85.8685	0.1413	101.87
					17	97.75302	85.0655	0.1493	102.07
					18	97.51325	84.2734	0.1573	102.27
					19	97.25887	83.4925	0.1651	102.49
					20	96.98956	82.7230	0.1728	102.72
					21	96.70503	81.9649	0.1804	102.96
					22	96.40500	81.2184	0.1878	103.22
					23	96.08924	80.4837	0.1952	103.48
					24	95.75754	79.7607	0.2024	103.76
					25	95.40973	79.0497	0.2095	104.05
					26	95.04568	78.3505	0.2165	104.35
					27	94.66527	77.6634	0.2234	104.66
					28	94.26844	76.9882	0.2301	104.99
					29	93.85515	76.3250	0.2367	105.33
					30	93.42541	75.6738	0.2433	105.67
					31	92.97926	75.0345	0.2497	106.03
					32	92.51679	74.4071	0.2559	106.41
					33	92.03810	73.7915	0.2621	106.79
					34	91.54335	73.1876	0.2681	107.19
					35	91.03275	72.5953	0.2740	107.60
					36	90.50652	72.0145	0.2799	108.01
					37	89.96493	71.4450	0.2856	108.44
					38	89.40830	70.8867	0.2911	108.89
					39	88.83697	70.3394	0.2966	109.34
					40	88.25133	69.8028	0.3020	109.80
					41	87.65179	69.2768	0.3072	110.28
					42	87.03887	68.7612	0.3124	110.76
					43	86.41288	68.2557	0.3174	111.26
					44	85.77452	67.7599	0.3224	111.76
					45	85.12428	67.2737	0.3273	112.27
					46	84.46275	66.7967	0.3320	112.80
					47	83.79054	66.3285	0.3367	113.33
					48	83.10829	65.8689	0.3413	113.87
					49	82.41667	65.4175	0.3458	114.42
					50	81.71633	64.9739	0.3503	114.97
					51	81.00811	64.5375	0.3546	115.54
					52	80.29262	64.1082	0.3589	116.11
					53	79.57066	63.6853	0.3631	116.69
					54	78.84299	63.2685	0.3673	117.27
					55	78.11041	62.8572	0.3714	117.86
					56	77.37370	62.4509	0.3755	118.45
					57	76.63369	62.0491	0.3795	119.05
					58	75.89120	61.6513	0.3835	119.65
					59	75.14704	61.2569	0.3874	120.26
					60	74.40205	60.8652	0.3913	120.87
					61	73.65696	60.4758	0.3952	121.48
					62	72.91198	60.0887	0.3991	122.09
					63	72.16720	59.7036	0.4030	122.70
					64	71.42273	59.3207	0.4068	123.32
					65	70.67865	58.9400	0.4106	123.94
					66	69.93509	58.5613	0.4144	124.56
					67	69.19213	58.1848	0.4182	125.18
					68	68.44988	57.8103	0.4219	125.81
					69	67.70843	57.4379	0.4256	126.44
					70	66.96789	57.0675	0.4293	127.07
					71	66.22836	56.6991	0.4330	127.70
					72	65.48994	56.3328	0.4367	128.33
					73	64.75272	55.9685	0.4403	128.97
					74	64.01680	55.6061	0.4439	129.61
					75	63.28229	55.2457	0.4475	130.25
					76	62.54928	54.8873	0.4511	130.89
					77	61.81787	54.5308	0.4547	131.53
					78	61.08815	54.1762	0.4582	132.18
					79	60.36022	53.8235	0.4618	132.82
					80	59.63417	53.4727	0.4653	133.47
					81	58.91011	53.1238	0.4688	134.12
					82	58.18813	52.7768	0.4722	134.78
					83	57.46832	52.4315	0.4757	135.43
					84	56.75076	52.0882	0.4791	136.09
					85	56.03557	51.7466	0.4825	136.75
					86	55.32282	51.4068	0.4859	137.41
					87	54.61261	51.0688	0.4893	138.07
					88	53.90503	50.7326	0.4927	138.73
					89	53.20016	50.3982	0.4960	139.40
					90	52.49811	50.0655	0.4993	140.07
					91	51.79894	49.7345	0.5027	140.73
					92	51.10275	49.4052	0.5059	141.41
					93	50.40963	49.0777	0.5092	142.08
					94	49.71966	48.7518	0.5125	142.75
					95	49.03293	48.4276	0.5157	143.43
					96	48.34951	48.1050	0.5189	144.11
					97	47.66949	47.7841	0.5222	144.78
					98	46.99294	47.4649	0.5254	145.46
					99	46.31996	47.1472	0.5285	146.15

Table A continued

Age %AL	Percent Surviving	Remaining Life	CAD Ratio	Prob. Life	Age %AL	Percent Surviving	Remaining Life	CAD Ratio	Prob. Life
100	45.65061	46.8312	0.5317	146.83	200	4.22433	21.4876	0.7851	221.49
101	44.98497	46.5167	0.5348	147.52	201	4.07030	21.2818	0.7872	222.28
102	44.32312	46.2039	0.5380	148.20	202	3.92035	21.0767	0.7892	223.08
103	43.66514	45.8926	0.5411	148.89	203	3.77442	20.8722	0.7913	223.87
104	43.01109	45.5828	0.5442	149.58	204	3.63244	20.6685	0.7933	224.67
105	42.36105	45.2747	0.5473	150.27	205	3.49436	20.4655	0.7953	225.47
106	41.71509	44.9680	0.5503	150.97	206	3.36011	20.2632	0.7974	226.26
107	41.07329	44.6628	0.5534	151.66	207	3.22965	20.0615	0.7994	227.06
108	40.43570	44.3592	0.5564	152.36	208	3.10291	19.8605	0.8014	227.86
109	39.80240	44.0570	0.5594	153.06	209	2.97983	19.6602	0.8034	228.66
110	39.17345	43.7564	0.5624	153.76	210	2.86035	19.4605	0.8054	229.46
111	38.54891	43.4572	0.5654	154.46	211	2.74440	19.2616	0.8074	230.26
112	37.92886	43.1594	0.5684	155.16	212	2.63194	19.0633	0.8094	231.06
113	37.31334	42.8631	0.5714	155.86	213	2.52290	18.8656	0.8113	231.87
114	36.70243	42.5683	0.5743	156.57	214	2.41722	18.6685	0.8133	232.67
115	36.09618	42.2748	0.5773	157.27	215	2.31483	18.4722	0.8153	233.47
116	35.49464	41.9828	0.5802	157.98	216	2.21568	18.2764	0.8172	234.28
117	34.89788	41.6922	0.5831	158.69	217	2.11971	18.0812	0.8192	235.08
118	34.30595	41.4029	0.5860	159.40	218	2.02685	17.8867	0.8211	235.89
119	33.71890	41.1150	0.5888	160.12	219	1.93704	17.6928	0.8231	236.69
120	33.13678	40.8285	0.5917	160.83	220	1.85022	17.4996	0.8250	237.50
121	32.55964	40.5434	0.5946	161.54	221	1.76634	17.3069	0.8269	238.31
122	31.98754	40.2596	0.5974	162.26	222	1.68532	17.1148	0.8289	239.11
123	31.42051	39.9771	0.6002	162.98	223	1.60711	16.9234	0.8308	239.92
124	30.85860	39.6959	0.6030	163.70	224	1.53165	16.7325	0.8327	240.73
125	30.30187	39.4161	0.6058	164.42	225	1.45888	16.5422	0.8346	241.54
126	29.75034	39.1375	0.6086	165.14	226	1.38873	16.3526	0.8365	242.35
127	29.20406	38.8603	0.6114	165.86	227	1.32115	16.1635	0.8384	243.16
128	28.66307	38.5843	0.6142	166.58	228	1.25607	15.9750	0.8402	243.98
129	28.12741	38.3095	0.6169	167.31	229	1.19344	15.7871	0.8421	244.79
130	27.59711	38.0361	0.6196	168.04	230	1.13320	15.5998	0.8440	245.60
131	27.07221	37.7639	0.6224	168.76	231	1.07529	15.4130	0.8459	246.41
132	26.55274	37.4929	0.6251	169.49	232	1.01965	15.2268	0.8477	247.23
133	26.03873	37.2231	0.6278	170.22	233	0.96622	15.0411	0.8496	248.04
134	25.53021	36.9546	0.6305	170.95	234	0.91495	14.8560	0.8514	248.86
135	25.02721	36.6873	0.6331	171.69	235	0.86577	14.6714	0.8533	249.67
136	24.52975	36.4211	0.6358	172.42	236	0.81864	14.4873	0.8551	250.49
137	24.03787	36.1562	0.6384	173.16	237	0.77348	14.3040	0.8570	251.30
138	23.55157	35.8924	0.6411	173.89	238	0.73026	14.1209	0.8588	252.12
139	23.07089	35.6298	0.6437	174.63	239	0.68891	13.9385	0.8606	252.94
140	22.59584	35.3684	0.6463	175.37	240	0.64937	13.7568	0.8624	253.76
141	22.12644	35.1081	0.6489	176.11	241	0.61160	13.5755	0.8642	254.58
142	21.66271	34.8489	0.6515	176.85	242	0.57554	13.3947	0.8661	255.39
143	21.20467	34.5909	0.6541	177.59	243	0.54114	13.2144	0.8679	256.21
144	20.75232	34.3340	0.6567	178.33	244	0.50835	13.0345	0.8697	257.03
145	20.30567	34.0782	0.6592	179.08	245	0.47711	12.8552	0.8714	257.86
146	19.86475	33.8235	0.6618	179.82	246	0.44737	12.6766	0.8732	258.68
147	19.42955	33.5700	0.6643	180.57	247	0.41909	12.4983	0.8750	259.50
148	19.00008	33.3175	0.6668	181.32	248	0.39221	12.3206	0.8768	260.32
149	18.57635	33.0660	0.6693	182.07	249	0.36669	12.1432	0.8786	261.14
150	18.15836	32.8157	0.6718	182.82	250	0.34247	11.9666	0.8803	261.97
151	17.74612	32.5664	0.6743	183.57	251	0.31952	11.7902	0.8821	262.79
152	17.33962	32.3181	0.6768	184.32	252	0.29778	11.6145	0.8839	263.61
153	16.93886	32.0709	0.6793	185.07	253	0.27721	11.4393	0.8856	264.44
154	16.54383	31.8247	0.6818	185.82	254	0.25777	11.2642	0.8874	265.26
155	16.15455	31.5796	0.6842	186.58	255	0.23940	11.0902	0.8891	266.09
156	15.77099	31.3355	0.6866	187.34	256	0.22208	10.9162	0.8908	266.92
157	15.39315	31.0923	0.6891	188.09	257	0.20575	10.7429	0.8926	267.74
158	15.02103	30.8502	0.6915	188.85	258	0.19038	10.5698	0.8943	268.57
159	14.65461	30.6091	0.6939	189.61	259	0.17592	10.3975	0.8960	269.40
160	14.29388	30.3689	0.6963	190.37	260	0.16234	10.2255	0.8977	270.23
161	13.93882	30.1298	0.6987	191.13	261	0.14960	10.0537	0.8995	271.05
162	13.58943	29.8916	0.7011	191.89	262	0.13765	9.8831	0.9012	271.88
163	13.24568	29.6543	0.7035	192.65	263	0.12647	9.7125	0.9029	272.71
164	12.90755	29.4181	0.7058	193.42	264	0.11602	9.5423	0.9046	273.54
165	12.57504	29.1827	0.7082	194.18	265	0.10627	9.3719	0.9063	274.37
166	12.24811	28.9483	0.7105	194.95	266	0.09717	9.2028	0.9080	275.20
167	11.92675	28.7149	0.7129	195.71	267	0.08870	9.0338	0.9097	276.03
168	11.61092	28.4823	0.7152	196.48	268	0.08082	8.8659	0.9113	276.87
169	11.30062	28.2507	0.7175	197.25	269	0.07351	8.6978	0.9130	277.70
170	10.99580	28.0200	0.7198	198.02	270	0.06673	8.5307	0.9147	278.53
171	10.69644	27.7902	0.7221	198.79	271	0.06046	8.3635	0.9164	279.36
172	10.40252	27.5613	0.7244	199.56	272	0.05467	8.1964	0.9180	280.20
173	10.11400	27.3332	0.7267	200.33	273	0.04932	8.0312	0.9197	281.03
174	9.83085	27.1061	0.7289	201.11	274	0.04441	7.8639	0.9214	281.86
175	9.55304	26.8798	0.7312	201.88	275	0.03989	7.6983	0.9230	282.70
176	9.28054	26.6544	0.7335	202.65	276	0.03574	7.5341	0.9247	283.53
177	9.01330	26.4298	0.7357	203.43	277	0.03195	7.3685	0.9263	284.37
178	8.75130	26.2061	0.7379	204.21	278	0.02848	7.2054	0.9279	285.21
179	8.49450	25.9833	0.7402	204.98	279	0.02532	7.0423	0.9296	286.04
180	8.24285	25.7613	0.7424	205.76	280	0.02245	6.8786	0.9312	286.88
181	7.99632	25.5401	0.7446	206.54	281	0.01985	6.7141	0.9329	287.71
182	7.75486	25.3197	0.7468	207.32	282	0.01749	6.5526	0.9345	288.55
183	7.51844	25.1002	0.7490	208.10	283	0.01536	6.3919	0.9361	289.39
184	7.28701	24.8815	0.7512	208.88	284	0.01345	6.2286	0.9377	290.23
185	7.06053	24.6636	0.7534	209.66	285	0.01173	6.0686	0.9393	291.07
186	6.83895	24.4465	0.7555	210.45	286	0.01019	5.9102	0.9409	291.91
187	6.62223	24.2301	0.7577	211.23	287	0.00882	5.7505	0.9425	292.75
188	6.41032	24.0146	0.7599	212.01	288	0.00761	5.5854	0.9441	293.59
189	6.20316	23.7999	0.7620	212.80	289	0.00653	5.4265	0.9457	294.43
190	6.00073	23.5859	0.7641	213.59	290	0.00558	5.2652	0.9473	295.27
191	5.80295	23.3727	0.7663	214.37	291	0.00474	5.1097	0.9489	296.11
192	5.60980	23.1603	0.7684	215.16	292	0.00401	4.9488	0.9505	296.95
193	5.42120	22.9486	0.7705	215.95	293	0.00337	4.7937	0.9521	297.79
194	5.23711	22.7377	0.7726	216.74	294	0.00282	4.6312	0.9537	298.63
195	5.05748	22.5275	0.7747	217.53	295	0.00234	4.4786	0.9552	299.48
196	4.88226	22.3181	0.7768	218.32	296	0.00193	4.3238	0.9568	300.32
197	4.71139	22.1094	0.7789	219.11	297	0.00158	4.1708	0.9583	301.17
198	4.54481	21.9014	0.7810	219.90	298	0.00129	3.9960	0.9600	302.00
199	4.38248	21.6941	0.7831	220.69	299	0.00104	3.8364	0.9616	302.84

309

Table A continued

<table>
<tr><th colspan="5" style="text-align:center">Iowa Type curve L1</th></tr>
<tr><th>Age
%AL</th><th>Percent
Surviving</th><th>Remaining
Life</th><th>CAD
Ratio</th><th>Prob.
Life</th></tr>
<tr><td>300</td><td>0.00083</td><td>3.6806</td><td>0.9632</td><td>303.68</td></tr>
<tr><td>301</td><td>0.00065</td><td>3.5614</td><td>0.9644</td><td>304.56</td></tr>
<tr><td>302</td><td>0.00051</td><td>3.4018</td><td>0.9660</td><td>305.40</td></tr>
<tr><td>303</td><td>0.00040</td><td>3.1998</td><td>0.9680</td><td>306.20</td></tr>
<tr><td>304</td><td>0.00030</td><td>3.0998</td><td>0.9690</td><td>307.10</td></tr>
<tr><td>305</td><td>0.00023</td><td>2.8910</td><td>0.9711</td><td>307.89</td></tr>
<tr><td>306</td><td>0.00017</td><td>2.7350</td><td>0.9726</td><td>308.74</td></tr>
<tr><td>307</td><td>0.00012</td><td>2.6663</td><td>0.9733</td><td>309.67</td></tr>
<tr><td>308</td><td>0.00009</td><td>2.3885</td><td>0.9761</td><td>310.39</td></tr>
<tr><td>309</td><td>0.00006</td><td>2.3328</td><td>0.9767</td><td>311.33</td></tr>
<tr><td>310</td><td>0.00004</td><td>2.2494</td><td>0.9775</td><td>312.25</td></tr>
<tr><td>311</td><td>0.00003</td><td>1.8328</td><td>0.9817</td><td>312.83</td></tr>
<tr><td>312</td><td>0.00002</td><td>1.4994</td><td>0.9850</td><td>313.50</td></tr>
<tr><td>313</td><td>0.00001</td><td>1.4994</td><td>0.9850</td><td>314.50</td></tr>
<tr><td>314</td><td>0.00001</td><td>0.5006</td><td>0.9950</td><td>314.50</td></tr>
<tr><td>315</td><td>0.00000</td><td>0.0000</td><td>1.0000</td><td>315.00</td></tr>
</table>

<table>
<tr><th colspan="5" style="text-align:center">Iowa Type curve L2</th></tr>
<tr><th>Age
%AL</th><th>Percent
Surviving</th><th>Remaining
Life</th><th>CAD
Ratio</th><th>Prob.
Life</th></tr>
<tr><td>0</td><td>100.00000</td><td>100.0000</td><td>0.0000</td><td>100.00</td></tr>
<tr><td>1</td><td>99.99981</td><td>99.0003</td><td>0.0100</td><td>100.00</td></tr>
<tr><td>2</td><td>99.99889</td><td>98.0013</td><td>0.0200</td><td>100.00</td></tr>
<tr><td>3</td><td>99.99658</td><td>97.0035</td><td>0.0300</td><td>100.00</td></tr>
<tr><td>4</td><td>99.99221</td><td>96.0077</td><td>0.0399</td><td>100.01</td></tr>
<tr><td>5</td><td>99.98516</td><td>95.0145</td><td>0.0499</td><td>100.01</td></tr>
<tr><td>6</td><td>99.97481</td><td>94.0242</td><td>0.0598</td><td>100.02</td></tr>
<tr><td>7</td><td>99.96060</td><td>93.0375</td><td>0.0696</td><td>100.04</td></tr>
<tr><td>8</td><td>99.94197</td><td>92.0548</td><td>0.0795</td><td>100.05</td></tr>
<tr><td>9</td><td>99.91840</td><td>91.0764</td><td>0.0892</td><td>100.08</td></tr>
<tr><td>10</td><td>99.88940</td><td>90.1027</td><td>0.0990</td><td>100.10</td></tr>
<tr><td>11</td><td>99.85449</td><td>89.1340</td><td>0.1087</td><td>100.13</td></tr>
<tr><td>12</td><td>99.81324</td><td>88.1706</td><td>0.1183</td><td>100.17</td></tr>
<tr><td>13</td><td>99.76522</td><td>87.2128</td><td>0.1279</td><td>100.21</td></tr>
<tr><td>14</td><td>99.71004</td><td>86.2608</td><td>0.1374</td><td>100.26</td></tr>
<tr><td>15</td><td>99.64733</td><td>85.3148</td><td>0.1469</td><td>100.31</td></tr>
<tr><td>16</td><td>99.57673</td><td>84.3749</td><td>0.1563</td><td>100.37</td></tr>
<tr><td>17</td><td>99.49792</td><td>83.4414</td><td>0.1656</td><td>100.44</td></tr>
<tr><td>18</td><td>99.41060</td><td>82.5142</td><td>0.1749</td><td>100.51</td></tr>
<tr><td>19</td><td>99.31448</td><td>81.5936</td><td>0.1841</td><td>100.59</td></tr>
<tr><td>20</td><td>99.20931</td><td>80.6796</td><td>0.1932</td><td>100.68</td></tr>
<tr><td>21</td><td>99.09483</td><td>79.7722</td><td>0.2023</td><td>100.77</td></tr>
<tr><td>22</td><td>98.97083</td><td>78.8715</td><td>0.2113</td><td>100.87</td></tr>
<tr><td>23</td><td>98.83711</td><td>77.9775</td><td>0.2202</td><td>100.98</td></tr>
<tr><td>24</td><td>98.69348</td><td>77.0903</td><td>0.2291</td><td>101.09</td></tr>
<tr><td>25</td><td>98.53978</td><td>76.2098</td><td>0.2379</td><td>101.21</td></tr>
<tr><td>26</td><td>98.37585</td><td>75.3359</td><td>0.2466</td><td>101.34</td></tr>
<tr><td>27</td><td>98.20157</td><td>74.4687</td><td>0.2553</td><td>101.47</td></tr>
<tr><td>28</td><td>98.01682</td><td>73.6081</td><td>0.2639</td><td>101.61</td></tr>
<tr><td>29</td><td>97.82151</td><td>72.7541</td><td>0.2725</td><td>101.75</td></tr>
<tr><td>30</td><td>97.61555</td><td>71.9066</td><td>0.2809</td><td>101.91</td></tr>
<tr><td>31</td><td>97.39888</td><td>71.0654</td><td>0.2893</td><td>102.07</td></tr>
<tr><td>32</td><td>97.17137</td><td>70.2306</td><td>0.2977</td><td>102.23</td></tr>
<tr><td>33</td><td>96.93262</td><td>69.4024</td><td>0.3060</td><td>102.40</td></tr>
<tr><td>34</td><td>96.68183</td><td>68.5811</td><td>0.3142</td><td>102.58</td></tr>
<tr><td>35</td><td>96.41791</td><td>67.7675</td><td>0.3223</td><td>102.77</td></tr>
<tr><td>36</td><td>96.13962</td><td>66.9622</td><td>0.3304</td><td>102.96</td></tr>
<tr><td>37</td><td>95.84571</td><td>66.1660</td><td>0.3383</td><td>103.17</td></tr>
<tr><td>38</td><td>95.53422</td><td>65.3801</td><td>0.3462</td><td>103.38</td></tr>
<tr><td>39</td><td>95.20560</td><td>64.6040</td><td>0.3540</td><td>103.60</td></tr>
<tr><td>40</td><td>94.85656</td><td>63.8399</td><td>0.3616</td><td>103.84</td></tr>
<tr><td>41</td><td>94.48666</td><td>63.0879</td><td>0.3691</td><td>104.09</td></tr>
<tr><td>42</td><td>94.09481</td><td>62.3485</td><td>0.3765</td><td>104.35</td></tr>
<tr><td>43</td><td>93.68001</td><td>61.6224</td><td>0.3838</td><td>104.62</td></tr>
<tr><td>44</td><td>93.24139</td><td>60.9099</td><td>0.3909</td><td>104.91</td></tr>
<tr><td>45</td><td>92.77820</td><td>60.2115</td><td>0.3979</td><td>105.21</td></tr>
<tr><td>46</td><td>92.28984</td><td>59.5275</td><td>0.4047</td><td>105.53</td></tr>
<tr><td>47</td><td>91.77585</td><td>58.8581</td><td>0.4114</td><td>105.86</td></tr>
<tr><td>48</td><td>91.23588</td><td>58.2034</td><td>0.4180</td><td>106.20</td></tr>
<tr><td>49</td><td>90.66975</td><td>57.5637</td><td>0.4244</td><td>106.56</td></tr>
<tr><td>50</td><td>90.07738</td><td>56.9390</td><td>0.4306</td><td>106.94</td></tr>
<tr><td>51</td><td>89.45886</td><td>56.3292</td><td>0.4367</td><td>107.33</td></tr>
<tr><td>52</td><td>88.81436</td><td>55.7344</td><td>0.4427</td><td>107.73</td></tr>
<tr><td>53</td><td>88.14419</td><td>55.1543</td><td>0.4485</td><td>108.15</td></tr>
<tr><td>54</td><td>87.44876</td><td>54.5889</td><td>0.4541</td><td>108.59</td></tr>
<tr><td>55</td><td>86.72360</td><td>54.0412</td><td>0.4596</td><td>109.04</td></tr>
<tr><td>56</td><td>85.98432</td><td>53.5016</td><td>0.4650</td><td>109.50</td></tr>
<tr><td>57</td><td>85.21661</td><td>52.9790</td><td>0.4702</td><td>109.98</td></tr>
<tr><td>58</td><td>84.42626</td><td>52.4703</td><td>0.4753</td><td>110.47</td></tr>
<tr><td>59</td><td>83.61413</td><td>51.9751</td><td>0.4802</td><td>110.98</td></tr>
<tr><td>60</td><td>82.78113</td><td>51.4931</td><td>0.4851</td><td>111.49</td></tr>
<tr><td>61</td><td>81.92824</td><td>51.0239</td><td>0.4898</td><td>112.02</td></tr>
<tr><td>62</td><td>81.05647</td><td>50.5673</td><td>0.4943</td><td>112.57</td></tr>
<tr><td>63</td><td>80.16690</td><td>50.1229</td><td>0.4988</td><td>113.12</td></tr>
<tr><td>64</td><td>79.26062</td><td>49.6903</td><td>0.5031</td><td>113.69</td></tr>
<tr><td>65</td><td>78.33876</td><td>49.2691</td><td>0.5073</td><td>114.27</td></tr>
<tr><td>66</td><td>77.40247</td><td>48.8591</td><td>0.5114</td><td>114.86</td></tr>
<tr><td>67</td><td>76.45290</td><td>48.4597</td><td>0.5154</td><td>115.46</td></tr>
<tr><td>68</td><td>75.49123</td><td>48.0707</td><td>0.5193</td><td>116.07</td></tr>
<tr><td>69</td><td>74.51863</td><td>47.6915</td><td>0.5231</td><td>116.69</td></tr>
<tr><td>70</td><td>73.53626</td><td>47.3220</td><td>0.5268</td><td>117.32</td></tr>
<tr><td>71</td><td>72.54528</td><td>46.9616</td><td>0.5304</td><td>117.96</td></tr>
<tr><td>72</td><td>71.54685</td><td>46.6099</td><td>0.5339</td><td>118.61</td></tr>
<tr><td>73</td><td>70.54209</td><td>46.2667</td><td>0.5373</td><td>119.27</td></tr>
<tr><td>74</td><td>69.53212</td><td>45.9315</td><td>0.5407</td><td>119.93</td></tr>
<tr><td>75</td><td>68.51802</td><td>45.6039</td><td>0.5440</td><td>120.60</td></tr>
<tr><td>76</td><td>67.50085</td><td>45.2835</td><td>0.5472</td><td>121.28</td></tr>
<tr><td>77</td><td>66.48165</td><td>44.9701</td><td>0.5503</td><td>121.97</td></tr>
<tr><td>78</td><td>65.46140</td><td>44.6632</td><td>0.5534</td><td>122.66</td></tr>
<tr><td>79</td><td>64.44107</td><td>44.3624</td><td>0.5564</td><td>123.36</td></tr>
<tr><td>80</td><td>63.42158</td><td>44.0675</td><td>0.5593</td><td>124.07</td></tr>
<tr><td>81</td><td>62.40383</td><td>43.7781</td><td>0.5622</td><td>124.78</td></tr>
<tr><td>82</td><td>61.38866</td><td>43.4938</td><td>0.5651</td><td>125.49</td></tr>
<tr><td>83</td><td>60.37687</td><td>43.2142</td><td>0.5679</td><td>126.21</td></tr>
<tr><td>84</td><td>59.36924</td><td>42.9392</td><td>0.5706</td><td>126.94</td></tr>
<tr><td>85</td><td>58.36648</td><td>42.6683</td><td>0.5733</td><td>127.67</td></tr>
<tr><td>86</td><td>57.36928</td><td>42.4013</td><td>0.5760</td><td>128.40</td></tr>
<tr><td>87</td><td>56.37827</td><td>42.1378</td><td>0.5786</td><td>129.14</td></tr>
<tr><td>88</td><td>55.39407</td><td>41.8776</td><td>0.5812</td><td>129.88</td></tr>
<tr><td>89</td><td>54.41722</td><td>41.6204</td><td>0.5838</td><td>130.62</td></tr>
<tr><td>90</td><td>53.44823</td><td>41.3659</td><td>0.5863</td><td>131.37</td></tr>
<tr><td>91</td><td>52.48759</td><td>41.1138</td><td>0.5889</td><td>132.11</td></tr>
<tr><td>92</td><td>51.53574</td><td>40.8639</td><td>0.5914</td><td>132.86</td></tr>
<tr><td>93</td><td>50.59305</td><td>40.6160</td><td>0.5938</td><td>133.62</td></tr>
<tr><td>94</td><td>49.65990</td><td>40.3699</td><td>0.5963</td><td>134.37</td></tr>
<tr><td>95</td><td>48.73660</td><td>40.1252</td><td>0.5987</td><td>135.13</td></tr>
<tr><td>96</td><td>47.82345</td><td>39.8818</td><td>0.6012</td><td>135.88</td></tr>
<tr><td>97</td><td>46.92069</td><td>39.6395</td><td>0.6036</td><td>136.64</td></tr>
<tr><td>98</td><td>46.02855</td><td>39.3981</td><td>0.6060</td><td>137.40</td></tr>
<tr><td>99</td><td>45.14722</td><td>39.1574</td><td>0.6084</td><td>138.16</td></tr>
</table>

Table A continued

		Iowa Type curve L2					Iowa Type curve L2		
Age %AL	Percent Surviving	Remaining Life	CAD Ratio	Prob. Life	Age %AL	Percent Surviving	Remaining Life	CAD Ratio	Prob. Life
100	44.27685	38.9174	0.6108	138.92	200	2.03522	15.5013	0.8450	215.50
101	43.41757	38.6777	0.6132	139.68	201	1.93217	15.3014	0.8470	216.30
102	42.56950	38.4383	0.6156	140.44	202	1.83299	15.1022	0.8490	217.10
103	41.73271	38.1990	0.6180	141.20	203	1.73762	14.9037	0.8510	217.90
104	40.90725	37.9597	0.6204	141.96	204	1.64596	14.7058	0.8529	218.71
105	40.09316	37.7203	0.6228	142.72	205	1.55792	14.5086	0.8549	219.51
106	39.29046	37.4807	0.6252	143.48	206	1.47341	14.3121	0.8569	220.31
107	38.49913	37.2408	0.6276	144.24	207	1.39235	14.1162	0.8588	221.12
108	37.71916	37.0006	0.6300	145.00	208	1.31465	13.9209	0.8608	221.92
109	36.95049	36.7599	0.6324	145.76	209	1.24023	13.7263	0.8627	222.73
110	36.19309	36.5187	0.6348	146.52	210	1.16899	13.5323	0.8647	223.53
111	35.44688	36.2769	0.6372	147.28	211	1.10086	13.3388	0.8666	224.34
112	34.71179	36.0346	0.6397	148.03	212	1.03574	13.1460	0.8685	225.15
113	33.98772	35.7916	0.6421	148.79	213	0.97355	12.9539	0.8705	225.95
114	33.27458	35.5480	0.6445	149.55	214	0.91421	12.7622	0.8724	226.76
115	32.57226	35.3037	0.6470	150.30	215	0.85763	12.5712	0.8743	227.57
116	31.88064	35.0587	0.6494	151.06	216	0.80372	12.3809	0.8762	228.38
117	31.19961	34.8130	0.6519	151.81	217	0.75242	12.1909	0.8781	229.19
118	30.52904	34.5667	0.6543	152.57	218	0.70363	12.0016	0.8800	230.00
119	29.86880	34.3198	0.6568	153.32	219	0.65727	11.8128	0.8819	230.81
120	29.21877	34.0721	0.6593	154.07	220	0.61326	11.6247	0.8838	231.62
121	28.57881	33.8239	0.6618	154.82	221	0.57152	11.4372	0.8856	232.44
122	27.94878	33.5751	0.6642	155.58	222	0.53198	11.2501	0.8875	233.25
123	27.32855	33.3258	0.6667	156.33	223	0.49456	11.0635	0.8894	234.06
124	26.71799	33.0759	0.6692	157.08	224	0.45918	10.8774	0.8912	234.88
125	26.11696	32.8256	0.6717	157.83	225	0.42576	10.6920	0.8931	235.69
126	25.52533	32.5748	0.6743	158.57	226	0.39424	10.5068	0.8949	236.51
127	24.94297	32.3237	0.6768	159.32	227	0.36453	10.3224	0.8968	237.32
128	24.36975	32.0722	0.6793	160.07	228	0.33657	10.1384	0.8986	238.14
129	23.80555	31.8205	0.6818	160.82	229	0.31028	9.9550	0.9004	238.96
130	23.25024	31.5686	0.6843	161.57	230	0.28560	9.7721	0.9023	239.77
131	22.70370	31.3165	0.6868	162.32	231	0.26246	9.5896	0.9041	240.59
132	22.16582	31.0643	0.6894	163.06	232	0.24079	9.4076	0.9059	241.41
133	21.63648	30.8120	0.6919	163.81	233	0.22053	9.2259	0.9077	242.23
134	21.11558	30.5598	0.6944	164.56	234	0.20161	9.0448	0.9096	243.04
135	20.60301	30.3077	0.6969	165.31	235	0.18397	8.8641	0.9114	243.86
136	20.09867	30.0556	0.6994	166.06	236	0.16754	8.6844	0.9132	244.68
137	19.60247	29.8038	0.7020	166.80	237	0.15228	8.5045	0.9150	245.50
138	19.11431	29.5522	0.7045	167.55	238	0.13812	8.3251	0.9167	246.33
139	18.63410	29.3008	0.7070	168.30	239	0.12500	8.1465	0.9185	247.15
140	18.16176	29.0499	0.7095	169.05	240	0.11287	7.9682	0.9203	247.97
141	17.69721	28.7993	0.7120	169.80	241	0.10168	7.7901	0.9221	248.79
142	17.24037	28.5492	0.7145	170.55	242	0.09137	7.6127	0.9239	249.61
143	16.79117	28.2996	0.7170	171.30	243	0.08189	7.4361	0.9256	250.44
144	16.34953	28.0505	0.7195	172.05	244	0.07320	7.2596	0.9274	251.26
145	15.91540	27.8020	0.7220	172.80	245	0.06525	7.0831	0.9292	252.08
146	15.48870	27.5542	0.7245	173.55	246	0.05799	6.9073	0.9309	252.91
147	15.06937	27.3070	0.7269	174.31	247	0.05138	6.7316	0.9327	253.73
148	14.65737	27.0605	0.7294	175.06	248	0.04537	6.5571	0.9344	254.56
149	14.25262	26.8148	0.7319	175.81	249	0.03993	6.3823	0.9362	255.38
150	13.85508	26.5698	0.7343	176.57	250	0.03501	6.2089	0.9379	256.21
151	13.46470	26.3256	0.7367	177.33	251	0.03058	6.0360	0.9396	257.04
152	13.08142	26.0823	0.7392	178.08	252	0.02661	5.8619	0.9414	257.86
153	12.70519	25.8399	0.7416	178.84	253	0.02305	5.6900	0.9431	258.69
154	12.33597	25.5983	0.7440	179.60	254	0.01988	5.5176	0.9448	259.52
155	11.97372	25.3576	0.7464	180.36	255	0.01707	5.3436	0.9466	260.34
156	11.61838	25.1179	0.7488	181.12	256	0.01457	5.1747	0.9483	261.17
157	11.26991	24.8791	0.7512	181.88	257	0.01238	5.0016	0.9500	262.00
158	10.92827	24.6412	0.7536	182.64	258	0.01045	4.8330	0.9517	262.83
159	10.59341	24.4043	0.7560	183.40	259	0.00877	4.6630	0.9534	263.66
160	10.26528	24.1684	0.7583	184.17	260	0.00731	4.4945	0.9551	264.49
161	9.94385	23.9335	0.7607	184.93	261	0.00605	4.3264	0.9567	265.33
162	9.62907	23.6995	0.7630	185.70	262	0.00497	4.1579	0.9584	266.16
163	9.32089	23.4666	0.7653	186.47	263	0.00405	3.9888	0.9601	266.99
164	9.01926	23.2347	0.7677	187.23	264	0.00327	3.8211	0.9618	267.82
165	8.72414	23.0037	0.7700	188.00	265	0.00261	3.6609	0.9634	268.66
166	8.43549	22.7738	0.7723	188.77	266	0.00207	3.4854	0.9651	269.49
167	8.15324	22.5449	0.7746	189.54	267	0.00162	3.3147	0.9669	270.31
168	7.87736	22.3169	0.7768	190.32	268	0.00125	3.1479	0.9685	271.15
169	7.60779	22.0900	0.7791	191.09	269	0.00095	2.9841	0.9702	271.98
170	7.34447	21.8640	0.7814	191.86	270	0.00071	2.8238	0.9718	272.82
171	7.08736	21.6391	0.7836	192.64	271	0.00052	2.6728	0.9733	273.67
172	6.83640	21.4151	0.7858	193.42	272	0.00038	2.4734	0.9753	274.47
173	6.59153	21.1920	0.7881	194.19	273	0.00026	2.3842	0.9762	275.38
174	6.35270	20.9699	0.7903	194.97	274	0.00018	2.2217	0.9778	276.22
175	6.11983	20.7489	0.7925	195.75	275	0.00012	2.0826	0.9792	277.08
176	5.89288	20.5287	0.7947	196.53	276	0.00008	1.8740	0.9813	277.87
177	5.67178	20.3095	0.7969	197.31	277	0.00005	1.6985	0.9830	278.70
178	5.45647	20.0911	0.7991	198.09	278	0.00003	1.4979	0.9850	279.50
179	5.24687	19.8738	0.8013	198.87	279	0.00002	0.9971	0.9900	280.00
180	5.04292	19.6573	0.8034	199.66	280	0.00001	0.4948	0.9951	280.49
181	4.84456	19.4417	0.8056	200.44	281	0.00000	0.0000	1.0000	281.00
182	4.65171	19.2270	0.8077	201.23					
183	4.46429	19.0132	0.8099	202.01					
184	4.28225	18.8002	0.8120	202.80					
185	4.10549	18.5881	0.8141	203.59					
186	3.93396	18.3768	0.8162	204.38					
187	3.76756	18.1663	0.8183	205.17					
188	3.60622	17.9567	0.8204	205.96					
189	3.44987	17.7478	0.8225	206.75					
190	3.29841	17.5398	0.8246	207.54					
191	3.15178	17.3326	0.8267	208.33					
192	3.00988	17.1261	0.8287	209.13					
193	2.87264	16.9205	0.8308	209.92					
194	2.73998	16.7155	0.8328	210.72					
195	2.61180	16.5113	0.8349	211.51					
196	2.48802	16.3079	0.8369	212.31					
197	2.36856	16.1051	0.8389	213.11					
198	2.25333	15.9031	0.8410	213.90					
199	2.14225	15.7018	0.8430	214.70					

Table A continued

Age %AL	Iowa Type curve L3 Percent Surviving	Remaining Life	CAD Ratio	Prob. Life	Age %AL	Iowa Type curve L3 Percent Surviving	Remaining Life	CAD Ratio	Prob. Life
0	100.00000	100.0000	0.0000	100.00	100	43.81420	30.0256	0.6997	130.03
1	100.00000	98.9984	0.0100	100.00	101	42.61133	29.8590	0.7014	130.86
2	100.00000	97.9984	0.0200	100.00	102	41.43386	29.6934	0.7031	131.69
3	100.00000	96.9984	0.0300	100.00	103	40.28232	29.5279	0.7047	132.53
4	100.00000	95.9984	0.0400	100.00	104	39.15710	29.3620	0.7064	133.36
5	100.00000	94.9984	0.0500	100.00	105	38.05846	29.1952	0.7080	134.20
6	100.00000	93.9984	0.0600	100.00	106	36.98648	29.0269	0.7097	135.03
7	100.00000	92.9984	0.0700	100.00	107	35.94118	28.8566	0.7114	135.86
8	100.00000	91.9984	0.0800	100.00	108	34.92241	28.6838	0.7132	136.68
9	99.99994	90.9985	0.0900	100.00	109	33.92995	28.5082	0.7149	137.51
10	99.99965	89.9988	0.1000	100.00	110	32.96348	28.3293	0.7167	138.33
11	99.99892	88.9994	0.1100	100.00	111	32.02260	28.1470	0.7185	139.15
12	99.99747	88.0007	0.1200	100.00	112	31.10681	27.9610	0.7204	139.96
13	99.99501	87.0028	0.1300	100.00	113	30.21559	27.7709	0.7223	140.77
14	99.99120	86.0061	0.1399	100.01	114	29.34835	27.5768	0.7242	141.58
15	99.98571	85.0108	0.1499	100.01	115	28.50446	27.3784	0.7262	142.38
16	99.97817	84.0172	0.1598	100.02	116	27.68325	27.1757	0.7282	143.18
17	99.96820	83.0255	0.1697	100.03	117	26.88404	26.9688	0.7303	143.97
18	99.95545	82.0361	0.1796	100.04	118	26.10613	26.7575	0.7324	144.76
19	99.93952	81.0491	0.1895	100.05	119	25.34879	26.5420	0.7346	145.54
20	99.92003	80.0648	0.1994	100.06	120	24.61134	26.3223	0.7368	146.32
21	99.89660	79.0834	0.2092	100.08	121	23.89304	26.0986	0.7390	147.10
22	99.86885	78.1053	0.2189	100.11	122	23.19321	25.8710	0.7413	147.87
23	99.83641	77.1305	0.2287	100.13	123	22.51117	25.6397	0.7436	148.64
24	99.79891	76.1593	0.2384	100.16	124	21.84624	25.4048	0.7460	149.40
25	99.75597	75.1919	0.2481	100.19	125	21.19779	25.1667	0.7483	150.17
26	99.70725	74.2283	0.2577	100.23	126	20.56520	24.9254	0.7507	150.93
27	99.65238	73.2689	0.2673	100.27	127	19.94787	24.6813	0.7532	151.68
28	99.59104	72.3138	0.2769	100.31	128	19.34526	24.4346	0.7557	152.43
29	99.52289	71.3629	0.2864	100.36	129	18.75682	24.1855	0.7581	153.19
30	99.44761	70.4166	0.2958	100.42	130	18.18205	23.9342	0.7607	153.93
31	99.36486	69.4748	0.3053	100.47	131	17.62050	23.6810	0.7632	154.68
32	99.27435	68.5377	0.3146	100.54	132	17.07172	23.4262	0.7657	155.43
33	99.17576	67.6053	0.3239	100.61	133	16.53530	23.1700	0.7683	156.17
34	99.06876	66.6778	0.3332	100.68	134	16.01087	22.9125	0.7709	156.91
35	98.95305	65.7552	0.3424	100.76	135	15.49809	22.6541	0.7735	157.65
36	98.82826	64.8376	0.3516	100.84	136	14.99663	22.3948	0.7761	158.39
37	98.69405	63.9251	0.3607	100.93	137	14.50621	22.1351	0.7786	159.14
38	98.55001	63.0178	0.3698	101.02	138	14.02657	21.8749	0.7813	159.87
39	98.39571	62.1158	0.3788	101.12	139	13.55745	21.6145	0.7839	160.61
40	98.23067	61.2193	0.3878	101.22	140	13.09814	21.3549	0.7865	161.35
41	98.05433	60.3285	0.3967	101.33	141	12.64995	21.0938	0.7891	162.09
42	97.86608	59.4436	0.4056	101.44	142	12.21119	20.8338	0.7917	162.83
43	97.66522	58.5648	0.4144	101.56	143	11.78221	20.5741	0.7943	163.57
44	97.45097	57.6925	0.4231	101.69	144	11.36286	20.3149	0.7969	164.31
45	97.22245	56.8269	0.4317	101.83	145	10.95300	20.0564	0.7994	165.06
46	96.97867	55.9685	0.4403	101.97	146	10.55253	19.7986	0.8020	165.80
47	96.71856	55.1177	0.4488	102.12	147	10.16132	19.5416	0.8046	166.54
48	96.44093	54.2749	0.4573	102.27	148	9.77929	19.2854	0.8071	167.29
49	96.14450	53.4407	0.4656	102.44	149	9.40634	19.0303	0.8097	168.03
50	95.82788	52.6156	0.4738	102.62	150	9.04239	18.7761	0.8122	168.78
51	95.48963	51.8003	0.4820	102.80	151	8.68735	18.5230	0.8148	169.52
52	95.12819	50.9952	0.4900	103.00	152	8.34117	18.2710	0.8173	170.27
53	94.74196	50.2010	0.4980	103.20	153	8.00375	18.0202	0.8198	171.02
54	94.32930	49.4184	0.5058	103.42	154	7.67504	17.7706	0.8223	171.77
55	93.88854	48.6481	0.5135	103.65	155	7.35497	17.5221	0.8248	172.52
56	93.41800	47.8906	0.5211	103.89	156	7.04346	17.2750	0.8273	173.27
57	92.91602	47.1466	0.5285	104.15	157	6.74047	17.0290	0.8297	174.03
58	92.38099	46.4168	0.5358	104.42	158	6.44590	16.7844	0.8322	174.78
59	91.81137	45.7017	0.5430	104.70	159	6.15971	16.5410	0.8346	175.54
60	91.20570	45.0018	0.5500	105.00	160	5.88181	16.2989	0.8370	176.30
61	90.56264	44.3178	0.5568	105.32	161	5.61213	16.0580	0.8394	177.06
62	89.88101	43.6501	0.5635	105.65	162	5.35059	15.8185	0.8418	177.82
63	89.15978	42.9992	0.5700	106.00	163	5.09713	15.5803	0.8442	178.58
64	88.39810	42.3654	0.5763	106.37	164	4.85165	15.3433	0.8466	179.34
65	87.59534	41.7491	0.5825	106.75	165	4.61407	15.1076	0.8489	180.11
66	86.75108	41.1505	0.5885	107.15	166	4.38429	14.8731	0.8513	180.87
67	85.86515	40.5699	0.5943	107.57	167	4.16224	14.6399	0.8536	181.64
68	84.93760	40.0075	0.5999	108.01	168	3.94780	14.4080	0.8559	182.41
69	83.96877	39.4633	0.6054	108.46	169	3.74089	14.1773	0.8582	183.18
70	82.95922	38.9375	0.6106	108.94	170	3.54139	13.9477	0.8605	183.95
71	81.90980	38.4299	0.6157	109.43	171	3.34919	13.7195	0.8628	184.72
72	80.82158	37.9406	0.6206	109.94	172	3.16419	13.4924	0.8651	185.49
73	79.69591	37.4695	0.6253	110.47	173	2.98628	13.2664	0.8673	186.27
74	78.53435	37.0163	0.6298	111.02	174	2.81532	13.0416	0.8696	187.04
75	77.33872	36.5808	0.6342	111.58	175	2.65120	12.8180	0.8718	187.82
76	76.11102	36.1628	0.6384	112.16	176	2.49379	12.5955	0.8740	188.60
77	74.85345	35.7620	0.6424	112.76	177	2.34297	12.3741	0.8763	189.37
78	73.56839	35.3779	0.6462	113.38	178	2.19859	12.1539	0.8785	190.15
79	72.25836	35.0102	0.6499	114.01	179	2.06054	11.9347	0.8807	190.93
80	70.92603	34.6585	0.6534	114.66	180	1.92866	11.7166	0.8828	191.72
81	69.57415	34.3222	0.6568	115.32	181	1.80282	11.4995	0.8850	192.50
82	68.20555	34.0009	0.6600	116.00	182	1.68287	11.2835	0.8872	193.28
83	66.82314	33.6939	0.6631	116.69	183	1.56867	11.0686	0.8893	194.07
84	65.42982	33.4008	0.6660	117.40	184	1.46008	10.8546	0.8915	194.85
85	64.02853	33.1208	0.6688	118.12	185	1.35694	10.6416	0.8936	195.64
86	62.62216	32.8534	0.6715	118.85	186	1.25911	10.4296	0.8957	196.43
87	61.21358	32.5979	0.6740	119.60	187	1.16643	10.2186	0.8978	197.22
88	59.80558	32.3536	0.6765	120.35	188	1.07874	10.0086	0.8999	198.01
89	58.40088	32.1198	0.6788	121.12	189	0.99591	9.7994	0.9020	198.80
90	57.00209	31.8957	0.6810	121.90	190	0.91776	9.5913	0.9041	199.59
91	55.61170	31.6808	0.6832	122.68	191	0.84415	9.3841	0.9062	200.38
92	54.23208	31.4739	0.6853	123.47	192	0.77492	9.1778	0.9082	201.18
93	52.86543	31.2746	0.6873	124.27	193	0.70992	8.9723	0.9103	201.97
94	51.51383	31.0820	0.6892	125.08	194	0.64899	8.7677	0.9123	202.77
95	50.17916	30.8955	0.6910	125.90	195	0.59197	8.5641	0.9144	203.56
96	48.86315	30.7141	0.6929	126.71	196	0.53872	8.3612	0.9164	204.36
97	47.56735	30.5372	0.6946	127.54	197	0.48907	8.1592	0.9184	205.16
98	46.29316	30.3639	0.6964	128.36	198	0.44288	7.9580	0.9204	205.96
99	45.04176	30.1936	0.6981	129.19	199	0.39999	7.7578	0.9224	206.76

Table A continued

Iowa Type curve L3

Age %AL	Percent Surviving	Remaining Life	CAD Ratio	Prob. Life
200	0.36026	7.5582	0.9244	207.56
201	0.32353	7.3595	0.9264	208.36
202	0.28966	7.1615	0.9284	209.16
203	0.25850	6.9645	0.9304	209.96
204	0.22992	6.7681	0.9323	210.77
205	0.20377	6.5725	0.9343	211.57
206	0.17991	6.3778	0.9362	212.38
207	0.15822	6.1836	0.9382	213.18
208	0.13855	5.9905	0.9401	213.99
209	0.12079	5.7978	0.9420	214.80
210	0.10480	5.6061	0.9439	215.61
211	0.09047	5.4149	0.9459	216.41
212	0.07767	5.2249	0.9478	217.22
213	0.06630	5.0351	0.9496	218.04
214	0.05624	4.8464	0.9515	218.85
215	0.04739	4.6580	0.9534	219.66
216	0.03964	4.4710	0.9553	220.47
217	0.03291	4.2830	0.9572	221.28
218	0.02708	4.0975	0.9590	222.10
219	0.02208	3.9121	0.9609	222.91
220	0.01782	3.7278	0.9627	223.73
221	0.01422	3.5450	0.9646	224.54
222	0.01122	3.3592	0.9664	225.36
223	0.00872	3.1789	0.9682	226.18
224	0.00668	2.9970	0.9700	227.00
225	0.00503	2.8161	0.9718	227.82
226	0.00371	2.6401	0.9736	228.64
227	0.00268	2.4627	0.9754	229.46
228	0.00189	2.2830	0.9772	230.28
229	0.00129	2.1123	0.9789	231.11
230	0.00085	1.9470	0.9805	231.95
231	0.00054	1.7776	0.9822	232.78
232	0.00033	1.5907	0.9841	233.59
233	0.00018	1.4996	0.9850	234.50
234	0.00010	1.2994	0.9870	235.30
235	0.00005	1.0990	0.9890	236.10
236	0.00002	0.9977	0.9900	237.00
237	0.00001	0.4959	0.9950	237.50
238	0.00000	0.0000	1.0000	238.00

Iowa Type curve L4

Age %AL	Percent Surviving	Remaining Life	CAD Ratio	Prob. Life
0	100.00000	100.0000	0.0000	100.00
1	100.00000	99.0000	0.0100	100.00
2	100.00000	98.0000	0.0200	100.00
3	100.00000	97.0000	0.0300	100.00
4	100.00000	96.0000	0.0400	100.00
5	100.00000	95.0000	0.0500	100.00
6	100.00000	94.0000	0.0600	100.00
7	100.00000	93.0000	0.0700	100.00
8	100.00000	92.0000	0.0800	100.00
9	100.00000	91.0000	0.0900	100.00
10	100.00000	90.0000	0.1000	100.00
11	100.00000	89.0000	0.1100	100.00
12	100.00000	88.0000	0.1200	100.00
13	100.00000	87.0000	0.1300	100.00
14	100.00000	86.0000	0.1400	100.00
15	100.00000	85.0000	0.1500	100.00
16	100.00000	84.0000	0.1600	100.00
17	100.00000	83.0000	0.1700	100.00
18	100.00000	82.0000	0.1800	100.00
19	100.00000	81.0000	0.1900	100.00
20	100.00000	80.0000	0.2000	100.00
21	100.00000	79.0000	0.2100	100.00
22	100.00000	78.0000	0.2200	100.00
23	100.00000	77.0000	0.2300	100.00
24	99.99999	76.0000	0.2400	100.00
25	99.99995	75.0000	0.2500	100.00
26	99.99979	74.0002	0.2600	100.00
27	99.99940	73.0004	0.2700	100.00
28	99.99862	72.0010	0.2800	100.00
29	99.99721	71.0020	0.2900	100.00
30	99.99491	70.0036	0.3000	100.00
31	99.99136	69.0061	0.3099	100.01
32	99.98616	68.0097	0.3199	100.01
33	99.97887	67.0146	0.3299	100.01
34	99.96897	66.0212	0.3398	100.02
35	99.95590	65.0297	0.3497	100.03
36	99.93905	64.0406	0.3596	100.04
37	99.91775	63.0542	0.3695	100.05
38	99.89130	62.0707	0.3793	100.07
39	99.85898	61.0907	0.3891	100.09
40	99.81999	60.1143	0.3989	100.11
41	99.77353	59.1421	0.4086	100.14
42	99.71878	58.1743	0.4183	100.17
43	99.65489	57.2113	0.4279	100.21
44	99.58099	56.2533	0.4375	100.25
45	99.49620	55.3009	0.4470	100.30
46	99.39964	54.3541	0.4565	100.35
47	99.29042	53.4133	0.4659	100.41
48	99.16768	52.4788	0.4752	100.48
49	99.03052	51.5508	0.4845	100.55
50	98.87810	50.6295	0.4937	100.63
51	98.70957	49.7151	0.5028	100.72
52	98.52410	48.8077	0.5119	100.81
53	98.32089	47.9076	0.5209	100.91
54	98.09917	47.0147	0.5299	101.01
55	97.85817	46.1293	0.5387	101.13
56	97.59718	45.2513	0.5475	101.25
57	97.31548	44.3809	0.5562	101.38
58	97.01238	43.5180	0.5648	101.52
59	96.68719	42.6626	0.5734	101.66
60	96.33923	41.8149	0.5819	101.81
61	95.96778	40.9748	0.5903	101.97
62	95.57209	40.1424	0.5986	102.14
63	95.15133	39.3177	0.6068	102.32
64	94.70457	38.5008	0.6150	102.50
65	94.23074	37.6919	0.6231	102.69
66	93.72862	36.8912	0.6311	102.89
67	93.19675	36.0988	0.6390	103.10
68	92.63340	35.3153	0.6468	103.32
69	92.03658	34.5411	0.6546	103.54
70	91.40395	33.7767	0.6622	103.78
71	90.73280	33.0228	0.6698	104.02
72	90.02010	32.2803	0.6772	104.28
73	89.26241	31.5501	0.6845	104.55
74	88.45601	30.8332	0.6917	104.83
75	87.59685	30.1307	0.6987	105.13
76	86.68071	29.4438	0.7056	105.44
77	85.70325	28.7740	0.7123	105.77
78	84.66015	28.1223	0.7188	106.12
79	83.54726	27.4903	0.7251	106.49
80	82.36077	26.8791	0.7312	106.88
81	81.09741	26.2900	0.7371	107.29
82	79.75459	25.7242	0.7428	107.72
83	78.33065	25.1828	0.7482	108.18
84	76.82500	24.6665	0.7533	108.67
85	75.23825	24.1762	0.7582	109.18
86	73.57239	23.7123	0.7629	109.71
87	71.83081	23.2751	0.7672	110.28
88	70.01839	22.8646	0.7714	110.86
89	68.14144	22.4806	0.7752	111.48
90	66.20766	22.1226	0.7788	112.12
91	64.22597	21.7898	0.7821	112.79
92	62.20638	21.4810	0.7852	113.48
93	60.15975	21.1948	0.7881	114.19
94	58.09754	20.9294	0.7907	114.93
95	56.03106	20.6828	0.7932	115.68
96	53.96924	20.4539	0.7955	116.45
97	51.92044	20.2413	0.7976	117.24
98	49.89268	20.0436	0.7996	118.04
99	47.89334	19.8594	0.8014	118.86

Table A continued

Age %AL	Percent Surviving	Remaining Life	CAD Ratio	Prob. Life
100	45.92922	19.6873	0.8031	119.69
101	44.00648	19.5257	0.8047	120.53
102	42.13058	19.3728	0.8063	121.37
103	40.30620	19.2270	0.8077	122.23
104	38.53722	19.0867	0.8091	123.09
105	36.82670	18.9500	0.8105	123.95
106	35.17687	18.8153	0.8118	124.82
107	33.58913	18.6811	0.8132	125.68
108	32.06415	18.5458	0.8145	126.55
109	30.60191	18.4080	0.8159	127.41
110	29.20175	18.2667	0.8173	128.27
111	27.86244	18.1207	0.8188	129.12
112	26.58234	17.9693	0.8203	129.97
113	25.35938	17.8117	0.8219	130.81
114	24.19124	17.6477	0.8235	131.65
115	23.07537	17.4769	0.8252	132.48
116	22.00912	17.2993	0.8270	133.30
117	20.98977	17.1152	0.8288	134.12
118	20.01462	16.9247	0.8308	134.92
119	19.08103	16.7283	0.8327	135.73
120	18.18649	16.5265	0.8347	136.53
121	17.32859	16.3200	0.8368	137.32
122	16.50514	16.1093	0.8389	138.11
123	15.71409	15.8950	0.8410	138.90
124	14.95359	15.6780	0.8432	139.68
125	14.22200	15.4587	0.8454	140.46
126	13.51785	15.2379	0.8476	141.24
127	12.83984	15.0162	0.8498	142.02
128	12.18685	14.7940	0.8521	142.79
129	11.55789	14.5718	0.8543	143.57
130	10.95212	14.3502	0.8565	144.35
131	10.36880	14.1293	0.8587	145.13
132	9.80734	13.9096	0.8609	145.91
133	9.26707	13.6914	0.8631	146.69
134	8.74754	13.4748	0.8653	147.47
135	8.24831	13.2601	0.8674	148.26
136	7.76897	13.0474	0.8695	149.05
137	7.30912	12.8368	0.8716	149.84
138	6.86841	12.6284	0.8737	150.63
139	6.44648	12.4223	0.8758	151.42
140	6.04296	12.2184	0.8778	152.22
141	5.65750	12.0168	0.8798	153.02
142	5.28973	11.8175	0.8818	153.82
143	4.93928	11.6205	0.8838	154.62
144	4.60575	11.4258	0.8857	155.43
145	4.28876	11.2333	0.8877	156.23
146	3.98790	11.0431	0.8896	157.04
147	3.70273	10.8551	0.8914	157.86
148	3.43284	10.6692	0.8933	158.67
149	3.17776	10.4855	0.8951	159.49
150	2.93706	10.3038	0.8970	160.30
151	2.71026	10.1242	0.8988	161.12
152	2.49689	9.9466	0.9005	161.95
153	2.29648	9.7710	0.9023	162.77
154	2.10855	9.5973	0.9040	163.60
155	1.93260	9.4256	0.9057	164.43
156	1.76816	9.2557	0.9074	165.26
157	1.61474	9.0875	0.9091	166.09
158	1.47185	8.9212	0.9108	166.92
159	1.33901	8.7567	0.9124	167.76
160	1.21574	8.5939	0.9141	168.59
161	1.10158	8.4327	0.9157	169.43
162	0.99604	8.2732	0.9173	170.27
163	0.89868	8.1153	0.9188	171.12
164	0.80905	7.9590	0.9204	171.96
165	0.72670	7.8043	0.9220	172.80
166	0.65120	7.6511	0.9235	173.65
167	0.58215	7.4993	0.9250	174.50
168	0.51912	7.3492	0.9265	175.35
169	0.46174	7.2003	0.9280	176.20
170	0.40962	7.0529	0.9295	177.05
171	0.36239	6.9069	0.9309	177.91
172	0.31971	6.7622	0.9324	178.76
173	0.28123	6.6190	0.9338	179.62
174	0.24665	6.4769	0.9352	180.48
175	0.21565	6.3361	0.9366	181.34
176	0.18794	6.1966	0.9380	182.20
177	0.16324	6.0585	0.9394	183.06
178	0.14130	5.9216	0.9408	183.92
179	0.12188	5.7854	0.9421	184.79
180	0.10473	5.6510	0.9435	185.65
181	0.08965	5.5174	0.9448	186.52
182	0.07643	5.3853	0.9461	187.39
183	0.06489	5.2540	0.9475	188.25
184	0.05486	5.1232	0.9488	189.12
185	0.04616	4.9946	0.9501	189.99
186	0.03866	4.8665	0.9513	190.87
187	0.03222	4.7393	0.9526	191.74
188	0.02671	4.6138	0.9539	192.61
189	0.02203	4.4877	0.9551	193.49
190	0.01806	4.3643	0.9564	194.36
191	0.01472	4.2412	0.9576	195.24
192	0.01192	4.1200	0.9588	196.12
193	0.00959	3.9995	0.9600	197.00
194	0.00767	3.8755	0.9612	197.88
195	0.00608	3.7582	0.9624	198.76
196	0.00479	3.6357	0.9636	199.64
197	0.00374	3.5160	0.9648	200.52
198	0.00289	3.4031	0.9660	201.40
199	0.00222	3.2792	0.9672	202.28

Iowa Type curve L4

Age %AL	Percent Surviving	Remaining Life	CAD Ratio	Prob. Life
200	0.00168	3.1725	0.9683	203.17
201	0.00126	3.0634	0.9694	204.06
202	0.00094	2.9360	0.9706	204.94
203	0.00069	2.8187	0.9718	205.82
204	0.00050	2.6998	0.9730	206.70
205	0.00036	2.5553	0.9744	207.56
206	0.00025	2.4596	0.9754	208.46
207	0.00017	2.3818	0.9762	209.38
208	0.00012	2.1659	0.9783	210.17
209	0.00008	1.9990	0.9800	211.00
210	0.00005	1.8985	0.9810	211.90
211	0.00003	1.8312	0.9817	212.83
212	0.00002	1.4971	0.9850	213.50
213	0.00001	1.4948	0.9851	214.49
214	0.00001	0.4959	0.9950	214.50
215	0.00000	0.0000	1.0000	215.00

Table A continued

Iowa Type curve L5

Age %AL	Percent Surviving	Remaining Life	CAD Ratio	Prob. Life
0	100.00000	100.0000	0.0000	100.00
1	100.00000	99.0000	0.0100	100.00
2	100.00000	98.0000	0.0200	100.00
3	100.00000	97.0000	0.0300	100.00
4	100.00000	96.0000	0.0400	100.00
5	100.00000	95.0000	0.0500	100.00
6	100.00000	94.0000	0.0600	100.00
7	100.00000	93.0000	0.0700	100.00
8	100.00000	92.0000	0.0800	100.00
9	100.00000	91.0000	0.0900	100.00
10	100.00000	90.0000	0.1000	100.00
11	100.00000	89.0000	0.1100	100.00
12	100.00000	88.0000	0.1200	100.00
13	100.00000	87.0000	0.1300	100.00
14	100.00000	86.0000	0.1400	100.00
15	100.00000	85.0000	0.1500	100.00
16	100.00000	84.0000	0.1600	100.00
17	100.00000	83.0000	0.1700	100.00
18	100.00000	82.0000	0.1800	100.00
19	100.00000	81.0000	0.1900	100.00
20	100.00000	80.0000	0.2000	100.00
21	100.00000	79.0000	0.2100	100.00
22	100.00000	78.0000	0.2200	100.00
23	100.00000	77.0000	0.2300	100.00
24	100.00000	76.0000	0.2400	100.00
25	100.00000	75.0000	0.2500	100.00
26	100.00000	74.0000	0.2600	100.00
27	100.00000	73.0000	0.2700	100.00
28	100.00000	72.0000	0.2800	100.00
29	100.00000	71.0000	0.2900	100.00
30	100.00000	70.0000	0.3000	100.00
31	100.00000	69.0000	0.3100	100.00
32	100.00000	68.0000	0.3200	100.00
33	100.00000	67.0000	0.3300	100.00
34	100.00000	66.0000	0.3400	100.00
35	100.00000	65.0000	0.3500	100.00
36	100.00000	64.0000	0.3600	100.00
37	100.00000	63.0000	0.3700	100.00
38	100.00000	62.0000	0.3800	100.00
39	100.00000	61.0000	0.3900	100.00
40	100.00000	60.0000	0.4000	100.00
41	100.00000	59.0000	0.4100	100.00
42	100.00000	58.0000	0.4200	100.00
43	100.00000	57.0000	0.4300	100.00
44	99.99999	56.0000	0.4400	100.00
45	99.99994	55.0000	0.4500	100.00
46	99.99975	54.0001	0.4600	100.00
47	99.99925	53.0004	0.4700	100.00
48	99.99814	52.0010	0.4800	100.00
49	99.99600	51.0021	0.4900	100.00
50	99.99221	50.0040	0.5000	100.00
51	99.98600	49.0071	0.5099	100.01
52	99.97639	48.0117	0.5199	100.01
53	99.96220	47.0185	0.5298	100.02
54	99.94206	46.0279	0.5397	100.03
55	99.91441	45.0405	0.5496	100.04
56	99.87749	44.0569	0.5594	100.06
57	99.82938	43.0779	0.5692	100.08
58	99.76802	42.1041	0.5790	100.10
59	99.69121	41.1362	0.5886	100.14
60	99.59667	40.1747	0.5983	100.17
61	99.48202	39.2205	0.6078	100.22
62	99.34487	38.2739	0.6173	100.27
63	99.18277	37.3356	0.6266	100.34
64	98.99333	36.4061	0.6359	100.41
65	98.77418	35.4858	0.6451	100.49
66	98.52303	34.5750	0.6543	100.57
67	98.23767	33.6740	0.6633	100.67
68	97.91601	32.7829	0.6722	100.78
69	97.55607	31.9021	0.6810	100.90
70	97.15593	31.0314	0.6897	101.03
71	96.71371	30.1710	0.6983	101.17
72	96.22749	29.3209	0.7068	101.32
73	95.69515	28.4812	0.7152	101.48
74	95.11423	27.6521	0.7235	101.65
75	94.48180	26.8339	0.7317	101.83
76	93.79419	26.0269	0.7397	102.03
77	93.04688	25.2320	0.7477	102.23
78	92.23432	24.4498	0.7555	102.45
79	91.34990	23.6817	0.7632	102.68
80	90.38589	22.9290	0.7707	102.93
81	89.33357	22.1932	0.7781	103.19
82	88.18348	21.4761	0.7852	103.48
83	86.92572	20.7796	0.7922	103.78
84	85.55036	20.1056	0.7989	104.11
85	84.04805	19.4561	0.8054	104.46
86	82.41051	18.8327	0.8117	104.83
87	80.63117	18.2373	0.8176	105.24
88	78.70573	17.6712	0.8233	105.67
89	76.63271	17.1357	0.8286	106.14
90	74.41381	16.6318	0.8337	106.63
91	72.05424	16.1600	0.8384	107.16
92	69.56276	15.7209	0.8428	107.72
93	66.95171	15.3145	0.8469	108.31
94	64.23671	14.9407	0.8506	108.94
95	61.43633	14.5989	0.8540	109.60
96	58.57147	14.2885	0.8571	110.29
97	55.66476	14.0085	0.8599	111.01
98	52.73982	13.7577	0.8624	111.76
99	49.82051	13.5346	0.8647	112.53

Iowa Type curve L5

Age %AL	Percent Surviving	Remaining Life	CAD Ratio	Prob. Life
100	46.93011	13.3373	0.8666	113.34
101	44.09070	13.1641	0.8684	114.16
102	41.32246	13.0124	0.8699	115.01
103	38.64318	12.8800	0.8712	115.88
104	36.06787	12.7639	0.8724	116.76
105	33.60849	12.6614	0.8734	117.66
106	31.27390	12.5692	0.8743	118.57
107	29.06982	12.4843	0.8752	119.48
108	26.99903	12.4035	0.8760	120.40
109	25.06161	12.3237	0.8768	121.32
110	23.25529	12.2421	0.8776	122.24
111	21.57580	12.1561	0.8784	123.16
112	20.01734	12.0636	0.8794	124.06
113	18.57295	11.9629	0.8804	124.96
114	17.23495	11.8528	0.8815	125.85
115	15.99530	11.7326	0.8827	126.73
116	14.84589	11.6023	0.8840	127.60
117	13.77886	11.4620	0.8854	128.46
118	12.78675	11.3126	0.8869	129.31
119	11.86267	11.1549	0.8885	130.15
120	11.00040	10.9900	0.8901	130.99
121	10.19442	10.8194	0.8918	131.82
122	9.43990	10.6442	0.8936	132.64
123	8.73269	10.4657	0.8953	133.47
124	8.06922	10.2851	0.8971	134.29
125	7.44648	10.1035	0.8990	135.10
126	6.86191	9.9216	0.9008	135.92
127	6.31332	9.7403	0.9026	136.74
128	5.79883	9.5601	0.9044	137.56
129	5.31678	9.3815	0.9062	138.38
130	4.86569	9.2049	0.9080	139.20
131	4.44419	9.0305	0.9097	140.03
132	4.05101	8.8585	0.9114	140.86
133	3.68493	8.6889	0.9131	141.69
134	3.34475	8.5217	0.9148	142.52
135	3.02930	8.3570	0.9164	143.36
136	2.73741	8.1948	0.9181	144.19
137	2.46795	8.0350	0.9197	145.03
138	2.21975	7.8775	0.9212	145.88
139	1.99168	7.7223	0.9228	146.72
140	1.78262	7.5693	0.9243	147.57
141	1.59146	7.4184	0.9258	148.42
142	1.41710	7.2697	0.9273	149.27
143	1.25848	7.1229	0.9288	150.12
144	1.11456	6.9781	0.9302	150.98
145	0.98432	6.8353	0.9316	151.84
146	0.86680	6.6942	0.9331	152.69
147	0.76105	6.5549	0.9345	153.55
148	0.66616	6.4174	0.9358	154.42
149	0.58128	6.2815	0.9372	155.28
150	0.50557	6.1473	0.9385	156.15
151	0.43826	6.0146	0.9399	157.01
152	0.37861	5.8835	0.9412	157.88
153	0.32592	5.7538	0.9425	158.75
154	0.27953	5.6257	0.9437	159.63
155	0.23884	5.4989	0.9450	160.50
156	0.20328	5.3734	0.9463	161.37
157	0.17231	5.2493	0.9475	162.25
158	0.14545	5.1263	0.9487	163.13
159	0.12224	5.0047	0.9500	164.00
160	0.10227	4.8844	0.9512	164.88
161	0.08516	4.7653	0.9523	165.77
162	0.07057	4.6471	0.9535	166.65
163	0.05818	4.5302	0.9547	167.53
164	0.04771	4.4147	0.9559	168.41
165	0.03891	4.3000	0.9570	169.30
166	0.03155	4.1865	0.9581	170.19
167	0.02543	4.0737	0.9593	171.07
168	0.02037	3.9615	0.9604	171.96
169	0.01621	3.8498	0.9615	172.85
170	0.01280	3.7422	0.9626	173.74
171	0.01004	3.6334	0.9637	174.63
172	0.00782	3.5230	0.9648	175.52
173	0.00604	3.4139	0.9659	176.41
174	0.00462	3.3095	0.9669	177.31
175	0.00350	3.2085	0.9679	178.21
176	0.00263	3.1045	0.9690	179.10
177	0.00196	2.9948	0.9701	179.99
178	0.00144	2.8958	0.9710	180.90
179	0.00105	2.7856	0.9721	181.79
180	0.00075	2.6999	0.9730	182.70
181	0.00053	2.6130	0.9739	183.61
182	0.00037	2.5268	0.9747	184.53
183	0.00026	2.3843	0.9762	185.38
184	0.00017	2.3819	0.9762	186.38
185	0.00012	2.1660	0.9783	187.17
186	0.00008	1.9991	0.9800	188.00
187	0.00005	1.8987	0.9810	188.90
188	0.00003	1.8316	0.9817	189.83
189	0.00002	1.4977	0.9850	190.50
190	0.00001	1.4959	0.9850	191.50
191	0.00001	0.4971	0.9950	191.50
192	0.00000	0.0000	1.0000	192.00

Table B

		Iowa Type curve SO					Iowa Type curve SO		
Age %AL	Percent Surviving	Remaining Life	CAD Ratio	Prob. Life	Age %AL	Percent Surviving	Remaining Life	CAD Ratio	Prob. Life
0	100.00000	100.0000	0.0000	100.00	100	50.00000	39.7589	0.6024	139.76
1	99.97910	99.0208	0.0098	100.02	101	49.30481	39.3125	0.6069	140.31
2	99.92921	98.0700	0.0193	100.07	102	48.60973	38.8674	0.6113	140.87
3	99.85617	97.1414	0.0286	100.14	103	47.91486	38.4238	0.6158	141.42
4	99.76252	96.2321	0.0377	100.23	104	47.22030	37.9817	0.6202	141.98
5	99.64988	95.3403	0.0466	100.34	105	46.52615	37.5409	0.6246	142.54
6	99.51946	94.4646	0.0554	100.46	106	45.83253	37.1014	0.6290	143.10
7	99.37223	93.6038	0.0640	100.60	107	45.13953	36.6634	0.6334	143.66
8	99.20898	92.7570	0.0724	100.76	108	44.44726	36.2266	0.6377	144.23
9	99.03038	91.9234	0.0808	100.92	109	43.75582	35.7912	0.6421	144.79
10	98.83704	91.1022	0.0890	101.10	110	43.06532	35.3570	0.6464	145.36
11	98.62946	90.2929	0.0971	101.29	111	42.37587	34.9241	0.6508	145.92
12	98.40814	89.4948	0.1051	101.49	112	41.68756	34.4925	0.6551	146.49
13	98.17349	88.7076	0.1129	101.71	113	41.00051	34.0621	0.6594	147.06
14	97.92592	87.9306	0.1207	101.93	114	40.31482	33.6330	0.6637	147.63
15	97.66579	87.1634	0.1284	102.16	115	39.63059	33.2050	0.6679	148.21
16	97.39345	86.4058	0.1359	102.41	116	38.94793	32.7783	0.6722	148.78
17	97.10922	85.6572	0.1434	102.66	117	38.26695	32.3527	0.6765	149.35
18	96.81340	84.9174	0.1508	102.92	118	37.58775	31.9282	0.6807	149.93
19	96.50628	84.1861	0.1581	103.19	119	36.91044	31.5050	0.6850	150.50
20	96.18813	83.4629	0.1654	103.46	120	36.23513	31.0828	0.6892	151.08
21	95.85922	82.7475	0.1725	103.75	121	35.56191	30.6618	0.6934	151.66
22	95.51979	82.0398	0.1796	104.04	122	34.89091	30.2418	0.6976	152.24
23	95.17008	81.3394	0.1866	104.34	123	34.22223	29.8229	0.7018	152.82
24	94.81032	80.6462	0.1935	104.65	124	33.55598	29.4051	0.7059	153.41
25	94.44074	79.9598	0.2004	104.96	125	32.89226	28.9884	0.7101	153.99
26	94.06155	79.2801	0.2072	105.28	126	32.23118	28.5727	0.7143	154.57
27	93.67296	78.6069	0.2139	105.60	127	31.57286	28.1581	0.7184	155.16
28	93.27517	77.9400	0.2206	105.94	128	30.91740	27.7444	0.7226	155.74
29	92.86837	77.2792	0.2272	106.28	129	30.26492	27.3318	0.7267	156.33
30	92.45276	76.6244	0.2338	106.62	130	29.61553	26.9201	0.7308	156.92
31	92.02851	75.9753	0.2402	106.98	131	28.96933	26.5095	0.7349	157.51
32	91.59582	75.3319	0.2467	107.33	132	28.32644	26.0998	0.7390	158.10
33	91.15485	74.6939	0.2531	107.69	133	27.68697	25.6910	0.7431	158.69
34	90.70578	74.0612	0.2594	108.06	134	27.05104	25.2832	0.7472	159.28
35	90.24878	73.4337	0.2657	108.43	135	26.41876	24.8764	0.7512	159.88
36	89.78402	72.8112	0.2719	108.81	136	25.79024	24.4704	0.7553	160.47
37	89.31165	72.1937	0.2781	109.19	137	25.16561	24.0654	0.7593	161.07
38	88.83183	71.5809	0.2842	109.58	138	24.54497	23.6613	0.7634	161.66
39	88.34472	70.9729	0.2903	109.97	139	23.92844	23.2580	0.7674	162.26
40	87.85047	70.3693	0.2963	110.37	140	23.31615	22.8557	0.7714	162.86
41	87.34924	69.7703	0.3023	110.77	141	22.70820	22.4542	0.7755	163.45
42	86.84117	69.1755	0.3082	111.18	142	22.10472	22.0536	0.7795	164.05
43	86.32640	68.5851	0.3141	111.59	143	21.50584	21.6538	0.7835	164.65
44	85.80509	67.9987	0.3200	112.00	144	20.91166	21.2548	0.7875	165.25
45	85.27737	67.4164	0.3258	112.42	145	20.32232	20.8567	0.7914	165.86
46	84.74338	66.8381	0.3316	112.84	146	19.73794	20.4594	0.7954	166.46
47	84.20327	66.2636	0.3374	113.26	147	19.15864	20.0629	0.7994	167.06
48	83.65716	65.6929	0.3431	113.69	148	18.58455	19.6672	0.8033	167.67
49	83.10519	65.1259	0.3487	114.13	149	18.01580	19.2723	0.8073	168.27
50	82.54749	64.5625	0.3544	114.56	150	17.45251	18.8782	0.8112	168.88
51	81.98420	64.0027	0.3600	115.00	151	16.89481	18.4849	0.8152	169.48
52	81.41545	63.4463	0.3655	115.45	152	16.34285	18.0923	0.8191	170.09
53	80.84136	62.8933	0.3711	115.89	153	15.79674	17.7005	0.8230	170.70
54	80.26206	62.3436	0.3766	116.34	154	15.25662	17.3094	0.8269	171.31
55	79.67768	61.7972	0.3820	116.80	155	14.72263	16.9191	0.8308	171.92
56	79.08834	61.2540	0.3875	117.25	156	14.19491	16.5295	0.8347	172.53
57	78.49416	60.7138	0.3929	117.71	157	13.67360	16.1406	0.8386	173.14
58	77.89528	60.1768	0.3982	118.18	158	13.15883	15.7525	0.8425	173.75
59	77.29180	59.6427	0.4036	118.64	159	12.65076	15.3651	0.8463	174.37
60	76.68386	59.1116	0.4089	119.11	160	12.14953	14.9783	0.8502	174.98
61	76.07156	58.5834	0.4142	119.58	161	11.65528	14.5923	0.8541	175.59
62	75.45503	58.0580	0.4194	120.06	162	11.16817	14.2069	0.8579	176.21
63	74.83439	57.5353	0.4246	120.54	163	10.68836	13.8223	0.8618	176.82
64	74.20976	57.0154	0.4298	121.02	164	10.21598	13.4383	0.8656	177.44
65	73.58124	56.4981	0.4350	121.50	165	9.75122	13.0549	0.8695	178.05
66	72.94896	55.9835	0.4402	121.98	166	9.29422	12.6723	0.8733	178.67
67	72.31303	55.4714	0.4453	122.47	167	8.84515	12.2902	0.8771	179.29
68	71.67356	54.9619	0.4504	122.96	168	8.40418	11.9089	0.8809	179.91
69	71.03067	54.4548	0.4555	123.45	169	7.97149	11.5282	0.8847	180.53
70	70.38447	53.9502	0.4605	123.95	170	7.54724	11.1481	0.8885	181.15
71	69.73508	53.4479	0.4655	124.45	171	7.13163	10.7686	0.8923	181.77
72	69.08260	52.9480	0.4705	124.95	172	6.72483	10.3898	0.8961	182.39
73	68.42714	52.4504	0.4755	125.45	173	6.32704	10.0116	0.8999	183.01
74	67.76882	51.9551	0.4804	125.96	174	5.93845	9.6340	0.9037	183.63
75	67.10774	51.4619	0.4854	126.46	175	5.55926	9.2570	0.9074	184.26
76	66.44402	50.9710	0.4903	126.97	176	5.18968	8.8806	0.9112	184.88
77	65.77777	50.4822	0.4952	127.48	177	4.82992	8.5048	0.9150	185.50
78	65.10909	49.9955	0.5000	128.00	178	4.48022	8.1297	0.9187	186.13
79	64.43809	49.5109	0.5049	128.51	179	4.14079	7.7551	0.9224	186.76
80	63.76487	49.0284	0.5097	129.03	180	3.81187	7.3811	0.9262	187.38
81	63.08956	48.5478	0.5145	129.55	181	3.49372	7.0077	0.9299	188.01
82	62.41225	48.0693	0.5193	130.07	182	3.18660	6.6349	0.9337	188.63
83	61.73305	47.5926	0.5241	130.59	183	2.89078	6.2627	0.9374	189.26
84	61.05207	47.1179	0.5288	131.12	184	2.60655	5.8911	0.9411	189.89
85	60.36941	46.6451	0.5335	131.65	185	2.33421	5.5201	0.9448	190.52
86	59.68518	46.1741	0.5383	132.17	186	2.07408	5.1497	0.9485	191.15
87	58.99949	45.7049	0.5430	132.70	187	1.82651	4.7800	0.9522	191.78
88	58.31244	45.2375	0.5476	133.24	188	1.59186	4.4109	0.9559	192.41
89	57.62413	44.7719	0.5523	133.77	189	1.37054	4.0424	0.9596	193.04
90	56.93468	44.3080	0.5569	134.31	190	1.16296	3.6747	0.9633	193.67
91	56.24418	43.8458	0.5615	134.85	191	0.96962	3.3077	0.9669	194.31
92	55.55274	43.3853	0.5661	135.39	192	0.79102	2.9417	0.9706	194.94
93	54.86047	42.9265	0.5707	135.93	193	0.62777	2.5767	0.9742	195.58
94	54.16747	42.4693	0.5753	136.47	194	0.48054	2.2129	0.9779	196.21
95	53.47385	42.0137	0.5799	137.01	195	0.35012	1.8510	0.9815	196.85
96	52.77971	41.5596	0.5844	137.56	196	0.23748	1.4917	0.9851	197.49
97	52.08514	41.1072	0.5889	138.11	197	0.14383	1.1375	0.9886	198.14
98	51.39027	40.6562	0.5934	138.66	198	0.07079	0.7952	0.9920	198.80
99	50.69519	40.2068	0.5979	139.21	199	0.02090	0.5000	0.9950	199.50

Table B continued

	Iowa Type curve S0			
Age %AL	Percent Surviving	Remaining Life	CAD Ratio	Prob. Life
200	0.00000	0.0000	1.0000	200.00

	Iowa Type curve S1			
Age %AL	Percent Surviving	Remaining Life	CAD Ratio	Prob. Life
0	100.00000	100.0000	0.0000	100.00
1	99.99975	99.0002	0.0100	100.00
2	99.99824	98.0017	0.0200	100.00
3	99.99449	97.0054	0.0299	100.01
4	99.98766	96.0120	0.0399	100.01
5	99.97697	95.0222	0.0498	100.02
6	99.96169	94.0366	0.0596	100.04
7	99.94116	93.0559	0.0694	100.06
8	99.91476	92.0803	0.0792	100.08
9	99.88188	91.1105	0.0889	100.11
10	99.84198	90.1467	0.0985	100.15
11	99.79453	89.1893	0.1081	100.19
12	99.73904	88.2386	0.1176	100.24
13	99.67505	87.2950	0.1271	100.29
14	99.60210	86.3585	0.1364	100.36
15	99.51978	85.4296	0.1457	100.43
16	99.42771	84.5082	0.1549	100.51
17	99.32552	83.5946	0.1641	100.59
18	99.21285	82.6890	0.1731	100.69
19	99.08937	81.7914	0.1821	100.79
20	98.95479	80.9020	0.1910	100.90
21	98.80882	80.0208	0.1998	101.02
22	98.65118	79.1478	0.2085	101.15
23	98.48164	78.2832	0.2172	101.28
24	98.29995	77.4270	0.2257	101.43
25	98.10590	76.5791	0.2342	101.58
26	97.89930	75.7397	0.2426	101.74
27	97.67997	74.9086	0.2509	101.91
28	97.44773	74.0860	0.2591	102.09
29	97.20244	73.2717	0.2673	102.27
30	96.94397	72.4657	0.2753	102.47
31	96.67219	71.6680	0.2833	102.67
32	96.38701	70.8786	0.2912	102.88
33	96.08832	70.0973	0.2990	103.10
34	95.77605	69.3243	0.3068	103.32
35	95.45014	68.5593	0.3144	103.56
36	95.11053	67.8023	0.3220	103.80
37	94.75719	67.0532	0.3295	104.05
38	94.39009	66.3121	0.3369	104.31
39	94.00922	65.5787	0.3442	104.58
40	93.61458	64.8531	0.3515	104.85
41	93.20617	64.1350	0.3586	105.14
42	92.78401	63.4246	0.3658	105.42
43	92.34815	62.7216	0.3728	105.72
44	91.89862	62.0259	0.3797	106.03
45	91.43547	61.3376	0.3866	106.34
46	90.95878	60.6564	0.3934	106.66
47	90.46861	59.9823	0.4002	106.98
48	89.96505	59.3153	0.4068	107.32
49	89.44819	58.6551	0.4134	107.66
50	88.91814	58.0018	0.4200	108.00
51	88.37500	57.3552	0.4264	108.36
52	87.81891	56.7152	0.4328	108.72
53	87.24999	56.0818	0.4392	109.08
54	86.66838	55.4548	0.4455	109.45
55	86.07422	54.8341	0.4517	109.83
56	85.46768	54.2197	0.4578	110.22
57	84.84891	53.6115	0.4639	110.61
58	84.21809	53.0093	0.4699	111.01
59	83.57540	52.4131	0.4759	111.41
60	82.92102	51.8228	0.4818	111.82
61	82.25514	51.2382	0.4876	112.24
62	81.57797	50.6594	0.4934	112.66
63	80.88971	50.0862	0.4991	113.09
64	80.19057	49.5185	0.5048	113.52
65	79.48078	48.9563	0.5104	113.96
66	78.76056	48.3994	0.5160	114.40
67	78.03015	47.8477	0.5215	114.85
68	77.28977	47.3013	0.5270	115.30
69	76.53969	46.7599	0.5324	115.76
70	75.78013	46.2236	0.5378	116.22
71	75.01136	45.6922	0.5431	116.69
72	74.23364	45.1657	0.5483	117.17
73	73.44723	44.6439	0.5536	117.64
74	72.65240	44.1269	0.5587	118.13
75	71.84942	43.6144	0.5639	118.61
76	71.03858	43.1065	0.5689	119.11
77	70.22014	42.6031	0.5740	119.60
78	69.39441	42.1041	0.5790	120.10
79	68.56167	41.6094	0.5839	120.61
80	67.72221	41.1190	0.5888	121.12
81	66.87633	40.6328	0.5937	121.63
82	66.02433	40.1507	0.5985	122.15
83	65.16651	39.6726	0.6033	122.67
84	64.30319	39.1985	0.6080	123.20
85	63.43467	38.7284	0.6127	123.73
86	62.56125	38.2621	0.6174	124.26
87	61.68327	37.7996	0.6220	124.80
88	60.80103	37.3408	0.6266	125.34
89	59.91485	36.8857	0.6311	125.89
90	59.02506	36.4342	0.6357	126.43
91	58.13198	35.9863	0.6401	126.99
92	57.23592	35.5418	0.6446	127.54
93	56.33723	35.1008	0.6490	128.10
94	55.43622	34.6632	0.6534	128.66
95	54.53322	34.2289	0.6577	129.23
96	53.62857	33.7979	0.6620	129.80
97	52.72259	33.3700	0.6663	130.37
98	51.81561	32.9454	0.6705	130.95
99	50.90797	32.5239	0.6748	131.52

Table B continued

Age %AL	Iowa Type curve S1 Percent Surviving	Remaining Life	CAD Ratio	Prob. Life		Age %AL	Iowa Type curve S1 Percent Surviving	Remaining Life	CAD Ratio	Prob. Life
100	50.00000	32.1054	0.6789	132.11		200	0.00000	0.0000	1.0000	200.00
101	49.09203	31.6900	0.6831	132.69						
102	48.18439	31.2775	0.6872	133.28						
103	47.27741	30.8679	0.6913	133.87						
104	46.37144	30.4612	0.6954	134.46						
105	45.46678	30.0574	0.6994	135.06						
106	44.56378	29.6563	0.7034	135.66						
107	43.66277	29.2580	0.7074	136.26						
108	42.76408	28.8623	0.7114	136.86						
109	41.86803	28.4693	0.7153	137.47						
110	40.97494	28.0789	0.7192	138.08						
111	40.08515	27.6911	0.7231	138.69						
112	39.19897	27.3058	0.7269	139.31						
113	38.31673	26.9230	0.7308	139.92						
114	37.43875	26.5427	0.7346	140.54						
115	36.56534	26.1647	0.7384	141.16						
116	35.69681	25.7892	0.7421	141.79						
117	34.83349	25.4160	0.7458	142.42						
118	33.97567	25.0450	0.7495	143.05						
119	33.12367	24.6764	0.7532	143.68						
120	32.27779	24.3099	0.7569	144.31						
121	31.43833	23.9457	0.7605	144.95						
122	30.60559	23.5836	0.7642	145.58						
123	29.77986	23.2237	0.7678	146.22						
124	28.96142	22.8659	0.7713	146.87						
125	28.15058	22.5101	0.7749	147.51						
126	27.34760	22.1563	0.7784	148.16						
127	26.55277	21.8046	0.7820	148.80						
128	25.76636	21.4548	0.7855	149.45						
129	24.98864	21.1070	0.7889	150.11						
130	24.21987	20.7611	0.7924	150.76						
131	23.46032	20.4171	0.7958	151.42						
132	22.71023	20.0749	0.7993	152.07						
133	21.96985	19.7346	0.8027	152.73						
134	21.23944	19.3961	0.8060	153.40						
135	20.51922	19.0593	0.8094	154.06						
136	19.80943	18.7243	0.8128	154.72						
137	19.11030	18.3910	0.8161	155.39						
138	18.42203	18.0594	0.8194	156.06						
139	17.74486	17.7295	0.8227	156.73						
140	17.07899	17.4013	0.8260	157.40						
141	16.42460	17.0747	0.8293	158.07						
142	15.78191	16.7496	0.8325	158.75						
143	15.15109	16.4262	0.8357	159.43						
144	14.53232	16.1043	0.8390	160.10						
145	13.92578	15.7840	0.8422	160.78						
146	13.33163	15.4651	0.8453	161.47						
147	12.75001	15.1478	0.8485	162.15						
148	12.18109	14.8319	0.8517	162.83						
149	11.62500	14.5175	0.8548	163.52						
150	11.08187	14.2045	0.8580	164.20						
151	10.55181	13.8929	0.8611	164.89						
152	10.03495	13.5827	0.8642	165.58						
153	9.53139	13.2739	0.8673	166.27						
154	9.04122	12.9665	0.8703	166.97						
155	8.56453	12.6603	0.8734	167.66						
156	8.10138	12.3555	0.8764	168.36						
157	7.65185	12.0520	0.8795	169.05						
158	7.21599	11.7498	0.8825	169.75						
159	6.79383	11.4488	0.8855	170.45						
160	6.38542	11.1491	0.8885	171.15						
161	5.99078	10.8506	0.8915	171.85						
162	5.60991	10.5533	0.8945	172.55						
163	5.24281	10.2573	0.8974	173.26						
164	4.88947	9.9624	0.9004	173.96						
165	4.54986	9.6687	0.9033	174.67						
166	4.22395	9.3761	0.9062	175.38						
167	3.91168	9.0847	0.9092	176.08						
168	3.61300	8.7944	0.9121	176.79						
169	3.32781	8.5052	0.9149	177.51						
170	3.05603	8.2171	0.9178	178.22						
171	2.79756	7.9301	0.9207	178.93						
172	2.55227	7.6442	0.9236	179.64						
173	2.32003	7.3594	0.9264	180.36						
174	2.10070	7.0755	0.9292	181.08						
175	1.89410	6.7928	0.9321	181.79						
176	1.70005	6.5110	0.9349	182.51						
177	1.51836	6.2303	0.9377	183.23						
178	1.34882	5.9506	0.9405	183.95						
179	1.19118	5.6719	0.9433	184.67						
180	1.04521	5.3942	0.9461	185.39						
181	0.91063	5.1175	0.9488	186.12						
182	0.78716	4.8418	0.9516	186.84						
183	0.67448	4.5671	0.9543	187.57						
184	0.57229	4.2934	0.9571	188.29						
185	0.48022	4.0207	0.9598	189.02						
186	0.39790	3.7491	0.9625	189.75						
187	0.32495	3.4785	0.9652	190.48						
188	0.26096	3.2088	0.9679	191.21						
189	0.20547	2.9404	0.9706	191.94						
190	0.15802	2.6731	0.9733	192.67						
191	0.11812	2.4072	0.9759	193.41						
192	0.08524	2.1429	0.9786	194.14						
193	0.05884	1.8800	0.9812	194.88						
194	0.03831	1.6195	0.9838	195.62						
195	0.02303	1.3624	0.9864	196.36						
196	0.01234	1.1094	0.9889	197.11						
197	0.00551	0.8648	0.9914	197.86						
198	0.00176	0.6420	0.9936	198.64						
199	0.00025	0.5000	0.9950	199.50						

Table B continued

Age %AL	Percent Surviving	Remaining Life	CAD Ratio	Prob. Life	Age %AL	Percent Surviving	Remaining Life	CAD Ratio	Prob. Life
0	100.00000	100.0000	0.0000	100.00	100	50.00000	25.3441	0.7466	125.34
1	100.00000	99.0000	0.0100	100.00	101	48.80904	24.9503	0.7505	125.95
2	100.00000	98.0000	0.0200	100.00	102	47.61897	24.5614	0.7544	126.56
3	99.99998	97.0000	0.0300	100.00	103	46.43065	24.1772	0.7582	127.18
4	99.99992	96.0001	0.0400	100.00	104	45.24498	23.7977	0.7620	127.80
5	99.99977	95.0002	0.0500	100.00	105	44.06281	23.4227	0.7658	128.42
6	99.99946	94.0005	0.0600	100.00	106	42.88502	23.0523	0.7695	129.05
7	99.99890	93.0010	0.0700	100.00	107	41.71246	22.6862	0.7731	129.69
8	99.99797	92.0019	0.0800	100.00	108	40.54600	22.3245	0.7768	130.32
9	99.99652	91.0032	0.0900	100.00	109	39.38646	21.9670	0.7803	130.97
10	99.99438	90.0052	0.0999	100.01	110	38.23468	21.6137	0.7839	131.61
11	99.99134	89.0079	0.1099	100.01	111	37.09148	21.2644	0.7874	132.26
12	99.98717	88.0116	0.1199	100.01	112	35.95767	20.9192	0.7908	132.92
13	99.98160	87.0165	0.1298	100.02	113	34.83402	20.5778	0.7942	133.58
14	99.97435	86.0227	0.1398	100.02	114	33.72131	20.2403	0.7976	134.24
15	99.96509	85.0306	0.1497	100.03	115	32.62030	19.9066	0.8009	134.91
16	99.95348	84.0405	0.1596	100.04	116	31.53172	19.5766	0.8042	135.58
17	99.93914	83.0525	0.1695	100.05	117	30.45629	19.2502	0.8075	136.25
18	99.92167	82.0669	0.1793	100.07	118	29.39470	18.9274	0.8107	136.93
19	99.90065	81.0840	0.1892	100.08	119	28.34762	18.6080	0.8139	137.61
20	99.87563	80.1042	0.1990	100.10	120	27.31571	18.2921	0.8171	138.29
21	99.84613	79.1278	0.2087	100.13	121	26.29958	17.9795	0.8202	138.98
22	99.81167	78.1549	0.2185	100.15	122	25.29984	17.6702	0.8233	139.67
23	99.77175	77.1860	0.2281	100.19	123	24.31706	17.3642	0.8264	140.36
24	99.72583	76.2213	0.2378	100.22	124	23.35178	17.0613	0.8294	141.06
25	99.67362	75.2609	0.2474	100.26	125	22.40452	16.7615	0.8324	141.76
26	99.61381	74.3058	0.2569	100.31	126	21.47577	16.4648	0.8354	142.46
27	99.54659	73.3557	0.2664	100.36	127	20.56550	16.1714	0.8383	143.17
28	99.47113	72.4109	0.2759	100.41	128	19.67561	15.8802	0.8412	143.88
29	99.38684	71.4719	0.2853	100.47	129	18.80502	15.5922	0.8441	144.59
30	99.29314	70.5389	0.2946	100.54	130	17.95470	15.3070	0.8469	145.31
31	99.18942	69.6121	0.3039	100.61	131	17.12467	15.0246	0.8498	146.02
32	99.07508	68.6919	0.3131	100.69	132	16.31553	14.7450	0.8526	146.74
33	98.94953	67.7784	0.3222	100.78	133	15.52747	14.4679	0.8553	147.47
34	98.81215	66.8720	0.3313	100.87	134	14.76071	14.1935	0.8581	148.19
35	98.66236	65.9727	0.3403	100.97	135	14.01545	13.9217	0.8608	148.92
36	98.49956	65.0809	0.3492	101.08	136	13.29187	13.6523	0.8635	149.65
37	98.32317	64.1968	0.3580	101.20	137	12.59010	13.3854	0.8661	150.39
38	98.13260	63.3205	0.3668	101.32	138	11.91024	13.1209	0.8688	151.12
39	97.92728	62.4522	0.3755	101.45	139	11.25237	12.8588	0.8714	151.86
40	97.70666	61.5921	0.3841	101.59	140	10.61650	12.5990	0.8740	152.60
41	97.47019	60.7403	0.3926	101.74	141	10.00264	12.3416	0.8766	153.34
42	97.21735	59.8970	0.4010	101.90	142	9.41080	12.0863	0.8791	154.09
43	96.94761	59.0622	0.4094	102.06	143	8.84086	11.8332	0.8817	154.83
44	96.66048	58.2362	0.4176	102.24	144	8.29274	11.5823	0.8842	155.58
45	96.35548	57.4190	0.4258	102.42	145	7.76631	11.3335	0.8867	156.33
46	96.03215	56.6106	0.4339	102.61	146	7.26140	11.0868	0.8891	157.09
47	95.69007	55.8112	0.4419	102.81	147	6.77784	10.8421	0.8916	157.84
48	95.32881	55.0208	0.4498	103.02	148	6.31538	10.5994	0.8940	158.60
49	94.94799	54.2395	0.4576	103.24	149	5.87399	10.3583	0.8964	159.36
50	94.54723	53.4673	0.4653	103.47	150	5.45277	10.1199	0.8988	160.12
51	94.12622	52.7042	0.4730	103.70	151	5.05201	9.8830	0.9012	160.88
52	93.68462	51.9502	0.4805	103.95	152	4.67119	9.6479	0.9035	161.65
53	93.22216	51.2055	0.4879	104.21	153	4.30993	9.4147	0.9059	162.41
54	92.73860	50.4699	0.4953	104.47	154	3.96784	9.1833	0.9082	163.18
55	92.23370	49.7434	0.5026	104.74	155	3.64452	8.9536	0.9105	163.95
56	91.70727	49.0261	0.5097	105.03	156	3.33952	8.7257	0.9127	164.73
57	91.15914	48.3179	0.5168	105.32	157	3.05239	8.4994	0.9150	165.50
58	90.58920	47.6187	0.5238	105.62	158	2.78265	8.2749	0.9173	166.27
59	89.99734	46.9286	0.5307	105.93	159	2.52981	8.0519	0.9195	167.05
60	89.38350	46.2474	0.5375	106.25	160	2.29334	7.8306	0.9217	167.83
61	88.74764	45.5752	0.5442	106.58	161	2.07272	7.6109	0.9239	168.61
62	88.08976	44.9118	0.5509	106.91	162	1.86740	7.3927	0.9261	169.39
63	87.40990	44.2573	0.5574	107.26	163	1.67683	7.1761	0.9282	170.18
64	86.70813	43.6114	0.5639	107.61	164	1.50044	6.9609	0.9304	170.96
65	85.98455	42.9742	0.5703	107.97	165	1.33764	6.7473	0.9325	171.75
66	85.23928	42.3456	0.5765	108.35	166	1.18785	6.5351	0.9346	172.54
67	84.47253	41.7254	0.5827	108.73	167	1.05048	6.3243	0.9368	173.32
68	83.68447	41.1136	0.5889	109.11	168	0.92493	6.1148	0.9389	174.11
69	82.87533	40.5101	0.5949	109.51	169	0.81058	5.9069	0.9409	174.91
70	82.04540	39.9149	0.6009	109.91	170	0.70686	5.7003	0.9430	175.70
71	81.19498	39.3277	0.6067	110.33	171	0.61316	5.4950	0.9450	176.50
72	80.32439	38.7485	0.6125	110.75	172	0.52887	5.2911	0.9471	177.29
73	79.43401	38.1773	0.6182	111.18	173	0.45341	5.0885	0.9491	178.09
74	78.52423	37.6138	0.6239	111.61	174	0.38619	4.8871	0.9511	178.89
75	77.59548	37.0580	0.6294	112.06	175	0.32664	4.6870	0.9531	179.69
76	76.64822	36.5098	0.6349	112.51	176	0.27418	4.4881	0.9551	180.49
77	75.68294	35.9691	0.6403	112.97	177	0.22825	4.2906	0.9571	181.29
78	74.70016	35.4357	0.6456	113.44	178	0.18833	4.0941	0.9591	182.09
79	73.70042	34.9096	0.6509	113.91	179	0.15387	3.8990	0.9610	182.90
80	72.68429	34.3907	0.6561	114.39	180	0.12438	3.7049	0.9630	183.70
81	71.65238	33.8788	0.6612	114.88	181	0.09935	3.5123	0.9649	184.51
82	70.60530	33.3738	0.6663	115.37	182	0.07833	3.3206	0.9668	185.32
83	69.54371	32.8756	0.6712	115.88	183	0.06086	3.1303	0.9687	186.13
84	68.46828	32.3841	0.6762	116.38	184	0.04651	2.9418	0.9706	186.94
85	67.37970	31.8992	0.6810	116.90	185	0.03491	2.7532	0.9725	187.75
86	66.27869	31.4208	0.6858	117.42	186	0.02565	2.5667	0.9743	188.57
87	65.16598	30.9488	0.6905	117.95	187	0.01840	2.3810	0.9762	189.38
88	64.04234	30.4830	0.6952	118.48	188	0.01284	2.1955	0.9780	190.20
89	62.90852	30.0234	0.6998	119.02	189	0.00866	2.0138	0.9799	191.01
90	61.76532	29.5699	0.7043	119.57	190	0.00563	1.8286	0.9817	191.83
91	60.61354	29.1222	0.7088	120.12	191	0.00348	1.6494	0.9835	192.65
92	59.45400	28.6805	0.7132	120.68	192	0.00203	1.4704	0.9853	193.47
93	58.28754	28.2444	0.7176	121.24	193	0.00110	1.2909	0.9871	194.29
94	57.11498	27.8140	0.7219	121.81	194	0.00054	1.1111	0.9889	195.11
95	55.93719	27.3891	0.7261	122.39	195	0.00023	0.9347	0.9907	195.93
96	54.75503	26.9697	0.7303	122.97	196	0.00008	0.7497	0.9925	196.75
97	53.56935	26.5555	0.7344	123.56	197	0.00002	0.4994	0.9950	197.50
98	52.38103	26.1466	0.7385	124.15	198	0.00000	0.0000	1.0000	198.00
99	51.19096	25.7429	0.7426	124.74					

319

Table B continued

	Iowa Type curve S3						Iowa Type curve S3			
Age %AL	Percent Surviving	Remaining Life	CAD Ratio	Prob. Life	Age %AL	Percent Surviving	Remaining Life	CAD Ratio	Prob. Life
0	100.00000	100.0000	0.0000	100.00	100	50.00000	19.7687	0.8023	119.77
1	100.00000	99.0050	0.0099	100.01	101	48.43931	19.3896	0.8061	120.39
2	100.00000	98.0050	0.0199	100.01	102	46.88077	19.0175	0.8098	121.02
3	100.00000	97.0050	0.0299	100.01	103	45.32653	18.6525	0.8135	121.65
4	100.00000	96.0050	0.0399	100.01	104	43.77872	18.2943	0.8171	122.29
5	100.00000	95.0050	0.0499	100.01	105	42.73945	17.7270	0.8227	122.73
6	100.00000	94.0050	0.0599	100.01	106	40.71078	17.5854	0.8241	123.59
7	100.00000	93.0050	0.0699	100.01	107	39.19477	17.2463	0.8275	124.25
8	100.00000	92.0050	0.0799	100.01	108	37.69341	16.9133	0.8309	124.91
9	99.99999	91.0050	0.0899	100.01	109	36.20864	16.5863	0.8341	125.59
10	99.99998	90.0050	0.0999	100.01	110	34.74235	16.2653	0.8373	126.27
11	99.99996	89.0050	0.1099	100.01	111	33.29636	15.9499	0.8405	126.95
12	99.99991	88.0051	0.1199	100.01	112	31.87242	15.6402	0.8436	127.64
13	99.99984	87.0051	0.1299	100.01	113	30.47221	15.3358	0.8466	128.34
14	99.99973	86.0052	0.1399	100.01	114	29.09733	15.0369	0.8496	129.04
15	99.99955	85.0054	0.1499	100.01	115	27.74927	14.7431	0.8526	129.74
16	99.99927	84.0056	0.1599	100.01	116	26.42947	14.4543	0.8555	130.45
17	99.99886	83.0060	0.1699	100.01	117	25.13924	14.1705	0.8583	131.17
18	99.99826	82.0065	0.1799	100.01	118	23.87982	13.8915	0.8611	131.89
19	99.99742	81.0072	0.1899	100.01	119	22.65232	13.6171	0.8638	132.62
20	99.99626	80.0081	0.1999	100.01	120	21.45776	13.3474	0.8665	133.35
21	99.99464	79.0093	0.2099	100.01	121	20.29707	13.0820	0.8692	134.08
22	99.99257	78.0110	0.2199	100.01	122	19.17104	12.8211	0.8718	134.82
23	99.98980	77.0131	0.2299	100.01	123	18.08037	12.5643	0.8744	135.56
24	99.98620	76.0159	0.2398	100.02	124	17.02566	12.3117	0.8769	136.31
25	99.98158	75.0194	0.2498	100.02	125	16.00737	12.0631	0.8794	137.06
26	99.97573	74.0237	0.2598	100.02	126	15.02588	11.8184	0.8818	137.82
27	99.96840	73.0291	0.2697	100.03	127	14.08145	11.5775	0.8842	138.58
28	99.95930	72.0357	0.2796	100.04	128	13.17423	11.3403	0.8866	139.34
29	99.94813	71.0437	0.2896	100.04	129	12.30426	11.1068	0.8889	140.11
30	99.93451	70.0534	0.2995	100.05	130	11.47150	10.8768	0.8912	140.88
31	99.91805	69.0648	0.3094	100.06	131	10.67577	10.6502	0.8935	141.65
32	99.89831	68.0784	0.3192	100.08	132	9.91684	10.4270	0.8957	142.43
33	99.87481	67.0943	0.3291	100.09	133	9.19434	10.2071	0.8979	143.21
34	99.84701	66.1128	0.3389	100.11	134	8.50784	9.9903	0.9001	143.99
35	99.81435	65.1343	0.3487	100.13	135	7.85682	9.7767	0.9022	144.78
36	99.77620	64.1590	0.3584	100.16	136	7.24067	9.5661	0.9043	145.57
37	99.73190	63.1873	0.3681	100.19	137	6.65871	9.3585	0.9064	146.36
38	99.68073	62.2194	0.3778	100.22	138	6.11018	9.1537	0.9085	147.15
39	99.62192	61.2559	0.3874	100.26	139	5.59427	8.9518	0.9105	147.95
40	99.55468	60.2969	0.3970	100.30	140	5.11008	8.7526	0.9125	148.75
41	99.47816	59.3429	0.4066	100.34	141	4.65670	8.5561	0.9144	149.56
42	99.39145	58.3942	0.4161	100.39	142	4.23313	8.3622	0.9164	150.36
43	99.29363	57.4513	0.4255	100.45	143	3.83835	8.1708	0.9183	151.17
44	99.18371	56.5144	0.4349	100.51	144	3.47129	7.9819	0.9202	151.98
45	99.06070	55.5839	0.4442	100.58	145	3.13085	7.7955	0.9220	152.80
46	98.92355	54.6603	0.4534	100.66	146	2.81592	7.6114	0.9239	153.61
47	98.77119	53.7439	0.4626	100.74	147	2.52536	7.4297	0.9257	154.43
48	98.60251	52.8349	0.4717	100.83	148	2.25801	7.2501	0.9275	155.25
49	98.41639	51.9339	0.4807	100.93	149	2.01271	7.0728	0.9293	156.07
50	98.21171	51.0411	0.4896	101.04	150	1.78829	6.8977	0.9310	156.90
51	97.98729	50.1569	0.4984	101.16	151	1.58361	6.7245	0.9328	157.72
52	97.74199	49.2815	0.5072	101.28	152	1.39749	6.5535	0.9345	158.55
53	97.47464	48.4153	0.5158	101.42	153	1.22881	6.3845	0.9362	159.38
54	97.18408	47.5585	0.5244	101.56	154	1.07645	6.2174	0.9378	160.22
55	96.86915	46.7115	0.5329	101.71	155	0.93930	6.0522	0.9395	161.05
56	96.52871	45.8745	0.5413	101.87	156	0.81629	5.8889	0.9411	161.89
57	96.16165	45.0477	0.5495	102.05	157	0.70638	5.7274	0.9427	162.73
58	95.76687	44.2314	0.5577	102.23	158	0.60855	5.5678	0.9443	163.57
59	95.34330	43.4256	0.5657	102.43	159	0.52185	5.4097	0.9459	164.41
60	94.88992	42.6307	0.5737	102.63	160	0.44532	5.2535	0.9475	165.25
61	94.40574	41.8468	0.5815	102.85	161	0.37808	5.0988	0.9490	166.10
62	93.88982	41.0740	0.5893	103.07	162	0.31927	4.9460	0.9505	166.95
63	93.34129	40.3124	0.5969	103.31	163	0.26810	4.7945	0.9521	167.79
64	92.75933	39.5622	0.6044	103.56	164	0.22380	4.6446	0.9536	168.64
65	92.14318	38.8234	0.6118	103.82	165	0.18565	4.4963	0.9550	169.50
66	91.49216	38.0961	0.6190	104.10	166	0.15299	4.3494	0.9565	170.35
67	90.80566	37.3803	0.6262	104.38	167	0.12519	4.2042	0.9580	171.20
68	90.08316	36.6761	0.6332	104.68	168	0.10169	4.0602	0.9594	172.06
69	89.32423	35.9835	0.6402	104.98	169	0.08195	3.9178	0.9608	172.92
70	88.52851	35.3024	0.6470	105.30	170	0.06549	3.7768	0.9622	173.78
71	87.69574	34.6329	0.6537	105.63	171	0.05188	3.6365	0.9636	174.64
72	86.82577	33.9749	0.6603	105.97	172	0.04070	3.4980	0.9650	175.50
73	85.91855	33.3284	0.6667	106.33	173	0.03160	3.3614	0.9664	176.36
74	84.97412	32.6933	0.6731	106.69	174	0.02427	3.2256	0.9677	177.23
75	83.99263	32.0695	0.6793	107.07	175	0.01842	3.0912	0.9691	178.09
76	82.97434	31.4569	0.6854	107.46	176	0.01381	2.9562	0.9704	178.96
77	81.91963	30.8555	0.6914	107.86	177	0.01020	2.8255	0.9717	179.83
78	80.82896	30.2651	0.6973	108.27	178	0.00743	2.6924	0.9731	180.69
79	79.70293	29.6856	0.7031	108.69	179	0.00532	2.5620	0.9744	181.56
80	78.54224	29.1169	0.7088	109.12	180	0.00374	2.4331	0.9757	182.43
81	77.34768	28.5588	0.7144	109.56	181	0.00258	2.3023	0.9770	183.30
82	76.12018	28.0113	0.7199	110.01	182	0.00174	2.1723	0.9783	184.17
83	74.86076	27.4741	0.7253	110.47	183	0.00114	2.0525	0.9795	185.05
84	73.57053	26.9472	0.7305	110.95	184	0.00073	1.9245	0.9808	185.92
85	72.25073	26.4303	0.7357	111.43	185	0.00045	1.8109	0.9819	186.81
86	70.90268	25.9233	0.7408	111.92	186	0.00027	1.6848	0.9832	187.68
87	69.52779	25.4261	0.7457	112.43	187	0.00016	1.4994	0.9850	188.50
88	68.12758	24.9384	0.7506	112.94	188	0.00009	1.2768	0.9872	189.28
89	66.70364	24.4600	0.7554	113.46	189	0.00004	1.2480	0.9875	190.25
90	65.25765	23.9910	0.7601	113.99	190	0.00002	0.9965	0.9900	191.00
91	63.79136	23.5309	0.7647	114.53	191	0.00001	0.4936	0.9951	191.49
92	62.30659	23.0797	0.7692	115.08	192	0.00000	0.0000	1.0000	192.00
93	60.80523	22.6373	0.7736	115.64					
94	59.28922	22.2033	0.7780	116.20					
95	57.76056	21.7777	0.7822	116.78					
96	56.22128	21.3603	0.7864	117.36					
97	54.67347	20.9508	0.7905	117.95					
98	53.11923	20.5492	0.7945	118.55					
99	51.56069	20.1552	0.7984	119.16					

320

Table B continued

Age %AL	Iowa Type curve S4 Percent Surviving	Remaining Life	CAD Ratio	Prob. Life
0	100.00000	100.0000	0.0000	100.00
1	100.00000	99.0000	0.0100	100.00
2	100.00000	98.0000	0.0200	100.00
3	100.00000	97.0000	0.0300	100.00
4	100.00000	96.0000	0.0400	100.00
5	100.00000	95.0000	0.0500	100.00
6	100.00000	94.0000	0.0600	100.00
7	100.00000	93.0000	0.0700	100.00
8	100.00000	92.0000	0.0800	100.00
9	100.00000	91.0000	0.0900	100.00
10	100.00000	90.0000	0.1000	100.00
11	100.00000	89.0000	0.1100	100.00
12	100.00000	88.0000	0.1200	100.00
13	100.00000	87.0000	0.1300	100.00
14	100.00000	86.0000	0.1400	100.00
15	100.00000	85.0000	0.1500	100.00
16	100.00000	84.0000	0.1600	100.00
17	100.00000	83.0000	0.1700	100.00
18	100.00000	82.0000	0.1800	100.00
19	100.00000	81.0000	0.1900	100.00
20	100.00000	80.0000	0.2000	100.00
21	100.00000	79.0000	0.2100	100.00
22	100.00000	78.0000	0.2200	100.00
23	100.00000	77.0000	0.2300	100.00
24	100.00000	76.0000	0.2400	100.00
25	100.00000	75.0000	0.2500	100.00
26	100.00000	74.0000	0.2600	100.00
27	99.99999	73.0000	0.2700	100.00
28	99.99998	72.0000	0.2800	100.00
29	99.99997	71.0000	0.2900	100.00
30	99.99994	70.0000	0.3000	100.00
31	99.99990	69.0001	0.3100	100.00
32	99.99982	68.0001	0.3200	100.00
33	99.99971	67.0002	0.3300	100.00
34	99.99953	66.0003	0.3400	100.00
35	99.99925	65.0005	0.3500	100.00
36	99.99884	64.0008	0.3600	100.00
37	99.99824	63.0011	0.3700	100.00
38	99.99738	62.0017	0.3800	100.00
39	99.99615	61.0024	0.3900	100.00
40	99.99445	60.0035	0.4000	100.00
41	99.99210	59.0049	0.4100	100.00
42	99.98892	58.0067	0.4199	100.00
43	99.98465	57.0092	0.4299	100.01
44	99.97901	56.0124	0.4399	100.01
45	99.97162	55.0165	0.4498	100.02
46	99.96204	54.0217	0.4598	100.02
47	99.94977	53.0283	0.4697	100.03
48	99.93418	52.0365	0.4796	100.04
49	99.91455	51.0466	0.4895	100.05
50	99.89007	50.0590	0.4994	100.06
51	99.85976	49.0740	0.5093	100.07
52	99.82255	48.0921	0.5191	100.09
53	99.77721	47.1138	0.5289	100.11
54	99.72235	46.1394	0.5386	100.14
55	99.65644	45.1696	0.5483	100.17
56	99.57779	44.2049	0.5580	100.20
57	99.48452	43.2458	0.5675	100.25
58	99.37460	42.2931	0.5771	100.29
59	99.24585	41.3473	0.5865	100.35
60	99.09588	40.4092	0.5959	100.41
61	98.92218	39.4792	0.6052	100.48
62	98.72208	38.5582	0.6144	100.56
63	98.49276	37.6469	0.6235	100.65
64	98.23128	36.7457	0.6325	100.75
65	97.93460	35.8555	0.6414	100.86
66	97.59959	34.9769	0.6502	100.98
67	97.22304	34.1104	0.6589	101.11
68	96.80170	33.2567	0.6674	101.26
69	96.33234	32.4163	0.6758	101.42
70	95.81171	31.5897	0.6841	101.59
71	95.23664	30.7775	0.6922	101.78
72	94.60402	29.9799	0.7002	101.98
73	93.91087	29.1975	0.7080	102.20
74	93.15439	28.4306	0.7157	102.43
75	92.33195	27.6794	0.7232	102.68
76	91.44115	26.9441	0.7306	102.94
77	90.47988	26.2251	0.7377	103.23
78	89.44630	25.5223	0.7448	103.52
79	88.33893	24.8360	0.7516	103.84
80	87.15666	24.1661	0.7583	104.17
81	85.89877	23.5127	0.7649	104.51
82	84.56495	22.8757	0.7712	104.88
83	83.15535	22.2550	0.7775	105.25
84	81.67059	21.6505	0.7835	105.65
85	80.11173	21.0620	0.7894	106.06
86	78.48036	20.4894	0.7951	106.49
87	76.77853	19.9325	0.8007	106.93
88	75.00878	19.3910	0.8061	107.39
89	73.17417	18.8646	0.8114	107.86
90	71.27816	18.3531	0.8165	108.35
91	69.32473	17.8562	0.8214	108.86
92	67.31826	17.3735	0.8263	109.37
93	65.26353	16.9048	0.8310	109.90
94	63.16571	16.4496	0.8355	110.45
95	61.03029	16.0077	0.8399	111.01
96	58.86308	15.5786	0.8442	111.58
97	56.67012	15.1621	0.8484	112.16
98	54.45766	14.7578	0.8524	112.76
99	52.23211	14.3653	0.8563	113.37

Age %AL	Iowa Type curve S4 Percent Surviving	Remaining Life	CAD Ratio	Prob. Life
100	50.00000	13.9843	0.8602	113.98
101	47.76789	13.6144	0.8639	114.61
102	45.54234	13.2552	0.8674	115.26
103	43.32988	12.9065	0.8709	115.91
104	41.13692	12.5679	0.8743	116.57
105	38.96971	12.2390	0.8776	117.24
106	36.83429	11.9196	0.8808	117.92
107	34.73647	11.6093	0.8839	118.61
108	32.68174	11.3077	0.8869	119.31
109	30.67527	11.0146	0.8899	120.01
110	28.72184	10.7298	0.8927	120.73
111	26.82583	10.4528	0.8955	121.45
112	24.99122	10.1834	0.8982	122.18
113	23.22147	9.9214	0.9008	122.92
114	21.51964	9.6665	0.9033	123.67
115	19.88827	9.4184	0.9058	124.42
116	18.32942	9.1769	0.9082	125.18
117	16.84465	8.9417	0.9106	125.94
118	15.43505	8.7126	0.9129	126.71
119	14.10123	8.4894	0.9151	127.49
120	12.84334	8.2719	0.9173	128.27
121	11.66107	8.0599	0.9194	129.06
122	10.55370	7.8531	0.9215	129.85
123	9.52012	7.6515	0.9235	130.65
124	8.55885	7.4547	0.9255	131.45
125	7.66805	7.2626	0.9274	132.26
126	6.84561	7.0751	0.9292	133.08
127	6.08913	6.8919	0.9311	133.89
128	5.39599	6.7130	0.9329	134.71
129	4.76336	6.5381	0.9346	135.54
130	4.18829	6.3672	0.9363	136.37
131	3.66766	6.2000	0.9380	137.20
132	3.19830	6.0365	0.9396	138.04
133	2.77697	5.8766	0.9412	138.88
134	2.40041	5.7200	0.9428	139.72
135	2.06540	5.5667	0.9443	140.57
136	1.76872	5.4165	0.9458	141.42
137	1.50724	5.2695	0.9473	142.27
138	1.27792	5.1254	0.9487	143.13
139	1.07782	4.9841	0.9502	143.98
140	0.90412	4.8456	0.9515	144.85
141	0.75416	4.7096	0.9529	145.71
142	0.62540	4.5763	0.9542	146.58
143	0.51548	4.4456	0.9555	147.45
144	0.42222	4.3171	0.9568	148.32
145	0.34356	4.1910	0.9581	149.19
146	0.27765	4.0672	0.9593	150.07
147	0.22279	3.9456	0.9605	150.95
148	0.17745	3.8260	0.9617	151.83
149	0.14024	3.7084	0.9629	152.71
150	0.10994	3.5927	0.9641	153.59
151	0.08545	3.4791	0.9652	154.48
152	0.06582	3.3675	0.9663	155.37
153	0.05023	3.2575	0.9674	156.26
154	0.03796	3.1488	0.9685	157.15
155	0.02838	3.0430	0.9696	158.04
156	0.02099	2.9383	0.9706	158.94
157	0.01535	2.8342	0.9717	159.83
158	0.01108	2.7337	0.9727	160.73
159	0.00790	2.6329	0.9737	161.63
160	0.00555	2.5360	0.9746	162.54
161	0.00385	2.4350	0.9756	163.44
162	0.00262	2.3435	0.9766	164.34
163	0.00176	2.2443	0.9776	165.24
164	0.00116	2.1465	0.9785	166.15
165	0.00075	2.0466	0.9795	167.05
166	0.00047	1.9680	0.9803	167.97
167	0.00029	1.8792	0.9812	168.88
168	0.00018	1.7221	0.9828	169.72
169	0.00010	1.6999	0.9830	170.70
170	0.00006	1.5000	0.9850	171.50
171	0.00003	1.5002	0.9850	172.50
172	0.00002	1.0006	0.9900	173.00
173	0.00001	0.5018	0.9950	173.50
174	0.00000	0.0000	1.0000	174.00

Table B continued

Age %AL	Iowa Type curve S5 Percent Surviving	Remaining Life	CAD Ratio	Prob. Life
0	100.00000	100.0000	0.0000	100.00
1	100.00000	99.0000	0.0100	100.00
2	100.00000	98.0000	0.0200	100.00
3	100.00000	97.0000	0.0300	100.00
4	100.00000	96.0000	0.0400	100.00
5	100.00000	95.0000	0.0500	100.00
6	100.00000	94.0000	0.0600	100.00
7	100.00000	93.0000	0.0700	100.00
8	100.00000	92.0000	0.0800	100.00
9	100.00000	91.0000	0.0900	100.00
10	100.00000	90.0000	0.1000	100.00
11	100.00000	89.0000	0.1100	100.00
12	100.00000	88.0000	0.1200	100.00
13	100.00000	87.0000	0.1300	100.00
14	100.00000	86.0000	0.1400	100.00
15	100.00000	85.0000	0.1500	100.00
16	100.00000	84.0000	0.1600	100.00
17	100.00000	83.0000	0.1700	100.00
18	100.00000	82.0000	0.1800	100.00
19	100.00000	81.0000	0.1900	100.00
20	100.00000	80.0000	0.2000	100.00
21	100.00000	79.0000	0.2100	100.00
22	100.00000	78.0000	0.2200	100.00
23	100.00000	77.0000	0.2300	100.00
24	100.00000	76.0000	0.2400	100.00
25	100.00000	75.0000	0.2500	100.00
26	100.00000	74.0000	0.2600	100.00
27	100.00000	73.0000	0.2700	100.00
28	100.00000	72.0000	0.2800	100.00
29	100.00000	71.0000	0.2900	100.00
30	100.00000	70.0000	0.3000	100.00
31	100.00000	69.0000	0.3100	100.00
32	100.00000	68.0000	0.3200	100.00
33	100.00000	67.0000	0.3300	100.00
34	100.00000	66.0000	0.3400	100.00
35	100.00000	65.0000	0.3500	100.00
36	100.00000	64.0000	0.3600	100.00
37	100.00000	63.0000	0.3700	100.00
38	100.00000	62.0000	0.3800	100.00
39	100.00000	61.0000	0.3900	100.00
40	100.00000	60.0000	0.4000	100.00
41	100.00000	59.0000	0.4100	100.00
42	100.00000	58.0000	0.4200	100.00
43	100.00000	57.0000	0.4300	100.00
44	100.00000	56.0000	0.4400	100.00
45	100.00000	55.0000	0.4500	100.00
46	99.99999	54.0000	0.4600	100.00
47	99.99998	53.0000	0.4700	100.00
48	99.99996	52.0000	0.4800	100.00
49	99.99993	51.0000	0.4900	100.00
50	99.99987	50.0001	0.5000	100.00
51	99.99976	49.0001	0.5100	100.00
52	99.99958	48.0002	0.5200	100.00
53	99.99928	47.0004	0.5300	100.00
54	99.99880	46.0006	0.5400	100.00
55	99.99803	45.0009	0.5500	100.00
56	99.99685	44.0015	0.5600	100.00
57	99.99503	43.0022	0.5700	100.00
58	99.99232	42.0034	0.5800	100.00
59	99.98831	41.0051	0.5899	100.01
60	99.98250	40.0074	0.5999	100.01
61	99.97418	39.0107	0.6099	100.01
62	99.96247	38.0152	0.6198	100.02
63	99.94620	37.0213	0.6298	100.02
64	99.92390	36.0295	0.6397	100.03
65	99.89372	35.0402	0.6496	100.04
66	99.85338	34.0542	0.6595	100.05
67	99.80012	33.0721	0.6693	100.07
68	99.73061	32.0948	0.6791	100.09
69	99.64087	31.1232	0.6888	100.12
70	99.52630	30.1585	0.6984	100.16
71	99.38154	29.2017	0.7080	100.20
72	99.20049	28.2541	0.7175	100.25
73	98.97629	27.3169	0.7268	100.32
74	98.70131	26.3916	0.7361	100.39
75	98.36721	25.4796	0.7452	100.48
76	97.96496	24.5821	0.7542	100.58
77	97.48497	23.7007	0.7630	100.70
78	96.91718	22.8366	0.7716	100.84
79	96.25125	21.9912	0.7801	100.99
80	95.47669	21.1655	0.7883	101.17
81	94.58312	20.3608	0.7964	101.36
82	93.56050	19.5778	0.8042	101.58
83	92.39937	18.8176	0.8118	101.82
84	91.09114	18.0807	0.8192	102.08
85	89.62837	17.3676	0.8263	102.37
86	88.00503	16.6787	0.8332	102.68
87	86.21677	16.0143	0.8399	103.01
88	84.26116	15.3744	0.8463	103.37
89	82.13791	14.7589	0.8524	103.76
90	79.84903	14.1676	0.8583	104.17
91	77.39893	13.6002	0.8640	104.60
92	74.79456	13.0564	0.8694	105.06
93	72.04530	12.5356	0.8746	105.54
94	69.16299	12.0371	0.8796	106.04
95	66.16179	11.5605	0.8844	106.56
96	63.05793	11.1049	0.8890	107.10
97	59.86957	10.6697	0.8933	107.67
98	56.61637	10.2540	0.8975	108.25
99	53.31926	9.8572	0.9014	108.86

Age %AL	Iowa Type curve S5 Percent Surviving	Remaining Life	CAD Ratio	Prob. Life
100	50.00000	9.4783	0.9052	109.48
101	46.68073	9.1168	0.9088	110.12
102	43.38363	8.7716	0.9123	110.77
103	40.13043	8.4422	0.9156	111.44
104	36.94207	8.1276	0.9187	112.13
105	33.83821	7.8273	0.9217	112.83
106	30.83701	7.5404	0.9246	113.54
107	27.95470	7.2663	0.9273	114.27
108	25.20544	7.0043	0.9300	115.00
109	22.60107	6.7539	0.9325	115.75
110	20.15098	6.5142	0.9349	116.51
111	17.86209	6.2849	0.9372	117.28
112	15.73884	6.0653	0.9393	118.07
113	13.78323	5.8550	0.9415	118.85
114	11.99497	5.6533	0.9435	119.65
115	10.37163	5.4599	0.9454	120.46
116	8.90886	5.2743	0.9473	121.27
117	7.60064	5.0960	0.9490	122.10
118	6.43950	4.9247	0.9508	122.92
119	5.41688	4.7601	0.9524	123.76
120	4.52331	4.6016	0.9540	124.60
121	3.74875	4.4491	0.9555	125.45
122	3.08282	4.3021	0.9570	126.30
123	2.51503	4.1605	0.9584	127.16
124	2.03504	4.0239	0.9598	128.02
125	1.63279	3.8920	0.9611	128.89
126	1.29869	3.7647	0.9624	129.76
127	1.02371	3.6416	0.9636	130.64
128	0.79951	3.5225	0.9648	131.52
129	0.61846	3.4074	0.9659	132.41
130	0.47370	3.2958	0.9670	133.30
131	0.35913	3.1878	0.9681	134.19
132	0.26940	3.0830	0.9692	135.08
133	0.19988	2.9814	0.9702	135.98
134	0.14662	2.8828	0.9712	136.88
135	0.10628	2.7872	0.9721	137.79
136	0.07610	2.6942	0.9731	138.69
137	0.05380	2.6037	0.9740	139.60
138	0.03753	2.5157	0.9748	140.52
139	0.02582	2.4299	0.9757	141.43
140	0.01751	2.3458	0.9765	142.35
141	0.01169	2.2647	0.9774	143.26
142	0.00768	2.1862	0.9781	144.19
143	0.00497	2.1056	0.9789	145.11
144	0.00315	2.0333	0.9797	146.03
145	0.00197	1.9517	0.9805	146.95
146	0.00120	1.8833	0.9812	147.88
147	0.00072	1.8054	0.9819	148.81
148	0.00042	1.7379	0.9826	149.74
149	0.00024	1.6664	0.9833	150.67
150	0.00014	1.4996	0.9850	151.50
151	0.00007	1.4993	0.9850	152.50
152	0.00004	1.2488	0.9875	153.25
153	0.00002	0.9983	0.9900	154.00
154	0.00001	0.4971	0.9950	154.50
155	0.00000	0.0000	1.0000	155.00

Table B continued

	Iowa Type curve S6			
Age %AL	Percent Surviving	Remaining Life	CAD Ratio	Prob. Life
0	100.00000	100.0000	0.0000	100.00
1	100.00000	99.0000	0.0100	100.00
2	100.00000	98.0000	0.0200	100.00
3	100.00000	97.0000	0.0300	100.00
4	100.00000	96.0000	0.0400	100.00
5	100.00000	95.0000	0.0500	100.00
6	100.00000	94.0000	0.0600	100.00
7	100.00000	93.0000	0.0700	100.00
8	100.00000	92.0000	0.0800	100.00
9	100.00000	91.0000	0.0900	100.00
10	100.00000	90.0000	0.1000	100.00
11	100.00000	89.0000	0.1100	100.00
12	100.00000	88.0000	0.1200	100.00
13	100.00000	87.0000	0.1300	100.00
14	100.00000	86.0000	0.1400	100.00
15	100.00000	85.0000	0.1500	100.00
16	100.00000	84.0000	0.1600	100.00
17	100.00000	83.0000	0.1700	100.00
18	100.00000	82.0000	0.1800	100.00
19	100.00000	81.0000	0.1900	100.00
20	100.00000	80.0000	0.2000	100.00
21	100.00000	79.0000	0.2100	100.00
22	100.00000	78.0000	0.2200	100.00
23	100.00000	77.0000	0.2300	100.00
24	100.00000	76.0000	0.2400	100.00
25	100.00000	75.0000	0.2500	100.00
26	100.00000	74.0000	0.2600	100.00
27	100.00000	73.0000	0.2700	100.00
28	100.00000	72.0000	0.2800	100.00
29	100.00000	71.0000	0.2900	100.00
30	100.00000	70.0000	0.3000	100.00
31	100.00000	69.0000	0.3100	100.00
32	100.00000	68.0000	0.3200	100.00
33	100.00000	67.0000	0.3300	100.00
34	100.00000	66.0000	0.3400	100.00
35	100.00000	65.0000	0.3500	100.00
36	100.00000	64.0000	0.3600	100.00
37	100.00000	63.0000	0.3700	100.00
38	100.00000	62.0000	0.3800	100.00
39	100.00000	61.0000	0.3900	100.00
40	100.00000	60.0000	0.4000	100.00
41	100.00000	59.0000	0.4100	100.00
42	100.00000	58.0000	0.4200	100.00
43	100.00000	57.0000	0.4300	100.00
44	100.00000	56.0000	0.4400	100.00
45	100.00000	55.0000	0.4500	100.00
46	100.00000	54.0000	0.4600	100.00
47	100.00000	53.0000	0.4700	100.00
48	100.00000	52.0000	0.4800	100.00
49	100.00000	51.0000	0.4900	100.00
50	100.00000	50.0000	0.5000	100.00
51	100.00000	49.0000	0.5100	100.00
52	100.00000	48.0000	0.5200	100.00
53	100.00000	47.0000	0.5300	100.00
54	100.00000	46.0000	0.5400	100.00
55	100.00000	45.0000	0.5500	100.00
56	100.00000	44.0000	0.5600	100.00
57	100.00000	43.0000	0.5700	100.00
58	100.00000	42.0000	0.5800	100.00
59	100.00000	41.0000	0.5900	100.00
60	100.00000	40.0000	0.6000	100.00
61	100.00000	39.0000	0.6100	100.00
62	100.00000	38.0000	0.6200	100.00
63	99.99999	37.0000	0.6300	100.00
64	99.99998	36.0000	0.6400	100.00
65	99.99996	35.0000	0.6500	100.00
66	99.99991	34.0000	0.6600	100.00
67	99.99981	33.0001	0.6700	100.00
68	99.99960	32.0001	0.6800	100.00
69	99.99917	31.0003	0.6900	100.00
70	99.99835	30.0005	0.7000	100.00
71	99.99682	29.0010	0.7100	100.00
72	99.99405	28.0018	0.7200	100.00
73	99.98917	27.0031	0.7300	100.00
74	99.98079	26.0053	0.7399	100.01
75	99.96681	25.0089	0.7499	100.01
76	99.94405	24.0145	0.7599	100.01
77	99.90793	23.0230	0.7698	100.02
78	99.85194	22.0356	0.7796	100.04
79	99.76716	21.0539	0.7895	100.05
80	99.64167	20.0798	0.7992	100.08
81	99.45998	19.1156	0.8088	100.12
82	99.20251	18.1639	0.8184	100.16
83	98.84525	17.2277	0.8277	100.23
84	98.35961	16.3103	0.8369	100.31
85	97.71260	15.4150	0.8459	100.41
86	96.86741	14.5451	0.8545	100.55
87	95.78452	13.7039	0.8630	100.70
88	94.42320	12.8943	0.8711	100.89
89	92.74358	12.1187	0.8788	101.12
90	90.70910	11.3793	0.8862	101.38
91	88.28921	10.6775	0.8932	101.68
92	85.46213	10.0142	0.8999	102.01
93	82.21749	9.3897	0.9061	102.39
94	78.55859	8.8037	0.9120	102.80
95	74.50386	8.2556	0.9174	103.26
96	70.08766	7.7443	0.9226	103.74
97	65.35972	7.2683	0.9273	104.27
98	60.38401	6.8261	0.9317	104.83
99	55.23615	6.4156	0.9358	105.42

	Iowa Type curve S6			
Age %AL	Percent Surviving	Remaining Life	CAD Ratio	Prob. Life
100	50.00000	6.0351	0.9396	106.04
101	44.76385	5.6826	0.9432	106.68
102	39.61599	5.3560	0.9464	107.36
103	34.64028	5.0535	0.9495	108.05
104	29.91234	4.7733	0.9523	108.77
105	25.49614	4.5135	0.9549	109.51
106	21.44141	4.2724	0.9573	110.27
107	17.78251	4.0486	0.9595	111.05
108	14.53787	3.8406	0.9616	111.84
109	11.71079	3.6471	0.9635	112.65
110	9.29090	3.4668	0.9653	113.47
111	7.25642	3.2986	0.9670	114.30
112	5.57680	3.1415	0.9686	115.14
113	4.21548	2.9945	0.9701	115.99
114	3.13259	2.8568	0.9714	116.86
115	2.28740	2.7276	0.9727	117.73
116	1.64039	2.6063	0.9739	118.61
117	1.15475	2.4921	0.9751	119.49
118	0.79749	2.3845	0.9762	120.38
119	0.54002	2.2830	0.9772	121.28
120	0.35833	2.1870	0.9781	122.19
121	0.23284	2.0963	0.9790	123.10
122	0.14806	2.0103	0.9799	124.01
123	0.09207	1.9288	0.9807	124.93
124	0.05595	1.8512	0.9815	125.85
125	0.03319	1.7778	0.9822	126.78
126	0.01921	1.7077	0.9829	127.71
127	0.01084	1.6402	0.9836	128.64
128	0.00595	1.5773	0.9842	129.58
129	0.00318	1.5157	0.9848	130.52
130	0.00165	1.4575	0.9854	131.46
131	0.00083	1.4036	0.9860	132.40
132	0.00040	1.3749	0.9863	133.37
133	0.00019	1.3419	0.9866	134.34
134	0.00009	1.2775	0.9872	135.28
135	0.00004	1.2494	0.9875	136.25
136	0.00002	0.9994	0.9900	137.00
137	0.00001	0.4994	0.9950	137.50
138	0.00000	0.0000	1.0000	138.00

Table C

	Iowa Type curve R1					Iowa Type curve R1			
Age %AL	Percent Surviving	Remaining Life	CAD Ratio	Prob. Life	Age %AL	Percent Surviving	Remaining Life	CAD Ratio	Prob. Life
0	100.00000	100.0000	0.0000	100.00	100	52.89519	36.7257	0.6327	136.73
1	99.74192	99.2593	0.0074	100.26	101	52.15288	36.2413	0.6376	137.24
2	99.48020	98.5191	0.0148	100.52	102	51.40644	35.7603	0.6424	137.76
3	99.21484	97.7812	0.0222	100.78	103	50.65605	35.2826	0.6472	138.28
4	98.94584	97.0457	0.0295	101.05	104	49.90189	34.8082	0.6519	138.81
5	98.67319	96.3125	0.0369	101.31	105	49.14417	34.3372	0.6566	139.34
6	98.39691	95.5815	0.0442	101.58	106	48.38308	33.8695	0.6613	139.87
7	98.11700	94.8528	0.0515	101.85	107	47.61883	33.4051	0.6659	140.41
8	97.83345	94.1262	0.0587	102.13	108	46.85164	32.9439	0.6706	140.94
9	97.54628	93.4019	0.0660	102.40	109	46.08172	32.4859	0.6751	141.49
10	97.25548	92.6796	0.0732	102.68	110	45.30930	32.0312	0.6797	142.03
11	96.96107	91.9595	0.0804	102.96	111	44.53462	31.5797	0.6842	142.58
12	96.66305	91.2415	0.0876	103.24	112	43.75790	31.1314	0.6887	143.13
13	96.36142	90.5255	0.0947	103.53	113	42.97940	30.6862	0.6931	143.69
14	96.05620	89.8116	0.1019	103.81	114	42.19937	30.2442	0.6976	144.24
15	95.74739	89.0997	0.1090	104.10	115	41.41805	29.8053	0.7019	144.81
16	95.43500	88.3897	0.1161	104.39	116	40.63572	29.3695	0.7063	145.37
17	95.11905	87.6816	0.1232	104.68	117	39.85262	28.9368	0.7106	145.94
18	94.79953	86.9755	0.1302	104.98	118	39.06904	28.5071	0.7149	146.51
19	94.47648	86.2711	0.1373	105.27	119	38.28526	28.0805	0.7192	147.08
20	94.14988	85.5687	0.1443	105.57	120	37.50154	27.6569	0.7234	147.66
21	93.81977	84.8680	0.1513	105.87	121	36.71818	27.2362	0.7276	148.24
22	93.48615	84.1691	0.1583	106.17	122	35.93546	26.8186	0.7318	148.82
23	93.14904	83.4719	0.1653	106.47	123	35.15368	26.4039	0.7360	149.40
24	92.80845	82.7764	0.1722	106.78	124	34.37314	25.9921	0.7401	149.99
25	92.46439	82.0825	0.1792	107.08	125	33.59414	25.5832	0.7442	150.58
26	92.11689	81.3903	0.1861	107.39	126	32.81698	25.1772	0.7482	151.18
27	91.76597	80.6996	0.1930	107.70	127	32.04198	24.7741	0.7523	151.77
28	91.41163	80.0105	0.1999	108.01	128	31.26944	24.3738	0.7563	152.37
29	91.05389	79.3229	0.2068	108.32	129	30.49969	23.9763	0.7602	152.98
30	90.69276	78.6367	0.2136	108.64	130	29.73303	23.5817	0.7642	153.58
31	90.32821	77.9521	0.2205	108.95	131	28.96980	23.1898	0.7681	154.19
32	89.96022	77.2689	0.2273	109.27	132	28.21032	22.8006	0.7720	154.80
33	89.58873	76.5872	0.2341	109.59	133	27.45491	22.4142	0.7759	155.41
34	89.21370	75.9071	0.2409	109.91	134	26.70390	22.0305	0.7797	156.03
35	88.83506	75.2285	0.2477	110.23	135	25.95763	21.6495	0.7835	156.65
36	88.45275	74.5515	0.2545	110.55	136	25.21641	21.2712	0.7873	157.27
37	88.06668	73.8761	0.2612	110.88	137	24.48060	20.8955	0.7910	157.90
38	87.67678	73.2024	0.2680	111.20	138	23.75051	20.5225	0.7948	158.52
39	87.28297	72.5305	0.2747	111.53	139	23.02648	20.1521	0.7985	159.15
40	86.88515	71.8603	0.2814	111.86	140	22.30885	19.7842	0.8022	159.78
41	86.48324	71.1919	0.2881	112.19	141	21.59795	19.4190	0.8058	160.42
42	86.07713	70.5254	0.2947	112.53	142	20.89412	19.0563	0.8094	161.06
43	85.66673	69.8609	0.3014	112.86	143	20.19768	18.6961	0.8130	161.70
44	85.25194	69.1984	0.3080	113.20	144	19.50898	18.3385	0.8166	162.34
45	84.83266	68.5379	0.3146	113.54	145	18.82834	17.9833	0.8202	162.98
46	84.40879	67.8795	0.3212	113.88	146	18.15608	17.6307	0.8237	163.63
47	83.98023	67.2234	0.3278	114.22	147	17.49255	17.2805	0.8272	164.28
48	83.54688	66.5695	0.3343	114.57	148	16.83806	16.9327	0.8307	164.93
49	83.10863	65.9179	0.3408	114.92	149	16.19292	16.5874	0.8341	165.59
50	82.66538	65.2687	0.3473	115.27	150	15.55747	16.2445	0.8376	166.24
51	82.21704	64.6218	0.3538	115.62	151	14.93201	15.9040	0.8410	166.90
52	81.76351	63.9775	0.3602	115.98	152	14.31686	15.5659	0.8443	167.57
53	81.30468	63.3357	0.3666	116.34	153	13.71231	15.2301	0.8477	168.23
54	80.84048	62.6966	0.3730	116.70	154	13.11867	14.8966	0.8510	168.90
55	80.37080	62.0600	0.3794	117.06	155	12.53623	14.5655	0.8543	169.57
56	79.89555	61.4262	0.3857	117.43	156	11.96528	14.2367	0.8576	170.24
57	79.41465	60.7952	0.3920	117.80	157	11.40609	13.9101	0.8609	170.91
58	78.92801	60.1669	0.3983	118.17	158	10.85895	13.5858	0.8641	171.59
59	78.43556	59.5415	0.4046	118.54	159	10.32411	13.2637	0.8674	172.26
60	77.93721	58.9190	0.4108	118.92	160	9.80182	12.9438	0.8706	172.94
61	77.43289	58.2995	0.4170	119.30	161	9.29235	12.6261	0.8737	173.63
62	76.92254	57.6830	0.4232	119.68	162	8.79592	12.3105	0.8769	174.31
63	76.40608	57.0695	0.4293	120.07	163	8.31275	11.9970	0.8800	175.00
64	75.88346	56.4591	0.4354	120.46	164	7.84307	11.6854	0.8831	175.69
65	75.35463	55.8518	0.4415	120.85	165	7.38707	11.3759	0.8862	176.38
66	74.81952	55.2477	0.4475	121.25	166	6.94493	11.0683	0.8893	177.07
67	74.27809	54.6468	0.4535	121.65	167	6.51684	10.7626	0.8924	177.76
68	73.73030	54.0491	0.4595	122.05	168	6.10295	10.4585	0.8954	178.46
69	73.17611	53.4546	0.4655	122.45	169	5.70340	10.1562	0.8984	179.16
70	72.61549	52.8635	0.4714	122.86	170	5.31832	9.8553	0.9014	179.86
71	72.04841	52.2756	0.4772	123.28	171	4.94781	9.5559	0.9044	180.56
72	71.47486	51.6911	0.4831	123.69	172	4.59195	9.2577	0.9074	181.26
73	70.89482	51.1099	0.4889	124.11	173	4.25081	8.9605	0.9104	181.96
74	70.30827	50.5321	0.4947	124.53	174	3.92444	8.6642	0.9134	182.66
75	69.71523	49.9577	0.5004	124.96	175	3.61284	8.3683	0.9163	183.37
76	69.11567	49.3868	0.5061	125.39	176	3.31601	8.0726	0.9193	184.07
77	58.50963	48.8192	0.5118	125.82	177	3.03391	7.7767	0.9222	184.78
78	67.89711	48.2551	0.5174	126.26	178	2.76646	7.4802	0.9252	185.48
79	67.27813	47.6945	0.5231	126.69	179	2.51357	7.1825	0.9282	186.18
80	66.65272	47.1373	0.5286	127.14	180	2.27508	6.8830	0.9312	186.88
81	66.02091	46.5836	0.5342	127.58	181	2.05081	6.5810	0.9342	187.58
82	65.38275	46.0334	0.5397	128.03	182	1.84053	6.2758	0.9372	188.28
83	64.73828	45.4867	0.5451	128.49	183	1.64396	5.9664	0.9403	188.97
84	64.08756	44.9435	0.5506	128.94	184	1.46075	5.6520	0.9435	189.65
85	63.43064	44.4038	0.5560	129.40	185	1.29047	5.3318	0.9467	190.33
86	62.76760	43.8675	0.5613	129.87	186	1.13261	5.0053	0.9499	191.01
87	62.09850	43.3348	0.5667	130.33	187	0.98656	4.6722	0.9533	191.67
88	61.42343	42.8056	0.5719	130.81	188	0.85156	4.3337	0.9567	192.33
89	60.74247	42.2799	0.5772	131.28	189	0.72632	3.9947	0.9601	192.99
90	60.05571	41.7576	0.5824	131.76	190	0.61061	3.6510	0.9634	193.66
91	59.36327	41.2389	0.5876	132.24	191	0.50457	3.3204	0.9668	194.32
92	58.66524	40.7236	0.5928	132.72	192	0.40831	2.9854	0.9701	194.99
93	57.96175	40.2118	0.5979	133.21	193	0.32197	2.6518	0.9735	195.65
94	57.25290	39.7035	0.6030	133.70	194	0.24565	2.3204	0.9768	196.32
95	56.53884	39.1986	0.6080	134.20	195	0.17949	1.9914	0.9801	196.99
96	55.81969	38.6972	0.6130	134.70	196	0.12359	1.6660	0.9833	197.67
97	55.09560	38.1992	0.6180	135.20	197	0.07806	1.3460	0.9865	198.35
98	54.36672	37.7046	0.6230	135.70	198	0.04300	1.0358	0.9896	199.04
99	53.63319	37.2134	0.6279	136.21	199	0.01848	0.7468	0.9925	199.75

Table C continued

<table>
<tr><td colspan="5" align="center">Iowa Type curve R1</td></tr>
<tr><td>Age
%AL</td><td>Percent
Surviving</td><td>Remaining
Life</td><td>CAD
Ratio</td><td>Prob.
Life</td></tr>
<tr><td>200</td><td>0.00456</td><td>0.5000</td><td>0.9950</td><td>200.50</td></tr>
<tr><td>201</td><td>0.00000</td><td>0.0000</td><td>1.0000</td><td>201.00</td></tr>
</table>

	Iowa	Type curve	R2	
Age %AL	Percent Surviving	Remaining Life	CAD Ratio	Prob. Life
0	100.00000	100.0000	0.0000	100.00
1	99.90517	99.0944	0.0091	100.09
2	99.80707	98.1913	0.0181	100.19
3	99.70561	97.2900	0.0271	100.29
4	99.60070	96.3927	0.0361	100.39
5	99.49224	95.4972	0.0450	100.50
6	99.38016	94.6044	0.0540	100.60
7	99.26435	93.7142	0.0629	100.71
8	99.14472	92.8266	0.0717	100.83
9	99.02117	91.9418	0.0806	100.94
10	98.89359	91.0598	0.0894	101.06
11	98.76190	90.1806	0.0982	101.18
12	98.62598	89.3042	0.1070	101.30
13	98.48574	88.4306	0.1157	101.43
14	98.34106	87.5600	0.1244	101.56
15	98.19184	86.6923	0.1331	101.69
16	98.03796	85.8276	0.1417	101.83
17	97.87933	84.9659	0.1503	101.97
18	97.71581	84.1072	0.1589	102.11
19	97.54731	83.2516	0.1675	102.25
20	97.37369	82.3992	0.1760	102.40
21	97.19485	81.5499	0.1845	102.55
22	97.01065	80.7038	0.1930	102.70
23	96.82099	79.8609	0.2014	102.86
24	96.62573	79.0212	0.2098	103.02
25	96.42474	78.1849	0.2182	103.18
26	96.21790	77.3519	0.2265	103.35
27	96.00508	76.5223	0.2348	103.52
28	95.78615	75.6960	0.2430	103.70
29	95.56096	74.8732	0.2513	103.87
30	95.32938	74.0539	0.2595	104.05
31	95.09128	73.2381	0.2676	104.24
32	94.84651	72.4258	0.2757	104.43
33	94.59492	71.6171	0.2838	104.62
34	94.33638	70.8120	0.2919	104.81
35	94.07074	70.0105	0.2999	105.01
36	93.79784	69.2128	0.3079	105.21
37	93.51754	68.4187	0.3158	105.42
38	93.22967	67.6284	0.3237	105.63
39	92.93409	66.8419	0.3316	105.84
40	92.63064	66.0593	0.3394	106.06
41	92.31914	65.2805	0.3472	106.28
42	91.99946	64.5056	0.3549	106.51
43	91.67141	63.7346	0.3627	106.73
44	91.33483	62.9677	0.3703	106.97
45	90.98955	62.2047	0.3780	107.20
46	90.63541	61.4458	0.3855	107.45
47	90.27222	60.6910	0.3931	107.69
48	89.89982	59.9403	0.4006	107.94
49	89.51803	59.1939	0.4081	108.19
50	89.12668	58.4516	0.4155	108.45
51	88.72557	57.7136	0.4229	108.71
52	88.31454	56.9798	0.4302	108.98
53	87.89341	56.2505	0.4375	109.25
54	87.46198	55.5255	0.4447	109.53
55	87.02008	54.8049	0.4520	109.80
56	86.56753	54.0888	0.4591	110.09
57	86.10413	53.3772	0.4662	110.38
58	85.62971	52.6701	0.4733	110.67
59	85.14408	51.9677	0.4803	110.97
60	84.64707	51.2699	0.4873	111.27
61	84.13847	50.5768	0.4942	111.58
62	83.61813	49.8884	0.5011	111.89
63	83.08585	49.2048	0.5080	112.20
64	82.54146	48.5260	0.5147	112.53
65	81.98479	47.8521	0.5215	112.85
66	81.41567	47.1831	0.5282	113.18
67	80.83392	46.5191	0.5348	113.52
68	80.23938	45.8601	0.5414	113.86
69	79.63191	45.2061	0.5479	114.21
70	79.01133	44.5573	0.5544	114.56
71	78.37752	43.9135	0.5609	114.91
72	77.73032	43.2750	0.5672	115.28
73	77.06961	42.6417	0.5736	115.64
74	76.39526	42.0137	0.5799	116.01
75	75.70717	41.3910	0.5861	116.39
76	75.00523	40.7737	0.5923	116.77
77	74.28934	40.1618	0.5984	117.16
78	73.55943	39.5553	0.6044	117.56
79	72.81544	38.9544	0.6105	117.95
80	72.05732	38.3590	0.6164	118.36
81	71.28502	37.7691	0.6223	118.77
82	70.49853	37.1849	0.6282	119.18
83	69.69785	36.6063	0.6339	119.61
84	68.88299	36.0335	0.6397	120.03
85	68.05401	35.4663	0.6453	120.47
86	67.21095	34.9049	0.6510	120.90
87	66.35390	34.3493	0.6565	121.35
88	65.48296	33.7995	0.6620	121.80
89	64.59828	33.2555	0.6674	122.26
90	63.70000	32.7174	0.6728	122.72
91	62.78831	32.1852	0.6781	123.19
92	61.86342	31.6590	0.6834	123.66
93	60.92558	31.1386	0.6886	124.14
94	59.97507	30.6242	0.6938	124.62
95	59.01217	30.1157	0.6988	125.12
96	58.03725	29.6132	0.7039	125.61
97	57.05065	29.1167	0.7088	126.12
98	56.05279	28.6261	0.7137	126.63
99	55.04412	28.1415	0.7186	127.14

325

Table C continued

Iowa Type curve R2

Age %AL	Percent Surviving	Remaining Life	CAD Ratio	Prob. Life
100	54.02510	27.6629	0.7234	127.66
101	52.99624	27.1902	0.7281	128.19
102	51.95810	26.7235	0.7328	128.72
103	50.91125	26.2627	0.7374	129.26
104	49.85632	25.8078	0.7419	129.81
105	48.79396	25.3588	0.7464	130.36
106	47.72486	24.9157	0.7508	130.92
107	46.64974	24.4784	0.7552	131.48
108	45.56937	24.0469	0.7595	132.05
109	44.48452	23.6211	0.7638	132.62
110	43.39604	23.2011	0.7680	133.20
111	42.30477	22.7867	0.7721	133.79
112	41.21160	22.3778	0.7762	134.38
113	40.11743	21.9745	0.7803	134.97
114	39.02321	21.5767	0.7842	135.58
115	37.92987	21.1842	0.7882	136.18
116	36.83841	20.7971	0.7920	136.80
117	35.74981	20.4151	0.7958	137.42
118	34.66508	20.0383	0.7996	138.04
119	33.58525	19.6665	0.8033	138.67
120	32.51131	19.2996	0.8070	139.30
121	31.44431	18.9375	0.8106	139.94
122	30.38528	18.5801	0.8142	140.58
123	29.33517	18.2274	0.8177	141.23
124	28.29510	17.8790	0.8212	141.88
125	27.26603	17.5349	0.8247	142.53
126	26.24893	17.1950	0.8281	143.19
127	25.24478	16.8590	0.8314	143.86
128	24.25449	16.5270	0.8347	144.53
129	23.27898	16.1986	0.8380	145.20
130	22.31913	15.8737	0.8413	145.87
131	21.37516	15.5526	0.8445	146.55
132	20.44967	15.2339	0.8477	147.23
133	19.54162	14.9185	0.8508	147.92
134	18.65230	14.6060	0.8539	148.61
135	17.78236	14.2961	0.8570	149.30
136	16.93241	13.9886	0.8601	149.99
137	16.10298	13.6833	0.8632	150.68
138	15.29456	13.3802	0.8662	151.38
139	14.50757	13.0789	0.8692	152.08
140	13.74239	12.7793	0.8722	152.78
141	12.99932	12.4812	0.8752	153.48
142	12.27861	12.1844	0.8782	154.18
143	11.58045	11.8889	0.8811	154.89
144	10.90498	11.5943	0.8841	155.59
145	10.25227	11.3006	0.8870	156.30
146	9.62235	11.0077	0.8899	157.01
147	9.01519	10.7154	0.8928	157.72
148	8.43072	10.4235	0.8958	158.42
149	7.86883	10.1322	0.8987	159.13
150	7.32937	9.8411	0.9016	159.84
151	6.81214	9.5504	0.9045	160.55
152	6.31692	9.2599	0.9074	161.26
153	5.84347	8.9696	0.9103	161.97
154	5.39151	8.6796	0.9132	162.68
155	4.96076	8.3899	0.9161	163.39
156	4.55091	8.1004	0.9190	164.10
157	4.16166	7.8113	0.9219	164.81
158	3.79266	7.5226	0.9248	165.52
159	3.44361	7.2345	0.9277	166.23
160	3.11416	6.9469	0.9305	166.95
161	2.80398	6.6601	0.9334	167.66
162	2.51274	6.3740	0.9363	168.37
163	2.24009	6.0890	0.9391	169.09
164	1.98570	5.8050	0.9419	169.81
165	1.74922	5.5222	0.9448	170.52
166	1.53029	5.2407	0.9476	171.24
167	1.32853	4.9607	0.9504	171.96
168	1.14356	4.6822	0.9532	172.68
169	0.97498	4.4053	0.9559	173.41
170	0.82235	4.1301	0.9587	174.13
171	0.68519	3.8568	0.9614	174.86
172	0.56299	3.5854	0.9641	175.59
173	0.45521	3.3159	0.9668	176.32
174	0.36123	3.0485	0.9695	177.05
175	0.28040	2.7832	0.9722	177.78
176	0.21198	2.5201	0.9748	178.52
177	0.15520	2.2592	0.9774	179.26
178	0.10918	2.0007	0.9800	180.00
179	0.07298	1.7451	0.9825	180.75
180	0.04561	1.4923	0.9851	181.49
181	0.02596	1.2435	0.9876	182.24
182	0.01287	0.9996	0.9900	183.00
183	0.00508	0.7657	0.9923	183.77
184	0.00128	0.5547	0.9945	184.55
185	0.00007	0.5003	0.9950	185.50
186	0.00000	0.0000	1.0000	186.00

Iowa Type curve R3

Age %AL	Percent Surviving	Remaining Life	CAD Ratio	Prob. Life
0	100.00000	100.0000	0.0000	100.00
1	99.98452	99.0154	0.0098	100.02
2	99.96768	98.0320	0.0197	100.03
3	99.94939	97.0498	0.0295	100.05
4	99.92954	96.0690	0.0393	100.07
5	99.90802	95.0896	0.0491	100.09
6	99.88474	94.1117	0.0589	100.11
7	99.85958	93.1352	0.0686	100.14
8	99.83241	92.1605	0.0784	100.16
9	99.80311	91.1874	0.0881	100.19
10	99.77155	90.2161	0.0978	100.22
11	99.73759	89.2466	0.1075	100.25
12	99.70109	88.2791	0.1172	100.28
13	99.66191	87.3136	0.1269	100.31
14	99.61990	86.3502	0.1365	100.35
15	99.57488	85.3890	0.1461	100.39
16	99.52671	84.4301	0.1557	100.43
17	99.47520	83.4736	0.1653	100.47
18	99.42019	82.5195	0.1748	100.52
19	99.36149	81.5679	0.1843	100.57
20	99.29891	80.6190	0.1938	100.62
21	99.23227	79.6728	0.2033	100.67
22	99.16136	78.7294	0.2127	100.73
23	99.08598	77.7890	0.2221	100.79
24	99.00592	76.8515	0.2315	100.85
25	98.92096	75.9170	0.2408	100.92
26	98.83088	74.9858	0.2501	100.99
27	98.73545	74.0578	0.2594	101.06
28	98.63445	73.1331	0.2687	101.13
29	98.52763	72.2118	0.2779	101.21
30	98.41475	71.2941	0.2871	101.29
31	98.29557	70.3799	0.2962	101.38
32	98.16982	69.4694	0.3053	101.47
33	98.03725	68.5627	0.3144	101.56
34	97.89760	67.6598	0.3234	101.66
35	97.75059	66.7608	0.3324	101.76
36	97.59596	65.8658	0.3413	101.87
37	97.43343	64.9748	0.3503	101.97
38	97.26271	64.0880	0.3591	102.09
39	97.08351	63.2054	0.3679	102.21
40	96.89555	62.3270	0.3767	102.33
41	96.69853	61.4530	0.3855	102.45
42	96.49214	60.5833	0.3942	102.58
43	96.27608	59.7182	0.4028	102.72
44	96.05003	58.8575	0.4114	102.86
45	95.81369	58.0015	0.4200	103.00
46	95.56673	57.1501	0.4285	103.15
47	95.30882	56.3034	0.4370	103.30
48	95.03964	55.4614	0.4454	103.46
49	94.75883	54.6243	0.4538	103.62
50	94.46607	53.7920	0.4621	103.79
51	94.16099	52.9647	0.4704	103.96
52	93.84325	52.1423	0.4786	104.14
53	93.51246	51.3250	0.4867	104.33
54	93.16827	50.5128	0.4949	104.51
55	92.81029	49.7057	0.5029	104.71
56	92.43813	48.9038	0.5110	104.90
57	92.05139	48.1072	0.5189	105.11
58	91.64965	47.3158	0.5268	105.32
59	91.23249	46.5299	0.5347	105.53
60	90.79948	45.7494	0.5425	105.75
61	90.35018	44.9744	0.5503	105.97
62	89.88412	44.2050	0.5579	106.21
63	89.40083	43.4413	0.5656	106.44
64	88.89983	42.6833	0.5732	106.68
65	88.38061	41.9311	0.5807	106.93
66	87.84267	41.1848	0.5882	107.18
67	87.28547	40.4446	0.5956	107.44
68	86.70847	39.7104	0.6029	107.71
69	86.11111	38.9824	0.6102	107.98
70	85.49283	38.2607	0.6174	108.26
71	84.85304	37.5454	0.6245	108.55
72	84.19116	36.8366	0.6316	108.84
73	83.50659	36.1345	0.6387	109.13
74	82.79872	35.4392	0.6456	109.44
75	82.06693	34.7507	0.6525	109.75
76	81.31063	34.0693	0.6593	110.07
77	80.52919	33.3950	0.6660	110.40
78	79.72202	32.7281	0.6727	110.73
79	78.88853	32.0686	0.6793	111.07
80	78.02814	31.4167	0.6858	111.42
81	77.14030	30.7725	0.6923	111.77
82	76.22450	30.1362	0.6986	112.14
83	75.28024	29.5080	0.7049	112.51
84	74.30707	28.8879	0.7111	112.89
85	73.30461	28.2761	0.7172	113.28
86	72.27252	27.6727	0.7233	113.67
87	71.21053	27.0780	0.7292	114.08
88	70.11845	26.4919	0.7351	114.49
89	68.99618	25.9147	0.7409	114.91
90	67.84370	25.3464	0.7465	115.35
91	66.66112	24.7872	0.7521	115.79
92	65.44864	24.2371	0.7576	116.24
93	64.20660	23.6963	0.7630	116.70
94	62.93546	23.1648	0.7684	117.16
95	61.63582	22.6427	0.7736	117.64
96	60.30844	22.1301	0.7787	118.13
97	58.95423	21.6270	0.7837	118.63
98	57.57425	21.1333	0.7887	119.13
99	56.16973	20.6493	0.7935	119.65

Table C continued

Iowa Type curve R3					Iowa Type curve R4			
Age %AL	Percent Surviving	Remaining Life	CAD Ratio	Prob. Life	Age %AL	Percent Surviving	Remaining Life	CAD Ratio	Prob. Life
100	54.74208	20.1748	0.7983	120.17	0	100.00000	100.0000	0.0000	100.00
101	53.29286	19.7098	0.8029	120.71	1	99.99917	99.0013	0.0100	100.00
102	51.82380	19.2543	0.8075	121.25	2	99.99821	98.0023	0.0200	100.00
103	50.33681	18.8084	0.8119	121.81	3	99.99710	97.0033	0.0300	100.00
104	48.83395	18.3718	0.8163	122.37	4	99.99581	96.0046	0.0400	100.00
105	47.31746	17.9446	0.8206	122.94	5	99.99432	95.0060	0.0499	100.01
106	45.78970	17.5266	0.8247	123.53	6	99.99261	94.0076	0.0599	100.01
107	44.25318	17.1178	0.8288	124.12	7	99.99064	93.0095	0.0699	100.01
108	42.71054	16.7180	0.8328	124.72	8	99.98839	92.0116	0.0799	100.01
109	41.16453	16.3271	0.8367	125.33	9	99.98581	91.0139	0.0899	100.01
110	39.61801	15.9449	0.8406	125.94	10	99.98287	90.0166	0.0998	100.02
111	38.07390	15.5713	0.8443	126.57	11	99.97952	89.0196	0.1098	100.02
112	36.53519	15.2060	0.8479	127.21	12	99.97570	88.0230	0.1198	100.02
113	35.00491	14.8489	0.8515	127.85	13	99.97137	87.0267	0.1297	100.03
114	33.48610	14.4997	0.8550	128.50	14	99.96646	86.0310	0.1397	100.03
115	31.98179	14.1582	0.8584	129.16	15	99.96090	85.0358	0.1496	100.04
116	30.49498	13.8242	0.8618	129.82	16	99.95463	84.0411	0.1596	100.04
117	29.02861	13.4972	0.8650	130.50	17	99.94755	83.0470	0.1695	100.05
118	27.58555	13.1771	0.8682	131.18	18	99.93959	82.0536	0.1795	100.05
119	26.16856	12.8636	0.8714	131.86	19	99.93064	81.0609	0.1894	100.06
120	24.78027	12.5562	0.8744	132.56	20	99.92061	80.0689	0.1993	100.07
121	23.42315	12.2548	0.8775	133.25	21	99.90936	79.0779	0.2092	100.08
122	22.09951	11.9588	0.8804	133.96	22	99.89679	78.0878	0.2191	100.09
123	20.81147	11.6680	0.8833	134.67	23	99.88275	77.0987	0.2290	100.10
124	19.56094	11.3820	0.8862	135.38	24	99.86710	76.1107	0.2389	100.11
125	18.34962	11.1003	0.8890	136.10	25	99.84968	75.1239	0.2488	100.12
126	17.17897	10.8227	0.8918	136.82	26	99.83032	74.1384	0.2586	100.14
127	16.05021	10.5486	0.8945	137.55	27	99.80883	73.1542	0.2685	100.15
128	14.96433	10.2778	0.8972	138.28	28	99.78501	72.1716	0.2783	100.17
129	13.92208	10.0098	0.8999	139.01	29	99.75865	71.1905	0.2881	100.19
130	12.92397	9.7443	0.9026	139.74	30	99.72953	70.2111	0.2979	100.21
131	11.97027	9.4808	0.9052	140.48	31	99.69738	69.2336	0.3077	100.23
132	11.06104	9.2190	0.9078	141.22	32	99.66196	68.2580	0.3174	100.26
133	10.19612	8.9586	0.9104	141.96	33	99.62298	67.2846	0.3272	100.28
134	9.37516	8.6993	0.9130	142.70	34	99.58013	66.3133	0.3369	100.31
135	8.59763	8.4408	0.9156	143.44	35	99.53311	65.3444	0.3466	100.34
136	7.86284	8.1829	0.9182	144.18	36	99.48157	64.3780	0.3562	100.38
137	7.16997	7.9253	0.9207	144.93	37	99.42514	63.4142	0.3659	100.41
138	6.51807	7.6680	0.9233	145.67	38	99.36345	62.4533	0.3755	100.45
139	5.90611	7.4107	0.9259	146.41	39	99.29610	61.4953	0.3850	100.50
140	5.33296	7.1534	0.9285	147.15	40	99.22264	60.5405	0.3946	100.54
141	4.79745	6.8961	0.9310	147.90	41	99.14264	59.5889	0.4041	100.59
142	4.29836	6.6388	0.9336	148.64	42	99.05561	58.6408	0.4136	100.64
143	3.83446	6.3814	0.9362	149.38	43	98.96106	57.6964	0.4230	100.70
144	3.40449	6.1242	0.9388	150.12	44	98.85847	56.7557	0.4324	100.76
145	3.00720	5.8673	0.9413	150.87	45	98.74727	55.8191	0.4418	100.82
146	2.64136	5.6107	0.9439	151.61	46	98.62690	54.8866	0.4511	100.89
147	2.30572	5.3546	0.9465	152.35	47	98.49675	53.9585	0.4604	100.96
148	1.99908	5.0993	0.9490	153.10	48	98.35620	53.0349	0.4697	101.03
149	1.72022	4.8448	0.9516	153.84	49	98.20459	52.1160	0.4788	101.12
150	1.46794	4.5915	0.9541	154.59	50	98.04125	51.2020	0.4880	101.20
151	1.24106	4.3395	0.9566	155.34	51	97.86547	50.2930	0.4971	101.29
152	1.03836	4.0890	0.9591	156.09	52	97.67652	49.3894	0.5061	101.39
153	0.85865	3.8402	0.9616	156.84	53	97.47365	48.4911	0.5151	101.49
154	0.70069	3.5932	0.9641	157.59	54	97.25609	47.5985	0.5240	101.60
155	0.56322	3.3481	0.9665	158.35	55	97.02304	46.7116	0.5329	101.71
156	0.44495	3.1052	0.9689	159.11	56	96.77368	45.8307	0.5417	101.83
157	0.34453	2.8645	0.9714	159.86	57	96.50717	44.9559	0.5504	101.96
158	0.26059	2.6262	0.9737	160.63	58	96.22265	44.0873	0.5591	102.09
159	0.19170	2.3902	0.9761	161.39	59	95.91925	43.2252	0.5677	102.23
160	0.13638	2.1570	0.9784	162.16	60	95.59608	42.3696	0.5763	102.37
161	0.09313	1.9265	0.9807	162.93	61	95.25224	41.5207	0.5848	102.52
162	0.06042	1.6988	0.9830	163.70	62	94.88682	40.6787	0.5932	102.68
163	0.03668	1.4746	0.9853	164.47	63	94.49889	39.8437	0.6016	102.84
164	0.02038	1.2542	0.9875	165.25	64	94.08753	39.0157	0.6098	103.02
165	0.00998	1.0401	0.9096	166.04	65	93.65182	38.1949	0.6181	103.19
166	0.00404	0.8341	0.9917	166.83	66	93.19084	37.3813	0.6262	103.38
167	0.00118	0.6440	0.9936	167.64	67	92.70366	36.5752	0.6342	103.58
168	0.00017	0.4996	0.9950	168.50	68	92.18937	35.7764	0.6422	103.78
169	0.00000	0.0000	1.0000	169.00	69	91.64709	34.9851	0.6501	103.99
					70	91.07592	34.2014	0.6580	104.20
					71	90.47502	33.4252	0.6657	104.43
					72	89.84356	32.6566	0.6734	104.66
					73	89.18073	31.8957	0.6810	104.90
					74	88.48579	31.1422	0.6886	105.14
					75	87.75801	30.3963	0.6960	105.40
					76	86.99674	29.6579	0.7034	105.66
					77	86.20134	28.9270	0.7107	105.93
					78	85.37129	28.2034	0.7180	106.20
					79	84.50608	27.4870	0.7251	106.49
					80	83.60532	26.7778	0.7322	106.78
					81	82.66866	26.0755	0.7392	107.08
					82	81.69587	25.3801	0.7462	107.38
					83	80.68667	24.6912	0.7531	107.69
					84	79.64019	24.0091	0.7599	108.01
					85	78.55460	23.3340	0.7667	108.33
					86	77.42712	22.6665	0.7733	108.67
					87	76.25416	22.0075	0.7799	109.01
					88	75.03161	21.3579	0.7864	109.36
					89	73.75505	20.7189	0.7928	109.72
					90	72.42015	20.0916	0.7991	110.09
					91	71.02281	19.4771	0.8052	110.48
					92	69.55955	18.8763	0.8112	110.88
					93	68.02768	18.2901	0.8171	111.29
					94	66.42545	17.7192	0.8228	111.72
					95	64.75218	17.1642	0.8284	112.16
					96	63.00838	16.6254	0.8337	112.63
					97	61.19577	16.1030	0.8390	113.10
					98	59.31727	15.5971	0.8440	113.60
					99	57.37696	15.1076	0.8489	114.11

327

Table C continued

Iowa Type curve R4

Age %AL	Percent Surviving	Remaining Life	CAD Ratio	Prob. Life
100	55.38004	14.6344	0.8537	114.63
101	53.33268	14.1770	0.8582	115.18
102	51.24196	13.7350	0.8626	115.74
103	49.11568	13.3080	0.8669	116.31
104	46.96222	12.8953	0.8710	116.90
105	44.79042	12.4963	0.8750	117.50
106	42.60935	12.1104	0.8789	118.11
107	40.42821	11.7368	0.8826	118.74
108	38.25614	11.3747	0.8863	119.37
109	36.10212	11.0236	0.8898	120.02
110	33.97478	10.6825	0.8932	120.68
111	31.88233	10.3508	0.8965	121.35
112	29.83244	10.0277	0.8997	122.03
113	27.83215	9.7124	0.9029	122.71
114	25.88782	9.4043	0.9060	123.40
115	24.00508	9.1027	0.9090	124.10
116	22.18878	8.8069	0.9119	124.81
117	20.44302	8.5163	0.9148	125.52
118	18.77112	8.2303	0.9177	126.23
119	17.17567	7.9483	0.9205	126.95
120	15.65853	7.6700	0.9233	127.67
121	14.22090	7.3948	0.9261	128.39
122	12.86339	7.1225	0.9288	129.12
123	11.58601	6.8526	0.9315	129.85
124	10.38833	6.5850	0.9341	130.59
125	9.26945	6.3195	0.9368	131.32
126	8.22813	6.0560	0.9394	132.06
127	7.26282	5.7945	0.9421	132.79
128	6.37174	5.5349	0.9447	133.53
129	5.55286	5.2774	0.9472	134.28
130	4.80402	5.0221	0.9498	135.02
131	4.12291	4.7691	0.9523	135.77
132	3.50709	4.5187	0.9548	136.52
133	2.95402	4.2712	0.9573	137.27
134	2.46101	4.0266	0.9597	138.03
135	2.02527	3.7854	0.9621	138.79
136	1.64387	3.5476	0.9645	139.55
137	1.31370	3.3136	0.9669	140.31
138	1.03149	3.0834	0.9692	141.08
139	0.79375	2.8572	0.9714	141.86
140	0.59682	2.6349	0.9737	142.63
141	0.43685	2.4167	0.9758	143.42
142	0.30983	2.2025	0.9780	144.20
143	0.21164	1.9924	0.9801	144.99
144	0.13815	1.7863	0.9821	145.79
145	0.08525	1.5845	0.9842	146.58
146	0.04899	1.3871	0.9861	147.39
147	0.02564	1.1950	0.9880	148.20
148	0.01181	1.0089	0.9899	149.01
149	0.00451	0.8326	0.9917	149.83
150	0.00128	0.6719	0.9933	150.67
151	0.00021	0.5480	0.9945	151.55
152	0.00001	0.5087	0.9949	152.51
153	0.00000	0.0000	1.0000	153.00

Iowa Type curve R5

Age %AL	Percent Surviving	Remaining Life	CAD Ratio	Prob. Life
0	100.00000	100.0000	0.0000	100.00
1	100.00000	98.9993	0.0100	100.00
2	100.00000	97.9993	0.0200	100.00
3	100.00000	96.9993	0.0300	100.00
4	100.00000	95.9993	0.0400	100.00
5	100.00000	94.9993	0.0500	100.00
6	100.00000	93.9993	0.0600	100.00
7	100.00000	92.9993	0.0700	100.00
8	100.00000	91.9993	0.0800	100.00
9	100.00000	90.9993	0.0900	100.00
10	100.00000	89.9993	0.1000	100.00
11	100.00000	88.9993	0.1100	100.00
12	100.00000	87.9993	0.1200	100.00
13	100.00000	86.9993	0.1300	100.00
14	100.00000	85.9993	0.1400	100.00
15	100.00000	84.9993	0.1500	100.00
16	100.00000	83.9993	0.1600	100.00
17	100.00000	82.9993	0.1700	100.00
18	100.00000	81.9993	0.1800	100.00
19	100.00000	80.9993	0.1900	100.00
20	100.00000	79.9993	0.2000	100.00
21	100.00000	78.9993	0.2100	100.00
22	100.00000	77.9993	0.2200	100.00
23	100.00000	76.9993	0.2300	100.00
24	100.00000	75.9993	0.2400	100.00
25	100.00000	74.9993	0.2500	100.00
26	100.00000	73.9993	0.2600	100.00
27	100.00000	72.9993	0.2700	100.00
28	100.00000	71.9993	0.2800	100.00
29	100.00000	70.9993	0.2900	100.00
30	100.00000	69.9993	0.3000	100.00
31	100.00000	68.9993	0.3100	100.00
32	100.00000	67.9993	0.3200	100.00
33	100.00000	66.9993	0.3300	100.00
34	100.00000	65.9993	0.3400	100.00
35	99.99998	64.9993	0.3500	100.00
36	99.99995	63.9993	0.3600	100.00
37	99.99989	62.9993	0.3700	100.00
38	99.99977	61.9994	0.3800	100.00
39	99.99954	60.9996	0.3900	100.00
40	99.99916	59.9998	0.4000	100.00
41	99.99854	59.0002	0.4100	100.00
42	99.99758	58.0007	0.4200	100.00
43	99.99612	57.0016	0.4300	100.00
44	99.99401	56.0027	0.4400	100.00
45	99.99100	55.0044	0.4500	100.00
46	99.98684	54.0067	0.4599	100.01
47	99.98120	53.0097	0.4699	100.01
48	99.97368	52.0137	0.4799	100.01
49	99.96384	51.0187	0.4898	100.02
50	99.95114	50.0251	0.4997	100.03
51	99.93499	49.0331	0.5097	100.03
52	99.91470	48.0430	0.5196	100.04
53	99.88951	47.0550	0.5295	100.05
54	99.85855	46.0694	0.5393	100.07
55	99.82089	45.0866	0.5491	100.09
56	99.77549	44.1069	0.5589	100.11
57	99.72121	43.1306	0.5687	100.13
58	99.65684	42.1582	0.5784	100.16
59	99.58107	41.1899	0.5881	100.19
60	99.49249	40.2261	0.5977	100.23
61	99.38962	39.2672	0.6073	100.27
62	99.27089	38.3136	0.6169	100.31
63	99.13466	37.3655	0.6263	100.37
64	98.97921	36.4234	0.6358	100.42
65	98.80275	35.4876	0.6451	100.49
66	98.60337	34.5584	0.6544	100.56
67	98.37911	33.6360	0.6636	100.64
68	98.12785	32.7208	0.6728	100.72
69	97.84733	31.8132	0.6819	100.81
70	97.53512	30.9134	0.6909	100.91
71	97.18856	30.0219	0.6998	101.02
72	96.80476	29.1389	0.7086	101.14
73	96.38056	28.2650	0.7174	101.26
74	95.91248	27.4005	0.7260	101.40
75	95.39673	26.5459	0.7345	101.55
76	94.82918	25.7018	0.7430	101.70
77	94.20535	24.8687	0.7513	101.87
78	93.52043	24.0472	0.7595	102.05
79	92.76930	23.2378	0.7676	102.24
80	91.94656	22.4413	0.7756	102.44
81	91.04658	21.6582	0.7834	102.66
82	90.06358	20.8891	0.7911	102.89
83	88.99168	20.1347	0.7987	103.13
84	87.82505	19.3955	0.8060	103.40
85	86.55794	18.6721	0.8133	103.67
86	85.18490	17.9650	0.8203	103.97
87	83.70084	17.2747	0.8273	104.27
88	82.10122	16.6015	0.8340	104.60
89	80.38218	15.9458	0.8405	104.95
90	78.54068	15.3080	0.8469	105.31
91	76.57472	14.6882	0.8531	105.69
92	74.48341	14.0865	0.8591	106.09
93	72.26719	13.5032	0.8650	106.50
94	69.92791	12.9382	0.8706	106.94
95	67.46899	12.3915	0.8761	107.39
96	64.89548	11.8631	0.8814	107.86
97	62.21420	11.3528	0.8865	108.35
98	59.43371	10.8605	0.8914	108.86
99	56.56439	10.3861	0.8961	109.39

Table C continued

Age %AL	Percent Surviving	Remaining Life	CAD Ratio	Prob. Life
100	53.61839	9.9293	0.9007	109.93
101	50.60957	9.4898	0.9051	110.49
102	47.55343	9.0676	0.9093	111.07
103	44.46694	8.6623	0.9134	111.66
104	41.36834	8.2737	0.9173	112.27
105	38.27696	7.9015	0.9210	112.90
106	35.21285	7.5455	0.9245	113.55
107	32.19655	7.2056	0.9279	114.21
108	29.24865	6.8814	0.9312	114.88
109	26.38945	6.5728	0.9343	115.57
110	23.63847	6.2796	0.9372	116.28
111	21.01406	6.0014	0.9400	117.00
112	18.53286	5.7379	0.9426	117.74
113	16.20943	5.4887	0.9451	118.49
114	14.05572	5.2531	0.9475	119.25
115	12.08071	5.0302	0.9497	120.03
116	10.29003	4.8185	0.9518	120.82
117	8.68570	4.6162	0.9538	121.62
118	7.26591	4.4205	0.9558	122.42
119	6.02505	4.2280	0.9577	123.23
120	4.95374	4.0342	0.9597	124.03
121	4.03925	3.8343	0.9617	124.83
122	3.26602	3.6237	0.9638	125.62
123	2.61654	3.3991	0.9660	126.40
124	2.07253	3.1600	0.9684	127.16
125	1.61653	2.9104	0.9709	127.91
126	1.23390	2.6579	0.9734	128.66
127	0.91519	2.4093	0.9759	129.41
128	0.65554	2.1656	0.9783	130.17
129	0.44994	1.9267	0.9807	130.93
130	0.29276	1.6926	0.9831	131.69
131	0.17779	1.4638	0.9854	132.46
132	0.09844	1.2408	0.9876	133.24
133	0.04783	1.0246	0.9898	134.02
134	0.01903	0.8184	0.9918	134.82
135	0.00536	0.6306	0.9937	135.63
136	0.00070	0.5001	0.9950	136.50
137	0.00000	0.0000	1.0000	137.00

329

Table D

		Iowa Type curve 01					Iowa Type curve 01		
Age %AL	Percent Surviving	Remaining Life	CAD Ratio	Prob. Life	Age %AL	Percent Surviving	Remaining Life	CAD Ratio	Prob. Life
0	100.00000	100.0000	0.0000	100.00	100	50.00000	50.0000	0.5000	150.00
1	99.50000	99.5000	0.0050	100.50	101	49.50000	49.5000	0.5050	150.50
2	99.00000	99.0000	0.0100	101.00	102	49.00000	49.0000	0.5100	151.00
3	98.50000	98.5000	0.0150	101.50	103	48.50000	48.5000	0.5150	151.50
4	98.00000	98.0000	0.0200	102.00	104	48.00000	48.0000	0.5200	152.00
5	97.50000	97.5000	0.0250	102.50	105	47.50000	47.5000	0.5250	152.50
6	97.00000	97.0000	0.0300	103.00	106	47.00000	47.0000	0.5300	153.00
7	96.50000	96.5000	0.0350	103.50	107	46.50000	46.5000	0.5350	153.50
8	96.00000	96.0000	0.0400	104.00	108	46.00000	46.0000	0.5400	154.00
9	95.50000	95.5000	0.0450	104.50	109	45.50000	45.5000	0.5450	154.50
10	95.00000	95.0000	0.0500	105.00	110	45.00000	45.0000	0.5500	155.00
11	94.50000	94.5000	0.0550	105.50	111	44.50000	44.5000	0.5550	155.50
12	94.00000	94.0000	0.0600	106.00	112	44.00000	44.0000	0.5600	156.00
13	93.50000	93.5000	0.0650	106.50	113	43.50000	43.5000	0.5650	156.50
14	93.00000	93.0000	0.0700	107.00	114	43.00000	43.0000	0.5700	157.00
15	92.50000	92.5000	0.0750	107.50	115	42.50000	42.5000	0.5750	157.50
16	92.00000	92.0000	0.0800	108.00	116	42.00000	42.0000	0.5800	158.00
17	91.50000	91.5000	0.0850	108.50	117	41.50000	41.5000	0.5850	158.50
18	91.00000	91.0000	0.0900	109.00	118	41.00000	41.0000	0.5900	159.00
19	90.50000	90.5000	0.0950	109.50	119	40.50000	40.5000	0.5950	159.50
20	90.00000	90.0000	0.1000	110.00	120	40.00000	40.0000	0.6000	160.00
21	89.50000	89.5000	0.1050	110.50	121	39.50000	39.5000	0.6050	160.50
22	89.00000	89.0000	0.1100	111.00	122	39.00000	39.0000	0.6100	161.00
23	88.50000	88.5000	0.1150	111.50	123	38.50000	38.5000	0.6150	161.50
24	88.00000	88.0000	0.1200	112.00	124	38.00000	38.0000	0.6200	162.00
25	87.50000	87.5000	0.1250	112.50	125	37.50000	37.5000	0.6250	162.50
26	87.00000	87.0000	0.1300	113.00	126	37.00000	37.0000	0.6300	163.00
27	86.50000	86.5000	0.1350	113.50	127	36.50000	36.5000	0.6350	163.50
28	86.00000	86.0000	0.1400	114.00	128	36.00000	36.0000	0.6400	164.00
29	85.50000	85.5000	0.1450	114.50	129	35.50000	35.5000	0.6450	164.50
30	85.00000	85.0000	0.1500	115.00	130	35.00000	35.0000	0.6500	165.00
31	84.50000	84.5000	0.1550	115.50	131	34.50000	34.5000	0.6550	165.50
32	84.00000	84.0000	0.1600	116.00	132	34.00000	34.0000	0.6600	166.00
33	83.50000	83.5000	0.1650	116.50	133	33.50000	33.5000	0.6650	166.50
34	83.00000	83.0000	0.1700	117.00	134	33.00000	33.0000	0.6700	167.00
35	82.50000	82.5000	0.1750	117.50	135	32.50000	32.5000	0.6750	167.50
36	82.00000	82.0000	0.1800	118.00	136	32.00000	32.0000	0.6800	168.00
37	81.50000	81.5000	0.1850	118.50	137	31.50000	31.5000	0.6850	168.50
38	81.00000	81.0000	0.1900	119.00	138	31.00000	31.0000	0.6900	169.00
39	80.50000	80.5000	0.1950	119.50	139	30.50000	30.5000	0.6950	169.50
40	80.00000	80.0000	0.2000	120.00	140	30.00000	30.0000	0.7000	170.00
41	79.50000	79.5000	0.2050	120.50	141	29.50000	29.5000	0.7050	170.50
42	79.00000	79.0000	0.2100	121.00	142	29.00000	29.0000	0.7100	171.00
43	78.50000	78.5000	0.2150	121.50	143	28.50000	28.5000	0.7150	171.50
44	78.00000	78.0000	0.2200	122.00	144	28.00000	28.0000	0.7200	172.00
45	77.50000	77.5000	0.2250	122.50	145	27.50000	27.5000	0.7250	172.50
46	77.00000	77.0000	0.2300	123.00	146	27.00000	27.0000	0.7300	173.00
47	76.50000	76.5000	0.2350	123.50	147	26.50000	26.5000	0.7350	173.50
48	76.00000	76.0000	0.2400	124.00	148	26.00000	26.0000	0.7400	174.00
49	75.50000	75.5000	0.2450	124.50	149	25.50000	25.5000	0.7450	174.50
50	75.00000	75.0000	0.2500	125.00	150	25.00000	25.0000	0.7500	175.00
51	74.50000	74.5000	0.2550	125.50	151	24.50000	24.5000	0.7550	175.50
52	74.00000	74.0000	0.2600	126.00	152	24.00000	24.0000	0.7600	176.00
53	73.50000	73.5000	0.2650	126.50	153	23.50000	23.5000	0.7650	176.50
54	73.00000	73.0000	0.2700	127.00	154	23.00000	23.0000	0.7700	177.00
55	72.50000	72.5000	0.2750	127.50	155	22.50000	22.5000	0.7750	177.50
56	72.00000	72.0000	0.2800	128.00	156	22.00000	22.0000	0.7800	178.00
57	71.50000	71.5000	0.2850	128.50	157	21.50000	21.5000	0.7850	178.50
58	71.00000	71.0000	0.2900	129.00	158	21.00000	21.0000	0.7900	179.00
59	70.50000	70.5000	0.2950	129.50	159	20.50000	20.5000	0.7950	179.50
60	70.00000	70.0000	0.3000	130.00	160	20.00000	20.0000	0.8000	180.00
61	69.50000	69.5000	0.3050	130.50	161	19.50000	19.5000	0.8050	180.50
62	69.00000	69.0000	0.3100	131.00	162	19.00000	19.0000	0.8100	181.00
63	68.50000	68.5000	0.3150	131.50	163	18.50000	18.5000	0.8150	181.50
64	68.00000	68.0000	0.3200	132.00	164	18.00000	18.0000	0.8200	182.00
65	67.50000	67.5000	0.3250	132.50	165	17.50000	17.5000	0.8250	182.50
66	67.00000	67.0000	0.3300	133.00	166	17.00000	17.0000	0.8300	183.00
67	66.50000	66.5000	0.3350	133.50	167	16.50000	16.5000	0.8350	183.50
68	66.00000	66.0000	0.3400	134.00	168	16.00000	16.0000	0.8400	184.00
69	65.50000	65.5000	0.3450	134.50	169	15.50000	15.5000	0.8450	184.50
70	65.00000	65.0000	0.3500	135.00	170	15.00000	15.0000	0.8500	185.00
71	64.50000	64.5000	0.3550	135.50	171	14.50000	14.5000	0.8550	185.50
72	64.00000	64.0000	0.3600	136.00	172	14.00000	14.0000	0.8600	186.00
73	63.50000	63.5000	0.3650	136.50	173	13.50000	13.5000	0.8650	186.50
74	63.00000	63.0000	0.3700	137.00	174	13.00000	13.0000	0.8700	187.00
75	62.50000	62.5000	0.3750	137.50	175	12.50000	12.5000	0.8750	187.50
76	62.00000	62.0000	0.3800	138.00	176	12.00000	12.0000	0.8800	188.00
77	61.50000	61.5000	0.3850	138.50	177	11.50000	11.5000	0.8850	188.50
78	61.00000	61.0000	0.3900	139.00	178	11.00000	11.0000	0.8900	189.00
79	60.50000	60.5000	0.3950	139.50	179	10.50000	10.5000	0.8950	189.50
80	60.00000	60.0000	0.4000	140.00	180	10.00000	10.0000	0.9000	190.00
81	59.50000	59.5000	0.4050	140.50	181	9.50000	9.5000	0.9050	190.50
82	59.00000	59.0000	0.4100	141.00	182	9.00000	9.0000	0.9100	191.00
83	58.50000	58.5000	0.4150	141.50	183	8.50000	8.5000	0.9150	191.50
84	58.00000	58.0000	0.4200	142.00	184	8.00000	8.0000	0.9200	192.00
85	57.50000	57.5000	0.4250	142.50	185	7.50000	7.5000	0.9250	192.50
86	57.00000	57.0000	0.4300	143.00	186	7.00000	7.0000	0.9300	193.00
87	56.50000	56.5000	0.4350	143.50	187	6.50000	6.5000	0.9350	193.50
88	56.00000	56.0000	0.4400	144.00	188	6.00000	6.0000	0.9400	194.00
89	55.50000	55.5000	0.4450	144.50	189	5.50000	5.5000	0.9450	194.50
90	55.00000	55.0000	0.4500	145.00	190	5.00000	5.0000	0.9500	195.00
91	54.50000	54.5000	0.4550	145.50	191	4.50000	4.5000	0.9550	195.50
92	54.00000	54.0000	0.4600	146.00	192	4.00000	4.0000	0.9600	196.00
93	53.50000	53.5000	0.4650	146.50	193	3.50000	3.5000	0.9650	196.50
94	53.00000	53.0000	0.4700	147.00	194	3.00000	3.0000	0.9700	197.00
95	52.50000	52.5000	0.4750	147.50	195	2.50000	2.5000	0.9750	197.50
96	52.00000	52.0000	0.4800	148.00	196	2.00000	2.0000	0.9800	198.00
97	51.50000	51.5000	0.4850	148.50	197	1.50000	1.5000	0.9850	198.50
98	51.00000	51.0000	0.4900	149.00	198	1.00000	1.0000	0.9900	199.00
99	50.50000	50.5000	0.4950	149.50	199	0.50000	0.5000	0.9950	199.50

Table D continued

Iowa Type curve 01					Iowa Type curve 02			
Age %AL	Percent Surviving	Remaining Life	CAD Ratio	Prob. Life	Age %AL	Percent Surviving	Remaining Life	CAD Ratio	Prob. Life
200	0.00000	0.0000	1.0000	200.00	0	100.00000	100.0000	0.0000	100.00
					1	99.43868	99.1126	0.0089	100.11
					2	98.87721	98.6726	0.0133	100.67
					3	98.31559	98.2334	0.0177	101.23
					4	97.75384	97.7950	0.0220	101.80
					5	97.19199	97.3575	0.0264	102.36
					6	96.63003	96.9208	0.0308	102.92
					7	96.06800	96.4849	0.0352	103.48
					8	95.50589	96.0498	0.0395	104.05
					9	94.94372	95.6155	0.0438	104.62
					10	94.38150	95.1821	0.0482	105.18
					11	93.81923	94.7496	0.0525	105.75
					12	93.25692	94.3179	0.0568	106.32
					13	92.69459	93.8870	0.0611	106.89
					14	92.13222	93.4570	0.0654	107.46
					15	91.56984	93.0279	0.0697	108.03
					16	91.00744	92.5997	0.0740	108.60
					17	90.44502	92.1725	0.0783	109.17
					18	89.88259	91.7461	0.0825	109.75
					19	89.32016	91.3206	0.0868	110.32
					20	88.75771	90.8962	0.0910	110.90
					21	88.19526	90.4727	0.0953	111.47
					22	87.63280	90.0501	0.0995	112.05
					23	87.07034	89.6286	0.1037	112.63
					24	86.50788	89.2081	0.1079	113.21
					25	85.94542	88.7886	0.1121	113.79
					26	85.38295	88.3703	0.1163	114.37
					27	84.82048	87.9530	0.1205	114.95
					28	84.25802	87.5367	0.1246	115.54
					29	83.69555	87.1217	0.1288	116.12
					30	83.13308	86.7077	0.1329	116.71
					31	82.57061	86.2950	0.1371	117.29
					32	82.00815	85.8834	0.1412	117.88
					33	81.44568	85.4731	0.1453	118.47
					34	80.88321	85.0640	0.1494	119.06
					35	80.32074	84.6562	0.1534	119.66
					36	79.75827	84.2497	0.1575	120.25
					37	79.19580	83.8445	0.1616	120.84
					38	78.63334	83.4406	0.1656	121.44
					39	78.07087	83.0382	0.1696	122.04
					40	77.50840	82.6372	0.1736	122.64
					41	76.94593	82.2376	0.1776	123.24
					42	76.38346	81.8395	0.1816	123.84
					43	75.82099	81.4429	0.1856	124.44
					44	75.25852	81.0478	0.1895	125.05
					45	74.69606	80.6544	0.1935	125.65
					46	74.13359	80.2625	0.1974	126.26
					47	73.57112	79.8723	0.2013	126.87
					48	73.00865	79.4838	0.2052	127.48
					49	72.44618	79.0970	0.2090	128.10
					50	71.88371	78.7120	0.2129	128.71
					51	71.32125	78.3288	0.2167	129.33
					52	70.75878	77.9475	0.2205	129.95
					53	70.19631	77.5681	0.2243	130.57
					54	69.63385	77.1906	0.2281	131.19
					55	69.07138	76.8151	0.2318	131.82
					56	68.50892	76.4417	0.2356	132.44
					57	67.94645	76.0703	0.2393	133.07
					58	67.38399	75.7011	0.2430	133.70
					59	66.82154	75.3341	0.2467	134.33
					60	66.25909	74.9693	0.2503	134.97
					61	65.69664	74.6069	0.2539	135.61
					62	65.13420	74.2468	0.2575	136.25
					63	64.57177	73.8892	0.2611	136.89
					64	64.00936	73.5340	0.2647	137.53
					65	63.44696	73.1814	0.2682	138.18
					66	62.88457	72.8314	0.2717	138.83
					67	62.32221	72.4840	0.2752	139.48
					68	61.75987	72.1395	0.2786	140.14
					69	61.19757	71.7977	0.2820	140.80
					70	60.63530	71.4589	0.2854	141.46
					71	60.07308	71.1230	0.2888	142.12
					72	59.51091	70.7901	0.2921	142.79
					73	58.94880	70.4604	0.2954	143.46
					74	58.38676	70.1338	0.2987	144.13
					75	57.82481	69.8105	0.3019	144.81
					76	57.26295	69.4906	0.3051	145.49
					77	56.70121	69.1741	0.3083	146.17
					78	56.13959	68.8611	0.3114	146.86
					79	55.57812	68.5517	0.3145	147.55
					80	55.01681	68.2460	0.3175	148.25
					81	54.45568	67.9441	0.3206	148.94
					82	53.89477	67.6460	0.3235	149.65
					83	53.33410	67.3519	0.3265	150.35
					84	52.77370	67.0618	0.3294	151.06
					85	52.21359	66.7758	0.3322	151.78
					86	51.65382	66.4940	0.3351	152.49
					87	51.09442	66.2165	0.3378	153.22
					88	50.53544	65.9434	0.3406	153.94
					89	49.97692	65.6748	0.3433	154.67
					90	49.41890	65.4107	0.3459	155.41
					91	48.86144	65.1513	0.3485	156.15
					92	48.30460	64.8966	0.3510	156.90
					93	47.74843	64.6467	0.3535	157.65
					94	47.19301	64.4016	0.3560	158.40
					95	46.63840	64.1615	0.3584	159.16
					96	46.08467	63.9264	0.3607	159.93
					97	45.53191	63.6964	0.3630	160.70
					98	44.98019	63.4716	0.3653	161.47
					99	44.42961	63.2520	0.3675	162.25

Table D continued

Age %AL	Percent Surviving	Iowa Type curve 02 Remaining Life	CAD Ratio	Prob. Life	Age %AL	Percent Surviving	Iowa Type curve 02 Remaining Life	CAD Ratio	Prob. Life
100	43.88026	63.0376	0.3696	163.04	200	9.87552	47.2309	0.5277	247.23
101	43.33224	62.8285	0.3717	163.83	201	9.73330	46.9137	0.5309	247.91
102	42.78565	62.6247	0.3738	164.62	202	9.59295	46.5928	0.5341	248.59
103	42.24059	62.4264	0.3757	165.43	203	9.45444	46.2680	0.5373	249.27
104	41.69720	62.2334	0.3777	166.23	204	9.31771	45.9397	0.5406	249.94
105	41.15557	62.0458	0.3795	167.05	205	9.18273	45.6076	0.5439	250.61
106	40.61584	61.8637	0.3814	167.86	206	9.04944	45.2720	0.5473	251.27
107	40.07814	61.6870	0.3831	168.69	207	8.91780	44.9329	0.5507	251.93
108	39.54259	61.5156	0.3848	169.52	208	8.78778	44.5903	0.5541	252.59
109	39.00935	61.3497	0.3865	170.35	209	8.65934	44.2443	0.5576	253.24
110	38.47853	61.1891	0.3881	171.19	210	8.53243	43.8949	0.5611	253.89
111	37.95031	61.0339	0.3897	172.03	211	8.40702	43.5422	0.5646	254.54
112	37.42481	60.8838	0.3912	172.88	212	8.28307	43.1863	0.5681	255.19
113	36.90220	60.7390	0.3926	173.74	213	8.16055	42.8272	0.5717	255.83
114	36.38262	60.5993	0.3940	174.60	214	8.03942	42.4650	0.5754	256.46
115	35.86624	60.4645	0.3954	175.46	215	7.91964	42.0997	0.5790	257.10
116	35.35322	60.3347	0.3967	176.33	216	7.80120	41.7312	0.5827	257.73
117	34.84370	60.2097	0.3979	177.21	217	7.68404	41.3599	0.5864	258.36
118	34.33786	60.0893	0.3991	178.09	218	7.56815	40.9856	0.5901	258.99
119	33.83584	59.9734	0.4003	178.97	219	7.45348	40.6084	0.5939	259.61
120	33.33782	59.8618	0.4014	179.86	220	7.34002	40.2284	0.5977	260.23
121	32.84393	59.7545	0.4025	180.75	221	7.22774	39.8456	0.6015	260.85
122	32.35435	59.6511	0.4035	181.65	222	7.11660	39.4601	0.6054	261.46
123	31.86922	59.5515	0.4045	182.55	223	7.00657	39.0719	0.6093	262.07
124	31.38869	59.4556	0.4054	183.46	224	6.89764	38.6810	0.6132	262.68
125	30.91290	59.3630	0.4064	184.36	225	6.78978	38.2875	0.6171	263.29
126	30.44199	59.2735	0.4073	185.27	226	6.68296	37.8915	0.6211	263.89
127	29.97610	59.1870	0.4081	186.19	227	6.57716	37.4930	0.6251	264.49
128	29.51535	59.1031	0.4090	187.10	228	6.47235	37.0921	0.6291	265.09
129	29.05986	59.0217	0.4098	188.02	229	6.36851	36.6887	0.6331	265.69
130	28.60975	58.9424	0.4106	188.94	230	6.26562	36.2830	0.6372	266.28
131	28.16512	58.8650	0.4114	189.86	231	6.16365	35.8750	0.6413	266.87
132	27.72606	58.7892	0.4121	190.79	232	6.06260	35.4646	0.6454	267.46
133	27.29268	58.7148	0.4129	191.71	233	5.96242	35.0521	0.6495	268.05
134	26.86504	58.6415	0.4136	192.64	234	5.86312	34.6372	0.6536	268.64
135	26.44322	58.5689	0.4143	193.57	235	5.76466	34.2203	0.6578	269.22
136	26.02729	58.4969	0.4150	194.50	236	5.66702	33.8013	0.6620	269.80
137	25.61729	58.4252	0.4157	195.43	237	5.57019	33.3802	0.6662	270.38
138	25.21326	58.3534	0.4165	196.35	238	5.47415	32.9570	0.6704	270.96
139	24.81526	58.2813	0.4172	197.28	239	5.37889	32.5319	0.6747	271.53
140	24.42329	58.2086	0.4179	198.21	240	5.28438	32.1047	0.6790	272.10
141	24.03737	58.1351	0.4186	199.14	241	5.19061	31.6757	0.6832	272.68
142	23.65752	58.0605	0.4194	200.06	242	5.09756	31.2448	0.6876	273.24
143	23.28374	57.9845	0.4202	200.98	243	5.00521	30.8120	0.6919	273.81
144	22.91600	57.9070	0.4209	201.91	244	4.91356	30.3774	0.6962	274.38
145	22.55431	57.8276	0.4217	202.83	245	4.82259	29.9410	0.7006	274.94
146	22.19862	57.7462	0.4225	203.75	246	4.73227	29.5029	0.7050	275.50
147	21.84892	57.6624	0.4234	204.66	247	4.64260	29.0631	0.7094	276.06
148	21.50515	57.5762	0.4242	205.58	248	4.55357	28.6216	0.7138	276.62
149	21.16729	57.4872	0.4251	206.49	249	4.46516	28.1784	0.7182	277.18
150	20.83526	57.3954	0.4260	207.40	250	4.37735	27.7336	0.7227	277.73
151	20.50902	57.3004	0.4270	208.30	251	4.29014	27.2872	0.7271	278.29
152	20.18851	57.2021	0.4280	209.20	252	4.20350	26.8393	0.7316	278.84
153	19.87365	57.1005	0.4290	210.10	253	4.11744	26.3898	0.7361	279.39
154	19.56438	56.9952	0.4300	211.00	254	4.03194	25.9389	0.7406	279.94
155	19.26062	56.8862	0.4311	211.89	255	3.94697	25.4865	0.7451	280.49
156	18.96230	56.7733	0.4323	212.77	256	3.86255	25.0326	0.7497	281.03
157	18.66932	56.6564	0.4334	213.66	257	3.77865	24.5773	0.7542	281.58
158	18.38161	56.5354	0.4346	214.54	258	3.69525	24.1207	0.7588	282.12
159	18.09908	56.4101	0.4359	215.41	259	3.61236	23.6627	0.7634	282.66
160	17.82163	56.2805	0.4372	216.28	260	3.52997	23.2034	0.7680	283.20
161	17.54919	56.1465	0.4385	217.15	261	3.44805	22.7428	0.7726	283.74
162	17.28166	56.0079	0.4399	218.01	262	3.36661	22.2808	0.7772	284.28
163	17.01894	55.8648	0.4414	218.86	263	3.28563	21.8176	0.7818	284.82
164	16.76094	55.7170	0.4428	219.72	264	3.20510	21.3533	0.7865	285.35
165	16.50757	55.5645	0.4444	220.56	265	3.12501	20.8877	0.7911	285.89
166	16.25873	55.4073	0.4459	221.41	266	3.04536	20.4209	0.7958	286.42
167	16.01432	55.2453	0.4475	222.25	267	2.96614	19.9530	0.8005	286.95
168	15.77426	55.0784	0.4492	223.08	268	2.88733	19.4840	0.8052	287.48
169	15.53845	54.9067	0.4509	223.91	269	2.80894	19.0138	0.8099	288.01
170	15.30680	54.7300	0.4527	224.73	270	2.73094	18.5425	0.8146	288.54
171	15.07921	54.5485	0.4545	225.55	271	2.65334	18.0702	0.8193	289.07
172	14.85559	54.3621	0.4564	226.36	272	2.57613	17.5968	0.8240	289.60
173	14.63585	54.1708	0.4583	227.17	273	2.49929	17.1224	0.8288	290.12
174	14.41990	53.9746	0.4603	227.97	274	2.42283	16.6470	0.8335	290.65
175	14.20766	53.7734	0.4623	228.77	275	2.34673	16.1706	0.8383	291.17
176	13.99903	53.5673	0.4643	229.57	276	2.27098	15.6933	0.8431	291.69
177	13.79393	53.3564	0.4664	230.36	277	2.19559	15.2150	0.8478	292.22
178	13.59228	53.1405	0.4686	231.14	278	2.12054	14.7358	0.8526	292.74
179	13.39398	52.9199	0.4708	231.92	279	2.04583	14.2557	0.8574	293.26
180	13.19897	52.6944	0.4731	232.69	280	1.97145	13.7747	0.8623	293.77
181	13.00715	52.4641	0.4754	233.46	281	1.89739	13.2928	0.8671	294.29
182	12.81846	52.2290	0.4777	234.23	282	1.82365	12.8101	0.8719	294.81
183	12.63280	51.9893	0.4801	234.99	283	1.75023	12.3265	0.8767	295.33
184	12.45012	51.7448	0.4826	235.74	284	1.67711	11.8421	0.8816	295.84
185	12.27033	51.4956	0.4850	236.50	285	1.60429	11.3570	0.8864	296.36
186	12.09336	51.2419	0.4876	237.24	286	1.53177	10.8710	0.8913	296.87
187	11.91915	50.9835	0.4902	237.98	287	1.45953	10.3843	0.8962	297.38
188	11.74762	50.7206	0.4928	238.72	288	1.38759	9.8967	0.9010	297.90
189	11.57870	50.4533	0.4955	239.45	289	1.31592	9.4085	0.9059	298.41
190	11.41233	50.1815	0.4982	240.18	290	1.24452	8.9196	0.9108	298.92
191	11.24845	49.9053	0.5009	240.91	291	1.17340	8.4299	0.9157	299.43
192	11.08699	49.6248	0.5038	241.62	292	1.10254	7.9396	0.9206	299.94
193	10.92789	49.3401	0.5066	242.34	293	1.03194	7.4486	0.9255	300.45
194	10.77109	49.0511	0.5095	243.05	294	0.96160	6.9568	0.9304	300.96
195	10.61654	48.7578	0.5124	243.76	295	0.89151	6.4645	0.9354	301.46
196	10.46418	48.4605	0.5154	244.46	296	0.82166	5.9715	0.9403	301.97
197	10.31395	48.1590	0.5184	245.16	297	0.75205	5.4780	0.9452	302.48
198	10.16580	47.8536	0.5215	245.85	298	0.68269	4.9837	0.9502	302.98
199	10.01967	47.5442	0.5246	246.54	299	0.61355	4.4890	0.9551	303.49

Table D continued

	Iowa Type curve O2					Iowa Type curve O3			
Age %AL	Percent Surviving	Remaining Life	CAD Ratio	Prob. Life	Age %AL	Percent Surviving	Remaining Life	CAD Ratio	Prob. Life
300	0.54464	3.9937	0.9601	303.99	0	100.00000	100.0000	0.0000	100.00
301	0.47596	3.4978	0.9650	304.50	1	99.17103	98.4323	0.0157	99.43
302	0.40751	3.0013	0.9700	305.00	2	98.34314	98.2567	0.0174	100.26
303	0.33926	2.5045	0.9750	305.50	3	97.51638	98.0855	0.0191	101.09
304	0.27124	2.0072	0.9799	306.01	4	96.69082	97.9187	0.0208	101.92
305	0.20342	1.5097	0.9849	306.51	5	95.86652	97.7564	0.0224	102.76
306	0.13581	1.0124	0.9899	307.01	6	95.04354	97.5985	0.0240	103.60
307	0.06840	0.5174	0.9948	307.52	7	94.22196	97.4452	0.0255	104.45
308	0.00119	0.5000	0.9950	308.50	8	93.40185	97.2964	0.0270	105.30
309	0.00000	0.0000	1.0000	309.00	9	92.58328	97.1522	0.0285	106.15
					10	91.76634	97.0127	0.0299	107.01
					11	90.95110	96.8778	0.0312	107.88
					12	90.13764	96.7475	0.0325	108.75
					13	89.32605	96.6220	0.0338	109.62
					14	88.51642	96.5012	0.0350	110.50
					15	87.70882	96.3852	0.0361	111.39
					16	86.90337	96.2739	0.0373	112.27
					17	86.10014	96.1673	0.0383	113.17
					18	85.29924	96.0656	0.0393	114.07
					19	84.50076	95.9686	0.0403	114.97
					20	83.70479	95.8765	0.0412	115.88
					21	82.91146	95.7891	0.0421	116.79
					22	82.12084	95.7065	0.0429	117.71
					23	81.33306	95.6286	0.0437	118.63
					24	80.54821	95.5555	0.0444	119.56
					25	79.76641	95.4872	0.0451	120.49
					26	78.98776	95.4236	0.0458	121.42
					27	78.21237	95.3646	0.0464	122.36
					28	77.44035	95.3103	0.0469	123.31
					29	76.67182	95.2607	0.0474	124.26
					30	75.90688	95.2156	0.0478	125.22
					31	75.14565	95.1751	0.0482	126.18
					32	74.38824	95.1391	0.0486	127.14
					33	73.63476	95.1075	0.0489	128.11
					34	72.88532	95.0803	0.0492	129.08
					35	72.14004	95.0574	0.0494	130.06
					36	71.39902	95.0388	0.0496	131.04
					37	70.66238	95.0243	0.0498	132.02
					38	69.93023	95.0139	0.0499	133.01
					39	69.20266	95.0076	0.0499	134.01
					40	68.47980	95.0052	0.0499	135.01
					41	67.76174	95.0067	0.0499	136.01
					42	67.04858	95.0119	0.0499	137.01
					43	66.34043	95.0208	0.0498	138.02
					44	65.63739	95.0332	0.0497	139.03
					45	64.93954	95.0490	0.0495	140.05
					46	64.24699	95.0682	0.0493	141.07
					47	63.55981	95.0907	0.0491	142.09
					48	62.87810	95.1162	0.0488	143.12
					49	62.20194	95.1447	0.0486	144.14
					50	61.53142	95.1761	0.0482	145.18
					51	60.86660	95.2102	0.0479	146.21
					52	60.20756	95.2469	0.0475	147.25
					53	59.55436	95.2861	0.0471	148.29
					54	58.90708	95.3276	0.0467	149.33
					55	58.26577	95.3713	0.0463	150.37
					56	57.63049	95.4171	0.0458	151.42
					57	57.00130	95.4649	0.0454	152.46
					58	56.37823	95.5144	0.0449	153.51
					59	55.76133	95.5655	0.0443	154.57
					60	55.15065	95.6182	0.0438	155.62
					61	54.54622	95.6722	0.0433	156.67
					62	53.94807	95.7274	0.0427	157.73
					63	53.35622	95.7837	0.0422	158.78
					64	52.77070	95.8410	0.0416	159.84
					65	52.19152	95.8990	0.0410	160.90
					66	51.61870	95.9576	0.0404	161.96
					67	51.05225	96.0168	0.0398	163.02
					68	50.49217	96.0763	0.0392	164.08
					69	49.93847	96.1360	0.0386	165.14
					70	49.39113	96.1958	0.0380	166.20
					71	48.85016	96.2556	0.0374	167.26
					72	48.31555	96.3151	0.0368	168.32
					73	47.78727	96.3743	0.0363	169.37
					74	47.26531	96.4331	0.0357	170.43
					75	46.74965	96.4912	0.0351	171.49
					76	46.24027	96.5487	0.0345	172.55
					77	45.73714	96.6053	0.0339	173.61
					78	45.24022	96.6609	0.0334	174.66
					79	44.74949	96.7154	0.0328	175.72
					80	44.26490	96.7687	0.0323	176.77
					81	43.78642	96.8207	0.0318	177.82
					82	43.31400	96.8712	0.0313	178.87
					83	42.84761	96.9202	0.0308	179.92
					84	42.38719	96.9676	0.0303	180.97
					85	41.93269	97.0132	0.0299	182.01
					86	41.48407	97.0569	0.0294	183.06
					87	41.04127	97.0987	0.0290	184.10
					88	40.60424	97.1384	0.0286	185.14
					89	40.17293	97.1759	0.0282	186.18
					90	39.74727	97.2112	0.0279	187.21
					91	39.32720	97.2442	0.0276	188.24
					92	38.91267	97.2748	0.0273	189.27
					93	38.50362	97.3029	0.0270	190.30
					94	38.09998	97.3285	0.0267	191.33
					95	37.70170	97.3514	0.0265	192.35
					96	37.30870	97.3716	0.0263	193.37
					97	36.92093	97.3890	0.0261	194.39
					98	36.53831	97.4036	0.0260	195.40
					99	36.16079	97.4153	0.0258	196.42

Table D continued

Age %AL	Iowa Type curve 03 Percent Surviving	Remaining Life	CAD Ratio	Prob. Life	Age %AL	Iowa Type curve 03 Percent Surviving	Remaining Life	CAD Ratio	Prob. Life
100	35.78829	97.4240	0.0258	197.42	200	14.45027	81.1438	0.1886	281.14
101	35.42076	97.4297	0.0257	198.43	201	14.32847	80.8293	0.1917	281.83
102	35.05812	97.4324	0.0257	199.43	202	14.20763	80.5125	0.1949	282.51
103	34.70031	97.4319	0.0257	200.43	203	14.08773	80.1935	0.1981	283.19
104	34.34726	97.4282	0.0257	201.43	204	13.96876	79.8722	0.2013	283.87
105	33.99891	97.4213	0.0258	202.42	205	13.85071	79.5487	0.2045	284.55
106	33.65519	97.4112	0.0259	203.41	206	13.73356	79.2230	0.2078	285.22
107	33.31603	97.3977	0.0260	204.40	207	13.61730	78.8951	0.2110	285.90
108	32.98137	97.3810	0.0262	205.38	208	13.50192	78.5651	0.2143	286.57
109	32.65114	97.3608	0.0264	206.36	209	13.38739	78.2329	0.2177	287.23
110	32.32527	97.3373	0.0266	207.34	210	13.27371	77.8987	0.2210	287.90
111	32.00370	97.3103	0.0269	208.31	211	13.16087	77.5623	0.2244	288.56
112	31.68637	97.2798	0.0272	209.28	212	13.04886	77.2238	0.2278	289.22
113	31.37321	97.2458	0.0275	210.25	213	12.93765	76.8833	0.2312	289.88
114	31.06415	97.2084	0.0279	211.21	214	12.82725	76.5407	0.2346	290.54
115	30.75914	97.1673	0.0283	212.17	215	12.71762	76.1962	0.2380	291.20
116	30.45811	97.1227	0.0288	213.12	216	12.60878	75.8496	0.2415	291.85
117	30.16099	97.0746	0.0293	214.07	217	12.50070	75.5010	0.2450	292.50
118	29.86773	97.0228	0.0298	215.02	218	12.39337	75.1506	0.2485	293.15
119	29.57826	96.9674	0.0303	215.97	219	12.28679	74.7981	0.2520	293.80
120	29.29252	96.9084	0.0309	216.91	220	12.18093	74.4438	0.2556	294.44
121	29.01046	96.8458	0.0315	217.85	221	12.07579	74.0876	0.2591	295.09
122	28.73202	96.7795	0.0322	218.78	222	11.97137	73.7295	0.2627	295.73
123	28.45712	96.7095	0.0329	219.71	223	11.86764	73.3696	0.2663	296.37
124	28.18573	96.6359	0.0336	220.64	224	11.76460	73.0078	0.2699	297.01
125	27.91777	96.5586	0.0344	221.56	225	11.66224	72.6442	0.2736	297.64
126	27.65320	96.4777	0.0352	222.48	226	11.56055	72.2788	0.2772	298.28
127	27.39195	96.3931	0.0361	223.39	227	11.45952	71.9116	0.2809	298.91
128	27.13398	96.3047	0.0370	224.30	228	11.35914	71.5427	0.2846	299.54
129	26.87923	96.2127	0.0379	225.21	229	11.25940	71.1720	0.2883	300.17
130	26.62764	96.1171	0.0388	226.12	230	11.16030	70.7995	0.2920	300.80
131	26.37916	96.0178	0.0398	227.02	231	11.06181	70.4255	0.2957	301.43
132	26.13374	95.9148	0.0409	227.91	232	10.96394	70.0496	0.2995	302.05
133	25.89133	95.8081	0.0419	228.81	233	10.86668	69.6721	0.3033	302.67
134	25.65188	95.6977	0.0430	229.70	234	10.77001	69.2930	0.3071	303.29
135	25.41533	95.5838	0.0442	230.58	235	10.67393	68.9122	0.3109	303.91
136	25.18165	95.4661	0.0453	231.47	236	10.57843	68.5299	0.3147	304.53
137	24.95077	95.3449	0.0466	232.34	237	10.48350	68.1459	0.3185	305.15
138	24.72266	95.2200	0.0478	233.22	238	10.38914	67.7603	0.3224	305.76
139	24.49727	95.0915	0.0491	234.09	239	10.29533	67.3731	0.3263	306.37
140	24.27454	94.9594	0.0504	234.96	240	10.20207	66.9845	0.3302	306.98
141	24.05444	94.8237	0.0518	235.82	241	10.10934	66.5943	0.3341	307.59
142	23.83692	94.6845	0.0532	236.68	242	10.01716	66.2025	0.3380	308.20
143	23.62194	94.5416	0.0546	237.54	243	9.92549	65.8093	0.3419	308.81
144	23.40946	94.3952	0.0560	238.40	244	9.83435	65.4146	0.3459	309.41
145	23.19942	94.2453	0.0575	239.25	245	9.74372	65.0184	0.3498	310.02
146	22.99180	94.0918	0.0591	240.09	246	9.65359	64.6207	0.3538	310.62
147	22.78654	93.9349	0.0607	240.93	247	9.56396	64.2217	0.3578	311.22
148	22.58362	93.7745	0.0623	241.77	248	9.47483	63.8211	0.3618	311.82
149	22.38298	93.6106	0.0639	242.61	249	9.38617	63.4192	0.3658	312.42
150	22.18460	93.4432	0.0656	243.44	250	9.29800	63.0159	0.3698	313.02
151	21.98843	93.2724	0.0673	244.27	251	9.21029	62.6112	0.3739	313.61
152	21.79443	93.0982	0.0690	245.10	252	9.12305	62.2051	0.3779	314.21
153	21.60257	92.9206	0.0708	245.92	253	9.03627	61.7977	0.3820	314.80
154	21.41282	92.7396	0.0726	246.74	254	8.94994	61.3890	0.3861	315.39
155	21.22513	92.5552	0.0744	247.56	255	8.86406	60.9789	0.3902	315.98
156	21.03947	92.3675	0.0763	248.37	256	8.77862	60.5675	0.3943	316.57
157	20.85582	92.1765	0.0782	249.18	257	8.69361	60.1549	0.3985	317.15
158	20.67412	91.9822	0.0802	249.98	258	8.60903	59.7410	0.4026	317.74
159	20.49436	91.7846	0.0822	250.78	259	8.52488	59.3258	0.4067	318.33
160	20.31650	91.5838	0.0842	251.58	260	8.44114	58.9094	0.4109	318.91
161	20.14050	91.3797	0.0862	252.38	261	8.35782	58.4916	0.4151	319.49
162	19.96634	91.1724	0.0883	253.17	262	8.27490	58.0728	0.4193	320.07
163	19.79398	90.9620	0.0904	253.96	263	8.19238	57.6527	0.4235	320.65
164	19.62340	90.7483	0.0925	254.75	264	8.11026	57.2314	0.4277	321.23
165	19.45456	90.5316	0.0947	255.53	265	8.02854	56.8088	0.4319	321.81
166	19.28744	90.3117	0.0969	256.31	266	7.94719	56.3852	0.4361	322.39
167	19.12201	90.0887	0.0991	257.09	267	7.86623	55.9604	0.4404	322.96
168	18.95824	89.8626	0.1014	257.86	268	7.78564	55.5345	0.4447	323.53
169	18.79610	89.6334	0.1037	258.63	269	7.70543	55.1074	0.4489	324.11
170	18.63556	89.4013	0.1060	259.40	270	7.62558	54.6792	0.4532	324.68
171	18.47660	89.1661	0.1083	260.17	271	7.54610	54.2498	0.4575	325.25
172	18.31920	88.9280	0.1107	260.93	272	7.46697	53.8194	0.4618	325.82
173	18.16332	88.6869	0.1131	261.69	273	7.38819	53.3880	0.4661	326.39
174	18.00895	88.4428	0.1156	262.44	274	7.30976	52.9554	0.4704	326.96
175	17.85605	88.1958	0.1180	263.20	275	7.23168	52.5218	0.4748	327.52
176	17.70460	87.9460	0.1205	263.95	276	7.15394	52.0871	0.4791	328.09
177	17.55459	87.6933	0.1231	264.69	277	7.07653	51.6514	0.4835	328.65
178	17.40598	87.4377	0.1256	265.44	278	6.99945	51.2147	0.4879	329.21
179	17.25875	87.1794	0.1282	266.18	279	6.92270	50.7769	0.4922	329.78
180	17.11289	86.9182	0.1308	266.92	280	6.84627	50.3382	0.4966	330.34
181	16.96836	86.6542	0.1335	267.65	281	6.77016	49.8985	0.5010	330.90
182	16.82515	86.3876	0.1361	268.39	282	6.69436	49.4578	0.5054	331.46
183	16.68324	86.1181	0.1388	269.12	283	6.61888	49.0161	0.5098	332.02
184	16.54260	85.8460	0.1415	269.85	284	6.54370	48.5735	0.5143	332.57
185	16.40322	85.5712	0.1443	270.57	285	6.46883	48.1299	0.5187	333.13
186	16.26508	85.2937	0.1471	271.29	286	6.39425	47.6855	0.5231	333.69
187	16.12814	85.0137	0.1499	272.01	287	6.31998	47.2400	0.5276	334.24
188	15.99241	84.7310	0.1527	272.73	288	6.24599	46.7937	0.5321	334.79
189	15.85785	84.4457	0.1555	273.45	289	6.17229	46.3464	0.5365	335.35
190	15.72445	84.1579	0.1584	274.16	290	6.09888	45.8983	0.5410	335.90
191	15.59219	83.8675	0.1613	274.87	291	6.02575	45.4492	0.5455	336.45
192	15.46105	83.5744	0.1643	275.57	292	5.95290	44.9993	0.5500	337.00
193	15.33101	83.2793	0.1672	276.28	293	5.88032	44.5486	0.5545	337.55
194	15.20206	82.9814	0.1702	276.98	294	5.80801	44.0970	0.5590	338.10
195	15.07418	82.6812	0.1732	277.68	295	5.73597	43.6445	0.5636	338.64
196	14.94736	82.3784	0.1762	278.38	296	5.66420	43.1912	0.5681	339.19
197	14.82157	82.0733	0.1793	279.07	297	5.59269	42.7371	0.5726	339.74
198	14.69680	81.7658	0.1823	279.77	298	5.52144	42.2821	0.5772	340.28
199	14.57304	81.4560	0.1854	280.46	299	5.45044	41.8264	0.5817	340.83

Table D continued

Iowa Type curve O3				
Age %AL	Percent Surviving	Remaining Life	CAD Ratio	Prob. Life
300	5.37970	41.3698	0.5863	341.37
301	5.30921	40.9124	0.5909	341.91
302	5.23896	40.4543	0.5955	342.45
303	5.16895	39.9955	0.6000	343.00
304	5.09919	39.5358	0.6046	343.54
305	5.02967	39.0753	0.6092	344.08
306	4.96038	38.6142	0.6139	344.61
307	4.89132	38.1523	0.6185	345.15
308	4.82250	37.6896	0.6231	345.69
309	4.75390	37.2263	0.6277	346.23
310	4.68552	36.7623	0.6324	346.76
311	4.61737	36.2975	0.6370	347.30
312	4.54943	35.8321	0.6417	347.83
313	4.48172	35.3659	0.6463	348.37
314	4.41422	34.8990	0.6510	348.90
315	4.34693	34.4315	0.6557	349.43
316	4.27984	33.9634	0.6604	349.96
317	4.21297	33.4946	0.6651	350.49
318	4.14630	33.0251	0.6697	351.03
319	4.07984	32.5549	0.6745	351.55
320	4.01357	32.0842	0.6792	352.08
321	3.94750	31.6128	0.6839	352.61
322	3.88163	31.1408	0.6886	353.14
323	3.81595	30.6682	0.6933	353.67
324	3.75046	30.1950	0.6981	354.19
325	3.68516	29.7212	0.7028	354.72
326	3.62005	29.2468	0.7075	355.25
327	3.55513	28.7717	0.7123	355.77
328	3.49038	28.2962	0.7170	356.30
329	3.42582	27.8200	0.7218	356.82
330	3.36144	27.3432	0.7266	357.34
331	3.29723	26.8660	0.7313	357.87
332	3.23320	26.3881	0.7361	358.39
333	3.16934	25.9098	0.7409	358.91
334	3.10565	25.4309	0.7457	359.43
335	3.04213	24.9514	0.7505	359.95
336	2.97878	24.4714	0.7553	360.47
337	2.91560	23.9909	0.7601	360.99
338	2.85258	23.5098	0.7649	361.51
339	2.78972	23.0283	0.7697	362.03
340	2.72702	22.5463	0.7745	362.55
341	2.66448	22.0638	0.7794	363.06
342	2.60209	21.5808	0.7842	363.58
343	2.53986	21.0973	0.7890	364.10
344	2.47779	20.6133	0.7939	364.61
345	2.41587	20.1288	0.7987	365.13
346	2.35409	19.6439	0.8036	365.64
347	2.29247	19.1585	0.8084	366.16
348	2.23099	18.6727	0.8133	366.67
349	2.16966	18.1864	0.8181	367.19
350	2.10848	17.6995	0.8230	367.70
351	2.04743	17.2124	0.8279	368.21
352	1.98653	16.7247	0.8328	368.72
353	1.92576	16.2367	0.8376	369.24
354	1.86514	15.7482	0.8425	369.75
355	1.80465	15.2593	0.8474	370.26
356	1.74429	14.7700	0.8523	370.77
357	1.68407	14.2803	0.8572	371.28
358	1.62399	13.7901	0.8621	371.79
359	1.56403	13.2996	0.8670	372.30
360	1.50420	12.8087	0.8719	372.81
361	1.44450	12.3174	0.8768	373.32
362	1.38493	11.8257	0.8817	373.83
363	1.32549	11.3336	0.8867	374.33
364	1.26616	10.8413	0.8916	374.84
365	1.20697	10.3484	0.8965	375.35
366	1.14789	9.8553	0.9014	375.86
367	1.08893	9.3618	0.9064	376.36
368	1.03010	8.8680	0.9113	376.87
369	0.97138	8.3738	0.9163	377.37
370	0.91278	7.8793	0.9212	377.88
371	0.85429	7.3845	0.9262	378.38
372	0.79592	6.8894	0.9311	378.89
373	0.73767	6.3939	0.9361	379.39
374	0.67952	5.8983	0.9410	379.90
375	0.62149	5.4024	0.9460	380.40
376	0.56357	4.9062	0.9509	380.91
377	0.50575	4.4100	0.9559	381.41
378	0.44805	3.9135	0.9609	381.91
379	0.39045	3.4170	0.9658	382.42
380	0.33295	2.9208	0.9708	382.92
381	0.27557	2.4249	0.9758	383.42
382	0.21828	1.9301	0.9807	383.93
383	0.16110	1.4377	0.9856	384.44
384	0.10402	0.9522	0.9905	384.95
385	0.04704	0.5000	0.9950	385.50
386	0.00000	0.0000	1.0000	386.00

Iowa Type curve O4				
Age %AL	Percent Surviving	Remaining Life	CAD Ratio	Prob. Life
0	100.00000	100.0000	0.0000	100.00
1	98.87130	100.4034	-0.0040	101.40
2	97.74568	100.5538	-0.0055	102.55
3	96.62338	100.7160	-0.0072	103.72
4	95.50465	100.8899	-0.0089	104.89
5	94.38974	101.0757	-0.0108	106.08
6	93.27892	101.2734	-0.0127	107.27
7	92.17248	101.4831	-0.0148	108.48
8	91.07069	101.7048	-0.0170	109.70
9	89.97385	101.9385	-0.0194	110.94
10	88.88226	102.1843	-0.0218	112.18
11	87.79625	102.4421	-0.0244	113.44
12	86.71613	102.7119	-0.0271	114.71
13	85.64223	102.9936	-0.0299	115.99
14	84.57489	103.2871	-0.0329	117.29
15	83.51443	103.5922	-0.0359	118.59
16	82.46120	103.9090	-0.0391	119.91
17	81.41555	104.2371	-0.0424	121.24
18	80.37782	104.5764	-0.0458	122.58
19	79.34834	104.9267	-0.0493	123.93
20	78.32747	105.2878	-0.0529	125.29
21	77.31554	105.6593	-0.0566	126.66
22	76.31289	106.0409	-0.0604	128.04
23	75.31983	106.4324	-0.0643	129.43
24	74.33669	106.8334	-0.0683	130.83
25	73.36379	107.2435	-0.0724	132.24
26	72.40141	107.6624	-0.0766	133.66
27	71.44985	108.0896	-0.0809	135.09
28	70.50937	108.5247	-0.0852	136.52
29	69.58025	108.9671	-0.0897	137.97
30	68.66272	109.4166	-0.0942	139.42
31	67.75702	109.8724	-0.0987	140.87
32	66.86334	110.3343	-0.1033	142.33
33	65.98189	110.8016	-0.1080	143.80
34	65.11284	111.2737	-0.1127	145.27
35	64.25634	111.7503	-0.1175	146.75
36	63.41253	112.2307	-0.1223	148.23
37	62.58152	112.7143	-0.1271	149.71
38	61.76340	113.2007	-0.1320	151.20
39	60.95826	113.6893	-0.1369	152.69
40	60.16614	114.1795	-0.1418	154.18
41	59.38708	114.6707	-0.1467	155.67
42	58.62110	115.1626	-0.1516	157.16
43	57.86820	115.6544	-0.1565	158.65
44	57.12835	116.1457	-0.1615	160.15
45	56.40153	116.6360	-0.1664	161.64
46	55.68767	117.1247	-0.1712	163.12
47	54.98671	117.6115	-0.1761	164.61
48	54.29856	118.0957	-0.1810	166.10
49	53.62313	118.5769	-0.1858	167.58
50	52.96030	119.0547	-0.1905	169.05
51	52.30995	119.5286	-0.1953	170.53
52	51.67195	119.9983	-0.2000	172.00
53	51.04616	120.4633	-0.2046	173.46
54	50.43241	120.9232	-0.2092	174.92
55	49.83055	121.3777	-0.2138	176.38
56	49.24040	121.8264	-0.2183	177.83
57	48.66179	122.2690	-0.2227	179.27
58	48.09455	122.7052	-0.2271	180.71
59	47.53847	123.1347	-0.2313	182.13
60	46.99337	123.5572	-0.2356	183.56
61	46.45905	123.9725	-0.2397	184.97
62	45.93532	124.3802	-0.2438	186.38
63	45.42197	124.7803	-0.2478	187.78
64	44.91881	125.1724	-0.2517	189.17
65	44.42562	125.5565	-0.2556	190.56
66	43.94221	125.9322	-0.2593	191.93
67	43.46837	126.2995	-0.2630	193.30
68	43.00390	126.6582	-0.2666	194.66
69	42.54859	127.0083	-0.2701	196.01
70	42.10225	127.3494	-0.2735	197.35
71	41.66467	127.6816	-0.2768	198.68
72	41.23566	128.0048	-0.2800	200.00
73	40.81502	128.3189	-0.2832	201.32
74	40.40256	128.6238	-0.2862	202.62
75	39.99808	128.9194	-0.2892	203.92
76	39.60140	129.2058	-0.2921	205.21
77	39.21233	129.4828	-0.2948	206.48
78	38.83069	129.7505	-0.2975	207.75
79	38.45630	130.0088	-0.3001	209.01
80	38.08898	130.2577	-0.3026	210.26
81	37.72857	130.4973	-0.3050	211.50
82	37.37488	130.7275	-0.3073	212.73
83	37.02776	130.9483	-0.3095	213.95
84	36.68704	131.1598	-0.3116	215.16
85	36.35257	131.3620	-0.3136	216.36
86	36.02418	131.5549	-0.3155	217.55
87	35.70172	131.7386	-0.3174	218.74
88	35.38506	131.9130	-0.3191	219.91
89	35.07403	132.0784	-0.3208	221.08
90	34.76850	132.2346	-0.3223	222.23
91	34.46834	132.3818	-0.3238	223.38
92	34.17339	132.5201	-0.3252	224.52
93	33.88355	132.6494	-0.3265	225.65
94	33.59867	132.7699	-0.3277	226.77
95	33.31862	132.8816	-0.3288	227.88
96	33.04330	132.9846	-0.3298	228.98
97	32.77258	133.0790	-0.3308	230.08
98	32.50634	133.1649	-0.3316	231.16
99	32.24447	133.2423	-0.3324	232.24

Table D continued

Age %AL	Iowa Type curve 04 Percent Surviving	Remaining Life	CAD Ratio	Prob. Life	Age %AL	Iowa Type curve 04 Percent Surviving	Remaining Life	CAD Ratio	Prob. Life
100	31.98687	133.3114	-0.3331	233.31	200	17.19183	112.1281	-0.1213	312.13
101	31.73341	133.3721	-0.3337	234.37	201	17.09700	111.7473	-0.1175	312.75
102	31.48401	133.4247	-0.3342	235.42	202	17.00264	111.3647	-0.1136	313.36
103	31.23856	133.4691	-0.3347	236.47	203	16.90876	110.9802	-0.1098	313.98
104	30.99696	133.5055	-0.3351	237.51	204	16.81534	110.5940	-0.1059	314.59
105	30.75912	133.5340	-0.3353	238.53	205	16.72237	110.2061	-0.1021	315.21
106	30.52493	133.5546	-0.3355	239.55	206	16.62984	109.8165	-0.0982	315.82
107	30.29432	133.5675	-0.3357	240.57	207	16.53776	109.4252	-0.0943	316.43
108	30.06719	133.5727	-0.3357	241.57	208	16.44610	109.0323	-0.0903	317.03
109	29.84346	133.5703	-0.3357	242.57	209	16.35487	108.6377	-0.0864	317.64
110	29.62304	133.5604	-0.3356	243.56	210	16.26405	108.2415	-0.0824	318.24
111	29.40585	133.5432	-0.3354	244.54	211	16.17365	107.8437	-0.0784	318.84
112	29.19181	133.5187	-0.3352	245.52	212	16.08364	107.4445	-0.0744	319.44
113	28.98086	133.4869	-0.3349	246.49	213	15.99403	107.0436	-0.0704	320.04
114	28.77290	133.4481	-0.3345	247.45	214	15.90481	106.6413	-0.0664	320.64
115	28.56787	133.4023	-0.3340	248.40	215	15.81597	106.2375	-0.0624	321.24
116	28.36569	133.3496	-0.3335	249.35	216	15.72751	105.8322	-0.0583	321.83
117	28.16631	133.2900	-0.3329	250.29	217	15.63942	105.4255	-0.0543	322.43
118	27.96965	133.2236	-0.3322	251.22	218	15.55169	105.0174	-0.0502	323.02
119	27.77564	133.1507	-0.3315	252.15	219	15.46432	104.6079	-0.0461	323.61
120	27.58423	133.0712	-0.3307	253.07	220	15.37730	104.1971	-0.0420	324.20
121	27.39534	132.9853	-0.3299	253.99	221	15.29062	103.7849	-0.0378	324.78
122	27.20893	132.8929	-0.3289	254.89	222	15.20429	103.3714	-0.0337	325.37
123	27.02493	132.7943	-0.3279	255.79	223	15.11829	102.9566	-0.0296	325.96
124	26.84329	132.6895	-0.3269	256.69	224	15.03262	102.5404	-0.0254	326.54
125	26.66395	132.5786	-0.3258	257.58	225	14.94728	102.1230	-0.0212	327.12
126	26.48685	132.4617	-0.3246	258.46	226	14.86225	101.7044	-0.0170	327.70
127	26.31195	132.3389	-0.3234	259.34	227	14.77754	101.2846	-0.0128	328.28
128	26.13919	132.2103	-0.3221	260.21	228	14.69314	100.8635	-0.0086	328.86
129	25.96853	132.0758	-0.3208	261.08	229	14.60904	100.4413	-0.0044	329.44
130	25.79992	131.9357	-0.3194	261.94	230	14.52525	100.0178	-0.0002	330.02
131	25.63330	131.7901	-0.3179	262.79	231	14.44174	99.5933	0.0041	330.59
132	25.46864	131.6389	-0.3164	263.64	232	14.35853	99.1675	0.0083	331.17
133	25.30588	131.4823	-0.3148	264.48	233	14.27560	98.7407	0.0126	331.74
134	25.14499	131.3204	-0.3132	265.32	234	14.19296	98.3127	0.0169	332.31
135	24.98593	131.1532	-0.3115	266.15	235	14.11059	97.8837	0.0212	332.88
136	24.82864	130.9809	-0.3098	266.98	236	14.02849	97.4536	0.0255	333.45
137	24.67310	130.8035	-0.3080	267.80	237	13.94666	97.0225	0.0298	334.02
138	24.51927	130.6210	-0.3062	268.62	238	13.86510	96.5903	0.0341	334.59
139	24.36710	130.4336	-0.3043	269.43	239	13.78380	96.1570	0.0384	335.16
140	24.21655	130.2413	-0.3024	270.24	240	13.70275	95.7228	0.0428	335.72
141	24.06761	130.0442	-0.3004	271.04	241	13.62195	95.2876	0.0471	336.29
142	23.92022	129.8424	-0.2984	271.84	242	13.54141	94.8514	0.0515	336.85
143	23.77435	129.6360	-0.2964	272.64	243	13.46111	94.4142	0.0559	337.41
144	23.62997	129.4251	-0.2943	273.43	244	13.38105	93.9761	0.0602	337.98
145	23.48705	129.2096	-0.2921	274.21	245	13.30122	93.5372	0.0646	338.54
146	23.34556	128.9897	-0.2899	274.99	246	13.22163	93.0972	0.0690	339.10
147	23.20547	128.7653	-0.2877	275.77	247	13.14227	92.6564	0.0734	339.66
148	23.06674	128.5368	-0.2854	276.54	248	13.06314	92.2146	0.0779	340.21
149	22.92935	128.3039	-0.2830	277.30	249	12.98423	91.7720	0.0823	340.77
150	22.79326	128.0670	-0.2807	278.07	250	12.90555	91.3284	0.0867	341.33
151	22.65846	127.8259	-0.2783	278.83	251	12.82708	90.8841	0.0912	341.88
152	22.52491	127.5808	-0.2758	279.58	252	12.74882	90.4389	0.0956	342.44
153	22.39259	127.3318	-0.2733	280.33	253	12.67077	89.9929	0.1001	342.99
154	22.26147	127.0788	-0.2708	281.08	254	12.59294	89.5460	0.1045	343.55
155	22.13152	126.8221	-0.2682	281.82	255	12.51530	89.0984	0.1090	344.10
156	22.00273	126.5615	-0.2656	282.56	256	12.43787	88.6500	0.1135	344.65
157	21.87507	126.2971	-0.2630	283.30	257	12.36064	88.2008	0.1180	345.20
158	21.74851	126.0292	-0.2603	284.03	258	12.28360	87.7508	0.1225	345.75
159	21.62303	125.7576	-0.2576	284.76	259	12.20676	87.3000	0.1270	346.30
160	21.49862	125.4825	-0.2548	285.48	260	12.13010	86.8486	0.1315	346.85
161	21.37524	125.2039	-0.2520	286.20	261	12.05364	86.3963	0.1360	347.40
162	21.25288	124.9219	-0.2492	286.92	262	11.97735	85.9434	0.1406	347.94
163	21.13152	124.6364	-0.2464	287.64	263	11.90126	85.4897	0.1451	348.49
164	21.01113	124.3477	-0.2435	288.35	264	11.82534	85.0354	0.1496	349.04
165	20.89170	124.0557	-0.2406	289.06	265	11.74960	84.5803	0.1542	349.58
166	20.77321	123.7605	-0.2376	289.76	266	11.67403	84.1246	0.1588	350.12
167	20.65564	123.4620	-0.2346	290.46	267	11.59864	83.6681	0.1633	350.67
168	20.53897	123.1605	-0.2316	291.16	268	11.52341	83.2111	0.1679	351.21
169	20.42318	122.8560	-0.2286	291.86	269	11.44836	82.7533	0.1725	351.75
170	20.30826	122.5483	-0.2255	292.55	270	11.37347	82.2949	0.1771	352.29
171	20.19419	122.2377	-0.2224	293.24	271	11.29874	81.8359	0.1816	352.84
172	20.08096	121.9242	-0.2192	293.92	272	11.22417	81.3763	0.1862	353.38
173	19.96853	121.6078	-0.2161	294.61	273	11.14976	80.9160	0.1908	353.92
174	19.85691	121.2886	-0.2129	295.29	274	11.07551	80.4551	0.1954	354.46
175	19.74608	120.9666	-0.2097	295.97	275	11.00141	79.9937	0.2001	354.99
176	19.63601	120.6419	-0.2064	296.64	276	10.92746	79.5316	0.2047	355.53
177	19.52671	120.3143	-0.2031	297.31	277	10.85366	79.0690	0.2093	356.07
178	19.41814	119.9842	-0.1998	297.98	278	10.78001	78.6058	0.2139	356.61
179	19.31030	119.6515	-0.1965	298.65	279	10.70651	78.1420	0.2186	357.14
180	19.20317	119.3162	-0.1932	299.32	280	10.63315	77.6777	0.2232	357.68
181	19.09675	118.9784	-0.1898	299.98	281	10.55993	77.2128	0.2279	358.21
182	18.99101	118.6380	-0.1864	300.64	282	10.48686	76.7473	0.2325	358.75
183	18.88594	118.2953	-0.1830	301.30	283	10.41392	76.2813	0.2372	359.28
184	18.78154	117.9501	-0.1795	301.95	284	10.34111	75.8149	0.2419	359.81
185	18.67779	117.6025	-0.1760	302.60	285	10.26845	75.3478	0.2465	360.35
186	18.57467	117.2526	-0.1725	303.25	286	10.19591	74.8804	0.2512	360.88
187	18.47218	116.9004	-0.1690	303.90	287	10.12351	74.4123	0.2559	361.41
188	18.37030	116.5459	-0.1655	304.55	288	10.05123	73.9438	0.2606	361.94
189	18.26903	116.1892	-0.1619	305.19	289	9.97908	73.4748	0.2653	362.47
190	18.16834	115.8303	-0.1583	305.83	290	9.90706	73.0053	0.2699	363.01
191	18.06824	115.4693	-0.1547	306.47	291	9.83517	72.5353	0.2746	363.54
192	17.96871	115.1061	-0.1511	307.11	292	9.76339	72.0649	0.2794	364.06
193	17.86974	114.7408	-0.1474	307.74	293	9.69174	71.5940	0.2841	364.59
194	17.77132	114.3735	-0.1437	308.37	294	9.62021	71.1226	0.2888	365.12
195	17.67344	114.0042	-0.1400	309.00	295	9.54879	70.6508	0.2935	365.65
196	17.57609	113.6329	-0.1363	309.63	296	9.47749	70.1785	0.2982	366.18
197	17.47927	113.2595	-0.1326	310.26	297	9.40631	69.7058	0.3029	366.71
198	17.38295	112.8843	-0.1288	310.88	298	9.33524	69.2327	0.3077	367.23
199	17.28714	112.5072	-0.1251	311.51	299	9.26428	68.7592	0.3124	367.76

Table D continued

Iowa Type curve 04

Age %AL	Percent Surviving	Remaining Life	CAD Ratio	Prob. Life	Age %AL	Percent Surviving	Remaining Life	CAD Ratio	Prob. Life
300	9.19343	68.2852	0.3171	368.29	400	2.49382	19.4943	0.8051	419.49
301	9.12270	67.8107	0.3219	368.81	401	2.42945	18.9976	0.8100	420.00
302	9.05206	67.3360	0.3266	369.34	402	2.36512	18.5007	0.8150	420.50
303	8.98154	66.8608	0.3314	369.86	403	2.30082	18.0038	0.8200	421.00
304	8.91112	66.3852	0.3361	370.39	404	2.23656	17.5067	0.8249	421.51
305	8.84081	65.9092	0.3409	370.91	405	2.17233	17.0096	0.8299	422.01
306	8.77060	65.4328	0.3457	371.43	406	2.10813	16.5123	0.8349	422.51
307	8.70048	64.9561	0.3504	371.96	407	2.04397	16.0150	0.8399	423.01
308	8.63047	64.4790	0.3552	372.48	408	1.97983	15.5176	0.8448	423.52
309	8.56056	64.0015	0.3600	373.00	409	1.91574	15.0200	0.8498	424.02
310	8.49075	63.5236	0.3648	373.52	410	1.85167	14.5224	0.8548	424.52
311	8.42103	63.0454	0.3695	374.05	411	1.78764	14.0247	0.8598	425.02
312	8.35141	62.5668	0.3743	374.57	412	1.72364	13.5268	0.8647	425.53
313	8.28188	62.0878	0.3791	375.09	413	1.65966	13.0290	0.8697	426.03
314	8.21244	61.6086	0.3839	375.61	414	1.59573	12.5310	0.8747	426.53
315	8.14309	61.1290	0.3887	376.13	415	1.53182	12.0329	0.8797	427.03
316	8.07384	60.6490	0.3935	376.65	416	1.46794	11.5348	0.8847	427.53
317	8.00468	60.1687	0.3983	377.17	417	1.40409	11.0366	0.8896	428.04
318	7.93560	59.6881	0.4031	377.69	418	1.34027	10.5383	0.8946	428.54
319	7.86661	59.2072	0.4079	378.21	419	1.27649	10.0399	0.8996	429.04
320	7.79771	58.7260	0.4127	378.73	420	1.21273	9.5415	0.9046	429.54
321	7.72889	58.2444	0.4176	379.24	421	1.14900	9.0430	0.9096	430.04
322	7.66016	57.7625	0.4224	379.76	422	1.08530	8.5444	0.9146	430.54
323	7.59151	57.2803	0.4272	380.28	423	1.02162	8.0458	0.9195	431.05
324	7.52294	56.7979	0.4320	380.80	424	0.95798	7.5471	0.9245	431.55
325	7.45445	56.3151	0.4368	381.32	425	0.89436	7.0484	0.9295	432.05
326	7.38604	55.8321	0.4417	381.83	426	0.83078	6.5495	0.9345	432.55
327	7.31772	55.3487	0.4465	382.35	427	0.76722	6.0507	0.9395	433.05
328	7.24947	54.8651	0.4513	382.87	428	0.70369	5.5518	0.9445	433.55
329	7.18130	54.3811	0.4562	383.38	429	0.64018	5.0530	0.9495	434.05
330	7.11320	53.8970	0.4610	383.90	430	0.57670	4.5542	0.9545	434.55
331	7.04518	53.4125	0.4659	384.41	431	0.51325	4.0553	0.9594	435.06
332	6.97724	52.9277	0.4707	384.93	432	0.44982	3.5567	0.9644	435.56
333	6.90937	52.4427	0.4756	385.44	433	0.38642	3.0582	0.9694	436.06
334	6.84157	51.9575	0.4804	385.96	434	0.32305	2.5600	0.9744	436.56
335	6.77384	51.4720	0.4853	386.47	435	0.25970	2.0625	0.9794	437.06
336	6.70619	50.9862	0.4901	386.99	436	0.19637	1.5665	0.9843	437.57
337	6.63860	50.5002	0.4950	387.50	437	0.13307	1.0738	0.9893	438.07
338	6.57109	50.0139	0.4999	388.01	438	0.06980	0.5938	0.9941	438.59
339	6.50364	49.5274	0.5047	388.53	439	0.00655	0.5000	0.9950	439.50
340	6.43627	49.0406	0.5096	389.04	440	0.00000	0.0000	1.0000	440.00
341	6.36896	48.5536	0.5145	389.55					
342	6.30171	48.0664	0.5193	390.07					
343	6.23453	47.5790	0.5242	390.58					
344	6.16742	47.0912	0.5291	391.09					
345	6.10037	46.6033	0.5340	391.60					
346	6.03339	46.1152	0.5388	392.12					
347	5.96647	45.6268	0.5437	392.63					
348	5.89961	45.1382	0.5486	393.14					
349	5.83281	44.6494	0.5535	393.65					
350	5.76607	44.1604	0.5584	394.16					
351	5.69939	43.6712	0.5633	394.67					
352	5.63278	43.1818	0.5682	395.18					
353	5.56622	42.6921	0.5731	395.69					
354	5.49971	42.2024	0.5780	396.20					
355	5.43327	41.7123	0.5829	396.71					
356	5.36688	41.2221	0.5878	397.22					
357	5.30055	40.7317	0.5927	397.73					
358	5.23428	40.2411	0.5976	398.24					
359	5.16806	39.7503	0.6025	398.75					
360	5.10189	39.2594	0.6074	399.26					
361	5.03578	38.7682	0.6123	399.77					
362	4.96972	38.2769	0.6172	400.28					
363	4.90371	37.7854	0.6221	400.79					
364	4.83776	37.2937	0.6271	401.29					
365	4.77186	36.8018	0.6320	401.80					
366	4.70601	36.3098	0.6369	402.31					
367	4.64020	35.8177	0.6418	402.82					
368	4.57445	35.3253	0.6467	403.33					
369	4.50875	34.8328	0.6517	403.83					
370	4.44310	34.3400	0.6566	404.34					
371	4.37749	33.8472	0.6615	404.85					
372	4.31193	33.3543	0.6665	405.35					
373	4.24642	32.8611	0.6714	405.86					
374	4.18096	32.3678	0.6763	406.37					
375	4.11554	31.8743	0.6813	406.87					
376	4.05017	31.3807	0.6862	407.38					
377	3.98485	30.8869	0.6911	407.89					
378	3.91956	30.3931	0.6961	408.39					
379	3.85433	29.8990	0.7010	408.90					
380	3.78913	29.4049	0.7060	409.40					
381	3.72398	28.9106	0.7109	409.91					
382	3.65888	28.4160	0.7158	410.42					
383	3.59381	27.9215	0.7208	410.92					
384	3.52879	27.4268	0.7257	411.43					
385	3.46381	26.9319	0.7307	411.93					
386	3.39887	26.4369	0.7356	412.44					
387	3.33397	25.9418	0.7406	412.94					
388	3.26911	25.4466	0.7455	413.45					
389	3.20430	24.9511	0.7505	413.95					
390	3.13952	24.4557	0.7554	414.46					
391	3.07478	23.9601	0.7604	414.96					
392	3.01008	23.4643	0.7654	415.46					
393	2.94542	22.9684	0.7703	415.97					
394	2.88079	22.4725	0.7753	416.47					
395	2.81621	21.9764	0.7802	416.98					
396	2.75166	21.4802	0.7852	417.48					
397	2.68714	20.9839	0.7902	417.98					
398	2.62267	20.4875	0.7951	418.49					
399	2.55823	19.9909	0.8001	418.99					

Table D continued

Age %AL	Percent Surviving	Iowa Type curve SQ Remaining Life	CAD Ratio	Prob. Life
0	100.00000	100.0000	0.0000	100.00
1	100.00000	99.5000	0.0050	100.50
2	100.00000	98.5000	0.0150	100.50
3	100.00000	97.5000	0.0250	100.50
4	100.00000	96.5000	0.0350	100.50
5	100.00000	95.5000	0.0450	100.50
6	100.00000	94.5000	0.0550	100.50
7	100.00000	93.5000	0.0650	100.50
8	100.00000	92.5000	0.0750	100.50
9	100.00000	91.5000	0.0850	100.50
10	100.00000	90.5000	0.0950	100.50
11	100.00000	89.5000	0.1050	100.50
12	100.00000	88.5000	0.1150	100.50
13	100.00000	87.5000	0.1250	100.50
14	100.00000	86.5000	0.1350	100.50
15	100.00000	85.5000	0.1450	100.50
16	100.00000	84.5000	0.1550	100.50
17	100.00000	83.5000	0.1650	100.50
18	100.00000	82.5000	0.1750	100.50
19	100.00000	81.5000	0.1850	100.50
20	100.00000	80.5000	0.1950	100.50
21	100.00000	79.5000	0.2050	100.50
22	100.00000	78.5000	0.2150	100.50
23	100.00000	77.5000	0.2250	100.50
24	100.00000	76.5000	0.2350	100.50
25	100.00000	75.5000	0.2450	100.50
26	100.00000	74.5000	0.2550	100.50
27	100.00000	73.5000	0.2650	100.50
28	100.00000	72.5000	0.2750	100.50
29	100.00000	71.5000	0.2850	100.50
30	100.00000	70.5000	0.2950	100.50
31	100.00000	69.5000	0.3050	100.50
32	100.00000	68.5000	0.3150	100.50
33	100.00000	67.5000	0.3250	100.50
34	100.00000	66.5000	0.3350	100.50
35	100.00000	65.5000	0.3450	100.50
36	100.00000	64.5000	0.3550	100.50
37	100.00000	63.5000	0.3650	100.50
38	100.00000	62.5000	0.3750	100.50
39	100.00000	61.5000	0.3850	100.50
40	100.00000	60.5000	0.3950	100.50
41	100.00000	59.5000	0.4050	100.50
42	100.00000	58.5000	0.4150	100.50
43	100.00000	57.5000	0.4250	100.50
44	100.00000	56.5000	0.4350	100.50
45	100.00000	55.5000	0.4450	100.50
46	100.00000	54.5000	0.4550	100.50
47	100.00000	53.5000	0.4650	100.50
48	100.00000	52.5000	0.4750	100.50
49	100.00000	51.5000	0.4850	100.50
50	100.00000	50.5000	0.4950	100.50
51	100.00000	49.5000	0.5050	100.50
52	100.00000	48.5000	0.5150	100.50
53	100.00000	47.5000	0.5250	100.50
54	100.00000	46.5000	0.5350	100.50
55	100.00000	45.5000	0.5450	100.50
56	100.00000	44.5000	0.5550	100.50
57	100.00000	43.5000	0.5650	100.50
58	100.00000	42.5000	0.5750	100.50
59	100.00000	41.5000	0.5850	100.50
60	100.00000	40.5000	0.5950	100.50
61	100.00000	39.5000	0.6050	100.50
62	100.00000	38.5000	0.6150	100.50
63	100.00000	37.5000	0.6250	100.50
64	100.00000	36.5000	0.6350	100.50
65	100.00000	35.5000	0.6450	100.50
66	100.00000	34.5000	0.6550	100.50
67	100.00000	33.5000	0.6650	100.50
68	100.00000	32.5000	0.6750	100.50
69	100.00000	31.5000	0.6850	100.50
70	100.00000	30.5000	0.6950	100.50
71	100.00000	29.5000	0.7050	100.50
72	100.00000	28.5000	0.7150	100.50
73	100.00000	27.5000	0.7250	100.50
74	100.00000	26.5000	0.7350	100.50
75	100.00000	25.5000	0.7450	100.50
76	100.00000	24.5000	0.7550	100.50
77	100.00000	23.5000	0.7650	100.50
78	100.00000	22.5000	0.7750	100.50
79	100.00000	21.5000	0.7850	100.50
80	100.00000	20.5000	0.7950	100.50
81	100.00000	19.5000	0.8050	100.50
82	100.00000	18.5000	0.8150	100.50
83	100.00000	17.5000	0.8250	100.50
84	100.00000	16.5000	0.8350	100.50
85	100.00000	15.5000	0.8450	100.50
86	100.00000	14.5000	0.8550	100.50
87	100.00000	13.5000	0.8650	100.50
88	100.00000	12.5000	0.8750	100.50
89	100.00000	11.5000	0.8850	100.50
90	100.00000	10.5000	0.8950	100.50
91	100.00000	9.5000	0.9050	100.50
92	100.00000	8.5000	0.9150	100.50
93	100.00000	7.5000	0.9250	100.50
94	100.00000	6.5000	0.9350	100.50
95	100.00000	5.5000	0.9450	100.50
96	100.00000	4.5000	0.9550	100.50
97	100.00000	3.5000	0.9650	100.50
98	100.00000	2.5000	0.9750	100.50
99	100.00000	1.5000	0.9850	100.50

Age %AL	Percent Surviving	Iowa Type curve SQ Remaining Life	CAD Ratio	Prob. Life
100	100.00000	0.5000	0.9950	100.50
101	0.00000	0.0000	1.0000	101.00

APPENDIX II

Moments of Iowa Curves

MOMENTS OF IOWA CURVES ABOUT ORIGIN AND MEASURES BASED ON THEM

Disp.	First (= m1)	Second (= m2)	Third (= m3)	Fourth (= m4)	Standard Deviation	Variance	Skewness	Kurtosis
SC	1.00000000	1.33333333	2.00000000	3.20000000	.577350	.333333	.000000	1.800000
S.5	1.00000000	1.27784595	1.83353784	2.81841014	.527111	.277846	.000000	1.960333
SO	1.00000000	1.22235856	1.66707568	2.43682027	.471549	.222359	.000000	2.078878
S.5	1.00000000	1.13629045	1.55887135	2.19510681	.431614	.186290	.000000	2.229248
S1	1.00000000	1.15022234	1.45066702	1.95339935	.387585	.150222	.000000	2.306903
S1.5	1.00000000	1.12318723	1.36956169	1.77678417	.350980	.123187	.000000	2.481751
S2	1.00000000	1.09615212	1.28845636	1.60017499	.310084	.096152	.000000	2.516138
S3	1.00000000	1.05951252	1.17853757	1.36657022	.243952	.059513	.000000	2.680903
S4	1.00000000	1.03013597	1.09040791	1.18335151	.173597	.030136	.000000	2.792057
S5	1.00000000	1.01394242	1.04182727	1.08421333	.118078	.013943	.000000	2.874479
S6	1.00000000	1.00567162	1.01701487	1.03412405	.075310	.005672	.000000	2.930992
SQ	1.00000000	1.00000000	1.00000000	1.00000000	.000000	.000000	.******	*.******
L	.99990815	1.39611377	2.35128904	4.48680495	.629522	.396297	.425741	2.921068
L.5	.99998340	1.33414106	2.11998972	3.80499242	.578078	.334174	.370172	2.954860
L1	1.00005865	1.27216835	1.88869040	3.12317989	.521585	.272051	.259709	2.718173
L1.5	1.00003038	1.22775011	1.74203268	2.75267465	.477168	.227689	.293929	2.907191
L2	1.00000211	1.18333187	1.59547495	2.38216940	.428168	.183328	.335771	2.982889
L3	.99998446	1.11093944	1.35421219	1.79033184	.333122	.110971	.333635	5.181884
L4	1.00000000	1.05460596	1.16885020	1.35783418	.233679	.054606	.155531	3.376855
L5	1.00000000	1.02671068	1.08194035	1.17010556	.163434	.026711	.171590	3.655762
R.5	1.00000794	1.27527118	1.81477714	2.75939412	.524648	.275255	(.005822)	2.004623
R1	1.00001588	1.21720902	1.62955427	2.31878823	.460023	.217177	(.047403)	2.199973
R1.5	1.00000755	1.17657685	1.50847694	2.05089976	.420193	.176562	(.081924)	2.451512
R2	.99999922	1.13594467	1.38739961	1.78301128	.368709	.135946	(.166230)	2.655858
R2.5	.99999955	1.10670959	1.30378797	1.60897914	.326665	.106710	(.219870)	2.993431
R3	.99999988	1.07747431	1.22017632	1.43494699	.278343	.077475	(.322565)	3.180305
R4	1.00000491	1.04247625	1.12107532	1.23813191	.206074	.042466	(.430118)	3.476015
R5	.99999266	1.01799845	1.05284832	1.10442086	.134213	.018013	(.233699)	3.228619
O2	.99552944	1.47720000	2.71419780	5.72284053	.697224	.486121	.661696	3.182123
O3	.98611535	1.79472215	4.36045313	12.25299058	.906807	.822299	1.688332	3.975167
O4	1.00263468	2.21210014	6.59166726	22.21111357	1.098555	1.206824	2.171693	4.178637
Exp	1.00000000	2.00000000	6.00000000	24.00000000	1.000000	1.000000	4.000000	9.000000

Index

ISBN 0-8138-2457-5